DEBATING THE
Roman de la rose

Routledge Medieval Texts

Routledge Medieval Texts makes the literary masterworks of the Middle Ages available in volumes translated by leading scholars. Suiting the needs of both general and advanced readers, each book contains an edition of the original with facing English translation. Based on the best available manuscripts, originals are presented in accurate, conservative versions, with minimal editorial or linguistic apparatus. Faithful, line-by-line translations in modern, colloquial English serve all audiences, from readers with no knowledge of the original language to those who need help with difficult constructions or unfamiliar vocabulary. Each volume features an introduction with a full discussion of important literary and critical questions, including the life of the author and the place of the work within either the authorial oeuvre or genre; the work's literary value and importance; the source materials drawn upon; the influence exerted on other writers; the manuscript tradition and printed history; and a select bibliography listing previous editions and major critical and historical studies. While the series includes texts from all medieval languages and literary traditions, important works from French, German, Italian, Occitan, Latin, and Hispanic literatures are its principal focus. Routledge Medieval Texts is overseen by an editorial board of eminent medievalists.

General Editors
Teresa Kennedy, Mary Washington College
R. Barton Palmer, Clemson University

Editorial Board
William W. Kibler, University of Texas
Norris J. Lacy, Pennsylvania State University
Giuseppe Mazzotta, Yale University
John M. Hill, United States Naval Academy
Stephen K. Wright, Catholic University of America

Series Titles
Eustache Deschamps
Selected Poems
Edited by Ian S. Laurie and Deborah M. Sinnreich-Levi
Translated by David Curzon and Jeffrey Fiskin

Walther von der Vogelweide
The Single-Stanza Lyrics
Edited and translated by Frederick Goldin

Alain Chartier
The Quarrel of the Belle dame sans mercy
Edited and translated by Joan E. McRae

Debating the *Roman de la rose*
A Critical Anthology
Edited by Christine McWebb
Introduction and Latin translations by Earl Jeffrey Richards

DEBATING THE
Roman de la rose

A CRITICAL ANTHOLOGY

EDITED BY
CHRISTINE McWEBB

Introduction and Latin translations by Earl Jeffrey Richards

Routledge
Taylor & Francis Group
New York   London

Routledge is an imprint of the
Taylor & Francis Group, an informa business

Routledge
Taylor & Francis Group
270 Madison Avenue
New York, NY 10016

Routledge
Taylor & Francis Group
2 Park Square
Milton Park, Abingdon
Oxon OX14 4RN

© 2007 by Taylor & Francis Group, LLC
Routledge is an imprint of Taylor & Francis Group, an Informa business

Printed in the United States of America on acid-free paper
10 9 8 7 6 5 4 3 2 1

International Standard Book Number-10: 0-415-96765-1 (Hardcover)
International Standard Book Number-13: 978-0-415-96765-5 (Hardcover)

Library of Congress Cataloging-in-Publication Data

Debating the Roman de la rose : a critical anthology / edited by Christine McWebb ;
    introduction and Latin translations by Earl Jeffrey Richards.
        p. cm.
    Includes bibliographical references and index.
    ISBN 0-415-96765-1 (hardback : alk. paper)
    1. Jean, de Meun, d. 1305? Roman de la rose. 2. Guillaume, de Lorris, fl. 1230.
Roman de la rose. 3. Romances--History and criticism. I. McWebb, Christine. II.
Richards, Earl Jeffrey.

PQ1529.D5 2006
841'.108--dc22   2006029608

Visit the Taylor & Francis Web site at
http://www.taylorandfrancis.com

and the Routledge Web site at
http://www.routledge-ny.com

for Anna and Benjamin

Contents

Preface

Guillaume de Lorris and Jean de Meun's conjoined *Roman de la rose* is without a doubt one of the foundational works of French medieval literature. We would be hard pressed to name a work that has enjoyed the same popularity and renown as the famous, or infamous, *Roman de la rose,* with over 300 extant manuscripts. This work has provoked much controversy, debate, and scholarship in the past as well as today. The present volume contextualizes the *Roman* by focusing on its reception from 1340 to 1410, thus broadening the framework of the *querelle* about the *Roman de la rose* (1401–1402). More precisely, I provide the reader with a global and comprehensive picture of the kinds of reactions evoked by this work, in particular by Jean de Meun's late thirteenth-century continuation of the *Roman* begun by Guillaume de Lorris.

A succinct overview of the *Roman de la rose* is in order here. It is comprised of two fundamentally different parts. In the first 4000 lines, written by Guillaume de Lorris in 1236, the narrator embarks on a dream voyage during which he falls in love with a rose, enclosed and protected by a walled garden. The protagonist's narration plunges the reader into an ocean of courtly conventions as the frame of the allegorical dream vision sets up a fierce battle between seductive sexual forces. These are personified by allegories called Fair Welcoming, Venus, Openness, and Pity on the one hand, and their moral counterparts evoked by virginal modesty and chastity on the other, among whom are to be counted Danger, Shame, Fear, Jealousy, and Foul Mouth. Because it represents female virginity, the rosebud, which must not be plucked, is protected and defended as the most valued and precious object in the hierarchy of female virtues. Furthermore, Guillaume de Lorris depicts the lover's sufferings and longings, his enduring yet vain efforts (most clearly seen in the second part of the text) to conquer the heart and body of the young maid, epitomized in the Rose. All the courtly topoi designed to enchant the medieval reader with the magic of a springtime world are present. But Lorris's text ends rather abruptly upon a scene in which Jealousy has locked the Rose in a tower in order to secure her from the Lover's advances. The poem remained at this point for about forty years, until, around 1275, the scholastically trained Jean de Meun, deploying a markedly different literary rhetoric, added another 17,000 lines.[1]

With Jean de Meun the tone moves from the courtly to the philosophical, thus reflecting the interests of late thirteenth-century scholasticism. Although Meun continues the narration of the protagonist's love quest, the reader now begins to find that it is all too easy to lose the narrative thread, interrupted as it is by a flood of digressions in the form of philosophical dissertations. The allegory of courtly love becomes a battle between various allegories, some of whom, such as the tellingly named Genius and Nature were added by Meun to Lorris's story. In the course of these exchanges, subjects such as love, friendship, and fortune's arbitrariness, as well as several politicized issues, are treated. We are reminded of the main plot only from time to time, and are forced to wait until the very end of the text for it to return to the forefront of the narration, when the Rose nears her final destiny, that is defeat: after multiple attacks on the fortress built by Jealousy, the lover plucks the rosebud.

The *Roman de la rose* retained its popularity through the fourteenth century and still enjoyed influence in the early fifteenth century, as the Debate about the *Roman de la rose* attests.[2] Apparently, in response to a conversation in early 1401 about the merits of Jean de Meun's *Roman de la rose* between the Provost of Lille, Jean de Montreuil, Christine de Pizan, and an unnamed "notable clerc," Jean de Montreuil composed the famous *Opusculum gallicum,* a laudatory treatise on Jean de Meun's *Roman* which, unfortunately, is lost to us today. The resulting correspondence about the *Roman*—in Christine de Pizan's eyes a very questionable piece of work—triggered the first known epistolary debate in the French literary world. In response to her opponent, Christine sent a countertreatise in which she rebuked primarily the obscene language used by various allegories in the *Roman,* such as Reason, as well as the defamation of women expressed by the Duenna, the Jealous Husband, and Genius. Jean de Montreuil, in turn, obtained the support of his colleague Gontier Col, who avidly attacked Christine in two epistles openly asking her to withdraw statements which, in his mind, constituted an insult to the greatest literary work of contemporary times. Christine did no such thing and, quite to the contrary of her adversaries' demands, dared to place the Debate in the public sphere by publishing the correspondence exchanged up to that point (early 1402).

This compilation was sent to Queen Isabeau de Bavière accompanied by a letter asking for her support. This notable event in the Debate was met with further exchanges of arguments, threats, and refutations, yet the participants during the two or three years of the Debate never reached a productive conclusion, unwilling as they were to shift their respective points of view. Pierre-Yves Badel's description of the Debate as "un dialogue de sourds" [a dialogue of the deaf][3] summarizes fittingly the participants' frustration surrounding this exchange. Jean de Montreuil had already described the correspondence in terms of frustration and Christine herself echoed this resignation in her last letter to Pierre Col toward the end of the Quarrel when she announced her withdrawal from it: "Non mie tairé pour doubte de mesprendre quant a oppinion, combien que faulte d'engin et de savoir me toult biau stile, mais mieulx me plaist excerciter en autre matiere a ma plaisance" [Nor do I silence myself for fear of being slandered because of my opinions, though I lack intelligence and a beautiful style. I simply wish to turn my attention to a topic which is more to my liking.][4] Clearly, Christine felt the Debate had become a waste of time for someone who had more important things to do.[5] Yet, in her subsequent works she would return to it repeatedly and obsessively.

Christine's insistence does not stem entirely from the strength of her convictions. It is my stance that she and the other participants in the Debate, or the Quarrel as it has commonly been termed since Arthur Piaget's chronology,[6] viewed their exchange as an ongoing intellectual debate which existed before them and continued to exist after 1403, albeit in different forms of literary expression. When we reinsert the Debate into a broader intellectual framework that extends beyond the limited scope of events between 1401 and 1403, it seems only reasonable for Christine to continue to defend her views: Her refusal to continue to engage in the epistolary exchange created a potential for expressing her views by different literary means as did many writers who were interested in the *Roman* before her.

In addition to making the texts in question accessible to an English-speaking public, it is my aim here to lift the Debate proper out of this overly narrow contextually misleading and constricting domain. I intend to demonstrate that the epistolary exchange was but one element, albeit a crucial or perhaps the central one, in a much longer and more wide-ranging polemic surrounding this seminal text of the High Middle Ages. Pierre-Yves Badel has already done this with his reception history of the *Roman de la rose* in the fourteenth century, since he included a broad spectrum of excerpts in his work intended for a francophone readership. I broaden the scope of the *Roman* discussion by resituating what modern criticism has defined as a single, canonical literary moment, placing the Quarrel in its more "natural" environment, one that includes the other important, known comments on the *Roman* by contemporaries or near-contemporaries of Christine and her interlocutors.

The anthology begins with Petrarch's crucial statement in his two epistles (1340 and repeated in 1366) criticizing the *Roman de la rose*, and ends with Laurent de Premierfait's comments on the *Roman* in his *De casibus virorum illustrium* dated 1409 and Christine de Pizan's remarks in the *Livre de fais d'armes et de chevalerie* (1410), a span of about seventy years.[7] This chronologically arranged critical anthology, which traces the diachronic and synchronic commentary Jean de Meun's work provoked, argues for reconsideration of this important medieval critical event and demonstrates why such rethinking is of considerable importance. The significance of the epistolary exchange, however, should not, in a leap of reforming zeal, be underestimated, and it receives its just due, both in Earl Jeffrey Richards's introduction and in the amount of space devoted to its original documents and their translations into English. *Roman* passages mentioned by the authors in this anthology are available in their original and in translation on the website of the MARGOT (Moyen Age et Renaissance: Groupe de recherche—Ordinateurs et Textes) research project run by the Department of French Studies at the University of Waterloo, located at http://margot.uwaterloo.ca/ (please see my User Guide for more details).

This project would not have come to completion without the help and the generosity of many people. I am deeply grateful to my colleagues who permitted me to reprint those texts by Christine de Pizan, which have already been edited and in some cases translated. I thank the following research libraries for their assistance and their permission to reproduce transcriptions of their manuscripts: the British Library, the Bibliothèque nationale de Paris, the Bibliothèque Mazarine, and the Bibliothèque royale de Belgique. My deepest gratitude goes to my colleague Earl Jeffrey Richards who wrote the introduction and translated the Latin passages into English. Countless e-mails and telephone calls kept our discussion of the topic alive and helped to move the project forward. I thank Delbert Russell and Thelma Fenster for reading drafts of the preface, their insightful comments and help with many difficult translation passages and Donald Bruce for his helpful feedback and continuous support. My research assistants Robbin Cogan, Larissa Sloutsky, and Joan Smeaton helped to move the project along with diligence and dedication. I thank Lee McWebb, Gudrun Schnell, Franziska Schnell and Roland Schnell for their expression of interest and support. Finally, I would like to thank the University of Alberta, the University of Waterloo, and the Social Sciences and Humanities Research Council of Canada for their financial assistance.

Notes

1. It is commonly accepted today that Jean de Meun continued the *Roman de la rose* and finished it between 1269 and 1278. On this topic see *Le roman de la rose*, ed. Félix Lecoy (Paris: Champion, 1965), vi–viii.
2. I use the phrase "debate about the *Roman de la rose*" in its widest sense, comprising the ongoing discussion of Jean de Meun's work from Petrarch (1340) to Laurent de Premierfait's *De casibus virorum illustrium* in 1409 and Christine de Pizan's remarks in the *Livre de fais d'armes et de chevalerie* in 1410. To distinguish between the larger debate and the actual debate epistles I will refer to the latter as either "Debate Epistles," "Quarrel," or "Debate."
3. Pierre-Yves Badel, *Le roman de la rose au XIVe siècle. Etude de la réception de l'oeuvre* (Geneva: Droz, 1980), 414; my translation.
4. Chap. 3.7, 188 for the original and 191 for the English translation.

5. At an unknown date, but undoubtedly before October 2, 1402, Pierre Col refutes one by one Christine's and Jean Gerson's arguments in a letter addressed to Christine (chap. 3.6). Her response to Pierre's letter dates from October 2, 1402, which he will only receive, however, on October 30. Pierre Col, in turn sends his reaction to this letter to Christine, of which, unfortunately only a fragment has survived and which consequently cannot be dated.

6. Arthur Piaget, "Chronologie es Epistres sur le Roman de la rose," in *Etudes romanes dédiées à Gaston Paris* (Paris: Bouillon, 1891), 114–22.

7. Please see the User Guide for a more complete justification of these chronological boundaries.

User Guide

Due to the hybrid nature of this work, as critical edition and translation, as well as anthology, the information contained in this user guide will serve as a road map for the reader to navigate his or her way through this volume. It was a challenging task to grasp and to organize with coherence the ongoing and long-lasting pluralistic reaction to the seminal work which was the *Roman de la rose*. The central aim of this endeavor, as explained in the preface, is to broaden the chronological and thematic delimitations of what has been called the Debate about the *Roman de la rose* ever since Arthur Piaget coined this term in 1891.

In his introduction, Earl Jeffrey Richards aptly demonstrates that although the actual Debate epistles do indeed create a coherent whole through the very nature of the epistolary exchange, it was certainly all too easy if not also logical for scholars to succumb to the inherent chronology of this exchange, turning Christine de Pizan's compilation of the correspondence into an oeuvre in its own right. However, we have now advanced far enough in Christinian scholarship that the Debate correspondence begs for reexamination: We must look beyond the borders of the oeuvre she created by publishing her dossier of epistles in 1402. To be sure, it is not only the chronology that needs expanding, but, as argued by Jeffrey Richards in the introduction, the issues in question during the epistolary exchange need to be recontextualized into a much broader sociopolitical framework. For the French-speaking reader this has already been undertaken primordially by Pierre-Yves Badel and Eric Hicks.[1]

When Petrarch bluntly declared that Italian writers and rhetoricians surpassed their French counterparts in ability, style, and skill, he not only afforded French clerics the opportunity to engage in a transnational debate on the literary value and superiority of their own culture, but he confirmed for us today that the nascent Italian humanism indeed began to slowly penetrate French culture during his time and through his writings. The flourishing interest and defense of the *Roman de la rose* can be explained, in part at least, by the birth of a new literary culture, first in Italy and subsequently in France. Chapter 1, therefore, must begin with Petrarch's verse epistle as the opening statement to the ensuing debate about the *Roman de la rose*. The excerpts in this chapter are meant to offer representative examples of the kind of reception Jean de Meun's continuation of Guillaume de Lorris's work provoked; I certainly do not claim to provide a complete picture of its reception. Since the core of the larger debate still remains the Debate epistles, in chapter 1 I have chosen only those authors whom I consider representative of specific thematic categories, namely those which will be relevant in the Debate epistles themselves. The dominant issues here are expressions of admiration of and reference to the *Roman* as an uncontested literary authority, in particular in the field of rhetoric and eloquence. Further, the question of the role of the mendicant orders was already of some urgency at the time of Jean de Meun's composition of the conjoined *Roman* and would continue to occupy clerical lawmakers well into the fifteenth century. The excerpts dealing with antifeminism and the infamous discourse of the Jealous Husband in Jean de Meun's work provide a counterargument to Christine de Pizan's forceful defenses of the virtues and strengths of the female. Lastly, it is important to include the rare critical voice of the *Roman*, which could be heard long before Christine, Jean Gerson, and Pierre d'Ailly.

In chapter 2 we move from clericalism to courtly discourse where the moral code of courtly lyricism is upheld by such writers as Eustache Deschamps, Philippe de Mézières, and of course Christine de Pizan herself. This chapter is nicely dovetailed by the Debate Epistles which follow the exact order suggested by Christine in her manuscript British Library Harley 4431 dedicated to the Queen of France. By the time the reader gets to the actual epistles, the broader contextualization of the first two chapters will allow him or her to read the letters in a different light, couched in a multiplicity of arguments and voices rather than as an isolated, stand alone oeuvre. The plurality of voices is what makes up the chapter following the correspondence as it lists those excerpts that are closely linked to the actual Quarrel, with contributions by Jean de Montreuil, Pierre Col, Christine de Pizan, and last but not least Jean Gerson. I would like to point out here that in the framework of the Debate the hitherto ignored *Jardin amoureux* by Pierre d'Ailly must be included in this list. Not only was Pierre d'Ailly a recipient of some of Jean de Montreuil's letters, but, more to the point, he contributed to the Debate with his rewriting of Guillaume de Lorris's *Garden of Delight*, all the while targeting the second author with very overt criticism by inserting his own *Garden of Delight* into a Christian, almost mythical or visionary context.

In the final chapter, I attempt to bring this polemic full circle by first listing Christine de Pizan's critical comments of the *Roman* in her later prose works and poems, and second by adding Laurent de Premierfait's comment from his *De casibus virorum illustrium* to the collection. De Premierfait fittingly ties many of the threads of the debate together, starting with his choice of text, which is Boccaccio's work on famous women to which Christine refers many times, notably in her *Livre de la cité des dames*. Moreover, Boccaccio was a great Italian influence on French writers of the fifteenth century and thus links Italian and French humanism long before the French Renaissance. It should not be forgotten that de Premierfait was a colleague and friend of Jean de Montreuil, and that he would without any doubt have been quite familiar with Jean Gerson and his often very severe views.

Now I will move on to more practical concerns: each excerpt is prefaced with a brief biographical and sociocultural contextualization. Ample information on existing editions, translations, and secondary sources can be found in the endnotes. My decision to include a particular text in either its entirety or only a certain portion of it, was motivated by its importance and pertinence to those issues involved in the Debate which I have outlined above. In order to afford the reader quick and easy access to the *Roman de la rose* passages to which the authors refer, I have made these available in their original and in English translation on the website of the MARGOT (Moyen Age et Renaissance: Groupe de recherche—Ordinateurs et Textes) research project run by the Department of French Studies at the University of Waterloo. The web address is: http://margot.uwaterloo.ca/. The excerpts are searchable either by keyword or exact phrase in both Middle High French and English or by corresponding page numbers (please see the website itself for further instructions on how to use it). Following Félix Lecoy's lead, I also used manuscript Bibliothèque nationale f. fr. 1573 for the transcription of the passages from the *Roman de la rose*. On the website, references are to folio and line numbers for the original passage and to line numbers for the translation into English. Because the *Roman* passages are available online, I have not included any bibliographical references to Lecoy's edition in this volume. However, references to Lecoy's edition have been included in the website. In addition to providing scholars with this critical anthology and the *Roman* passages for research purposes, I also offer instructors a tool to use in the classroom where they will be able to access simultaneously the commentary on the *Roman* (in book format) as well as the targeted *Roman* passages themselves (in electronic format). The website can be used free of charge. Passages are not subject to copyright. We do ask, however, that the website is cited in any ensuing publications and its authors given due credit.

Note

1. *Le Débat sur le Roman de al rose* (Geneva: Slatkine Reprints, 1996).

Introduction:
Returning to a "Gracious Debate":
The Intellectual Context of the Epistolary
Exchange of the Debate about the
Roman de la Rose

Earl Jeffrey Richards

The Debate about the *Roman de la Rose* has been a recurrent, almost perennial topic in literary history since the late nineteenth century. Two very modern difficulties arise in talking about the Debate: first, a misconception about its cohesion that stems from the tendency to structure the Debate dialectically, and second, the tendency to endorse either the medieval critics or the medieval advocates of the *Roman* as a function of contemporary interpretations of the *Roman* itself. Some contemporary scholars, particularly from the pro-*Roman* faction, have tended not to question their own critical assumptions, whereas Christine de Pizan specialists, including myself, while defending her censure of Jean de Meun in the Debate, have invariably been forced to explain how their analysis of Christine squares with their assessment of the *Roman*.[1] The urgent methodological question is whether it is possible to assess the Debate independently of whether one supports or condemns the *Roman* itself, and whether it is possible to overcome this almost classic scholarly impasse. In order to get beyond this impasse one needs to be prepared to leave behind the dialectical focus and look at the Debate from within a wider intellectual historical context. It is precisely this endeavor which lies at the heart of this book.

While Christine's writings remain without a doubt crucial to the Debate, their significance stems initially from her self-appointed role as the first "editor" of the Debate documents, and second from her attempt to conduct what she terms as a gracious and nonhateful debate. Thus she creates a forum where judgments of literary merit of one specific work can be pondered. Although this is not shared by her opponents and, in fact, is not always practiced by Christine herself, her collection of letters on the *Roman* says as much about her own poetic values as it does about the actual course and context of the Debate itself. In her opening letter to Guillaume de Tignonville, she pointedly refers to "le debat gracieux et non haineux" [this gracious and amicable debate].[2] In the letter concluding her "edition" of the epistles on the *Roman*, she uses the same terms when she writes to Pierre Col, "Si feray fin a mon dittié du debat non hayneux commencié, continué et finé par maniere de soulas sans indignacion a personne" [Herewith, I close my ditty of this amicable debate, which I started, carried, and ended without wishing to offend anyone].[3]

In addition to the repetiton of "non hayneux," the other significant terms here are *dittié* and *soulas*. The first of these terms, *dittié* (which survives in the English word *ditty* and is the term Christine uses for her famous poem about Joan of Arc), can mean anything from "composition" to "treatise," but essentially signals that Christine saw the epistolary exchange as a new kind of writing: it is here that she establishes her own shift from lyric to prose. The second term, *soulds* (which survives in English *solace*, whose original and now obsolete meaning "delight, amusement," reflects its meaning for Christine), is closely tied to the humanist notion of literary *otium*,[4] and will be invoked again by Christine at the beginning of *Le livre de la Cité des Dames*, when she says (with tongue firmly in cheek) that she sought some diversion or amusement from her serious study and consequently skimmed through the misogynist writings of Mathéolus, "me pensay qu'en maniere de solas le visiteroye" [thinking that I would peruse it for some amusement].[5] The second use of *so(u)las* undoubtedly alludes to the first, and in both cases Christine is appealing to an ideal of literary sophistication typical of her favorite Italian authors, Dante and Petrarch.

The erudite grace and amiability which Christine strove to instill in her letters has escaped scholarly notice because one of Christine's opponents, Gontier Col, misconstrued her criticisms as an "invective": "[t]u as nouvellement escript par maniere de invective aucunement contre ce que mon maistre, enseigneur et familier, feu maistre Jehan de Meun...fist et compila ou livre de la *Rose*..." [you recently expressed yourself in the form of an invective against the *Roman de la rose* composed and compiled by my defunct master, teacher, and friend Jean de Meun...].[6] This passage from Gontier Col is in fact the first recorded occurrence of the term *invective* in French, although every standard scholarly lexicon for French claims that Christine herself was the first to use the term at the beginning of her 1404 biography of Charles V, where she speaks of "ma nouvelle invective, en laquelle j'espoire tractier des vertus et proprietés de noblece de courage, chevalerie, et sagece..." [my new invective in which I hope to treat the virtues and properties of nobility of heart, of knighthood, and wisdom ...].[7] Following Godefroy in his dictionary of Old French, who defined the word in the one case as a "lively discourse," every other standard lexicographer hesitates to assign its traditional meaning to Christine's use of the term invective. In fact, as is widely recognized, Christine's biography of Charles V is a thinly veiled critique of the decline of the monarchy under Charles VI and of the corruption of the princes of the blood, and she uses "invective" with its precise connotations for her moralist argument.

The word *invective* in French goes back to its use in classical Latin, and in evaluating the Debate documents one cannot forget the fundamentally bilingual nature of literary culture in the Paris of Christine's day, which particularly thrived in the royal chancery, the universities, and the monasteries of the capital. Classical and postclassical Latin usage coexisted with the vernacular in these quarters. Any literate clerk of the time knew of Sallust's invective against Cicero and Ammelianus's invective against Rufinus. When Gontier Col uses the term, however, he was specifically thinking of Petrarch's use of the term in such celebrated works as the *Invectiva contra medicum,* the *Invectiva contra quendam magni status hominem,* and above all, the *Invectiva contra eum qui maledixit Italie.* Petrarch more or less revived and popularized the term in humanist circles (and its reception per se can be seen in 1397, for example, when Pietro Paolo Vergerio the Elder composed an *Invectiva contra Carolum Malatestam*). The fact that Gontier Col identifies Christine's critique of the *Roman* as an invective demonstrates that he understood her arguments as a continuation of Petrarch's criticisms of the *Roman* and of French literary culture in general, and that he understood the protonationalism of Petrarch's thought.[8] After all, the first literary debate or *certamen* arose with Petrarch's claim that poets and orators were not to be found outside of Italy, a claim which, as will be seen, may have been the most significant challenge which the supporters of the *Roman* wished to address.[9] Petrarch's crucial statement serves as the starting point for the compilation of *Roman* commentary assembled in this book.[10]

Christine did not rise to Gontier's challenge, for his term *invective* distorts her position as part of a clever rhetorical move. Her opponents in the Debate call her critique an invective in order to discredit her by characterizing her as a peevish female autodidact. The linguistic restraint of her calm, indeed serene, response, forgoes the inflammatory style of misogynist texts and thereby focuses all the more sharply and objectively on the real, day-to-day violence perpetrated on women, but without confusing this real violence with verbal violence. Her tactic suggests that she initially hesitated to engage in a full-blown Petrarchan-style *certamen* on the *Roman*—even though many of her subsequent works, especially the *Livre de la Cité des Dames*— continue the debate. Given the profundity of Christine's literary culture, it should hardly be surprising that she took this tack.

Her intellectual depth is confirmed by two atypical phrases which she uses in the course of the Debate, namely the *gloses d'Orliens* and *arguemistes*: her comparison of Jean de Meun's promise of a gloss to the "glosses of Orléans" (an allusion to the use of hair-splitting legal arguments, cultivated at the faculty of law in Orléans),[11] and her term *arguemiste* (with the double meaning of alchemy, the traditional translation of this term, and *algorism* or arithmetic in Arabic numerals, the actual and hitherto overlooked meaning of the term) to describe Jean de Meun's verbal pyrotechnics. Moreover, her cover letter for the epistles, addressed to Queen Isabeau, makes her moral and rhetorical position quite clear:

> [p]ourréz entendre la diligence, desir et voulenté ou ma petite puissance s'estent a soustenir par deffenses veritables contre aucunes oppinions a honnesteté contraires, et aussi l'onneur et louenge des femmes (laquelle pluseurs cleres et autres se sont efforciéz par leurs ditiéz d'amenuisier, qui n'est chose loisible a souffrir ne soustenir).
>
> [hearing them, you will see the diligence, desire, and will with which I defend myself as much as I can against dishonorable opinions, and where I defend the honor and praise of women (which many clerics and others make a point of diminishing in their works; this ought not to be tolerated, nor is it sustainable)][12]

Christine's moral defense of women, to use Rosalind Brown-Grant's apt phrase, underscores the dignity of her position.[13]

Before going any further, however, a brief summary of recent scholarship on the Debate may be helpful. The most serious scholarly effort hitherto to expand the "documentary basis" of the Debate was undertaken by Eric Hicks in his 1977 edition who, while endorsing the original chronology proposed by Arthur Piaget in 1891, adds material to his compilation such as excerpts from works by Jean Gerson and Christine which had traditionally been ignored in defining the chronology of the Debate. Other scholars have sought to enlarge the pertinent documents in the Quarrel to include Gerson's sermon "Considerate lilia" from August 25, 1401. It does not name the *Roman* but advances the same arguments leveled against the *Roman* shortly thereafter:

> Quarto, plurimus ei de honesto ac bono sit sermo contra illos qui ignominiosas partes corporis et actus nefandos non solum aperta impudentia nominare audent sed impudentiori animositate hoc ex Rationis persona licere fieri defendunt; non considerantes quod haec dicendo corruunt in errorem Begardorum et Turelipinorum qui de nulla re naturaliter data erubescendum esse dicebant; quemadmodum et Cynici philosophi more canum dicebant esse vivendum palam in nuditate et exercitione membrorum pudendorum; quos inculpat Tullius in *De officiis* tractans

de pulchro et decoro; et Seneca praecepit: turpia ne dixeris, paulatim enim pudor rerum per verba dediscitur; et Apostolus: corrumpunt bonos mores colloquia prava.[14]

[Fourth, my word to him concerning the honest and good and against those who dare to name the shameful parts of the body and criminal acts not only with open impudence but who also with shameless animosity defend that this be allowed to happen with the support of the person of Reason, without considering that those who say this run into the error of the Beghards and the Turlepines who are said not to blush regarding any topic presented as being natural. In the same way the Cynic philosophers were said to have lived openly in the manner of dogs in nudity and in the use of their genitals, which Cicero criticizes in *De officiis* when he discusses the beautiful and the fitting; and Seneca teaches, do not speak of ugly things, for the shame regarding reality is taught little by little through words, and the Apostle teaches that improper speech corrupts good behavior.]

This suggestion, first made by Max Liebermann in 1962, was further elaborated upon by Pierre-Yves Badel in 1980 who argued that this sermon and the series of sermons commonly titled "Poenitemini" were a response to the lost treatise, the *opusculum gallicum,* by Jean de Montreuil from April 1401 which, since Piaget, has traditionally been taken as the first document of the Debate.[15]

In addition, in the introduction to my translation of Christine's *Livre de la cité des dames*, the *Book of the City of Ladies*,[16] I expanded on Hicks's claim by arguing that Christine's use of Reason, Rectitude, and Justice in the *City of Ladies* to present a methodical defense of women's political legitimacy suggests that Christine took issue with the literary subversion of "reason" in the *Roman*,[17] and that her vindication of reason was at the same time a vindication of the rights of women. This makes perfect sense in a climate where the Salic Law had only recently—1390—been invoked and by no less than Jean de Montreuil:

Estque verum, et in antiquissimis libris ac regestris reperitur, dictam constitutionem seu legem factam fuisse priusquam Francia regem haberet christianum, et Karoli magni imperatoris et regis Francie auctoritate firmatam; quequidem lex, salica nominate, a Romanis trahens ortum, cum plerisque non parum ad hec facientibus, determinative hoc modo concludit: Nulla portio hereditatis mulieri veniat, sed ad virilem sexum tota terre hereditas perveniat.[18]

[And it is also true that it [the Salic law] is found in the most ancient books and chronicles, that this constitution or law was made before France had a Christian king, and that it was confirmed by the authority of the emperor and French King Charlemagne. This particular law, called the Salic, takes its origins from the Romans, who with many other topics accomplished not inconsiderable things in this regard, and definitely resolved it in this way: No portion of an inheritance will go to a woman, but the entire inheritance of the land will go to a male.]

Further, as Sarah Hanley observed, Jean de Montreuil's three polemical treatises against the English (written between 1413 and 1416)[19] not only defend the claims of the French Valois kings by invoking (fraudulently) the Salic Law, but also answer arguments advanced by Christine in the *Cité des Dames*.[20] The point is well taken because it shows that it was not the specific issue of female political legitimacy, but the topic of political legitimacy in general, which was a moving force behind Montreuil's defense of the *Roman* and Christine's criticism of it. Political legitimacy in France during the Hundred Years War meant justifying Valois claims to the throne, which in turn meant defending the exclusion of women from political power. Jean de Meun's celebrated claims, made at the midpoint of the conjoined *Roman*, namely that he will continue not only the unfinished work of Gulliaume de Lorris, but also the tradition of love poetry going back to the Latin poets, taken together with Chrétien de Troyes's claims in the prologue of *Cligès* that the literary culture of Greece has now arrived in France, via Rome, and would remain there forever, tend to confuse French cultural dominance and French political legitimacy.[21] This perhaps unexpected *conjointure* assumed a new poignancy with the Avignon Papacy. One could argue then that Petrarch's subsequent rejection of the *Roman*, to which I will turn in a moment, stemmed from both a cultural and a political judgment prompted by his desire to see the Papacy return to Rome.

As for Christine, she saw the ideal of French cultural legitimacy as secondary to the question of women's political legitimacy.[22] For her, this very specific question of female political legitimacy raises not only legal, but theological issues: if the Virgin Mary shares dominion with her Son, which all theological authors were prepared to grant, then is Mary not only the Queen of Mercy but also the Queen of Justice? And if Mary is the Queen of Justice, then she implicitly founds a female order of Melchisedech, and thus supplies an heretical theological basis for the admission of women to the priesthood. The issue of female political legitimacy is thus closely linked to the question of the *Roman's* heresy,[23] of the *Roman's* misogyny, of the morality of poetry, of French literary nationalism, and of the duplicity of language.

In the third book of the *Cité des Dames*, Christine has Lady Justice proclaim the Virgin Mary, Queen of Heaven, as the Queen of the City of Ladies, thus making Mary the Queen of Justice. This gesture was preeminently political because male claims to ecclesiastical office had been (and still are) based on the Pauline belief (Hebrews 6:20) that Melchisedech, the priest-king in Genesis 14:18 whose name meant "king of justice," prefigured Christ, the King of Justice. Thus, to make Mary the Queen of Justice was not simply an act of piety, but also an act of political defiance. The Debate about the *Roman* therefore first and foremost represents a cross-section of political opinions, of the political fault lines at the court of Charles VI. These were heavily influenced by the simultaneous revival of interest in the rights of Aristotle and St. Thomas Aquinas in the 1370s.

Indeed, if one takes a cue from Sarah Hanley that Jean de Montreuil's treatises were the last documents of the Debate, perhaps one might also say that his original invocation of the Salic Law in 1390 for all intents actually initiates the Debate, at least in France. In fact, however, the debate began much earlier, and not in France, but in Italy, as Christine McWebb argues by way of the excerpts in this edition beginning with Petrarch. In 1340, Petrarch was invited to be crowned poet laureate—, either from the Sorbonne or the Roman senate, —and he preferred finally to be crowned in Rome, in 1341. At this same time, while considering the invitation from the Sorbonne, Petrarch wrote a verse epistle to the Duke of Milan, Guido Gonzaga, in which he dismissed the claims of French literary superiority, doubtlessly cherished by the Sorbonne, based on the transfer of literary culture from Italy to France, the *translatio studii* topos which, as is well known, Jean de Meun cites at the midpoint of the conjoined *Roman*. In his epistle to Guido Gonzaga, Petrarch commends the eloquence of Italy over that of all other nations, including France, which claimed Jean de Meun as its witness for its literary preeminence.[24] In 1366, in a celebrated passage from a later prose epistle,[25] this one written to Urban V urging him to return the Papacy to Rome, Petrarch, more uncompromising than ever, amplified his earlier remarks, noting that orators and poets were not to be sought outside of Italy.[26]

Put concisely, the *Roman de la Rose* had become politicized into an emblem of French cultural supremacy during both the Avignon Papacy and the Hundred Years War. The proponents of the *Roman* were not necessarily defending Jean de Meun as much as they were supporting French political claims. While all the male participants of the Debate had theological training—indeed Jean Gerson, Pierre d'Ailly, and Jean de Montreuil had all been students at the College of Navarre—it is significant and hardly coincidental that the most ardent defenders of the *Roman*—Jean de Montreuil and Gontier Col—were all active as jurists for the French royal house. Their defense of Jean de Meun goes hand in hand with a support of the French monarchy against English polemics in favor of succession to the throne through a female line and against Italian polemics dismissing French cultural dominance.

Christine's objections to the *Roman* dovetail obviously with the criticisms offered by Pierre d'Ailly and Jean Gerson. As historians have long recognized, these two churchmen were strongly influenced by the thought of William of Ockham, not only in matters regarding conciliar theory and papal power,[27] a topic distant from the *Roman*, but also in questions regarding the nature of, and logic behind, allegorical signification. The studied prolixity of the *Roman*, with its never-ending excurses and the unfulfilled promise of gloss, must have irritated these two clerics who subscribed to the principle of Ockham's Razor ("Pluralitas non est ponenda sine necessitate" [pluralities should not be posited unnecessarily] or "Entia non sunt multiplicanda sine necessitate" [(separate abstract) beings (i.e., abstractions) should not be multiplied without necessity]). Pierre d'Ailly even went so far as to compose his own version of the Garden of Delight which enacts the Christian soul's yearning for her beloved, God.[28] And Gerson, in a frequently cited observation, accurately depicts the veritable celebration of contradiction in Jean de Meun:

> Propterea opus illud chaos informe recte nominatur, et babilonica con-fusio et brodium quoddam almanicum et Protheus in omnes se formas mutans—tale demum cui dici possit illud pueris decontatum: "Conveniet nulli qui secum dissidet ipse."
>
> [For this reason that work is rightly called a formless chaos, a Baby-lonian confusion, some kind of German soup, and a Proteus changing himself into every shape, precisely that which can be said that schoolboys should avoid, "something which disagrees with itself can never agree with anyone else."][29]

The proverb that Gerson quotes, touches on the question of contraries—oth-erwise cited as "Nulli conveniet, sibi qui contrarius ipsi/Extat" [whatever shows itself as contrary to itself can agree with no one.][30] The importance for Gerson of this principle of noncontradiction is repeated when he observes indignantly, "Nécessité n'a loy. Diex! quelle doctrine—non pas doctrine, mais blaspheme et heresie!" [Necessity has no law. God! What a doctrine—not a doctrine, but rather blasphemy and heresy!][31] And this position is entirely consistent with Ockham's position, consequently raising the question as to what extent Gerson's various writings on the *Roman* can be connected to other intellectual currents at both the royal court and at the University of Paris in the late 1390s and early 1400s. For instance, when Gerson asks, "[l]equel est pis: ou d'ung crestien clere preschier en la persone d'ung Sarrasin contre la foy, ou qu'il amenast le Sarrazin qui parlast ou escripst?"[which is worse: If, in the guise of a Saracen, a Christian cleric were to preach against faith, or if he were actually to bring the Saracen, who would himself speak or write?],[32] he is clearly adhering to the line of Thomas Aquinas in *De unitate intellectus contra Averroistas*. Gerson associates, rightly or wrongly, Jean de Meun's verbal play with the Averroists whom Thomas had attacked over a century earlier. Gerson's rejection of the

Roman as a piece of heresy could not have been more vehement, especially when the Thomist underpinnings of his arguments are clear.[33]

Yet, Gerson's remarks about the celebration of contradiction in the *Roman* make reference to further contemporary events which were highly significant for the Parisian university community. Just before the Lover at the end of Jean de Meun's part of the *Roman de la Rose* finally takes possession of his Rose, he comments on the long promised gloss or commentary on his allegory. He implies that if one will understand love, one must recognize its antithetical nature because contraries comment reciprocally on each other:

> Ainsinc va des contreres choses,
> Les unes sont des autres gloses;
> Et qui l'une en veust defenir,
> De l'autre li doit souvenir,
> Ou ja, par nule antancion,
> N'i metra diffinicion;
> Car qui des .ii. n'a cognoissance,
> Ja n'i cognoistra differance,
> San quoi ne peut venir en place
> Diffinicion que l'an face.

[And so it goes with contraries: the one glosses the other, and whoever wants to define one of them must bear the other in mind, for otherwise, it is impossible to offer any definition at all. For whoever does not have knowledge of the two will never know the difference between them, without which one can never apply whatever definition one makes.][34]

This passage has been the subject of an enormous body of scholarly commentary, specifically because its discussion of contraries corresponds to the central notion of the indeterminacy of language in postmodernist thought. Such a postmodernist reading, while suitably identifying the central thematic and rhetorical role of equivocation and evasive ambiguity in Jean's part of the *Roman*, diverts attention from the linguistic and historical context of Jean's passage and of Gerson's response to it. Jean uses the word *contraire* in its original Latin sense of "contradictory" rather than its extended meanings of "repugnant" or "abhorrent." When he says *contraires choses*, he seems in fact to echo the prominent term *veritates contrarie* or *contrary truths* which appears in the prologue to the 219 condemnations issued by the Bishop of Paris, Étienne Tempier on March 7, 1277. Until 1268, Tempier had been the Chancellor of the Sorbonne, and he issued his first condemnation of various "errors" in the university curriculum in 1270. Many contemporary scholars tend to see in the Debate about the *Roman* confirmation of the multiplicity of possible interpretations of the work (and of literary works in general), a veritable corroboration of postmodernist criticisms of logocentrism.[35] While potentially anachronistic, this currently popular interpretation in fact recalls the theory of "double truth" in Paris denounced by Tempier. While these famous condemnations appear at first glance far removed from the Debate about the *Roman*, they are related to the fate of Thomist thought in Parisian intellectual circles, both in the 1270s and the period immediately preceding the Debate itself.

Thomas Aquinas, who returned to the Sorbonne in 1268, explained at the opening of his *Quæstiones disputatæ de veritate* (written 1256–59 in response to developments which would climax in the condemnations of 1270 and 1277) that "quaecumque different ratione ita se habent quod unum illorum potest intelligi sine altero" [things differ in such a way that the one of them can be understood without the other]. The phrase articulates the exact opposite position of Jean at the end of the *Roman*. In this same passage by Jean, the phrase "par moye antencion" alludes to the phrase *auctoris intentio* or "author's intention," specifically coined and *only* used by Thomas Aquinas at the beginning of the *Summa contra gentiles* (now dated to the early 1260s) and in the *De perfectione spiritualis vitae* (1270). All of these works were written in Paris within less than ten years of each other and somewhat earlier than the dating of the late 1270s for the composition of the second part of the *Roman de la Rose*.[36]

Christine echoes Gerson's critique about the Proteus-like mutability of meaning in the *Roman* when, in the last letter of her collection, to Pierre Col, she compares Jean de Meun's work with the *livres des arguemistes*, traditionally taken to mean "the books of the alchemists":

> Scez comme il va de celle lecture? Ainsi comme des livres des arguemistes: les uns les lisent et entendent d'une maniere, les autres qui les lisent les entendent tout au rebours; et chacun cuide trop bien entendre.
>
> [Do you know how it goes with such a reading? It is like the books of the alchemists: There are those who read and understand them in one way, and others who read them and understand in the completely opposite way, and everyone thinks he understands them well.][37]

The remarkable fact about Christine's term *arguemistes* (which she uses repeatedly) is that it is well and truly her own invention, found nowhere else in all of medieval French literature, and that it is not only a neologism, but also a veritable *portemanteau* word in Lewis Carroll's strictest sense, for it blends the standard term in Old French *alchemiste* (which sometimes appears as *arquemiste*) with the verb *argumenter*, "to present sophistic arguments" (related to the rhetorical topos regarding poetic conceits or *argutia*) and *algorisme* (variant: "argorisme," arithmetic calculations with Arabic numerals).[38] Jean de Meun does indeed practice what Rimbaud would term centuries later *l'alchimie*

du verbe, and his verbal pyrotechnics (and, after all, it is a historical fact that alchemists experimented with fireworks) have never been and could never be denied by anyone. But if one examines the meaning of Jean de Meun's writings, the results are indeed reminiscent of the difficulties which late medieval people first had when they began to calculate with Arabic numerals: some would say Jean means this, the others would say that he means exactly the opposite—and this interpretative impasse was doubtless his intention in the first place. It is worth noting then that Jean de Meun may have played with contradictions in his work as an implicit plea for intellectual freedom as a protest against the intellectual climate in Paris, and consequently against intellectual censorship (mirrored in the 1270 and 1277 condemnations of Étienne Tempier).

The subtlety of Christine's neologism *arguemiste* recalls a similarly complicated and concentrated erudition in her allusions to medieval jurisprudence. When she compares Jean de Meun's unfulfilled promise of a gloss with the destructive glosses of Orléans, she was referring to a highly critical (if not sophistic) method of legal argumentation. As these two examples show, Christine was motivated in the Debate to evaluate the *Roman* in the widest possible intellectual context of her time, and if one ignores how she defined her own literary context with reference to the theology, jurisprudence, and "natural science" of her age, one will fail to appreciate the profound intellectual provocation of her work not only in her letters but also in her subsequent works as evidenced by the excerpts in chapter 4.

Because Jean de Meun's part of the *Roman* was viewed for decades either as the expression of a nascent "bourgeois" mentality or as a "witting retelling of the story of the Fall," as a medieval Christian allegory *generis sui*, most scholars in the past—with the notable exceptions of Alan M. F. Gunn and Franz Walter Müller[39]—were hardly inclined to think of Jean's continuation of the *Roman* in the context of the Averroist controversies at the University of Paris or as contemporary with the late works of Thomas Aquinas.[40] For future *Roman* scholars the challenge will be to situate Jean's work more precisely within the intellectual context of the turbulent 1270s, as Christine McWebb has begun to do, because although False Seeming claims that he has no intention of speaking against any living man, of course that is precisely what he is doing.[41] False Seeming's cover-up is part of an oblique continuation of the antifraternal polemic as he ostentatiously adopts the stance of anticlericalism, targeting in particular the mendicant orders. He makes his position quite clear when he goes on to recount two factual cases of the University's involvement in this debate. First, he insists on Guillaume de Saint-Amour's unjust condemnation to exile by papal decree as a consequence of speaking out publicly about the preaching friars' lack of adherence to their vows.[42] As an example of the University's vigilance against monastic subversion, he then brings up the banning of the *Liber introductorius ad Evangelium aeternum* published in 1255 by the Franciscan Gérard de Borgo San Donnino in which he announces the coming of a new Scripture. Both instances attest to the waning acceptance of the academic and communal involvement by the preaching friars on the one hand and the rise of semireligious and revolutionary sects on the other.[43]

This said, passages in Jean de Meun's work which borrow from Aristotle will now need to be evaluated within the context of Thomas's own efforts to defend the study of Aristotle and at the same time to draw a clear distinction between Aristotle's philosophy and that of the Averroists, particularly evident in *De unitate intellectus contra Averroistas*.[44] The surviving influence of the antifraternal controversy was felt for centuries at the Sorbonne, and it should not surprise us that the participants in the *Roman* Debate not only understood the implications of this polemic for Jean de Meun, but also responded, if only after a century, to Jean's treatment of the mendicants.[45] This delayed reaction served as an argument in favor of the *Roman*'s orthodoxy for some of its supporters: after all, so the argument went, if the *Roman* were indeed so truly heretical, why did it take so long for these criticisms to be raised? The major weakness of this claim is that medieval French writers who cite the *Roman* positively, and whose works are excerpted in chapter 1, were hardly major figures by any stretch of the imagination. Dante seems to have been the first important writer to dismiss the *Roman* when he speaks of the generation of semen in the male body and pointedly avoids using the word *testicles* as Jean de Meun had done, but speaks instead of a place where silence is more fair than speech.[46] Surely Dante's implicit rejection and Petrarch's explicit repudiation of the *Roman* should remind us that the *Roman*'s orthodoxy was questioned at a fairly early date. These are dovetailed by Guillaume de Digulleville in the second version of the *Pèlerinage de vie humaine* and the *Song of Songs*.[47]

As part of understanding the Debate of the *Roman*, it is important to reconstruct the specific intellectual connections between Jean de Meun's work and the antifraternal and anti-Averroist controversies of the 1270s.[48] The issues raised during this turbulent period resurfaced in the last decades of the fourteenth century, in part because the French royal court under Charles V took particular interest in cultivating Thomist political philosophy and in reviving interest in Aristotle. In the early 1370s, Nicole Oresme authored commentaries on major works by Aristotle (*Le livre de ethiques d'Aristote* [1372], *Le livre de politiques d'Aristote* [1374], *Le livre de yconomique d'Aristote* [ca.1374], and *Le Livre du ciel et du monde* [1377]). The works of Thomas Aquinas's most famous pupil Aegidius Romanus (Gilles de Rome) were also translated for Charles V. At the very same time Charles V was encouraging the revival of Aristotelian philosophy, he was active in renewing interest in Thomist thought as well. The most striking evidence for the resurgence of the popularity of the Angelic Doctor at the court in Paris was the construction of a royal chapel at the Couvent St. Jacques to house the right arm of the saint, sent there expressly by Pope Urban V in July 1369. Interestingly enough, Jean de Meun was also buried in the Couvent St. Jacques—he left the Dominicans there his house, which was just across the street, in exchange for burial in the convent. He also left them a chest, which they supposed was filled with gold, but which was filled with slate tiles instead, all having geometric designs. The Dominicans were so angry when discovering this deception that they disinterred Jean's body, provoking an outcry which forced them to rebury him in the convent church. The same convent church, destroyed in the French Revolution, sheltered Jean's tomb and the royal chapel with the relic of the Angelic Doctor.[49] This perhaps ironic (and literally physical) juxtaposition of two of the most influential intellectuals of Paris in the 1270s must have created for contemporaries a reciprocal and tangible glossing in stone: Jean's grave "comments" on the royal chapel dedicated to Thomas's relic, and vice versa.

Thus it was hardly a coincidence that the debate about the *Roman* began at a time when the same Thomist doctrines formulated contemporary to the second part of the *Roman* attracted renewed interest at both the University of Paris and the royal court. In focusing on understanding the debate within this context, it is striking that Thomas demanded hermeneutic clarity where Jean prefers equivocation. The issue is not whether Thomas's semiotic philosophy is to be preferred to Jean's, but that the contest and competition between these two semiotic positions could not have been more clearly defined. While Thomas's theological views regarding the creation of women epitomize the Church's misogyny,[50] his views of signification provide a powerful instrument against the portrayal of women favored by Jean de Meun, where verbal ambiguity and hedging effectively ridicule the historical position and experience of women. While the lines of opposition and the issues of political legitimacy, misogyny, and heresy were clearly delineated, Christine, perhaps paradoxically, still insists on speaking of a "gracious" debate, and this because she hopes to reconcile the opponents (who were, it should be repeated, actually mostly all old college friends) in the name of a higher ideal of reason. It is as though Christine recognized the potential impasse of the Debate itself and sought to overcome it by appealing to a truly idealized and most likely impossible notion of a literary republic, to a literary cosmopolitanism which has yet to be realized.

Notes

1.   The most noteworthy modern defenders of the Roman—whose defense of this work goes hand in hand with a rejection of all criticisms leveled against it—include D.W. Robertson, *Preface to Chaucer* (Princeton, NJ: Princeton University Press, 1962); John V. Fleming, *The Roman de la rose. A Study in Allegory and Iconography* (Princeton, NJ: Princeton University Press,

1969); Pierre-Yves Badel, *Le Roman de la Rose au XIVe siècle. Étude de la réception de l'œuvre* (Geneva: Droz, 1980); David Hult, *Self-Fulfilling Prophecies: Readership and Authority in the First Roman de la rose* (Cambridge, UK: Cambridge University Press, 1986); Sylvia Huot, *The Romance of the Rose and Its Medieval Readers: Interpretation, Reception, Manuscript Transmission* (Cambridge, UK: Cambridge University Press, 1993); Douglas Kelly, *Internal Difference and Meanings in the Roman de la rose* (Madison: University of Wisconsin Press, 1995); Alastair Minnis, *Magister Amoris, The Roman de la Rose and Vernacular Hermeneutics* (Oxford: Oxford University Press, 2001). See also the references in note 35.

2. See chap. 4.2, 216 and 217 (page numbers refer first to the original and then to the translation).

3. See chap. 3.7, 188 and 199.

4. This is the term also used by Gontier Col and Jean de Montreuil when they refer to the latter's prolonged stay in Germany.

5. *La città delle dame*, ed. Patricia Caraffi and Earl Jeffrey Richards (Milan: Luni Editrice, 1997), 40, my translation.

6. See chap. 3.3, 114 and 115.

7. *Le livre des fais et bonnes meurs su sage roy Charles V*, 2 vols., ed. Suzanne Solente (1936–40; Geneva: Slatkine Reprints, 1977), 1:6; my translation.

8. See William J. Kennedy, *The Site of Petrarchism, Early Modern National Sentiment in Italy, France and England* (Baltimore: Johns Hopkins University Press, 2003).

9. For more detailed information, see Pier Giorgio Ricci, "La cronologia dell'ultimo 'certamen' petrarchesco," *Studi Petrarcheschi* 4 (1951): 47–59.

10. See chap. 1.1.

11. See my two articles on this topic: Richards, "Glossa Aurelianensis est quae destruit textum: Medieval Rhetoric, Thomism and Humanism in Christine de Pizan's Critique of the Roman de la Rose," *Cahiers de Recherches Médiévales (XIIe–XVe s.)* 5 (1998): 247–63; and "Christine de Pizan and Medieval Jurisprudence," *Contexts and Continuities, Proceedings of the Fourth International Colloquium on Christine de Pizan* (July 2000), ed. Angus J. Kennedy et al. (Glasgow: University of Glasgow Press, 2002), 747–66.

12. See chap. 3.1, 108–110 and 109–111.

13. Rosalind Brown-Grant, *Christine de Pizan and the Moral Defense of Women. Reading Beyond Gender* (Cambridge, UK: Cambridge University Press, 1999).

14. "Sermon Considerate Lilia" in *Jean Gerson. Œuvres complètes, vol. 5, L'œuvre oratoire*, ed. Msgr. *Glorieux* (Paris: Desclée, 1960-), 163; my translation.

15. For excerpts from these sermons, see chap. 4.10.

16. Earl Jeffrey Richards, *The Book of the City of Ladies* (New York: Persea, 1982).

17. A cogent argument for the link between reason and the vindication of women's rights is found in Karen Green, *The Woman of Reason: Feminism, Humanism and Political Thought* (Cambridge, UK: Polity Press, 1995).

18. In *Opera. L'œuvre historique et polémique*, ed. N. Grévy, E. Ornato, G. Ouy (Turin: Giappichelli, 1975), 2: 226–27; my translation.

19. Ibid., 2:160–313.

20. Sarah Hanley, "Identity Politics and Rulership in France: Female Political Place and the Fraudulent Salic Law in Christine de Pizan and Jean de Montreuil," in *Changing Identities in Early Modern France*, ed. Michael Wolfe (Durham, NC: Duke University Press, 1997), 78–94.

21. Michelle A. Freeman, *The Poetics of Translatio Studii and Conjointure: Chretien de Troyes's "Cligès"* (Lexington KY: French Forum Publishers, 1979).

22. I have treated these issues in detail in a forthcoming essay, "Political Thought as Improvisation: Female Regency and Mariology in Late Medieval French Thought," in *Virtue, Liberty, and Toleration: Political Ideas of European Women, 1400–1800*, ed. Jacqueline Broad and Karen Green (Brussels: Brepols).

23. This aspect has been long neglected but recently reintroduced into the scholarly discussion by

Christine McWebb in, "Heresy and Debate: Reading the Roman de la Rose," *Aevum* 77 (2003): 545–56.

24. See Earl Jeffrey Richards, *Dante and the Roman de la rose: An Investigation into the Vernacular Narrative Context of the Commedia* (Tübingen: Niemeyer,1981), 62.

25. *Seniles* 9.i.

26. Grover Furr, "France vs. Italy, French Literary Nationalism in 'Petrarch's Last Controversy' and a Humanist Dispute of ca. 1395," *Proceedings of the Patristic, Medieval and Renaissance Conference*, 4 (1979): 115–25.

27. See Bernard Guenée, "Pierre d'Ailly (1351–1420)," in *Entre l'église et l'état: quatre vies de prélats français à la fin du moyen âge (XIIIe–XVe siècle)* (Paris: Gallimard, 1987), 125–299; and Paul J. J. M. Bakker, "Syncategorèmes, concepts, équivocité: Deux questions anonymes, conservées dans le ms. Paris, B.N., lat. 16401, liées à la sémantique de Pierre d'Ailly (c. 1350–1420)," *Vivarium* 34 (1996): 76–131; Louis B. Pascoe, "Theological Dimensions of Pierre d'Ailly's Teaching on the Papal Plenitude of Power," *Annuarium Historiae Conciliorum* 11 (1979): 357–66; and "Pierre d'Ailly: histoire, schisme et Antichrist," in *Genèse et débuts du Grand Schisme d'Occident*, ed. Michel Hayez (Paris: CNRS, 1980), 615–22.

28. See chap. 4.4.

29. This is from Gerson's letter "Talia de me", chap. 4.9, 356 and 357.

30. This proverb is otherwise recorded by Hans Walther, *Proverbia sententiaeque latinitatis medii ac recentioris aevi... aus dem Nachlass von Hans Walther,* 3 vols., ed. P.G. Schmidt (Göttingen, Germany: Vandenhoeck & Ruprecht, 1982–86), no. 18982a: "Nulli conveniet, sibi qui contrarius ipsi/Extat, ut, unde calor prodiit, inde gelet," cited from a fourteenth-century manuscript in Göttingen, Philol. 130, "Poletychon" [recte: "Polytychon"].

31. See chap. 4.5, 292 and 293.

32. Chap. 4.5, 288 and 289.

33. We must not forget that Gerson was eager in theory to burn every copy of the *Roman*—for which he has been justly criticized—as he was in fact to burn heretics like Jan Hus, for which, strangely, he has rarely been reproached—and the parallel between burning books and burning human beings was later made by Heinrich Heine, "Dies war ein Vorspiel nur, dort wo man Bücher verbrennt, verbrennt man auch am Ende Menschen" [this was only a prelude: where one first burns books, one ends up burning people] *Almansor* (1821), l: 243, my translation.

34. My translation.

35. Kevin Brownlee and Sylvia Huot, ed. *Rethinking the Romance of the Rose: Text, Image, Reception* (Philadelphia: University of Pennsylvania Press, 1992); Sylvia Huot, *The Romance of the Rose and Its Medieval Readers: Interpretation, Reception, Manuscript Transmission* (Cambridge, UK: Cambridge University Press, 1993); Susan Stakel, *False Roses: Structures of Duality and Deceit in Jean de Meun's Roman de la rose* (Stanford, CA: Anma Libri, 1991); Marilynn Desmond, "The Querelle de la Rose and the Ethics of Reading," in *Christine de Pizan: A Casebook*, ed. Barbara K. Altmann and Deborah L. McGrady (New York: Routledge, 2003), 167–80; David F. Hult, "The Roman de la rose, Christine de Pizan, and the querelle des femmes," in *The Cambridge Companion to Medieval Women's Writing*, ed. Carolyn Dinshaw and David Wallace (Cambridge, UK: Cambridge University Press, 2003), 184–94; and Daniel Heller-Roazen, *Fortune's Face: The Roman de la Rose and the Poetics of Contingency* (Baltimore: Johns Hopkins University Press, 2003).

36. *Summa Contra Gentiles*, lib. 1 cap. 2 title 'Quae sit in hoc opere auctoris intentio' [The Author's Intention in This Work].

37. Chap. 3.7, 154, 155–157.

38. Pierre-Yves Badel, "Lectures alchimiques du Roman de la Rose," *Chrysopoeia: Revue de la Société d'Étude de l'Histoire de l'Alchimie* 5 (1992–96): 173–90.

39. Alan M. F. Gunn, *The Mirror of Love, A Reinterpretation of "The Romance of the Rose,* (Lubbock: Texas Technical Press, 1952); Franz Walter Müller, *Der Rosenroman und der lateinische Averroismus des 13. Jahrhunderts* (Frankfurt: Klostermann, 1947).

Introduction

40. The best studies of the controversies at the University of Paris during the thirteenth century have been assembled in the indispensable volume Albert Zimmermann, ed., *Die Auseinandersetzungen an der Pariser Universität im XIII. Jahrhundert* (Berlin: Walter de Gruyter, 1976); and J. M. M. H. Thijssen, *Censure and Heresy at the University of Paris 1200–1400* (Philadelphia: University of Pennsylvania Press, 1998). Of specific relevance for the composition of the second part of the *Roman* and the thought of Thomas Aquinas, is Édouard-Henri Wéber, "Les discussions de 1270 à l'université de Paris et leur influence sur la pensée philosophique de S. Thomas d'Aquin," *Die Auseinandersetzungen*, 2285–2316.

41. In Christine McWebb, "Heresy and Debate."

42. For a full account of Guillaume de Saint-Amour's involvement in this polemic, see John Moorman, *A History of the Franciscan Order. From Its Origin to the Year 1517* (Oxford: Clarendon Press, 1968), 127–31; and Michel-Marie Dufeil, *Guillaume de Saint-Amour et la polémique universitaire parisienne, 1250–1259* (Paris: Picard, 1972). A succinct account of this case in the context of vernacular poetry can be found in Renate Blumenfeld-Kosinski, "Satirical Views of the Beguines in Northern French Literature," in *New Trends in Feminine Spirituality. The Holy Women of Liège and Their Impact*, ed. Juliette Dor (Brussels: Brepols, 1999), 237–49.

43. Jean de Meun is not alone in voicing his criticism of the growing semireligious movement. In the vernacular tradition, it is first and foremost the poet Rutebeuf who has nothing but ridicule and mockery reserved for the Beguines, in particular in his Diz des Beguines. For an analysis of his poetry, see Renate Blumenfeld-Kosinski, "Satirical Views of the Beguines."

44. Wéber has identified three distinct competing positions on the teaching of Aristotle. As complicated as it is to pin down Jean's meaning on any one topic, one accepted fact is that Jean's critique of the mendicant orders corresponds to his sympathies for Guillaume de Saint-Amour in his attacks on the Dominicans and Franciscans, "Les discussions de 1270."

45. See Penn R. Szittya, "The Antifraternal Tradition in Middle English," *Speculum* 52 (1977): 287–313.

46. *Purg.* 25.43–44, "ov'è più bello / tacer che dire."

47. For the relevant excerpts, see chap. 1.E.

48. For examples of commentary exchanged on this issue in the context of the debate about the *Roman*, see chap. 1.C.

49. The best documentation remains Célestin Douais, *Les reliques de saint Thomas d'Aquin, Textes originaux* (Paris: Librairie Ch. Poussielgue, 1903). See also Étienne Delaruelle, "La translation des reliques de Saint Thomas d'Aquin à Toulouse (1369) et la politique universitaire d'Urbain V," *Bulletin de littérature ecclésiastique* 56 (1955): 129–46, reprinted 1999. Constant Mews (Monash University, Melbourne) and I are in the process of reediting these materials.

50. Aquinas, *Summa* 1.2.92.

Chapter One

Italian Humanism and French Clericalism in the Fourteenth Century[1]

Since it is Jean de Meun's part of the *Roman de la rose* which is of concern to me, I have limited my selection of references almost exclusively to his work. This said, however, there are numerous fourteenth-century writers—the anonymous author of the *Echecs amoureux*, for instance—who do not make a distinction between the two parts that constitute the *Roman*, but consider it as a whole, a "Miroir de vie humaine" [Mirror of/for human life]. The *Echecs* is a commentary on the mythography and the narrative in both sections of the *Roman*.[2] Also important to mention here, of course, is the *Remaniement de Gui de Mori*, a complete rewriting of both sections of the *Roman* in a purely courtly spirit.[3]

A. The Beginning of the debate about the *Roman de la rose*

1. Francesco Petrarch (1304–74)

The polemic between French and Italian intellectuals, Petrarch, Jean de Montreuil, Nicolas de Clamanges, and others, did not evolve only around the literary quality of contemporary writers, but, as argued by E. Jeffrey Richards in the Introduction, was grounded in the political controversy of the Avignon Papacy. As Jeffrey Richards states,

In 1340, Petrarch was invited to be crowned poet laureate—either from the Sorbonne or the Roman senate—and he preferred finally to be crowned in Rome, in 1341. At this same time, while considering the invitation from the Sorbonne, Petrarch wrote a verse epistle to the Duke of Milan, Guido Gonzaga, in which he dismissed the claims of French literary superiority, doubtless cherished by the Sorbonne, based on the transfer of literary culture from Italy to France, the *translatio studii* topos which, as is well known, Jean de Meun cites at the midpoint of the conjoined *Roman*. In his epistle to Guido Gonzaga, Petrarch commends the eloquence of Italy over that of all other nations, including France, which claimed Jean de Meun as its witness for its literary preeminence.[4]

Petrarch's comment on the *Roman de la rose* confirms that this work had assumed a representative and authorial status which he counters with examples from the Greek and Roman literary canons. In 1366, Petrarch, more uncompromising than ever, repeated his earlier statement from 1340 that orators and poets were not to be sought outside of Italy ("oratores et poete extra Italiam non querantur").[5] I consequently consider Petrarch's verse epistle to Guido Gonzago the starting point of the debate about the *Roman de la rose*.[6]

1340: Verse Epistle III.30[7]

Text:

> Itala quam reliquias superet facundia linguas,
> Vir praestans, Graiam, praeter, (si fama sequenda est
> Et Cicero) nullam excipio, brevis iste libellus
> 4   Testis erit, clara eloquio quem gallia caelo
> Attolitque favens, summisque aequare laborat
> Silicet hic vulgo recitat sua somnia Gallus.

Translation:

> O illustrious man, how Italian eloquence conquers all other languages—besides the Greek one, I make exception of none [other], if rumor is to be believed as well as Cicero—this short little book of yours will be a witness, which France, famous for eloquence, has nurtured and borne to heaven and strives to make
> 5   equal to the greatest [works]; that is, a Frenchman recites here his dream-visions in the vernacular.

B. The Roman as *Auctoritas*

From the time of its publication and during the entire fourteenth century, both parts of the *Roman de la rose* were frequently cited as exemplary models of rhetorical skill, eloquence, and stylistic beauty. The examples shown below demonstrate the widespread admiration for the linguistic quality of this work within clerical circles.

1. Gilles li Muisis (1272–1353)

Gilles li Muisis[8] was a Benedictine abbot at the monastery of Saint-Martin de Tournai who, after he tragically became blind at the age of 80, composed a collection of French verses titled *Registre* (1346),[9] wherein he expresses his thoughts on many practices, moral or otherwise, of his day. Conscious of his own lack of literary and rhetorical skill, li Muisis admires the *Roman de la rose* and its authors for the work's clarity, beauty, and completeness. He mentions the *Roman* several times in his writing: Li Muisis does not distinguish between the two authors of the *Roman*, but speaks of its composers in the plural. It certainly is puzzling why a Benedictine abbot who holds Christian morality in high esteem would praise Jean de Meun's doctrinally controversial text. The answer is most probably that li Muisis, like some of his contemporaries, though referring to the *Roman*'s subject matter as "noble," focused less on content than on rhetorical eloquence. And on that score, Jean de Meun's composition can undoubtedly be praised as a model of its kind, which is an argument even Christine de Pizan readily acknowledges when, for instance, she marvels in her letter addressed to Pierre Col, "Et vrayement moy mesmes me suis maintes fois merveillee que si grant dicteur cessast a si pou d'œuvre,—non obstant que plusieurs qui luy sont favourables luy veulent imposer des dictiez mesmes de saint Augustin." [And, truly, as for myself, I have often wondered at the fact that such a great poet had stopped at so few works, albeit that several of his supporters would like to attribute to him even the poems of Saint Augustine.][10]

Given that the laudatory tone in theme and style is repeated in all three references to the work,[11] for brevity's sake, I quote only two of the three excerpts in which li Muisis refers to the *Roman*. In the first excerpt, li Muisis laments his loss of eyesight, which deprives him of much of the pleasure and learning he could otherwise acquire through reading. The *Roman de la rose* is mentioned alongside the poetry of the Hermit of Molliens as one of the most beautiful and noble works ever written:

1346: Li Méditations[12]

Text:

Une matère m'est venue:
En men coer l'ay lonc temps tenue;
Se le seusse mettre par lettre,
4   Volentiers l'i fecisse mettre;
Mès les boins faiseurs je redoubte
Qui sèvent le manière toute
De biaus dis faire et trouver.
8   Or voroi-ge bien esprouver
Si je les porrois siwir
Et leurs manières consiwir.
Bien y convient et sens et paine;
12   A chou plaisance les amaine;
Au faire mettent estudie,
Par quoy leur œvre soit prisie.
De biaus dis siert-on les signeurs
16   Par tous les païs les grigneurs
Et les gens de toutes manières,
Par quoy se facent boines chières
En tous les lieus où sont ensamble.
20   C'est moult grans oèvre, ce me samble,
Et ot-on volentiers ces dis.
Si laist-on souvent les mesdis
Et moult de parolles malvaises,
24   Qui moult souvent tollent les aises
Des compaignies asanlées,
Dont y viènent souvent mellées;
Se moèvent wères et descors;
28   S'en convient faire accors,
Amendes et pélerinages;
Et tout vient des malvais corages
Et chou que de vins trop on prent,
32   Et li sages tels gens reprent;
Leur compaignie s'est malvaise,
Souvent les compagnons mésaise.
Toutes si faites choses viènent
36   Des fols gens qui les maintiènent.
Pour chou fait-il boin biaus dis dire
Pour oster tous courous et yre,
As diners faire liement

Translation:

A subject has entered my mind which I kept in my heart for a long
time. If only I had known how to put it in words, I gladly would
have done so. However, I fear the composers, who know so well the
way to rhyme and compose beautifully. Now, I would prove myself
5   if only I could imitate them and their methods. Wisdom and pain
are both a part of it, and will guide them to playful pleasure. They
apply themselves to learning to compose, which is why their work
is appreciated. Lords and common folk everywhere are followed by
beautiful poems, which is why wherever people are together, there
10   is merriment. It seems to me that this is a very grand achievement,
and one gladly hears these poems. Thus, medisance is often ignored,
as are the many evil words which very often destroy the lightheart-
edness of gatherings, where evil words can frequently be found. If
retribution and discord leave, accords, restitutions, and pilgrimages
15   come about. Evil forces and too much wine are the cause, and the
wise rebuke such people: their company is evil, their guests often
disagreeable. All such things come from the foolish people who uphold them. For this reason, good and beautiful poems are recited to
diffuse all strife and discord; at midday meals and suppers, alliances
20   are formed. In this way, poets live more agreeably, and their words
of wisdom are better delivered. For this I would gladly undertake a
valliant deed—however, with the lot given to me by God, and with
my time, which will end and pass, I can neither write nor read, and
have nothing to make me laugh, for I have lost my eyesight, so that
25   I cannot read a book. And I have no longer the need to get drunk on
wine, anger, or thought. I do, however, have the need to meditate in
order to occupy my time well. When I cannot study, I find paintings
in the soul. It is for this reason that I cure my agony through thinking, if I can, and from it take the same pleasure as I would from
30   reading. Further, I take pleasure in a little penance. Being vicious
is an evil life, for vice is no friend of the soul. The good-doers of
the past who left the wordly life did good works, and left them to
teach both the stupid and the wise. There are many beautiful books
which guide people to live a holy life. I was able to find even more
35   beautiful things in the *Roman de la rose*.[13] Blessed are those who
composed it! They proved their wisdom well, for the subject is very
noble, a pleasure to read, and very clear. What can I say about the
verses of the Hermit,[14] all of which I would gladly read every day,
if only I could. This would be time beautifully spent. One must take
40   pleasure in reading them, for they steer many people to the path

40   Et à soupers tout ensement.
        Ensi poet-on plus aise vivre,
        Ses sens avoir plus à délivre.
        Pour chou feroi-ge volentiers
44   Cose vaillant, entrementiers
        Que m'est de Dieu donnet espasse
        Et que mes temps finist et passe,
        Escrire point ne puis, ne lire,
48   Et que n'ay matère de rire
        Pour le lumière qu'ay pierdue
        Par mes excès de me vewe,
        Si que lire ne puis en livre.
52   Si n'ay mestier que je m'enyvre
        De vins, de courous, de penser.
        S'ay mestier de mi pourpenser
        Pour me temps bien ensonnyer
56   Quand je ne puis estudyer,
        Pour à l'âme trouver penture;
        Dont convient que je mache cure
        De penser, se puis, et de faire
60   Chou que poroit à lisans plaire,
        Et ausi que j'aie plaisance
        En faisant un pau de penanche.
        Wiseus estre, c'est maise vie,
64   Car à l'âme n'est pas amie.
        Li boin faseur, ou temps passet,
        Qui dou siècle sont trespasset,
        Ont fait et laisciet biaus ouvrages
68   Pour ensignier et sots et sages.
        S'en appèrent moult de biel livre
        Qui saintement font les gens vivre.
        J'ay pau trouvet plus bielle chose,
72   Que c'est dou romanc de le Rose;
        Bénit soient qui le trouvèrent,
        Leur sens en grant bien esprouvérent,
        Car noble moult est li matère,
76   Au lire plaisans et bien clère.
        Des viers dou Renclus que diroie?
        Que moult volentiers, se pooie,
        Les liroie trèstous les jours.
80   En chou seroit biaus li séjours.

of restitution. One can take many a good example from them. And
they are elegant to listen to, for they make the heart rejoice for all
the good and the wisdom that one finds there. Never was such a
work created. If one applied oneself well, knowledge would be well
45   served in meditating all day long and in illuminating one's heart
well. He who would put his understanding there would find beautiful things. It has been composed for those of all ranks: how vices
are refuted, and how one ought to comport oneself if one wishes
to attain a good end. It is true that this knowledge is very good and
50   worth more than great possessions....[15]

Now I have spoken much about these works, their composers, and the use of poetry of the Hermit and of the *Rose*, which are
undoubtedly very beautiful things, of friar Jaquemon Bochet, who
in his book makes many reprimands in order that sinners may repent
55   and promise their hearts to God entirely, and of other things of
which I have made mention and pronounced my opinion.

I will now return to myself, for I know well that I will die and
am always on the path of death. I have no posterity left here, and
there will be no one left alive.

Au lire doit-on avoir joye,
Car il mettent bien gens en voie
D'amender trèstous leur affaire.
84   On y prent maint boin exemplaire.
Si sont gracieux à oïr,
Car il font les coers esjoïr
Dou bien et dou sens k'on y treuve.
88   Onques ne fut faite tel oèvre.
S'on y mettoit bien sen entente,
Au savoir che seroit grant rente
Pour trèstous les jours ruminer
92   Et sen coer bien illuminer.
Qui sen sens bien y metteroit,
Des bielles choses trouveroit.
De tous estas ens est trouvet,
96   Comment visces sont réprouvet,
Comment on se doit maintenir,
Qui voelt à boine fin venir;
Et s'est, voir, moult boins li savoirs:
100   Assés vault mieuls que grans avoirs…
Or ai moult parlé del ouvrage,
Des faseurs et de leur usage
Des viers dou Renclus, de la Rose,
104   Qui sont chiertes moult bielle chose,
De frère Jaquemon Bochet
Qui en sen livre maint nochet
Fait as pékeurs pour repentir
108   Leur coer à Dieu avoir entir,
D'autres choses dont mention
Ay fait et dit m'entencion.

Or à my retourner volrai;
112   Car je sai bien que je morrai
Et que je vois tous jours morant;
Et si n'ay chi nul demorant:
Aussi n'ara nuls qui ait vie.

1346: Li Estas—Des Prélas[16]

In what follows, li Muisis interrupts a satirical account of the practices and exaggerated concern with worldly things on the part of prelates, in order to praise once again the beauty of the *Roman de la rose*:

Text:

Tout ainsi que les lays voic clergiet maintenir,
Et en tous leurs maintiens leur coustume tenir,
Et à l'anchien tempore nuls ne voelt revenir:
4   Fort est k'à l'amour Dieu nuls puist ensi venir.

Car Dieus voelt des vrais coers avoir recongnisance,
Et voelt que cescuns ait des peckiés repentance
Et k'en li seulement mache sen espérance;
8   Autrement des peckiés ne fera délivrance.

Laye gent, si con lune, se cangent et se muent,
Et les boines doctrines pluseur souvent respuent.
Las! il ne sèvent mie comment leur âmes tuent,
12   Quant les virtus en visces trèstous les jours transmuent.

Je n'oc parler dou siècle nulle gent autrement.
Cescuns dist ceste note qui va malvaisement;
A tous lés, en tous cas, on voit empirement;
16   Il n'est nulle nouvelle de nul amendement.

Tout ainsi que li lune se clartet a pierdue;
Se met chius as ténèbres, qui le bien en mal mue,
Et s'il savoit comment de grasce se desnue,
20   Jamais ne chiesseroit, se seroit revenue.

Comment oseroit nuls dire le véritet,
De che siècle qui keurt le grant iniquitet,
K'on en dist, k'on en ot, dont tout boin ont pitet,
24   Comment de pluseurs sont anchien temps despitet?

C'est voirs; li gent présent ne l'oseroient dire,
Car il touke cescun et nul ne se remire.
Grant folie seroit de faire dont escrire
28   Chou dont li consience remorderoit au lire.

Translation:

The Social Ranks—Of the Prelates

Just as the clergy sees the laypeople maintain their ways and uphold their customs in all respects, and just as no one wishes to return to the old ways, it is difficult for anyone to achieve God's love in this way. For God wishes to know our true hearts, and wishes us all to
5   repent of our sins and to place our hope in Him alone; otherwise He will not deliver us from our sins. Layfolk, like the moon, change and transform, and many of them often scoff at good doctrines. Alas, they do not know how they are killing their souls, when nearly every day they transform virtues into vices. I have never heard it spoken
10   differently of the worldly life. Everyone sings this evil melody. In any case, one sees deterioration in every corner. There is no news of improvement. Just as the moon has lost its brightness, it [the worldly life] descends into darkness, which transforms good into evil. And if it knew how to free itself of mercy, it would never leave,
15   and would never come back. How would anyone dare tell the truth of the worldly life, which is built on great inequality? Whatever one may say or hear about it, one pities all the good people. How the old times are despised by many! It is true: today, people would not dare say it, for it would affect everyone and no one would recover.
20   It would be great folly to write about something that would torment one's conscience when reading it. All these occurrences, which one sees today in all regions, come from the heart. This is not excusable, not in any country. All men and women aspire to the worldly life. Clergy and layfolk attend the school of this treacherous wordly life,
25   whose words are worthless. The worldly life has instructed the weak too well, for it makes all hearts vain and it causes the good to flee. Today one sees all vices reign—great pride, great envy, and great avarice; anger, hatred, oppression, and all other evil—treacheries so great that they cause prejudice. And what can one say of the great
30   gluttony which is such a great friend of the stomach? Nothing is spared when it comes to the chestful of food which one always likes to be richly filled. Formerly, lust was practiced discreetly; now it is done in too much abundance. The present fashion shows it, it really does seem to me: "What do you want? Here I am," without further
35   ado. I have heard tell of great strife: Is it not true, then, that every-day people succumb to sin? Do they all obey this disorder? Every day they have reason to fall. If I told all that of which I have heard

Dou coer viènent trèstoutes ches adiventions,
K'on voit aujourdui faire par toutes régions.
Escuser ne s'en puet, voir, nulle nations;
32   Au siècles tout et toutes ont les intentions.

Clergiet et li gent laye trèstout vont à l'escolle
De ce siècle trayte, riens n'i vault li parolle.
Li siècles a trop bien d'iaus instruire le molle,
36   Car tous les coers fait vains et fait que bien s'envolle.

Comment voit-on rengier au jour dui trèstous visces,
Grans orghieus, grans envies et ches grans avarisces,
Courous, haynes, praices et tous autres malisces,
40   Trekeries si grant qui font les préjudisces?

Et que poroit-on dire de le grant gloutrenie,
Au ventre k'on voit iestre si grandement amie?
Pour le kierté des vivres on ne s'espargne mie
44   K'on ne voelt que tous jours soit taule bien garnie.

Luxure fasoit-on jadis privéement;
Or le fait-on par trop abandonnéement.
Abit présent démonstrent, che sanle vraiment:
48   «Que voes-tu? je sui chi». sans autre parlement.

A l'oyr ay grant duel: k'es-ce dont dou véir
Les gens trèstous les jours en peckiés enkéir,
A ches désordenances tous, toutes obéir?
52   Véant ont tous les jours ocquoison de kéir.

L'estat de toutes gens trop bien dire poroie,
Se de chou que j'oc dire, parler m'enhardisoie.
Par chou que je ne voic, escusés en seroie;
56   Se me dient aucun que trop bien je feroie.

Mais je redoubte trop à faire mention
Sous ches parfais trouveurs qui leur entention
De tous estas ont fait et déclaration:
60   Tost tenroit-on me dist à grand présumption.

tell, I could say more than enough about all groups of people, and I would terrify myself in speaking about it. Since I cannot see, I will
40 be excused from it, even if someone tells me I would to it well. But I am too afraid to make mention of it in the presence of perfect composers, who have expressed their opinion on all groups of people: I would then be accused of great presumption. Never, anywhere, has such a thing as the book of the Hermit or of the *Roman de la rose*
45 been composed. All their poems are so clear, that there is no need to expound upon them. One has never seen such a beautiful thing revealed. They speak about everything and about all men and women. *and yet this debate* Their poems can cause great fear in many people; they spare no one, if one listens well. And to hear them, people must assemble along
50 major roads. It distresses me that their beautiful poems are getting little attention. No living man can say anything about the work *universal* except that the worldly life gets worse every day. Those who wish to speak the truth cannot deny this. The composer of the *Rose*, and the Recluse did only too well: with their poems many people have
55 gained understanding and fear; carefully and with wisdom, they criticize all groups of people. Whoever reads them frequently will derive great pleasure from them.

Dou livre dou Renclus, dou Rommant de la Rose
Onques mais en remans ne fu trouvet tel cose.
Tout leur dit sont si cler que mestier n'ont de glose;
64   Si bielle cose voir onques ne fu desclose.

Il parollent de tout et de tous et de toutes;
En leurs dis pueent prendre moult de gens des grans doubtes;
Il n'espargnent nullui, se tu bien les ascoutes;
68   Pour oïr, se doit-on assanner par grans routes.

Leurs biaus dis dont me poise, moult petit on remire,
Se ne peut homs vivans sour l'ouvrage riens dire,
Fors chou que tous les jours li siècles trop empire;
72   Nuls qui voelt dire voir, ne le puet escondire.

Li trouveur de la Rose, li Renclus trop bien fisent;
Par leur dis moult de gens sens et crémeur acquisent;
Sagement, soutieument tous les estas reprisent;
76   Grande plaisance prendent chil qui souvent les lisent.

2. Pierre Ceffons[17]

Pierre Ceffons (Petrus de Ceffons Clarevallensis), a Cistercian monk at Clair-vaux, is the only known Latin writer pre-Debate to mention the *Roman* favor-ably. Though today he and his works have been clouded by obscurity, in his time Ceffons was a well-known and renowned theologian who wrote most of his works during the second half of the fourteenth century and whose works are crucial for understanding Cistercian history. In addition, he published texts on early humanism and dabbled in the mathematical sciences. In his *Lectura super IV libros Sententiarium*, written in 1353[18]—a theological commentary on the Sentences of Lombardus—there are two references (of which I quote only one), and in the *Centilogium,*[19] one reference, to the *Roman.*[20] In the first instance Jean de Meun's text is used as an *auctoritas* for the author's use of Alain de Lille's description of Fortune; the second one praises Lucretia's steadfast defense of chastity, which is quoted on pages 26 of this chapter:

1353: Centilogium

Text:

> «Est rupes maris in medio quam verberat equor etc.». Vide ibi de Fortuna et eius domo, libro .8; et ibi videtur [sumpsisse] de dictis suis ille qui fecit opus *De Rosa*. Vide in utroque domum Fortune.

Translation:

> "There is a cliff in the middle of the sea against which the ocean lashes." See here the passage concerning Fortune and its house in book eight, and there you will see that the author who wrote the *Rose* took some of his sayings. Look at both houses of Fortune.

3. *Raoul de Presles (1315–82)*

De Presles was an advocate by profession and a contemporary of Pierre Cef-fons. Primarily a compiler, he uses the *Roman* several times as an *auctoritas* in his commentary on his translation of Augustine's *De civitate dei.* De Presles's reputation as a literary man is due principally to this translation, which was commissioned by Charles V later in the author's life. As we can discern from the autobiographical comments inserted in his work, it was only with much reticence that he tackled this laborious task, which took him four years to com-plete (1371–75).[21] In addition to the two references to the *Roman*, de Presles also includes "Mehum" [Meun] among the list of venerable authors and doc-tors, which is contained in manuscript BN fr. 22912. According to Jeanette Beer, this list of "indisputably scholarly accomplishments" was motivated by several objectives: first, it "provided public justification for the scholar-king's taste in translators. Perhaps it also served to advertise items with which Raoul's public was not particularly familiar…."[22] Once again, Jean de Meun, as was befitting the illustrious figure he had become, is mentioned in order to attest to the literary quality of de Presles's own work.

1375: Commentary on the Translation of De civitate dei[23]

In this first excerpt, it becomes apparent that clerical culture had begun to shift away from Latin *auctores* toward references to vernacular texts, which are coming to assume the same authorial credibility as their Latin predeces-sors or contemporaries. As Pierre-Yves Badel notes, "Il est intéressant de voir s'ébaucher, en cette seconde moitié du XIVᵉ siècle, un premier travail critique sur un texte vulgaire" [It is interesting to see that in this second half of the fourteenth century critical work is undertaken for the first time on a text in the vernacular].[24]

Text:
> Voye Alain en *Anticlaudiano* en son VIIIme livre duquel Maistre
> Jehan du Mehun ou livre de la rose ou chapitre de Fortune print
> son texte et sa sentence, et semble qu'il ne fist que le translater en
> ce pas. Car ou Alain dit: «Est rupis in medio maris quem verberat
> equor». Maistre Jehan du Mehun dit: «Une roche est sur la mer
> seans ice», en poursuivant le latin de Alain.

Translation:

> See Alain in the eighth book of *Anticlaudianus*, from which Mas-
> ter Jean de Meun took his text and his statement in the *Book of the
> Rose*'s chapter on Fortune. And he seems merely to have translated
> Alain at this juncture. For where Alain says, "Est rupis in medio
> maris quem verberat equor," Master Jean de Meun says, "Une roche
> est sur la mer seans ice," [There is a rock in the sea] following
> Alain's Latin.[25] Jean de Meun borrows this commonplace metaphor
> for Fortune's fickleness from Alain de Lille's *Anticlaudianus*.

1375: Commentary on the Translation of De civitate dei[26]

The following excerpt is part of a long exposition on the *Cité de Dieu* (IV,10), wherein de Presles explains the identity of Saturn:

Text:

        Et pour ce aucuns si l'appellent froit pour ce seulement qu'il nuist aux creatures humaines et aux biens terriens; et ce mot appellé froit qui est dist pour nuisant n'est pas mot nouvel ne nouvele inter-pretacion, quar de ce en [a en] exemple [en] Virgille qui dit: "Frigi-

5   dus, o pueri, fugite hinc, latet anguis in herba," lequel ver expose notablement et declaire maistre Jehan de Meun en son livre qu'il fist *De la Rose* ou chappitre du Jaloux ou il dit:

       Enffans qui cuilliés les flourettes
       Et les freses fresches et nettes,

10   Le froit serpent qui gist soubz l'erbe
       Fuiés, enffans, quar il enherbe
       Et emprisonne *(sic)* et envenime
       Toute rien qui de lui s'aprime etc.
         Encore n'est il pas figuré sans cause ancient….

Translation:

    And for this reason some define "cold" as merely harming human beings and earthly goods. And this word *cold*, which is said to be harmful, is neither a new word nor a new interpretation, since we have an example of it in Virgil: Frigidus, o pueri, fugite hinc,
5   latet anguis in herba, clearly exposing a serpent, and Master Jean de Meun proclaims in his book *Of the Rose* which he wrote, in the chapter of the Jealous Husband:

    Children who pick flowers
    And fresh, clean strawberries,
10   The cold serpent which lies beneath the grass
    Flee, children, for it enthralls
    And emprisons and poisons
    All that comes near, etc.
        Again, this is not evoked without an old meaning….

C. The Debate about the Mendicants

As E. Jeffrey Richards points out in the Introduction, academic heresy was a topic with which many a cleric or learned man was preoccupied in thirteenth-century Europe. Numerous texts and teachings fell victim to accusations, as shown by the example of Bishop Tempier's condemnations. Yet Jean de Meun's highly controversial continuation of the *Roman de la rose* escaped this fate, and it was not publicly criticized until the beginning of the fifteenth century. Even during the Quarrel, however, the text and its dead author were never publicly chastised. It is my view, as we have demonstrated above, that in order to shed some light on the reception of this popular work by the university community we must turn to the diatribe on mendicancy and lay piety of the ambiguous allegory, False Seeming. The vivacious interest in the "chapter" of False Seeming is evidenced by the numerous modifications of it by scribes, who as early as the end of thirteenth century added passages of up to one hundred lines in as many as sixty manuscripts, and who in one manuscript went so far as to insert a warning that not everyone should read this passage. It is obvious from these modifications that the *Roman* was also used as a weapon against the mendicants.[27] Evidently, then, there was a monastic effort to censure this portion of the *Roman*, though at the same time with a sort of connivance due to the unfaltering popularity of the work in clerical circles. As an example of the kind of commentary the passage of False Seeming provoked in the fourteenth century, I will cite two of the *Roman*'s great admirers, Philippe de Mézières and Jean le Fèvre.

1. Philippe de Mézières (1327–1405)

A contemporary of Raoul de Presles, Pierre Ceffons, and Eustache Deschamps, Philippe de Mézières's culture was, as pointed out by Pierre-Yves Badel, "celle des hommes de la génération de Charles V et des traducteurs royaux: passion pour l'histoire, la morale et, surtout, la morale politique" [that of the men of Charles V's generation and of the royal translators: with a passion for history, morals, and above all political morals].[28] De Mézières's most widely circulated work, *Le songe du Vieil Pèlerin* clearly reflects the author's political involvement and his hope for reform, since the date of publication coincides with the coming of age of Charles VI in 1389. At the same time, de Mézières actively participated in the ongoing debate at the University of Paris on the role of the mendicants and the semireligious, in particular the Beguines and the Beghards, as did many writers of his time, such as Gilles li Muisis, for example.[29] His cautious accusation of the mendicants' hypocrisy is the subject of the following excerpt.

1389: Le songe du vieil pèlerin[30]

Text:

Cy parle la chambriere des contrayres aus fins besans des mendians

«Et quant aux contrayres», dist la chambriere, «des fins besans de l'ordre des quatre mendians, bonne est leur doctrine publique, par laquelle il se puet dire un grant temps vrayment que es temps passez ilz ont la foy soustenue, par leur predication encontre

5   les hereses, et vaillamment defendue. Mais a present de leur secrete pratique et arquemie oultrageuse en admiracion de toutes autres arquemies, pour abregier ma relacion», dist la chambriere, «je m'en atens a la confession de leurs filles espirituelles et a l'opinion de l'Universite de Paris, qui cognoist bien les besans des mendiens, et

10   des mors et des vifz. Et qui vouldra plus a plain savoir des contraires des dessusdiz mendians, non pas des preudommes mais des forgeans foible monnoye en la nef, la ou l'en crye Mont Joye d'un a ung, si lise le romant de maistre Jehan de Meun; et la trouvera par maniere d'une estrange tragedie une riche et soutille arquemie, qui

15   ne s'acorde pas bien a la forge de ma maistresse Verite la royne. Quel merveille, car elle ne pourroit estre son amye. Et qui vouldra plus espicialment cognoistre la monnoye qui se forge en ceste premiere gerarchie, si lise le livre de saint Bernard de sa contemplacion, qu'il fait au pape Eugene. Et ce souffise assez brefment», dist

20   la chambriere, «des contraires de la premiere gerarchie du royaume de France, c'est assavoir de l'eglise, de laquelle il fault sobrement parler, pour reverence des personnes sacrees qui sont ou devroient estre vray mirouer reluisant comme jadis ilz estoient des troys gerarchies de la belle nef francoise, Souveraine appellee».

Translation:

        Here the lady in waiting speaks about the reprisal for the fine gold coins of the mendicants

        "And as to the reprisal," says the lady in waiting, "for the fine gold coins of the order of the four mendicants, their official doctrine is good, which can be said to reflect a great era in the past when they upheld and valliantly defended their faith with their predica-

5   tions against heresies. But at present, for their secret pratice and outrageous alchemy in admiration of all other alchemies, to shorten my account," said the lady in waiting, "I will defer to the confession of their spiritual daughter and to the opinion of the University of Paris, who knows well the gold of the mendicants, dead or alive.

10   And whoever would like to know more about the reprisal of the above-mentioned mendicants—not the noble men but the forgers of weak money in the nave, the place where one cries Mont Joie from one to the next—ought to read the romance by Master Jean de Meun. There he will find, by way of a strange tragedy, a rich and

15   subtle alchemy[31] which does not conform well to the forge of my mistress Truth, the queen. What a surprise, for she could not be his friend. And whoever would like to gain detailed knowledge about the money forged in the first hierarchy ought to read the book of contemplation by Saint Bernard, written for Pope Eugene. This is

20   enough," said the lady in waiting, "about the reprisals by the first hierarchy of the kingdom of France, namely the Church, of which one must speak modestly out of reverence for the holy people, who are or should be a true, bright mirror, as they were in former times of the three hierarchies of the beautiful French nave, called the

25   Sovereign."

2. Jean le Fèvre (ca. 1320–ca.1390)

The *Liber Lamentationum*, by Matheolus, the unhappily married and "biga-mous"[32] cleric from Boulogne-sur-Mer, was written at the latest in 1290.[33] Its immediate and long-lasting success persuaded Jean le Fèvre to undertake a translation into French, adding to the longstanding tradition of antinuptial discourse in the French clerical circles of the High and late Middle Ages.[34] In the passage below, Le Fèvre closely translates Matheolus's comments on hypocrisy and the sin of lechery committed by the Beguines:

1380–87: Les lamentations de Mathéole[35]

Text:

> Au jour d'hui soubs turlupinage
> Trouveroit on en tapinage
> Envie, dol, ipocrisie,
> 4   Pensée par fraude brisie,
> Especialment es beguines.
> D'ardoir ou deu d'amours sont dignes,
> Car il n'est si jolie chose,
> 8   Quant leur burlette est bien desclose
> Et elles sont bien a droit pointes
> Et dessoubs large robe jointes.
> Plus sont simples et precieuses,
> 12   Et tant plus sont luxurieuses.
> Elles font le catimini;
> Mais, par le verbo Domini!
> Elles cuevrent leur ribauldie
> 16   Du mantel de papelardie....
> Il a de bons estudians
> Es religions mendians.
> 20   Ja soit ce qu'aucunes gens dient,
> Qu'a leur seul proufit estudient,
> Je considere qu'il sont hommes
> Naturels, aussi que nous sommes.
> 24   Pour ce n'ay voulenté de mordre
> Sur les freres ne sur leur ordre.
> Pour briefté atant m'en delivre,
> Combien que Mahieu, en son livre,
> 28   En ait assés versifié
> Et leurs meurs diversifié.
> Si fist maistre Jehan de Meun;
> Tous les reproucha un et un,
> 32   Ou chapitre de Faulx Semblant.
> Je m'en tais, si m'en vois amblant
> Le chemin que j'ay commencié....

Translation:

> It seems that today under the Turlupines's disguise one finds
> envy, deceit, hypocrisy, and corrupt thought, especially among the
> Beguines. They are worthy of love's flames and affliction, for there
> is no prettier sight than when their heads are entirely uncovered,
5   and they are slender and pretty under their large dresses. They are
> as naive and dear as they are lascivious. They play hide-and-seek.
> And upon the Lord's word! They cover their ribaldry with the cloak
> of false devotion.... There are good students amidst the mendicants.
> Although some say that they study only to their own advantage. I
10   deem them to be Nature's men, just as we are. For this reason I do
> not wish to bite the friars, nor their orders. For brevity's sake, I will
> refer to Matheolus, who in his book spoke about this in rhyme, and
> detailed their customs, as did Master Jean de Meun. He criticized
> them one by one in the chapter of False Seeming. I will be silent
15   and depart hurriedly down the path on which I was engaged....

D. Antifeminism and the Jealous Husband

No other passage has retained the reader's attention and contributed to the success of the *Roman* as extensively as the speech of the Jealous Husband. The following texts are some examples attesting to its popularity.

1. Pierre Ceffons

In *Lectura super IV libros sententiarium*, Pierre Ceffons includes a brief summary of the *exemplum* of Lucretia, making reference to the lively antifeminist debate of the previous years.

1353: Lectura Super IV Libros Sententiarium[36]

Text:

>   De quo dicitur in opere *De Rosa*:
>   «Si n'est mais nulle Lucrece
>   Ne nulle Penelope en Grece,
> 4   Prude fame par saint Denis,
>   Don il est moins que de fenis».[37]
>   Et idem:
>   «Toutes estes, sereiz» etc.[38]

Translation:

>   As is stated in the work *Of the Rose*:
>   "There is no Lucretia, no Penelope in Greece; a noblewoman,
>   by Saint Denis, is rarer than a phoenix."
>   And:
> 5   "You women are all, will be…" etc.

2. Matheolus (ca. 1295–?) and Jean le Fèvre

Although Matheolus does not explicitly mention the *Roman de la rose* in his monumental tirade against women and the state of marriage, the *Liber Lamentationum*, the points of connection are all too evident, notably to the *Roman*'s passage of the Jealous Husband. Jean le Fèvre's translation of the *Lamentations de Mathéole* and the subsequent "refutation"[39] of his misogynist views in the *Livre de Leesce*[40] are an integral part of the ongoing *querelle des femmes*[41] to which Christine de Pizan reacts in the incipit of the *Livre de la cité des dames*. Lady Reason takes it upon herself to interpret Matheolus's misogynist and antimarriage tirade in book 1, chapter 2 of the *Cité*.[42]

3. Philippe de Mézières

In his *Livre de la vertu du sacrement de mariage*,[43] Philippe de Mézières mentions the *Roman* three times, discussing marriage and how to cure the husband who has gotten caught in its trap. The author admits to never having been married himself (fol. 90v° of the manuscript), yet undertakes the composition of this didactic treatise on marriage for married women. I will include two of the three references to the *Roman*:

*Le prologue tierch livre du Livre de la vertu du sacrement de mariage et du
reconfort des dames mariees*

Text:

        Cy commence la tierce face du miroir ou prologue proposé, c'est
le tierch livre du sacrement de mariage entre l'omme et la femme
et du confort des dames mariees, malcontentes et bien contentes. Et
premierement un prologue:…

5   Encores est assavoir que, [pour] aucune introduction du
reconfort des dames mariees et des seigneurs aussy, que estre
malcontent de son mariage n'est autre chose que une fievre continue et douloureuse passion qui aucunefois vault pis et fait plus
de mal que passion colique. Ce scevent ceulx [et celles] que Dieu
10   veuille conforter. Ceste passion est engendree d'umours corrumpus
coleriques, fleumatiques, melencoliques et habondance de sang
corrumpu, et aucunefois la passion vient par accident et dehors le
corps dont mains maulx en avient. Pour reconforter donques les
mariés et tous Crestiens qui seront passionnés d'aucune maladie,
15   cestui viel solitaire qui jusques cy a esté lapidaire et de son petit
pouoir a presenté les pierres precieuses de sa petite mercerie, pour
l'amour de Dieu et de son proisme par la bonté de Dieu devendra
phisicien et presentera aus dames mariees et a tous bons Crestiens
qui ne sont pas sains et averont passion .vij. manieres de medicines,
20   c'est assavoir: medicine preparative, linitive, purgative, confortative,
preservative, nutritive et vivificative. Et ne s'esmerveille nulz de
tant de medicines, car toutes sont necessaires a personnes qui sont
fort passionees et par especial ou fort loyen de mariage, duquel lyen
maistre Jehan de Meum en personne des maulx contens disoit ainsy,
25   «Ainsy m'aist saint Julien,/que mariage est mal lyen». Telx gens ont
bien mestier de reconfort qui sont plongié en desconfort.

Translation:

> Here begins the third side of the mirror or the proposed prologue, which is the third book of the sacrament of marriage between man and woman, and is for the comfort of married ladies, discontented and contented alike. First, a prologue:…

5 >   Further, it is important to know, as an introduction to the subject of helping married ladies and gentlemen, that dissatisfaction in marriage is nothing other than a continuous fever and a painful disease, no worse and no less painful than colic. The men and women whom God wishes to comfort know this. This passion is en-

10 > gendered by corrupt choleric, flegmatic, melancholic humors and by an abundance of corrupt blood, and sometimes this disease occurs by accident and comes from outside of the body, from which many evils stem. Thus, in order to comfort married people and all Christians who are assailed by some illness, this solitary old man—who

15 > up to now has been a stone cutter and whose modest power has been represented by the precious stones of his small workshop—will become a physician, and will present seven medical strategies to married ladies and to all good Christians who are not in good health and who suffer from disease; he will do so for the love of

20 > God and for the admiration of God's goodness: preparative, soothing, purgative, stimulating, preservative, nutritive, and energizing. And no one ought to be astonished that there are so many cures, for they are all necessary for people who are very ill, especially those within the strong bondage of marriage, of which Jean de Meun said,

25 > in the person of the unhappy man, "Thus Saint Julian put it to me that marriage is an evil bondage."[44] Those people are in dire need of help, who have fallen into desolation.

Le ve chapitre[45]

Although Philip de Mézières seemingly contradicts the misogynist views of the Jealous Husband in this passage, his *apologia* reminds us of the same literary strategy employed by Jean de Meun's narrator in the epic apology in his continuation of the *Roman*.

Text:

De .vij. manieres de fievres en especial dont les dames mariees malcontes souventefois sont tourmentees et les maris aussy, pour ce qu'il ont faulsé leur mariage…

5   O quelz traisons et orribles fais ont esté traitié et fais en ceste male guerre privee, dont mainte ame a esté dampnee, maint royaume perdu, maint preudomme mort par poisons et de glaive et mainte preudefemme estranglee, et tout pour l'appetit desordené, courous desmesuré, propre volenté desordenee et principaument la faulse jalousie enracinee, de laquelle le Jalous ou Livre de la Rose fort se

10   doloit et les passions d'icelle clerement demonstroit s'amie qu'il menti faulsement quant il parla outrageusement des sainctes dames mariees en diffamant leurs denrees, disant le faulz Jalous, «Toutes estes seres et fustes», *et cetera.* Ce fu mal dit, car il bourda. Mainte et maintes dames mariees ont esté, sont et seront qui leur mar-

15   iage ont gardé chastement, gardent et garderont, et mainte vierge, [vesves] et pucelle devant Dieu se trouvera nette et belle. Retournant donques au propos, les dessusdictes fievres .vij. et les .vij. maladies et orribles passions des malcontents de leur mariage avienent pour les transgressions des mariés qu'i font principaument contre leur

20   vray Espoulz immortel, dont les rebondes avienent a l'espouse mortele et au mari mortel.

Translation:

Of seven different fevers by which, in particular, dissatisfied married ladies are often tormented, as are their husbands, for having betrayed their marriage....

5   Oh, what treason and horrible deeds have been done in this evil private war in which many a soul has been damned, many a kingdom lost, many a nobleman killed by poison and by sword, and many a noblewoman strangled—and all this for inordinate appetite, exaggerated anger, one's own inordinate will, and, principally, ingrained false jealousy, about which the Jealous Husband in the

10   Book of the Rose cries bitterly, and the passions of which he has clearly demonstrated to his friend, to whom he lied gravely when he spoke outrageously of holy married women defaming their worth. The false Jealous Husband says about women, "You all are, will be, and were..." etc.[46] This was badly stated, for he lied. There are and

15   will be many married women who keep their marriage chaste, they do so now and will continue to do so, and there are many virgins, widows, and maidens who will arrive pure and beautiful before God. To return to our topic, then, the above-mentioned seven fevers and seven illnesses and horrible passions of those who are dissatis-

20   fied in their marriage occur because of the transgressions of their spouses, who act principally against their true, immortal Husband; the consequences of this reverberate upon the mortal wife and the mortal husband.

4. Le Mesnagier de Paris (anonymous; ca. 1393)

A rich bourgeois householder wrote this treatise on the management of the household and on female virtue and duty, for his much younger wife. Consisting of three books with topics ranging from how to treat servants to how to effectively expunge fleas from the home and clothes, and from recipes for Christian morality, the *Mesnagier* offers rich findings on fourteenth-century bourgeois living in Paris. The anonymous author refers to the *Roman* in the context of instructing his wife on female chastity. One cannot help but wonder why he mentions such a controversial book as possible reading material for his young wife, a question which no doubt would have entered Christine de Pizan's mind.[47]

Text: [48]

Modèles de chasteté féminine

20. Adont Brut le conseillier et Colatin le mary d'icelle Lucresse, et tous ses amis, plourans et doulans, prindrent celle espee qui estoit sanglante, et sur le sanc jurerent par le sanc Lucresse que jamaiz ne fineroient jusques atant qu'ilz avroient Tarquin et son filz destruit; et
5   le poursuivront a feu et a sanc et a toute sa lignee boutee hors, si que jamaiz nul n'en vendra a dignité.
21. Et tout ce fut tantost fait; car ilz la porterent enmy la ville de Romme et esmeurent tellement le peuple que chascun jura la destruction de l'empereur Tarquin et de son filz, et a feu et a sang.
10   Et adonc fermerent les portes afin que nul n'issist pour aller adviser l'emprereur de leur emprise, et s'armerent et yssirent deshors, alant vers l'ost de l'empereur comme tous forcenez. Et quant ilz approcherent de l'empereur et il ouy le bruit et tumulcte et vit les gens, pouldres, et fumees des chevaulx, avec ce que l'en lui dist, il et son
15   filz s'enfuirent en desertz, chetifz et desconfortez.
22. Sur quoy le *Rommant de la Rose* dist ainsi: «N'onc puis Rommains pour ce desroy/Ne vouldrent faire a Romme roy».
23. Ainsi avez vous deux examples, l'un de garder honnestement son vesvaige ou sa virginité ou pucellaige, l'autre de garder son
20   mariaige ou chasteté. En saichiez que richesse, beaulté de corps et de viaire, lignaige et toutes les autres vertus sont peries et anichillees en femme qui a taiche ou souspeçon contre l'une d'icelles vertus. Certes, en ces cas tout est pery et effacié, tout est cheu sans jamais relever, puis que une seule foiz femme est souspeçonnee ou
25   renommee au contraire. Et encore supposé que la renommee soit a tort, si ne peut jamais icelle renommee estre effacee. Et veez en quel peril perpetuel une femme met son honneur et l'onneur du lignaige de son mary et de ses enfants quant elle n'eschieve le parler de tel blasme, ce qui est legier a faire

Translation: [49]

Models of Female Chastity

Then Brutus the counselor and Collatine, the husband of this same Lucretia, and all her friends, weeping and mourning, took the sword, all stained with blood, and swore upon the blood of Lucretia that they would never rest until they had destroyed Tarquin and his
5   son, and pursued him with fire and bloodshed, and cast forth all his race, so that none henceforth might rise to any honor. They moved quickly to make true on their resolution, for they carried her body through the town of Rome, and thereby moved the people so that each man swore to destroy the Emperor Tarquin and his son by fire
10   and by bloodshed. Then they shut the gates that none might go forth to warn the emperor of their intent, and they armed themselves and sallied forth, hurrying like mad folk to the place where the emperor's army lay. And when they drew near to the emperor and he heard the noise and the tumult and saw the people covered with dust, and
15   saw the smoke of the horses, and heard what people told him, then he and his son fled, fearful and in disarray. About which the *Romance of the Rose* says, "After this trouble, the Romans never again wanted to crown a king in Rome."[50]
       Here, then, are two examples: one, maintaining the honor
20   of one's widowhood, virginity, or maidenhood; the other, keeping chastity in marriage. And know that riches, beauty of body and face, lineage, and all other qualities are destroyed in a woman who is tarnished or who raises suspicion with regard to one of the aforementioned virtues. In such a case, all is irrevocably lost, and she will
25   fall, never to rise again: for it suffices a woman to attract suspicion only once to create a bad reputation. And even supposing that she was suspected wrongly, never can this ill reputation be wiped away. See, then, in what unending danger a woman places her honor, and the honor of her husband's line and that of her children, when she
30   does not succeed in preventing others from spreading such blame about her, which is so easy to do.

E. The Early Opponents

The large number of extant manuscripts dating from the fourteenth century attests to the great popularity of the *Roman de la rose* during the first hundred years after its composition. Most saw the text as a masterpiece of rhetorical and allegorical achievment, and if they had critical comments to make about the content of Jean de Meun's continuation, these were rarely voiced. The reception of the work seemed overwhelmingly positive and enthusiastic, and, as we have seen, the work quickly rose to the status of authorial text for other learnèd writers. At least two dissenting voices can be heard, however:

1. Guillaume de Digulleville (1295–1358)

Guillaume de Digulleville lived as a Cistercian monk in the abbey of Chaalis, Ile-de-France, from 1326 until his death. Joan B. Williamson describes his literary activity: "He is known for his dream-allegory moral poems. Inspired by Jean de Meun's *Roman de la rose* and perhaps by other allegories, he created a trilogy on the Pilgrimage of Life theme, in which divine grace, nature, and the virtues and vices are personified."[51] More than an inspiration, the *Roman* seems to have been at the root of the genesis of de Digulleville's trilogy.[52] In fact, the scribes of manuscript Arras 845 feel the need to point out the intertexual link between the two works: «Chi s'ensieut li *Pelerinages*, qui est uns biaux miroirs de sauvement, et le compila uns grans clers en divinité, moines de l'abbie de Chaalis. Et est fais par poeterie, comme li *Livres de le Roze*, qui est en grant partie de philozofie, mes cilz pelerinages est de theologie» [Here follow the *Pèlerinages*, a beautiful mirror for salvation, compiled by a great cleric in divinity, a monk of the abbey of Chaalis. It is composed in poetic form, like the *Book of the Rose*, which is to a large extent a book of philosophy; this pilgrimage, however, is one of theology].[53] The three works are the *Pèlerinage de vie humaine* (1330–31), followed by a retraction of his praise of the *Roman* in a second version (1355). In his revision he omits the verses which attest to his reading of the *Roman* where he applauds the obscene use of the metaphor of the pilgrim. To preclude any further criticism directed at him he makes sure to defend himself against accusations of having praised Jean de Meun and his work. This is followed, between 1355 and 1358, by the *Pèlerinage de l'âme*. The excerpts here attest to the author's initial admiration of the *Roman* and to his subsequent refutation of the work.

1350: Pèlerinage de vie humaine[54]

Text:

>   Une vision veul nuncier
>   Qui en dormant m'avint l'autrier.
>   En veillant avoie leü,
> 4 Consideré et bien veü
>   Le biaus *Roumans de la Rose.*
>   Bien croi que ce fu la chose
>   Qui plus m'esmut a ce songier
> 8 Que ci aprés vous veuil nuncier.

Translation:

>   I wish to tell you of a vision which came to me in my sleep
>   the day before yesterday. When I was awake, I had read, consid-
>   ered, and examined well the beautiful *Roman de la rose.* I strongly
>   believe that this was in fact what led me to this dream, which I wish
>   to recount to you below.

1350: Pèlerinage de vie humaine

In the following excerpt, Reason laments her fate and reminds the reader of the way she was treated in the *Roman de la rose.*

Text:

>   Amour charnel (tout) hors m'enchace
>   Et me fait (tost) vuidier la place;
>   Ce verrez vous tout sans glose
> 4 Ou *Rommans* qui est *de la Rose.*

Translation:

>   Carnal love has chased me away, and has led me to vacate my
>   dwelling. This you will see without elaboration in the *Roman* which
>   is *Of the Rose.*

1355: Pèlerinage de vie humaine[55]

The following excerpt is from the second *Pèlerinage,* dated 1355, which according to Edmond Faral enjoyed considerably less popularity than the first
one.[56] The lines at the beginning of the first excerpt, where the narrator traces
his dream back to his reading of the *Roman,* have been omitted in this revised
version of the *Pèlerinage.* Moreover, here Venus is depicted as the primordial
sin from which the pilgrim must protect himself. In contrast to the first version, where Venus complains about the chastity of people of the Church, in

the revision it is precisely this statement which is maligned, through the voice of the allegory herself. Venus finds herself here in dialogue with the narrator, the pilgrim.

Text:

```
         [Q]uant sçay que en nul jour
         Je ne pourroie avoir s'amour,
         (c.à.d. l'amitié de Chasteté)
4        Je mesdi de li bien souvent
         Et faiz mesdire par ma gent,
         Si com il appert sens glose
         En mon Romans dit [de] la Rose,
8        Ou Faus Semblant le fais nommer
         Pas mon notaire et appeler;
         Et la cause est car approchier
         Ne me laisse a lui ne touchier.
12       Pourquoi, dis je, dis estre tien
         Le romans qu'as dit? Que scay bien
         Qui le fist et comment eut nom.
         Du dire, dist elle, ai raison.
16       Quar je le fis et il est mien,
         Et ce puis je prouver très bien,
         Car du premier jucques au bout
         Sans discontinuer par tout
20       Il n'y a fors de moi parlé,
         Ce tant seulement excepté
         Que mon clerc escrivain embla
         Et en estranges champs soia,
24       De quoi maintes gens ont cuidié
         Que en sa terre l'eust soié;
         Mes non fist, ains partie grant
         Il en embla en autrui champ;
28       Dont il avint que, quant il soioit
         Et que en un sac tout boutoit
         Pour ce qu'il le vouloit celer
         Et droit n'avoit de l'emporter,
32       D'un Normant haut escrié fu,
         Qui de loing l'avoit apparceu:
         «Ha, dist il, n'est pas raison
         De faire fais d'autrui moisson»!
36       Celui tantost s'en affui,
```

Translation:

> "[W]hen I know I will never have her [Chastity's] love, I
> speak ill of it quite often, and have my people do the same, as is the
> case, without going into detail, in my *Romance of the Rose*, where
> False Seeming names it through my scribe. The reason is that I am
>
> 5   not allowed to either approach or touch her." "Why," I say, "do you
> say that this romance is yours when you know full well who wrote
> it and what his name is. I am right in saying this, I say, because I
> created it and it is mine, and I can prove this very well, for from
> beginning to end it speaks about me, so much so that my cleric
>
> 10   writer left and scythed in foreign fields, which led many people to
> believe that he had scythed on his own land. This was not so, but
> for the most part he went off to someone else's field. And he stuffed
> everything into a bag, because he wanted to hide it but did not have
> the right to take it away. He was uncovered by a Norman who yelled
>
> 15   loudly after having perceived him from afar: 'Ha, he said, it is not
> right to collect someone else's harvest!' The former fled instantly,
> but was so stupefied that he did not take along the crook. He spoiled
> my romance, which displeases me greatly, for I did not want him
> in it except to write about me. As I had told him, he was to write
>
> 20   something of his own. Because he had been decried for having fled,
> he never liked Normans, which he showed in the romance in saying
> that Evil Mouth had fled from Normandy. He lied about that, as he
> did when he maligned the religious in my favor for hating Chastity
> and chasing her everywhere." I said: "You and your writer, you are
>
> 25   full of evil, for he who bad mouths another does not have a good
> mouth."

?

Mes pas ne fu tant esbay
Que le larrecin n'aportast
Et en mon romans ne l'entast,
40   Laquel chose moult me desplut,
Car je vousisse que n'eüst
Fors seulement de moi escript,
Si com je li avoie dit,
44   Ou, au moins, qu'i n'y eüst rien
Mis, fors tant seulement du sien.
Or fu, pour ce que escrié
Fu de ce qu'il avoit emblé,
48   Onques puis Normant il n'ama,
Si com ou roumans moustra,
Disant que de Normandie
Estoit Male Bouche affuie;
52   Dont il menti aussi com fist
Quant des religieux mesdist
A ma faveur, pour ce que hé
Et parsui partout Chasteté.
56   Toi donc, dis [je], et ton escrivain
Estes de grant mauvestié plain;
Car, quicunques d'autrui mesdit,
Bonne bouche n'a pas, ce cuit.

2. The Song of Songs

The second opponent is the anonymous author of a commentary and translation of the *Song of Songs*, dating from the end of the thirteenth or the beginning of the fourteenth century:

Commentary on the Song of Songs [57]

Text:

> [Car] rimer wel, douce pucelle
> En cui mes cuers est et repose,
> Pour vostre amour rime novelle
4 > Tele com mes cuers le propose:
> P[lu]s plaisans assés et plus belle
> Et plus vraie, bien dire l'ose,
> Et plus honeste que n'est celle
8 > Dou *Roumant* c'on dist [*de*] *la Rose*.

Translation:

> In order to rhyme well, sweet maiden in whom my heart rests, for your love rhymes anew, as my heart suggests: more pleasant and more beautiful and more true, I dare say, and more honest than that of the *Roman* called *Of the Rose*.

Notes

1. My selection of authors who have commented on Jean de Meun's section of the *Roman de la rose* is largely based on Pierre-Yves Badel's outstanding scholarly work, *Le roman de la rose au XIVe siècle. Etude de la réception de l'œuvre* (Geneva: Droz, 1980). I thank the Editions Droz for granting me permission to reproduce the excerpts. All translations are my own unless otherwise stated.

2. For precise examples of the textual proximity between the *Echecs amoureux* and the *Roman de la rose*, I refer to the critical edition by Christine Kraft, *Die Liebesgarten-Allegorie der 'Echecs amoureux'* (Frankfurt/Main: Peter Lang, 1977).

3. For a discussion of the nature of the rewriting, I refer to Lori Walters's article, "Gui de Mori's Rewriting of Faux Semblant in the Tournai *Roman de la Rose*," in *The Medieval Opus: Imitation, Rewriting, and Transmission in the French Tradition*, ed. Douglas Kelly (Amsterdam: Rodopi, 1996), 261–76; and Lori Walters, "Illuminating the Rose: Gui de Mori and the Illustrations of MS 101 of the Municipal Library, Tournai," in *Rethinking the Romance of the Rose: Text, Image, Reception*, ed. Kevin Brownlee and Sylvia Huot (Philadelphia: University of Pennsylvania Press, 1992), 167–200.

4. Introduction, 9.

5. Petrarch, *Seniles* 9.1.

6. To remind the reader, I use the phrase "debate about the *Roman de la rose*" in its widest sense, comprising the ongoing discussion of Jean de Meun's work from Petrarch (1340) to Laurent de Premierfait's *De casibus virorum illustrium* in 1409 and Christine de Pizan's remarks in the *Livre de fais d'armes et de chevalerie* in 1410. To distinguish between the larger debate and the actual Debate epistles I will refer to the latter as either "Debate Epistles," "Quarrel," or "Debate."

7. In Domenico Rossetti, ed., *Poesi minori del Petrarca* (Milan, 1831), 2:342–45. Also quoted by Ernest Langlois in *Les manuscrits du Roman de la rose, Description et Classement* (Geneva: Slatkine Reprints, 1974), 203. Translation by Earl Jeffrey Richards in *Dante and the Roman de la rose* (Tübingen: Niemeyer, 1981), 62.

8. For further biographical details and a succinct analysis of his works, see Langlois, *La vie en France au moyen âge. De la fin du XIIe au milieu du XIVe siècle d'après des moralistes du temps* (Geneva: Slatkine Reprints, 1970), chap. 5, 2:321–73.

9. Kervyn de Lettenhove, ed. *Poésies de Gilles li Muisis*, 2 vols. (Louvain, Belgium: Lefever, 1882). This edition proves to be mediocre, as pointed out by Langlois (chap. 5, 2:322) and P.-Y. Badel (1980, n. 52, 74). Unfortunately, it is the only one available of the single extant manuscript, which is owned by a private collector. See Langlois, chap 5, n. 4, 322.

10. Chap. 3.7, 148 and 149.

11. For the third reference to the *Roman de la rose*, I refer to de Lettenhove's edition, 1:114–15.

12. Ibid. 1:84–94.

13. Although in the introduction to his edition de Lettenhove attributes this intertextual reference to Guillaume de Lorris's portion of the *Roman de la rose*, there is no explicit indication that would limit it only to this part of the work (1:11).

14. Gilles li Muisis mentions the Reclus de Molliens (early thirteenth century) several times in his poetry, usually alongside the *Roman de la rose*, as an incontestable authority on Christian morality. The Reclus de Molliens has been identified as Barthelemy, a monk of the abbey of Saint-Fuscien-au-Bois who went into seclusion at the church of Sainte-Marie de Molliens-Vidame. He composed two didactic poems, the *Roman de carité* and *Miserere*. As Roberta Krueger points out: "Skillful allegorization, alliteration, assonance, and word play enliven the Reclus de Molliens's stern condemnation of human foibles"; "Reclus de Molliens," in William W. Kibler and Grover A. Zinn, eds., *Medieval France. An Encyclopaedia* (New York: Garland, 1995) 784.

15. This passage is followed by a laudatory list praising the literary accomplishments of lay and religious authors such as the friar minor Bochet, as well as Guillaume de Machaut, Jacques de

Vitri, Jehan de le Mote, and Collart Haubiert. It is interesting to note that once again the *Roman de la rose* is mentioned alongside or rather followed by the verses of the Hermit.

16. De Kettenhove, 1:353–57.

17. For more detailed information on the author, I refer to D. Trapp, "Peter Ceffons of Clairvaux." *Recherches de théologie ancienne et médiévale* 24 (1957): 101–54 ; and to Badel, 1980, 165–72.

18. To my knowledge, this text has not yet been edited, and is available only in manuscript form (MS Troyes BM 62).

19. This text can be found in MS Troyes BM 859, fols 1ro–58vo and MS Troyes BM 930, fols 17ro–67ro.

20. The excerpts are quoted in Badel, 1980, 170–71.

21. For more biographical information I refer to Robert Bossuat, "Raoul de Presles" In *Histoire littéraire de la France* (Paris: Imprimerie nationale, 1973), 40:1–16.

22. "Patronage and the Translator: Raoul de Presles's *La cité de Dieu* and Calvin's *Institution de la religion Chrestienne* and *Institutio religionis Christianae*," in *Translation and Transmission of Culture between 1300 and 1600,* ed. Jeanette Beer and Kenneth Lloyd-Jones (Kalamazoo, MI: Medieval Institute Publications, 1995), 91–142;99.

23. P.-Y. Badel mentions manuscripts BN fr. 20105, 20106, and 22912. The latter served as source text for the transcription of folios 3ro to 5vo by Jeanette Beer in her article "Patronage and the Translator." She checked this manuscript against the later one at the British Library, RO17Fiii. Until now the only edited version available has been that of Le Comte A. De Laborde in vol. 1 of *Les manuscrits à peintures de la Cité de Dieu de Saint Augustin*, 3 vols. (Paris: Rahir, 1909), which, according to Beer, contains many mistakes (133). More recently, portions of BN fr. 221912, fols 3vo–4ro were transcribed by William Hinkle in an appendix—*The fleurs de lis of the Kings of France, 1283–1488* (Carbondale: Southern Illinois University Press), 162–65—unfortunately also full of inaccuracies and an incomplete transcription. As an appendix to her article, Beer provides a transcription of folios 3ro to 5vo. The first reference to the Roman is quoted in the original and in translation in the article (96–97), which I have reproduced here with slight modifications in the translation. For a succinct summary of Raoul de Presles's activities as a translator, I refer to Léopold Delisle, *Recherches sur la librairie de Charles V, Roi de France, 1337–1380. Partie II: Inventaire général des livres ayant appartenu aux Rois Charles V et Charles VI et à Jean, Duc de Berry* (Amsterdam: van Heusden, 1967), 107–114. In addition, I refer to the following works for further information about the author and analyses of his translation: vol. 1, chaps. 3 and 4 of *Les manuscrits à peintures* titled "Raoul de Praelles et sa famille" and "Traduction et Commentaires de Raoul de Praelles," respectively; Charity Cannon Willard, "Raoul de Presles's Translation of Saint Augustine's *De civitate dei,*" in *Medieval Translators and Their Craft,* ed. Jeanette Beer (Kalamazoo, MI: Medieval Institute Publications, 1989), 329–46.

24. 178 (my translation).

25. This quote refers to the following passage in the *Roman de la rose*: "Une roche est en mer seanz,/Bien parfont, el milieu leanz,/Qui sus la mer en haut se lence,/Contre cui la mers grouce et tence./Li flot la hurtent et debatent/Qui tous jours a li se combatent/Et maintes foiz tant i cotissent/Que toute en mer l'ensevelissent;/Aucune foiz se redespueille/De l'eaue qui toute la mueille/Si com li flos arrier se tire,/Donc saut en l'air et se respire" [There is a rock in the sea, deeply anchored offshore, which rises high above the sea, against which it thunders and fights. The sea hits it incessantly, and often so fiercely that it is entirely drowned. Sometimes the rock casts the water away anew, which covers it completely, and the water retreats, so that it can jump in the air to breathe]. See also the excerpt by Pierre Ceffons in this chapter, number B.2.

26. Quoted in Badel, 1980, 175.

27. See this chapter, C for the passages in question. As early as the end of the thirteenth century, up to one hundred verses were added, appearing in sixty mss (for example, in manuscript BN fr. 1569 which can be found in Ernest Langlois's edition of the *Roman de la rose* (Paris: Firmin

Didot, 1914–24), 3:311–26: after verse 11315 there is a reference to Augustine's *Des uevres des moines*, discussing the cases in which mendicancy ought to be licit. Following verse 11568, ten verses are added where False Seeming praises himself for being his followers' spiritual guidance and for having received a pontifical decree, then following verse 11902, sixteen verses are added where False Seeming praises the "fols princes" [foolish princes] who favor him and threatens those who despise him. In three manuscripts, Bruxelles BR 1101 for instance, there is a warning after verse 11222 not to read without precaution verses 11223–980 (see Langlois, 3:396).

28. Badel, 1980, 386; my translation.

29. See Langlois, *La vie en France au moyen âge*, chap. 5, 2:343–48. For a more detailed discussion of the controversy surrounding the mendicant orders, I refer to the introduction.

30. The excerpt is quoted in G. W. Coopland's edition *Le songe du vieil pelerin*, 2 vols. (Cambridge, UK: Cambridge University Press, 1969), 1:625 (book 2, chap. 166). Reprinted with the permission of Cambridge University Press.

31. The art or the science of alchemy seemed to attract much attention during the end of Middle Ages. As we have seen in the Introduction, Christine de Pizan herself refers to the alchemists when she compares the *Roman* to the *livres des arguemistes* (see Introduction, 14).

32. This adjective was coined by the ecumenical Council of Lyon, held May 1 to July 17, 1274, on the reformation of clerical customs. Thereafter, married clerics were forbidden to wed either a nonvirgin, a widow, or a prostitute. This was Mathelous's plight, of course, for he had chosen as his wife a widow by the name of Perrette or Perrenelle. This choice was met with canonical degradation and chastisement, and he was relieved of his clerical duties, rights, and privileges. See Langlois, *La vie en France au moyen âge*, chap. 5, 2:242–43, for more details of this "unfortunate" event in the author's life.

33. An excellent edition of the Latin text and its translation and of the *Livre de Leesce* was prepared by A. G. van Hamel, *Les lamentations de Matheolus et le Livre de Leesce de Jehan Le Fèvre, Edition accompagnée de l'original latin des Lamentations*, 2 vols. (Paris: Bouillon, 1892, 1905). My quotes are taken from this edition. For a detailed analysis of the *Lamentations* I refer to Langlois, *La vie en France au moyen âge*, 2:241–90. Van Hamel claims 1298 to be the date of publication of the *Liber Lamentationum*, but P.-Y. Badel confirms 1290 as the last possible publication date, based on new manuscript evidence which has surfaced since van Hamel's edition (see Badel, 1980, 178). Langlois also accepts the earlier publication date precisely because of the historical references made in the above-mentioned passage: "C'est au synode national de Paris, présidé par le légat Benoit Caëtani en 1290, qu'eut lieu la passe d'armes décisive entre les partisans et les adversaires des Mendiants sur la question des confessions...[L]e principal orateur, après l'évêque d'Amiens, fut Jacques de Boulogne, évêque de Thérouanne, le propre patron de notre Bigame.... Je pense en conséquence que les *Lamenta*, certainement écrits avant 1292, l'ont été probablement en 1290 ou très peu après, sous le coup de l'émotion produite par le synode" (n.1, 265) [It is during the national synod of Paris, chaired by the legate Benoit Caëtani in 1290, that arms were definitively raised between the partisans and the adversaries of the Mendicants on the question of confession.... The principal orator, after the Bishop of Amiens, was Jacques de Boulogne, Bishop of Thérouanne, who was the patron of our Bigamous.... I think, therefore, that the *Lamenta* were certainly written before 1292, probably in 1290 or shortly thereafter, as a result of the emotion produced by the synod] (my translation). For more information on Jean le Fèvre and his works I refer to Geneviève Hasenohr-Esnos's edition of the *Respit de la mort, Respit de la mort par Jean le Fèvre* (Paris: Picard, 1969).

34. The translation dates from between 1380 and 1387. Though mainly a literal translation, le Fèvre often adapts the original to his own views on the state of marriage and clergy.

35. Van Hamel, vol. 2, lines 1765–1801.

36. Quoted in Badel, 1980, 171.

37. The passage is actually misquoted by Ceffons, who seems to have combined two quotes. In manuscript BN fr. 1573 the passage continues after line 2 above: "Si n'est il mes nule Lucrece,/Ne Penelope nule en Grece/Ne preude fame nule en terre,/Se l'en les savoit bien requerre" [There

is no Lucretia, no Penelope in Greece, no Noblewoman on earth, and if one searched well for them.] See http://margot.uwaterloo.ca

38. One might argue here that there is no need to complete the sentence, since this couplet had probably attained the status of proverb by the time of Ceffons: "Toutes estes, serez ou fustes/De fet ou de voulente, pustes!" [You women are all, will be, or were, by act or will, sluts!].

39. According to Renate Blumenfeld-Kosinski in "Jean Le Fevre's *Livre de Leesce*: Praise or Blame of Women?" *Speculum* 69, 3 (1994): 705–25, and Karen Pratt in "The Strains of Defense: The Many Voices of Jean Lefèvre's *Livre de Leesce*," in *Gender in Debate from the Early Middle Ages to the Renaissance*, ed. Thelma S. Fenster and Clare A. Lees (New York: Palgrave, 2002), 113–34, the sincerity of his *apologia* is more than questionable. Both scholars argue that rather than refuting the misogyny he committed in translating Matheolus's *Lamentations*, he presents "a tongue-in-cheek approach" full of "male irony," as Pratt puts it (113–14).

40. According to van Hamel, the *Livre de Leesce* has survived in six manuscripts (the *Lamentations* appears in eleven; four contain both works), attesting to the widespread popularity of the author's writings.

41. For a discussion of the *querelle des femmes* in the context of Jean le Fèvre's *Livre de Leesce*, see Renate Blumenfeld-Kosinski, "Jean Le Fevre's *Livre de Leesce*," in which she includes a useful bibliography on the background information of the *querelle des femmes*; see also Karen Pratt, "The Strains of Defense." Further, though theoretically now dated, I also refer to Joan Kelly, "Early Feminist Theory and the *Querelle des femmes*, 1400–1789," in *Women, History, and Theory: The Essays of Joan Kelly*, ed. Joan Kelly (Chicago: University of Chicago Press, 1984), 65–109.

42. For the exact passage and its translation, see chap 5.2.

43. I quote from the edition *Le livre de la vertu du sacrement de mariage* by Joan B. Williamson (Washington, D.C.: Catholic University of America Press, 1993), 219, which uses BN fr. 1175 as its base manuscript. This manuscript is the only extant one of the text. The third reference to the *Roman* is located on pages 43–44 of the edition and constitutes the prologue to book 1.

44. In manuscript BN fr. 1573, the lines read, "Mariages est maus liens,/Ainsit m'aïst sainz Juliens" (fol. 74vo), http://margot.uwaterloo.ca.

45. *Le livre de la vertu*, 241.

46. This is the same quote cited by Pierre Ceffons in his *Lectura super IV libros Sententiarium* (D.1) and points to the proverbial nature of this infamous couplet.

47. Unfortunately, the majority of the secondary literature produced on this work focuses on book 3, which lists contemporary recipes, cooking and gardening tips. The list of scholarly work on the content of books 1 and 2 is therefore limited. I refer to Roberta Krueger, "'Nouvelles choses': Social Instability and the Problem of Fashion in the *Livre du chevalier de La Tour Landry*, the *Ménagier de Paris*, and Christine de Pizan's *Livre des trois vertu*," in *Medieval Conduct*, ed. Kathleen Ashley and Robert Clark (Minneapolis, MN: University of Minnesota Press, 2001), 49–85; and Janet Ferrier, "Seulement pour vous endoctriner: The Author's Use of Exempla in *Le Menagier de Paris*," *Medium Aevum* 48 (1979): 77–89.

48. The edition I used is by Georgina E. Brereton, *Le mesnagier de Paris* (Paris: Livres de poche, 1994), 148–50. The work survives in three manuscripts: BN fr. 12477, BN nouvelles acquisitions françaises 6739, and Bibliothèque Royale, Bruxelles 10310–10311. Brereton's edition is based mainly on BN fr. 12477.

49. My translation is based on Eileen Power, trans., *The Goodman of Paris (Le ménagier de Paris). A Treatise on Moral and Domestic Economy by a Citizen of Paris*, c. 1393. (London: Routledge, 1992), 70–71. In an effort to retain as much authenticity as possible, Power translates the text with certain stylistic, lexical, and orthographic characteristics of Middle High English, which I have taken the liberty of modernizing in my own translation.

50. Power uses Chaucer's *Legend of Good Women* for the translation of this quote: "Ne never was ther king in Rome toun/Sin thilke day" (ll. 1869–70).

51. *Medieval France. An Encyclopaedia*.

52. See Badel, 1980, 362.

53.   Quoted in Badel, 1980, 362. The translation is mine.
54.   The excerpts from the 1350 work are quoted in Badel, 1980, 362 and 363–64. There is one edition of Digulleville's *Pèlerinage* by J. J. Stürzinger, *Le pèlerinage de la vie humaine de Guillaume de Deguileville* (London: Nichols and Sons for the Roxburghe Club, 1893). For further study on the author and his works, I refer to Langlois, *La vie en France au moyen âge. Enseignements, méditations, et controverses d'après des écrits français à l'usage des laïcs*, chap. 5, 4:199–268; Edmond Faral, *Histoire littéraire de la France* (Paris: Imprimerie nationale, 1962), 39:1–132; and, for an analysis of the manuscript miniatures, Paule Amblard, *Le pèlerinage de vie humaine: le songe très chrétien de l'abbé Guillaume de Digulleville: ouvrage réalisé à partir du manuscrit 1130 de la Bibliothèque Sainte-Geneviève à Paris* (Paris: Flammarion, c1998).
55.   Quoted in Badel, 1980, 368–69, based on the manuscript BN fr. 12466, of which there is no edition as of yet.
56.   Edmond Faral, *Histoire littéraire de la France.*
57.   The text is quoted in Badel, 1980, 370, based on manuscript BN fr. 14966.

Chapter Two

The Defense of Courtly Discourse and Morals

A. The Poets' Reaction

There is no question that the *Roman de la rose* was seen as the courtly dream-allegory par excellence. Writers such as Guillaume de Machaut, Jean Froissart, and Eustache Deschamps clearly use both parts as a model to be imitated. Machaut (who in a sense represents the generation of courtly writers who preceded Christine) admires the *Roman* in his *Voir Dit*. Both he and Froissart borrow extensively from its courtly tradition in all their works, and admire the *Roman* for its poetic beauty in the context of courtly discourse.[1]

Eustache Deschamps, a contemporary of Christine's who was very much admired by her and by Philippe de Mézières,[2] borrows heavily from Jean de Meun in several of his works, first and foremost in his *Miroir de mariage*, which in many ways constitutes a "response to and a recasting of the *Roman de la rose*."[3] Although he does not explicitly imitate the *Roman*, he speaks about the same themes, such as obscene language and the prolonged metaphor of the pilgrim, Nature and the forge of love, the complaint that humans do not follow the path of Nature, his views on astrology, the power of Fortune, the Golden Age, marriage, and so forth. Deschamps explicitly praises Chaucer for having translated the *Roman*. He dedicates the following *ballade* to Geoffrey Chaucer upon sending the latter some of his works, and, according to William Calin, this *ballade* contains the first reference to Chaucer by a poet from the continent.[4]

1. Eustache Deschamps (ca.1346–ca.1406)[5]

Ballade de moralitez[6]

Text:

CCLXXXV: Autre Balade
O Socrates plains de philosophie,
Seneque en meurs et Anglux en pratique,
4   Ovides grans en ta poeterie,
Bries en parler, saiges en rethorique,
Aigles treshaulz, qui par ta theorique
Enlumines le regne d'Eneas,
8   L'Isle aux Geans, ceuls de Bruth, et qui as
Semé les fleurs et planté le rosier,
Aux ignorans de la langue pandras,
Grant translateur, noble Geffroy Chaucier.

12   Tu es d'amours mondains Dieux en Albie:
Et de la Rose, en la terre Angelique,
Qui d'Angela saxonne, est puis flourie
Angleterre, d'elle ce nom s'applique
16   Le derrenier en l'ethimologique;
En bon anglès le livre translatas;
Et un vergier ou du plant demandas
De ceuls qui font pour eulx auctorisier,
20   A ja longtemps que tu edifias
Grant translateur, noble Geffroy Chaucier.

A toy pour ce de la fontaine Helye
Requier avoir un buvraige autentique,
24   Dont la doys est du tout en ta baillie,
Pour rafrener d'elle ma soif ethique,
Qui en Gaule seray paralitique
Jusques a ce que tu m'abuveras.
28   Eustaces sui, qui de mon plant aras:
Mais pran en gré les euvres d'escolier
Que par Clifford de moy avoir pourras,
Grant translateur, noble Gieffroy Chaucier.

32   L'Envoy:
Poete hault, loenge destruye,
En ton jardin ne seroye qu'ortie:
Considere ce que j'ay dit premier,
36   Ton noble plant, ta douce mélodie.
Mais pour sçavoir, de rescripre te prie,
Grant translateur, noble Geffroy Chaucier.

Translation:
Ballade 285

  O, Socrates, full of philosophy, Seneca for morality, for
practical life an Aulus Gallius, a great Ovid in your poetry; brief in
speech, wise in the art of writing, lofty Eagle, who by your science
enlighten the kingdom of Aeneas, the island of Giants, of Brutus,
5 who have sown there the flowers and planted the rose-tree for
those who are ignorant of French; great translator, noble Geoffrey
Chaucer.

  You are the god of earthly love in Albion; and in the Angelic
land, (which from the Saxon lady Angela has flowered into Angle-
10 land—from her this name is now applied as the last in the series
of names) you translate the Book of the Rose; and long since you
have set up an orchard, for which you have asked plants of those
who make in order to be authorities; great translator, noble Geoffrey
Chaucer.

15 From you therefore, I have sought an authentic drink from the
fountain of Helicon whose stream is entirely under your control, to
quench from it my feverish thirst; I, who will be paralyzed in Gaul
until you give me drink. I am Eustace; you shall have some of my
plants; accept graciously the schoolboy works which you
20 will receive from me by Clifford;[7] great translator, noble Geoffrey
Chaucer.

The Envoi:
  High poet, glory of the esquires, in your garden I should be
only a nettle: bear in mind what I said first of your noble plants,
25 your sweet music; for me to realize this, I pray you reply; great
translator, noble Geoffrey Chaucer.

2.   *Philippe de Mézières (1327–1405)*

In the following excerpt, the allegory called Lechery complains about the
corruption of her natural forge by Sodomites and Gomorrians. It is within this
context that she refers to the same complaint by the allegory Nature in Jean de
Meun's *Roman de la rose.*

1389: Le songe du vieil pèlerin[8]

Text:

> Comment la vieille, Luxure figuree, se plaint a la royne Verite
> de ceulx qui en corrompant sa forge naturelle forgent les vilz et hor-
> ribles besans contre nature.
>
> «Encores», dist la vieille Luxure, «dame royne, et non pas

5   sans laermes je me plains a vous ou ciel et en la terre de mes faulx
arquemistes qui ont faulcie ma forge. Or fussent ilz trahinez tous et
penduz par la gorge, c'est assavoir de ceulx et celles dont saint Paul
l'appostre en ses epystres publiquement se complaint, et Nature ma
maistresse ou Livre de la Rose aigrement se douloit. Helas»!

10   dist la vieille regulee Luxure, « de ceste tresvile ordure es royaumes
d'occident, forgeant mes fins besans, jadis je estoie quipte et bien
asseuree. Mais aujourduy en pleurant». «Helas»! je le dy: ma forge
est bestournee. Les tresmaleureux chetis Gomorriens, pires que
Juifz et priviez de Paradis, laissierent mes beaux houtiz et les

15   precieux vaisseaux de ma sainte forge ordonnee, et forgerent besans
ors, pourriz et puans et sans aloy, qui n'ont point de duree. Or leur
en preigne ainsi», dist la vieille, «comme il fist a l'empereur Noy-
ron, qui prist l'abbit d'une femme et se fist espouser a un homme, et
le tint comme son baron et villement ma belle forge faulsa».

Translation:

How the duenna, Lechery, complains to Queen Truth about those who, by corrupting her natural forge, are forging vile and horrible coins against Nature.

"Moreover," said old Lechery, "Lady Truth, it is not with-
5   out tears that I complain to you in the sky and on earth about my false alchemists, who have betrayed my forge. May all those about whom Saint Paul publicly complains in his epistles and about whom Nature, my mistress, cries bitterly in the Romance of the Rose be delivered and hanged by their throats. Alas!" said the old regular
10   Lechery, "in the past I was quite confident and assured about this very vile rubbish in the kingdoms of the West, continuing to forge my fine gold coins. But nowadays I cry about it. Alas! I say: my forge has been turned upside down. The very unfortunate criminals, the Gomorrians, worse than Jews and forbidden in Paradise, left my
15   beautiful tools and the precious vessels of my holy, orderly forge and forged gold coins, rotten and stinking and without alloy, which will not last. Now it is filled with them, said the duenna, like the emperor Neron, who dressed as a woman and married a man and kept him as his baron and vilely betrayed my forge.

B. Christine de Pizan : The debate before the Debate

1. 1399: L'epistre au dieu d'amours[9]

Since Eric Hicks's edition of the Debate correspondence, it has been established
that the *Epistre au dieu d'amours* cannot be considered the first "document" of
the Debate Epistles, as Ch. F. Ward would have it.[10] As Earl Jeffrey Richards
has tried to show in the Introduction, it becomes more and more apparent that
it is misleading at best to speak about the Debate—that is, the exchange of
letters between the participants in this Quarrel—as a literary endeavor with
a fixed beginning and end. Therefore, I will treat the *Epistre* as only one example of Christine's continuous effort to refute this instrumental work, albeit
an important effort and a crucial one for the evolution of her career as a writer
and author.[11] Because the content of this particular poem is so closely related
to issues dealt with in the later correspondence, I have decided to reproduce
it in its entirety.[12]

In their translation, Fenster and Carpenter Erler have chosen to translate
the decasyllabic lines of the *Epistre au dieu d'Amours* into unrhymed lines of
iambic pentameter. I am reproducing their translation with slight modifications.
More significant changes are listed in the appendix.

Text:
Ci commence l'Epistre au dieu d'Amours

51r°	Cupido, dieu par la grace de lui,
	Roy des amans, sans ayde de nullui,
	Regnant en l'air du ciel tres reluisant,
4	Filz de Venus, la deesse poissant,
	Sire d'amours et de tous ses obgez,
	A tous noz vrays loyaulx servans subgez:
	Salut, amour, familiarité.
8	Savoir faisons en generalité
	Qu'a nostre court sont venues complaintes
	Par devant nous et moult piteuses plaintes
	De par toutes dames et damoiselles,
12	Gentilz femmes, bourgoises et pucelles,
	Et de toutes femmes generaument,
51v°	Nostre secours requerant humblement,
	Ou se ce non du tout desheritees
16	De leur honneur seront et ahontees.
	Si se plaignent les dessusdites dames
	Des grans extors, des blames, des diffames,
	Des traÿsons, des oultrages tres griefs,

Translation:

Letter of the God of Love

           Cupid, a god by virtue of his grace,
The king of lovers, his alone that charge,
Who reigns amid the space of radiant skies;
4   Son of Venus, the powerful goddess!
The lord of love and all that he surveys,
To all our true and loyal servitors:
Greetings and love and affable respects.
8   To one and all about we make it known
That here, before our court, complaints have come
To us, and plaints so very piteous,
From women, both the young and older ones,
12   From noble ladies, maidens, merchants' wives,
From all of womankind, wherever found,
Most humbly asking us to intervene.
Failing our help, they will be completely shorn
16   Of every shred of dignity, and shamed.
The ladies mentioned here above complain
Of damage done, of blame and blemished name,
And of betrayals, very grievous wrongs,

[handwritten marginal note:] need to save the dignity of all women from The Rose!

20   Des faulcetez et de mains autres griefs
      Que chacun jour des desloyaulx reçoivent,
      Qui les blament, diffament, et deçoivent.
            Sur tous pays se complaignent de France,
24   Qui jadis fu leur escu et deffence,
      Qui contre tous de tort les deffendoit,
      Comme il est droit et si com faire doit
      Noble pays ou gentillece regne.
28   Mais a present elles sont en ce regne,
      Ou jadis tant estoient honnourees,
      Plus qu'autre part des faulx deshonorees,
      Et meismement, dont plus griefment se deulent,
32   Des nobles gens qui plus garder les seulent.
      Car a present sont plusieurs chevaliers
      Et escuyers mains duis et coustumiers
      D'elles traÿr par beaulx blandissemens.
36   Si se faignent estre loyaulx amans
      Et se cueuvrent de diverse faintise;
            Si vont disant que griefment les atise
      L'amour d'elles, qui leurs cuers tient en serre,
40   Dont l'un se plaint, a l'autre le cuer serre,
      L'autre pleure par semblant et souspire,
      Et l'autre faint que trop griefment empire,
      Par trop amer tout soit descouloué
44   Et presque mort et tout alengouré.
      Si jurent fort et promettent et mentent
      Estre loyaulx, secrés, et puis s'en vantent.
      D'aler souvent et de venir se peinent,
48   Par ces moustiers ja et la se pormeinent
      En regardant, s'apuyent sur autelz
      Par faulx semblans; mains en y a de telz.
      Par mi rues leurs chevaulx esperonnent,
52   Gays et mignos a cliquettes qui sonnent.
      Moult font semblant d'en estre embesongnez,
      Mulles, chevaulx n'y sont pas espargnez.
      Diligens sont de bailler leurs requestes;
56   Moult enquierent ou sont nopces et festes,
      La vont plusieurs mignos, jolis et cointes.
      Si font semblant de sentir de noz pointes
      Si qu'a peines les peuent endurer!

20   Of falsehoods uttered, many other griefs,   *issue of loyalty*
    Endured each day from those disloyal men
    Who blame and shame, defame and deceive them.
        Above all other lands their plaint is of France,
24   Defense and shield to them in former days,
    Protecting them from harm on every side;
    That is right, that is what a noble land must do,
    A country in which gentle breeding rules.
28   But now in France, the place where in the past   *related*
    Women were honored so, those men who are false   *specifically to*
    Dishonor them, more than in other lands,   *the turmoil in*
    Especially—and here they grieve the more—   *France @ the*
32   The noblemen, who used to champion them.   *time*
    For such are many knights these days, and squires
    Who have less experience and training at
    Betraying them through pretty flatteries.
36   The loyal lovers' pose they strike is false.
    Hiding behind their myriad deceits,
    They go declaring that a woman's love
    Inflames them sorely, keeps their hearts locked up;
40   The first laments, the second's heart is wrenched,
    The next pretends to fill with tears, and sighs;
    Another claims to sicken horribly:
    Because of love's travail he is grown quite pale,
44   Now perishing, now very nearly dead.
    Swearing their fervent oaths, they lie and vow
    To be discreet and true, and then they crow.
    Sparing themselves no pain to come and go,
48   They promenade in church and peer about,[13]   *fashionable almost to be*
    Bending their knees upon the altar steps   *over dramatic about the*
    In fake devotion: many are like that!   *temptations etc of*
    They spur their horses up and down the streets   *love + women*
52   Jaunty and handsome, jingling as they go.
    They make a show of great activity,
    And spare no horse or mule. Then, ever so
    Attentively, they tender their requests,
56   Inquiring for the weddings and the feasts[14]
    At which those polished, ardent, gallant swains,
    Display how much they feel our arrows' cut,
    So much that they can barely stand the pain!

60   Autres mettent grant peine a procurer
            Par messages ou par quelque acointance
            De mettre a fin ce que leur faulx cuer pense.
            Par tieulx maintiens en plus de mile guises
64   Les faulx amans se cueuvrent de faintises;
            C'est assavoir les desloyaulx qui heent
            Foy, loyauté, et a decevoir beent.
                    Car les loyaulx ne sont pas en ce conte,
68   Et ceulx doit on amer et tenir conte,
            Car decevoir en nul cas ne vouldroyent;
            Je leur deffens. Pour ce consens qu'ilz ayent
            De noz doulx biens savoureux bonne part,
72   Car a mes gens largement en depart,
            Et ceulx tiennent mes vrays commandemens,
            Justes, loyaulx, et bons enseignemens.
            Si leur deffens villennie et meffait,
76   Et leur commands poursuivre honneur de fait,
            Estre loyaulx, secrés, et voir disans,
            Larges, courtois, et fuïr mesdisans,
                    Humbles et doulx, jolis et assesmez,
80   Fermes et frans, poursuivre a estre amez,
            Armes suivir a ceulx qu'il appartient
            Los acquerir. Qui en ce point se tient,
            Sache pour vray que ne lui fauldray mye
84   A lui donner dame belle et amie;
            Car quant ainsi je suis d'aucun servy,
            Guerdon lui rens comme il a desservy.
            Mais se bien vient a ces faulx d'aventure,
88   N'est pas droit bien, combien que je l'endure,
            Car en tous cas le bien est moult petit,
            Quant il est pris sans desir n'appetit.
                    Et que vauldroit a homs descouragé
92   Grans viandes, ypocras ou saugé,
            Puisque saveur nulle ou peu y aroit?
            Mais a cellui qui desirant seroit
            De pain faitis ou d'une miche blanche,
96 52rᵒ   S'ataindre y peut, Dieux scet comme il la tranche
            Joyeusement et de grant cuer s'en paist!
            Ainsi de toute riens desiree est.
                    Ainsi se trop ne sant apperceües,
100   Sont maintes fois les dames deceües.

60   Still other would-be lovers strive and strain,
        Sending their messengers or coming around,
        To get the thing their feigning hearts intend.
        Maintaining thus a thousand masquerades,
64   These suitors hide behind their false parades;
        That is to say, those traitors who detest   ∴ women put in moral
        Fidelity or faith, who aim to trick.   danger
            The loyal are not numbered in that count,
68   It is those one ought to love and count upon;   ∆ shows Ø all men are
        In no case would they want to practice fraud,   this way
        For I forbid it. So I grant to them
        Good portion of our sweet and tasty store,
72   Because I give abundantly to those
        Who are mine, and they uphold my true commands,[15]
        My just, sincere, and worthy tutelage.
        Thus I forbid them evil or misdeed,
76   Ordering them to strive for real esteem,
        To be sincere, discreet, speak truthfully,
        Be giving, courtly, flee from gossipers;   def of a good man
        Be humble, gentle, loving, and refined.
80   Be steady, noble, seek to be well-loved,
        And let all those deserving of acclaim
        Take weapons up. Whoever holds to that,
        Let him know, surely I will not fail to grant
84   A beautiful, sweet lady-love to him,
        For when I am served by someone in such wise,
        I render him reward as he is deserved.
        If good, though, comes by chance to those who are false,
88   It is not a good thing that is true, although I may
        Put up with it; indeed, there is paltry gain
        When one partakes with little appetite.
            To one without much interest what would
92   Exquisite fare, sage wine or spiced, be worth?
        For him they would have no taste, or just a bit.
        But to that man who might have coveted
        A simple bread or but a bite of white,
96   If he succeeds, God knows how joyfully
        He slices it and feasts with all his heart!
        For that is what he desires above all else.
            If women, therefore, do not step cautiously,
100   They will be deluded time and time again;

Car simples sont, n'y pensent se bien non,
Dont il avient souvent, vueillent ou non,
Qu'amer leur fault ceulx qui si les deçoivent:
104   Traÿes sont ains qu'elles l'apperçoivent!
Mais quant ainsi les ont enveloppees
Les desloyaulx qui les ont attrappees,
Or escoutez comment ilz s'en chevissent:
108   Ne leur souffit ce qu'ainsi les traÿssent,
Ains ont compains de leur male aliance;
Si n'y remaint ne fait ne couvenance
Qui ne soit dit l'un a l'autre; et, trop plus
112   Qu'ilz n'ont de bien, se vantent que reclus
Sont devenus en la chambre leur dames
Dont sant amez. Puis jurent corps et ames
Comment du fait il leur est avenu,
116   Et que couchié bras a bras y ont nu.
Les compaignons ce dient es tavernes,
Et les nobles font leurs parts et leur cernes
En ces grans cours de noz seigneurs les ducs,
120   Ou cheus le roy, ou ailleurs espandus.
Et la tiennent de tieulx plais leur escoles!
Plusieurs y a qui deussent leur paroles
En bons contes drecier sans bourderie
124   A raconter pris de chevalerie;
Mais aux grans feus a ces soirs, ou sur couches
La rigolent l'un l'autre, et par reprouches
S'entredient: «Je sçay bien de tes fais:
128   Tele t'aimë, et tu le jolis fais
Pour seue amour, mais plusieurs y ont part;
Tu es receu quant un autre s'en part»!
La diffament les envïeux la belle
132   Sans achoison ne nul amal savoir d'elle.
Et lors cellui qui en est rigollé
Monstre semblant qu'il en soit adolé;
Mais moult lui plaist de ce qu'on l'en rigolle,
136   Et de son beq mainte parole volle
Qui blasme vault, combien qu'il s'en excuse;
En excusant celle nomme et accuse,
Et fait semblant de celer et couvrir
140   Ce qu'i lui plaist a dire et descouvrir.
        D'autres y a qui le rigol commencent

For women have no guile, and think but good;
And so it happens often, willed or not,
They love the very men deceiving them;
104 Betrayed before they have even noticed it!
And when those men have got them all wrapped up,
Those cads who have got their women neatly trapped,
Listen to how they make a game of it:
108 Not satisfied with just betraying them,
They have partners in their nasty liaison,
No deed performed or promise made can fail
To be retold around; the less they have had,
112 The more they boast of having been shut in
The chambers of ladies who have loved them.
They swear on soul and body how events
Turned out for them, whatever the circumstance,
116 And claim that naked, arm in arm, they lay.
Their cohorts talk of it in every inn,
And nobles share the news in huddled groups
In courts belonging to the dukes, our lords,
120 Or yet before the king, or elsewhere spread.
To stuff like that their learnèd discourse comes!
Many of them should turn their talk instead
Toward telling fitting tales without bold lies,
124 Stories that show the worth of chivalry.
But lolling at those toasty evening fires,
They rib each other, and by means of taunts
Exchanged, they say: "I know what you are about:
128 Your sweetheart is such a one, you play the beau
To have her love; but many get their share,
For you are greeted as another parts!"
The lady's slandered by the envious,
132 Who have no cause, who know no ill of her.
And then the object of their taunting glee
Contrives a great display of dole and pain;
And yet, their teasing pleases him quite well.
136 Many a guilty word comes flying from
His chirping throat, though he makes an excuse;
As he is excused, she is named and she is accused,
And he pretends to hide and cover up
140 The very things he gladly bares to all!
        Others exist who prompt the raillery

A celle fin que les autres s'avancent
D'eulx rigoler et d'eulx ramentevoir
144 Ce qu'ilz veulent a tous faire savoir.
Si s'en rient, et tout en accusant,
Se vont du fait lachement excusant.
Si en y a qui se sont mis en peine
148 C'on les amast, mais perdu ont leur peine,
Si sont honteux dont ilz sont refusé.
Ne veulent pas qu'on croye que musé
Ayent en vain. Pour ce de ce se vantent
152 C'onques n'avint; et s'en cellui lieu hantent
Pour aucun cas ou par quelque acointance,
De tout l'ostel compteront l'ordonnance
Pour enseignes de confermer leur bourdes.
156 La sont dictes maintes paroles lourdes,
Et qui dire ne les veult mie appertes
Les monstre au doy par paroles couvertes.
La sont femmes moult laidement nommees
160 Souventes fois, et sans cause blamees,
Et mesmement d'aucunes grans maistresses,
Tout ayent ilz brunes ou blondes tresses.
Dieux, quieulx parleurs! Dieux, quelles assemblees,
164 Ou les honneurs des dames sont emblees!
Et quel prouffit vient d'ainsi diffamer
A ceulx mesmes qui se deussent armer
Pour les garder et leur honneur deffendre?
168 Car tout homme doit avoir le cuer tendre
Envers femme, qui est sa chiere mere
Et ne lui est ne diverse n'amere,
Ainçois souëve, doulce, et amiable,
172 A son besoing piteuse et secourable,
Qui tant lui a fait et fait de services,
52v° Et de qui tant les œuvres sont propices
A corps d'omme souëvement nourrir.
176 A son naistrë, au vivre, et au mourir
Lui sont femmes aydans et secourables
Et piteuses, doulces, et serviables.
Si est cellui mau congnoissant et rude
180 Qui en mesdit, et plain d'ingratitude.
Ancor dis je que trop se desnature
Homme qui dit diffame, ne laidure,

Just so the rest will take the lead, begin
To tease them and remind them of the things
144　　That from the first they hoped to advertise.
Laughing at that, accusing all the while,
They give some lame excuse for what they have done.
　　　　Now certain others there have toiled away
148　　At being loved, and yet their labor is lost.
They feel ashamed of having been refused
And do not want others thinking that their time
Was spent in vain. That is why they boast and claim
152　　They were not spurned; and should they be about
Her place on business or just visiting,
They will tell about the way the household is run
By way of proof, confirming all their lies.
156　　How many vulgar things are uttered there;
Whoever wants to shun straightforward words
Through innuendo points them out the more.
　　　　And there, quite shabbily, are women named
160　　So many times and blamed without a cause,
　　　And in particular some mistresses
Of note: the fair-haired and brunette alike.
　　　　Good God, what gossips, God, what gatherings,
164　　At which a lady's honor is stripped away!
And where, in slander, is the profit for
The very men who ought to arm themselves
To guard the ladies and defend their names?
168　　For every man must have a tender heart
Toward woman, she who is his mother dear,
Who is never wicked, pitiless toward him,
But rather, she is pleasant, gentle, sweet;
172　　When he's in need, she understands and helps.
She is done and does so many services
For him; how right her ministrations are,
Gently to serve the creature needs of man.
176　　At birth, in life, and at his time of death,
Women, always willing, help and assist.
Compassionate and kind, obliging him.
The man who slanders them is merciless,
180　　An ingrate, lacking any thought of thanks.
So I repeat: that man too much distorts
His nature, who rehearses ugly slurs,

Ne reprouche de femme en la blamant,
184   N'une ne deux ne tout generaument.
Et supposé qu'il en y ait de nices,
Ou remplies de plusieurs divers vices,
Sans foy n'amour ne nulle loyauté,
188   Fieres, males, plaines de cruauté,
Ou pou constans, legieres, variables,
Cautilleuses, faulces et decevables:
Doit on pour tant toutes miettre en fermaille,
192   Et tesmoigner qu'il n'est nulle qui vaille?
        Quant le hault Dieu fist et forma les angelz,
Les cherubins, ceraphins, et archangelz,
N'en y ot il de mauvais en leurs fais?
196   Doit on pour tant anges nommer mauvais?
Mais qui male femme scet, si s'en gard,
Sans diffamer ne le tiers ne le quart,
Ne trestoutes en general blamer,
200   Ne tous leurs meurs femenins diffamer.
Car moult en fu, est et sera de celles
Qui a louer font com bonnes et belles,
Et ou vertus et graces sont trouvees,
204   Sens et valeur en bonté esprouvees.
Et de blasmer celles qui le mains valent,
Ceulx qui se font, encor dis je qu'ilz falent
S'ilz les nomment, disant qui elles sont,
208   Ou demeurent, quoy ne quieulx leurs fais sont,
Car le pecheur on ne doit diffamer,
Ce nous dit Dieux, n'en publique blamer.
Les vices bien peut on et les pechez
212   Tres fort blamer, sans ceulx qui entechez
En sont nommer, ne diffamer nullui;
Le tesmongne l'escript ou je le lui.
De tieulx parleurs en y a a grans sommes,
216   Dont grant honte est tel vice en gentilz hommes.
Je di a ceulx qui en sont entechié,
Non mie a ceulx qui n'y ont nul pechié,
Car maint y a des nobles si vaillans
220   Qui mieulx perdre vouldroient leur vaillans
Que de tieulx fais restez ne reprouvez
Fussent pour riens, n'en tel cas pris prouvez.
        Mais les mauvais dont je fais mencion,

Or blames a woman, thus reproaching her,
184   Whether it is one, or two, or womankind.
Now, if some women are the foolish kind,
Brimming with sin of every stamp and type,
And lacking faith and love and loyalty,
188   Or puffed-up, evil, filled with cruelty,
Inconstant, loose, and low and fickle types,
Or scheming, false, or practicing deceit—
Must we, because of that, imprison all,
192   And testify that none deserves respect?
        When God on high the angels made and formed,
Cherubim, seraphim, and archangels,
Now were there not some bad ones in the lot?
196   Because of that must one call angels bad?
The man who knows an evil woman should
Keep clear of her, and not defame all
Of womankind, or charge them all,
200   Decrying every trait that's feminine.
For many do and did and will exist
        Who should be praised as good and courteous,
In whom are grace and virtue to be found,
204   Whose goodness proves their wisdom and their worth.
Blaming the ones whose worth is less than that—
I say once more that those who do so err
If they name names, revealing who they are,
208   Or where they live, or what and which the deeds,
Because the sinner must not be defamed,
So God commands, nor publicly reproved.
The vices and the sins may be condemned
212   Most forcefully, without repeating names
Of those affected, or defaming them.
The Scripture that I read attests to that.
Great hordes of gossipers like that exist;
216   In gentlemen such vice is cause for shame.
I speak to those alone who bear this taint,
And not to those who have not any sin,
For many are the nobles, rich in worth,
220   Who would rather lose their worldly wealth than be
Accused of or denounced for such deeds, not
For anything, nor captured in the act.
        But wicked men, of whom I am speaking here,

[handwritten margin note: don't blame all women for Sara's sins]

224   Qui n'ont bon fait ne bonne entencion,
        Ne prennent pas au bon Hutin exemple
        De Vermelles, ou bonté ot si ample
        C'onques nulz homs n'y sçot que reproucher,
228   Ne nul mesdit en diffamant n'ot cher.
        Souvrainement porta honnour aux femmes,
        Ne pot ouÿr d'elles blasme ou diffames.
        Chevalier fu preux, sage, et bien amé;
232   Pour ce fu il et sera renommé.
                Le bon Otte de Grançon le vaillant,
        Qui pour armes tant s'ala travaillant,
        Courtois, gentil, preux, bel et gracïeux
236   Fu en son temps; Dieux en ait l'ame es cieulx!
        Car chevalier fu moult bien enteché.
        Qui mal lui fist, je tiens qu'il fist peché,
        Nonobstant ce que lui nuisi Fortune.
240   Mais de grever aux bons elle est commune,
        Car en tous cas je tiens qu'il fu loyaulx,
        D'armes plus preus que Thelamon Ayaulx.
        Onc ne lui plot personne diffamer,
244   Les dames volt servir, prisier, amer.
                D'autres plusieurs furent bons et vaillans;
        Estre doivent exemple aux deffaillans.
        Encor en est maint, il est bien mestiers,
248   Qui des vaillans suivent les bons sentiers.
        Honneur les duit, vaillance les y maine,
        A acquerir pris et loz mettent peine.
        Des nobles meurs blen entechez se perent;
252   Par leurs beaulx fais leur vaillances apperent
        En ce royaume, ailleurs, et oultre mer.
53r°   Mais je me tais d'eulz et leurs noms nommer
        C'on ne deïst que ce fust flaterie,
256   Ou qu'il peüst tourner a vanterie.
        Et tieulx doivent gentilz hommes par droit
        Estre, autrement gentillece y faudroit.
                Si se plaignent les dessusdites dames
260   De plusieurs clercs qui leur surmettent blasmes.
        Dictiez en font, rimes, proses et vers,
        En diffamant leurs meurs par moz divers.
        Si les baillent en matiere aux premiers,
264   A leurs nouveaulx et jeunes escoliers,

224   Who haven't good intentions or good deeds,
         Do not find in Hutin de Vermeilles[16] a man
         To imitate; such goodness was in him
         That no one could reproach a thing he did,
228   Nor was he fond of scandalmongering.
         He honored ladies' names especially,
         And could not hear them blamed or vilified.
         A brave, genteel, belovèd knight was he;
232   For that he was and ever will be famed.
              Good Othe de Grandson,[17] valiant man and brave,
         Who labored long at arms; a courteous
         And gracious knight, who in his time was fine
236   And fair and bold; God keep his soul above!
         He had been endowed with knighthood's qualities.
         Whoever did him wrong did sin, I say.
         And never mind that Fortune did him ill—
240   She commonly brings harm to good men, too—
         Because I hold that he was true, more brave
         At arms than Ajax, son of Telamon.[18]
         And slander never made him glad; he wished
244   To serve the ladies, love and treasure them.
             Now, many other men were good and brave,
         Examples for all those who are faltering.
         There still are many more (they are needed so)
248   Who follow in the paths of worthy men.
         For honor guides them, valor leads the way.
         They do their best to earn esteem and praise;
         It is clear they have been endowed with noble ways—
252   By deeds they do their bravery is revealed,
         In France, in other lands, and overseas.
         But I refrain from naming them right here
         Lest people say it is only flattery,
256   Or lest it be employed in boastfulness.
         Now they are gentlemen, correctly called,
         Or gentle breeding is nowhere to be found.
             The ladies mentioned here above complain
260   Of many clerks who place much blame on them,
         Composing tales in rhyme, in prose, in verse,
         In which they scorn their ways with words diverse;
         They give these texts out to their youngest lads,
264   To schoolboys who are young and new in class,

En maniere d'exemple et de doctrine
Pour retenir en aage tel doctrine.
      En vers dient, Adam, David, Sanson,
268   Et Salomon, et autres a foison
Furent deceu par femme main et tart:
Et qui sera dont li homs qui s'en gard?
Li autre dit que moult sont decevables,
272   Cautilleuses, faulces et pou valables.
      Autres dient que trop sont mençongieres,
Variables, inconstans et legieres.
D'autres plusieurs grans vices les accusent
276   Et blasment moult, sans qu'en riens les excusent.
Et ainsi font clercs et soir et matin,
Puis en françois leurs vers, puis en latin,
Et se fondent dessus ne sçay quieulx livres,
280   Qui plus dient de mençonge q'uns yvres.
Ovide en dit, en un livre qu'il fist,
Assez de maulx, dont je tiens qu'il meffist,
Qu'il appella le *Remede d'Amour*s,
284   Ou leur met sus de moult villaines mours,
Ordes, laides, plaines de villennie.
Que tieulx vices ayent je le lui nie;
Au deffendre par hataille je gage
288   Contre tous ceulx qui getter vouldront gage.
Voire, j'entens des femmes honorables;
En mes comptes ne mes les non valables.
Si ont les clercs appris trés leur enfance
292   Cellui livret en premiere scïence
De gramairë, et aux autres l'apprennent
A celle fin qu'a femme amer n'emprennent.
Mais de ce sant folz et perdent leur peine,
296   Ne l'empescher si n'est fors chose vaine,
Car entre moy et ma dame Nature,
Ne souffrerons, tant com le monde dure,
Que cheries et amees ne soient,
300   Malgré tous ceulx qui blamer les vouldroient,
Et qu'a plusieurs meismes qui plus les blament
N'ostent les cuers et ravissent et emblent.
Sans nul frauder ne faire extorcion,
304   Mais tout par nous et nostre impression,
Ja n'en seront hommes si accointez

Examples given to indoctrinate
So they will retain such doctrine when they are grown.
   Thus, "Adam, David, Samson, Solomon," [19]

268   They say in verse, "a score of other men,
Were all deceived by women morn and night;
So who will be the man who can escape?"
"They're treacherous," another clerk opines,

272   "And false and cunning; they're no good at all."
   "They're dreadful liars," other men pronounce,
"They're faithless, fickle, they are low and loose."
Of many other wrongs they stand accused

276   And blamed; in nothing can they be excused.
And that is what clerks are up to noon and night,
With verses now in Latin, now in French,
They base their words on I do not know what books, —

280   Which tell more lies than any drunkard does.
Now Ovid, in a book he wrote, sets down
Profuse affronts; I say that he did wrong.
He titled it *Remedia amoris*:[20]

284   There he ascribes to women nasty ways,
Repulsive, sordid, filled with wickedness.
That women have such vices I deny;
I take up arms in my defense of them

288   Against all those who would throw the challenge down.
It is honorable women I would defend;
I put no worthless women in my tales.
Now, since their childhood days the clerks have read

292   That book in grammar class, the subject that
One studies first. They teach it to the rest
In hopes they will not seek out a woman's love.
They are foolish, though, their effort is thrown away.

296   Such obstacles are but a vain attempt:
Between my lady Nature and myself,
We will not accept, as long as life endures,
That women be not cherished well and loved,

300   In spite of all who would censure them, or will,
We hinder women who would steal the hearts
Of just those very men who blame them most.
Engaging in no fraud or fakery,

304   But simply through persuasion on our part,
No more will men be taught as they have been

             Par soubtilz clercs ne pour tous leurs dictiez,
             Nonobstant ce que mains livres en parlent
308   Et les blasment, qui assez pou y valent.
                     Et s'aucun dit qu'on doit les livres croire
             Qui furent fais d'ommes de grant memoire
             Et de grant sens, qui mentir n'en daignerent,
312   Qui des femmes les malices prouverent,
             Je leur respons que ceulx qui cë escriprent
             En leurs livres, je treuve qu'ilz ne quistrent
             En leurs vies fors femmes decevoir.
316   N'en povoient yceulx assez avoir,
             Et tous les jours vouloient des nouvelles,
             Sans loyauté tenir, nez aux plus belles.
             Qu'en ot David et Salomon le roy?
320   Dieu s'en courça et pugni leur desroy.
                     D'autres plusieurs, et mesmement Ovide,
             Qui tant en volt, puis diffamer les cuide,
             Et tous les cleres, qui tant en ont parlé,
324   Plus qu'autre gent en furent affollé,
                     Non pas d'une seule mais d'un miller.
             Et se tel gent orent dame ou mouller
             Qui ne feïst du tout a leur vouloir,
328   Ou qui meïst peine a les decevoir,
             Quel merveille? Car il n'est nulle doubte
             Que quant uns homs en tel vilté se boute,
             Il ne va pas querant les vaillans dames,
332 53v°   Ne les bonnes, prisiees, preudes femmes.
             Ne les congnoit, ne il n'en a que faire,
             Fors ceulx ne veult qui sont de son affaire.
             De fillettes se pare et de pietaille.
336   Est il digne d'avoir chose qui vaille,
             Un villottier qui toutes met en conte
             Et puis cuide trop bien couvrir sa honte,
             Quant plus n'en peut et qu'il est ja vielx homs,
340   D'elle traÿr par ses soubtilz raisons?
                     Mais qui blasmast seulement les donnees
             Aux grans vices et les abandonnees,
             Et conseillast a elles non suivir
344   Comme ilz ont fait, bien s'en pourroit suivir,
             Et ce seroit chose moult raisonnable,
             Enseignement juste et digne et louable,

By learnèd clerks, nor by all of their verse,
Regardless of the many books that speak
308 Of women, blaming them: their value is slim.
        For if it is said we must believe those books
Composed by men of excellent renown,
Who never stooped so low to tell a lie,
312 Who proved the evil things that women do,
My answer is that those who wrote such things
In books of theirs sought nothing while they lived
Except to trick their women, so I find.
316 For never could they get enough of them,
And every day they wanted fresh supplies,
Loyal not even to the loveliest.
Take David, or take Solomon the king:[21]
320 God grew enraged and punished their excess.
        And many others—Ovid comes to mind—
Who desired many, then he slandered them.
All of those clerks, who had so much to say,
324 Were smitten even more than other men,
And with a thousand—not with one alone!
Now if those men had mistresses or wives
Who failed to do entirely as they wished,
328 Who may have taken pains to play them false,
What wonder is that? For there is no doubt at all
That if a man will wallow in such filth,
He will not go out and find the worthy ones:
332 The women who are good, esteemed, and prized.
He does not know that kind, nor deal with them.
He wants just those who share his vulgar tastes,
Embellishing himself with whores and tarts.
336 Does he deserve to have a valued thing,
This rake who thinks they are all for his delight,
Then thinks, when he is grown old and impotent
That he has concealed his shame so very well,
340 Betraying her with learnèd arguments?
        If just those women could be brought to blame
Who are given to debauchery and vice,
And counseled to renounce the life they have led,
344 Then good result could certainly ensue;
And that would be a reasonable course,
A worthy lesson, just and laudable,

Sans diffamer toutes generaument.
348   Et a parler quant au decevement,
Je ne sçay pas penser ne concevoir
Comment femme puist homme decevoir:
Ne le va pas ne cercher ne querir,
352   Ne sus son lieu prier ne requerir;
Ne pense a lui, ne ne lui en souvient
Quant decevoir l'omme et tempter la vient.
Tempter comment? Voire, par tel maniere
356   Qu'il n'est peine qui ne lui soit legiere
A endurer ne faissel a porter.
A autre riens ne se veult deporter
Fors a pener a elles decevoir,
360   Pour y mettre cuer et corps et avoir.
Et par lonc temps dure la triolaine,
Souventes fois avient, et celle peine,
Nonobstant ce que moult souvent ilz faillent
364   A leurs esmes ja soit ce qu'ilz travaillent.
Et de ceulx parle Ovide en son traictié
De l'*Art d'amours,* car pour la grant pitié
Qu'il ot de ceulx compila il un livre
368   Ou leur escript et enseigne a delivre
Comment pourront les femmes decevoir
Par faintises et leur amour avoir.
Si l'appella *Livre de l'Art d'amours,*
372   Mais n'enseigne condicions ne mours
De bien amer mais ainçois le contraire.
Car homs qui veult selon ce livre faire
N'amera ja, combien qu'il soit amez.
376   Et pour cë est li livres mau nommez,
Car c'est *Livre d'Art de grant decevance,*
Tel nom lui don, *et de faulce apparence!*
       Et comment dont quant fraisles et legieres
380   Et tournables, nices et pou entieres
Sont les femmes, si comme aucuns clercs dient,
Quel besoing dont est il a ceulx qui prient
De tant pour ce pourchacer de cautelles?
384   Et pour quoy tost ne s'i accordent elles
Sans qu'il faille art n'engin a elles prendre?
Car pour chastel pris ne faut guerre emprendre,
Et mesmement poëte si soubtil

Without dispraising all in general.
348   And now, speaking about deceptiveness,
       I cannot imagine, nor yet comprehend,
       Just how a woman might deceive a man:
       It is not she who goes pursuing him,
352   Nor calls upon or asks for him at home,
       Nor dwells on thoughts of him incessantly,
       Since he comes around to tempt her and deceive.
       And how does he entice?—In such a way,
356   Indeed, that all exertion seems quite small
       To him, and every burden light to bear.
       No other recreation does he seek
       Except his striving toward beguiling her,
360   Employing all his body, heart, and wealth.
       This torment, with its toil and moil, goes on
       For very long, repeated many times,
       Despite the fact that men may often fail
364   At their pursuit, however much they strive.
              Now Ovid speaks of men like that in his
       Ars amatoris; the pity that he felt
       For them encouraged him to write a book
368   In which he taught them and did openly
       Elucidate a way to trick the girls
       By means of subterfuge, and have their love.
       And then he called the book *Ars amatoris,*
372   Although it does not teach the terms or ways
       Of loving well, but quite the opposite.
       The man who would behave as in that book
       Will never love, however he is loved.
376   Because of that its title is misconceived,
       Its subject is *The Art of Great Deceit,*
       Of False Appearances—I dub it that!
              But now, if women are such easy marks,
380   If they are the fickle, foolish, faithless lot
       That certain clerks maintain they are, then why
       Must men pursuing them resort to schemes,
       To clever subterfuge and trickery?
384   And why do not women yield more readily,
       Without the need for guile to capture them?
       A castle taken needs no further war,
       And surely not from such a learnèd bard

388   Comme Ovide, qui puis fu en exil.
        Et Jehan de Meun ou *Rommant de la Rose:*
      Quel lonc procés! Quel difficile chose!
      Et scïences et cleres et obscures
392   Y mist il la, et de grans aventures!
      Et que de gent supploiez et rouvez,
      Et de peines et de baras trouvez
      Pour decevoir sans plus une pucelle—
396   S'en est la fin, par fraude et par cautelle!
      A foible lieu fault il dont grant assault?
      Comment peut on de pres faire grant sault?
      Je ne sçay pas ne vëoir ne comprendre
400   Que grant peine faille a foible lieu prendre,
      Në art, n'engin, ne grant soubtiveté.
      Dont convient il tout de neccessité,
      Puisque art couvient, grant engin et grant peine
404   A decevoir femme noble ou villaine,
      Qu'elz ne soient mie si variables,
      Comme aucuns dit, n'en leur fais si muables.
        Et s'on me dit li livre en sont tuit plain
408   (C'est le respons a maint dont je me plain!),
      Je leur respons que les livres ne firent
      Pas les femmes, ne les choses n'i mirent
      Que l'en y list contre elles et leurs meurs.
412   Si devisent a l'aise de leurs cuers
54r°   Ceulx qui plaident leur cause sans partie;
      Sans rabatre comptent, et grant partie
      Prennent pour eulx, car de leger offendent
416   Les batailleurs ceulx qui ne se deffendent.
      Mais se femmes eussent li livre fait,
      Je sçay de vray qu'aultrement fust du fait,
      Car bien scevent qu'a tort sont encoulpees.
420   Si ne sont pas les pars a droit coppees,
      Car les plus fors prennent la plus grant part,
      Et le meilleur pour soy qui pieces part.
        Encor dient li felon mesdisant,
424   Qui les femmes vont ainsi desprisant,
      Que toutes sont faulces, seront et furent,
      N'onques ancor nulle loyauté n'urent,
      Et que teles, amans, qui qu'elles soient,
428   Toutes treuvent quant les femmes essayent.

388   As Ovid, later exiled from his land.
           And Jean de Meun's *Roman de la rose*,   haha!
       Oh what a long affair! How difficult!
       The erudition clear and murky both
392   That he put there, with those great escapades!
       So many people called upon, implored,
       So many efforts made and ruses found
       To trick a virgin—that, and nothing more!
396   And that is the aim of it, through fraud and schemes!
       A great assault for such a feeble place?
       How can one leap that far so near the mark?
       I cannot imagine or make sense of it,
400   Such force applied against so frail a place,
       Such ingenuity and subtlety.
       Then necessarily it must be thus:
       Since craft is needed, cleverness and toil,
404   To gull a peasant or a noble born,
       Then women must not have such fickle wills
       As some declare, nor waver in their deeds.
           Should it be said that books are filled with tales
408   Of just such women (I deplore that charge!),
       To this I say that books were not composed
       By women, nor did they record the things
       That we may read against them and their ways.
412   Yet men write on, quite to their hearts' content,
       The ones who plead their case without debate.
       They give no quarter, take the winner's part
       Themselves, for readily do quarrelers
416   Attack all those who do not defend themselves.
       If women, though, had written all those books,
       I know the works would read quite differently,
       For well do women know this blame is wrong.
420   The parts are not apportioned equally,
       Because the strongest take the largest cut
       And he who slices it can keep the best.
           And still the nasty scandalmongers say,
424   Who go about disdaining women thus,
       That all are false, have been, will always be;[22]
       Never have any had much loyalty;
       And suitors find, who try the ladies out,
428   That all are false, no matter who they are.

A toutes fins leur est le tort donné:
Qui qu'ait meffait, sur elles est tourné.
      Mais c'est maudit, et on voit le rebours,
432   Car quant a ce qui affiert a amours,
Trop de femmes y ont esté loyales,
Sont et seront, nonobstant intervalles
Ou faulcetez, baras ou tricheries
436   C'on leur ait fait, et maintes menteries.
Que fu jadis Medee au faulx Jason?
Tres loyalë! Et lui fist la toison
D'or conquerir par son engin soubtil,
440   Dont il acquist loz plus qu'autre cent mil.
Par elle fu renommé dessur tous,
Si lui promist que loyal ami doulx
Seroit tout sien, mais sa foy lui menti
444   Et la laissa pour autre et s'en parti.
      Que fu Dido, roÿne de Cartage?
De grant amour et de loyal courage
Vers Eneas, qui exillé de Troye,
448   Aloit par mer, las, despris et sans joye,
Presque peri, lui et ses chevaliers.
Recueilli fu, dont lui estoit mestiers,
De la belle, qu'il faulcement deceut.
452   Car a tres grant honneur elle receut
Lui et ses gens, et trop de bien lui fist;
Mais puis aprés vers elle tant meffist,
Nonobstant ce que lui eust foy promise
456   Et donnee s'amour, voire en faintise.
Si s'en parti, ne puis ne retourna,
Et autre part la sienne amour tourna;
Dont a la fin celle, pour s'amistié,
460   Mourut de dueil, dont ce fu grant pitié.
      Peneloppe la femmë Ulixés,
Qui raconter vouldroit tout le procés
De la dame, trop trouveroit a dire
464   De sa bonté, ou il n'ot que redire.
Tres belle fu, requise et bien amee,
Noble, sage, vaillant et renommee.
D'autres plusieurs, et tant que c'est sans nombre,
468   Furent et sont et seront en ce nombre.
Mais je me tais adés d'en plus compter,

For every reason women are accused;
No matter who has done wrong, women are blamed.
    How wrong that is! It is just the opposite,
432   For when it comes to matters of the heart,
So many women have been true in love;
They are and will be so, despite the times
They may have had to suffer many lies,
436   Along with ruses, falsehood, trickery.
Medea toward false Jason, how was she?[23]
So very true! And by her subtle craft
He won the golden fleece, through which he was
440   More famous than a hundred thousand men,
Through her he was renowned above the rest.
He promised his would be a loyal love,
Completely hers, but then he broke his word
444   And went away and sought another's arms.
    Dido, the Queen of Carthage, what of her?[24]
She showed great love, she kept her loyalty,
Both for Aeneas, fugitive from Troy,
448   Who crossed the seas worn out, bereft, and sad,
He nearly perished, he and all his crew.
She welcomed him when he was most in need,
That lovely woman whom he then deceived.
452   With very great distinction she received
Aeneas and his men, treating them well.
But afterward he did her so much wrong,
For though he had pledged his faith to her, and had
456   Bestowed his love (indeed, in pure pretense),
Aeneas left her, never to return,
And turned his love away, toward someone else;
And so, because she was in love with him,
460   The grieving Dido died; how pitiful!
    Then there is Penelope, Ulysses' wife:[25]
Whoever thought he would tell about the trials
That she endured would find a lot to say
464   About her goodness, far above reproach.
She was belovèd, beautiful, desired,
And noble, wise, and worthy, much renowned.
Others, so many that they're numberless,
468   Have been and are and will be in the count.
But now I hold my tongue, recount no more,

Car lonc procés seroit a raconter.
Si ne sont pas femmes si desloyales
472   Comme aucun dit, ains sont plusieurs loyales.
Mais il avient, et c'est de commun cours,
C'on les deçoit et traÿst en amours.
Et quant ainsi se treuvent deceües,
476   Les aucunes des plus apperceües
S'en retrayent; de ce font grant savoir.
Doivent elles dont de ce blasme avoir?
Est ce doncques se Dieu vous doint santé,
480   Mal ne folour, barat, ne faulceté?
Nennil, certes, ains est grant sens ainçois!
      Mais je congnois de voir et apperçois
Que se amans tenissent verité,
484   Foy, loyauté, sans contrarïeté,
Vers leur dames feïssent leur devoir,
Comme amant doit faire par droit devoir,
Je croy que pou ou nulle faulseroit,
488   Et que toute femme loyal seroit.
      Mais pour ce que plusieurs faulcent et mentent,
Et en maint lieux par desloyauté hantent,
Leur faulce l'en, et c'est tout par leur coulpe
492   Se on leur fait de tout autel pain souppe.
      Et aucuns sont qui jadis en mes las
Furent tenus, mais ilz sont d'amer las
54v° Ou par viellece ou deffaute de cuer.
496   Si ne veulent plus amer a nul fuer,
Et couvenant m'ont de tous poins nÿé,
Moy et mon fait guerpy et renÿé,
Comme mauvais serviteurs et rebelles.
500   Et tele gent racomptent tieulx nouvelles
Communement, et se plaignent et blasment
Moy et mon fait, et les femmes diffament
Pour ce que plus ne s'en peuent aydier,
504   Ou que leur cuers veulent de moy vuider.
Si les cuident faire aux autres desplaire
Par les blasmer, mais ce ne peuent faire.
      Je hé tel gent trop plus que autre riens, certes,
508   Et les paye souvent de leurs dessertes.
Car en despit de leurs males paroles,
Eulx assotter d'aucunes femmes folles

For that accounting would be long to give.
Thus, women are not quite so insincere
472   As some maintain; in fact, many are true.
And yet it happens, all too commonly,
That they can be deceived, betrayed in love.
And finding, then, that they have been deceived,
476   The women who are most prudent soon withdraw;
In that they are only demonstrating sense.
Should they be blamed for fickleness instead?
Does God so freely give out idle traits,
480   Such evil, foolishness, deceit, and guile?
Why no, indeed! Withdrawing shows great sense!
        But I can truly see and recognize
That if all lovers were to hold to truth,
484   To faith and loyalty, without dispute,
Behaving toward their ladies as they should,
Just as a lover ought to do, by rights,
I think that few women or none would cheat,
488   And every woman would act faithfully.
Because so many men, though, cheat and lie,
Go calling here and there, disloyally,
They are tricked in turn; from their own recipe
492   They are made to eat the self-same humble pie!
        Now some out there were held once in my snares,
But they have become worn out, too tired to love,
Because they are either old or lacking pluck.
496   Refusing love again at any price,
Rejecting every sort of pact with me,
They have turned their backs on me and what I do,
Like wicked and rebellious servitors.
500   Their kind then tell their stories everywhere,
To everyone, they soon complain, and blame
The work I do and me, slurring women,
Because they can no longer love, or else
504   It is that they wish to rid their hearts of me.
They think that men will not desire women
If they condemn them; there, they cannot succeed.
        I hate such people more than anyone,
508   And often pay them just the wage they have earned.
Because, despite the evil words they say,
I make them fall for trifling women, those

De peu d'onneur, males, mau renommees,

512   Je fais yceulx; de tel gent sont amees.
Si ne remaint en eulx plume a plumer:
Bien les scevent a leur droit reclamer.
La sont surpris et bien enveloppé

516   Ceulx qui le mieulx cuident estre eschappé.
Comme il affiert sont tel gent avoyé;
Si leur est bien tout meschief employé.
Et ancor pis, car ceulx qui plus souvent

520   Vont.les femmes par grant soing decevant,
Et qui le plus s'en peinent et travaillent,
N'il ne leur chault qu'il leur couste ou qu'ilz baillent,
Ne quel peinë ilz doyent endurer

524   Pour a grant soing leur vouloir procurer,
Tant qu'ilz tant font par malices prouvees,
Par faulx semblans, par choses controuvees,
Qu'ilz attrayent plusieurs a leurs cordelles

528   Par leurs engins et par faulces cautelles,
Et puis aprés s'en moquent et s'en vantent,
            Et vont disant que femmes se consentent
Legierement, com legieres et fraisles,

532   Et qu'on ne doit avoir fiance en elles.
C'est mal jugié et trop male sentence
De trestoutes pour tant mettre en la dance!
Mais s'aucunes attrayent en tel guise,

536   Quel merveille! Ne fu pas par faintise,
Par faulx consaulx, par traÿson bastie,
Par parlemens, engins et foy mentie,
La grant cité de Troye jadis prise,

540   Qui tant fu fort, et toute en feu esprise?
Et tous les jours par engins et desrois
Ne traÿst on et royaumes et roys?
Trop deçoivent les beaulx blandissemens;

544   Tous en sont plains et livres et romans.
Si n'est pas dont chose a trop merveiller
Quant pour mentir, pener et traveiller,
On peut vaincrë une chose simplete,

548   Une ignorant petite femmellette.
Et fust ores maliciëuse et sage,
Si n'est ce pas en ce grant vassellage
A homme agu, de grant malice plain,

Of little honor, tarts of base repute—
512   Such are the men by whom that type is loved.
Those men have not a feather left to pluck,
Women like that know how to claim their due.
The men are victims, caught and swallowed up—
516   And they are the ones who thought they would get away!
They are led along in just the way that fits;
Misfortune brought their way is well-deserved.
And yet there is even worse: The very men
520   Who often work with care at their deceits,
Who most persistently do strain and strive,
Without a thought to cost nor what they will give,
Nor to the hardship they must surely bear
524   To get, by dint of effort, what they want
(Who practice every proven wicked trick,
Dissembling art, invented scheme, and ploy,
So they succeed in roping in a score
528   Through their chicanery and stratagems)
Are just the ones who later laugh and boast
        And claim aloud that women give themselves
Ever so readily, like easy marks;
532   Thus one should have no confidence in them!
Their judgment is poor, the understanding very bad,
Including all within their merry dance.
And if some women act deceitfully,
536   No wonder! Was not it through counterfeit,
Through false advice and treason well-designed,
Through counsels, craftiness, and perjured faith
That Troy, that city strong and great, was seized
540   Of old, and put entirely to the torch?
And every day, by craft and treachery,
Are not there kings and kingdoms both betrayed?
Fine flattery deceives so very well,
544   And books and stories amply bear the proof.
So hardly is there cause for wonder when,
By lying, struggling with his might and main,
A man may best a naïve, trusting thing:
548   A woman, simple and unassuming.
But if she is slyly clever and malign,
Is it not when she is in the vassalage
Of some unpleasant man who is filled with spite,

552 Qui peine y met comme il en est tout plain?
         Et ainsi sont les femmes diffamees
     De plusieurs gens, et a grant tort blasmees
     Et de bouchë et en plusieurs escrips;
556 Ou qu'il soit voir ou non, tel est le cris.
         Mais qui qu'en ait mesdit ou mal escript,
     Je ne truys pas en livre n'en escript
     Qui de Jhesus parle ne de sa vie
560 Ou de sa mort pourchaciee d'envie,
     N'Euvangile, qui nul mal en tesmoigne,
     Mais maint grant bien, mainte haulte besongne,
     Grant prudence, grant sens et grant constance,
564 Parfaicte amour, en foy grant arrestance,
     Grant charité, fervante voulenté,
     Ferme et entier courage entalenté
     De Dieu servir, et grant semblant en firent,
568 Car mort ne vif oncques ne le guerpirent;
     Fors des femmes fu du tout delaissié
     Le doulx Jhesus, navré, mort et blecié.
         Toute la foy remaint en une femme.
572 Si est trop fol qui d'elles dit diffame,
     Ne fust ores que pour la reverence
     De la haute Roÿne, en remembrance
55rº De sa bonté, qui tant fu noble et digne
576 Que du filz Dieu porter Elle fu digne.
     Grant honneur fist a femme Dieu le Pere,
     Qui faire en volt son espouse et sa mere,
     Temple de Dieu a la Trinité, jointe.
580 Bien estre doit femme joyeuse et cointe
     Qui autele comme Celle forme a,
     Car oncques Dieux nulle riens ne forma
     De dignité semblable, n'aussi bonne,
584 Fors seulement de Jhesus la personne.
     Si est trop folz qui de riens les ramposne
     Quant femmë est assise en si hault trosne
     Coste son filz, a la dextre du Pere.
588 C'est grant honneur a femenine mere.
     Si ne trouvons qu'onques les deprisast
     Le bon Jhesus, mais amast et prisast.
         Dieu la forma a sa digne semblance,
592 Et lui donna savoir et congnoissance

552 Who dishes out all the pain that he has?
    And women are defamed in just that way
By many people, and they are wrongly blamed
In utterance; in many writings, too;
556 Whether true or not, that is what is claimed.
    And yet, whoever is said or written ill
Of women, only good is said of them
In books that speak of Jesus, of His life,
560 Or of His death, pursued so jealously;
The Gospel speaks no ill of them, but all
Record their high responsibilities,
Great prudence, great good sense, great constancy,
564 Their perfect love, their lasting faithfulness,
Their ample charity, their fervent will.
With firm and steadfast hearts and minds they longed
To serve the Lord, as they indeed did show,
568 For never did they leave Him, live or dead;
Except for by women, all alone was
Sweet Jesus left—wounded, dead, and stricken.
In just one woman all the faith remained.
572 How foolish is the man who sullies them,
If only for the reverence due to her,
The Queen of Heaven, in remembrance of
Her goodness; so noble and dignified,
576 She earned the right to bear the Son of God!
Thus God the Father honored woman so,
Who made of her His mother and His spouse;
God's Temple to the Trinity was joined.
580 A woman should be glad and filled with joy
Since she resembles her and has her form;
For God has never formed another thing
Of equal dignity, nor quite as good,
584 Excepting Jesus's own humanity.
How foolish, then, is he who charges them,
When woman's seated on so high a throne
Beside her Son, and to the Father's right,
588 An honor to maternal womankind.
We find that women never were disdained
By Jesus, rather were they loved and prized.
    Now, God created her resembling Him;
592 He gave to her intelligence and skill

Pour soy sauver, et don dentendement.
Si lui donna forme moult noblement
Et fu faite de moult noble matere,
596   Car ne fu pas du limon de la tere,
Mais seulement de la coste de l'omme,
Lequel corps ja estoit, s'en est la somme,
Le plus noble des choses terrïennes.
600   Et les vrayes histoires ancïennes
De la Bible, qui ne peut mençonge estre,
Nous racontent qu'en Paradis terrestre
Fu formee femme premierement,
604   Non pas l'omme. Mais du decevement
Dont on blasme dame Eve nostre mere,
Dont s'ensuivi de Dieu sentence amere,
Je di pour vray qu'onque Adam ne deceut
608   Et simplement de l'ennemi conceut
La parole qu'il lui donna a croire.
Si la cuida estre loyale et voire.
En celle foy de lui dire s'avance,
612   Si ne fu donq fraude ne decevance,
Car simplece, sans malice celee,
Ne doit estre decevance appellee.
Nul ne deçoit sans cuider decevoir,
616   Ou autrement decevance n'est voie.
          Quieulx grans maulx donc en peuent estre dis?
Par desservir n'ont elles Paradis?
De quieulx crimes les peut on accuser?
620   Et s'aucuns folz a leur amour muser
Veulent, a eulx par quoy mal en couviengne,
N'en peuent mais; qui est sage s'en tiengne.
Qui est deceu et cuidoit decevoir
624   Fors lui tout seul n'en doit le blasme avoir.
Et se sur ce je vouloie tout dire,
Doubte aroie d'encourir d'aucuns l'ire.
Car moult souvent pour dire verité
628   Mautalent vient, et contrarïeté.
Pour ce ne vueil faire comparoisons;
Haineuses sont a la fois tieulx raisons.
Si me souffist de louer sans blamer,
632   Car on peut bien quelque riens bon clamer
Sans autre riens nommer mauvais ou pire.

To save her soul, and judgment and good sense.
When God created her he gave her form
Majestic, made of very noble stuff:
596 For not from earthly mud was she derived,
But made uniquely from the rib of man,
Whose body was, all told, among the things
Of earth, the noblest one that had been made.
600 The old and trusted stories that are found
Within the Bible—certainly not lies—
Relate that woman was the first to be
Created in the earthly Paradise,
604 Not man. Now as to the deceitful act
For which our mother Eve is brought to blame,
Upon which followed God is harsh punishment,
I say she never did play Adam false,
608 In innocence she took the enemy's
Assertion, which he led her to believe.
Accepting it as true, sincerely said,
She went to tell her mate what she had heard.
612 No fraudulence was there, no planned deceit,
For guilelessness, which has no hidden spite,
Must not he labeled as deceptiveness.
For none deceives without intending to,
616 Or else it is not really called deceit.
        What evils can be said of womankind?
And is not Paradise their recompense?
What awful crimes can one accuse them of?
620 And if some foolish men prefer to play
At love—and may they gain but ill from it—
They cannot do else; yet let the wise refrain;
For he who planned deceit but was instead
624 Deceived has but himself alone to blame.
And if, on this, I were to say it all,
I would fear incurring wrath from certain ones,
For very often speaking out the truth
628 Creates ill feeling and hostility.
So I do not want to make comparisons:
Comparisons, at times, just cause more hate.
Let me be satisfied to praise not blame,
632 For one can call some people good without
Comparing, saying who is bad or worse.

Car son bon droit aucune foiz empire
Cellui qui blasme autrui pour s'aloser;
636 Si se vault mieulx du dire repposer.
Pour ce m'en tais. Si en soit chacun juge:
Si justement selon verité juge,
Si trouvera, se vient a droit juger,
640 Que leur plus grant maulx peut pou domager.
        N'occïent gent, ne blecent, ne mahaignent,
Ne traÿsons ne pourchacent n'emprennent.
Feu ne boutent, ne desheritent gent,
644 N'empoisonnent, n'emblent or në argent.
Ne deçoivent d'avoir ne d'eritage
N'en faulx contras, et ne portent dommage
Aux royaumes, aux duchez, n'aux empires.
648 Mal ne s'ensuit gueres, mesmes des pires.
Communement une ne fait pas rigle.
        Car qui vouldra par histoire ou par Bible
Me remprover par moy donner exemple
652 D'une ou de deux ou de plusieurs ensemble
        Qui ont esté reprouvees et males,
Encore en sont celles met ennormales.
55v° Car je parle selon le commun cours,
656 Car moult pou sont qui usent de tieulx tours.
        Et s'on me veult dire que mie enclines
Condicions et taches femenines
Ne sont a ce, n'a user de batailles,
660 N'a gent tuer, në a faire fouailles
Pour bouter feu, në a tieulx choses faire,
Pour ce nul preu, louange, ne salaire
Ne leur en peut ne doit appartenir
664 D'elles souffrir de telz cas n'abstenir,
Mais sauve soit la grace des diseurs,
Je consens bien qu'elles n'ont pas les cuers
Enclins a ce, ne a faiz de tel affaire!
668 Car nature de femme est debonnaire,
Moult piteuse, paoureuse et doubtable,
Humble, doulce, coye, et moult charitable,
Amiable, devote, en paix honteuse,
672 Et guerre craint, simple et religïeuse.
Et en courrous tost appaise son yre,
Ne peut vëoir cruauté ne martire.

> For he who blames another just to praise
> Himself casts doubt on his integrity.

636 It is certainly far better not to speak.
And so I hold my tongue. Let each one judge,
And, heeding truth, adjudicate the case.
He will find, if he will try it honestly,

640 Her greatest fault can cause but little harm.
She does not kill or wound or mutilate,
Or foster any treasonous misdeeds;
Or dispossess another; set afire

644 Or poison; pilfer silver, steal one's gold;
Or cheat of wealth or one's inheritance
Through bogus contracts; nor does she bring harm
To empires or to duchies or to realms.

648 Ill barely follows, even from the worst.
Commonly, one alone will not prove the rule.
And so, whoever would search history
Or in the Bible just to prove me wrong,

652 With instances of one or two or more
Who have been immoral women and corrupt,
Will find those cases are abnormal ones.
I am speaking of the great majority,

656 For very few are those who use such tricks.
And if there is someone who would say to me
That women's traits and qualities are not
Inclined toward things like that—toward making war,

660 Or murdering, or fashioning the torch
To start the blaze, or any of these things—
And thus no special credit, praise, or pay
Belongs to them, nor can nor should apply,

664 For struggling to abstain from all of that,
With due respect to those who hold this view,
I quite agree, indeed, that women's hearts
Are not so made, disposed toward wickedness!

668 For woman's nature is but sweet and mild,
Compassionate and fearful, timorous
And humble, gentle, sweet, and generous,
And pleasant, pious, meek in time of peace,

672 Afraid of war, religious, plain at heart.
When angry, quickly she allays her ire,
Nor can she bear to see brutality

[handwritten note:] yes, there are corrupt women, but they aren't the norm

Et teles sont par nature sans doubte
676   Condicions de femme, somme toute.
Et celle qui ne les a d'aventure,
Contre le droit toute se desnature,
Car cruauté fait en femme a reprendre,
680   Ne l'en n'i doit fors toute doulceur prendre.
        Et puisqu'elz n'ont meurs ne condicions
A faire fais de sanc n'occisions,
N'a autres grans pechez lais et orribles,
684   Dont sont elles ignocens et paysibles,
Voire, des grans et innormes pechez;
Car chacun est d'aucun vice tachez,
Si ne seront doncques pas encoulpees
688   Des grans meffais ou ne sont attrappees.
Si n'en aront n'en peine në en coulpe
Punicion, puisqu'elles n'y ont courpe,
Dont dire puis (ce n'est pas heresie)
692   Que moult leur fist le hault Dieu courtoisie
D'elles former sans les condicions
        Qui mettent gens a griefs perdicions.
Car des desirs s'en ensuivent les fais
696   Dont maint portent sur leur armes grief fais.
Si vault trop mieulx c'on n'ait pas le desir
Dont l'acomplir souvent fait mort gesir.
Qui soustenir vouldroit seroit herite
700   Que qui tempté n'est n'a point de merite
De non pecher et de soy abstenir.
Teles raisons ne font a soustenir,
Car nous veons par les sains le contraire:
704   Saint Nicolas n'eüst sceu peché faire,
Onq ne pecha n'oncques n'en fu tempté;
N'autres plusieurs n'en orent voulenté.
Je di pecher quant est mortellement,
708   Pecher povoient ilz veniellement.
Si sont tous ceulx appellez prëesleus,
Predestinez et de Dieu esleüs.
        Par ces raisons conclus et vueil prouver
712   Que grandement femmes a approuver
Font et louer, et leurs condicions
Recommander, qui inclinacions
N'ont aux vices qui humaine nature

Or suffering. It is clear those qualities
676   By nature make a woman's character.
And she who is lacking them by accident
Corrupts her nature, goes against the grain.
In women, cruelty is to be reproved,
680   And gentleness alone should be approved.
      Now since it is not their temper or their way
To kill or bring about some bloody act,
Nor have they other ugly, awful sins;
684   They are innocent of them, completely free,
Indeed, of flagrant and enormous sins.
Now each of us is tainted by some sin,
But women will not be marked as culpable
688   For great misdeeds in which they are not ensnared.
Nor will they have, through suffering or pain,
The punishment for sins that are not theirs.
Thus I can say, and it is no heresy,
692   That God on high did them a courtesy
When He created them without those traits
      That lead one into grave calamity.
For from desires those same pursuits are born
696   Whose hardships leave their mark on many souls.
It is better, then, by far to lack desire,
Whose satisfying often causes death.
A heretic alone would take the view
700   That one not tempted merits no reward
For not committing sins, for self-restraint.
That sort of thinking cannot be sustained:
The lives of saints confirm the opposite.
704   Saint Nicholas could not have known sin's way;[26]
He never sinned, nor was he tempted to.
And many others never had the wish.
When wrong is mortal then I call it sin;
708   Indeed, they could have sinned but venially.
So all of those are called the chosen few,
Predestined people, God's elected ones.
      It is my conclusion, and I want to prove,
712   That women do so very much to be
Applauded, and therefore I recommend
Their traits, which show no inclination toward
The vices that scathe human character

[handwritten margin note:] ∴ no need to talk about how hard it is to resist (women's) temptation if that's not important

716   Va domagiant et grevant creature.
         Par ces preuves justes et veritables
         Je conclus que tous hommes raisonnables
         Doivent femmes prisier, cherir, amer,
720   Et ne doivent avoir cuer de blamer
         Elles de qui tout homme est descendu.
         Ne leur soit pas mal pour le bien rendu,
         Car c'est la riens ou monde par droiture
724   Que homme aime mieulx et de droite nature.
         Si est moult lait et grant honte a blasmer
         La riens qui soit que l'en doit plus amer
         Et qui plus fait a tout homme de joye.
728   Homs naturel sans femme ne s'esjoye:
         C'est sa mere, c'est sa seur, c'est s'amie,
         Et pou avient que a homs soit ennemie.
         C'est son droit per qui a lui est semblable,
732   La riens qui plus lui peut estre agreable.
         Në on n'y peut pris ne los conquester
         A les blamer, mais grant blame acquester.
         N'il n'est blame si lait ne si nuisant
736   Comme tenu estre pour mesdisant,
         Voire, ancor plus especiallement
         De diffamer femmes communement.
         C'est un vice diffamable et villain;
740   Je le deffens a homme quant je l'aim.
  56r°   Si s'en gard donc trestout noble courage,
         Car bien n'en peut venir, mais grant domage,
         Honte, despit et toute villenie;
744   Qui tel vice a n'est pas de ma mesgnie.
                 Or ay conclus en tous cas mes raisons
         Bien et a droit; n'en desplaise a nulz homs.
         Car se bonté et valour a en femme,
748   Honte n'est pas a homme ne diffame,
         Car il est né et fait d'autel merrien.
         Se mauvaise est, il ne peut valoir rien,
         Car nul bon fruit de mal arbre ne vient.
752   Telle qu'elle est ressembler lui couvient,
         Et se bonne est, il en doit valoir mieulx,
         Car aux meres bien ressemblent les fieulx.
         Et se j'ay dit d'elles bien et louange,
756   Comme il est vray, ne l'ay fait par losange

716   And bring to human beings pain and woe.
        So, through these just, veracious arguments
        I demonstrate that reasonable men
        Should value women, love and cherish them;
720   And should not have a mind to deprecate
        The female sex, from whom each man is born.
        Let none repay them evil for their good,
        For woman, rightly, is that single soul
724   Whom man loves deeply and through natural law. (Mother - son)
        How shabby, then, how scandalous it is
        To blame the being one ought most to love,
        And who affords each man the greatest joy.
728   Without a woman, he who is natural
        Is sad, for she is his mother, sister, love.
        And rarely is she enemy to him,
        For she is his kindred soul, so much like him,
732   The being most compatible with him.
        Nor can one conquer, honor, or esteem
        By blaming her, for blame alone is won.
        No blame so foul or damaging exists
736   As being thought a bearer of false tales,
        And that is more especially the case
        When women as a group are criticized.
        For that is a shameful and a vulgar flaw,
740   Which I forbid to any man I love.
        Let every noble heart avoid it, then,
        For good cannot come of it, but harm alone,
        Humiliation, every baseness, shame;
744   Who has that vice is not of my domain.
            I have shown my thinking now on every point
        Justly and well; let no man be displeased.
        For if in women there is good and worth,
748   That is surely no disgrace or shame to man!
        For he is born and made of equal clay:
        If she is bad, then he can have no worth,
        For no good fruit can come from rotten trees.
752   He must resemble her just as she is,
        And if she is good, he must be worth the more,
        For mothers give their likeness to their sons.
        And if I have said fine things in praise of them,
756   As truth allows, it was not flattery,

[handwritten margin note: bringing down women only also brings down men]

N'a celle fin que plus orgueil en aient,
Mais tout affin que toudis elles soient
Curïeuses de mieulx en mieulx valoir,
760   Sans les vices que l'en ne doit avoir.
Car qui plus a grant vertu et bonté,
En doit estre moins d'orgueil surmonté,
Car les vertus si enchacent les vices.
764   Et s'il est des femmes aucunes nices,
Cest epistre leur puist estre doctrine.
Le bien prennent pour loyale doctrine,
Le mal laissent. Les bonnes vueillent en ce
768   Prendre vouloir d'avoir perseverance,
Si en aront preu, joye, honneur et loz,
Et Paradis a la fin, dire l'oz.
           Pour ce conclus en diffinicion
772   Que des mauvais soit fait punicion,
Qui les blasment, diffament et acusent,
Et qui de faulx desloyaulx semblans usent
Pour decevoir elles. Si soient tuit
776   De nostre court chacié, bani, destruit,
Et entredis et escommenïé,
Et tous noz biens si leur soient nïé;
C'est bien raison qu'on les excommenie.
780   Et commandons de fait a no mesgnie
Generaument, et a noz officiers,
A noz sergens et a tous noz maciers,
A noz prevosts et maires et baillis
784   Et vicaires, que tous ceulx maubaillis
Et villenez soient tres laidement,
Injurïez, punis honteusement,
Pris et liez, et justice en soit faite,
788   Sans plus souffrir nulle injure si faite,
Ne plus ne soit enduré tel laidure.
Nous le voulons ainsi et c'est droiture.
Accompli soit sans faire aucun delais.
792   Donné en l'air en nostre grant palais,
Le jour de may la sollempnee feste
Ou les amans nous font mainte requeste,
L'an de grace mil trois cent quatre vins
796   Et dix et neuf, presens dieux et divins.
           Par le dieu d'Amours puissant

Nor so that they might puff themselves with pride,
But to that end that always they may be
Desirous of increasing their own worth,
760   Avoiding vices one ought not to have;
Whoever has great virtue and is good
Is necessarily less gripped by pride,
For thus do virtues drive our vices out.
764   And if some foolish women are about,
May this epistle be enlightening,
And may they take the good as loyal creed,
Leaving the bad. Let worthy women find
768   In these remarks the will to persevere,
And they will have honor, joy, esteem, and gain,
And they will earn Paradise, I dare maintain.
       With this in mind I give my final word:
772   Let punishment be dealt to the corrupt,
Who level blame, accuse, calumniate,
And who employ their false appearances
In order to deceive. And thus let all
776   Be banished from our court, chased out, brought low,
Banned from all rites and excommunicated.
May all our favors be denied to them;
Their interdiction is appropriate.
780   And we command emphatically to all
The members of our court, our officers,
Our process servers, and our men-at-arms;
Our provosts, mayors, and our magistrates
784   And deputies, that all such men must be
Treated contemptuously, fully shamed,
Thoroughly ruined, punished in disgrace
And seized and bound. Justice be done to them!
788   No more shall we endure such injuries,
And no more let such villainy be borne.
We wish it thus, and it is right and just.
So may it be enforced without delay.
792   Enacted in our palace in the sky
This day in May, the solemn festival
When lovers make many requests of us,
The year of grace, in thirteen ninety-nine,
796   And witnessed by the gods and deities.
       From the mighty God of Love,

                A la relacion de cent
                Dieux et plus de grant povoir,
800   Confermans nostre vouloir:
                      Jupiter, Appollo et Mars,
                Vulcan, par qui Pheton fu ars;
                Mercurïus, dieu de lengage,
804   Eolus, qui vens tient en cage.
                Neptunus, le dieu de la mer,
                Glaucus, qui mer fait escumer,
                Les dieux des vaulx et des montaignes,
808   Des grans forests et des champaignes.
                Et les dieux qui par nuit obscure
                S'en vont pour querir aventure.
                Pan, dieu des pastours, Saturnus,
812   Nostre mere la grant Venus,
                Pallas, Juno et Lathona,
                Cerés, Vesta, Anthigona,
                Aurora, Thetis, Arecusa,
816   Qui le dieu Pluto encusa,
                Minerve la bateillerresse,
   56vº   Et Dyane la chassarresse,
                Et d'autres dieux no conseiller
820   Et deesses plus d'un miller.
                      Cupido le dieu d'Amours,
                Cui amans font leurs clamours.
                      Explicit l'Epistre au dieu d'Amours

Reported to a hundred
Gods and more, whose power is vast,
800   Making our wishes firmly known:
           Jupiter, Apollo, and Mars,
       And Vulcan, by whom Phaeton burned,
       And Mercury, the god of tongues,[27]
804   Aeolus, he who cages winds,
       And Neptune, god of all the seas,
       And Glaucus, he who churns the foam,
       The gods of mountaintop and vale,
808   The gods of the great woods and plains,
       And gods who in the dark of night
       Go forth on their adventuring;
       And Saturn; Pan, the shepherd's god;
812   Our mother, greatest Venus;
       Pallas, Juno, and Latona,
       Vesta, Antigone, Aurora,
       Thetis, Arethusa, Ceres,
816   By whom god Pluto was accused,[28]
       Minerva, woman warrior,
       Diana, goddess of the hunt,
       And other gods, our counselors,
820   A thousand goddesses and more.
           Cupid, the God of Love, to whom
       All lovers send their doleful cries.
           Here ends the Letter of the God of Love.

2. *1399–1400: Les enseignemens moraux que Cristine donne a son filz*[29]

The *Enseignemens* contain 113 moral dicta, expressed in quatrains, written in the second person and addressed to Christine's son Jean. As Roberta Krueger proclaims, "The maternal speaker offers traditional advice without comment. There is no authorial portrait, although the counsel that one should not 'diffame' women or read Ovid's *Ars amatoria* or the *Roman de la rose* distinguish the *Enseignemens* as Christine's."[30] It is this particular advice to her son which is reproduced here.

Text:

264v° Se tu veulx fuir le danger
     D'amours et du tout l'estranger,
     Eslongne toy de la personne
4   A qui ton cuer le plus se donne.

     Se bien veulx et chastement vivre,
     De la rose ne lis le livre
     Ne Ovide de l'Art d'amer,
8   Dont l'exemple fait a blasmer.

     Se tu veulx lire des batailles
     Et des regnes les commencailles,
     Si lis Vincent et autres mains,
12   Le fait de troye et des rommains.

     Pour devocion acquerir
     Se tu veulx es livres querir,
     Saint Bernard et aultres aucteurs
16   Te seront en ce fait docteurs.

     S'en amours tu as ton vouloir
     Et veulx amer pour mieulz valoir,
     Ne t'en mez tele rage ou pis
20   Que tu en puisses valoir pis.

Translation:

The Moral Teachings Given by Christine to Her Son

If you wish to flee the danger
Of love and chase it away entirely,
Distance yourself from the person
4   To whom your heart gives itself the most.

If you wish to live well and chastely,
Do not read the book of the Rose,
Nor Ovid's *Ars amatoris*,
8   Which is an example that incites reproach.

If you wish to read about battles
And the beginnings of reigns,
Read Saint Vincent and many others,[31]
12   The deeds of Troy and of the Romans.

he's the one who led her/guided her

In order to acquire piousness,
If you wish to seek it in books,
Saint Bernard and other theologians
16   Will be your masters in this matter.[32]

If your desire is for love
And you wish to love in order to increase your worth,
Do not allow yourself to endure such pain
20   That you will be worth less for it.

3. 1400: Le livre du débat de deux amans[33]

The love debate, which has just over 2000 lines, is humbly dedicated to the
Duke of Orléans,[34] an arbiter in the matter presented before him. At the end
of the poem, after a lengthy debate between Christine, two other ladies, and a
squire concerning the dangers of foolish love, the author/narrator intervenes,
when it becomes clear that a judgment cannot be rendered and that a mediator
is needed.[35]

Text:

A Knight Complains about the Pains of Love and Jealousy

63v°	«Fuyez, fuyez,
	Yceste amour, jeunes gens! et voyez
	Comment on est pour lui mal avoyez!
4	Ses promesses, pour Dieu, point ne croyez,
	Car son attente
	Couste plus chier que ne fait nulle rente.
	Nul ne s'i met, qu'aprés ne s'en repente,
8	Car trop en est perilleuse la sente,
	Sachés sans doubte,
	Et moult en est de leger la foy route.
	C'est un trespas obscur, ou ne voit goute
12	Cil qui s'i fiert et nissement s'i boute,
	N'est pas mençonge;
	Tant de meschiefs en vient, que c'est un songe,
	Si tient plus court que l'esparvier la longe,
16	Et mal en vient, le plus de ce respon ge,
	C'est fait prouvé.
	Croyez cellui qui bien l'a esprouvé:
	Si ne suis je mie pour tant trouvé
20	Sage en ce cas, mais nice et reprouvé,
	C'est mon dalmage.
	Mais a la fois, un fol avise un sage,
	Et qui esté a en lointain voyage
24	Peut bien compter comment on s'i hebarge,
	En mainte guise.
	Qui s'i vouldra mirer, je l'en avise,
	Car tous les jours avient par tel devise,
28	Mais du peril ne se gaite ny vise
	L'amant musart,

Translation:

"Flee, flee
From this love, young people! And see
How ill-guided one is because of it!
4   Do not believe its promises, by God,
For its expectations
Are more costly than any other loan.
No one commits to it without later regretting it,
8   For this path is too perilous,
Be certain of it,
Too fickle is the road of this faith.
It is an obscure pathway, where one sees not a thing;
12   He who trusts it and stupidly stumbles onto it,
This is no lie,
Will encounter so much misfortune that it is a dream
Which is shorter than the leash of a ladyhawk,
16   And evil comes of it, this I guarantee:
It is a proven fact.
Believe one who has experienced it thoroughly:
And in this case I was not
20   Considered wise, but stupid and disdainful,
This is the damage I suffer.
But sometimes a foolish person counsels a wise one,
And whoever has traveled to faraway places
24   Can well recount how to hide oneself,
Under many guises.
Whoever would like to follow my example, I recommend it,
For every day this is the story of the foolish lover
28   Who does not look out for peril
And puts his life in this hazardous state,

Qui sa vie met en si fait hasart,

64r°   Et n'escheve le grant feu et tout s'art;

32   Ainçois le suit et celle amour de s'art

L'amant esprent

Par le plaisir qui a amer le prent.

Si le tient si qu'il ne scet s'il mesprent

36   Ou s'il fait bien, et, s'aucun l'en reprent,

Il s'en courrouce

Ne gre n'en scet; tant a plaines de mousse

Ses oreilles, qui de raison escousse

40   Sont si que ouÿr lui semble chose doulce

De chose amere,

Et sa marrastre il retient pour sa mere;

Felicité lui semble estre misere,

44   Et de misere et servage se pere;

Est il bien bugle?

Ainsi amours fait devenir avugle

Le fol amant, qui se cueuvre d'un cruble

48   Et bien cuide veoir en temps de nuble

Le cler souleil,

Et juge bon ce qu'il lui plaist a l'ueil,

Ainsi est il. Pour tant, dire ne vueil

52   Ce que je di pour ce que n'aye vueil

D'amours servir,

Ne pour blasmer qui s'i veult asservir,

Mais pour dire comme il s'i fault chevir

56   Qui a amours veult loyauté pleuvir

De cuer certains.

Ainsi, ma dame, et vous, beau doulx compains,

Ouÿr pouez que l'amant a trop mains

60   De ses plaisirs, s'il est a droit attains,

Qu'il n'a de joye;

Ce scevent ceulx qu'amours destraint et loye

En ses lïens, ou maint homme foloye.

64   Savoir le doy, car griefment m'en douloye

Quant en ce point

Estoye pris; encor n'en suis je point

Quitte du tout, dont dessoubz mon pourpoint

68   Couvertement ay souffert maint dur point

A grant hachee.

Mais je ne croy que a nul si bien en chee

And cannot escape the great fire where all will burn;
Instead, he follows it, and this love will burn him.
32   The lover is set ablaze by the pleasure
That pushes him to love.
If it happens that he does not know he is erring
Or if he is lucky and someone criticizes him,
36   He gets irritated;
He does not know to be thankful. His ears are so full of
Moss that when shaken by reason
He thinks he hears sweet things
40   Rather than bitter ones,
And he will mistake his godmother for his mother;
Bliss will seem misery to him
And he will pair up with misery and servitude;
44   Is he a young bull?
This is how love blinds
The foolish lover who covers himself with a sieve,[36]
And who is convinced that in times of fog
48   He sees the clear sun.
And judges well what is to his eye's liking,
Thus it is. However, I do not wish to say
What I say because I do not wish
52   To serve love,
Nor to insult anyone who wishes to become its servant,
But to say how one must act
If one wishes to swear loyalty to love   ✳
56   Out of a steadfast heart.
Therefore, my lady, and you, beautiful sweet friend,
Can hear that the lover has far fewer
Pleasures, if he is directly affected,
60   Than he has joy;
Those entrapped by love and kept in its trap,
Where many a man becomes a fool, know this.
I must know, for painfully I did hurt
64   When I was taken to that place;
I am not yet free of it,
For under my cloak I hide
The sufferings of many a cruel blow
68   By a large ax.
Yet I do not believe that whoever has fallen so far
Ought to suffer such a punishment

64r°   Que tel peine ne lui soit approuchee,
72   Com je vous ay ycy dicte et preschee;
            Ce n'est pas fable».
                    Quant le courtois chevalier aimable
            Ot finee sa parole nottable
76   Que li plusieurs tendroient veritable
            Et bien comptee,
            Dite a beaulx trais, ne peu ne trop hastee,
            La dame adont, qui bien l'ot escoutee,
80   Recommença et dit, «Se j'ay nottee
            Vostre parole,
            Bien a son droit Amours a dure escolle
            Tient les amans, qui n'est doulce ne molle,
84   Sicom j'entens, et qui maint homme affolle
            Sans achoison.
            Mais quant a moy, tiens que mie foison
            Ne sont d'amans pris en tele prison,
88   Tout non obstant que plusieurs leur raison
            Vont racontant,
            Puis ça puis la, aux dames, mais pour tant
            N'y ont le cuer, ne ne sont arrestant
92   En un seul lieu, combien qu'assez gastant
            A longue verve
            De leur mos vont; mais que nul s'i asserve
            Si durement ne croy, ne que ja serve
96   Si loyaument de pensee si serve
            Amours et dame;
            Et sauve soit vostre grace, par m'ame,
            Ne croy que nul espris de tele flame
100   Soit qu'il ait tant de griefs doulours pour femme.
            Mais c'est un compte
            Assez commun, que aux femes in racompte
            Pour leur donner a croire, et tout ne monte
104   Chose qui soit; et celle qui aconte
            A tel lengage,
            A la parfin on la tient a pou sage.
            Et quant a moy, tiens que ce n'est que usage
108   D'ainsi parler d'amours par rigolage
            Et passer temps,
            Et s'il fu voir, ce que dire j'entens,
            Qu'ainsi fussent vray en l'anciën temps

As I have declared and preached here;

72   This is not a fable."
          When the kind, courtly knight
     Finished his illustrious speech—
     Which some would consider truthful

76   And well recounted,
     Told in beautiful phrases, neither too slow nor too fast—
     The lady who listened to him well,
     Spoke again and said, "If I have understood

80   Your speech,
     Justifiably, Love keeps lovers
     In a trying school, which is neither sweet nor soft—
     I understand it thus—and which makes many a man foolish

84   Without justification.
     As for me, however, I think there are not many lovers
     Who are captured in such a prison,
     Although there are some who go about *that of foolishness from love*

88   Telling ladies this and that,
     But their hearts are not in it, neither are they loyal
     To one single place, so that their words
     Go far in causing damage; yet I do not believe

92   That many are greatly subservient to their words; if they are not
          already loyal
     In thought, how can they be so to
     Love and ladies;

96   And with all due respect, by my soul,
     I do not believe anyone is so incensed
     That he endures such hurtful pains for a woman.
     That is a tale

100   Quite common told to women
     In order to make them believe it is
     The most valuable thing there is,
     And she who succumbs to such language

104   Is considered to be not very wise in the end.
     As for me, I think that to speak about love like this
     Is merely a custom, to laugh,
     And to pass the time,

108   And if it is true, what I hear tell,
     That it was thus in ancient times,
     More than a century ago,
     I think

112   Li amoureux, il a plus de cent ans,
        Au mien cuidier
        Que ce n'avint, ce n'est ne d'ui ne d'yer
        Qu'ainsi attains soient; mais par plaidier
116   Et bien parler se scevent bien aydier
        Li amoureux,
        Et se jadis et mors et langoureux
        Ilz en furent, et mains maulx doulereux
120   Endurerent mesmes les plus eureux,
        Comme vous dites,
        Je croy qu'adés leurs douleurs sont petites.
        Mais es rommans sont trouvees escriptes
124   A droit souhaid et proprement descriptes
        A longue prose.
        Bien en parla le Rommant de la Rose
        A grant proces, et auques ainsi glose
128   Ycelle amour, com vous avez desclose
        En ceste place,
        Ou chapitre Raison, qui moult menace,
        Le fol amant, qui tel amour enlace,
132   Et trop bien dit que pou vault et tost passe
        La plus grant joye
        D'icelle amour, et conseille la voye
        De s'en oster; et bien dit toutevoye
136   Que c'est chose qui trop l'amant desvoye,
        Et dur flëaulx,
        Et que c'est la desloyauté loyaulx
        Et loyauté qui est trop desloyaulx,
140   Un grant peril ou nobles et royaulx,
        Et toute gent
        Sont perillé s'ilz en vont approuchant.
        Ainsi fu dit....»

112   That this was never so, not today and not yesterday,
        That lovers were affected thus,
        But by pleading and speaking eloquently,
        Lovers know well how to help themselves.
116   And if in former times they were dying and languishing,
        And even the happiest endured
        Many hurtful pains,
        As you say,
120   I think that now their pains are small.
        In romances one can find them written
        To one's desire and properly described
        In long prose.
124   The *Roman de la rose* spoke of them well
        At length, and detailed
        Such a love as you have disclosed.
        In this work,
128   In the chapter of Reason she greatly threatens
        The Foolish Lover, who is entangled in such love,
        And she says all too clearly that it is not worth much, and that
        The greatest joy will pass quickly
132   From this love, and she tells of the path
        To use to escape it; and she says
        That in any case it is a thing which misleads
        The lover too much
136   And is a cruel burden to bear,
        And that it is loyal disloyalty
        And loyalty which is too disloyal,
        A great peril, where nobles, royals,
140   And all people
        Are in danger if they come close to it."

Notes

1. For a detailed analysis of the points of connection between Guillaume de Machaut and the *Roman de la rose* I refer to Pierre-Yves Badel, *Le Roman de la Rose au XIVe siècle. Étude de la réception de l'œuvre* (Geneva: Droz, 1980), 82–94; Karl D. Uitti, "From Clerc to Poète: The Relevance of the *Romance of the Rose* to Machaut's World," in *Machaut's World: Science and Art in the Fourteenth Century*, ed. Madeleine Pelner Cosman and Bruce Chandler (New York: New York Academy of Sciences, 1978), 209–16; and Sylvia Huot, "Reliving the *Roman de la rose*: Allegory and Irony in Machaut's *Voir-Dit*," in *Chaucer's French Contemporaries. The Poetry/Poetics of Self and Tradition*, ed. R. Barton Palmer (New York: AMS P, 1999), 47–70.
2. Let us not forget that Christine dedicates one of her poems to him, the *Epistre a Eustace Morel*, written on February 10, 1403. For the most recent edition of this poem, see Jean-François Kosta-Théfaine, "*L'Epistre a Eustace Morel* de Christine de Pisan," *Le moyen français* 38 (1996): 79–91. See also E. Jeffrey Richards, "The Lady Wants to Talk: Christine de Pizan's *Epistre a Eustace Mourel*," in *Eustache Deschamps, French Courtier-Poet. His Work and His World*, ed. Deborah M. Sinnreich-Levi (New York: AMS Press, 1998), 109–22.
3. Discussed in Sylvia Huot, 1998, "The *Miroir de mariage*: Deschamps Responds to the *Roman de la rose*," in *Eustache Deschamps, French Courtier-Poet*, 131–144.
4. William Calin, 1998, "Deschamps's 'Ballade to Chaucer' Again, or the Dangers of Intertextual Medieval Comparatism," in *Eustache Deschamps, French Courtier-Poet*, 73–84; 75.
5. For a general biographical overview, I refer to the introduction of Deschamps, *Oeuvres complètes*, 11 vols, ed. Auguste Queux de Saint-Hilaire and Gaston Raynaud (Paris: Didot, 1878–1903), repr., New York: Johnson Reprint Corporation, 1966).
6. *Oeuvres complètes*, 2:138–39. Most of Deschamps prolific literary output has been preserved in a single manuscript compiled a few years after his death, BN fr. 840. For further analysis of this ballade, see William Calin, "Deschamps's 'Ballade to Chaucer'" which I used for the transcription and the translation of the passage with slight modifications in the translation. Reprinted with permission of AMS Press.
7. Calin, "Deschamps 'Ballade to Chaucer,'" 76.The messenger was Sir Lewis Clifford, who is mentioned as "l'amoureux Cliffort" in the refrain of another one of Deschamps's ballades (no. 536, 3:376–376). As a soldier and negotiator, Clifford was a member of Chaucer's circle. Moreover, he was a protégé and intimate of the very highest echelons in both England and France.
8. The excerpt is quoted in G. W. Coopland's edition, *Le songe du vieil pelerin*, 2 vols (Cambridge, UK: Cambridge University Press, 1969), 340–41.
9. I thank Thelma Fenster and Mary Carpenter Erler for permitting me to reproduce their edition and translation of this text which appears in *Poems of Cupid, God of Love*. Christine de Pizan's *Epistre au dieu d'Amours and Dit de la Rose*, Thomas Hoccleve's *The Letter of Cupid, with George Sewell's The Proclamation of Cupid*, ed. Thelma S. Fenster and Mary Carpenter Erler (Leiden: Brill, 1990). The extant manuscripts (containing Christine's collected works) are:
    a. Chantilly Condé 492 (anc. 1667)
    b. Bibliothèque Nationale fonds français 12779 (Mouchet, suppl. fr. 6259)
    c. BN f.fr. 604, anc. 7087, de la Mare 413
    d. BN f.fr. 835 (anc. 7217, Dupuy 466, Rigault 593)
    e. British Library Harley 4431 (fols 51ro–56vo) (base manuscript)
    According to Thelma Fenster and Mary Carpenter Erler, "A sixth manuscript, Westminster Abbey MS 21 (siglum W), contains the *Epistre au dieu d'Amours*, the *Dit de la Pastoure*, and a *Jeu a vendre*, but it is a miscellaneous collection of works by divers hands and not a 'book' of Christine's poems...." In addition to these manuscripts, Fenster and Carpenter Erler mention an early printed edition of the *Epistre*, the whereabouts of which are not known. It is titled *Le contre roman de la Rose nommé le gratia dei*, and was once held by the Biblioteca Colombina in Seville. However, according to Roy, it was stolen and sold to M. le baron Pichon in 1884 (in *Poems of Cupid*, n.28, 20 and in Roy, vol. 2, ix). Maurice Roy was the first to prepare an

edition of this text, in vol. 2 of his *Oeuvres poétiques de Christine de Pisan*, vols.1–28 (1886, 1891, 1896; repr., New York: Johnson, 1965), using BN f. Fr. 835 as his base manuscript. For a description of the extant manuscripts, their classification and justification for changing to Harley 4431 as base manuscript, I refer to Fenster and Carpenter Erler's edition, 20–25. For a list of variants in BN f. Fr. 835, see 79 (MS D).

10. See Hicks, *Le débat sur le Roman de la rose* (Geneva: Slatkine, 1996), xxix. Eric Hicks, and many Christine-scholars after him, have shown convincingly that despite the repeated mention of the *Roman* in the *Epistre*, and despite the plea to the Court of Love to counteract uncourtly behavior by men, this poem cannot be considered the cause for the ensuing correspondence that was to be called the Quarrel (see in particular Hicks, *Le débat*, xxviii–xxxii, and Fenster and Carpenter Erler, 3–5). With respect to Fenster and Carpenter Erler's introduction to their edition/translation, I would like to point out that the *Epistre* was indeed not the first text to openly criticize Jean de Meun's *Roman*, as the editors claim (3). Let us not forget Guillaume de Digulleville's second version of his *Pèlerinage de vie humaine* (1355), in which he openly refutes the *Roman* and corrects the laudatory comments of his initial composition (chap.1.1).

11. For a discussion of this issue, see James Laidlaw's important contributions, "Christine de Pizan: A Publisher's Progress," *Modern Language Review* 82.1 (1987): 37–75; and "Christine de Pizan: An Author's Progress," *Modern Language Review* 78, no.3 (1983): 532–50.

12. In addition to the introduction to Fenster and Carpenter Erler's edition, I refer to the following works for critical analyses of this poem: Claire Nouvet, "Writing (in) Fear," in *Gender and Text in the Later Middle Ages*, ed. Jane Chance (Gainesville: University Press of Florida, 1996), 279–305; Thelma Fenster, "Did Christine Have a Sense of Humor? The Evidence of the *Epistre au dieu d'amours*," in *Reinterpreting Christine de Pizan*, ed. E. Jeffrey Richards (Athens: University of Georgia Press, 1992), 23–36; Kevin Brownlee, "Discourses of the Self: Christine de Pizan and the *Rose*," *Romanic Review*, 79, no.1 (1988): 199–221; Charity Cannon Willard, "A New Look at Christine de Pizan's *Epistre au dieu d'Amours*," in *Seconda Miscellanea di studi e ricerche sul Quattrocento francese*, ed. Jonathan Beck and Gianni Mombello (Chambéry/Turin: Centre d'études franco-italien, 1981), 71–92; and Eric Hicks, *Le débat sur le Roman de la rose*, xxviii–xxxii.

13. The advice to promenade about here and there is reminiscent of Ovid's prescriptions in the *Art of Love* where "he counsels the would-be seducer to seek out women in public places, such as the temple, theater, and the like" (*Poems of Cupid*, 82). More importantly, the same advice is given by the duenna to the Lover in the *Roman de la rose*.

14. See note 13.

15. The commandments refer to the Ten Commandments of the God of Love pronounced in Guillaume de Lorris's *Roman de la rose*.

16. As explained by Fenster and Carpenter Erler, "Hutin de Vermeille, knight and chamberlain to King Charles V, was married to Marguerite de Bourbon, daughter of Louis I of Bourbon." Christine praises him again in the *Débat de deux amans* of which I include an excerpt (chap. 2,B3).

17. Ibid., 83: "Oton de Grandson was both a poet and a chevalier. The chivalric deeds that Christine praises probably refer to his participation in many military campaigns." Again, she praises his goodness also in the *Débat* where he is mentioned alongside Hutin de Vermeille.

18. Ibid., 83: "Thelamon Ayaulx, Telamonius Ajax, or Ajax, son of Telamon… was a Greek hero of the Trojan War whom Christine mentions in other of her works, such as the *Epistre d'Othea* and the *Mutacion de Fortune*. The construction of Thelamon Ayaulx derives from the Latin patronymic, Telamonius Ajax, meaning Ajax, son of Telamon. Heroes were often known by such patronymics…."

19. As noted by Fenster and Carpenter Erler, *Poems of Cupid*, 84: "In the letters of the *Debate of the Rose* Pierre Col, Christine, and Jean Gerson repeatedly mention what they see as the misdeeds of the two kings."

20. Christine uses the title in its French version in the singular, *le Remede d'Amours*.

21.   Fenster and Carpenter Erler, *Poems of Cupid*, 84.

22.   The allusion once again to the proverbial couplet in Jean de Meun's *Roman* is all too apparent here: "Toutes estes, serez ou fustes/De fet ou de voulente, pustes!"

23.   Christine "uses the example of Medea in an unqualified way," as she will again in the *Livre de la cité des dames* and the *Mutacion de Fortune*. In the *Mutacion* for instance the "emphasis is on the harm that can be done by Love, which blinds even the most learned, who do not perceive their folly" (Fenster and Carpenter Erler, 86).

24.   Again, as in the *exemplum* of Medea and Jason, Dido is deceived by Aeneas who broke his promise to marry her. Christine recounts Dido's tragedy in the *Mutacion de Fortune* as well.

25.   The courage of Penelope who never lost faith in her husband's return is mentioned repeatedly by Christine; for example, in the *Livre de la cité des dames*.

26.   As explained by Fenster and Carpenter Erler, 87, "In choosing St. Nicholas of Myra as an exemplar the God of Love [Christine] names one of the most popular saints of the Middle Ages. His cult became widely known in the West in the tenth century. In addition to being the subject of plays in both French and Latin, the story of St. Nicholas is told on the south portal and in four stained-glass windows of the cathedral at Chartres. Other iconographic representations survive, including stained-glass cycles, carvings, frescoes, and the like."

27.   As Fenster and Carpenter Erler, 88, point out, "Mercury was the god of eloquence, as well as of science and the arts."

28.   Fenster and Carpenter Erler, 88: "The goddesses and heroines named by the God of Love beginning at this line are either protectors of marriage (Juno), devoted and/or self-sacrificing mothers (Latona, Ceres, Aurora, Thetis) or sisters (Antigone), or notably chaste or concerned with chastity (Arethusa, Minerva, Diana, Vesta). Many suffered because of, or for the sake of, a man." See Fenster and Carpenter Erler, 88 for detailed accounts of their deeds. Many of these female figures reappear in Christine's subsequent works.

29.   The only existing edition is that of M. Roy (3:27–44). Again, for reasons of consistency I have used manuscript Harley 4431 as the base manuscript. The *Enseignemens* were one of Christine's most popular texts and were widely copied. A great number of manuscripts of this text are extant; they are too numerous to all be mentioned in detail. Roy used the following four manuscripts as his base manuscripts, which appear to be part of the same family: BN f.fr. 1551, 1623, 2239, 825 (see 3: iv–ix for details); my translation.

30.   Roberta Krueger, "Christine's Anxious Lessons. Gender, Morality, and the Social Order from the *Enseignemens* to the *Avision*," in *Christine de Pizan and the Categories of Difference*, ed. Marilynn Desmond (Minneapolis: University of Minnesota Press, 1998), 16–40; 19. See also: Nathalie Nabert, "Christine de Pizan, Jean Gerson et le gouvernement des âmes," in *Au champ des escriptures*, ed. Eric Hicks, Diego Gonzalez, and Philippe Simon (Paris: Champion, 2000), 251–68; E. Jeffrey Richards, "Rejecting Essentialism and Gendered Writing: The Case of Christine de Pizan," in *Gender and Text in the Later Middle Ages*, ed. Jane Chance (Gainesville: University Press of Florida, 1996), 96–131.

31.   Saint Vincent of Lérins (H c.450) was a Gallo-Roman saint and the chief theologian of the Abbey of Lérins. Before joining the monastic life he may possibly have been a soldier. During his time as an ordained priest he acquired a preeminent reputation in scriptural learning and dogma.

32.   Saint Bernard is considered the theological authority on piety as evidenced in Philippe de Mézières's *Songe du vieil pelerin* (chap. 1.C). Moreover, Christine praises him once again in her letter to Pierre Col (chap. 3.7, 174 and 175).

33.   The most recent existing edition is that of Barbara Altmann, *The Love Debate Poems of Christine de Pizan* (*Le livre du Debat de deux amans, Le livre des Trois jugements, Le Livre du Dit de Poissy*) (Gainesville: University Press of Florida, 1998). Reprinted with the permission of the University of Florida Press. The translation is my own. For detailed remarks on manuscript listings and descriptions, see Altmann's introduction to the edition, in particular pp. 36–61. This work survives in seven manuscripts:

        a. Brussels, Bibliothèque Royale 11034

      b. BN f.fr. 1740

      c. BN f. fr. 835, 606, 836, 605 (the debate appears in the first volume, f.fr. 835 (fols 52ro–64r)

      d. Chantilly Condé 492 (fols 51vo–67ro)

      e. BN f.fr. 12779 (fols 50ro–65ro)

      f. BN f.fr. 604 (which is thought to be a copy of d) 39vo–51vo

      g. Harley 4431 (fols 58vo–71ro) (base manuscript)

34.   Christine's patron and judge for this poem was Louis I, son of King Charles V and younger brother of the future Charles VI to whom Christine also dedicates the *Epistre Othea* and the *Dit de la rose*. He is mentioned several times in her lyric poetry as well. C. C. Willard, *Christine de Pizan. Her Life and Works* (New York: Persea Books, 1984), 166, suggests, "It may ... have been partially with her son's interests in mind that she made a great effort to gain the patronage of the duke of Orleans." As it turns out, however, her son Jean is later placed in the service of the Duke of Burgundy instead.

35.   For a complete synopsis of the poem, see Barbara Altmann, *The Love Debate Poems*, 7–9. The following works offer critical analyses of the *Livre du débat de deux amans*: Barbara Altmann, "Hearing the Text, Reading the Image: Christine de Pizan's *Livre du Debat de DeuxAmans*," in *Au champ des escriptures*, 693–708; "Trop peu en sçay: The Reluctant Narrator in Christine de Pizan's Works on Love," in Chaucer's *French Contemporaries: The Poetry/Poetics of Self and Tradition*, ed. Barbara Altmann and Barton Palmer (New York: AMS Press, 1999), 217–49; and Charity Cannon Willard, "A Re-examination of *Le Debat de deux amans*," *Les bonnes feuilles* 3 (1974): 73–88.

36.   As noted by Barbara Altmann in her edition, "The word *cruble* is troublesome...the context is still that of the irrational lover blinded by the force of emotion.... In the Supplement to [Frédéric Godefroy's *Dictionnaire de l'ancienne langue française et de tous les dialectes*, 10 vols. (1881–1902; repr. Nendeln/Liechtenstein: Kraus Reprint, 1969)], however, he lists *cruble* as a variation on *crible*, a sieve, with our passage from *Deux amans* as his only example. Given that other vowels in this quatrain have been adapted at line's end to fit the rhyme, this solution seems likely. The lover would thus be putting on ... a sieve as a hat against the sun he believes he sees even in cloudy weather. Such ridiculous attire would be appropriate for someone so besotted that he cannot see reason," 144–45.

Chapter Three

The Debate Epistles (1401–1402)

The order of the actual epistolary exchange between Christine de Pizan and her adversaries, Jean de Montreuil, Gontier and Pierre Col is determined by my base manuscript, British Library MS Harley 4431. This manuscript is part of a series of three copies of the epistles which have been produced after October 2, 1402, the date of Christine's long reply to Pierre Col. In addition to the Harley manuscript there are Berkeley, University of California UCB 109 and Paris, BN fr. 835.[1] Since up to now Christine scholars allowed Christine's position, and only her position, to define the Quarrel, her last version of the letters in the Quarrel ought to be the most important documents we need to consider. However, as Jeffrey Richards has also shown in the Introduction, my approach to the Quarrel is not defined by Christine's letters alone, and this cannot be stressed enough, but rather by the comprehensive intellectual context of the circles which she, Gerson, and the other participants in this exchange frequented. The Quarrel is in fact but one (albeit a significant) element of the ongoing discussion among jurists and theologians at the court of Charles VI. At the same time, however, Christine's own "last" word in the Quarrel *was* the Harley version of the letters, and it is for this reason that the Harley manuscript must be preferred as base manuscript.[2]

Up to now, the English-speaking reader had to rely on Joseph L. Baird and John R. Kane's translation of the Debate Epistles dating from 1978.[3] In addition to the frequently unreliable translation of the Debate Epistles, this edition contains a twenty-five page introduction which in many respects also needs to be extensively revised in light of research that has been undertaken since the date of its publication. For the sake of brevity I will only point out its most notable shortcomings. It goes without saying that the references to scholarly works in the introduction itself as well as in the annexed bibliography are now dated and in many cases no longer valid. A lot has been done since the crucial works by John V. Fleming, *The Roman de la Rose: A Study in Allegory and Iconography*[4] and D.W. Robertson, *A Preface to Chaucer.*[5] Though these works

107

are still useful in many ways, their misogynist views of Christine de Pizan and her role in the debate are often questioned in today's scholarship. Further, A. Piaget's and P. Potansky's treatment of the chronology of the correspondence between the participants of the debate which dates from 1891 has long been revised by Eric Hicks in his edition of the text.[6] Baird and Kane use C. F. Ward's 1911 edition of the debate correspondence titled *The Epistles on the Roman de la rose and Other Documents in the Debate* as a basic text for the French documents despite its flaws, which the two authors point out themselves.[7] Evidently, Ward's edition has been rendered obsolete by Hicks's recent and revised edition of the Quarrel.

1. February 1, 1402: Letter from Christine de Pizan to Queen Isabeau de Bavière (1371–1435)

Text:

237r° CI COMMENCE LE LIVRE DES EPISTRES DU DEBAT SUS *LE ROMMANT DE LA ROSE* ENTRE NOTABLES PERSONNES: LE PREVOST DE LILLE, MAISTRE GONTIER COL, MAISTRE PIERRE COL, SON FRERE ET CRISTINE DE PIZAN[8]

La premiere epistre, a la royne de France
Cristine
     A tres excellant, tres haulte et tres redoubtee princesse, ma dame Ysabel de Baviere, par la grace de Dieu royne de France

5   Tres haulte, tres puissant et tres redoubtee dame, toute humble recommandacion mise avant tout œuvre. Et comme j'aye entendu que vostre Tres Noble Excellence se delicte a oïr lire dictiéz de choses vertueuses et bien dites—laquelle chose est accroiscement de vertus et de bonnes meurs a vostre noble personne, car si comme

10   dit un sage: «Vertus avec vertus, sagece avec noblece rendent la personne reverend» (qui puet estre entendue parfaite)—, et, ma tres redoubtee, pour ce que tele vertu est trouvee en vostre noble entendement, est chose convenable que dictiéz de choses esleues vous soient presentéz comme a souveraine. Pour tant, moy simple et

15   ignorant entre les femmes, vostre humble chamberiere soubz vostre obeissance, desireuse de vous servir se tant valoye en la confiance de vostre benigne humilité, suis meue a vous envoyer les presentes epistres, esquieulx, ma tres redoubtee dame—s'il vous plaist moy tant honnorer que ouyr les daigniéz—, pourréz entendre la dili-

20   gence, desir et voulenté ou ma petite puissance s'estent a soustenir par deffenses veritables contre aucunes oppinions a honnesteté con-

Translation:

HERE BEGINS THE BOOK OF THE EPISTLES OF THE DE-
BATE ABOUT *THE ROMAN DE LA ROSE* BETWEEN THE
ILLUSTRIOUS PERSONS THE PROVOST OF LILLE, MASTER
GONTIER COL; MASTER PIERRE COL, HIS BROTHER; AND
CHRISTINE DE PIZAN

The First Epistle, to the Queen of France
Christine

     To the most excellent, very noble, and venerated princess, my
Lady Isabeau de Bavière,[9] Queen of France, by the Grace of God.

5   Very noble, very powerful, and venerated Lady, I humbly recommend this entire work to you. I have heard that your very noble
Excellency delights in listening to eloquent works about virtuous
things which will increase the virtue and good habits of your noble
person. As a wise man once said, "Virtue coupled with virtue and
10   wisdom with generosity will make a person revered" (this can easily
be understood). My venerated Lady, since such virtue is what you
aspire to, it is appropriate that distinguished works be presented
to you as they are to rulers. For this reason, I, simple and ignorant
among women, your humble lady in waiting,[10] at your service—de-
15   siring to serve you if your kind humility will allow it—wish to send
you these epistles, in which, my venerated Lady, if you will honor
me by hearing them, you will see the diligence, desire, and will
with which I defend myself as much as I can against dishonorable
opinions, and where I defend the honor and praise of women (which
20   many clerics and others make a point of diminishing in their works;
this ought not to be tolerated, nor is it sustainable). And as weak as

traires, et aussi l'onneur et louenge des femmes (laquelle pluseurs
cleres et autres se sont efforciéz par leurs dictiéz d'amenuisier, qui
n'est chose loisible a souffrir ne soustenir). Et combien que foible
25   soye pour porter tel charge contre si soubtilz maistres, non obstant
ce, comme de verité meue—ainsi comme je sçay de certaine science
leur bon droit estre digne de deffence—, mon petit entendement
a voulu et veult soy emploier, come ycy appert et en autres miens
dictiéz, a debatre leurs contraires et accusans. Si suppli humblement
30   Vostre Digne Haultece que a mes raisons droiturieres, non obstant
que ne les sache conduire et mener par si beau lengage comme autre
mieulx le feroit, y vueillez adjouster foy et donner faveur de plus
dire se plus y sçay. Et tout soit fait vostre saige et benigne correction.
35   Tres haulte et tres excellant, ma tres redoubtee dame, je pry la
vraye Trinité que vous octroit bonne vie et longue, et acomplissement
de tous voz bons desirs.
          Escript la veille de la Chandeleur, l'an mil •IIII• et ung.
          La toute vostre tres humble creature,
40   Cristine de Pizan

my position may be in pronouncing such accusations against such skilled masters, I am motivated by truth. Thus, my limited intelligence[11] wishes to continue to make itself useful, as I have already

25 done in some of my other poems,[12] by debating their arguments and accusations, although I am fully aware that they have the right to defend themselves. I beg humbly, worthy Highness, that you faithfully support my righteous reasons, although I cannot express myself as eloquently as others might, and permit me to say more about this

30 matter. All this will be done with your wise and kind approval.

Very noble, very excellent, and most venerated Lady, I ask the Holy Trinity to grant you a good and long life and the fulfillment of all your good wishes.

Written on the eve of Candlemas, in the year 1401.[13]

35 Your most humble servant,

Christine de Pizan

2. *September 13, 1401: Christine's Explanatory Letter*[14]

Text:

237v°   COMME ja pieça paroles feussent meues entre mon seigneur
le prevost de Lisle, maistre Jehan Jonhannes, et Cristine de Pizan
touchans traictiéz et livres de plusieurs materes, esquelles paroles
le dit prevost ramentut *Le Rommant de la Rose* en lui attribuant tres
5   grant et singuilere louange et grant digneté, de laquel chose en repli-
quant et assignant plusieurs raisons la dite Cristine dist que, sauve
sa reverence, si grant louange ne lui appertenoit aucunement selon
son avis:

     ITEM, après plusieurs jours envoya le dit prevost a Cristine la
10   coppie d'une epistre, laquelle adreçoit a un sien amy notable clere,
lequel, meu de raison, estoit de la meisme oppinion de la dite contre
le dit rommant, et pour lui ramener avoit le dit prevost escript la
dicte epistre moult notablement aourne de belle rethorique, et pour
estre en .ii. pars valable, envoya a la dite Cristine ycellui;

15   ITEM, comme Cristine, veu et consideré la dicte epistre,
rescript au dit prevost, si comme cy après pourra estre veu;

     ITEM, comme après ces choses venist a congnoissance a
nottable personne, maistre Gontier Col, que la dicte Cristine avoit
escript contre *Le Rommant de la Rose,* lequel, comme inaniméz
20   contre elle, lui escript la present epistre qui s'ensuit:

Translation:

> When, recently, words were exchanged between the provost of Lille, Master Jean Johannes, and Christine de Pizan about treatises and books on several subjects, the provost called to mind the *Roman de la rose*, attributing to it great and singular praise and dignity. To this
>
> 5 Christine responded with several arguments stating that, with all due respect, in her mind this great praise was quite unfounded:

- Some days later, the provost sent a copy of a letter to Christine and to a friend of his, <u>an illustrious cleric, who, motivated</u> by <u>reason, shared her opinion against the said romance</u>. In order to

10 convince him of his opinion, the provost had adorned his letter with beautiful rhetoric, and, to kill two birds with one stone, sent it to Christine as well.

- The aforementioned Christine, who saw and reflected upon this letter, replied to the provost, as may be seen below.

15 - The fact that Christine had written against the *Roman de la rose* came to the attention of a distinguished person, Master Gontier Col, who, being in disagreement with her, wrote her the following letter:

3. September 13, 1401: Gontier Col Asks Christine to Send Him a Copy of Her Reply to Jean de Montreuil's Treatise

Text:

237vº Maistre Gontier Col

A prudent, honoree et sçavent damoiselle Cristine

Femme de hault et eslevé entendement, digne d'onneur et
recommandacions grans. J'ay ouy parler par la bouche de plusieurs
5   et notables cleres que entre tes autres estudes et œuvres vertueuses
moult a louer (comme j'entens par leur relacion), tu as nouvellement
escript par maniere de invective aucunement contre ce que mon
maistre, enseigneur et familier, feu maistre Jehan de Meun—vray
catholique, sollempnel maistre et docteur en son temps en sainte
10   theologie, philosophe tres parfont et excellant sachant tout ce qui a
entendement humain est scible, duquel la gloire et renommee vit et
vivra es aages avenir entre les entendemens par ses merites levéz,
par grace de Dieu et œuvre de nature—, fist et compila ou livre
de la *Rose.* Et comme dient les relateurs ou referandaires de ceste
15   chose, t'efforces et estudies de le reprendre et chargier de faultes en
ta dicte œuvre nouvelle: laquelle chose me vient a grant amiracion
et merveille inestimable, et a ce non croire me meut l'experience
et exercite de toy d'avoir sceu, leu et entendu lui ou dit livre et en
ses autres fais en françois, et autres plusieurs et divers docteurs,
20   aucteurs et poetes.
    238rº   Et pour ce //[15] que les denonciateurs de ceste chose tiennent et
gardent—les aucuns par aventure comme envieux sur les fais du dit
feu maistre Jehan de Meun—ta dicte invective comme chose singu-
liere et haultement composee, ediffiee et conduite a leur plaisir et
25   intencion, si que de eulx n'en puis avoir coppie ne original. Te pry et
requier sur l'amour que as a science que ta dicte œuvre tele que elle
est me vueilles envoyer par cest mien message ou autre tel comme
il te plaira, affin que sur ce je puisse labourer et moy employer a
soustenir mon maistre et ses fais: dont il ne fust ja besoing que moy
30   ne autre mortel s'en meslast s'il fust en vie, laquelle mieulx am-
eroye avoir esté en mon temps que estre empereur des Rommains
presentement.

Et pour toy ramener a vraye verité et que plus avant saches
et congnoisses les fais du dit de Meun, pour toy donner matiere de
35   plus escripre contre lui se bon te semble, ou a tes satalites—qui en
ce fait t'ont boutee pour ce que touchier n'y osoient ou ne savoient,
mais de toy veulent faire chappe a pluye pour dire que plus y sauroi-
ent que une femme et plus reprimer la renommee indeficient entre

Translation:

> Master Gontier Col
>
> To the wise, honorable, and learned Lady Christine
>
> Woman of high intelligence, worthy of honor and great es-
> teem! I have heard from the mouth of several illustrious clerics that
5 among your other (they tell me) highly praised studies and virtuous
> works, you recently expressed yourself in the form of an invec-
> tive against the *Roman de la rose* composed and compiled by my
> defunct master, teacher, and friend Jean de Meun, a true Catholic,
> in his time a solemn master and doctor of holy theology; a thorough
10 philosopher and a most learned humanist, whose glory and repu-
> tation will continue to live on due to the recognition of his high mer-
> its, by the grace of God and by the work of Nature. And, as I was
> told by those who recounted these matters to me, in your new work
> you attempt to contradict him and to accuse him of errors. I am very
15 much astonished by this because from what I have heard about you,
> I cannot believe that you have read and understood this book or his
> other works in French, nor those written by several other masters,
> authors, and poets.
>
>   And since the messengers of this matter consider your in-
20 vective to be outstanding, elegantly written for their pleasure and
> reflection (some perhaps out of envy for the defunct Master Jean
> de Meun), I can obtain from them neither a copy nor the original.
> Therefore, out of your love for knowledge, I beseech you to send
> me a copy of your work, either returning it with this messenger or
25 at your convenience, so that I may put my efforts toward supporting
> my master and his arguments. If he were still living today—which I
> would prefer over being Emperor of Rome—it would not be neces-
> sary for me or any other mortal being to become involved in this
> matter.
>
30   In order to remind you of the veritable truth and so that you
> may better know the works of de Meun—which may indeed give
> you or your satellites more material to contradict him (it was they
> who encouraged you in this in the first place, since they themselves
> would never have dared or known how to do it. Instead they wish
35 to use you as a buffer, so that they may say they knew more about
> this than a woman, further tarnishing the unjustified ill reputation of
> such a man)—I hastily and publicly send you a small excerpt of the
> *Tresor*, which he compiled to be read by his detractors and others

40   les mortelx d'un tel homme—, t'envoye patentement et hastivement
un pou de *Tresor* que il compila pour estre de ses envieux et des
autres congneu a sa mort (lequel est incorrect par faulte d'escripvain
qui pas ne l'entendi, comme il y pert, et n'ay eu espace ne loisir
de le veoir ne corriger au lonc pour la haste et ardeur que j'ay de
veoir ton dessus dit œuvre, et mesmement qu'il est a supposer que
45   bien sauras les faultes de l'excripvain corriger brieve compilacion
corrigier et entendre). Et quant en ce qu'il fist du livre de la *Rose,*
ou plus a lectres et sentences estranges et diverses (l'as voulu ou osé
chargier, corriger et reprendre, comme ilz dient), une chose ne vueil
oublier ne passer soubz dissimulacion: que se de ce ne te rappelles
50   et desdis, je, confiant de bonne et vraye justice et que verité qui ne
quiert angles sera o moy —combien que en grans autres occupa-
cions soye de present astraint et aye esté le temps passé—, entre-
prendray le soustenir contre tes et autres escrips quelconques.
          Escript hastivement, present Jehan de .iiii. Mares, Jehan
Porcher, conseilliers, et Guillaume de Neauville, secretaire du roy
55   nostre sire, le mardi .xiiie. jour de septembre, l'an mil .IIII^C. et un.
          Le tien, tant comme loy d'amistié peut souffire,
          Gontier Col
          Secretaire du roy nostre sire

after his death. (This book is incorrect due to the errors of a scribe
40   who apparently did not understand it. I have had neither the time nor
the leisure to read and correct it at length because I so ardently wish
to see your aforementioned work, and also because I presume that
you will soon be able to understand and correct the scribe's errors
in that compilation.) And where the book of the *Rose* is concerned,
45   which contains many extraordinary lessons (which, they say, you
wished or dared to correct and criticize), I wish to make one thing
very clear: Regardless of how preoccupied I may be and have always been with other matters, if you do not revoke and retract what
you have said, I, relying on good and true justice and searching for
50   the truth, will undertake to defend him against your own writings
and those of any other person.

Written in haste and in the presence of Jean de Quatre Mares,
Jean Porchier, counselors,[16] and of Guillaume de Neauville, secretary to Our Lord the King, on Tuesday, September 13, 1401.

Yours, as much as the law of friendship can bear,
55   Gontier Col
Secretary to Our Lord the King

4. June/July 1401: Christine's Reaction to Jean de Montreuil's Treatise on the Roman de la rose

Text:

238r° CRISTINE

A moult souffisant et sçavent personne, maistre Jehan Jonhannez,
secretaire du roy nostre sire, et Prevost de Lille.

　　　Reverence, honneur avec recommandacion, a vous mon
5 238v° seigneur le prevost de Lille, tres cher sire et maistre, sage // en
meurs, ameur de science, en clergie fondé et expert de rethorique,
de par moy Cristine de Pizan, femme ignorant d'entendement et de
sentement leger—pour lesquelles choses vostre sagece aucunement
n'ait en despris la petitece de mes raisons, ains vueille supployer
10　　par la consideracion de ma femenine foiblece. Et comme il vous ait
pleu de vostre bien, dont vous merci, moy envoyer un petit traictié
ordené par belle rethorique et voirsemblables raisons (lequel est
de voz diz fait en reprennant, comme il me semble, aucuns blasmeurs de la compilacion du *Rommant de la Rose* en aucunes pars et
15　　moult soustenant et approuvant l'ouevre et les aucteurs d'icelle et
par especial Meun). Je, ayant leu et considéré vostre dicte prose et
compris l'effet selon la legiereté de mon petit engine—combien que
a moy ne soit adreçant ne response ne requiert, mais meue par oppinion contraire a voz dis accordant a l'especial clerc soubtil a qui
20　　vostre dicte espistre s'adrece—, vueil dire, divulguer et soustenir
magnifestement que, sauve vostre bonne grace, a grant tort et sans
cause donnéz si parfaicte louange a celle dicte œuvre, qui mieulx
puet estre appellee droicte oysiveté que œuvre utile, a mon jugement
et combien que moult reprenéz les contredisans, et dites que «grant
25　　chose est d'ainsi comprendre ce que un autre dit tesmongne; mieulx
a construit et mis sus par grant estude et a lonc trait», etc., ne me
soit imputé a presompcion d'oser repudier et reprendre aucteur si
sollempnel et tant soubtil; mais soit nottée la ferme et grant oppinion qui me muet contre aucunes particularitéz qui ou dit sont
30　　comprises—et, au fort, chose qui est dicte par oppinion et non de
loy commandee se puet redarguer sans prejudice. Et combien que
ne soie en science apprise ne stillee de lengage soubtil (dont sache
user de belle arenge et mos pollis bien ordenéz qui mes raisons
rendissent luisans), pour tant ne lairay a dire materiellement et en
35　　gros vulgar l'oppinion de mon entente, tout ne la sache proprement
exprimer en ordre de paroles aournees.

　　　Mais pourquoy ay je dit devant que «mieulx peut estre appellee oysiveté… »? Sans faille, il me semble que toute chose

Translation:

Christine

To a most skillful and learned person, Master Jean Johannes, Secretary to Our Lord the King and provost of Lille.

5   To my lord the provost of Lille, with reverence, honor, and esteem. Dear lord and master who is wise in morals, steeped in learning, a trained clergyman, and an expert in rhetoric: I, Christine de Pizan, an ignorant woman of inadequate opinion—for this your wisdom may well hold the insignificance of my arguments in disdain—beg you to take into consideration my female weak-

10   ness. Since you had the kindness, for which I thank you, to send me a small treatise[17] adorned with beautiful rhetoric and convincing arguments (where you say, it seems to me, that you can find no fault with any aspect of the compilation of the *Roman de la rose*, which you support and approve as you do its authors, in particular de

15   Meun), I, having read and reflected upon it and having understood it within the limits of my small intelligence, will reply because of my disagreement with you, although this treatise was not addressed to me, nor do you require my response. Rather, I agree with the skilled cleric to whom your text is addressed,[18] and wish to divulge

20   and maintain openly that, with all due respect, you are mistaken in according unlimited praise to this work, which, I think, instead of being labeled useful should be called a work of idleness. As much as you reprimand your opponents and say that "it is important to understand that which is shown by another text if it is better written,

25   longer, and well founded," etc., I shall not be accused of presumption for daring to repudiate and criticize this famous and very skilled author. However, take heed of my firm disagreement with certain elements which you express in your treatise. In truth, a mere assertion not rightfully justified can be contradicted without bias. Although

30   I am neither learned nor eloquent in style (beautiful phrases and polite, elegant words would certainly make my arguments shine), I will nevertheless express my opinion plainly and in simple French, even if I cannot express it properly in adorned speech.

       Yet why did I say earlier that this book "ought rather be called

35   a work of idleness…"? Without a doubt, it seems to me that a thing without use for anyone, regardless of how painstakingly it was done, may be called idle or worse than idle, even more so if it turns out to be harmful. When, some time ago and after I had acquired

40   sans preu, non obstant soit elle traicté, faicte et accomplie a grant
      labeur et peine, peut estre appellee oyseuse ou pis que oyseuse de
      tant comme plus mal en ensuit. Et comme ja pieça pour la grant
      renommee commune du dit rommans desiray le veoir, aprés que
      congnoissence m'ot un petit fait entendre choses soubtilles, le leu et
      consideray au lonc et au lé le mieulx que le sceu comprendre. Vray
45   est que pour la matiere qui en aucunes pars n'estoit a ma plaisance
      m'en passoye oultre comme coq sur brese: si ne l'ay planté veu.
      Neantmainz demoura en ma memoire aucunes choses traictees en
      lui que mon jugement condamna moult et ancore ne peut approuver
      pour contraire louange d'autre gent. Bien est vray que mon petit
50   entendement y considere grant joliveté, en aucunes pars, tres sol-
      lempnellement parler de ce qu'il veult dire—et par moult beaulx
      termes et vers gracieux et bien leomines: ne mieulx ne pourroit estre
239rº dit plus soubtilment ne par plus // mesuréz trais de ce que il volt
      traictier. Mais en accordant a l'oppinion ement en aucunes pars—et
55   mesmement ou personnage que il claime Raison, laquelle nomme
      les secréz membres plainement par nom, et a ce que son oppinion
      soustenéz et communiqués que ainsi doye raisonnablement estre
      fait, et alleguéz que es choses que Dieu a faites n'a nulle laidure
      et par consequant n'en doit le nom estre eschivé, je dy et confesse
60   que voirement crea Dieu toutes choses pures et netes venans de soy,
      n'adonc en l'estat d'ignocence ne eust esté laidure les nommer;
      mais par la polucion de pechié devint homme inmonde, dont ancore
      nous est demouré pechié original. Ce tesmoingne l'Escripture
      saincte. Si comme par comparoison puis alleguer: Dieux fist Lucifer
65   bel sur tous anges et lui donna nom tres sollempnel et bel, qui puis
      fu par son peché ramené a orrible laidece; par quoy le nom, tout soit
      il de soy tres bel, si donne il orreur aux oyans pour l'imprecion de la
      personne.
           Encore proposéz que Jhesu Crist, «en parlant des pecheresses,
70   les appella *meretrix*», etc. Et que il les appellast par cellui nom
      vous puis souldre que cellui nom de *meretrix* n'est mie deshonneste
      a nomer selon la vilté de la chose—et plus vilment pourroit estre
      dit mesmes en latin. Et que honte doye estre aboutee en parlant en
      publique des choses dont nature mesmes se hontoye, je dis que,
75   sauve la reverence de l'aucteur et la vostre, grant tort comettez
      contre la noble vertu de honte, qui de sa nature reffraint les gou-
      liardises et deshonnestetés en dis et fais; et que ce soit grant vice et
      hors ordre de pollicie honneste et de bonnes meurs appert en mains

40   sufficient knowledge to understand such things, I wished to read this
     romance because of its great reputation, I read and thought about it
     at great length and tried to the best of my ability to understand it.
     It is true that I skipped the passages which were not to my liking,
     just as a rooster skips over hot embers: therefore, I did not read it
     in its entirety.[19] Nevertheless, I remember some things in it which
45   I condemn very much. Moreover, I cannot approve of the praise
     coming from others for this work. It is also true that my limited un-
     derstanding finds great beauty in many parts of the work, where he
     solemnly expresses what he wishes to say in very beautiful phrases
     and graceful leonine rhymes.[20] What he wished to say, he could not
50   have said more skillfully, nor in a better rhyme. But in agreeing with
     the opinion which you contradict, there is no doubt in my mind that
     he sometimes speaks dishonorably, as when he speaks about the
     character whom he calls Reason, who calls the secret parts plainly
     by their names.[21] You openly proclaim his view as logical and
55   invoke—rightfully, I admit—that there is no ugliness in all things
     which God created, and consequently their names need not be hid-
     den, because all things coming from Him are pure and clean, since
     in the state of innocence there was no ugliness in naming them. Yet
     through the corruption of sin mankind was ruined, and original sin
60   has remained (as is shown in Holy Scripture). If I may argue by
     analogy: God made Lucifer the most beautiful among the angels and
     gave him a solemn and beautiful name, which was later reduced to
     terrible ugliness through his sin. As a result, the name, beautiful as it
     may be in itself, terrifies those who hear it because of its association
65   with the person.

     You also quote Jesus Christ who, "when He spoke of the fe-
     male sinners, called them *meretrix*," etc.[22] That He called them thus
     can be explained: It is not shameful to say the word *meretrix*, be-
     cause it refers to an abject thing; words more abject than this could
70   be used, even in Latin. What is shameful, however, is to speak in
     public of things of which Nature herself would be ashamed. With all
     due respect for the author and for you, I must say that you sin great-
     ly against the noble virtue of shame, which by definition restrains
     obscenities and disgrace in word and deed. That this is a great vice
75   and against honorable government and good custom[23] is written in
     many places in Holy Scripture. And the word "which was merely
     called relics"[24] must be repudiated. I grant you, it is not the word
     which causes the disgrace of the thing, but the thing which renders
     the word disgraceful. It is for this reason, in my feeble opinion, that

80   lieux de l'Escripture sainte, et que ne doye estre repudiéz le nom
      «ne que se reliques feussent nommées». Je vous confesse que le
      nom ne fait la chose deshonneste de la chose, mais la chose fait le
      nom deshonneste. Pour ce, selon mon foible avis, en doit estre parlé
      sobrement—et non sans neccessité—pour fin d'aucun cas particu-
85   lier, comme de maladie ou autre honneste neccessaire. Et si comme
      naturellement les mucierent noz premiers parens, devons faire en
      fait et en parole.
             Et encore ne me puis taire de ce, dont trop suis mal contempt:
      que l'office de Raison, laquelle il meismes dit fille de Dieu, doye
90   mettre avant tele parole et par maniere de proverbe comme je ay
      notte en ycellui chapitre, la ou elle dit a l'Amant que «en la guerre
      amoureuse vault mieulx decevoir que deceuz estre». Et vraiement je
      ose dire que la Raison maistre Jehan de Meun renia son Pere a cellui
      mot, car trop donna autre doctrine, et que mieulx vaulsist l'un que
95   l'autre, s'ensuivroit que tous .ii. fussent bonz: qui ne puet estre et
      je tiens par oppinion contraire que mains est mal, a realment parler,
      estre deceu que decevoir car trop est pire le vice de propre malice
      que cellui de simple ignorance.
             Or alons oultre en considerant la matiere ou maniere de parler,
100   qui au bon avis de plusieurs fait a reprochier. Beau Sire Dieux! quel
      orribleté! quel deshonnesteté et divers reprouvéz enseignemens
239vº recorde ou chapitre de la Vielle! Mais pour Dieu! qui y pourra //
      notter fors ennortemens sophistes tous plains de laidure et toute vil-
      laine memoire? Hahay! entre vous qui belles filles avéz et bien les
105   desiréz entroduire a vie honneste, bailléz leur, bailléz et queréz *Le
      Romant de la Rose* pour apprendre a discerner le bien du mal—que
      dis je! mais le mal du bien! Et a quel utilité ne a quoy prouffite aux
      oyans tant ouyr de laidures? Puis ou chapitre de Jalousie, pour Dieu!
      quieulx grans biens y peuent estre nottéz, n'a quel besoing recorder
110   les deshonnestetés et laides paroles qui asséz sont communes en la
      bouche des maleureux passionnéz d'icelle maladie? Quel bon ex-
      emple ne introducion peut estre ce? Et la laidure qui la est recordee
      des femmes, dient plusieurs en lui excusant que c'est le Jaloux qui
      parle, et voirement fait ainsi comme Dieu par la bouche de Jher-
115   emie. Mais sans faille quieulxque addicions mençongeuses qu'il ait
      adjoustees, ne peuent—Dieu merci!—en riens amenrir ne rendre
      empirées les condicions des femmes. Hahay! et quant il me souvi-
      ent des faintises, faulx semblans et choses dissimulees en mariage et
      autre estat que l'en puet retenir d'icellui traictié, certes je juge que
120   moult sont beaulx et prouffitables recors a ouyr!

80   one must speak of these things only when absolutely necessary,
        such as in the case of an illness or for some other legitimate reason.
        Just as our first parents hid these parts naturally, so must we, in deed
        and in speech.

            I cannot yet be silent about that which dissatisfies me im-
85   mensely: He makes it Reason's task, whom he himself calls daugh-
        ter of God, to propound such speech, and in the form of a dictum,
        as I note in the passage where she says to the Lover that "in the war
        of love… it is better to deceive than to be deceived." In fact, I dare
        say that with this statement Master Jean de Meun's Reason has de-
90   nounced her Father because He Himself taught her a very different
        lesson. And it cannot be that both statements are valid; this would
        mean that both are good. I think the opposite is true: Clearly, to be
        deceived is not as bad as to deceive, for the vice of pure perfidy is
        much worse than that of simple ignorance.

95   Now let us consider further the subject matter or manner of
        speech to which many would reasonably object. Good God! What
        disgust! What disgrace! And the exhortations which he teaches in
        the passage of the Duenna! By God! Who could possibly find any-
        thing but specious advice in them, full of insults and baseness? Hey,
100   those of you who have beautiful daughters and wish to introduce
        them to an honorable life, give them—yes, ask for and give them—
        the *Roman de la rose* in order that they may learn how to distinguish
        good from bad. What am I saying? I mean bad from good! And to
        what end should anyone listen to such insults? Then, in the pas-
105   sage of the Jealous Husband, my God, what could possibly be the
        benefit of such shameful and insulting speech, frequently uttered by
        those poor souls afflicted by this illness? What good example can
        this possibly set? And the insults of women—which can be found in
        that passage and which many dismiss by pointing out that it is the
110   Jealous Husband speaking and that, indeed, this can be compared to
        God speaking through the mouth of Jeremiah![25] Yet surely, then, the
        other lies he added can in no way, God be thanked, lessen or worsen
        the situation for women. For when I remember the deceits, hypocri-
        sies, and lies that occur in marriage or any other state which can be
115   learned from this treatise, I certainly think that by comparison these
        are beautiful and good to hear!

            And the character whom he calls the priest Genius truly
        speaks wondrously: no doubt, Nature's works would have van-
        ished entirely long ago, had he not so highly recommended them!
120   By God, I would like to find someone who can explain to me the

Mais le personnage qu'il appelle le prestre Genius dit merveille: sans doubte les œuvres de Nature feussent ja pieça du tout
faillies se il tant ne les eust recommandées! Mais pour Dieu! qui est
cil qui me sceust declairier ou souldre a quoy peut estre prouffit-
125   able le grant procés plain de vitupere qu'il appelle sermon, comme
par derrision de saincte predicacion, qui dit que fait cellui Genius,
ou tant a de deshonnestetéz et de noms et de mos sophistez trouvéz
plus atisans les secréz de Nature—lesquieulx doivent estre teuz et
non nomméz. Et puis que point ne voit on descontinuer l'œuvre
130   qui par ordre commun faillir ne peut. Car se autrement fust, bon
seroit, pour le prouffit de generacion humaine, trouver et dire mos
et termes atisans et enflamens pour inanimer homme a continuer
l'œuvre.
        Encore plus fist l'aucteur, se bien en ay memoire, dont
135   trop ne me puis merveillier a quel fin. Car ou dit sermon il joint
avec, en maniere de figure, paradis et les joyes qui la sont. Bien
dit que en celluy yront les vertueux, et puis conclut que tous
entendent—hommes et femmes sans espargnier—a parfournir et
exerciter les œuvres de Nature; ne en ce ne fait excepcion de loy,
140   comme se il voulzist dire—mais dit plainement!—que ilz seront
sauvéz. Et par ce semble que maintenir vueille le peché de luxure
estre nul, ains vertu—qui est erreur et contre la loy de Dieu. Ha!
quel semence et quel doctrine! quans grans biens en peuent ensui-
vir! Je croy que maint en ont laissié le monde et entréz en religion
145   ou devenus hermites pour celle sainte lecture, ou retrais de male vie
et estre sauvés de tel ennortement, qui sans faille onque ne vint, dire
l'ose a qui qu'il desplaise, fors de courage corrompu et abandonné
a dissolucion et vice—qui puet estre cause de grant inconvenient et
240r°   peché. Et ancore, pour Dieu! regardons // oultre un petit: en quelle
150   maniere peut estre valable et a bonne fin ce que tant et si excessivement, impettueusement et tres nonveritablement il accuse, blasme
et diffame femmes de plusieurs tres grans vices et leurs meurs
tesmoigne estre plains de toute perversité; et par tant de repliques
et auques en tous personnages ne s'en peut saouler. Car se dire me
155   vouléz que ce face le Jaloux comme passionné. Je ne sçay entendre qu'il appartiengne a l'office de Genyus, qui tant recommande
et ennorte que l'en couche avec elles sans delaissier l'œuvre que
il tant loe; et cil mesmes dit sur tous personnages moult de grans
vituperes de elles, et dist de fait: «Fuyéz! fuyéz! fuyéz le serpent
160   venimeux»! Et puis si dist que on les continue sans delaissier. Si a
malement grant contradicion de commander a fuir ce que il volt que

advantage of the long speech full of venom that he calls a "sermon,"
as if to deride holy preaching—delivered, he says, by this so-called
Genius. In it such disgrace and specious words are used, fanning the
flames of Nature's secrets, which ought to remain tacit and not be
named, because it is impossible to see a work come to an end which
logically cannot end: if the opposite were true, it would be advantageous for the continuation of humankind to find and utter fiery
words and terms to encourage mankind to continue this work.

130   The author goes even further, if I remember correctly, though I
cannot for the life of me understand to what purpose. In this sermon he uses metaphor to associate paradise and the joys that can be
found there. He rightfully says that the virtuous will go there, and
then announces that all men and women, without exception, should
perform and carry out Nature's works—no exception made, as if he
135   wished to say (and, in fact, does say plainly)—that it is precisely
these people who will be saved. It seems that he wishes to maintain
that lechery is not a sin but, on the contrary, a virtue, which is wrong
and against the law of God. Ha! What a notion, and what a doctrine!
No good can possibly come of it! I think that many left the worldly
140   life and have chosen to enter the monastic one, becoming hermits
for the Holy Scripture, or have chosen to turn their backs on a sinful
life, saving themselves from this kind of exhortation which, I dare
tell those who will not like to hear it, will lead inevitably to immo-
rality, decay, and vice, possibly causing great misfortune and sin.

145   And there is more, my God! Let us look a little further! How
can his excessive, impetuous, and false accusations, insults, and
defamation of women—whom he accuses of several great vices and
perverse habits—possibly be valid and purposeful? His appetite for
such statements and examples seems insatiable. And if you wish
150   to tell me that the Jealous Husband says these things out of anger,
I do not understand why it is Genius's task to vehemently recommend and exhort that one share a bed with them [women] without
refraining from the work he so praises. At the same time, however,
he rants and raves about them, saying in fact, "Flee! Flee! Flee from
155   the venomous serpent!" Yet he goes on to say that one should not
cease to follow them. This is a flagrant contradiction, to command
one to flee from that which one is supposed to follow and follow
that from which he wishes one to flee. Since women are so perverse,
he should command men not to approach them at all, because one
160   should always avoid the risk of encountering misfortune.

And since he so strongly forbids men to confide in women,

on suive et suivir ce que il veult que on fuye. Mais puis que tant sont
perverses, ne les deust commander approcher aucunement; car qui
inconvenient redoubte, eschiver le doit.

165   Et pour ce que il tant deffent dire son secret a femme—qui
du savoir est si engrant, comme il recorde, dont je ne sçay ou
tous les deables trouva tant de fatras et de paroles gastées qui la
sont arengées par lonc proces—, mais je pry tous ceulx qui tant
le font autentique et tant y adjoustent foy qu'ilz me sachent a dire
170   quans ont veuz accuséz, mors ou pendus ou reprouchéz en rue par
l'encusement de leurs femes: si croy que cler les trouveront seméz.
Non obstant que bon conseil seroit et louable que un chacun tenist
son secret clos pour le plus seur, car de toute gent est il de vicieux;
et n'a pas moult, comme ouy raconter, que un fu accuséz et puis
175   pendus par soy estre descouvert a un sien compere en qui se fioit,
mais je croy que en la face de justice pou vont les clamées ne les
plaintes de tant orribles maulx, des grans desloyautéz et des grans
deableries que il dit que tant malicieusement et secretement scevent
femmes commettre. Si est voirement bien secret quant il n'appert a
180   nullui! Et comme autrefoiz ay dit sur ceste matiere en un mien dictié
appellé *L'Epistre au Dieu d'amours:* ou sont les contrées ou les royaumes qui par leurs grans iniquitéz sont exilliéz? Mais sans parler a
voulenté, disons de quieulx grans crimes peut on accuser meismes
les pires et qui plus deçoivent: que peuent elles faire, de quoy te
185   deçoivent? Se elles te demandent de l'argent de ta bourse, dont ne
le te emblent ou tolent elles pas: ne leur bailles mie se tu ne veulx!
Et se tu dis que tu en es assotéz, si ne t'en assote mie! Te vont elles
en ton hostel querir, ne prier ou prendre a force? Bon seroit savoir
comment elles te deçoivent.

190   Et ancore, tant supperfluement et laidement parla des femmes
mariées qui si deçoivent leurs maris—duquel estat ne pot savoir par
experience et tant en parla generaument: a quelle bonne fin pot ce
estre et quel bien ensuivre? N'y sçay entendre fors empeschement
de bien et de paix de mariage, et rendre les maris qui tant oyent de
195   babuises et fatras, se foy y adjoustent, souspeçonneux et pou amanz
leurs femmes. Dieux! quelle exortacion! comme elle est prouffit-
240v° able et vrayement puis que // en general ainsi toutes blasma, de
croire par ceste raison suis contrainte que oncques n'ot acoinctance
ne hantise de femme honnorable ne vertueuse, mais par plusieurs
200   femmes dissollues et de male vie hanter—comme font communement les luxurieux—, cuida ou faingni savoir que toutes teles
feussent, car d'autres n'avoit congnoissance et se seulement eust

who, he claims, are so eager to know their secrets[26]—though I do
not know where the devil he found such rubbish and tainted speech,
which he arranges in a long passage—I ask all those who believe
165 that this is true to tell me when they have seen a man accused or
killed, hanged, or reprimanded in the streets due to the indiscretion
of his wife. I think they will be hard to find. That being said, it is
always wise and noble to keep one's secrets hidden, because there
is perfidy everywhere. As I heard tell not long ago, for example,
170 there was someone who was accused and then hanged after being
denounced by a friend in whom he had confided. Yet I think that
neither the complaints nor the rumors of such terrible sins, disloy-
alties, and evil acts, which women purportedly commit in a mean
spirit of complicity, will go very far in the court of law. In the end,
175 a true secret is that which belongs to no one! I have already spoken
about this in one of my poems, *L'Epistre au Dieu d'Amour*:[27] Where
are the countries and kingdoms which have been exiled due to the
great injustices caused by women? Let us not speak arbitrarily: Of
which terrible crimes can even the worst and the most deceptive
180 be accused? Truly, what can they do to betray you? If they ask for
money from your purse, they will not simply steal it from you. So
do not give it to them if you do not wish to! And if you say that they
have made a fool of you, do not let them! Will they seek you out in
your place of lodging, pleading with you or taking you by force? It
185 would be nice to know how it is that they deceive you.

Moreover, he speaks unnecessarily and defamingly of married women who terribly betray their husbands, though he cannot
know about the married state from experience, and thus can only
speak about it in general terms. What good does this do, and what
190 can come of this? It can serve only to impede happiness and peace
in marriage and to render husbands suspicious, who hear so much
babbling and exaggeration and believe it, and it causes them to have
little love for their wives. My God, what a biased exhortation! And,
indeed, since he insults all women, I am forced to believe that he did
195 not know nor was he acquainted with any honorable and virtuous
woman, but, having known only fallen ones who led sinful lives,
as the lecherous tend to do, he thought he knew—or claimed to
know—that they must all be like this. And if he had only insulted
the dishonorable ones and counseled men to flee them, he would
200 have given a good lesson. But no, he accuses them all, without
exception. Since he thinks they are deprived of reason and accuses
them wrongfully, he himself should be blamed instead because he

blasmé les deshonnestes et conseillié elles fuir, bon enseignement
et juste seroit. Mais non! ains sans excepcion toutes les accuse.

205   Mais se tant oultre les mettes de raison se chargia l'aucteur de elles
accuser ou jugier nonveritablement, blasme aucun n'en doit estre
imputé a elles, mais a cellui qui si loing de verité dit la mençonge
qui n'est mie creable, comme le contraire appere manifestement.
Car se il et tous ses complices en ce cas l'eussent juré, a nul n'en

210   soit grief, il a esté, est et sera moult de plus valables femmes, plus
honnestes, mieulx moriginées et meismes plus sçavens, et dont
plus grant bien est ensuivi au monde que oncques ne fist de sa
personne—mesmement en pollicie mondaine et en meurs vertueux
tres enseignées—, et plusieurs qui ont esté cause du reconciliement

215   de leurs maris, et porté leurs affaires et leurs secréz et leurs passions doulcement et secretement, non obstant leur feussent leurs
maris rudes et mal amoureux. De ce treuve l'en asséz preuves en
la Bible et es autres anciennes histoires, comme Sarra, Rebecha,
Ester, Judith, et autres asséz; et mesmes en noz aages avons veu

220   en France moult de vaillans femmes, grans dames et autres de noz
dames de France: la saincte devote royne Jehanne, la royne Blanche,
la duchesse d'Orlians fille du roy de France, la duchece d'Anjou qui
ores est nommé royne de Cecile—qui tant orent beauté, chasteté,
honnesteté et savoir—, et autres asséz; et de mendres vaillans

225   preudefemmes, comme ma dame de la Ferté, femme messire Pierre
de Craon—qui moult fait a louer—, et asséz d'autres, qui trop seroit
longue narracion dire plus.

Et ne croiéz, chier sire, ne aucun autre n'ait oppinion, que je
die ou mette en ordre ces dites deffences par excusacion favourable

230   pour ce que femme sui: car veritablement mon motif n'est simplement fors soustenir pure verité si comme je la sçay de certaine
science estre au contraire des dictes choses de moy nyées. Et de
tant comme voirement suis femme, plus puis tesmoingnier en ceste
partie que cellui qui n'en a l'experience, ains parle par devinailles et

235   d'aventure.

Mais aprés toutes ces choses, par amours, soit consideré
quel est la fin du dit traictié. Car si comme dit un proverbe, «A
la fin sont terminées les choses». Si soit veu et notté a quoy peut
estre prouffitable la tres orrible et honteuse conclusion—que dis

240   je, honteuse!—mais tant deshonneste que je ose dire que personne
aucune amant vertus et honnesteté ne l'orra qui tout ne soit confus
de honte et abominé d'ainsi ouyr discerner et desjoindre et mectre
soubz deshonnestes ficcions ce que honte et raison doit reffraindre,

is so far from the truth; and his lie is not credible, since the contrary
is so obviously true. For if he and all his partisans in this case had
sworn that there were, are, and will be many worthy, honorable,
educated, and even knowledgeable women who bring more good
to the world than he ever did, even in worldly politics and in wise
virtue, no harm will be done to anyone. Similarly, there were many
who brought about reconciliation with their husbands and quietly
kept the secret of their dealings and confidences and suffering even
if their husbands were violent and bad lovers. Enough proof can be
found of this in the Bible and in other ancient stories, such as in the
lives of Sarah, Rebecca, Esther, Judith,[28] and many others. And even
nowadays, there are many courageous and noble ladies of France, *ex.*
such as the holy and pious Queen Jeanne, Queen Blanche, the *of*
Duchess of Orléans (daughter of the King of France), and the Duch- *honor-*
ess of Anjou, now Queen of Sicily.[29] They are beautiful, chaste, *able*
honorable, and knowledgeable, as are many others. Further, there *married*
are many courageous bourgeois ladies such as my Lady of Ferté, *women*
wife of Seigneur Pierre de Craon—she is to be praised—and others
too numerous to mention here.[30]

And you must believe me, dear sir, that I do not sustain these
opinions in favor of women simply because I am myself a woman.
For, to be sure, my purpose is simply to uphold the absolute truth
because I know from experience that the truth is contrary to those
things which I am denying. And as much as I am a woman, I am
much better able to speak of these things than one who has no experience in this matter, and who thus can go only by mere assumption
and guessing.

And then after all this, by God, let us consider the end of
this treatise! As a certain proverb says, "Things finish in the end."
Pay heed to the purpose of this very awful and shameful conclusion; what am I saying? Shameful? It is so shameful that I dare
say that no one who loves virtue and honor will hear this shameful
ruse without being ashamed and outraged, when Shame and Reason would not even allow decent people to think these disgraces,
let alone listen to them. What is worse, I dare say that no one who
loves virtue and honor will hear this shameful ruse without feeling
ashamed and outraged, when Shame and Reason…. So why praise a
text which no one will dare read nor tell in a proper setting—at the
table of queens, princesses, or bourgeois ladies, for whom it would
be appropriate to cover their faces, to blush with shame? And if you
wish to excuse him claiming that it pleased him to use such images

aux bien ordonéz, seulement le penser; encore plus, j'ose dire
245 241r° que personne aucune // amant vertus et honnesteté ne l'orra qui
tout ne soit confus de honte et abominé d'ainsi ouyr discerner et
desjoindre et mectre soubz deshonnestes ficcions ce que honte….
Et dont que fait a louer lecture qui n'osera estre leue ne parlée en
propre fourme a la table des roynes, des princesses et des vaillans
250   preudefemmes—a qui convendroit couvrir la face de honte rougie?
Et se tu le veulx excuser en disant que par maniere de jolie nouvelle
lui plot mectre la fin d'amours par telles figures. Je te respons que
en ce nulle estrangeté ne nous racompte ne apprent! Ne scet on
comment les hommes habitent aux femmes naturellement? Se il
255   nous narrast comment ours ou lyons ou oyseaux ou autre chose fust
et fust devenuz, ce seroit de matiere de rire pour la fable, mais nulle
nouvelleté en ce ne nous annonce. Sanz faille plus plaisamment et
trop plus doulcement et par plus courtois termes s'en feust passé,
et qui mieulx plairoient mesmes aux amans jolis et honnestes, et a
260   toute autre vertueuse personne.

Ainsi, selon ma petite capacité et foible jugement, sans plus
estre prolice en lengage, non obstant que asséz plus porroit estre dit
et mieulx, ne sçay considerer aucune utilité ou dit traictié; mais tant
m'y semble appercevoir que grant labeur fu prins sans aucun preu
265   non obstant que mon jugement confesse maistre Jehan de Meun
moult grant clerc soubtil et bien parlant, et trop meilleur œuvre
plus prouffitable et de sentement plus hault eust sceu mettre sus
se il s'i fust appliquié—dont fu domage—, mais je suppose que la
grant charnalité, peut estre, dont il fu rempli, le fist plus abonder a
270   voulenté que a bien prouffitable, comme par les opperacions communement sont congneues les inclinacions.

Non obstant ce, je ne repreuve mie *Le Rommant de la Rose*
en toutes pars. Car il y a de bonnes choses et bien dictes sans faille
et de tant est plus grant le peril car plus est adjoustee foy au mal
275   de tant comme le bien y est plus auttentique; et par ce ont maint
soubtil aucunes foiz semés de grans erreurs par les entremesler et
palier avec verité et vertus. Mais si comme dit son prestre Genyus:
«Fuiéz! fuyéz femme, le mal serpent mucié soubz l'orbe!», puis je
dire: «Fuiéz! fuiéz les malices couvertes soubz ombre de bien et de
280   vertu!»

Pour ce dis, en concluant, a vous sire tres chier, et a tous voz
aliéz et complices qui tant le louéz et si hault voulez magnifier que
a peu tous autres volumes vouléz et oséz abaissier devant lui, n'est
digne que louange lui soit imputée, sauve vostre bonne grace; et

for the end of his love tale for the sake of embellishing it, I respond
245   that he does not tell or teach us anything extraordinary whatsoever!
Is it not known how men and women customarily copulate? If he
had told us how bears, lions, or birds or other things behaved, and
how they were created, it would have been funny because of the
mockery, but he tells us nothing new. Surely, he could have used
250   more pleasant and more courtly expressions, which would have
pleased beautiful and honorable lovers better, as it would any other
virtuous person.

Therefore, according to my limited intelligence and weak
judgment and my lack of prolix language, though much more could
255   be said and could be better expressed, I do not find this treatise
useful in any way. Instead, it seems to me that great effort was
undertaken for little gain. Despite my judgment, I admit that Master
Jean de Meun was a very skilled and eloquent cleric who could
have created a much more useful doctrine had he applied himself to
260   it—which is a shame, but I suppose that instead of by usefulness, he
was guided by his great love for carnality, which consumed him. After all, it is known that our actions reveal our inclinations. This said,
I do not rebuke the *Roman de la rose* in its entirety, since without a
doubt, it contains good and well-said things. In fact, the danger is all
265   the greater because more credibility is given to the bad even if the
good holds more authority and truth. Through this many errors have
been planted, cleverly mixed in with truth and virtue. As his priest
Genius says, "Flee, flee from women, the evil serpents hidden under
the grass!" And he goes on: "Flee, flee the evil hidden beneath the
270   shadow of good and virtue!"

So in conclusion, I say to you, dear sir, and to all your allies
and partisans, who praise his work so highly that you are prepared
to dare elevate it above all others, with all due respect, it is not
worthy of such praise. You do not do other more worthy works
275   justice, because a work without usefulness, which is harmful for the
common good even if it is delightful and was painstakingly written, cannot be praised. Let us consider the example of the victori-
ous Romans who, in former times, attributed no praise or honor to
something which did not serve a public purpose. Then let us decide
280   whether we are able to crown this romance with laurels. After having considered these things and numerous others, I think it deserves
to be buried in flames rather than crowned with laurels, although
you claim it to be a "mirror for good living, a model for all estates
to lead a life of wise social and moral conduct."[31] With all due

285   grant tort faites aux valables: car œuvre sans utilité et hors bien
       commun ou propre—poson que elle soit delitable, de grant labeur
       et coust—ne fait a louer. Et comme anciennement les Rommains
       triumphans n'atribuassent louange aucune ne honneur a chose quel-
       conques se elle n'estoit a l'utilité de la chose publique, regardons a
290   leur exemplaire, se nous pourons couronner cestui rommant, mais
       je treuve, comme il me semble, ces dictes choses et asséz d'autres
       considerées, mieulx lui affiert ensevelissement de feu que couronne
241v° de laurier, non obstant que le // clamés «mirouer de bien vivre,
       exemple de tous estas de soy politiquement gouverner et vivre
295   religieusement et sagement»; mais au contraire, sauve vostre grace,
       je dis que c'est exortacion de vice confortant vie dissolue, doctrine
       plaine de decevance, voye de dampnacion, diffameur publique,
       cause de souspeçon et mescreantise, honte de plusieurs personnes,
       et peut estre d'erreur.

300   Mais je sçay bien que sur ce en l'excusant vous me respondréz
       que le bien y est ennorté pour le faire et le mal pour l'eschever. Si
       vous puis souldre par meilleur raison que nature humaine, qui de
       soy est encline a mal, n'a nul besoing que on lui ramentoive le pié
       dont elle cloche pour plus droit aler. Et quant a parler de tout le bien
305   qui ou dit livre peut estre notté, certes trop plus de vertueuses cho-
       ses, mieulx dites, plus autentiques et plus prouffitables—meismes
       en politiquement vivre et moralement—, sont trouvées en mains
       autres volumes fais de philosophes et docteurs de nostre foy, comme
       Aristote, Seneque, saint Paul, saint Augustin et d'autres—ce savéz
310   vous—, qui plus valablement et plainement tesmoignent et ensei-
       gnent vertus et fuyr vices que maistre Jehan de Meun n'eust sceu
       faire: mais si voulentiers ne sont veus ne retenus communement des
       charnelx mondains, pour ce que moult plaist au malade qui a grant
       soif quant le medecin lui ottroye que il boive fort, et tout voulentiers
315   pour la lecherie du boire se donne a croire que ja mal ne lui fera.
             Et si me rens bien certaine que vous—a qui Dieu l'ottroit—et
       tous autres par la grace de Dieu ramenéz a clarté et purté de nette
       conscience, sans soullieure ou polucion de peché ne entencion de
       lui, nettoyéz par pointure de contriction (laquelle œuvre et fait cler
320   veoir le secret de conscience et condampne propre voulenté comme
       juge de verité), feréz autre jugement du *Romant de la Rose* et voul-
       driéz, peut estre, que oncques ne l'eussiéz veu. Si souffist a tant.
             Et ne me soit imputé a folie, arrogance ou presompcion d'oser,
       moy femme, reprendre et redarguer aucteur tant soubtil et son œuvre
325   amenuisier de louange, quant lui, seul homme, osa entreprendre a
       diffamer et blasmer sans excercitacion tout un sexe.

285   respect: On the contrary, I call it an exhortation to vice, encouraging immoral life, a doctrine full of deceit; the path to damnation; a
public defamer. It gives rise to suspicion and idolatry, to shame for
many people, and possibly to heresy.[32]

I am convinced, however, since you protect him, that you will
290   reply that the good is there to exhort others to practice it, and the
bad is there to be avoided. If only I could persuade you that human
nature, which is in itself inclined to sinfulness, does not need to be
reminded of its limp in order to walk straight. And speaking of all
the good which can be noted in this work, certainly more virtu-
295   ous things, even things relating to social and moral conduct, can
be found in many other works by renowned philosophers such as
Aristotle, Seneca, Saint Paul, Saint Augustine, and so forth, who as
you know attest to and teach the virtues and to flee vices much more
effectively, eloquently, and profitably than ever was Jean de Meun
300   able to do. But what will be remembered above all are the carnal
pleasures, in the same way the invalid abuses his doctor's permission to drink, and out of gluttony believes that drinking will do him
no harm. I am certain that you—to whom God allows it—and all the
others onto whom God has bestowed clarity and a good conscience,
305   untarnished by sin or its intention, will do penitence (the purpose
of which is to bare the secrets of our conscience and to condemn
our own will as judge of truth) and will judge the *Roman de la rose*
properly and wish perhaps that you had never seen it. This will
suffice.

310   I should not be accused of madness, arrogance, or pretentiousness in that I, a woman, dared to criticize such a skilled author and
to diminish the praise of his work, when he alone dared to defame
and to insult, without exception,[33] an entire sex.

5. *September 15, 1401: Gontier Col's Reply to Christine de Pizan after She Had Sent Him a Copy of Her Letter to Jean de Montreuil*

Text:

241v° ITEM, comme la dicte Cristine eust envoyé la coppie de la dicte
epistre a maistre Gontier Col, lui renvoya l'epistre qui s'ensuit:
Maistre Gontier Col
A femme de hault entendement, damoiselle Cristine.

5   Pour ce que la Sainte Escripture nous enseigne et commande
242r° que quant on voit son amy errer ou faire faulte // on le doit corriger
et reprendre premierement a part, et se il ne se veult amender pour
celle fois que on le corrige devant gent, et se pour ce ne se veult corriger que on le tiengne *tanquam eunucus et publicanus.* Et je te aime
10   loyaument pour tes vertus et merites, t'ay premierement par une
mienne lettre, que avant yer t'envoyay, exortée, avisée et priée de
toy corriger et amender de l'erreur et magnifeste folie ou demence
trop grant a toy venue par presompcion ou oultrecuidance et comme
femme pacionnée en ceste matiere,—ne te desplaise se je dy voir.
15   Je, ensuivant le commandement divin, ayant de toy compassion par
amour charitable, te pry, conseille et requiers la seconde foiz par
ceste moye cedule que ton dessus dit erreur tu veuilles corriger, des-
dire et amender envers le tres excellant et inreprehensible docteur
en saincte divine Escripture, hault philosophe et en toutes les .vii.
20   ars liberaulx clerc tres parfond, que si orriblement oses et presumes
corriger et repprendre a sa grant charge—et aussi envers ses vrays
et loyaux disciples, mon seigneur le prevost de Lisle et moy et
autres—, et confesser ton erreur: et nous aurons pitié de toy et te
prendrons a merci en te baillant penitence salutaire. Et de ce, avec la
25   responce de mon autre lectre, te plaise moy ta bonne voulenté faire
savoir a ton ayse et loisir avant que je me mette en peine d'escripre
encontre tes faulses, sauve ta reverence, escriptures que de lui tu as
voulu escripre et si ores et autrefoiz quant je te escriray te appelle en
singulier, ne te desplaise ne le me imputes a arrogance ou orgueil:
30   car cest et a esté de tousjours ma maniere quant j'ay escript a mes
amis, especiallement quant sont lectréz.
            Dieux vueille briefment ramener ton cuer et entendement a
vraye lumiere et congnoiscence de verité! Car ce soit dommage se
plus demouroies en tel erreur soubz les tenebres d'ignorence.
35   Escript ce jeudi .xv°. jour de septembre.
Le tien Gontier Col

Translation:

Master Gontier Col

To Lady Christine, a woman of high intelligence.

Holy Scripture teaches and commands us to correct a friend who is in the wrong. First, we must take him aside and notify him
5 in private of his error. If he refuses to retract it, he must then be corrected publicly, and if he again refuses to retract, he must be held *tanquam eunucus et publicanus*.[34] Since I love you loyally for your virtues and merits, I sent you, the day before yesterday, a first letter in which I begged, exhorted, and advised you to retract your error
10 and manifest foolishness which was caused by your pretentiousness, as a woman passionate about this matter—be not angered with me for speaking the truth. I, following divine order, having compassion for you out of charitable love, ask, and advise you for the second time with this notification to correct and retract your accusation
15 against the excellent and irreprehensible master of Holy Scripture, renowned philosopher, and expert in all seven liberal arts, whom you so horribly dare to reprimand and criticize, as well as his true and loyal disciples—my lord the provost of Lille, myself, and others. Confess your error and we shall have mercy on you and grant
20 you salutary penitence. Together with your response to my other letter, I ask you to announce this intent at your convenience, before I see myself forced to write against your—with all due respect—erroneous views which you have written against him.

And if now or at any time when I write to you I address you in
25 the familiar, I ask you not to be offended nor to attribute it to arrogance on my part, for this is and has always been my custom when writing to friends, in particular when they are erudite.

Without delay, may God bring your heart and intellect to the true light and to the knowledge of truth, for it would be a shame if
30 you remained any longer in the darkness of error and ignorance.

Written this Thursday, September 15.

Yours,

Gontier Col

6. End of September, 1401: Christine Replies to the Above Letter from Gontier Col

Text:

242r°   Cristine

A tres nottable et souffisant personne, maistre Gontier Col, secretaire du roy nostre sire.

O clerc soubtil d'entendement philosophique, stilé es sciences,
5   prompt en polie rethorique et soubtile poetique, ne vueillez par
erreur volentaire reprendre et reprouver ma veritable oppinion justement meue pour tant se elle n'est a ta plaisance. Et comme
j'ay sceu par tes premieres lectres a moy envoyées tu desirant
242v° avoir la // coppie d'un petit traictié en maniere d'epistre de par
10   moy ja envoyé a sollempnel clerc, mon seigneur le prevost de Lisle
(ouquel est traictié et dit au lonc selon l'estendue de mon petit engin
l'oppinion de moy tenue, a la sienne contraire, de la grant louange
qu'il attribue a la compilacion du *Rommant de la Rose,* comme il
m'aparu par un sien dictié adrecant a un soubtil clerc docteur, sien
15   ami, contraire a sa dicte oppinion—a laquelle la moye confere). Et
pour vouloir emplir ton bon mandement le t'ay envoye; par quoy,
aprés la veue et visitacion d'icellui, comme ton erreur pointe et
touchee de verité, meu de impacience m'as escript tes .ii.ème lettres
plus injurieuses reprochant mon femenin sexe (lequel tu dis comme
20   passionné comme par nature et meu de folie et presompcion d'oser
corriger et reprendre si hault docteur, si gradué et tant solempnel
comme tu clames l'aucteur d'icellui). Et de ce moult m'ennortez
que je m'en desdie et repente, et merci piteuse sera ancore vers moy
estendue, ou se non de moy sera fait comme du publican, etc.

25   Ha! homme d'entendement ingenieus! ne seuffres a propre
voulenté tenir close la soubtilleté de ton engin! Regardes droit selon
voye theologienne la plus souveraine et tu tant ne condampneras
mes dis ainsi comme les ay escrips, et considereras se louange affiert es pas particuliers que ilz repprennent; et toutesfoiz bien soit de
30   toy notté en toutes pars quieulx choses je condampne et quelles non.
Et se tu tant desprises mes raisons pour la petitece de ma faculté
(laquelle tu me repproches de dire «comme femme», etc.). Saches
de voir que ce ne tiens je a villenie ou aucun reprouche, pour le reconfort de la noble memoire et continuelle experience de tres grant
35   foison vaillans femmes avoir esté et estre tres dignes de louange
et en toutes vertus apprises, auxquelles mieulx vouldroie ressembler que estre enrichi de tous les biens de fortune. Mais ancore se
a toutes fins veulx pour ce amenuisier mes vehementes raisons,

Translation:

Christine

To the illustrious and skilled Master Gontier Col, Secretary to the Lord Our King.

O skilled cleric, knowledgeable in philosophy, versed in the
5   sciences and in polite rhetoric and skillful poetics, I ask you not to
rebuke and reproach my truthful opinion simply because it is not to
your liking. You sent me a first letter asking for a copy of the little
epistolary treatise which I had already sent to the solemn cleric,
my lord the provost of Lille (in which, inasmuch as it was possible
10   with my limited intelligence, I contradicted him who greatly praises
the compilation of the *Roman de la rose* in a treatise addressed, I
think, to a skilled and learned cleric, a friend of his who does not
seem to share his opinion but whose views would be more in line
with my own).[36] In response to your kind request, I sent you a copy
15   of this treatise, which, after you had read it thoroughly, led you to
write me, with impatience, a second letter, in which you commit a
poignant error removed from the truth. You insult me still further
because I am a woman, which according to you makes me fickle,
mad, and pretentious, for daring to correct and to reprimand such a
20   reputable scholar as you claim this author to be. And you strongly
advise me to retract what I have said and to repent, in which case
mercy will still be bestowed upon me. If I do not, I shall share the
fate of the publican, etc.[37]

Ha! Man of ingenuity! Do not let your own willfulness blunt
25   the cleverness of your mind! Look straight down the path of holy
theology and you will not condemn my writings thus. Instead you
will judge whether praise is truly appropriate for those parts of the
Roman which my writings address. In any case, it would be good
of you to note precisely which parts I condemn and which ones I do
30   not. If in fact you so despise my arguments for my lack of intelligence (which you attribute to the fact that "I am a woman," etc.),
know that I consider precisely that point an insult to the memory
of all noble women, past and present, educated in all virtues, and
deserving of praise. I would rather be compared to them than to
35   receive all the wealth of this earth. Again, if you absolutely wish to
weaken my strong opinion, you should remember that a small knife
can rupture a large bag filled with goods. And do you not know that
a small weasel is able to attack and destroy a great lion? If you think

veuilles toy reduire a <u>memoire que une petite pointe de ganivet</u>

40   <u>ou coutellet peut percier un grant sac plain et enflé de materielles</u>
<u>choses</u>; et ne sces tu que une petite mostelle assault un grant lyon et
<u>a la foiz</u> le desconfit? Si ne cuides aucunement moy estre meue ne
desmeue par legiereté, par quoy soye tost desdite—ja soit ce que en
moy disant villenie me menaces de tes soubtilles raisons, lesquelles

45   choses sont communement espouentement aux couars; mais affin que tu puisses retenir en brief ce que plus au lonc ay autrefoiz
escript: Je dis derrechief et replique et triplique tant de foiz comme
tu vouldras que le dit intitulé *Le Rommant de la Rose,* non obstant
y ait de bonnes choses (et de tant y est le peril plus grant comme le

50   bien y est plus autentique, comme autrefoiz ay dit), mais pour ce
que nature humaine est plus dessendant au mal je dis que il peut

243r° estre cause de mauvaise et perverse exortacion en tres // abominables meurs confortant vie dissolue, doctrine plaine de decevance,
voye de dampnacion, diffameur publique, cause de souspeçon et

55   mescreantise et honte de plusieurs personnes, et peut estre d'erreur
et tres dehonneste lecture en plusieurs pars. Et tout ce je vueil et ose
tenir et maintenir par tout et devant tous publiquement et prouver
par lui mesmes, m'en rapporter et attendre au jugement de tous
justes preudes hommes theologiens et vrays catholiques, et gens de

60   honneste et salvable vie.
     La tienne,
     Cristine de Pizan[35]

that I am motivated only by fickleness, why are you so annoyed?
40   Is it not cowardly to threaten a simpler person when you yourself
are so skilled? In order to remind you briefly of what I have written
elsewhere in more detail, I shall tell you again and again, as often as
you like, that the text entitled *Le Roman de la rose*, though it contains good things (which actually makes it more perilous, because
45   the good in it is legitimate, as I have said before), can create bad and
perverse exhortations for the abominable morals of dissolute life,
because human nature is more inclined to sin. It is a doctrine full of
betrayal, leading its readers to the path of damnation; it is a public
defamer, giving cause for suspicion and lying and shame for many
50   people and sometimes providing for a dishonorable and erroneous
reading. All this I wish and dare to maintain, everywhere and before
everyone publicly, and am willing to submit my opinion to the judgment of just and noble theologians, genuine Catholics, and honorable persons.
55   Yours,
            Christine de Pizan

7. October 2, 1402: Christine's Response to Pierre Col[38]

Text:

243r° A maistre Pierre, secretaire du roy nostre sire

Pour ce que entendement humain ne peut estre eslevé jusques a haultesse de clere cognoiscence d'enterine verite attendre des choses occultes (par l'offuscacion grosse et terrestre qui l'empesche et tolt vraie clarté), convient par oppinion plus que de certainne science determiner des choses ymaginées plus voirs-amblables: pour celle cause sont esmeues souventes fois diverses questions—mesmement entre les plus soubtilz—par oppinions contraires, et chascun s'efforce de monstrer par vive raison son oppinion estre vraye. Et que l'experience en soit magnifeste est clere chose, ce pouons nous veoir par nous mesmes presentement, pour ce dy en parlant a toy, clerc soubtil, a qui aucune ignorence ne toult vif sentement et abilleté de lengage a demonstrer de toy les choses oppinées—, vueil que tu saches, tout soient tes raisons bien conduites a la fin de ton entencion contraires a la mienne oppinion, ycelles, non obstant la belle eloquence, ne meuvent en riens mon courage ne troublent mon sentement au contraire de ce que autrefois ay escript sus la matiere,—dont presentement et de nouvel me veulx poindre et renouveller les aguillonnemens ja a moy lanciéz par les escriptures d'autres sollempnelles personnes sus la matiere, dont tu m'as envoyé ta nouvelle escripture touchant certain debat pieca meu a cause de la compilacion du *Rommant de la Rose*. Et combien que occupée soy autre part, ne mon entencion n'estoit de plus escripre sur ce, encore te respondray en gros et rudement, selonc mon usaige, verité sans paliacion. Et comme je ne sceusse suivre ton bel stile, supployer vueilles le deffault et l'ignorance.

Tu m'escris a ton commencement que comme tu desirasses veoir de mes escriptures, te soit venu entre mains un certain mien epistre adressant a mon seigneur le prevost de Lisle, laquelle se commence: «Reverence honneur», etc. Si dis tost aprés que je m'efforce de reprendre ce «tres hault catholique, divin orateur»,

243v° etc., maistre Jehan de Meun, // ou livre de la *Rose* en aucunes particularitez, «pour lequel louer tu n'oseroies ouvrir ta bouche ne que ton pié avancier a entrer en une abisme». Mere Dieu! arestons cy un pou! Est il doncques pareil a Jhesu Crist ou a la Vierge, plus que saint Paul ou les docteurs de sainte Esglise, qui dis que ne le pourroye «souffisament louer pour y user tous mes membres se tous estoient devenus lengues», etc.? Toutefois est il vray, sauve ta reverence, que trop extreme et excessive louange donnee a crea-

[handwritten marginal notes: "this rime no exterded w/ greeting subsequent humble words"]

[handwritten right margin note: "she has to laud debate in itself as an exercise leading to the truth"]

Translation:

To Master Pierre, secretary to our Lord the King

Since human understanding cannot attain the height of absolute knowledge of the perfect truth of hidden things (due to the thick
worldly obscurity which hinders it from seeing the entire and true

5   meaning), it is appropriate to determine the truthfulness of imagined
things through opinion rather than through a certain knowledge. It
is for this reason that questions are often raised, even by the most
learned, which represent contradictory opinions and in which each
party attempts to show, through forceful reasoning, the truth of one's

10 own opinion. And that experience plays a part in this is obvious, as
we may see in our own current debate. O skilled cleric, whose keen
sentiment and rhetorical ability in expressing opinions is in no way
impeded by ignorance, I wish therefore to inform you that, regardless of the adverse nature of your arguments and the beauty of your

15 eloquence, I will not be shaken in my courage to continue to present
my views, though they are contrary to yours, as you know from my
earlier writings. Thus, I will continue to fend off the sharp attacks
with which I have already been targeted by other reputable persons'
writings on this matter, among them your latest letter on this debate

20 motivated by the compilation of the *Roman de la rose*. And although
I am occupied with other matters and my intent was not to continue
writing on this subject, I will nevertheless reply to you in my cus-
tomary simplistic manner of telling the truth without disguise. Since
I am unable to emulate your beautiful style, I ask you to take into

25 consideration this weakness and ignorance.

You begin your letter by saying that, in wishing to see one
of my letters, you had come across a certain epistle of mine which
was addressed to my lord, the provost of Lille, starting with "Reverence, honor," etc., wherein I go on to say that I attempt to criticize

30 this "very noble Catholic, divine orator," etc., Master Jean de Meun
in certain parts of his book of the *Rose*, "because to praise it [you]
would not dare to open [your] mouth, no more than to put [your]
foot forward towards an abyss." Mother of God! Let us stop here
for a moment! Does this mean he is like Jesus Christ or the Virgin

35 and greater than Saint Paul or the Holy Church Fathers, whom I
could not "praise enough even if all [my] body parts had turned
into tongues," etc.? At any rate, it is true, with all due respect, that
too much and excessive praise given to a human being will turn to
reproach and criticism. And since it is the pure truth which prompts

40   ture fait a reprendre et tourne a blasme. Et comme verité pure me
contraingne a toy respondre ce que plus voulentiers tairoie (pour ce
que la matiere n'est a ma plaisance), le feray selon mon rude stile.
Mais si comme m'escrips que je te pardonne se tu parles a moy par
'tu', samblablement te pry, comme ce soit le plus propre selon nos
45   ancians,—comme tu mesmes dis.

        Premierement tu proposes que sans raison je blasme ce qui
est dit ou dit *Rommant de la Rose* ou chapitre de Raison, la ou elle
nomme les secrés membres d'omme par leur droit nom; et relates ce
que autrefois ay respondu ailleurs, que «voirement crea Dieu toutes
50   choses bonnes… mais par la pollucion du peché de nos premiers
parens devint homme immonde»: et ay donné exemple de Lucifer,
dont le nom est bel et la personne orrible, et en concluant ay dit
que «le non ne fait pas la deshonnestetés de la chose, mais la chose
fait le non deshonneste». Et de ce cy dire tu dis que je ressemble le
55   pellican, qui s'occist de son bec. Si fais ta conclusion et dis après:
«Se la chose donc fait le non deshonneste, quel nom je puis bailler
a la chose qui ne soit deshonneste»? A ce je respondray sans passer
oultre grossement. Car je ne suis logicienne; ne a vraye verité dire
n'a ja besoing teles persuasions. Sans faille je confesse que je ne
60   pourroie en nulle maniere parler de deshonnesteté, de voulenté cor-
rompue ne affin de elle—quelconques nom que je lui baillasse, ou
fust aux secrés membres ou autre chose deshonneste—, que le nom
ne fust deshonneste. Et toutefois se pour certain cas de maladie ou
autre neccessité il convenoit declairier ou les membres ou quoy que
65   ce fust, et j'en parloye en maniere que on m'entendist et non nommer par propre nom, je ne parleroye point deshonestement: la cause
si est pour ce a la fin pour quoy je parleroye ne seroit pas deshonnestement et neantmains se te les nommoie par leur propre nom
et fust ores a cause bonne. Si parleroye je deshonnestement, car la
70   premiere intencion de la chose a ja fait le nom deshonneste dont
s'ensuit vraye ma premiere preposicion: «que la chose fait le nom
deshonneste, et non mie le nom la chose».

        Et a la question que tu me fais: «se je parloye des secrés mem-
bres d'un petit enfant», lequel est innocent (se je les oseroye bien
75   nommer pour ce que il est sans pollucion de peché), aincois que je
te responde. Aincois que question je te demande pour responce: se
un enfant petit est ramené a autelle innocence et en aussi esgal
estat ne plus ne moins que estoit Adam quant Dieu l'ot creé. Se tu
244r° dis oyl, // c'est faulx, car le petit enfant meurt a douleur ains que
80   il ait peché. Ce n'eust point fait Adam en l'estat d'innocence, car

40   me to respond to you, though I would much rather be silent (be-
       cause this matter is not to my liking), I will do so in my blunt style.
       And since you ask me to forgive you for your informal address, I,
       too, ask you to do the same, according to the custom of our forefa-
       thers, as you yourself say.

45   First, you suggest that I reprimand without justification that
       which is said in the passage of Reason in the *Roman de la rose*,
       where she calls the secret male parts by their proper names,[40] and
       you recount my earlier reply to you, that "it is true that God made
       all things good, but mankind became unclean through the corrup-
50   tion of original sin." I gave the example of Lucifer, whose name is
       beautiful but who as a person is abominable, concluding that "the
       name does not make the thing shameful, but it is the thing which
       makes the name shameful." And because of this you said that I
       resembled the pelican, who kills himself with his beak. This is
55   your conclusion, after which you go on to say, "If the thing causes
       the shame of the name, what name could I give to a thing which is
       shameful?" I will respond to this bluntly, for I am no logician, nor
       to be honest do I consider such rationalizations necessary. Indeed,
       I admit that I could not speak at all about shame, corrupted will, or
60   any such thing, regardless of the name I gave it—be it the secret
       parts or any other shameful thing—without causing the name, too,
       to become shameful. Nevertheless, if it were appropriate to pro-
       nounce the names of body parts or whatever other thing in order
       to describe a certain illness or out of some other necessity, and if
65   I could make myself understood without using the proper name, I
       would not speak at all shamefully, because the purpose for which
       I spoke would not be shameful. However, if I were to call them by
       their proper names, even for a good reason, I would speak shame-
       fully, because it is the initial intent of the thing which causes shame
70   in the first place. It follows, then, that my first proposition was true:
       "that the thing makes the word shameful and not at all the name the
       thing."
               And my answer to your question, "If I were to speak about
       the secret parts of a small child, who is innocent" (that is, whether I
75   dare to call these parts what they are, for a child is not yet corrupted
       by sin), would be in the form of another question: If a small child
       is truly this innocent, is he not then equal—no more, no less—to
       Adam when God first created him? If your answer is yes, you are
       wrong, for the small child dies in pain before it can sin. This is not
80   the case with Adam in his state of innocence, because it was his sin

de son peché fu engendré mort. Se tu me dis non, doncques te dis je
vraye ma proposicion: que tel honte nous est engendrée par la pollucion de nos premiers parens. Et ce que tu dis que «riens ne vault
tant repliquer du peché originel, car il vint de la desobeissance»,
85   je te confesse que de ce vint il. Mais tu me dis se la pollucion de
nos premiers parens fait le nom deshonneste des secrés membres,
doncques, ce dis tu, «par plus forte raison on ne devroit mie nommer
yceulx noz premiers parans. Car ce sont ceulx qui pecherent, et non
pas les membres». A ce je te feray pour responce un gros argument,
90   et vouldroie que bien le me soluces. Pour quoy fu ce que tantost que
nos premiers parans orent peché et congnoissance orent de bien et
de mal, ilz mucierent incontinent leurs secrés membres et se hon-
toyerent? Toutevoies n'en avoient encore usé. Je te demande pour
quoy ilz ne couvrirent leurs yeulx ou leur bouche, dont ils avoient
95   peché, et non pas les secrés membres? Et me semble que tres lors fu
née honte raisonnable, laquelle la Raison de ton maistre et toy et tes
complices voulez chacier et estroper. Si m'est avis que je ne me suis
point occise de mon bec, ainssi comme tu me condampnes.

       Comme je ne soye une seule en la tres bonne, vraye et juste op-
100   pinion raisonnable contre la compilacion du dit *Rommant de la Rose*
(pour les tres reprouvées exortacions qui y sont—non obstant tel bien
comme il y peut avoir), soit vraye chose que entre les autres bonnes
personnes concordans a ma dicte oppinion, avint, aprés que je os
escript mon epistre (laquelle tu dis que as veu),—vint a voulenté
115   pour l'acroissement de vertu et le destruisement de vice—de quoy le
dit de la Rose peut avoir empoisonné plusieurs cuers humains—pour
y obvier, tres vaillant docteur et maistre en theologie, souffissant,
digne, louable, clerc solempnel, esleu entre esleus, compila un œuvre
en brief conduite moult notablement par pure theologie, de quoy tu
120   m'escris en ton traictié que tu as «veue en maniere d'une plaidoirie
en la court de sainte Crestienté, en laquelle estoit justice canonique
establie come juge et les Vertus entour elle comme son conseil,
duquel le chief et comme chancelier estoit Entendement Soubtil,
joint par compagnie a dame Raison, Prudence, Science et autres
125   comme secretaires, Eloquence Theologienne comme avocat de la
court et le promoteur des causes estoit Conscience, lequel promoteur
ont fait lever et presenter une requeste pour Chasteté contenant ceste
fourme: «A justice la droituriere, tenant le lieu de Dieu en terre, et a
toute sa religieuse court devote et tres crestienne. Supplie humble-
130   ment et se complaint Chasteté, vostre feale subgete, que remede soit
mis et provision brieve sur les forfaitures intollerables, lesquelles

which caused death. If your answer is no, you are admitting that
my proposition is correct: That such shame was caused by the corruption of our first parents. Moreover, when you say that "nothing
warrants returning to the argument of original sin, because it was
85   caused by disobedience," I admit that this is so. But you tell me that
the corruption of our first parents caused the shame of the name of
the secret parts, as you say, "it is for that very reason one should
not name our first parents, because it is they who sinned and not the
body parts." I will respond to this with a complex problem which I
90   would like you to solve for me: Why was it that as soon as our first
parents had sinned and had knowledge of good and evil, they at
once covered their secret parts and were ashamed, though they had
not yet made use of them. I ask you, why did they not cover their
eyes or mouths, with which they had sinned, instead of their secret
95   parts? It seems to me that reasonable shame was born of this, which
your master's Reason, you, and your partisans wish to chase away
and quash. I think that I have not in the least killed myself with my
beak, as you would have it.

       Since I am not alone in this very good, true, just, and logical
100   opposition to the compilation of the *Roman de la rose* (prompted
by the terrible exhortations in it, despite all the good that it may
contain), it is true that among the other good persons who share
my opinion, it is thought that the *Rose* may have poisoned many
human hearts. After I wrote my epistle, which you said you had
115   seen, and which is intended to increase virtue and to destroy vice,
a very noble doctor and master of theology—a learned, dignified,
venerated cleric,[41] chosen from among the chosen—compiled a
brief work motivated by pure theology, which you in your treatise
consider "a sort of appeal to the court of Holy Christianity, where
120   Canonical Justice was established as judge and the virtues around it
as councilors, whose chancellor was Learned Understanding, joined
by the company of Lady Reason, Prudence, Knowledge, and others
as secretaries. Theological Eloquence was the court's advocate, and
the promoter of causes was Conscience, who presented a petition on
125   behalf of Chastity formulated as follows: 'To the righteous Justice,
keeper of God's place on earth, and to her entire devout court of
Christianity. Chastity, your loyal subject, begs you humbly and laments that remedy and immediate correction must be imposed on
the intolerable crimes committed incessantly against me by some-
130   one who calls himself the Foolish Lover.' This is followed by eight
or nine articles."[42]

m'a fait et ne cesse faire un qui se fait nommer le Fol Amoureux».
244vᵒ Et met après // huit ou nuef articles.

Et non obstant que a moy singulierement adreces le premier
135   proeme de ta devant dicte escripture (comme tu presumes a toy
estre legier repudier mes raisons pour mon ignorence, confiant en
ton bon sens et soubtilleté, m'est avis encore), tu oses ajoindre tes
reprehencions, teles comme tu les vuelx dire, aux dis de si notable
personne dessusdicte et de œuvre tant bien composée comme est la
140   sienne, pour ce que elle est contraire a l'oppinion en quoy tu erres.
Or avises, or avises si je porroye raisonnablement toy dire l'oprobre
que tu me dis en aucuns de tes chapistres en ceste maniere: «O
presompcion oultraigeuse! o tres fole oultrecuidance!», etc. Si n'est
mie mon entencion de moy charger deffendre contre toy en toutes
145   pars les questions proposées par dame Eloquence dessusdicte (car
il ne touche du tout au propos de ma premiere epistre), se n'est en
aucunes pars ou il touchera a la matiere dont tu me redargues: car
je m'en atens a cellui qui la dicte plaidoirie a composée, qui en pou
de paroles la sara mieux deffendre que toute ma vie ne saroie a son
150   droit resgarder. Mais tant en puis je bien dire que tu—qui mieulx le
cuides entendre que luy, plain de sagece et haulte clergie—le veulx
reprendre de ignorence. Bien dis pour plus courtoisement parler de
si nottable personne, que se bien y eust estudié le dit livre, d'autant
comme son entendement passe tous autres, de tant plus le louast et
155   prisast; ainsy—loués soit Dieux!—toy meismes le confesses sol-
lempnelle personne. Si est bon a croire et a presumer que tel homme
eust blasmee publiquement œuvre qu'il n'eust par avant bien avisee
et comprise!

Encore puis je bien respondre a ce que tu dis qu'il parle de Fol
160   Amoureux comme clerc d'armes (si comme cellui qui onques riens
ne senti), qu'il n'est ja neccessaire, pour parler proprement des choses, avoir l'experience. Et moult d'exemples t'en pourroient estre
donnés: tu meismes le sces—et trop plus de soubtilles choses et hors
le sentement naturel ont esté descriptes proprement—, que l'effect
165   d'amours n'est a entendre a homme soubtil et d'entendement; et toy
meismes confesses qu'il n'est necessaire avoir l'experience, et neantmains tu conclus que se il eust eu l'experience de Fol Amoureux,
autrement deist qu'il ne fait.

Je trespasse cy endroit aucuns articles de la sus dicte plaidoirie
170   de dame Eloquence pour ce que ce n'est a moy a moy a respondre:
et mesmement de ce que tu dis que maistre Jehan de Meun appella saintuaires ne me debatis je oncques car le taire en est le plus

And although you address the prologue of your aforementioned letter solely to me (since, confident in your abilities and skills, you assume, apparently, that it is easy to refute my reasoning because of my ignorance), you dare include the treatise of this illustrious person, whose work is so eloquently composed, in your unfounded reprobation, merely because it expresses an opinion which is contrary to your own. Now consider, consider whether I could not logically apply to you the slander which you have used against me several times: "O outrageous pretentiousness! O very foolish pride!" etc.[43] It is not my intention to take it upon myself to defend against your accusations all of the questions raised by Lady Eloquence in the work of this author, since he does not mention the topic of my first epistle, save for some parts where he touches upon the matter for which you criticize me. Instead I am confident that, with very few words, he will defend his work better than I could ever do in an entire lifetime. But I will say this much: You, who think you understand the work better than does he who is full of wisdom and high learning, accuse him of ignorance. You do say, in your attempt to speak more courteously of such an illustrious person, that if he had studied this book properly—in particular since his intelligence exceeds that of all others—he would have praised and appreciated it even more. Well then, God be praised, you, who yourself admit that he is a highly regarded person, would have us believe that such a man would publicly insult a work which he had not previously studied and understood!

Moreover, I can easily respond to what you have to say concerning the part where he speaks about the Foolish Lover as an ordained cleric (like someone who has never felt anything emotionally): that in order to speak about things properly, it is not necessary to have any experience. Many examples could be given of this: You yourself know that the effect of love cannot be understood by a learned man (many complex things have been described properly without being experienced naturally). Though you yourself admit that it is not necessary to have any experience in this, you conclude that, if indeed he had had the experience of the Foolish Lover, he would have spoken differently than he did.

At this point I will skip over some articles of the above-mentioned complaint by Lady Eloquence, because it is not up to me to respond to them. The same goes for your comment about Master Jean de Meun's definition of sanctuaries. I shall never discuss this, because the most honorable thing to do is simply to pass over it in

honneste. Mais pour ce que tu l'excuses et dis que ainsi se peuent
appeller, et selon loy et pour monstrer la folie au Fol Amoureux,
175   sans faille tu dis autrement que tu ne penses, sauve ta grace. Car tu
245r° sces bien que // oncques ne le dist en entencion de la chose peust estre appellée sainte, mais le dist par une maniere d'une desrision plus
aluchaint, et plus grant atisement aux luxurieux. (Au moins, quelque
entencion qu'il eust, sçay je bien qu'il sonne mal a ceulx qui ne se
180   delitent en tele charnalité.)

Je ne vueil mie passer oultre ce que tu dis que je ne doy mie
cuider ce que il dit en son *Testament*: «J'ay fait en ma jeunece maint
dit par vanité», qu'il entende de ce livre de la *Rose*. Et comme se tu
le sceusces, bien affermes que oncques ne s'en repenti ne dist pour
185   celle cause et toutefois ne l'excepta il mie de riens. Mais tu dis qu'il
entendi de balades, rondiaulx et virelaiz que nous n'avons mie. Ou
sont donques ces autres dictiez que il fist vains et folz? Merveilles
est que de si souverain dicteur n'ont esté sollempneement gardés:
car d'autres qui ne furent a lui a comparer est grant mencion faicte,
190   et des siens n'est personne en vie qui oncques en ouyst parler. Et
vrayement moy mesmes me suis maintes fois merveillée que si
grant dicteur cessast a si pou d'œuvre,—non obstant que plusieurs
qui luy sont favourables luy veulent imposer des dictiez mesmes
de saint Augustin. Mais toutefois se tu veulx dire que il s'en soit
195   teus pour eschiver gloire vaine et que voirement en fist plusieurs,
regardes ou prologue de Boece que il translata—ou il raconte les
translacions et escriptures que il a faites: si croy que il n'en oublia
nulles. (Ce dis je pour ceulx qui autres escriptures luy veulent at-
tribuer, combien que de ce n'ay je que faire.) Mais a nostre propos
200   vrayement je croy et tiens qu'il dist ce qui est dit en son *Testament*
purement pour cellui rommant, car il nous appert par celle parolle et
ne savons le contraire.

Tu viens a mon propos, et dis que dame Eloquence dit: «N'est
ce pas, fait elle, grant rage dire qu'on doye parler nuement et baude-
205   ment et sans vergongne, tant soyent deshonnestes les paroles au
jugement de toutes gens»? Puis tu dis a dame Eloquence que lui
impose mal reciter son fait principal, sur quoy elle fonde tous ses
argumens ensuians, mais tu excuses aprés son aucteur en l'accusant
d'ignorence, et dis ce que j'ay cy devant recité: que c'est, comme tu
210   tiens, par faute de le veoir et pou l'avoir estudié.

En faisant ta responce a dame Eloquence tu recites les paroles
que dist Raison ou dit rommant, qui sont teles en substance: qu'elle
peut bien nommer par propre nom les choses qui ne sont se bonnes

silence. However, since you excuse him and declare that his definition is legitimate to show the foolishness of the Foolish Lover, what
175   you say undoubtedly differs from what you think, with all due respect, because you know very well that he does not intend the thing
to be holy, but instead uses it as a sort of poignant mockery intended
for the excitement of the lecherous. (Whatever intention he may have
had, I am certain that it sounds sinful to those, at least, who take no
180   delight in such carnality.)

However, I shall not skip over your telling me not to believe
that when he states in his *Testament*,[44] "In my youth, I have written
many a text out of vanity," he is actually referring to the *Rose.* And
as if you knew this, you affirm that he never repented, nor did he
185   refer to this book in this context, and yet he certainly did not exclude
it. Instead, you claim that he was referring to his *ballades*, *rondels*,
and *virelais*,[45] which we no longer possess. Where are these poems,
then, which he composed out of vanity and foolishness? It is surprising that they have not been dutifully preserved, coming as they do
190   from such a noble poet, since of others who cannot measure up to
him there is great mention; yet of his own poems no living person
has ever heard. And, truly, as for myself, I have often wondered at
the fact that such a great poet had stopped at so few works, albeit
that several of his supporters would like to attribute to him even the
195   poems of Saint Augustine.[46] At any rate, if you wish to say that he
silenced himself in order to avoid vainglory and that in reality he did
compose more, look at Boethius's prologue, which he translated and
in which he mentions the translations and writings he had done.[47]
I do not think that he forgot any. (I say this for those who wish to
200   attribute other writings to him, although it is not actually necessary.)
As far as our own matter is concerned, I maintain that what he said
in his *Testament* referred only to this romance, because this is what is
evident from his speech and we can prove nothing to the contrary.

You then return to my topic and quote Lady Eloquence: "Is it
205   not, she says, a great outrage to claim that one must speak bluntly,
bawdily, and shamelessly, regardless of how shameful the words are
in the eyes of all others?" Then you say to Lady Eloquence that she
was forced to state erroneously her main argument, on which all her
ensuing arguments are based. Yet in what follows, you excuse her
210   author due to ignorance and repeat what I already said: that this happened, you maintain, for want of seeing and sufficiently studying the
Rose.

In your response to Lady Eloquence you quote the words of

non; et dis qu'il ne dit pas que on en doye parler, mais que on en
215   peut bien parler. Si te respondray cy un petit pour dame Eloquence
un pou grossement. Je sçay bien voirement que devoir est contrainte
et pouoir est volenté, mais toutefois par la maniere de parler de quoy
on use en tel cas, on n'en peut parler nuement ne oultreement sans
mesprendre (comme il est prouvé cy devant et ancore sera aprés) et
220   tu soustiens avec celle Raison que parler eut proprement ou en peut
sanz mesprendre, et alleugues que la sainte Escripture et la Bible
245v°   les nomme par propre non ou il eschiet. Si te // respons, beau doulz
ami: se la Bible les nomme ou la sainte Escripture, ce n'est mie
en tele maniere ne a tel propos, ains est la matiere trop loings de
225   aluchement charnel; et si n'est mie la Bible faicte d'un personnage
femenin qui s'apellast fille de Dieu, et si ne parle mie a Fol Amoureux ou elle puist atisier le feu.

Tu dis ancore que se le nom desplaist a aucuns, que il ne
desplait mie a tous: mais de ce te croi je moult bien! Car chose mal
230   faicte et mal dicte ne desplait mie a chacun. Et dis que ce dis tu pour
ce que dame Eloquence dit: «Tant soient les paroles deshonnestes
au resgart de toutes gens». Et cy endroit te prens tu a la cordelle ou
tu m'as cuidié prendre, quant tu dis que l'en ne doit mie prendre les
mos si a la letre: car tu scez bien que la plus grant partie est prise
235   pour le tout, et vrayement a la plus grant partie desplairoit ouyr
nommer en publique deshonnestetez.

Tu dis qu'il ne fault ja dire que bonne coustume deffent en
parler proprement, dont tu te tais, ce dis tu, «se la coustume est
bonne ou mauvaise»: si ne sçay pour quoy tu t'en tais se tu y scez
240   riens de bon, mais se au contraire penses, tu as fole oppinion, que
femmes ne l'ayent mie accoustumé. Ce dist dame Eloquence, comme tu dis: elle dist voir, et dommage seroit se autrement feust et que
tant de reprouche peust estre rapporté es autres contrées des femmes
de ce royaume! Car on dist ung proverbe commun: «A la lengue est
245   congneue l'affection»; car ycelle Raison que tu tant auctorises dit
que «ce n'est fors desacoustumance» en France: ce n'est mie desacoustumance, car oncques ne l'acoustumerent! Et dont vient que
elles ne l'ont acoustumé? Il vient de raisonnable honte, qui—Dieux
mercis!—n'est mie chaciee de leurs frons.
250   Encore dis qu'il peut estre que en autres pays les femmes les
nomment proprement: mais je ne sçay pour quoy tu fais tele consequence quant tu n'en scez riens, et si n'est mencion que en tout le
monde femmes ne hommes mesmement en parlent plainement et
en publique. Et si t'esbahis, ce dis tu, de la coustume que «femmes

215 Reason in this romance, which essentially can be summarized as
follows: that she has the right to call those things which are far from
good by their proper names. And you say that he does not say that
one *must* speak about them, but that one *may* speak about them. I
reply to you a bit clumsily in favor of Lady Eloquence. I know very
well that "must" is constraint and "may" is will, but nevertheless,
220 regardless of which verb one uses in this case, it is impossible to
speak about this matter bluntly or appropriately without erring (as
has already been proven and will be proven hereafter). And you
side with Reason, claiming that where possible she spoke properly,
without error, and you allege that Holy Scripture and the Bible call
225 these things by their proper names where it is appropriate. I respond
to you, dear kind friend: If the Bible or Holy Scripture names them,
it is not in the same way nor for the same intention. In the *Rose*
the focus of the matter is too much on carnal pleasure. Further, the
Bible neither uses a female character called daughter of God, nor
230 does this character speak to the Foolish Lover in situations where
she could easily kindle the flames of passion.

You also claim that though the name displeases some, it does
not displease all. This I believe well, because something poorly
done and poorly said does not displease everyone. And you say this
235 because of what Lady Eloquence has said: "The words are so terribly shameful in the eyes of everyone." Here you tie the cord you had
reserved for me around your own neck when you say that one must
not take the words literally, for you know very well that the greater
part of a thing is seen as the whole, and indeed it would displease
240 most people to hear that shameful things are pronounced publicly.

You say that one must never say that good custom forbids it
to name these things properly, so you keep silent and simply state,
"whether the custom is good or bad." I do not know why you keep
silent about this if you know something good about it, or (what
245 a foolish opinion) if, on the contrary, you think that women have
never adhered to this custom. Here, you quote Lady Eloquence, who
speaks the truth when she says that it would be a shame if this were
different, and women of this kingdom could then be reprimanded in
other countries! As a common proverb says, "One's moral disposi-
250 tion is expressed through language." And Reason, whom you respect
so much, says that "this [custom] is not uncommon" in France,
which is not true at all because it was never the custom! And why
is that so? Because of reasonable shame, which, thanks to God, has
certainly not been chased from women's attitudes.

255   nomment leurs secrés membres par leur propre nom, mais elles ne
       veulent nommer ceulx aux hommes». Je te respons ad ce que, sauve
       ta grace, certes non font femmes honorables mie en publique; et
       se aucunes femmes plus nomment les choses qui leur sont privées
       que celles qui leur sont plus estranges, tu ne t'en dois merveiller.
260   Mais tu, qui tant te debas et par tant de repliques que plainement se
       doivent nonmer par nom et que bien dist la Raison maistre Jehan
       de Meun, je te prie chierement—tu qui es son tres especial dis-
       ciple, comme tu dis—pour quoy ne les nommes plainement en ton
       escripture sans aler entour le pot? Il me semble que tu n'es pas bon
265   escolier, car tu n'en suis mie pas bien la doctrine de ton maistre. Qui
       te meut ad ce? Se tu dis que ce n'est mie la coustume, si as doubté
       d'en d'estre repris. Que te chault de celle coustume? Veulz tu vivre
       a oppinion de gent? Suis la bonne doctrine: si monstre aux autres
       qu'ilz doivent faire. Car toutes choses se commencent une fois. Et
270   se on t'en blasme au premier, tu seras aprés loué quant on reverra la
246r° coustume bonne // et belle. Ha! par Dieu! par Dieu! autrement va!
       Tu ne le peus nyer que honte ne t'en garde. Et ou est la Raison
       maistre Jehan de Meun? Elle a pou de puissance quant honte le
       desconfit. Benoite soit tele honte qui desconfit tele Raison! Et se
275   je te haysse je diroie: «Pleust a Dieu que tu l'eusses fait!», mais je
       t'aime pour ton bon sens et le bien que on dit de toy (non obstant ne
       te congnoisce): si ne vouldroie ta deshonneur. Car parler honneste-
       ment avec les vertus moult advient en bouche de louable personne.
          Il me semble que tu reprens la maniere de parler de dame
280   Eloquence, qui dit que mal garda Meun les rigles de rethorique, car
       il deust avoir regardé a qui Raison parloit, car c'estoit a Fol Amou-
       reux qui plus en pouoit estre embraséz: «ce que ne seroit un grant
       clerc philosophe ou theologien» ne peust estre amoureux. Mais si
       peut, comme tu dis: et donnes exemple de David, Salamon et autres.
285   Si me merveille moult de toy qui veulx autruy corriger du mesmes
       deffault en quoy tu de commun cours et enchés, et soustiens ou il
       te plaist ce que veulx confondre pour un autre. Il est bon assavoir
       que quant le vaillant preudomme parla de Fol Amoureux, il sup-
       posa que ycellui feust soubtrait de toute science quant ou cas de
290   Fole Amour—supposé que grant science feust en lui—, et quant
       il dit un grant clere theologien, il suppose que, la passion de Fole
       Amour n'y soit point: car il convient que son soubtil entendement,
       qui point ne erre, l'entendist ainsi ou plus soubtillement. Mais tu dis
       que un homme ne s'en mouvera ja a fole amour pour teles paroles.
295   Et on te dit qu'il y est ja meu puis qu'il est Fol Amoureux, mais

255   Then you state that it is possible that women
name these things properly, yet I do not understa'
such an argument, since you know nothing about it a.
mentioned nowhere that elsewhere women or even men na.
openly in public. And you are surprised, as you say, about the cu.
260   tom that "women refer to their secret parts by their proper names,
but they will not name those of men." With all due respect, I reply
that no honorable woman will ever do this in public. And if women
are more inclined to name that which is theirs and not that which is
foreign to them, you should not be surprised. Yet you, who debate
265   and defend the position that they should be named properly, sid-
ing with Master Jean de Meun's Reason, pray, tell me, you who are
his loyal disciple, as you yourself say, why do you not name them
openly in your writing instead of speaking around them? It seems to
me that you are not a good pupil because you do not emulate well
270   your master's doctrine. Why is this? If you say that this is not the
custom, is it because you are afraid of being reprimanded? Why do
you care about this custom? Do you wish to live by the opinions
of others? Emulate the good doctrine and show others what they
must do, because everything must begin somewhere. And though
275   you may be insulted for it initially, you will be praised later when
people see that the custom is good and beautiful. Ha, by God! By
God! otherwise, leave it alone. You cannot deny that shame keeps
you from it. And where is your Master Jean de Meun's Reason? She
has little power when shame defeats her. Blessed be such shame,
280   which destroys his Reason! And if I disliked you, I would say, "May
it please God that you have violated the custom!" But I am fond of
you for your common sense and for the good that is spoken of you
(though I do not know you). I would not wish you dishonor. For
speaking honorably and virtuously usually comes from the mouth of
285   a respectful person.

      It seems to me that you condemn the argument of Lady Elo-
quence, who says that de Meun observed poorly the rules of rhetoric
because he should have paid attention to Reason's interlocutor: It
was the Foolish Lover, who could be even more enticed by the state-
290   ment "that a great philosopher or theologian" could not be in love.
Yet you show that this is possible when you refer to the examples
of David, Solomon, and others. What amazes me greatly is that you
wish to correct others of the same error which you yourself commit, and uphold one argument where it pleases you, only to reverse
295   it later. It is good to know that when the vaillant nobleman spoke of

son embrasement en peut bien croistre. Tu dis que quant Raison les
nomma elle preschoit a l'Amant qu'il s'en otast du tout. Responce:
s'il est ainsi comme tu l'entens, et comme maistre Jehan de Meun
dist estre la fin d'amours—laquelle chose on pourroit debatre, que
300 ce ne soit mie rigle generale de tant tendre a celle fin—, Raison fist
a l'Amant ainsi comme se je parloie a une femme grosse ou a un
malade, et je lui ramentevoie pommes aigres ou poires nouvelles ou
autre fruit, que lui feust bien appetissant et contraire, et je lui disoie
que se il en mengeoit, ce lui nuiroit moult. Vrayement je tiens que
305 mieulx lui souvendroit et plus lui aroit penetré en son appetit les
choses nommées que la deffence faicte de non en mengier: et sert
au propos que autrefois ay dit. Et tu tant le reprens que on ne doit
ramentevoir a nature humaine le pié dont elle cloche.

Tu argues que maistre Jehan de Meun, «ou chapitre de Raison,
310 ne dessendi pas a parler des secrés membres pour affection qu'il
eust d'en parler», mais «pour monstrer la folie de ceulx qui dient
qu'il n'est licite d'en parler». Et sans faille se pour celle cause le
fist, il failly a son esme, quant par une tres grant folie fere il cuida
estaindre un tres grant sens. Si appert, ce dis tu, qu'il ne le fist mie
315 pour delit. Par ceste raison que « ailleurs ou il parle de l'œuvre de
nature, il l'appelle «gieu d'amours». Nous sommes bien! Hay! vray
Dieux! Tu dis merveilles! Ainsi pouroies tu dire que en la fin de son
livre il nenomme mie les deshonnestetés qui y sont par leurs propres
246v° noms! // Et voirement ne fait! Et que vault cela? Il les nomme par
320 mos poetiques entendables .C. fois et plus atisans et plus penetratiss
et plus deliteux a ceulx qui y sont enclins que se il les nommast par
leurs propres noms.

Tu dis oultre que qui lit et entent le dit rommant, «que il entendra que maistre Jehan de Meun ne devoit autrement parler qu'il
325 parla». Tu dis trop bien que il l'entende a ta guise. Scez comme il
va de celle lecture? Ainsi comme des livres des arguemistes: les
uns les lisent et entendent d'une maniere, les autres qui les lisent
les entendent tout au rebours; et chacun cuide trop bien entendre.
Et sur ce ilz œuvrent et apprestent fourniaulx, alembis et croisiaux
330 et entremelsent divers metaulx et matieres et soufflent fort, et pour
un petit de sublimacion ou congiel qui leur appert merveillable, ilz
cuident ataindre a merveilles. Et puis quant ils ont fait et fait et gasté
leur temps, ilz y scevent autant comme devant,—mais que coust et
despence et la maniere de distiller et de aucunes congellacions de
335 nulle utilité. Ainsi est il de toy et de moy et de plusieurs: tu l'entens
et le prens d'une maniere, et moy tout au rebours; tu recites, je

the Foolish Lover, he assumed that he was devoid of all knowledge about foolish love, providing that he had any knowledge at all, and when he said "a great theologian," he assumed that the passion of foolish love was completely absent because his learned understand-
300 ing, which does not err, would make him understand it thus or even more skillfully. You say that no man will succumb to foolish love from such words. The response is that the Foolish Lover has already done so, and his excitement could even increase. You say that when Reason named these parts, she was preaching to the Lover to refrain
305 completely from foolish love. My response: If it is as you say and this is what Master Jean de Meun claims is the objective of love (it is debatable whether aspiring even more to this objective should in fact be the general rule), Reason deals with the Lover in the same way as I would if I reminded a pregnant woman or a sick person
310 about sour apples or new pears, or other fruit which they would find appetizing but not agreeable, and if I told them that if they ate some they would be better nourished. Truly, I maintain that this would re- mind and tempt them more in their longing than if they were forbid- den to eat these things. This underscores my earlier argument which
315 you vehemently criticize: that one must not remind human nature of the foot with which it limps.

You claim that in the passage of Reason, Master Jean de Meun "did not lower himself to speak about the secret parts simply because it pleased him to do so," but "in order to demonstrate the
320 foolishness of those who say it is illicit to speak about them." If he truly did so for this reason, he undoubtedly failed in his objective when he committed the great error of assuming that he could leave out one very important meaning. When, elsewhere, he speaks of Nature's work as a "game of love," you say that he does not do so
325 out of cupidity. We are in good company! Ha! Dear God! You speak marvels! You could also say, then, that at the end of his book he does not call the disgraces which there are by their proper names! Because he truly does not! And what is the meaning of this? He names them poetically, which can be understood one hundred times
330 more easily and is more pleasing, more poignant, and more delight- ful to those who are so inclined than if he had called them by their proper names.

You go on to say that whoever reads and understands this romance "will understand that, indeed, Master Jean de Meun should
335 not speak at all differently than he did." Very well, as long as the reader understands it according to your wish. Do you know how

replique. Et quant nous avons fait et fait, tout ne vault riens; car la
matiere est tres deshonneste, ainsi comme aucuns arguemistes qui
cuident fere de fiens or. Le taire en feust bon, et mieulx me plairoit
340   non estre arguemiste en ceste partie, mais la deffence m'est convenable puis que je suis assaillie.

De ce que tu argues ensuyant contre la plaidoirie devant Justice par dame Eloquence a la charge du devant dit maistre, je l'en
lairay convenir. Car bien t'en sara convener quant lui plaira.

345   Tu relates ce que autrefois ay dit: que je ne me puis taire et
trop merveiller de ce que Raison dit que mesmes en la guerre amoureuse «mieulx vault decevoir que deceu estre». Et que j'argue qu'il
s'ensuiroit doncques estre tous deux estre bons: qui ne peut estre et
puis si jures ton serment que se me feusse deportee d'escripre cest
350   argument ce feust mon honneur. Et que c'est proposicion d'enfans
quant ilz arguent. Toutevoyes te promets je bien, quoy qu'il t'en
soit avis: je ne la pense mie a chanceller. Mais de ce que tu cuides
confondre mon argument de dire: Jhesu Crist dist que «mieulx feust
a Judas que il n'eust oncques esté que avoir trahi son maistre»,
355   vrayement je te respons que bon fu que Jhesu Crist morust et bon fu
que Judas nasquist; mais mieulx feust pour lui se il n'eust oncques
esté ne, pour cause de l'inconvenient de sa desesperance et la punicion de sa trahison. Et tu mesmes n'as pas tenu la rigle en toutes
tes solucions dont tu me veulx reprendre. Et merveilles interpretes
360   ce qui est dit clerement et a la lectre: « Il vault trop mieulx, biau
maistre, decevoir que estre deceu», —qui dis que c'est a dire que
il te greveroit moins faire semblant de moy amer pour toy aysier
de mon corps que se tu en perdoies ton «estude, sens, temps, ame,
corps et loz». C'est bien extremement parlé! Dont semble il qu'il
365   conviengne decevoir, ou perdre «sens, temps, ame», etc.! Sans
247r°   faille la faveur // que tu y as te fait bien loings aler querre ceste
extreme excusacion. Et toutefois ne met il point ces .ii. extremités
ensemble. Si te dis ancore de rechef que en la loy de Jhesu Crist et
selon sa doctrine, plus est deffendu decevoir son prochain que estre
370   deceu. C'est assavoir decevance frauduleuse, car par maniere de
parler peut estre dit decevance tele chose qui n'est mie grant vice).
Mais affin que je ne l'oublie, je diray ce dont je suis contente: c'est
que tu dis que tu as oppinion que oncques maistre Jehan de Meun ne
escript ce en son livre, et que c'est chose adjoustée. Bien appert que
375   tu parles a voulenté, sauve ta grace, car c'est du propre lengage et
tout un mesmes mettre et stile. Mais tu voulroyes bien qu'il ne l'eust
oncques dit! Tu peus bien hardiement dire que oncques de Raison,
fille de Dieu, n'yssi tel mot.

it goes with such a reading? It is like the books of the alchemists:[48]
There are those who read and understand them in one way, and
others who read and understand them in the completely opposite

340 way, and everyone thinks he understands them well. And with that
they work to prepare furnaces, alembics, and crucibles, mixing various metals and substances, breathing hard into the fire, and for a little
bit of sublime metal or residue, which seems marvelous to them,
they think they have perfected great wonders. Then, when they have

345 worked and wasted their time, they know as much as before, but at
what expense? All this, only to have developed entirely useless ways
of distilling and congealing. This is how you, I, and others are: You
understand this romance in one way and I in the opposite; you quote,
and I reply. And after we have done this over and over, it means

350 nothing, because the matter is very shameful, just as that of certain
alchemists who think they can change dung into gold. To pass over
this in silence would be good, and I would rather not be like the alchemists in this case, yet I must defend myself since I was attacked.

I will pass over your next argument against Lady Eloquence's
355 complaint about Master Jean de Meun, which she addresses to Justice, and I will leave it at the author's discretion. He will settle this
matter whenever it pleases him.

You repeat what I said previously, that I cannot be silent and
stop marveling about Reason's statement that in amorous war "it is
360 better to deceive than to be deceived." My argument is that it follows
that both are good, which is not possible. Then you swear on your
oath that abstaining from expressing my view, would have benefited
my honor, and that it is like children arguing. Nevertheless, make no
mistake, I promise you that, whatever your opinion may be, I do not
365 think of retracting mine. If you think you can crush my argument by
referring to Jesus Christ, who said that "it would have been better for
Judas had he never lived, than to betray his master," I reply, in fact,
that it was good that Jesus Christ died, and it was good that Judas
was born. Yet it would have been better if he had never been born,
370 because of the pain of his despair and the punishment for his betrayal. In all your conclusions, you yourself have not adhered to the principles for which you intend to criticize me. You interpret wondrously
that which is stated clearly and literally: "It is better, dear Master, to
deceive than to be deceived." This means that it would cause you less
375 pain to pretend that you loved me in order to enjoy my body than
if you lost your "learning, sense, time, soul, body and reputation"[49]
over it. That is quite something! It would seem, then, that either one
must deceive or lose "sense, time, soul," etc.! The advantage you

380   Ha! Decevance Frauduleuse! Mere de Trayson! Qui est ce qui
      t'ose mettre avant en nul cas? Et puis que nous y sommes entrés,
      pour Dieu que je m'y arreste un petit, non obstant la prolixité car
      on ne peut bonnement en brief comprendre moult de choses. Par ta
      foy, consideres un petit—tu qui as leues les histoires—, quel vice
      a tenu et tient en ce monde plus grant lieu a aydier a parfournir les
385   plus grans perversités: tu trouveras Decevance. Regardes se Decev-
      ance nous donna la mort premierement. Lis les histoires troyennes:
      tu trouveras les histoires selon Ovide et autres comment Discorde
      sema la graine de la guerre, mais jamais n'eust tout cueilli se dame
      Decevance n'y feust venue quant elle fist trahir et prendre la fort cité
390   de Troye; et tout est plain de ses fais, que trop seroient loncs a dire.
      Ha! Dieux! comme tout noble courage se doit bien garder d'avoir
      en soy si villain vice, qui passe tous autres en maniere de fait! Quel
      difference mettras tu entre Trahison et Decevance? Je n'y en sçay
      point, mais que l'un sonne pis que l'autre. Et se tu dis: donques s'en
395   vault il mieux aydier sus un autre que un autre s'en aydast sur soy.
      Je te dis de rechief que non fait: car selon la justice de Dieu cellui
      est plus punis qui injurie autrui que cellui qui est injuriés. Et disons
      ancore mesmement en cas d'amours, pour ce que la Raison maistre
      Jehan de Meun dit que «Mieulx vault», etc. Vrayement j'en diray
400   mon oppinion, et m'en tiengne a fole qui vouldra, tant hé Decev-
      ance. Je ay un seul filz—que Dieu me veuille conserver s'il lui
      plaist—, mais je ameroie mieulx qu'il feust parfaictement amoureux
      avec le sens que je espere que Dieux lui donra, comme ont hommes
      raisonnables, d'une femme bien condicionnée et sage qui amast
405   honneur—et lui en avenist ce que avenir lui en pourroit —, que je ne
      seroie que a son pouoir feust deceveur de toutes ou de plusieurs. Car
      je cuideroie que a plusieurs decevoir il peust plus tost perdre «sens,
      temps, ame, corps et loz»,[49] que de bien en amer une seule.
           Et cuides tu que je croie—par ta foy! que ce soit le plus grant
410   meschief qui puist avenir a jeunes hommes d'estre amoureux? (Mais
      que ce soit en bon lieu ou il ait honneur et sens, car qui ameroit une
247v° bergiere si vouldroit il brebis garder //—je ne le dis mie pour l'estat,
      mais pour les condicions pour monstrer que le cuer qui aime desire
      tousjours soy tourner aux meurs de ce ou il a mise s'amour—:
415   pour ce croy bien que ceulx qui amer veulent doivent moult eslire
      ou ilz mettront leur pensee, car la cuiday je que soit le peril.) Et
      ainsi cuides tu que je croye, tous ceulx qui ont esté ou sont bien
      amoureux, que toute leur felicité soit de tendre a coucher avec leurs
      dames? Certes ce ne croy je mie, car je croy que plusieurs ont ame
420   loyaument et parfaictement qui oncques n'y couchierent, ne onques

380   gain from this makes you go very far in seeking this extreme pre-
text, and in any case he never puts these two extremes side by side.
I tell you once more that according to Jesus Christ and His doctrine,
it is more strictly forbidden to deceive one's neighbor than to let
oneself be deceived. (This means fraudulent deceit, because, in a
manner of speaking, it could also simply mean deceit, which is not

385   a great vice.) So that I shall not forget, I shall say what I please: It
is your statement that Master Jean de Meun never did actually write
this in his book, but that it was in fact added. With all due respect,
it seems that you are speaking according to your wishes, because it
is his own language, in the same rhyme and style. You wish he had

390   never said it! You can say with certainty that Reason, daughter of
God, never pronounced such a thing.

          Ha! Fraudulent deceit! Mother of betrayal! Who would dare to
quote you in this case? And since we have entered into this matter,
by God, I shall stop here for a moment, despite the prolixity, be-

395   cause it is impossible to understand many things well if they are not
explained sufficiently. By your faith, consider briefly, you who have
read the legends, which vice has held and holds the greatest place
in this world and helps to perform the greatest perversities: you will
find that it is Deceit. Was it not Deceit who brought us death in the

400   first place? Read the Trojan legends! In those told by Ovid and others, you will find how Discord planted the seed of war, but he would
never have harvested everything if Lady Deceit had not arrived, betraying and overtaking the city of Troy. These facts are obvious, and
it is unnecessary to explain further. Ha! My God! Noble courage

405   must protect itself well from this evil vice, which surely surpasses
all others in deed. How would you differentiate between Betrayal
and Deceit? I do not know, but one sounds worse than the other. And
if you say that it is better to help oneself at the expense of another
than for another to help himself at one's own expense, I tell you at

410   once that this is not true, for according to God's justice the one who
hurts others is punished more severely than the one who is hurt. Let
us come back one more time to the case of love where Master Jean
de Meun's Reason says "It is better...." I will express my opinion
frankly about this, and whoever thinks I am foolish may do so, this

415   is how much I despise Deceit. I have only one son, may God protect
him; I would prefer him to fall in love—following the good sense
which one hopes God gave him and which sensible men have, with
a well brought up and wise woman who loves honor (it has happened before and could thus happen to him)—than to be capable

420   of deceiving all or many women. For in my mind, deceiving many

ne deceurent ne furent deceus, de qui estoit principale entencion que
leurs meurs en vausissent mieulx,—et pour celle amour devenoyent
vaillans et bien renommés, et tant que en leur viellesce ilz louoient
Dieu qu'ilz avoient esté amoureux. Ainsi ay je ouy dire que le disoit
425   mesmement le bon connestable messire Bertran de Claquin, messire
Morise de Tresguidi et mains autres chevalereux. Si ne perdoient
ceulx «sens, temps, ame, corps et loz». Je parle tant de ce loz pour
ce que tu m'as escript que je l'espluche bien. Or le t'ay espluché,
mais tu me feroies ycy plusieurs responces et diras que maistre
430   Jehan de Meun entendoit de ceulx qui en sont oultreement folz. Je
te respons que de toutes choses, bonnesment qui sont bonnes, peut
on mal user; mais puis qu'il vouloit descripre entierement amours,
il ne la deust mettre si extreme a une seule fin, voire fin si deshonnestement touchée. Tu me diras que je parle contre dame Eloquence
435   qui parle de Fol Amoureux dont Meun parle et je te dy que a estre
bien amoureux n'est point neccessaire estre fol, ne que on en perde
«sens, temps», etc. Tu me diras ancore que je conforte les jones a
estre amoureux: je te di que je ne lo point qu'ilz le soient, car toute
amour mondaine n'est que vanité, mais se l'un des .ii. convenoit,
440   c'est pis decevoir que estre bien amoureux, et pis en peut venir.
Mais pour ce que maistre Jehan de Meun, qui plusieurs choses bien
descript, ne descript mie la proprieté du deceveur, j'en parleray un
petit en rude stile pour aguiser l'appetit de ceulx qui se delitent. La
condicion du deceveur est menteur, parjure, faulz semblant, flateur,
445   traytre, fallacieux, malicieux, agaitant, couvert, et autres maulx
infinis. Et la fin qui lui en demeure, quant plus n'en peut: moqueur,
mesdisant, envieux et souspeconneux: tieulx en sont les tiltres. Mais
pour ce que j'ay parlé de ceulx qui aiment honorablement je puis
dire, ainsi comme tu dis de cellui qui composa la plaidoirie dessus-
450   dicte, qu'il ne senty oncques que fu fol amoureux, aussi croy je que
maistre Jehan de Meun ne senti oncques que fu honorable amoureux.
      Aprés tu repliques ce que dame Eloquence et moy disons par
grant admiracion de la grant deshonnesteté qui est ou chapitre de
455   la Vielle, et disons: «Qui y pourra notter fors toute laidure et vil
248r°   enseingnement //»? Et assés plus en disons que tu ne repliques. Et
pareillement ou chapistre de Jalousie. Et puis tu me fais un grant
sault sur ce ce que j'ay dit a la fin du dit mien espistre et ramennes
ceste part mal a propos, ne te desplaise. Et dis que j'ay dit que je
460   ne condampne pas l'aucteur ou aucteurs en toutes pars du dit livre,
comme, ce dis tu, «se je vouloie dire que je le condampnasse en ce
en quoy je le reprens», et dis que je me fais juge de ce que j'ay dit

would make him lose "sense, time, soul, body, and reputation" more than loving well one single woman.

    And do you truly believe, by your faith, that I think falling in love is the greatest misfortune which could befall young men?
425 (Though it had better occur in a good place where there is honor and sense, for he who loves a shepherdess must wish to herd sheep. I do not say this because of social estate, but because of the way it is with love, showing that the heart which loves will always desire to follow the customs of the person in whom it has placed its love.
430 I therefore firmly believe that those who wish to love must be very selective about their intentions, because I think that this is where the danger lies.) And do you also believe that I think that all those who have been or are in love will find their happiness in trying to bed their ladies? This, of course, is not at all what I believe, because I
435 think that many have loved loyally and well who have never bedded them nor deceived them, nor were deceived, and whose chief intention was to increase the worth of their own morals, and it is thanks to this kind of love that they have become noble and renowned, and even in their old age they praise God for having been in love. For
440 instance, I have heard tell that the good commander Sir Bertram of Guesclin,[50] Sir Morise of Tresguidi,[51] and several other knights said so. They did not lose "sense, time, soul, body and reputation." I speak at such length of this so-called reputation because you asked me to examine it well. Now I have examined it. But here you may
445 give me several responses, and will say that Master Jean de Meun referred only to those who were outrageously foolish. My reply to you is that, as with all things even those which are good can be misused. Since he wished exclusively to describe love, he should not have shown only one purpose, and such a disgraceful one to
450 boot. You will say that I contradict Lady Eloquence, who speaks of de Meun's Foolish Lover. I tell you that in order to love well it is not at all necessary to be foolish, nor to lose one's "sense, time, etc." You will then tell me that I encourage the young to fall in love, and to this I reply that this is not so, because any worldly love is nothing
455 but vanity. However, if we must allow for one of the two, I would say that it is worse to deceive than to love well, and worse can come of it. Yet since Master Jean de Meun, who, after all, describes many things well, never describes the character of the deceiver, I will speak about this a little in plain language in order to whet the ap-
460 petite of those who take delight in such things. The deceiver is a liar, pretender, flatterer, traitor; he is fallacious, malicious, instigating, insincere, and possesses endless other flaws. And the fate that will

par oppinion. Si te respons que en verité tu as mal cueilli les flours
de mon dictié et fait chappel mal acoustré et mal sorty, sauve ta
465   grace: car j'ay dit, non mie par oppinion mais de certaine science,
qu'il parla tres laidement et tres deshonnestement en plusieurs
pars, et tres mauvaise exortacion et le jugement de ce est legier a
faire, car il se preuve par lui mesmes. Si le puis et moy et chacun
qui entent françois condampner en celle partie, mais pour ce que
470   en toutes pars ne traicte mie de celle deshonnesteté, dis je que je
ne le condampne mie en toutes pars. Et tu repliques trop bien que
je voulroie avoir trouvé, comme je ay dit, qui me sceust souldre
souffisammant a quoy peuent estre bonnes tant de deshonnestetés:
et toutefois ne m'y fais tu nulle solucion, ains trespasses oultre sans
475   respondre a ce propos. Et come innanimés sans achoison me dis tu
tele vilennie comme cy s'ensuit «O presompcion oultraigeuse! O
tres folle oultrecuidance! O parole trop tost issue et sans advis de
bouche de femme, qui condampne homme de si hault entendement,
de si fervent estude, qui a si grant labeur et meure deliberacion a fait
480   si tres noble livre comme est cellui de la *Rose,* qui passe ainssy tous
autres qui oncques furent en lengaige ouquel il est escript son livre;
duquel, quant tu l'aras leu .C. fois se tu en entens la greigneur partie, tu n'employas oncques si bien ton temps ne ton entendement».
Responce: O homme, deceu par oppinion volantaire! Certes je te
485   pourroie respondre, et ne vueil, oprobrieusement,—non obstant que
par lais reprouches me travailles par petite reputacion et sans raison.
O entendement ofusqué! O congnoissance pervertie, aveuglée par
propre voulenté: qui juges venin angoisseux estre restorement de
mort; doctrine perverse estre salvable exemple; fiel amer, miel doul-
490   cereux; laidure orrible estre beauté solacieuse;—de qui une simple
femmellette, avec la doctrine de sainte Eglise, peut reprendre ton
erreur! Fuy et eschieves la doctrine perverse qui te pourroit mener a
dampnement, de laquelle, quant Dieu t'ara enluminé de vraye congnoiscence, tu aras orreur en toy retournant arriere remirant le pas ou
495   tu aras passé en voye de periller.
Tu dis pour moy reprouver que «Verité engendre hayne et
flaterie amys » (ce dit Terence). Et pour ce tu te doubtes que je le
vueille mordre, et me conseilles que je me garde mes dens; si saches
certainement que tu faus a cuider, sauve ta reverence: et pour ce que
500   mensonge decevable y a et faulte de verité, je ne le voulsisse mie
248v°   seulement mordre, // mais esrachier les tres grans mensonges falla-
cieuses qui y sont. Tu respons a dame Eloquence et a moy que maistre Jehan de Meun en son livre introduisi personnages, et fait chacun
parler selon ce que lui appartient. Et vrayement je te confesse bien

be his when he has finished is that he will be mocked and slandered.
He will be mistrusted and greeted with suspicion. Those are the
465 facts. Because I spoke of those who love honorably, I can say, just
as you claimed that the one who composed the above-mentioned
complaint will never understand foolish love, that Master Jean de
Meun will never understand honorable love.

Then you address the dismay we felt about the abominable
470 shame in the passage of the Duenna on which Lady Eloquence and
I commented, among other things which are not included in your
reply: "Who will remember anything other than appalling filth
and base teaching?" This comment also applies to the passage of
Jealousy. After that you leap to the very end of my epistle which, do
475 not be offended, you misquote. You quote me as saying that I do not
condemn the author or authors for the entire book as if I wished to
say that I condemn him only for that for which I criticize him, and
you say that I declare myself the judge based merely on opinion.
I reply that in reality you have done a poor job of harvesting the
480 flowers from my poem, and have made an ill-shaped garland out of
them, with all due respect, because it is not merely on the basis of
opinion but of knowledge and experience that I said that he spoke
in a very ugly and shameful manner in several places, creating evil
exhortations. And this is easy to confirm, because it can be proven
485 with his very words. Thus, you or I or anyone who understands
French can condemn him for this part. However, since he does not
speak about this disgrace throughout, I do not condemn him for
everything. And you reply all too well that I wished to find, as I said
myself, someone who could explain satisfactorily to what end so
490 many disgraces might be good. Yet you provide me with no solution, so I will pass over this matter without responding to it. And for
no reason, you insult me with the following words: "O extreme pretentiousness! O very foolish arrogance! O words uttered too quickly
and thoughtlessly by a woman's mouth, who condemns a man of
495 such high intelligence and fervent learning, who after great labor
and ripe deliberations created so noble a book as that of the *Rose*,
which surpasses all others ever created in the language in which he
wrote his book, and which, should you understand most of it after
having read it one hundred times, you will never before have put
500 your time or intelligence to such good use." My response: O man,
deceived by capricious opinion! Of course I could, but will not,
reply harshly despite your ugly reproaches accusing me of being
of little renown and devoid of reason. O offended intelligence! O
perverted knowledge blinded by one's own will, believing terrifying

505   que selon le gieu que on vuelt jouer il convient instrumens propres,
        mais la voulenté dou joueur les appreste tieulx comme il les luy
        fault. Toutefois certainement, ne te desplaise, il failli a bien introdui-
        ire ses personnages de commettre a aucuns autre chose que leur of-
        fice: comme a son prestre que il appelle Genius, qui tant commande
510   coucher avec les femmes et que on continue l'œuvre sans delaissier,
        et puis si dit que on fuye femme sur toute rien. Et en dit plus de mal
        ou autant de villenie comme nul qui y soit. Si ne sçay entendre qu'il
        appartiengne a son office ne a mains autres personnages qui de celle
        matiere parlent. Tu dis que ce fait le Jaloux comme son office et je
515   te dis que auques en tous personnages ne se peut taire de vituperer
        les femmes, qui, Dieux merci, ne sont de ce en riens empirées. Et de
        ce ay je assez parlé en mon autre epistre, sur quoy tu ne m'as gaires
        respondu. Si ne m'en pense cy endroit guaires a chargier.
               Puis que cellui livre de la *Rose* est tant necessaire et expedi-
520   ent pour doctrine de bien vivre tant prouffitablement, je te pry que
        tu me dies a quel prouffit du bien commun peut venir tant avoir
        assemblé de dissolucions que dist le personnage de la Vielle. Car
        se tu dire que c'est afin que on s'en garde, je cuide qu'il ait la plus
        grant partie de gens qui oncques n'orent que faire de teles deabler-
525   ies comme elle recorde, et ne scevent que ce peut estre: dont ne peut
        venir tel mal au prouffit du bien commun, dont la plus grant partie
        ne s'en empesche. Et je saroie voulentiers se toy mesmes, quant tu
        les as leues, se tu as plus a memoire la bonté de toy garder et vivre
        chastement, ou la dissolucion des paroles. Si est une merveilleuse
530   interpretacion que vous faites entre vous ses aliés, que telle orrible
        mauvaistié soit tournee a si grant bien. Et du Jaloux aussi, que tu
        dis qu'il parle comme jaloux. Je te dis que grant necessité estoit tel
        gastement de paroles malgracieuses pour le bien et introduction du
        bien commun. Si t'en fais pareille responce comme de la Vielle. Ce
535   que tu as dit en oultre de la cause, comme tu crois, qui fait parler le
        Jaloux tant de mal de femme, ne fait point a mon propos: pour ce le
        passe oultre.
               Oultre tu dis a dame Eloquence et a moy en repliquant par
        similitude que se un relate ce que un autre a dit, comme fait Saluste
540   qui recite la conjuracion de Catiline encontre la chose publique de
        Rome, ou Aristote qui recite opinions des ancians philosophes con-
        tenans erreurs, se ils sont cause de ce mesmes meffait,—comme «la
        sainte Escripture recite les abominables pechiés de Sodome et de
249r°   Gomore, ennorte elle pour tant yceulx ensuir»? Tu dis // trop bien,
545   ce te semble, et bien a propos. Mais je te demande se quant yceulx
        ou autres, ou la sainte Escripture recite tieulx choses, se il y a devant

505   venom to bring restoration from death, perverse doctrine to be an
example for salvation, bile to be sweet honey, and horrible ugliness
to be charming beauty! A simple little woman, with the help of Holy
doctrine, is able to criticize your erring ways! Flee and avoid the
perverse doctrine which could lead you to damnation and which you
510   will frown upon with horror once God has illuminated you with the
true knowledge, and you will turn around and see the path you were
treading on your way to peril.

        To reprimand me you say that "truth will give birth to hatred
and flattery to friends" (which is a quote by Terence).[52] Because
515   of this you fear that I will bite him, and you advise me to keep my
teeth to myself. Know, with all due respect, that you are mistaken:
It is because of the deceitful lies and lack of truth in this work that I
would like not only to bite him, but to tear out these extremely fallacious lies. You reply to Lady Eloquence and to me that Master Jean
520   de Meun introduces characters in his book who all speak according
to what they represent. I admit that, surely, one needs the appropriate tools for the game one wishes to play. Yet it is the player who
shapes them according to how he wishes to play the game. Certainly
then, do not be offended: He failed to introduce his characters in
525   such a way as to represent their duty alone. For example, the priest
whom he calls Genius, who insists that one ought to bed women
and continue Nature's work without interruption, then says that it
is imperative to flee from women. He says more evil and villainous
things than anyone else in this book, and I do not understand how
530   it is part of his duty nor that of any other character to speak thus.
You claim that the Jealous Husband is merely doing his duty, and I
tell you that almost all the characters are unable to stop slandering
women, who, thank God, are not in the least affected by this. I have
spoken enough about this in my other epistle, which you ignore
535   almost entirely.[53] So do not expect me to speak about it here.

        Since this book of the *Rose* is so necessary and advantageous
in furthering the doctrine of moral living, pray tell me how the
discourse of the Duenna contributes to this, consisting as it does of
nothing but dissoluteness. If you intend to say that its purpose is
540   to deter us from such dissoluteness, I think that the majority of all
people have never even heard of the sort of devilry as is recorded
here and do not know what it could be. Therefore, it is not possible
that such evil can benefit the common good, if most people are not
involved in such acts in the first place. Moreover, I would like to
545   know whether you yourself when you read this, retained more about
the morals of restraint and chaste living or about the dissoluteness

ou aprés personnages ou autres propos qui conforte et afferme par
moles paroles et atrayans que l'en trahisse ou que l'en soit herite, et
ainsi des autres maulx. Tu sces bien que nennil, car en quelque lieu
550   que tieulx maulx ou autres soient pareillement recités en livres, c'est
a la vituperacion de la chose, en tele maniere de lecture que elle
sonne desplaisammant a tous ceulx qui l'oyent. Et le prescheur dont
tu m'as escript qu'il ramentoit le pié dont on cloche en son sermon
(ce as tu dit pour ce que je dis que on ne le devoit ramentevoir a
555   nature pour plus droit aler). Commant le ramentoit il? Comment
dist il? «Mes enfans, joués, galés, tenés vous aise, c'est la voye de
paradis fait par Dieu»! Sire, non fait. Ains ramentoit ce pié de telle
maniere que il fait grant orreur aux oyans et on peut en tele maniere
dire: «Dieu te doint bon jour» qu'il sonne mal et rancune.

560   Et puis tu fais une maniere de complainte a Chasteté et dis
«Ha! dame! est ce le loyer que vous vouléz rendre a maistre Jehan
de Meun, qui tant vous a prisée et toutes autres vertus, et blasmé
tous vices, comment entendement le peut concevoir? Voire, fais tu,
comme entendement humain le peut concevoir»? Et puis après si dis
565   que je m'en soubsrie ja. Ha! que tu sçavoies bien que je m'en riroye
de ce bon mot! Car quant je pense aux beaulx enseingnemens de
chasteté et honnestes paroles qui y sont, vrayement je ay matiere de
moy rire de ce que tu dis. Puis après tu dis que «qui bien lit ce livre,
il y trouvera enseingnemens pour fuir tous vices et suivre toutes
570   vertus». Et puis tu recites aucuns enseingnemens, que tu dis qui y
sont. Et vrayement je te dis que aussi feras tu en la loy de Mahom-
met; se tu lis l'Alchoran tu y trouveras de tres bons poins de nostre
foy et de bien devoz, et te plairoit moult, mais c'est tout honny;
tout ensemble ne vault rien; la consequence en est toute gasté: a la
575   conclusion tient tout. Ne sces tu que au conseil mesmement, quoy
que on ait par proposé, on se tient a la conclusion dereniere? Et se
maistre Jehan de Meun, se je l'ose dire, eust parlé parmy son livre
de plusieurs choses a quoy nature humaine est encline et qui advien-
nent, et puis ramené au propos et fait sa conclusion en meurs de
580   bien vivre, tu eusses plus grant cause de dire que il le fist adfin de
bien; et car tu scez se un dicteur veult user d'ordre de rethorique, il
fait ses premisses de ce que il veult traictier, et puis entre de propos
en propos et parle de plusieurs choses s'il lui plaist, puis revient a
sa conclusion de ce pour quoy il a faite sa narracion: et vrayement
585   en ce cas ne failli de riens l'aucteur ou dit livre, car ignorance n'y a
lieu. Mais tu me diras que ce fist Lorris. Responce: «Je tiens tout un
mesme edifice» souffist pour responce a cest chapistre, non obstant

of her words. This is a wondrous interpretation which you and your allies propose, that such horrible sinfulness will turn into such great good! The same goes for the Jealous Husband who, you claim,

550 speaks in accordance with his [allegorical] significance. I have said that it was absolutely necessary to destroy such ungracious words for the common good, and I present the same reply here as I did with regard to the Duenna. And that which you state further, about what you believe makes the Jealous Husband defame women so

555 terribly, is not part of my argument. Therefore, I will pass over it in silence. Further, you reply to Lady Eloquence and to me by analogy that if one repeats what another has said—as does Sallust, who recounts the conspiracy of Catiline against Rome,[54] or Aristotle, who quotes erroneous opinions of the ancient philosophers—one

560 is guilty of the same error. For instance, is "Holy Scripture, when it recounts the abominable sins of Sodom and Gomorrah, guilty of exhorting men to commit these sins?" You seem to think that this argument is just and well presented. Yet I ask you, when these authors or others or even Holy Scripture recounts such things, has

565 there been or will there be a person who was or will be seduced by soft, alluring words to the point that he is proclaimed a traitor, a heretic, or any other such evil name? You know well that this is not so, because wherever these or equally evil words can be found, it is the disgust of the thing which, upon being read, sounds displeasing

570 to all those who hear it. And the preacher whom you mention as, in his sermon, having reminded the person about the foot with which he limps (you said this in response to my arguments that one must not remind Nature about this, so that she may walk straight).... How did he remind this person about it? What did he say? "My children:

575 play; amuse yourselves! This is the path to paradise that God has created!" Sir, it is not so. He called the foot to memory in such a manner that he instilled in his listeners great terror which one could even do with a phrase like "God bids you good day" making it sound evil and vengeful.

580 Then you make a sort of complaint to Chastity, saying, "Ha! My Lady! Are these the dues you wish to pay Jean de Meun, who held you and all the other virtues in such high esteem and who insulted all vices, as can easily be understood? Do you actually say 'as can easily be understood?'" Then you go on to say that I smile

585 about this. Ha! You knew very well that I would laugh about this insistent statement! Because when I think of the beautiful lessons of Chastity and the other honorable words it contains, truly, I have

y ayes dit maintes choses a ton propos que je passe oultre: car tout
vient a une fin. Et l'espluches tant comme bon te samblera.

590   249v°   // Tu as devant dit qu'il ne blasme pas les femmes, ains en dist
bien. Si m'en attens a la verité prouvée et dis que saint Ambroise
blasma plus le sexe femenin qu'il ne fait, car il dist que c'est un sexe
usagé a decevoir. Je te responderay a ce. Tu scez bien que quant les
docteurs ont parlé c'est a double entendement, et mesmes Jhesu

595   Crist en ses sermons. Si est bon asavoir que saint Ambroise ne le
dist oncques pour les personnes des femmes, car je croy que le bon
sire n'eust riens voulu blasmer fors vice; car bien savoit qu'il estoit
maintes saintes femmes, mais il voult dire que c'est un sexe dont
homme usageement desoit son ame. Ainsi comme Salamon qui dist:

600   «Mieulx vault le meffait d'un homme que le bienfait d'une femme».
Nous savons bien que c'est faulx a le prendre a la lectre, mais par
luy mesmes pouons prendre exemple—mieulx eust valu pour lui le
meffait d'un home, en tel cas peust avoir esté, que aucun bien qu'il
pot veoir en la femme dont il fu si fort amoureux qu'il en aoura les

605   ydoles. Et aussi le pot il dire par prophetie. Car mieulx nous vault
le meffait de Judas que le bienfait de Judich qui occist Olophernes,
ou d'une autre femme, mais tu dis merveilles aprés. Car tu affermes
vrayement que je les blasme plus qu'il ne fait quant je dis que se
on lisoit le livre de la *Rose* devant les roynes et princesses, que il

610   leur convendroit couvrir la face de honte rougie. Et puis si respons:
«Pour quoy rougiroient? Il semble que elles se tendroient pour
coulpables des vices que le jaloux recite des femmes». Ha! Dieux!
que c'est bien dit et bien rapporté! Tu ne te fais point de honneur
de rapporter chose que le contraire puist estre prouvé; c'est mal es-

615   tudié: quant je disoie que aux dames convendroit couvrir la face de
honte rougie, ce n'estoit point pour les paroles du Jaloux, aincois dis
d'ouyr les orribletés qui y sont en la fin tant abominables. De quoy
je disoie: «A quoy peut estre leue en leur presence»? Et de dire que
elles en rougiroient, je ne les blasme de riens, ains les loe d'avoir la

620   chaste vertu de honte.
        Tu respons aprés a dame Eloquence, pour ce que il est contenu
en sa complainte des diffamacions et vituperes que maistre Jehan de
Meun raconte de religion: et dis qu'il ne la blasma mie et vrayement je te respons que sauve ta grace; car comme il feust diffameur

625   publique il la diffame excessivement et sans riens excepter. Et bien
le scet entendre le bon catholique de tres religieuse voulenté, qui
bien en scet le tort reprendre. Et de ce m'atens a lui, car il ne touche
au propos de ma premiere epistre. Et comme tu mesmes dis que je

590

595

600

605

610

615

620

625

reason to laugh about what you have said. Then you say that "whoever reads this book well, will find lessons in it about fleeing vices and following all virtues." You quote certain lessons which you claim can be found in it. In fact, I tell you that the same can be said of the law of Mohamed: If you read the Koran, you will find in it very good and pious points concerning our faith, which will please you greatly. But this is flawed, and worth nothing. The logical consequence is completely tarnished, the conclusion does not hold up. Do you not know that even in the high council, despite what has been proposed earlier, it is always the final conclusion that is valid? And if Master Jean de Meun, dare I say, had spoken in his book about several things to which human nature was inclined, and had then returned to his conclusion about customs of moral living, you would have had a stronger argument when you said that he did so in order to promote virtue. Yet you know that if a writer wishes to use the rules of rhetoric, he first presents the premises of his topic, then he moves from argument to argument, and may discuss several topics if he is so inclined; then, in his conclusion, he always returns to the purpose of his discourse. In this case, in fact, the author of this book failed in nothing, because he is not lacking experience. You will tell me, however, that this was done by de Lorris. My response, "I consider this all the same edifice," will suffice as a response to this passage, although you have said many things to support your argument, which I will not go into because everything comes to an end. And you may examine this as closely as you like.

You said earlier that he does not insult women, but speaks well of them. I am awaiting proof of this, but you say only that Saint Ambrose insults the female sex more than he does, because he says that women are accustomed to deceiving. I shall reply to this. You know well that the theologians always imply a double meaning in their words, as did Jesus Christ in his preaching. I would like to point out that Saint Ambrose did in no way say this concerning all mortal women because, I think, this good man would have wished to reprimand nothing but vices, for he knew well that there were many holy women. What he wished to say was that frequently men use the female sex to deceive their own souls. As Solomon said, "A sin committed by a man is worth more than a good deed by a woman."[55] We know full well that it is wrong to take this literally, and we can take Saint Ambrose himself as example: To him, a sin committed by a man was worth more, because if he had not been so enamored with the woman he loved, so much so that he committed

630   te puis dire et tu peus dire voire, tu recites les bonnes nouvelles et
les vas cueillant ainsi comme il te plaist a ton propos, et laisses les
mauvaises.

De l'ennortement dont dame Eloquence se plaint (de
l'enseingnement de prendre le chastel de jalousie, dont elle dit qu'il
vouloit bouter chasteté hors de toutes femmes), tu en fais mervil-
635 250r° leuse responce en ce que tu dis que // ce est pour aviser les gardes
de «mieulx estouper les lieux par ou il peut estre pris, ou d'y mettre
milleurs gardes». Et puis tu dis que en toutes manieres de guerres
les assaillans ont l'aventage, mais que ilz soient avisés. Or parlons
un petit des guerres, a l'aventure entre toy et moy: je te dis qu'il
640   est aucune maniere de guerre que les assaillans ont l'avantage. Et
sces tu quant c'est? Quant le capitaine ou le conduiseur est plus
malicieux et duit de guerre, et il a a faire a foible partie et simple,
non usagiée de guerre. Encore y a il un aultre point qui souvent
nuit aux deffendeurs—supposé que ilz soient fors—: c'est trahison
645   ou faulz blandissement de ceulz mesmes en qui ilz se fioyent (par
ce fut pris jadis le fort chastel de Ylyon). Et du chastel assailli ne
saroies tu aultre conseiller comment les pertuis de trahison seroient estouppés, car ilz sont trop couvers. Maistre Jehan de Meun
enseingne comment le chastel de Jalousie sera assailli et pris: il ne
650   le fait point adfin que les deffendeurs estouppent le pertuis car il ne
parle point a eulx ne il n'est de leur conseil; ains conforte et ennorte
les assaillans en toutes manieres d'assault,—ainsi comme se je te
conseilloie la maniere de vaincre ton ennemi, ce ne seroit mie adfin
qu'il se gardast de toy. Se tu vuelx dire il ne l'enseingne pas, mais il
655   dit comment il fut pris, je te dis que qui raconteroit une malicieuse
maniere de faire faulse malicieuse ou comment on l'aroit faite, il
l'enseingneroit assés. Dont je dy certainnement que il ne le fist a
autre fin fors pour introduire les assaillans.

Aprés tu dis ce dont tu te prens trop bien au las—se le vou-
660   loies considerer quant tu amenes Ovide *De l'art d'amours* a ton
propos; et ancores l'epreuves—dont je te sçay bon gré—quant tu
dis que a tort en fu exillié. Tu dis que quant Ovide l'escript ce fu en
latin, lequel n'entendoient femmes, et que il le bailla seulement aux
assaillans pour apprendre a assaillir le chastel, et c'estoit la fin de
665   son livre; mais la jalousie des Rommains tres enorme l'exilla sans
raison pour celle cause, comme tu dis. Sans faille il me semble se tu
fusses bien avisié, n'amenasses ja cellui Ovide *De l'art d'amours* en
place pour excusacion de ton maistre. Mais de tant le peus tu bien
faire que c'est le pur fondement et principe de ce livre de la *Rose,*

idolatry, he might well have seen the good in her. One might also
quote prophecy: for Judas's sin is worth more to us than Judith's
good deed of slaying Holofernes, or that of any other woman.[56] You
amaze me when you go on to assert that I insult them more than
he does when I say that if the book of the *Rose* were read in front
of queens and princesses, they should cover their faces, red with
shame. And to this you respond, "Why blush? It seems that they
consider themselves guilty of the vices which the Jealous Husband
recounts of women." Ha! My God! How well said! You do not
increase your honor in the slightest by reporting things of which the
contrary can be proven. You studied this matter poorly, for when I
said that women should cover their faces, red with shame, I was in
no way speaking about the words of the Jealous Husband, but was
referring to the abominable things at the end of the book, about
which I said, "Why should it be read in their presence?" And in saying that they would blush, I do not insult them at all, rather I praise
them for possessing the chaste virtue of shame.

Then you respond to Lady Eloquence's complaint about Master Jean de Meun's defamation and slander of religion stating that he
in no way insults it. With all due respect, I reply to you that since,
in fact, he was a public defamer, he defames religion excessively,
sparing nothing. Any good devout Catholic will understand this and
will know to reprimand the error in this. This is what I would also
expect from him[57] because he does not address the subject of my
first epistle. Since you yourself say that we may be frank with one
another, I say that you recount the good messages and harvest them
for the convenience of your argument. The bad ones, on the other
hand, you leave out.

Your response to the encouragement about which Lady
Eloquence complains (namely, the lesson on capturing Jealousy's
castle, where chastity is supposed to be chased from all women)
strikes me as odd, for you claim that the guards were instructed in
this manner in order to "better block off the places where chastity
could be captured or to place better guards there." Then you say that
in any war the advantage is on the side of the assailants, providing
that they have been informed. Now, let us speak about war for a moment, namely, the situation between you and me: I tell you that the
advantage is on the side of the assailants only in some cases. And
do you know when that is? When the captain or general is malicious
and skilled in the ways of war, and when he is confronted with a
weak and simple opponent who is unaccustomed to war. Then there

670   lequel est mirouer et exemple de bien et chastement vivre, ainsi
       comme il l'a pris ou dit Ovide—, qui d'autre chose ne parle fors de
       chasteté! Ha! Dieux! comme il appert que ta pure voulenté aveugle
       ton bon sens quant tu dis que sans cause fu exillié, voire que les
       Rommains—lesquelx gouvernoient tous leurs fais par polixie sou-
675   verainement ordennée en cellui temps—le chacierent a tort, comme
       tu dis, pour cause de jalousie. Et comme tu dis après que Meun ne
       mist pas en son livre tant seulement *L'Art d'amours* que Ovide fist
       mais beaucoup d'autres aucteurs. Donques par ta raison
       mesmes est prouvé que Meun parle aux assaillans, comme Ovide
680 250v° que // il prent. Mais tu dis que «de tant comme il recite diverses
       manieres d'assaillir, de tant avise il plus les gardes du chastel de
       eulx deffendre». Voirement fait ainsi comme qui t'assauldroit pour
       toy occire—dont Dieux te gard!—: il t'apprendroit comment tu te
       deveroies deffendre! Il te feroit grant courtoisie! Bien l'en deveroies
685   mercier! Au moins ne peus tu nyer que il n'enseingne a faire mal
       aux assaillans, foibles ou fors que soient li deffendeur.
            Ancore ne me vueil mie taire que tu dis par jalousie et sans
       raison fu exillié Ovide. Quant les sages Rommains virent et apper-
       ceurent la perverse doctrine, et le venin angoisseux appresté pour
690   lancier es cuers des joenes a les attraire a dissolucion et oyseuse
       et les engins tendus a decevoir, prendre, suborner et soubstraire la
       virginité et chasteté de leurs filles et femes, eulx—a bonne cause
       dolens de telle doctrine semence, adont pour punicion voire plus pit-
       euse que souffisante—exillerent l'aucteur de tele doctrine. Et n'est
695   pas doubte que son livre ardirent ou le porent trouver, mais de male
       plante demeure toudis racine. Ha! livre mal nommé *L'Art d'amours!*
       Car d'amours n'est il mie mais art de faulse et malicieuse industrie
       de decevoir femmes peut il bien estre appellés. C'est belle doctrine!
       Est ce dont tout gaingnié que bien decevoir ces femmes? Qui sont
700   femmes? Qui sont elles? Sont ce serpens, loups, lyons, dragons,
       guievres ou bestes ravissables devourans et ennemies a nature
       humaine, qu'il conviengne faire art a les decevoir et prendre? Lisés
       donc l'*Art*: aprenés dont a faire engins! Prenés les fort! Decevés les!
       Vituperés les! Assaillés ce chastel! Gardés que nulles n'eschappe
705   entre vous, hommes, et que tout soit livré a honte! Et par Dieu, si
       sont elles vos meres, vos seurs, vos filles, vos femmes et vos amies;
       elles sont vous mesmes et vous mesmes elles. Or les decevés assés,
       car «il vault trop mieulx, beau maistre decevoir», etc.
            Je me ris de ce que tu dis que tu as presté ton livre de la *Rose*
710   a un home fol amoureux pour soy oster de fole amour, lequel lui a

670   is another aspect which often harms the defenders, assuming that
       they are strong, and that is treachery or betrayal by those whom they
       trust (this is precisely how Ilion's castle was captured long ago).[58]
       Moreover, neither you nor anyone else would know how to block
       the holes of treachery of this besieged castle, because they are so
675   well concealed. Master Jean de Meun teaches how Jealousy's castle
       will be besieged and taken. Yet his purpose is not to help the defend-
       ers protect the holes because he in no way addresses them, and his
       advice is not for them. Instead, he counsels the assailants in the
       many ways of assault. Thus, if I advised you on how to defeat your
680   enemy, I would not teach the enemy how to protect himself from
       you. If you wish to claim that he does not teach this, but that he
       merely tells us how the castle was taken, I tell you that whoever told
       of the malicious way of making counterfeit money, taught it well
       enough. Therefore, I say with certainty that he does so exclusively
685   to show the assailants a way into the castle.
           Then you bring Ovid's *The Art of Love* into your argument,
       falling into your own trap in saying that he was wrongfully exiled.
       You prove your own mistake, for which I am grateful. You say that
       when Ovid wrote this book, he did so in Latin, which women did
690   not understand, and that he only gave it to the assailants in order
       to teach them how to attack the castle. This was the purpose of
       his book. You claim that because of their tremendous jealousy the
       Romans exiled him wrongfully and without cause. Assuredly, it
       seems to me that had you been well informed, you would never have
695   brought Ovid's *The Art of Love* into the argument in your effort to
       excuse your master. You could not have done better, because it is
       the foundation of and the principle for this book of the *Rose*, which
       is a mirror and example of moral and chaste living, which is what
       Ovid said, too, who speaks of nothing but chastity! Ha! My God!
700   It seems that your common sense is blinded by your wishes when
       you say that he was exiled for no reason, that even the Romans, who
       governed all their matters by legal and orderly politics at that time,
       committed an error in chasing him away out of jealousy, as you
       claim. Further, you make the claim that in his book de Meun did
705   not only borrow from Ovid's *Art of Love* but also from many other
       authors. Hence, your reasoning itself proves that de Meun addresses
       the assailants, as did Ovid from whom he borrowed. Yet you say that
       "the more he recounts the many ways of attack, the more he teaches
       the guards of the castle to defend themselves." Indeed, this would
710   be like saying that if someone attacked you with the intent of killing

ja tant prouffité que tu lui as ouy jurer sa foy que c'est la chose qui
plus lui a aidié a s'en oster. Et tu dis que ce as tu dit pour ce que
je dis a la fin de mon espistre: «Quant en sont devenus hermites»?
Responce: et je te promet se tu eusses appresté a ton amy un livre
715   des devocions saint Bernard, ou aucune bonne legende introdui-
sant a sauvement et a demonstrer que il n'est que une seule amour
bonne—en laquelle on doit ficher son cuer et son affection, en la
maniere que Philosophie le demonstre a bone—, ou autre chose
semblable, tu lui eusses mieux fait son prouffit; mais prens toy garde
720   que ne lui ailles bailler l'instrument pour soy oster de la chaleur du
souleil et soy getter en une fournaise toute embrasée. Et je te diray
un aultre exemple sans mentir, puis que nous sommes es miracles du
Rommant de la Rose. J'ay ouy dire, n'a pas moult, a un de ces com-
paingnons de l'office dont tu es et que tu bien congnois, et homme
725   d'auctorité, que il congnoist un omme marié, lequel ajou//ste foy
251r°   au *Rommant de la Rose* comme a l'Euvangile; cellui est souverainnement jalous, et quant sa passion le tient plus aigrement il va
querre son livre et lit devant sa feme, et puis fiert et frappe sus et
dist: «Orde, tele comme quelle il dit, voir que tu me fais tel tour. Ce
730   bon sage homme maistre Jehan de Meun savoit bien que femmes
savoient faire»! Et a chacun mot qu'il treuve a son propos il fiert un
coup ou deux du pié ou de la paume. Si m'est avis que quiconques
s'en loue, celle povre femme le compere chier.

Il m'anuye si moult grant prolixité de lengage, car comme
735   ennuy est a moy mesmes, suppose que pourra estre aux lisans; mais
pour ce que il me convient repliquer les choses proposees, autrement ne seroit entendable, m'en esteut eslongner ma matiere; si me
soit pardonné de qui le tendra a anuy.

Encore ne te peus taire de la Vielle, et dis que quant elle parle
740   a Bel Accueil elle lui dit avant le coup:

Ne vous vueil pas en amour mettre,
mais se vousen voulés entremettre,
je vous en monstreray voulentiers, etc.

Et puis dit que elle lui presche adfin qu'il ne soit deceus.
745   Responce: vray Dieux! Comment est ce malicieuse maniere de
decevoir, de monstrer que ce que on fait et dit, quelque mal que ce
soit, que c'est a bonne fin et a cause bonne! Car il n'est si simple, se
il appercevoit la decevance, que il ne s'en gardast: si la fault couvrir
par cautelle, et le droit tour du malicieux deceveur est comencier
750   lengaige par bonne introite pour mieulx parfournir son malice. Si
n'est point d'excusance en ceste partie ce que tu as mis avant.

you (may God protect you), he would teach you how you should defend yourself! He would do you a great service! You should thank him for it! At least you cannot deny that he does not teach how to harm the assailants, regardless of how weak or strong the defenders

715 may be.

I cannot yet be silent about your argument that Ovid was exiled out of jealousy and without cause. When the wise Romans saw and took heed of the perverse doctrine and its dangerous poison—ready to be launched into the hearts of the young in order to attract

720 them to dissoluteness and idleness, their minds corrupted to deceive, to take and capture the virginity and chastity of their daughters and wives—they exiled the author of such a doctrine. Justifiably they had everything to fear from the dissemination of such a doctrine and therefore chose this as a punishment which showed pity and mercy.

725 And there is no doubt that they burnt his book wherever they could find it, yet of an evil plant the root will always remain. Ha! This book, wrongfully entitled *The Art of Love*! For it does not speak of love at all, and ought to be called the art of malicious and false labor of deceiving women. This is a beautiful doctrine indeed! Is

730 everything gained, then, when women are deceived? Which women? Who are they? Are they serpents, wolves, lions, dragons, vipers, or ravishing, devouring beasts and enemies of humans, that there must be an art to deceiving and conquering them? Then read the *Art*: learn to betray! Take them with force! Deceive them! Slander them!

735 Attack this castle! Make certain that none may escape from you, men, and that all will be delivered to shame! And, by God, they are your mothers, sisters, daughters, wives, and friends. They are you and you are they. Yet deceive them plenty, because "dear sir, it is better to deceive, etc."

740 It makes me laugh when you say that you loaned your book of the *Rose* to a foolish lover in order that he might cast foolish love aside; it seems he gained so much from it that you heard him swear that this was what helped him most in this endeavor. And you say that you mention this because I say at the end of my epistle, "When

745 did this make them hermits?" My response: I promise you that had you loaned your friend a book of devotions by Saint Bernard[59] or any other good legend intended to lead one to salvation and to show that there is only one good love in which one ought to place one's heart and affection, as Lady Philosophy shows Boethius,[60] you

750 would have helped him much more. Take care that you do not give him the tool to rid himself of the sun's warmth and to throw himself

Tu dis se il y a riens mal dit et a diffame de sexe femenin, que il n'en est que reciteur des autres aucteurs. Responce: je sçay bien que il n'est mie le premier qui ait mal dit, mais il l'acroist quant il le

755   recite.

Tu dis que ce estoit pour plus enseingnier les parties a garder le chastel. Responce: le mal admonnesté et loué a faire, n'est mie a supposer que ce soit adfin que on se gard.

Tu dis que il le fist aussi pour suire la matiere maistre Guil-

760   laume de Lorris. Responce: celluy qui suit le forvoyé ne fait mie a excuser se il se forvoie.

Tu dis que en ce faisant parle de toutes choses en leur estat au prouffit de creature humaine, tant a l'ame comme au corps. Responce: il ne fait point parler en commun de toutes choses en leur

765   estat; et aussi il parle de plusieurs aultrement que leur estat et au domage de l'ame et du corps, come il est ja prouvé.

Tu dis que «pour ce parla il de paradis et des vertus: pour les suivre». Responce: voire, mais il dit que vices sont vertus quant par ses personnages il loue mal faire, comme il est dit. Et de vertus

770   fait vice quant il dit tant de vitupere et doulereux mal de l'ordre de mariage, lequel est saint et approuvé,—et d'autres bons estas semblablement que il diffame generaument. Et mal parle de paradis quant il dist, combien que ce soit par mos un pou enveloppés—mais autant vault a dire—, que les luxurieux iront en paradis.

775 251vº   Et // ce fait il dire a Genyus, lequel escommenie de sa puissance (qui est nulle) ceulx qui excerciteront l'œuvre de Nature et les vices enseingne plus proprement qu'il ne fait les vertus.

Tu dis que «de tant comme il parle de vices et de vertus, d'enfer et de paradis pres a pres l'un de l'autre, monstre il plus la

780   beatitude des uns et la laidure des autres». Responce: la beatitude des uns ne monstre il mie quant il dit que les malfaiteurs yront. Et pour ce mesle il paradis avec les ordures dont il parle: pour donner plus grant foy a son livre. Mais se mieulx vuelx ouyr descripre paradis et enfer, et par plus soubtilz termes et plus haultement parlé de

785   theologie, plus proufitablement, plus poetiquement et de plus grant efficace, lis le livre que on appelle le Dant, ou le te fais exposer pour ce que il est en lengue flourentine souverainnement dicté: la oiras autre propos mieulx fondé plus soubtilment, ne te desplaise, et ou plus tu pourras prouffiter que en ton *Rommant de la Rose,*—et cent

790   fois mieulx composé; ne il n'y a comparoison, ne t'en courousses ja.

Tu dis que Genius ne promet mie paradis aux folz amoureux. Responce: deable lui faist promettre, quant il n'est mie a lui a livrer.

into a blazing furnace. And I will give you another example without
lying, since we are speaking about the wonders of the *Roman de
la rose*. I have heard tell that one of the colleagues of your office,
755   whom you know well and who is a man of authority, knows a married man who believes in the *Roman de la rose* as in the New Testament. He is terribly jealous, and when his passions make him writhe
he seeks his book and reads it in front of his wife, then he hits it and
says, "Vile woman, you are like the woman in the book and you be-
760   tray me. This good and wise man, Master Jean de Meun, knew well
what women were capable of!" And with every word which he found
to his liking he kicked or slapped her once or twice. I think that whoever is proud of this, his poor wife must pay dearly. I am annoyed by
such prolixity of language, and if it annoys me, it probably annoys
765   the readers. Yet because I must respond to the arguments which are
presented here—otherwise it would not make sense to extend the
matter—I beg forgiveness of those who also feel annoyed.

  You still cannot be quiet about the discourse of the Duenna and
quote right from the onset what she says to Fair Welcoming:
770   I do not wish to make you fall in love,
   But if you wish you to engage in it,
   I will gladly show you, etc.
  And then you say she preaches to him so that he may not be
deceived. My response: Dear God! What kind of a malicious means
775   of deception is this to show that what one does and says, no matter
how sinful, is acceptable if it is for a good cause! He is not so naïve
that once he realizes the deceit, he will not shield himself against it.
It will have to be carefully covered, and the malicious betrayer will
slyly begin his speech with the right introduction in order to better
780   deliver his malice. There is no excuse in this part for what you said
earlier.

  You claim that he says nothing evil about women and does not
defame them, but merely quotes other authors. My response: I know
full well that he is hardly the first to speak badly about them, but he
785   makes it worse by quoting other authors.

  You claim that he does this in order to better teach the adversaries to guard the castle. My response: It is hard to believe that
when evil is encouraged and praised, it is done with the purpose of
avoiding evil.

790   You claim that he did this because he wished to follow Master
Guillaume de Lorris's subject matter. My response: One who follows
those who stray cannot be blamed if he strays as well.

Mais tu dis que dame Eloquence lui met sus. Et il parle, ce dis tu, de
ceulx qui excerciteront bonnement les œuvres de Nature. Responce:
795   or viens tu a mon propos, Dieux merci! Vrayement il n'y met ne
bonnement ne mauvaisement, mais simplement, ceulx qui excerciteront les susdictes œuvres.

Et dis que ce n'est mie tout bien, ce fere bonnement et estre
fol amoureux. Responce: de ce bonnement ne parla il oncques en ce
800   pas; mais je te dis que ce est pis estre luxurieux en plusieurs lieux,
comme il veult enseingnier, que estre fort amoureux en un seul lieu.

Tu dis que Nature ne Genius n'ennortent pas estre fol amoureux, mais ilz ennortent suivre les œuvres susdictes, lesquelles sont
licites aux fins amoureux. Responce: doncques veulx tu dire, puis
805   que Nature ne l'ennorte, que estre fort amoureux est contre nature:
laquelle chose n'est mie, sauve ta grace; mais puis que il dit que
ilz sont licites aux fins, il convendroit savoir en quelle maniere les
convient affiner.

Tu dis que ce est pour continuer l'espece humaine et pour lais-
810   sier le mauvais peché que on ne doit nommer. Responce: sans cause
se debat tant de ce, car Dieu mercis, elle ne deffault point et est
chose gastée et fole d'ammonnester l'eaue que elle voise son cours;
ne l'autre peché qu'il veult dire n'est point renomme en France,
Dieux soit loués! l n'en convient ja mettre tel os en bouche de nulli.
815   Tu dis que combien que tu n'oses ne vueille dire que excerciter la dicte œuvre «hors de mariage ne soit pechés…». Responce,
sans passer oultre: voire, mais Dieux scet que toy—et d'autres
disciples comme toy, qui l'osast dire—en penses, mais il s'en fault
taire, et pour cause. Toutefois, ce dis tu, est il permis en mariage.
820   Responce: Dieux en soit loués! ce savons nous bien! Toutesfois ne
l'exprime point le livre de la *Rose* en nul endroit en tele maniere.
252r° Mais tu vuelx dire que ainsi l'entendi // maistre Jehan de Meun
quant il dist ou chapitre de la Vielle, cestui mot:

Pour ce sont fais les mariages,
825   par le conseil des plus sages,
pour oster dissolucion….

Responce: tu le me vas querre bien loings, et memes a propos ce
qui est dit bien hors propos; la Vielle ne preschoit mie a Bel Accueil
de mariage: elle s'en gardoit moult bien, ne chose que elle die ne
830   tourne a bonne fin. Et si croy que maistre Jehan de Meun ne fist
point dire a elle ce mot pour louer mariage. Car ce n'estoit mie
son office. Et te souviengne que tu as dit aultre part que ce n'estoit
pas Meun qui parloit: ce faisoient les personnages chacun en son
office,—mais c'estoit il qui dist ce bon mot. Et ce n'estoit il mie qui

795 You claim that by following de Lorris, he speaks of everything according to its order for the profit of humanity, in soul and body. My response: He does not always speak of everything the way it is in its natural order but also speaks of many things differently than what the natural order prescribes and to the detriment of body and soul, as has already been proven.

800 You claim that "he spoke of paradise and virtues in order that we might follow them." My response: This is true, but he presents vices as virtues when he praises the evil deeds of his characters, as has been said. And he turns virtues into vices when he so horribly slanders the state of marriage, which is holy and respected, and other similar states, which he defames sweepingly. And he slanders paradise
805 when he claims that the lecherous will go there; no matter how much he disguises it with words, this is the meaning of his words. And he lets Genius say this, who excommunicates by the power invested in him (which is worthless) those who will not[61] perform Nature's work; and he teaches vices much better than virtues.

810 You claim that "as much as he speaks about vices and virtues, hell and paradise in juxtaposition, he shows more effectively the beauty of certain ones and the ugliness of the others." My response: He in no way shows the beauty of certain ones when he says that wrongdoers will go there. And, therefore, he confuses paradise with the filth of
815 which he speaks only to attribute more credibility to his book. However, if you truly wish to hear better descriptions of paradise and hell, presented in more skilled terms of high theology, more efficiently and poetically, read the book which is called the Dante, where he [Dante] will explain it to you for what it truly is in eloquently written Floren-
820 tine language. There you will hear other—no offense—more skillfully argued points, from which you will benefit much more than from your *Roman de la rose*, not to mention that they are a hundred times better composed. I assure you, there is no comparison.[62]

You claim that Genius does not promise paradise to the foolish
825 lovers. My response: The devil makes him promise that which is not for him to grant. You say that Lady Eloquence misinterprets him and, according to you, he speaks of those who perform well the works of Nature. My response: Now you come to my point, thank God! In fact, he does not say "well" or "poorly," but simply those who perform
830 the above-mentioned tasks. And you say that to do it well and to be a foolish lover is hardly the same thing. My response: He never spoke of "well" in this passage, but I tell you that it is worse to be lecherous several times, as he wishes to teach us, than to be deeply in love only once.

835   parloit ou chapitre du Jaloux! Et ainsi as ton dit et ton desdit, et est
       bien loings du propos de Genius dont nous parlons, lequel ne pensa
       oncques a mariage, le bon home! Et aussi n'est ce mie ton oppin-
       ion, se Dieux m'ayst, quoy que tu dies. Et ancore pour ce que tant
       t'efforces de excuser Meun—et veulx gloser que ce vouloit il en-
840   tendre «que on peust excerciter la dicte œuvre licitement au moins
       en mariage»—, vient trop mal a propos que en tel estat on doye tant
       excerciter l'œuvre et si diligemment, et il, tant et si excessivement,
       blasme la vie que il dit estre en mariage, quant il dit que tant y a
       de conte qu'on que il n'eust nul quelque grant y eust volenté, qu'il
845   ne s'en deust tirer arriere—qui le croiroit—; et ainsi seroient mal
       continuées ces œuvres. Il deust avoir loué l'estat ou l'en les doit
       faire pour donner appetit a chacun que il se meist; mais il fait tout le
       contraire: si est trop mal a propos. Ne il n'appert que il l'entende en
       celle guise. Et toy mesmes, pour mieulx amender la besongne, dis
850   ensuivant (bien a propos de louer mariage pour confermer que pour
       ce le dist il), que saint Augustin dit: «Qui est sans femme espousée,
       il pense aux choses de Dieu pour lui plaire», mais cellui qui est
       «joint par mariage, pense les choses qui sont du monde»,—dont tu
       dis aprés que ce as tu dit pour ceulx qui veulent reprendre par leur
855   lengage, sans raison, aucteur quel qu'il soit, nottable et non repris
       par avant. Si as tres bien prouvé que maistre Jehan de Meun, quant
       il tant parloit de excerciter l'euvre de Nature, que il entendoit en
       mariage! Dieux, comment est ce bien prouvé! Voire, ainsi comme
       dit le proverbe commun des gloses d'Orliens, qui destruisent le
860   texte.
            Encore ne te peus tu taire, et fais une grant narracion pour
       tousjours excuser ton bon maistre: mais je ne pense mie a tout re-
       later mot a mot, car trop m'anuyeroit—et ja anuye de tant parler de
       cestui propos—, et aussi tout vient assez a une fin.
865   Tu dis que «pour ce que chacun n'a pas leu le livre de la
       Rose», tu reciteras les propres mos de Genyus, comme ilz sont ou
       livre. Si en recites voirement plusieurs de ceulx propos que il dit,
       mais tu en trespasses assés, et vais cueillant ca et la ceulx qui mieux
       te plaisent; et n'as talent de mettre arriere le bien que il dit que on
870 252v° rende l'autruy qui l'a, et que on // soit piteux et miscricors, et
       tieulx choses. Voire, et que on face les œuvres Dieu de par Dieu et
       on yra en paradis! Je croy que il vouloit suivre l'ordre et la secte des
       Turlupins, et ainssy mesloit venin avec miel et doulce liqueur avec
       fiel: veez la bien qui y est.
875   Je ne sçay a quoy tant nous debatons ces questions, car je croy

835   You claim that neither Nature nor Genius advises others to love foolishly, but to perform the above-mentioned tasks which are permissible for courtly lovers. My response: Do you wish therefore to say that since Nature advises this, it is against Nature to love strongly? This, of course, is not the case, with all due respect, yet

840   since he says that they are permissible for courtly lovers, it would be nice to know in what way they are courtly.

      You claim that their purpose is to continue the human race and to refrain from the terrible sin which must not be named. My response: There is no reason for this debate, because there is no need

845   for it, thank God. It is foolish and a waste of time to try to cause water to run against its natural course. Nor is the other sin of which he wishes to speak common in France, God be praised! It is never appropriate to put such a thing in anyone's mouth.

      You claim that you neither dare nor wish to say in any way

850   that performing this task "outside of marriage is not a sin…." My response, without passing over it: You are correct, yet God knows that you and others like you who dare utter it, also think about it. Yet for good reasons one must not speak of it. Nevertheless, you say that it is permitted in marriage. My response: God be praised! We know it

855   well! Yet nowhere does the book of the *Rose* express it in this way. You wish to say that Master Jean de Meun understood it thus when, in the passage of the Old Woman, we find this:

        For marriage was created
        By the council of the wisest

860   To cast aside dissoluteness….

My response: You go far to find this quotation in an argument which has nothing to do with the subject at hand, because the Duenna did in no way preach about marriage to Fair Welcoming. On the contrary, far from it. Whatever she says will never have a good

865   outcome. I think that Master Jean de Meun did by no means make her say this with the intent of praising marriage. This was not at all her task, and I remind you that you have said elsewhere that it was not de Meun who was speaking here, nor was it he who spoke in the passage of the Jealous Husband! So, you say one thing then

870   you contradict yourself, and we have lost track of Genius's argument, which was our topic. He did not have marriage in mind at all, the good man! This is not your own opinion, either; I do not care what you say, God help me. Moreover, you are so set in excusing de Meun, and wish to gloss over that which he said, "that one was

875   allowed to perform this task licitly in marriage at least." This does

ne toy ne moy ne avons talant de mouvoir nos oppinions. Tu dis
qu'il est bon. Je dy qu'il est mauvais. Or me soulz qu'il soit bon,
et quant toy avec tes autres complices arés assés debatu par vos
soubtilz raisons et tant pourrés faire que mal soit bien, je croiray

880   que *Le Rommant de la Rose* soit bon! Mais je sçay bien que il est
propre a ceulx qui veulent malicieusement vivre et mieux eulx
garder d'autruy que ilz ne veulent que autrui se garde d'eulx. Mais
a ceulx qui veulent bien et simplement vivre, sans trop envelopper
es voluptés du monde ne autruy decevoir ne que autre les decoive,

885   ce livre n'a mestier. Et vrayement je aimeroie mieulx estre du part
des oposites que de ses complices, car j'ay oppinion que mendre
part en ait le loup; et comme dit le bon preudomme qui composa la
playdoirie dessusdicte: «Pleust a Dieu que tele *Rose* n'eust oncques
esté plantée ou jardin de Crestianté!»—combien que tu te dies

890   estre de ces disciples. Et puis que le veulx estre, si le soyes; quant
a moy, je renonce a sa discipline, car je tends a autre que je cuide
estre plus prouffitable et qui mieulx m'est agreable et si ne suis
mie seule en celle oppinion; ne sçay pour quoy plus que aux autres
vous en prenés a moy entre vous ses disciples: ce n'est mie honneur

895   soy prendre a la plus foible partie. Il y a si grant foisson de sages
docteurs dignes de foy et plains de science, et vrayement si y a il
des grans princes de ce royaume et chevaliers et nobles et plusieurs
autres qui sont de la mesmes oppinion que je suis, et tiennent que ce
est lecture inutile et nonhonorable: pour quoy entre vous n'alés vous

900   derompre la grosse tige de l'arbre et faire tant que il soit estirpé et
esrachié, et la racine dont peut venir et sourdre la seve et liqueur
soit toute amortie, non mie vous prendre aux petites branches par
desseure qui n'ont force ne vertu, pour cuider tout estirper qui vous
en prenés a moy, qui ne suis fors comme la voix d'un petit gresillion

905   qui toutejour bat ses elles et fait grant noise, et tout est neant envers
le hault chant delitable des gracieux oysiaulx.

Mais tu dis que tu ne te peus «assés merveillier comment
personne ose blasmer non pas seullement lui, mais ceulx qui prisent
et aiment son livre de la *Rose*». Responce: je ne me puis asses mer-

910   veiller comment personne ose entreprendre louer cellui livre, ouquel
sont comprises saintes matieres souffisantes a mettre cuer humain
en dampnable erreur.

Tu dis que quant a toy, plus desires estre «repris pour prisier et
amer son livre que estre des trop soubtilz blasmeurs». Tu ressembles

915   en ceste partie celle qui dit que mieulx ameroyt estre *meretrix* appellee de cellui que elle aimoit par amours.

not make sense, because in the state of marriage one must perform
it diligently. Yet he so excessively insults married life, in saying that
there is so much strife in it, that there are not many who had enough
will not to withdraw from marriage. Who would believe that?

880   Hence, these tasks will be insufficiently continued. He should have
praised this state, as one must, to make it attractive so that people
will engage in it. But he does the opposite, which is entirely inap-
propriate. It does not seem that he understands it in this way. And
you yourself, to remedy the flaw (trying to praise marriage and show

885   that this was de Meun's view), quote Augustine: "He who is without
a wife thinks of divine things in order to please God," but one who
is "joined in marriage thinks of worldly things." And you claim that
you said this for those who for no reason wish to reprimand any
author who is illustrious and has never before been criticized. You

890   have proven very cleverly that when Master Jean de Meun spoke
repeatedly of performing Nature's task, he meant within the context
of marriage! My God, how this is well proven! This is indeed like
the proverb about the glosses of Orléans,[63] which ended up destroying the text.

895   And you still cannot be silent, but must add a long harangue
in your incessant attempt to excuse your good master. However, I
shall not consider repeating it word for word, because it would bore
me too much—and I am already very bored with this topic—and
besides, everything comes to an end eventually.

900   You claim that "because not everyone has read the book of
the *Rose*," you will quote the words of Genius as they appear in the
book. In fact, you quote some of his arguments, yet you skip many
others and collect those here and there which please you more. You
do not wish to neglect the good he mentions, for instance, that one

905   should forgive others and that one ought to be merciful, charitable,
and so forth. And even that one ought to do God's works through
God in order to go to paradise! I think that he wished to follow the
sect of the Turlupines[64] and thus mixed venom with honey and sweet
liquor with bile. Behold the good it contains.

910   I do not know why we continue to debate these questions
because I think that neither you nor I has the will to change our
position. You say that he is good. I say he is bad. Now show me who
is right, and when you and your other accomplices have sufficiently
debated this matter with your skillful reasoning, and when you have

915   shown that bad is good, I will believe that the *Roman de la rose* is
good! Yet I know very well that this work is for those who wish to

253r° Tu dis que sachent tuit que «il reste // ancore .vii. mille qui
sont tous preste de le deffendre». Responce: c'est rigle general que
mauvaise secte accroist voulentiers, aussi comme la mauvaise herbe,
920 mais en plusieurs choses la plus grant quantité ne fait mie pour tant
a presumer estre meilleur et se Dieu plaist, ja si grant assemblee
n'en sera faicte; ce n'est mie article de foy: tiengne chacun ce qu'il
vouldra.
Tu dis que se il eust esté «du temps de entre nous qui le blas-
925 mons, tu deisses que nous eussiens hayne particuliere a sa personne;
mais nous ne le veismes oncques: dont tu ne peus ymaginer dont ce
vient». Responce: pour ce que oncques ne le veismes, ne oncques
ne nous meffist, as tu mieulx cause de penser que droite vraye pure
verité nous meut; car le haineux ne doit estre creu. Se non, ce dis tu,
930 qu'il viengne de la «haultece du livre plus abile a recevoir les vens
des souffles envieux. Car l'ignorence n'en est point cause de tel y
a, ce dis tu, se n'est pour cause de pou lire le dit livre». Responce:
tu peus estre certain que le bon preudomme qui le blasme (dont
tu veulx dire que n'est mie par ignorence), il n'a aucune envie sur
935 cellui livre; car je croy que la haultece de sa tres eslevee vie ne lui
lairoit avoir envie de plus digne chose. Quant est de moy, non obstant mon ignorence, ny ay aucune envie. Et pour quoy aroie? Il ne
me fait ne froit ne chaut, ne mal ne bien ne toult ne donne; ne il ne
parle d'estat dont je soye pour quoy aye cause de indignacion, car je
940 ne suis mariée ne espoir estre, ne religieuse aussi, ne chose qu'il dy
ne me touche. Je ne suis Bel Accueil, ne je n'ay paour de la Vielle,
ne boutons n'ay a garder. Et si te promets que je aime beaulx livres
et soubtilz, et bien traictiés, et les quiers et les cerche et les lis voulentiers si rudement comme les sache entendre. Et si n'aime point
945 cellui de la *Rose,* la cause si est simplement et absoluement pour
ce que il est de tres mauvaise exortacion et deshonneste lecture, et
qui plus penetre en courage mal que bien; et peut estre, selon mon
jugement, cause de sa dampnacion et dampnement de vie a ceulx
qui l'oyent et qui se delictent, et d'actraire a deshonnestes meurs: si
950 te jure sur mon ame et par ma creance que autre cause ne me meut.
Et ce que tu dis aprés, que peut estre que le blasmons pour donner
plus grant appetit de le veoir, et ainsi seroit nostre oppinion bonne,
tu peus estre certain que ce n'est pas nostre motif!
Aprés tout ce, tu me appelles de plus grant valeur que je ne
955 sui, tienne mercy, et dis que tu me pries que je garde «l'onneur que
j'ay a garder; et que se on m'a louée pour ce que je ay tiré d'un vo-
let par sus les tours de Nostre Dame, que je ne tasche pas a ferir la

live sinfully, and it is better to keep them from others if they do not
wish that others be kept from them. But this book is not for those
who wish to live well and simply without excessively embracing
920   worldly temptation, nor for those who do not wish to deceive others or be deceived by others. And, truly, I would rather be counted
among the opponents of his accomplices, because in my opinion it
is the wolf who will get the smallest gain. As the good nobleman
stated, who composed the above-mentioned complaint, "Would that
925   it had pleased God for this *Rose* never to have been planted in the
garden of Christendom!" Nonetheless, you call yourself one of his
disciples. Since this is what you say, so be it. As for me, I give up,
because I wish to attend to other nicer and more beneficial matters. I
am not alone in my opinion, and do not understand why you pay me
930   so much attention since it is not exactly an honor to attack the weakest party. There are so many wise theologians worthy of trust and
very knowledgeable, and, indeed, there are so many great princes in
this kingdom, and knights, nobles, and others who share my opinion
and think that reading this book is useless and shameful. Why do
935   you not go after the big branch of the tree and rip it out and get to
the root, from which you may suck the sap, rather than attacking the
little twigs on top, who have neither power nor virtue. You attack
me, who am no stronger than the voice of a little cricket which does
not cease flapping its wings and making a lot of noise, which never-
940   theless can never rival the delightful song of the great noble birds.

   You say that you cannot cease to "marvel at how anyone can
dare insult not only him but those who praise and love his book of
the *Rose*." My response: I cannot cease to marvel at how anyone can
dare praise this book, which contains enough topics to condemn the
945   human heart to damning horrors.

   You claim that you would prefer to be "reprimanded for
promoting his book than to be part of a group of the most skilled
critics." In this you are just like the one who said she would prefer
to be called *meretrix* by the one whom she loved loyally.

950   You claim that everyone knows that "there are still seven
thousand who are ready to defend him." My response: It is common
knowledge that a bad sect grows readily like weed, yet the greatest
quantity does not necessarily imply better quality. And if it pleases
God, he will stop this profusion. This book is hardly a decree of
955   faith. Each one may maintain what he wishes.

   You claim that had he been "contemporary to those of us who
insult him, we would have hated him particularly, yet we never saw

lune d'un bougion pesant, et que me garde de ressembler le corbel,
qui pour ce que on loua son chant, commenca a chanter plus hault
960   et laissa cheoir la buchete». Responce: vrayement je ne pourroie
d'aucune chose respondre si proprement comme de mon propre fait:
si puis en ceste partie tesmoingnier verité de certainne science. Tu
m'anjoins ou accuses comme de presompcion de moy mesmes: si
te jure sur ma foy que oncques ne presumay avoir si hault lengage
965 253v° comme // sus les tours Nostre Dame—ne sçay comment plus hault
tacheroie—; ne pour cuider hault chanter ne me cherra ja buchete.
Car je repute mon fait et mon savoir de nulle grandeur; autre chose
n'y a quelconques fors tant—je le puis bien dire veritablement—,
que j'aime l'estude et vie solitaire; et par frequenter et exerciter
970   ycellui peut bien estre que iey ay cueilli des basses flourettes du jardin delicieux, non pas monté sur les haulx arbres pour cueillir de ce
beau fruit odorent et savoureux (non mie que l'appetit et la voulenté
n'y soit grant, mais foiblece d'entendement ne le me seuffre); et
mesmes pour l'oudour des flourettes dont j'ay fait graisles chap-
975   pellés, ceulx qui les ont voulu avoir—a qui ne les osasse ne peusse
veer—, se sont esmervilliéz de mon labour, non pour grandeur qui
y fait, mais pour le cas nouvel qui n'est accoustumé: si ne s'en sont
mie teus,—non obstant ait esté loing temps cele, et te promet que a
ma resqueste n'est magnifestés. Et se veulx dire que aucunes choses
980   aye faites ou non de singulieres personnes, ce a esté depuis que ja en
estoit commune renommée. (Ce ne dis je pour nulle excusance, car
il n'en est besoing, mais pour oster toute oppinion qui pourroit estre
que en mon fait presumasse aucune auctorité.)

Et supplie toy et tes consors en oppinion: ne me sachés mau-
985   vais gré pour cause de mes escriptures et du present debat sus le
livre de la *Rose*. Car d'aventure avint le commencement et non mie
de voulenté proposée, quelque oppinion que je y eusse, ainsi comme
tu le peus veoir en un petit traictié ou je devisay le premier motif
et le derrenier terme de nostre debat. Et trop me seroit grief estre
990   subgette a tele servitute que n'osasse respondre a autrui verité selon
ma conscience de chose qui ne puet tourner a prejudice; ains peut
aviser plus sage de plus avant penser que il n'a consideré par lonc
temps, car comme dist un commun proverbe: «A la fois avise un fol
un sage».
995   Et c'est neant que tu dis que l'Esglise sainte, ou tant a eu de
vaillans hommes depuis qu'il fu fait, l'a souffert par lonc temps
sans reprendre (attendoit que moy et les autres le venissions rep-
roucher!): car tu sces que toutes chose sont meues a certain temps,

him. You cannot fathom where this hatred comes from." My response: Since we never saw him, nor did he ever harm us, you ought
960   to have even more reason to believe that we were motivated by pure
truth, because an enemy must not be believed. If not that, you say,
then it must come from the "noble status of the book, which attracts
the winds of the envious. For ignorance is not entirely to blame,
you say, nor an inadequate reading of it." My response: You may
965   rest assured that the good nobleman who insults it (you concede,
in fact, that this is not done out of ignorance) has no desire to read
this book, because, I think, the esteem of his noble life would lead
him to read more dignified things. As for me, my ignorance notwithstanding, I, too, have no wish to read it. And why would I? It makes
970   me feel neither cold nor hot, neither bad nor good. It does not offer
me anything, nor does it speak about any state to which I belong. I
am not married, nor do I have the hope of marrying;[65] I am not clois-
tered. I am not Fair Welcoming, nor am I afraid of the Duenna, nor
do I have rosebuds to guard. I promise you that I love beautiful and
975   skillful books which are well written, and it is those books I seek
and read voluntarily as simple as my understanding of them may be.
The reason I do not like the book of the *Rose* is simply that it consists of bad exhortation and is disgraceful reading, encouraging evil,
not good. And, according to my judgment, it is cause for damnation,
980   as it condemns the lives of those who hear it, take pleasure in it,
and feel tempted by shameful morals. I swear upon my soul and my
faith that this is my opinion. And when you say later on that perhaps
we reprimand it in order to incite more interest in it, which would
mean that our opinion of it is good, you may rest assured that this is
985   not our goal!

          After all this, you attribute more praise to me than you should,
for which I am grateful, and you ask me to keep "the honor which
I have to protect, and that even if I have been praised for having
shot a little arrow over the towers of Notre-Dame, that I not attempt
990   to hit the moon with a heavy cannon, and that I be careful not to
resemble the raven, who began singing even louder when his song
was admired, which caused him to drop his mouthful of food." My
response: Indeed, I could not choose anyone but myself for the perfect answer to this, which will be supported by the truth of experi-
995   ence. You accuse me of pretentiousness, but I swear upon my faith
that I never had any ambition of possessing language as elevated as
the towers of Notre-Dame, nor would I know how to acquire it, nor
would I sing so high that I might drop my food. Because I attribute

ne riens n'est lonc envers l'espace des ans; et souvent avient que
1000 par une pointelette est cure une grant enflure. Conment a souffert
l'Esglise sainte demourer si lonc temps l'oppinion de la concepcion
de Nostre Dame—qui plus est chose nottable—sans en reprendre
nullui? Et n'a gaires que ce qui n'avoit oncques esté debatu est venu
avant par si grant esmeute: et si n'est ce pas article de foy; aussi
1005 n'est cecy. Si en croye chacun ce qui lui plaist le mieulx et quant a
moy, plus n'en pense faire escripture, qui que m'en escripse, car je
n'ay pas empris toute Saine a boire: ce que j'ay escript est escript.
Non mie tairé pour doubte de mesprendre quant a oppinion, combien que faulte d'engin et de savoir me toult biau stile, mais mieulx
1010 me plaist excerciter en autre matiere a ma plaisance.
        Si prie tous ceulx qui mes petis dictiés verront, que ilz
254v° vuellent supployer le deffault de mon savoir par consideracion de
la personne, // et prendre tout a bonne fin et entencion pure,—sans
laquelle ne vouldroie aucune chose mettre avant. Si feray fin a
1015 mon dittié du debat non hayneux commencié, continué et finé par
maniere de soulas sans indignacion a personne. Si pry la Benoite
Trinité, parfaite et enterine sapience, qui vueille toy et tous ceulx
par especial qui aiment science et noblesce de bonnes meurs enlu-
miner de si vraye clarté que estre puissent conduis a la joie celes-
1020 tille.
        Amen.
        Escript et compleit par moy, Cristine de Pizan, le .iie . jour
d'octobre, l'an mil .IIII[C] . et deux.
        Ta bien vueillant amie de science,
1025   Cristine

no grandeur to my knowledge; it is solely the result—and this I
admit freely—of my love of learning and of a life of solitude. From
regular practice, I have perhaps harvested the lesser flowers of the
garden of delight, but I did not climb into high trees to harvest the
sweet-smelling and sweet-tasting fruit (albeit that the appetite and
the wish for it are great, but the weakness of my intelligence does
not allow it). And yet, although I would never have dared to show
them, those who wished my slender garlands for the smell of the
little flowers were amazed at my labor, not because of its grandeur
but because of its novelty, to which they were not accustomed. They
were not silent about it, though it had been hidden for a long time,
and I promise you that they did not respect my wish. And if you
suggest that I did certain things for certain individuals, this happened after I already enjoyed a public reputation. (I do not say this
as an excuse, because there is no need for that, but to put an end to
any opinion which might insinuate that I presume to have a certain
authority.)

I beg you and your supporters not to hold a grudge against
me for my writings and for the present debate about the book of
the *Rose*, because this was the fruit of coincidence and not a certain
intention, whatever my opinions may have been, as you may see in
a little treatise where I lay out in full all the terms of our debate.[66] I
would suffer too much to be subjected to such servitude, so much
that I did not dare respond to others according to the truth of my
conscience for fear that it could be construed as prejudice against
me. It is possible to counsel a wiser person to think more deeply
than before, as is expressed by this common proverb: "Sometimes
the fool can counsel a wise one."

Your argument is unfounded, that the Holy Church—where
there have been many noble men since the book's composition—has
for so long tolerated it without reprimand and was waiting for me
and others to refute it, because you know that everything ripens
at a certain moment and nothing is long in relation to the passing
of time, and it often happens that a great boil is cured by a small
needle. How long the Holy Church tolerated the opinion concerning
the conception of Our Lady, which is surprising, without reprimand-
ing anyone? And that which had never been debated suddenly created such upheaval. It was not out of faith, nor is this. One always
believes that which is the most pleasing. As for me, I will write no
more about this, no matter who writes to me because I have not
undertaken to drink the entire Seine. What I have written is written.

1040   Nor do I silence myself for fear of being slandered because of my
opinions, though I lack intelligence and a beautiful style. <u>I simply
wish to turn my attention to a topic which is more to my liking</u>. I
ask that all those who see my significant works excuse my lack of
knowledge out of consideration for my person, and take it for what

1045   it is and for its good intention, without which I would never write
a thing. Herewith, I close my ditty of this amicable debate, which I
started, carried and ended without wishing to offend anyone. I pray
to the Blessed Trinity, perfect and of supernal wisdom, that you and
all those who love knowledge and the nobility of good behavior will

1050   be enlightened by true clarity, which will lead to celestial joy.
        Amen.
        Written and finished by me, Christine de Pizan, the second
day of October of the year 1402.
        Your well meaning friend in knowledge,

1055   Christine

Notes

1. For a detailed description of the manuscripts which contain the Debate Epistles, I refer to the introduction of Eric Hicks's edition, *Le débat sur le Roman de la rose* (Geneva: Slatkine Reprints, 1996), lviii–lxi, lxx–lxxii, and xcvii–xcix.
2. The Debate Epistles are on folios 237ro to 254ro.
3. Joseph L. Baird and John R. Kane, trans., *La querelle de la rose*. Letters and Documents (Chapel Hill, NC: North Carolina Studies in the Romance Languages and Literatures, 1978). In addition to Charles Frederick Ward's first (flawed) edition of the Debate Epistles, *The Epistles on the Romance of the Rose and Other Documents in the Debate* (Chicago: University of Chicago Press, 1911), Baird and Kane used manuscripts Paris, BN f. fr. 835 and 1563 for their translation. They also had access to Eric Hicks's forthcoming edition at the time. For Jean Gerson's treatise they relied on the text by Ernest Langlois, "Le traictié d'une vision faite contre le Ronmant de la rose." *Romania* 45 (1919): 23–48, and the translations of Jean de Montreuil's Latin letters are based on Ezio Ornato's edition, *Jean de Montreuil. Opera*, vol. 1 (Turin: Giappichelli, 1963).
4. John V. Fleming, *The Roman de la Rose: A Study in Allegory and Iconography* (Princeton, NJ: Princeton University Press, 1969).
5. D. W. Robertson, *A Preface to Chaucer* (Princeton, NJ: Princeton University Press, 1962).
6. Baird and Kane make reference to Piaget's article "Chronologie des Epistres sur le Roman de la Rose," in *Etudes romanes dédiées à Gaston Paris* (Paris: Bouillon, 1891), on page 12 of their work. Potansky's *Der Streit um den Rosenroman* (Munich: Fink, 1972) is mentioned on page 13. For the revised chronology, see Eric Hicks, *Le débat*, li–liv.
7. C. F. Ward, *The Epistles*, 28.
8. The variants with respect to manuscript Paris BN ms. fr. 12779 are indicated in appendix A. This manuscript dates from the beginning of the fifteenth century and was used by Eric Hicks as base manuscript for the debate epistles which occupy folios 141vo to 149ro. Orthographic changes are not noted. In Harley 4431 the letter from Christine de Pizan to the Queen can be found on fol. 237ro.
9. As is well known, manuscript British Library Harley 4431 was dedicated to Queen Isabeau de Bavière (1371–1435), wife of Charles VI for whom Christine had a great deal of admiration. The frontispiece of Harley 4431 depicts the scene where Christine in a humble position hands her manuscript to the queen. The importance of Charles VI's wife for Christine is confirmed by her famous *Epistre a la reine* (1405) and the later *Lamentations sur les maux de la France* (1410) where she addresses the queen symbolically in the role of "mother" of her children, that is, the citizens of France (see Bernard Ribémont, "Christine de Pizan et la figure de la mère," in *Christine de Pizan 2000. Studies on Christine de Pizan in Honour of Angus J. Kennedy*, ed. John Campbell and Nadia Margolis (Amsterdam: Rodopi, 2000), 149–62. For the edition of the *Epistre a la reine see Liliane Dulac, "L'Epistre a la reine,"* in *Christine de Pizan*, ed. Liliane Dulac and Jean Dufournet, special issue, *Revue des langues romanes* 92, no.2 (1988): 253–64; and for the *Lamentations*, Angus J. Kennedy, "La lamentacion sur les maux de la France de Christine de Pisan," in *Mélanges de la langue et littérature françaises du moyen âge et de la Renaissance offerts à Monsieur Charles Foulon*, vol. 10 (Paris: Institut de français, Université de Haute-Bretagne, 1980), 177–85.
10. See chap. 5.4, 412.
11. The *humilitas topos* was common for writers of Christine's time and not only limited to female writers. We find the same expressions or similar ones in the letters composed by Christine's male counterparts; for example, in Pierre Col's letter to Christine and Jean Gerson (see chap. 4.6, 306 and 307).
12. For Christine's other references to the *Roman de la rose*, prior to this epistle, see chap 2.B. In chronological order they are the *Epistre au dieu d'amours* (1399), *Les enseignemens moraux que Cristine donne a son filz* (1399–1400), and *Le livre du débat de deux amans* (1400).
13. The day of Candlemas, February 2, commemorates the occasion when the Virgin Mary in obedience to Jewish law, went to the Temple in Jerusalem both to be purified forty days after

the birth of her son and to present Jesus to God as her firstborn (Luke 2:22–38). The correct year however is 1402 instead of 1401: As Thelma Fenster and Mary Carpenter Erler explain, "Christine and her contemporaries dated the beginning of the year at the movable feast of Easter, following a practice introduced more than two centuries earlier by King Philip Augustus"; *Poems of Cupid, God of Love. Christine de Pizan's Epistre au dieu d'Amours and Dit de la rose, Thomas Hoccleve's the Letter of Cupid,* ed., trans. Thelma Fenster and Mary Carpenter Erler (Leiden: Brill, 1990), 129. Since this letter was composed in February, the year would actually be 1402.

14. These explanations led to Gontier Col's first letter to Christine. This explanatory note occupies fol. 237vo of Harley 4431.

15. // indicates the beginning of a new folio in the manuscript.

16. The first entry where Jean de Quatre Mares appears as counselor of the Parliament of Paris has been identified by Félix Aubert as November 24, 1386 in Archives Nationales, X.1a34, fol. 196vo and for Jean Porchier as April 27, 1387 in *Archives Nationales,* X.1a34, fol. 247vo; in *Le Parlement de Paris. De Philippe le Bel à Charles VII (1314–1422). Sa compétence, ses attributions* (Geneva: Slatkine, 1977, 341).

17. The small treatise refers to the *opusculum gallicum,* the treatise written by Jean de Montreuil about the *Roman* in May or June 1401, which is unfortunately lost to us today. Thanks to Christine's meticulous reply to this treatise, we have been provided, albeit implicitly, with a summary of its content.

18. The "especial clerc soubtil" has been identified as Nicolas de Clamanges (see Pierre-Yves Badel, *Le roman de la rose au XIVe siècle. Etude de la réception de l'œuvre* (Geneva: Droz, 1980), 412.

19. The fact that Christine admits that she did not read the *Roman* in its entirety will later on become a significant point of contention in Pierre Col's reply to both Christine and Jean de Gerson (see chap. 4.6, 336 and 339).

20. This term has been coined by Eustache Deschamps and designates a rhyme scheme where a rhyme covers a full syllable: see *Eustache Deschamps. Selected Poems,* ed. Ian S. Laurie and Deborah M. Sinnreich-Levi (New York: Routledge, 2002), 31.

21. Much has been written on Lady Reason's lengthy defense of naming the male and female genitalia without euphemism, starting with Alan Gunn, *The Mirror of Love. A Reinterpretation of The Romance of the Rose* (Lubbock, TX: Texas Technical Press, 1952); Daniel Poirion, "Les mots et les choses selon Jean de Meun," *L'information littéraire* 26 (1974): 7–11 and "De la signification selon Jean de Meun," in *Archéologie du signe,* ed. Lucie Brind'Amour and Eugene Vance (Toronto: Pontifical Institute of Medieval Studies, 1983), 165–85; John F. Fleming, *Reason and the Lover* (Princeton, NJ: Princeton University Press, 1984); David Hult, "Language and Dismemberment: Abelard, Origen, and the Romance of the Rose," in *Rethinking the Romance of the Rose. Text, Image, Reception,* ed. Kevin Brownlee and Sylvia Huot (Philadelphia: University of Pennsylvania Press, 1992), 101–30; Eric Hicks, "Situation du débat sur le *Roman de la rose,*" in *Une femme de lettres au moyen âge. Etudes autour de Christine de Pizan,* ed. Liliane Dulac and Bernard Ribémont (Orléans, France: Paradigme, 1995), 51–67; 56; David Hult, "Words and Deeds: Jean de Meun's *Romance of the Rose* and the Hermeneutics of Censorship," *New Literary History. A Journal of Theory and Interpretation* 28, no.2 (1997): 345–66; and A. J. Minnis, *Magister amoris. The Roman de le rose and Vernacular Hermeneutics* (Oxford: Oxford University Press, 2001), 119–63.

22. In Matt. 21:31: "Meretrices praecedent vos in regnum Dei" and in Luke, 15: 30: "Devoravit substantiam suam cum meretricibus." Etymology: Latin *meretric-, meretrix* prostitute, from *merēre* to earn.

23. Even though the expression *custom* may sound archaic, I frequently opted for this expression rather than using synonyms such as *practice.*

24. In her discussion on words and their meaning, Lady Reason stresses the arbitrariness of the sign and the absence of relation between word and thing as she admits that "coilles" ("cullions") could be called "reliques" ("relics") or vice versa. Let us not forget that *reliques* is the term used

later on in the narrative to describe the sacred, untouched vagina of the young virgin. For criti-
cal analyses of this passage, see Daniel Poirion, "Les mots et les choses selon Jean de Meun,"
Information littéraire 26 (1974): 7–11; and Christine McWebb, "Hermeneutics of Irony: Lady
Reason and the *Romance of the Rose*," *Dalhousie French Studies*, 69 (2004): 3–14.

25. According to the Book of Jeremiah of the Old Testament, the prophet began his career in 627–26,
     the thirteenth year of King Josiah's reign. It is told there that he responded to Yahweh's call to
     prophesy by protesting, "I do not know how to speak, for I am only a youth."

26. For a contextualization of the antifeminine tradition in the Middle Ages, I refer to Alcuin Blamires,
     The Case of Women in Medieval Culture (Oxford: Clarendon Press, 1997); and *Woman Defamed
     and Woman Defended: An Anthology of Medieval Texts*, ed. Alcuin Blamires, Karen Pratt, and
     Marx C. William (Oxford: Clarendon Press, 1992).

27. See chap. 2.B.1.

28. The list of female biblical exempla will appear again in some of Christine's subsequent works,
     most notably in the *Livre de la cité des dames* (book 2, chapters 31, 32, 38, 39).

29. The choice of contemporary women of power is not a coincidence. As pointed out in the
     introduction, Christine was very much aware of the consequences for female regency of the
     infamous Salic Law evoked by Jean de Montreuil. All three queens were living proof in one
     way or another of these consequences: Queen Jeanne has been identified by Eric Hicks as
     Jeanne d'Evreux (1310–71), third wife and widow of Charles IV. She bore her husband three
     daughters who were barred from the throne after the death of their father in 1328, thus opening
     the way for the ascension of Philippe VI to the throne. Queen Blanche has been incorrectly
     identifed by Suzanne Solente (Suzanne Solente, ed., *Le livre des fais et bonnes meurs su sage
     roy Charles V*, 2 vols [1936–40 ; repr. Geneva: Slatkine Reprints, 1977]) as Queen Blanche de
     Navarre (1331–98), second wife of Philippe VI. In the *Livre de la cité des dames* (I.13), however,
     the phrase "feu femme du roy Jehan" has been added to the description of this woman which
     would identify her as Bonne de Luxembourg, wife of Jean II, and the mother of Charles V and
     mother-in-law of Marie de Châtillon who died in 1349, a year before Jean II was crowned king.
     The confusion of Blanche and Bonne is understandable because of the third name: the Duchess
     of Orléans was Blanche of France (1328–93), wife of Philippe of Orléans and oldest surviving
     daughter of Charles IV and Jeanne d'Evreux. This would make her female heir to the throne
     through the female line. Like the other two, she is mentioned also in Earl Jeffrey Richards and
     Patrizia Caraffi ed. and trans., *Livre de la Cité des dames* (Milan: Luni Editrice, 1998), 1:13;
     Charity Cannon Willard and Eric Hicks, eds., *Livre des Trois vertus* (Paris: Champion, 1989),
     1:9, 23; and Eric Hicks and Thérèse Moreau, eds., *Livre des fais et bonnes meurs du sage roy
     Charles V* (Paris: Stock, 1997): for Jeanne d'Evreux, 3:xxxv, 254; Bonne de Luxembourg, 3:
     xliii, 273; Blanche de Navarre, queen of France, 3:l, 281; also see *Le débat*, 202.

30. According to Eric Hicks, my lady of Ferté was Jeanne de Chastillon, third daughter of Gaucher
     de Châtillon and the lady of Rosay in Thiérache. She married Pierre Craon, lord of Sablé and
     La Ferté-Bernard. In 1410, she took Louis II and Marie de Bretagne to court with the aim of
     recovering a portion of her possessions which had been confiscated after the assassination at-
     tempt on Clisson. She is said to have died in 1433 (*Le débat*, 203).

31. Jean de Meun proposes the term *Mirror for Lovers* as an alternative title for his continuation of
     the *Roman*. The term *mirror* inserts the *Roman* in the framework of the didactic genre alongside
     the numerous contemporary mirrors for princes and princesses. The reference here is to Jean
     de Monreuil's lost treatise; however, it does come up again in one of his Latin epistles, the *Ut
     sunt mores* (see chap. 4.1).

32. This is the first mention of a possible accusation of heresy by Christine which will become a
     recurrent threat uttered by her and Jean Gerson.

33. This word replaces *excepcion* in BN fr. 12779. Since *excercitacion* makes no sense here, I also
     used *exception* in the translation.

34. This is a misquote of "sciut ethnicus et publicanus" in Matt., 18:16–17.

35. The epistles about the *Roman de la Rose* of BN fr. 12779 end here with "Explicit les epistres
     sus *Le Rommant de la Rose*." Christine's correspondence with Pierre Col was added only later
     in manuscript Harley 4431.

36.   This friend is in all likelihood Pierre d'Ailly who, as we can see, does not share Jean de Montreuil's enthusiasm for the *Roman* (see chap. 4.4).

37.   See note 34.

38.   Pierre Col's letter was written in the summer of 1402 (see chap. 4.6). The correspondence between Christine and Pierre Col has been checked against manuscript Paris BN fr. 1563 (beginning of fifteenth century, the Debate epistles are on fols 178ro to 199ro) used by Eric Hicks as his base manuscript. This letter to Pierre Col was written on October 2, 1402 by Christine in response to Pierre Col's letter to her at the end of the summer of 1402. In that letter Pierre reacts to (a) Christine's epistle to Jean de Montreuil and (b) Jean Gerson's treatise against the *Roman de la Rose*. This first letter of Pierre's is not in Harley 4431 but it is in BN fr. 1563.

39.   This is a quote from the *Roman*, which the allegory of Reason in Jean Gerson's "Ecole de la raison" takes up: "Je vous deffens a tous ensemble la male escole d'iniquité,/car il y pert qui si assemble/temps, sens, purté, los, verité." [I forbid all of you the evil school of injustice, for he who frequents it will lose learning, sense, time, soul, body, and reputation]. For a complete edition of this dialogue of 149 lines including the "Complainte de la Conscience," I refer to Msgr. Palémon Glorieux, ed. *Jean Gerson. Oeuvres complètes*, 7 vols. (Paris: Desclée, 1960), 1:103–11; my translation.

40.   According to A. J. Minnis, the adjective "propre" and, in particular its adverb "proprement" in the context of language use and naming things, should be read in the sense of "literal" versus "figurative"; that is, "impropre," or "impropria." Whenever "proper" and "properly" are used in conjunction with naming things or speaking "properly," it is this connotation that is inferred. For a detailed study of these terms, I refer to A. J. Minnis, *Magister amoris,* chap. 3.

41.   The venerated cleric is Jean Gerson. His treatise condemning the *Roman* was published on May 18, 1402. Gerson also takes offense at the obscene language used by Jean de Meun's Lady Reason. Even years after the exchange of letters, in 1414, he reminds his readers of this controversial issue: "Considerons jouxte ces choses que furent jadis aucuns philosophes qui commandoient a aler nus comme chiens et bestes, a nommer toutes choses par leur propre nom sans honte; du quel fol erreur fu le compileur du vicieux Romant de la Rose." [Let us consider such things as philosophers who in former times commanded us to walk naked like dogs and beasts and to name all things by their proper name without shame. The compiler of the vicious *Roman de la rose* was guilty of this foolish error] (*Jean Gerson. Oeuvres complètes*, 1:97 "Considérons mon ame d'or en avant." The translation is mine). It is interesting to note that Gerson refers to Jean de Meun as a compiler and not as an author in his own right.

42.   Christine refers to Jean Gerson's treatise and Pierre Col's subsequent rebuttal (chap. 4.5,6).

43.   This intertextual remark as well those which follow are all quotes from Pierre Col's response to Christine and Jean Gerson in chap. 4.6.

44.   For an edition of this text see Silvia Buzzetti Gallarati, ed. *Le Testament Maistre Jehan de Meun: un caso letterario* (Alessandria, Italy: Ed. dell'Orso, 1989).

45.   In addition to the works listed by the author himself in the prologue to his translation of Boethius's *Consolation of Philosophy* (see note 47), are also his *Sept articles de la foy et proverbes dorés*: "Cy finist ce présent livre nommé les Sept articles de la foy et les Proverbes dorez, avec aucunes remonstrances que fait maistre Jehan de Meung au roy, son souverain seigneur. Imprimé à Paris le .XX. jour de septembre, l'an mil .V. cens et .III., pour Antoine Vé, marchant libraire...." [Here ends the present book titled the Sept articles de la foy et les Proverbes dorez, with exhortation from Master Jean de Meun to the King, his Sovereign Lord. Printed in Paris, the 20th day of September, 1503 for Antoine Vé, merchant bookseller] (published in Paris, 1503). According to Hicks and Lecoy, the *Tresor de Jean de Meun*, which is the alternate title of the *Sept articles*, is in reality the work of Jean Chapuis (see *Le débat*, 198–199 and Lecoy, 1:x, n. 1).

46.   To my knowledge, there is no indication of this attribution anywhere.

47.   "A ta royal majesté, trés noble prince, par la grace de Dieu roy de France, Philippe le Quart, je, Jehan de Meun, qui jadis ou Romant de la Rose, puis que Jalousie ot mis en prison Bel Acueil, enseignay la maniere du chastel prandre et de la rose cuillir, et translatay de latin en françoiz le livre de Vegece De chevalerie, et le livre des Merveilles d'Irlande, et la Vie et les Epistres maistre Pierre Abarrelart et Heloÿs sa femme, et le livre Aelied De espirituel amistié, envoye ores

Boece De consolacion, que je t'ay translaté de latin en françois, jaçoit ce que tu entendes bien latin, maiz toutevoies est moult plus legier a entendre le françoiz que le latin." [To your Royal Majesty, very Noble Prince, King of France through the mercy of God, Philippe IV, I, Jean de Meun, who previously taught the way to take the castle and to pick the rose in the *Roman de la rose* since Jalousy emprisoned Fair Welcoming, and I, who translated from Latin into French the book of Vegetius *De chevalerie* and the book of the *Merveilles d'Irlande*, the *Vie* and the *Epistres* by master Peter Abelard and Heloise his wife, and the book by Aelred *De espirituel amistié*, send you now Boethius's *De consolacion* which I have translated for you from Latin into French. Although you understand Latin well, it is nevertheless easier to understand French than Latin.]; Isabelle Bétemps, Michèle Guéret-Laferté, Nicolas Lenoir, Sylvain Louis, Jean Maurice, Carmelle Mira, eds., *La consolation de la Philosophie de Boèce. Dans une traduction attribuée à Jean de Meun d'après le manuscrit Leber 817 de la Bibliothèque municipale de Rouen* (Rouen, France: Les Publications de l'Université de Rouen, 2004), 5; my translation). As specified by the editors, two of the translations listed here are lost today, the translation of *De amicitia spirituali* by Aelred de Rievaulx and of the *Topographia hibernica* by Giraut de Barri, which Jean de Meun titles *Livre des Merveilles d'Irlande* (5, note 1).

48.   As pointed out by Eric Hicks, Christine knew the *Summa perfectionis* by Geber which she cites in her *Livre des faits et bonnes meurs du roi Charles V le Sage*, eds. Eric Hicks and Thérèse Moreau (Paris: Stock, 1997), 3:lxiv, 299. (See also *Le débat*, 223).

49.   See note 39.

50.   In Barbara Altmann, ed., *The Love Debate Poems of Christine de Pizan* (*Le livre du Debat de deux amans, Le livre des Trois jugements, Le Livre du Dit de Poissy*) (Gainesville: University Press of Florida, 1998), ll:1569–85: "Bertrand du Guesclin (1320–80) was a military hero who began his brilliant career in the siege of Rennes (1356–57). He was advisor to King Jean II and then high constable and commander in chief of France (1370–80) under Charles V. Du Guesclin's skill in using guerilla warfare tactics to curtail the English incursions into France and to deal with the brigands that plagued the country in the mid-fourteenth century enabled him to advance rapidly in the king's services. He is also reputed to have been a model of chivalric behavior and to have set a standard for knightly conduct" (149). For further information on du Guesclin see also Michael Jones, ed. *Letters, Orders and Musters of Bertrand du Guesclin 1357–1380* (New York: Boydell Press, 2004). Christine evidently was a great admirer of this man since she also dedicates several chapters to him in her *Livre des faits et bonnes moeurs du roi Charles V.* In addition, she traces a portrait of him in BN fr. 603, fol. 7ro et vo of the *Livre des fais d'armes* (see *Le débat*, 224).

51.   Maurice de Trésguidi (alt. Trisguidis, Terriguidis) was one of the Breton squires at the battle of Trente, see *Le débat*, 224–25.

52.   "Obsequium amicos, veritas odium parit" (Andros). Jean de Montreuil also refers to this quote in his epistle 119: "quoniam ab alio de stili ruditate et incomptu, ab alio de materia (que sue ratione veritatis nonnullis odium pareret)…." (chap. 4.1, 204 and 205).

53.   The "other epistle" Christine refers to is in all likelihood her long letter to Jean de Montreuil. Pierre Col did in fact respond to this letter in his reply to Christine and Jean Gerson at the end of the summer of 1402 (chap. 4.6).

54.   Jean de Meun used the same example in order to exonerate himself of having pronounced bawdy words. Lucius Sergius Catilina (108–62 BC) was an aristocrat in the late Roman Empire. His zealous pursuit of power drove him to attempt to overthrow the republic, albeit unsuccessfully.

55.   Eccli., XLII,14: "Melior est enim iniquitas viri quam mulier benefaciens."

56.   Judith like Esther is an example of a virtuous, beautiful widow who rescues her people through her female power of seduction when she enters Holofernes's tent and succeeds in cutting off the besieger's head after she gets him very drunk. Christine de Pizan repeatedly uses this story in her works to demonstrate female courage.

57.   Christine refers to Jean Gerson.

58. Ilion is of course the Hellenized name for the city of Troy.
59. Christine also recommends reading this book in her *Enseignements moraux* (chap. 2.B.2).
60. The Harley manuscript reads "bone" but MS fr. 12779 uses "Boethius." Christine repeatedly refers to Boethius's *Consolation of Philosophy* as an auctoritas, for instance in the *Le livre du chemin de long estude*, ed. Andrea Tarnowski (Paris: Lettres gothiques, 2000), ll:206–208, 278–94, 4125–130, 4636–643, 4841–860, 5117–128, 5955–960), as well as in *Le livre de l'advision Cristine*, ed. Christine Reno and Liliane Dulac (Paris: Champion, 2000), 63–103,132–33, 136, 138.
61. The negation "ne" has been omitted in the Harley manuscript. It needed to be translated as a negative, however, to preserve the correct meaning of Christine's statement.
62. Christine's admiration of Dante's works has long since been established by Jeffrey Richards and others; see in particular Richards, "Christine de Pizan and Dante: A Reexamination," *Archiv für das Studium der Neueren Sprachen und Literaturen* 222 (1985): 100–11. Further, I refer to Kevin Brownlee's reprinted article "Literary Genealogy and the Problem of the Father: Christine de Pizan and Dante," in *Dante Now: Current Trends in Dante Studies*, ed. Theodore J. Cachey (Notre Dame, IN: University of Notre Dame Press, 1995), 205–35; Sylvia Huot, "Seduction and Sublimation: Christine de Pizan, Jean de Meung and Dante," *Romance Notes* 25, no.3 (1985): 361–73; and Lionello Fiumi, "La fortune de Dante en France de Christine de Pisan à Saint-John Perse," *Bulletin de la Société d'Etudes dantesques du Centre universitaire méditerranéen* 16 (1967): 33–45. Moreover, in the *Chemin de longue etude* Christine explicitly mentions Dante as her source of the "chemin de lonc estude" as the place where all noble hearts and intelligent souls meet:

    > Mais le nom du plaisant pourpris
    > Oncques mais ne me fu appris,
    > Fors en tant que bien me recorde
    > Que Dant de Florence recorde
    > En son livre qu'il composa
    > Ou il moult beau stile posa ....

    [But the name of this pleasant enclosure, I never learned, because if my memory serves me correctly, Dante of Florence recorded it in his book which he composed and where he explained in a most beautiful style....] (in Andrea Tarnowski, ed. *Le chemin de longue étude* (Paris: Lettres gothiques, 2000),154, ll :1125–30; my translation).
63. According to Eric Hicks, the glosses of Orléans are an ancient proverb of which an example in Latin has been identified as cited by Le Roux de Lincy in 1307. See *Le débat*, 227 for a possible interpretation.
64. For further information on this sect in the context of the Quarrel, see Christine McWebb, "Heresy and Debate: Reading the Roman de la Rose," *Aevum* 77 (2003): 545–56.
65. Christine was widowed in 1390 when her husband, Etienne de Castel, died in an epidemic, probably the plague. He was thirty-four and Christine twenty-five years old.
66. See this chapter no.2.

Chapter Four

The Architectonics of Voices (1401–1404)

The following letters and excerpts are very much an integral part of the debate proper; however, Christine de Pizan did not include them in the compilation of manuscript Harley 4431. It is for this reason that I decided to present them in a separate chapter under separate headings. I include here, among other texts, Jean de Montreuil's Latin epistles dealing with the *Roman* as well as Jean Gerson's treatise against the *Roman de le rose* and excerpts from his series of sermons entitled *Poenitemini*.[1]

Note on Translations

All of Jean de Montreuil's epistles and Jean Gerson's treatise "Talia de me" were translated by Earl Jeffrey Richards. It was our aim to reproduce with as much accuracy as possible the complex syntax of the Latin originals. As a result, these translations are frequently characterized by long sentences with multiple subordinate clauses. This should not be viewed as a stylistic inadequacy, but rather as an attempt to remain as faithful as possible to Jean de Montreuil's and Jean Gerson's composition styles.

1. May–June/July, 1401: Epistles by Jean de Montreuil (1354–1418)[2]

This first group of epistles by Jean de Montreuil (epistles 103, 118, 119, 120, 121, and 122) was composed during the early summer months of 1401 and is included in the collection of letters prepared for Nicolas de Clamanges between 1405 and 1407 in manuscript Bibliothèque Nationale lat. 13062. These letters form a thematically homogeneous group as they all address Jean de Meun's *Roman de la rose* in one form or another. The addressee of epistle 103 is Pierre d'Ailly to whom the provost of Lille sent, together with this letter, the lost treatise on the *Roman*, the *opusculum gallicum*. It was composed at the end of May 1401, and offers explanations as to why Jean de Montreuil chose to read the *Roman de la rose*: he was motivated by his colleague and friend

Gontier Col who urged him enthusiastically to turn his attention to this work. The time seemed right as the provost had just returned from Germany and was enjoying what we would consider a sabbatical today, referred to during this time as an *otium*.[3]

Text:

Epistle 103[4]

67v°   Cum, ut dant sese res, nichil ut melius scribam occurrat, pater
              mi perquamreverendissime, ne esse velim rumorum dictator aut quia
              id supra et contra officium nostrum est, ut sic dicam, novellicans, en
              Gonthero nuper me hortante—quin potius impellente!—a me *Rose*
5   videri *Romantium,* cucurri legique quamavidissime, et actoris inge-
              nium quantum conicere datum est impetusque tulit, gallica scrip-
              tione, prout in annexo presentibus Vestra reverendissima videbit
              Paternitas, designavi.
                   Vestrum ergo fuerit, domine mi, an nimium aut minus debito
10   seu cum temperamento actorem laudaverim decernere, ac nichilomi-
              nus vestro huic adoptivo, modo altiores occupationes vestre sinant,
              intimare si quedam ad thesaurarium nostrum Lingonensem citra
              dies aliquot a me manans rescriptio, Vestre usque ad Dominationis
              lectionem deventa sit.
15   Valete et plaudite.

Translation:

Since, as things stand, it happens that I cannot write anything better, my most reverend father, nor would I wish to spread rumors, and since this goes above and against our office, as I would say, while I was clearing new ground with Gontier [Col] who recently

5   urged—in fact rather forced—me to look at the *Roman de la rose*, I ran through it and read it as diligently as possible. And in a French work, which you, most reverend father, will see attached to this letter, I describe how much material the author's genius was able to assemble and how much material his vigor as author supported.

10   It will be up to you, my Master, to determine whether I will have praised this author too much or less than what is due, or with balance, and then to indicate nonetheless to your adoptive son in this matter—should your loftier duties permit—whether a particular written reply stemming from me several days ago to our treasurer of

15   Langres has reached the reading of your Lordship.
Take care and send your approval.

***

The following letter was composed at the end of July or the beginning of
August, 1401. It was addressed to the same advocate to whom Jean de Montreuil
also sent epistle 122 in an effort to have a negative judgment against the *Roman
de la rose* overturned or at least modified.

Text:

Epistle 118[5]

84v°   Quo magis magisque perscrutor, vir acutissime, misteriorum
pondera ponderumque misteria operis illius profundi ac memorie
percelebris a magistro Johanne de Magduno editi, et ingenium accu-
ratius revolvitur artificis; totus quippe in ammirationem commoveor
5   et accendor quo instinctu quove spiritu seu mente tu precipue, qui
inter civiles actiones omni die versaris (que maxime ex electione
sana pendent et ubi precipitur tarde et cum gravitate de rebus ferre
sententiam), eundem disertissimum ac scientificissimum actorem
leviter nimis, scurriliterve aut inepte loquutum fuisse censuisti, et
10   quasi in pretorio causam ageres, nudiustertius contra mortuum verba
faciens, debachando iurgabaris, in inventione nichilominus atque
claritate proprietateque et elegantia magistrum Guillelmum de Lorris longius anteponens,—de quo tunc, certa motus consideratione,
85r°   exclamare // pretermisi, et nunc linquam.
15   Sed si amodo serio dixisse fatearis, «dic quo pignore certes:
veniam, ut ait Virgilius, quocumque vocaris», ut qui magistros et
benefactores meos ad extremum usque singultum non desero, aut
suo in honore—quoad potero—sinam ledi. Sin vero, ut potius reor,
ioco protuleris, aut forsan motus aliunde, non adeo feroces sumus
20   ut que sit in disputando libertas ignoremus, aut lingue vertibilitati
non noverimus indulgere; immo, quia altercando scitur veritas,
«aurumque probatur in fornace», de industria ingenuissimi doctoris
huius concedo disputare,—ita tamen ut nichil imposterum cum
obstinatione adversus imitatorem nostrum asseveres.
25   Vale, et intimato super hoc quid intendis: qui si pergis de
preceptore nostro ulterius male loqui, non est quod dissimulare
queamus. Hanc ex nunc pro diffidentia suscipito; sunt etenim, ne in
dubium revoces, pugilis et atlethe non pauci, qui scripto voceque et
manu pariter, ut est posse, causam istam defensabunt.

Translation:

          The more and more I examine, O most discerning man, the treasures of the mysteries and the mysteries of the treasures of this profound work, celebrated in memory, and composed by Jean de Meun, the more accurately the genius of its makers becomes appar-

5   ent. I am entirely moved to admiration, and intrigued by what instigation or by what spirit or mind you, who concern yourself daily with cases of civil law—which altogether depend on sound choice and where it is taught to bring judgment on matters slowly and with seriousness—have judged that this same most learned and most

10   knowledgeable author has spoken too lightly or scurrilously and foolishly, and as though you were prosecuting a case in the palace, speaking against a dead man the day before yesterday, and raging, you have reproached him, preferring all the while Master Guillaume de Lorris in matters of creativity, clarity, propriety, and elegance,

15   about whom, at the time, moved by a certain consideration, I failed to comment and from which I will now desist.

          But if you were to confess that you spoke seriously, "tell me what the stakes are for which you will fight, and I will go wherever you are summoned," as Virgil said,[6] for to the last breath I will not

20   desert my masters and benefactors, nor will I let them be wounded in their honor, as best as I can. However, if indeed, as I would rather judge, you said these things as a joke, or perhaps were motivated by someone else, we are not that savage that we forget what freedom is permitted in debates, or that we cannot indulge in verbal volubility;

25   on the contrary, since the truth becomes known through disputing, and "the gold is tested in the furnace,"[7] I will permit a judgment about the diligence of this most ingenuous doctor, provided, however, that you make no claims imposed with obstinancy against our imitator.[8]

30   Take care and inform me what you intend to do about this: If you proceed to speak further ill of our teacher, we are unable to conceal what this is. You may take this for distrust, or indeed, lest you doubt, there are many boxers and wrestlers who would, in writing and in speech, as well as with their hands, defend this cause.

***

This letter was composed at the same time as the previous one and was sent to a prelate together with a copy of the treatise on the *Roman de la rose*. It is interesting to note that Jean de Montreuil appeals to the "venerate father" (pater venerande) to keep his treatise in the vernacular a secret for fear of falling into ill repute. This fear was justified in his mind on the one hand because he chose to write it in French but probably also because de Montreuil felt leery about its controversial content. Consequently, he was not prepared to publicize his positive views on the *Roman*.

Text:

Epistle 119[9]

85r°   Ex quo nugis datum est meis tanti esse, pater reverende, quod eas
       Vestra Dominatio visere dignatur et expetit, ecce cum michi vestris
       obsecundare preceptis congruum sit pergrandisque arrogantia renu-
       ere, huiusmodi nugas vobis mitto, tali pacto, pater mi confidentis-
5   sime, ne cuiquam communicentur: quoniam ab alio de stili ruditate
       et incomptu, ab alio de materia (que sue ratione veritatis nonnullis
       odium pareret), aut de levitate scurrilitateve in eo quod vulgari
       sermone editum est reprehendi possem vel notari,—potissime quia
       genus assolet humanum potius ambigua depravare quam in
10 85v° partem // capere meliorem. Sed nichil est quod vestre fidelitatis
       prudentie non submitterem, alteri per omnia tanquam michi.
           Valete, fidentissime pater, et ut stulticias verbales meas
       sepenumero tulistis, ita has ineptias litterales benigniter supportate.

Translation:

  Since, most reverend father, so much estime has been given to my trifles that your Lordship requests and deigns to go and look at them, here they are, as it is fitting for me to act in compliance with your instructions and would be enormously arrogant to refuse. I

5 send trifles of this kind to you in the understanding, my most confident father, that they will be communicated to no one else because I could be reproached and censured in part due to their coarse and unpolished style, and in part due to their subject matter (because telling the truth provokes hate from several people)[10] or due to their

10 lightness and scurrility because they are written in the vernacular; above all because the human species is accustomed more to distort ambiguities than to take them in the best sense. But there is nothing I would not submit to the prudence of your loyalty, as if it were another me.

15 Take care, most faithful father, and since you have repeatedly born with my verbal silliness, in the same way kindly bear with this literary foolishness.

***

The addressee of this letter is Gontier Col to whom the provost sent at the same time a copy of epistle 118 as a call for help and support. The date of composition is the same as that of the previous two letters. The tone and content of this letter confirm the provost's fear of being accused of heresy. His partisan's support would therefore be very welcome indeed.

Text:

Epistle 120[11]

85v°   Scis me, consideratissime magister atque frater, iugi hortatu tuo et
       impulsu nobile illud opus magistri Johannis de Magduno, *Roman-*
       tium de Rosa vulgo dictum, vidisse: qui, quia de ammirabili arti-
       ficio, ingenio ac doctrina tecum sisto—et irrevocabiliter me fateor
5   permansurum—, a plurimis scolasticis non parve autoritatis viris,
       supraquam credibile tibi foret, male tractor et arguor amarissime, ut
       si ulterius defendere coner, plane me probare velint, ut dicunt, here-
       ticum. Nec pretendere prodest te totque viros alios valentes scienti-
       ficos et perdoctos illum tanti fecisse pene ut colerent, utque quam eo
10   carere mallent camisia et nichilominus nostris correctoribus ante-
       ponere suos emulos, qui, si quid reprehensionis inesset, adeo magni
       erant ut librum suum vivere nequaquam permisissent una hora. Nec
       eos iuvat insuper obsecrare—quod ius omne poscit—ut prius vide-
       ant notentque quamobcausam, qua dependentia et occasione dicat
15   res, quas personas introducat, quam damnetur tantus auctor; sed
       confestim verba intercipiunt mea interrumpuntque, ut labra movere
       vix audeam: quin michi anathematis obprobrium comminentur, ac
       ferme iudicent reum mortis.
            Quid vis dicam? Tantis, quod me magis urit, magistrum nos-
20   trum prosequuntur maledictis ut ignem potius quam lecturam
       meruisse attestentur, «seque inexpiabili scelere contaminare ex-
86r°   istimant si quitquam // audierint; cumque rursus iure humani-
       tatis submissius expostulo ut non prius damnent quam universa
       cognoverint», ostendendo quod «etiam sacrilegis et proditoribus
25   veneficis potestas defendendi sui datur», quodque «nec predamnari
       quemquam incognita causa licet», nichil agimus tamen, frater hon-
       oratissime, sed tempus terendo incassum acra verberamus, «nec est
       quod speremus posse aliquid impetrare, tanta est hominum pertina-
       cia». Hi sunt mores, ea dementia! «Timent enim ne, a nobis revicti,
30   manus dare aliquando, clamante ipsa veritate, cogantur. Obstrepunt
       igitur, ut ait Lactantius, et intercidunt ne audiant: oculos suos oppri-
       munt ne lumen videant quod offerimus», morem Judeorum adversus

Translation:

       You know, my most esteemed master and brother, that I was bound through your urging and instigation to read this noble work of Master Jean de Meun, called the *Roman de la rose* in the vernacular, [and that I] who agree with you regarding its admirable artifice,
5   innate qualities, and erudition—and I confess I will remain irrevocably convinced of this—who am badly treated and bitterly charged, more than you would believe, by many learned men of considerable authority, so that if I strove to defend myself further, they would openly intend to prove me a heretic, as they say. It is of no use to
10   claim that you and so many other powerful scholarly and erudite men value him so much that they worship him so that they would rather do without their shirt than be without him. And it is equally useless to adduce to our censors his enemies who were so powerful that they would not have permitted his book to exist for an hour if
15   there were anything worth censuring in it. Nor is it of any help to entreat them—what every law demands—to look and to note the background, context, and occasion in which he says what he does and which persons he introduces before condemning such an author, but instead they immediately cut short my words and interrupt them
20   so that I hardly dare to move my lips, indeed they threaten me with the reproach of anathema and practically judge me guilty of death.

       What do you want me to say? They pursue our master with such curses—which afflicts me more—that they claim he has deserved to be burnt rather than to be read,[12] "and they consider
25   themselves to be contaminated by an inexpiable crime if they hear anything [of it]," and if I once again urge them in the name of humanity more humbly "not to condemn before they know all the facts," noting "the right to defend oneself is even granted to the sacrilegious, to traitors and to poisoners," that "it is not permitted
30   to condemn anyone in advance before their case is known," we still achieve nothing, my most honored brother, but wasting time: we assail the air with our words in vain. "And there is no reason we can

Salvatorum Nostrum observantes, penes quem «inimici facti sunt judices».

35   Sic doctor noster emeritissimus condamnatur—quod vetant leges omnes—innocentissimus, non auditus, ab his qui profecto coram vivente mutire non temptassent; eundem tamen, et quod molestius ferendum est, male visum perscrutatumque et notatum, ignominiose despiciunt nostri correctores, execrantur et impugnant.

40   O arrogantiam, temeritatem, audaciam! opus tantum, tot diebus ac noctibus tantoque cum sudore et attentione digesta elaboratum et editum, hi qui superficietenus nec eodem contextu, aut ex integro se legisse profitentur, subito, instar eorum qui mense inter crapu- las omnia, ut libet et fert impetus, accusant, reprehendunt atque

45   damnant,—paulo magis ponderis in stateram ponentes tantum opus quam lucis unius cantilenam histrionis!

    Quorum pretextu in alterum istorum patronorum scriptotenus invexi, sicut videbis per eam quam tibi fert epistolam is baiulus.

    Tuum ergo erit, dux, princeps rectorque huius cepti, laudatissimum

50 86vº et amatissimum imitatorem tuum defensare, et hos malesanos et // deliros conculcare ac ratiunculas meas indigestas disertie tue acu- mine validare, comere et linire, quatenus ego, qui auxilii tui confi- dentia ac ingenii ope fretus, campus hunc duelli introii, alias non facturus. Scio enim quod ubi obdormientes tui sensus expergiscen-

55 tur, et calamus iacens excret se, «non prevalebunt adversus nos» isti veritatis inimici, sed eos, cum voles, non dubito efficies oves mittes, et mutos reddes per omnia tanquam truncos.

    Vale, nec amicos sinas, quoadpotes, sic iniuste, vafre, perniti- ose et inique pessundari.

hope to achieve anything, so great is the obstinancy of men." This is
their behavior, their madness! "For they fear lest, if reconquered by
35 us, they would at some time, with the truth itself being proclaimed,
be forced to surrender, and therefore they make a lot of noise, as
Lactantius says, so that they can interrupt us and not listen: They
shut their eyes in order not to see the light we bring," following the
practice of the Jews toward Our Savior in whose house "the enemies
40 have been turned into the judges."[13]

And thus our preeminent doctor is condemned—in violation
of all laws—utterly innocent, his case unheard, by those who during
his lifetime would most assuredly not have dared to grumble openly
and yet—what is more disturbing to bear—our censors despise him
45 shamefully, curse and impugn him whom they have poorly seen,
examined, and noted. The arrogance, the temerity, the audacity!
Those who declare to have read this work, elaborated and produced
over days and nights with so much sweat and systematic care,
superficially, out of context and anew, suddenly accuse, reproach,
50 and condemn it like hungover drunks who say whatever they please
at table, and placing it in the scales consider it hardly more weighty
than some actor's song composed in one day.

For these reasons I inveighed against another one of these law-
yers just as you can see in the letter which this carrier has brought
55 you. There it will be up to you as the leader, prince, and director of
this undertaking to defend such a praiseworthy and beloved imitator,
and to tread underfoot these sick and mad [critics] and to strengthen,
arrange in order, and overlay my half-baked reasonings with the
sharpness of your eloquence, inasmuch as I, relying on the confi-
60 dence of your help and the wealth of your genius, have entered this
battlefield, something I would otherwise not have done. For I know
that your senses, having fallen asleep, will wake up, that your idle
pen will set itself in motion, and that these enemies of truth "will
not prevail against us" but that you will doubtlessly turn them, as
65 you wish, into mild lambs, and that you will render them mute on
everything as though they had been amputated.

Take care and grant as much as you can that your friends not
be destroyed so unjustly, cleverly, perniciously and unfairly.

***

Eric Hicks speculates that the addressee of this letter is the same as that of epistle 119, in other words the *pater venerande* referred to here as *pater mi prestantissime*.[14] Together with this letter, which was composed at the same as the previous ones, the unidentified prelate also received a copy of the invective (epistle 118) and of epistle 120. Again, Jean de Montreuil insists on keeping the invective confidential.

Text:

Epistle 121[15]

86v°   Mee an fuerit inconsiderationis obtusitas, aut vestre id confidentia
        bonitatis faciat, vosmet iudicate, pater mi prestantissime, quod ego
        modicus magno, doctissimo non doctus, illiteratus litteratissimo, et
        demum stolidus circumspectissimo, sic de nugis rudimentisque meis
5   vobiscum loquor: ago conferoque, ut que nulli mortalium commu-
        nicaverim, scriptotenus habeatis. Sed ita est, pater reverende, error
        unus alium provocat facillime, et, ut inquit Claudianus, «suadet
        licentia luxum». Ego etiam, puerorum instar, ubi (quod in proverbio
        est) fit michi bonus vultus, illuc eo, illic sum, ibi ad tedium usque
10   dego, et incautus «linguam in fronte gerens», quidquid occurit pro-
        fero, animum liberrime detegendo per omnia proprio veluti confes-
        sori.
             Rursus igitur subiit mentem meam Paternitati Vestre mittere
        eam de qua pridie in domo vestra sermonem habuimus, satirice
15   invectionis formam tenentem epistolam: non ut transcribatur—hoc
        supplico, posco, obsecro requiroque—, sed solum eam Vestra
87r°   Dominatio pervideat, anamavertatque si // dispendiosa nimis—de
        quo formido inest—mordaxve aut insolens extiterit, et correctoris
        emendatorisque more, in margine mendas notet. Scio enim, quod
20   temperati minime est, me in utramque partem meorum affectuum
        fore pernimium vehementem, quoniam, ut Therentius causam
        signat, aut gaudio sumus prepediti nimio, aut egritudine; et, quod
        temeritatem non minuit, en, pater carissime, iterum circa eandem
        materiam ad quendam socium meum minutam[16] hanc (licet eidem
25   adhuc nequaquam transmissa sit) ipsi Dominationi Vestre vector
        deffert,—que non arrogantie, sed de vestra benignitate prudenti
        prestite michi audacie imputetur.

Translation:

You yourself must judge whether the dullness of my lack of forethought or my confidence in your goodness prompts me, my most outstanding father, to speak with you this way about my trifles and first lessons—here I am a modest man speaking with a great 5 one, an uneducated one with the most erudite, an illiterate with the most literate, and finally a stupid one with the most circumspect: I have written and brought together what I would have communicated to no mortal so that you could have this in writing. But it is such, reverend father, one error easily provokes a second, and as Claudia- 10 nus said, "license favors overindulgence." I, like the little boys, still remain (as in the proverb) where I am welcome, I go and stay there until boredom sets in and carrying my tongue in my face incautious- ly say whatever occurs to me, laying freely bare my mind regarding everything almost as though I were speaking to my confessor. 15 Thus once again it occurred to me to send to Your Father this letter, written satirically in the form of an invective, about which we had spoken yesterday in your home, not so that it would be recopied—I beg you, I entreat you, I implore you, I ask you not to do this—but only that your Lordship look at it and reflect whether 20 it is too damaging—which I fear—or biting or insolent, and note its defects in the margin following the practice of a corrector or emendator. For I know that it is hardly balanced, that I have been impassioned in all parts of my emotions, as Terence observed: either by too much joy or too much sadness we are fettered and, what does 25 not reduce temerity, here, dearest father, is once again the rough draft about the same material destined for one of my colleagues (although it has not yet been sent) which this carrier brings to your Lordship and which can be imputed not to my arrogance, but to my boldness regarding the goodness of your excellent prudence.

***

The last letter in this group was sent at the end of July or the beginning of August, 1401 to the advocate who also received the invective, epistle 118. In this letter Jean de Montreuil realizes that said advocate has abstained from further negative judgments of Jean de Meun's work. As the provost triumphantly proclaims: The truth will ultimately prevail.

Text:

Epistle 122[17]

87r°   Etsi facundissimus, si copiosus, si eloquens et abundans, sed («quod scribendi fons est») sapiens es, vir insignis, video tamen, veritate vincente ac pariter conscientia remordente, adversus satiricum illum perseverum magistrum Johannem de Magduno nichil te ulterius
5   «mutiere audere» aut disserere posse; ipsius quippe veritatis tanta vis est ut ei nullius rethoris industria sese equet: illo assentiente qui dicit: «Veritas manet in eternum», «falsa non durant».
         Redi ergo ipsius doctoris ac preceptoris carissimi in gratiam, nec quia facile prorupisti verearis. Ilico enim, cum voles, veniam
10   impetrando noster eris, modo de resipiscentia tua ex fideli promissione nullus apud nos scrupulus remaneat. Non enim latet nos quousque disputandi progrediatur licentia, et quod disputationi serotine sepenumero matutina contradicit. Scis insuper, vir experte, Originem et una Lactantium erravisse, et pariter Augustinum ple-
15 87v° rosque magni nominis atque fame alios revocasse // doctores.
         Non igitur pudeat nimis libere dicta et attemptata obnoxius reparare; forsan vero que damnas perfunctorie vidisti, nec recenter: que duo maxime iudicium perverterunt ac te precipitem dederunt in errorem,—non fidei quidem, vel iniquitatis aut malicie, sed in quem
20   nonnulli predictorum (ipsius de Magduno superficietenus viso pede) tecum ruunt. Neque presentem monitionem nostram parvipendas aut existimes caritate fraterna vacare, vel me gratis prioribus nostris in litteris te de amantissimis defensoribusque philosophi prelibati animadvertisse. Sunt enim quorum calcaria auro fulgent magnisque
25   dignitatibus potiuntur, qui pro tuicione nostri propositi «pulcram petunt, cum Marone, per vulnera mortem»; nec acceptius quidquam Deo agere putarent quam in eos irruere qui nostrum coarguunt instructorem de sillaba solum parvula sive coma.
         Atqui te quid facturum censeam a me queris? Id quod prophe-
30   ta simul et rex non erubuit suppliciter confiteri hortor dicas: «Delictum meum cognitum tibi feci, et iniusticiam meam non abscondi». Quod si tractatum superinde conficeres interim, per amicitiam

Translation:

> Though most eloquent, rich, articulate and affluent, your are also—and "here is the source of writing"[18]—wise, most excellent man, yet I realize that conquered by truth and equally bitten by conscience, you "do not dare to mutter"[19] anything or are unable to
>
> 5 argue against this most resolute satirical poet Jean de Meun; indeed, the force of this truth is such that the diligence of no speaker could equal him, guaranteed by him who said, "the truth abides forever"[20] and "the false does not last."[21]
>
> Therefore make your peace with this doctor and most dear
>
> 10 teacher, and do not fear because you burst forth so easily. For you will immediately be one of us when you obtain pardon, provided no scruple over your coming back to your senses remains among us regarding your faithful promise. For it is not hidden to us how far the license in argument can go, and that the morning's argu-
>
> 15 ment contradicts the evening's. And you know, learned man, that Origen and with him Lanctantius were mistaken and equally that the Church Fathers have corrected Augustine and many others of great name and fame.
>
> And thus may it not be shameful when one is guilty to cor-
>
> 20 rect things spoken or attempted too freely: perhaps in fact you have looked perfunctorily or not recently at what you condemn. These two factors have perverted your judgment and led you headlong into an error into which several of those mentioned before have rushed, along with you, not out of faith, iniquity or malice, but having only
>
> 25 superficially read Jean de Meun. Nor should you underestimate our present warning or think that it lacks brotherly love or that in my pervious letters I warned you without cause regarding the fervent supporters and defenders of the philosophy being tasted. For there are those whose spurs shine with gold and who possess high offices
>
> 30 who, in defending our argument, "will seek for all their wounds a beautiful death," as Virgil says; for they think they can do nothing more acceptable to God than rushing to attack those who refute our teacher for only a single syllable or punctuation mark.

nostram precor tedio tibi nequaquam adveniat, tuo huic mandare
quampiam preposito remissivam, que levatio presertim sit nostre
35   expectationis et tue intencionis nuncia in aliquo: cum psalmista, «
letabor ego super eloquia tua, quasi qui invenit spolia multa».

Vale.

And nevertheless you ask me what I think you should do?
35   I urge you to say what the prophet and at the same time king did not blush to confess humbly: "I have made known my crime to you and I have not hidden my injustice."[22] So that nothing in any way will happen to you because of an offense, I pray for the sake of our friendship that if you write a treatise on this subject in the
40   meantime, send some response to our argument to this man of yours which would principally be an alleviation of our expectation and a messenger of your intention in this matter. As the Psalmist says, "I will rejoice in your eloquence as someone who has found great spoils."[23]
45   Take care.

2. *February 1(?), 1402: Christine's Epistle to Guillaume de Tignonville*[24]

Guillaume de Tignonville was Provost of Paris from June 6, 1401 to 1408. As knight, counselor to the King, provost of Paris, and endowed with still further titles he seemed to have been the ideal supporter for Christine's cause. As pointed out by Eric Hicks, together with Marshal Boucicaut he was also one of the founders of the order "L'écu verd à la dame blanche" [White Lady on the Green Shield] of April 11, 1400 and belonged to the twenty-four ministers of the "Cour amoureuse."[25]

Text:

142r°   A mon tres chier seigneur, noble chevalier et saige, messire Guil-
        laume de Tygnonville, prevost de Paris.

            A vous mon seigneur le prevost de Paris, par la grace de Dieu
        et providence de vostre bon sens esleu a si digne siege et office
5   comme garde de si haulte justice, recommandacion avec obeissance
        premise de par moy Cristine, foible d'entendement et la mendre
        des femmes desireuses vie honneste. Savoir vous fais que soubz
        la fiance de vostre sagesce et valeur suis meue a vous segnefier le
        debat gracieux et non haineux meu par oppinions contraires entre
10   solempneles personnes: maistre Contier Col, a present general
        conseillier du roy nostre sire, et maistre Jehan Johannes, prevost de
        Lisle et secretaire du dit seigneur, duquel dit debat vous pourrés oïr
        les premisses par les epistres envoiees entre nous et par les mem-
        oires que de ce feront si aprés mencion; de laquelle chose, tres saige
15   prevost, je supplie vostre humilité que non obstant les labourieuses
        occupacions de plus grans et neccessaires negoces, vous plaise par
        maniere de soulas vouloir entendre les raisons de noz descors. Et
        avec ce suppli la bonne discrete consideracion de vostre savoir que
        vueille discuter et proprement eslire le bon droit de mon oppinion,
20   non obstant ne le saiche vivement divulguer ne mectre en termes
        consonans et propices a la deffense de mon dit droit, si comme autre
        mieulx le sauroit.

            Pour ce requier vous, tres sçavant, que par compassion de ma
        femmenine ignorance, vostre humblece s'encline a joindre a mes
25   dictes vraies oppinions par si que vostre saigesce me soit force,
        ayde, deffense et appuyal contre si notables et esleuz maistres,
        desquelx les subtiles raisons auroient en petit d'eure mis au bas ma
        juste cause par faulte de savoir soustenir; et par ce, comme bon droit
        ait mestier d'aide, soubz vostre aliance soye plus hardiement inani-
30   mee de continuer la guerre encommencee contre les diz puissans et
        fors. Et de ce vous plaise ne estre reffusant pour consideracion de

Translation:

To my dearest lord, noble and wise knight, Sir Guillaume de Tignonville, Provost of Paris.[26]

To my lord, provost of Paris, who by divine grace and in view of your own good judgment have been elected to such a high office
5 as the keeper of high justice, I, Christine, of little intelligence and the lowest of women desirous of leading an honest life, offer you my respect and obedience. I inform you that I wish to place this gracious and amicable debate about contrary opinions between solemn persons into the confidence of your wisdom: Master Gontier Col,
10 presently Council General to Our Lord the King, and Master Jean Johannes, provost of Lille and the said lord's secretary. You will be able to follow the premises of this debate which we exchanged and which is reported below. I appeal to your humility, very wise provost, that despite your more important and more urgent tasks you
15 agree to hear, for your pleasure, the reasons for our disagreements. Appealing to your knowledge and discretion, I ask that you deliberate and then justifiably favor my rightful opinion, although I do not know how to divulge it forcefully nor to express it in consonant and auspicious language, to defend my rights as others would be better
20 able to do.

Therefore, O very learned man, I ask that out of compassion for my female ignorance, your modesty will allow you to support me[27] in my correct opinions, in order that your wisdom will give me strength, defense, and support against such illustrious and distin-
25 guished masters, whose skillful arguments would crush my just cause in a second, due to my inability to defend it. For this reason and since righteousness is on our side, your alliance will encourage me to continue the war begun against these illustrious and distinguished men. Since you more than anyone are aware that your posi-
30 tion obliges you to support the weakest party if the cause is just, I ask you, out of consideration for my opponents' great and my small intelligence, not to refuse my request.

leur grant faculté et la moye petite, comme vostre bon sens soit
expert qu'il appertiengne a vostre office soustenir en tous cas la plus
142v° foible partie par si que cause ait // juste.

35   Aussi, chier seigneur, ne vous soit a merveille, pour ce que
mes autres dictiéz ay acoustuméz a rimoyer, cestui estre en prose.
Car comme la matiere ne le requiere autressy, est droit que je suive
le stille de mes assaillans, combien que mon petit sçavoir soit pou
respondant a leur belle eloquence.

40   Si vous octroit paradis cil qui toutes choses a crées.

Also, dear sir, please do not be surprised to find this work in prose, though my other works are usually in rhyme.[28] Since the mat-
35   ter requires it thus, it is correct to follow the style of my opponents, despite the fact that my limited knowledge does not permit me to match their beautiful eloquence.

May the One who created all things grant you paradise.

3. 1402: Christine's Poem Le dit de la rose[29]

There has been much speculation as to why Christine removed this poem from her later collections, which date between 1407 and 1410. Was this omission motivated by purely practical factors, or can we discern ideological strategies in her choice of works in a given collection? James Laidlaw argues that Christine simply did not want to give two copies of the *Dit* to her patron, the Duke of Orléans, to whom she had already presented a copy at the time of composition of this text.[30] Eric Hicks, on the other hand, suspects that Christine considered the mundane topic of this poem out of place among the more philosophical and ideologically driven epistles which made up the Quarrel. He claims: "la querelle avait pris une envergure telle qu'elle faisait oublier les contingences de ses origines mondaines: la prédication gersonienne dotait le traité de Christine de tout le prestige de l'Université; la réponse de Pierre Col lui donnait l'occasion de reprendre ses thèses et de les exposer avec plus d'ampleur. Le second traité de Christine sera donc versé au dossier de la querelle, et les 'epistres du débat sur *Le Roman de la Rose*' deviendront un véritable *livre*" ["the Quarrel had taken on such a scope that the contingencies of its mundane origins were for-gotten: Gerson's sermons endowed Christine's treatise with all the prestige of the University, Pierre Col's reply afforded her the opportunity to retract her theses and to expose them on a wider scale. Christine's second treatise will consequently be added to the dossier of the Quarrel and the 'Epistre du débat sur *Le Roman de la Rose*' will become an actual *book*.]"[31] Whatever the case may be, as with the *Epistre au dieu d'Amours*, the author's efforts to correct and counteract misogynist tendencies in courtly circles are at the heart of this dream vision.[32] Using the name of an actual chivalric order, the Order of the Rose, clearly creates an intertextual reference to the *Roman*. It is for this rea-son that the *Dit de la rose* must be considered a key component of the debate, and carries the same argumentative weight as Christine's letters themselves. Consequently, I have decided to reproduce it in its entirety.

Text:

74r° Cy commence le Dit de la Rose
A tous les princes amoureux
Et aux nobles chevalereux
4 Que vaillantise fait armer,
Et a ceulz qui seulent amer
Toute bonté pour avoir pris,
Et a tous amans bien apris
8 De ce royaume et autre part,
Partout ou vaillance s'espart;
A toutes dames renommées
Et aux damoiselles amées,
12 A toutes femmes honnorables,
Saiges, courtoises, agreables:
Humble recommandacion
De loyal vraye entencion.
16 Si fais savoir a tous vaillans,
Qui pour honneur sont travaillans,
Unes nouvelles merveilleuses,
Gracïeuses, non perilleuses,
20 Qui avenues de nouvel
Sont en beau lieu plain de revel.
Aussi est droiz que ceulz le sachent
Qui mauvaistié devers eulz sachent,
24 Afin qu'ilz amendent leurs fais
Pour estre avec les bons parfais.
Si fut voir qu'a Paris advint,
Present nobles gens plus de vint,
28 Joyeux et liez et senz esmois,
L'an quatre cens et un, ou mois
De janvier, plus de la moittié
Ains la date de ce dittié,
32 Du mois passé, quant ceste chose
            Advint en une maison close.
Ot assemblé de nobles gens,
Riches d'onnour et beaulx et gens.
36 Chevaliers y ot de renom
Et escuiers de vaillant nom:
Ne m'estuet ja leurs noms nommer,
Mais chascun les seult bons clamer.
40 Notables sont et renommez,

Translation:

	Here begins the Tale of the Rose
	To princes all inclined to love,
	To all the gallant noblemen
4	Inspired to arms by bravery;
	To those whose custom is to love
	All goodness, thus to earn esteem;
	To lovers bred in gentle ways,
8	Here in our realm, in other states,
	Wherever valor radiates;
	To ladies all of good renown,
	To all the maidens who are loved,
12	To women who are honorable,
	Gracious, well-bred, and courteous:
	A modest counsel is offered here,
	Given in true sincerity.
16	I bring to all the valorous,
	Who persevere for honor's sake,
	These wondrous tidings, pleasing news,
	No harmful, frightening report.
20	The word arrived quite recently
	In fine rooms filled with revelry.
	Those who would harm the festive guests
	By rights should hear of this event,
24	So they may remedy their ways
	To be as equals of the good.
	It came indeed to Paris, there,
	Before a noble group of more
28	Than twenty, carefree, happy.
	The year was fourteen hundred one,
	In January, one before
	The month in which this tale took place,
32	And more than half the month was out;[33]
	It happened in a house shut tight,
	Where noble folk had gathered, rich
	In honor, handsome, and well-bred.
36	Attending there were knights of note
	And squires renowned for chivalry.
	I need not state their names, but all
	Are used to calling them good men.
40	Their names are known, of sure repute,

Des plus prisiez et mieulx amez
Du tres noble duc d'Orlïens,
Qui Dieu gart de tous maulx lïens.
44   Si sont de son hostel tous ceulz,
Et n'y avoit pas un tout seulz
Qui n'aime, je croy, tous bons fais;
Lëans a assez de si fais.
48   Assemblez les ot celle part
Courtoisie, qui ne depart
De ceulz qui sont de gentil sorte.
La fu bien fermee la porte,
52   Car vouloient en ce lieu estre
Senz estranges gens privez estre,
Pour deviser a leur plaisir.
La fu appresté a loisir
56   Le soupper; si furent assis,
Joyeux et liez et non pensis.
Bien furent servis par les tables
De mez a leur gré delitables,
60   Car ne fu, j'en ose jugier,
Pas tout leur plaisir ou mangier,
Mais en la compaignie qui
De vraie et bonne amour nasqui.
64   Liez estoient et esbatans,
74vᵒ Gays et envoisiez et chantans
Tout au long de cellui souper,
Comme gent qui sont tout un per
68   Et amis vrais, sens estrangier.
La n'ot parlé a ce mangier
Fors de courtoisie et d'onnour,
Senz diffamer grant ne menour,
72   Et de beaulx livres et de dis,
Et de balades plus de dix.
Qui mieulx mieulx chascun devisoit,
Ou d'amours qui s'en avisoit,
76   Ou de demandes gracïeuses.
Viandes plus delicïeuses
N'y ot, com je croy, a leur goust,
Tout soyent d'assez petit coust,
80   Et de ris et de bonne chiere;
De ce n'orent ilz pas enchiere.

Most highly prized and loved by him,
Noble lord, Duke of Orléans
(God keep him from all evil ties!)
44   The company were of his court
And not a single one of them,
I deem, neglects to love good ways;
Many of them are formed that way.
48   They had been assembled in that place
By Courtesy, who never parts
From those who are nobly born and bred.
The door was closed and tightly shut
52   Because they wanted to be there
Without a stranger, privately,
Conversing as they pleased to do.
The supper was prepared to suit
56   Their taste; and so they sat to dine
With joy and cheer, not worrying.
At every table they were served
Such dishes as delighted them.
60   For I dare say, their pleasure came
Not only from the meal they had,
But from the company itself,
Gathered in true and loyal love.
64   Joyous were they, their spirits high,
Rejoicing, happy, singing out
Throughout that feast, like people all
Of equal mind, like friends who are true,
68   Without another in their midst.
They spoke of nought at dinner but
Of honor and of courtesy,
With neither great nor small traduced,
72   Of handsome books and poetry,
And there were more than ten ballades.
Each vied to write the best he could:
Some pondered love and wrote of it,
76   While others wrote gracious requests.
No more delicious food was there
To suit their taste, so I believe,
However small its cost might be,
80   Nor laughter nor delightful fare.
Of those they had no short supply.

Ainsi se firent longuement
En ce gracïeux parlement.
84   Mais Amours, ses loyaulx amis,
Qui a valeur se sont soubzmis,
Volt visiter droit en ce point.
Car alors seurvint tout a point,
88   Nonobstant les portes barrees
Et les fenestres bien sarrees,
Une dame de grant noblesse
Qui s'appella dame et deesse
92   De Loyauté, et trop belle yere!
La descendi a grant lumiere
Si que toute en resplent la sale.
Toute autre beauté si fut pale
96   Vers la sienne de corps, de vis,
            Et de beau maintien, a devis
Bien paree et bien attournee.
Si fu entour avironnee
100 De nymphes et de pucelletes,
Atout chappelles de fleurettes,
Qui chantoyent par grant revel
Hault et cler un motet nouvel
104 Si doulcement, pour voir vous dis,
Que bien sembloit que Paradis
Fut leur reduit et qu'el venissent
De ce lieu dont fors tous biens n'issent;
108 Celle deesse a tel maisgnie.
Devant la table a compaignie
Vint o les siennes bien parees.
Si tenoient couppes dorees,
112 Si comme pour faire en present
A celle gent nouvel present.
Adont fut la sale estourmie,
Il n'y ot personne endormie,
116 Tuit furent vëoir la merveille.
Il n'y ot cellui qui l'oreille
Ne tendist pour bien escouter
Que celle leur vouloit noter;
120 Chascun se tut pour y entendre.
Quant les pucelles a cuer tendre
Orent leur chançon affinee,

They passed a good long time that way,
Engaged in charming dinner talk.
84   But Love, to whom they had pledged themselves
So gallantly, desired just then
To call upon her loyal friends,
For there appeared quite suddenly,
88   Although the doors were barred and fast,
The windows drawn together tight,
A lady of nobility:
A lady, and the goddess called
92   Of Loyalty. How fair was she!
And there she came amidst great light,
The room resplendent everywhere.
Indeed, all other beauty paled
96   Compared with hers—her form, her face,
      Her bearing: beauty fetchingly
Arrayed and elegantly clad!
She came encircled round about
100   By nymphs and maidens, all of whom
Wore chaplets made of tiny blooms.
In joy they sang a new motet
In voices ringing loud and clear,
104   So sweetly sung, I tell you true,
It seemed that Paradise must be
Their home, and that they must have come
From there, the source of nought but good;
108   That is how the goddess's household is.
She came before the seated guests,
Her ladies handsomely attired,
With golden vases held outstretched,
112   As if to offer them as gifts
To that invited company.
At that the room became abuzz,
Now not a soul was slumbering
116   As everyone sought out the sight.
There was not one who did not strain
An ear to listen carefully
To what she wished him to know.
120   Each one grew still, to better hear.
And when the tenderhearted maids
Had finished singing out their song,

Adonc se prist la belle nee,
124   Qui d'elles dame et maistresse yere,
       A dire par belle maniere
       Ces parolles qui ci escriptes
       Sont en ces balades, et dittes.
128   Ne plus ne moins les ennorta,
75r°   Et les balades apporta:
              Balade
       Cil qui forma toute chose mondaine
132   Vueille tousdiz en santé maintenir
       Et en bauldour de grant leesse plaine
       Ceste belle compaignie, et tenir.
       Deesse suis, si me doit souvenir
136   De trestous bons et des bonnes et belles.
       Pour ce qu'ainsi il doit appartenir,
       Venue suis vous apporter nouvelles.

       De par le dieu d'Amours qui puet la peine
140   Des fins amans desmettre et defenir,
       Present nouvel gracïeux, d'odeur saine,
       Je vous apport, et salus sens fenir.
       Si m'escoutez et vueilliez retenir,
144   Car je vous di que de haultes querelles,
       Dont il pourra assez de biens venir,
       Venue suis vous apporter nouvelles.

       De Loyauté, deesse souveraine,
148   On m'appellë, et a mon seurvenir
       Je ne port pas de discorde la graine,
       Com fist celle qui Troyes fist bannir.
       Ains pour tousjours loyauté soustenir
152   Et pour oster les mauvaises favelles,
       Et les mauvaiz desloyaulx escharnir,
       Venue suis vous apporter nouvelles.
              Balade
156   Le dieu d'Amours par moy il vous presente
       Ces roses ci de voulenté entiere.
       Cueillies sont de tres loyal entente
       Es beaulx vergiers dont je suis courtilliere.
160   Si vous mande qu'a tres joyeuse chiere
       Preigniez le don; mais c'est par couvenant

The high-born lady, she who was
124 Mistress and lady both to them,
So graciously began to speak
The words that are recorded here,
In these ballades, and said aloud.
128 Exhorting them, no more no less,
She then presented these ballades:
Ballade
May He who fashioned every worldly thing
132 Guard well this handsome company, maintain
And keep all this group in health exulting,
In happiness replete with gay refrain.
Goddess am I, to me it thus pertains
136 To note good men, good ladies fair to view.
Because that is how these things should be arranged,
I have come to bring the news down here to you.

And from the god of Love to you I bring
140 This pleasant news, a breath of freshest air,
And with it, greetings past all reckoning,
From him who would end each courtly lover's pain.
So listen well, and let my words remain:
144 From high-placed talks from which there could ensue,
I tell you, many worthy goods and gains,
I have come to bring the news down here to you.

As Loyalty, the goddess governing,
148 I am addressed, and in my wake and train
I bring no seed of any quarreling,
Unlike that one who was the Trojans's bane.
Instead, loyalty ever to sustain,
152 To take away the evil slander, too,
To mock and ridicule disloyal swains,
I have come to bring the news down here to you.
Ballade
156 To you, through me, the god of Love presents
These roses, willingly, sincerely so,
For they were gathered, with loyal intent,
In lovely orchards where I tend their growth.
160 And thus he orders that with joyful glow
You take the gift; but then agree you must

Que desormais en trestoute maniere
Yrez l'onneur des dames soustenant.

164   Si veult qu'ainçoiz que nullui se consente
       A recevoir la rose belle et chiere,
       Qu'il face veu que jamaiz il n'assente
       Blasme ou mesdit en nesune maniere
168   De femme, qui son honneur tiengne chiere;
       Et pour ce a vous m'envoye maintenant;
       Si vouez tous qu'a parolle pleniere
       Yrez l'onneur des dames soustenant.

172   Chevaliers bons et tous de noble sente,
       Et tous amans, c'est bien droit qu'il affiere
       Qu'a ce veu ci vo cuer se represente;
       Amours le veult, si n'y mettez enchiere.
176   Mais ne soit pas de voulenté legiere,
       Car a l'estat de vous appartenant.
       Et si jurez que jusques a la biere
       Yrez l'onneur des dames soustenant.

180   En disant ces balades cy,
       La deesse, sienne mercy,
       Assist les couppes sur les tables.
       Dedens ot roses odorables,
184   Blanches, vermeilles, et trop belles,
       Et cueillies furent nouvelles.
       Et avecques ce presentoit,
       En beaulx rolez qu'elle gettoit,
188 75vº   Ceste balade qui recorde
       Qu'Amours veult qu'ainçois qu'on accorde
       A prendre la jolie rose,
       Que l'en face veu de la chose
192   Qui est en l'escript contenu,
       Et qu'il soit juré et tenu,
       Et qui tout ce vouldra vouer
       Et celle promesse advouer,
196   Hardiement preingne la rose
       Ou toute doulçour est enclose.
       Si oyez lire la balade
       Qu'apporta la deesse sade.

That from now on in every way you know,
The honor of all ladies is your trust.

164 The god desires that no one here consent
To have the dear and lovely rose bestowed
Unless he swears he never will assent
To any sort of blame or word that is low
168 Of woman, and he keeps her honor close.
And so, for that, to you he sends me thus;
All swear that with your strong and forthright vow
The honor of all ladies is your trust.

172 Good knights and all of you so eminent,
And lovers all, it is right and fitting now
That toward the vow your hearts show kind intent,
For Love thus wishes it; do not answer No.
176 But let your will in this not come and go
Because for your estate it is right and just,
And swear from now until toward the grave you bow
The honor of all ladies is your trust.

180 Engaged so in her balladry,
The goddess, thanks be said to her,
Before us put the vases down.
Each one held roses, fragrant ones,
184 Vermillion, white, quite beautiful,
And they had all been freshly plucked.
Along with this she offered us,
On handsome scrolls that she tossed out,
188 The same ballade that is noted here.
It states what Love requires before
One may agree to take the rose:
That is, that one should take the vow,
192 The one contained within the scroll,
Which must be sworn and firmly kept.
Now he who will accept those terms
And make that promise solemnly,
196 Let him so boldly take the rose
In which all sweetness is enclosed.
So listen now, hear the ballade,
The one the winsome goddess brought.

200   Balade
             A bonne Amour je fais veu et promesse,
             Et a la fleur qui est rose clamee,
             A la vaillant de Loyauté deesse,
204   Par qui nous est ceste chose informee,
             Qu'a tousjours mais la bonne renommee
             Je garderay de dame en toute chose,
             Ne par moy ja femme n'yert diffamee;
208   Et pour ce prens je l'Ordre de la Rose.

             Et si promet a toute gentillesse
             Qu'en trestous lieux et prisee et amee
             Dame sera de moy comme maistresse,
212   Et celle qui j'ay ma dame nommee
             Souveraine, loyauté confermee
             Je lui tendray jusques a la parclose.
             Et de ce ay voulenté affermee;
216   Et pour ce prens je l'Ordre de la Rose.

             Et si merci Amours et son humblesse,
             Qui nous a cy tel semence semee,
             Dont j'ay espoir que serons en l'adresse
220   De mieulx valoir; c'est bien chose informee
             Que de lui vint honneur tres renommee.
             Si defendray, s'aucun est qui dire ose,
             Chose par quoy dame estre puist blasmee;
224   Et pour ce prens je l'Ordre de la Rose.

             Princes haultains ou valeur est fermee,
             Faites le veu—bonté y est enclose.
             L'enseingne en vueil porter en mainte armee,
228   Et pour ce prens je l'Ordre de la Rose.

             Adonc furent en audiance
             Levez et, senz contrariance,
             Firent tous le beau veu louable,
232   Qui est gentil et honnorable.
             Quant nullui ne vit contredire,
             La deesse adonc prist a dire
             Ce rondelet, prenant congié;
236   Si n'y a pensé ne songié.

200	Ballade
	To Love I vow and promise solemnly,
	And to that flower, called a champion rose,
	And to the valiant goddess, Loyalty,
204	By means of whom to us this news appears
	To keep each lady's reputation clear
	Forevermore, in every way I know,
	And to be sure no woman's name is smeared;
208	And thus I take the Order of the Rose.[34]
	And so I promise with nobility
	That everywhere each lady I will revere
	As if she were a mistress prized by me.
212	To her whom I have named my sweetheart dear
	And sovereign love, my loyalty sincere
	I will offer her until we reach our close,
	For certainly in this I will persevere;
216	And thus I take the Order of the Rose.
	To Love, my thanks, and to his courtesy,
	For seeds that he has sown amongst us here,
	Through which we are moving forth, I hope to see,
220	To greater worth; a thing one often hears
	Is that from him came honor beyond peer.
	So I will forbid it, if there should be those
	Who would blame a lady by words they would dare speak;
224	And thus I take the Order of the Rose.
	Now lofty princes in whom worth inheres,
	Recite the vow, where goodness is enclosed.
	In many armies, its standard I will bear;
228	And thus I take the Order of the Rose.
	They stood, and publicly, without
	A word of disagreement said,
	They took the fine and worthy vow,
232	So noble and so honor-filled.
	As none was seen to disagree,
	The goddess then began to speak
	This rondelet, while taking leave;
236	No more did she reflect on it.

Rondel.
Or m'en vois dire les nouvelles
Au dieu d'Amours, qui m'envoya.

240   De ses belles roses nouvelles
Or m'en vois dire les nouvelles.

Adieu vous dy, tous ceulz et celles
Que bonne amour cy avoya.
244   Or m'en vois dire les nouvelles
Au dieu d'Amours, qui m'envoya.

Quant ce fut dit, lors s'envola
Celle deesse qui vint la.
248 76r°   Mais les nymphes, qui furent liez,
De leurs doulces voix deliez
Commencierent tel mellodie
(Ne cuidiez que mençonge die)
252   Quë il sembloit a leur doulz chant
Qu'angelz feussent, ou droit enchant.
              Ainsi parti de celle place
La deesse, qui de sa grace
256   Ot la compaignie esjoÿe—
Tel nouvelle leur ot gehie.
D'elle font feste et de ses choses,
Et tous se parent de ses roses,
260   Par teste, par braz, par poitrine,
En promettant foy enterine,
Si comme ou veu est devisié
Qu'ilz orent moult bien avisié.
264   Quant assez selon leur loisir
Orent esté en ce plaisir,
Chantans, rians a chiere lie,
Senz dueil et sens merencolie,
268   Partis s'en sont, congié ont pris,
Emportant la rose de pris.
Et je, qui n'oz pas le cuer noir,
Demouray en cellui manoir
272   Ou ot esté celle assemblee,
Ou je ne fus de riens troublee.
Tart fu ja et saison en l'eure
D'aler couchier, et bien fu heure.

> Rondel
> I will go now bearing back the news
> To Love, who sent me to this place.

240　　About his roses fresh and new
　　　　I will go now bearing back the news.

　　　　I bid farewell to you and you,
　　　　Whom worthy love has guided here.
244　　I will go now bearing back the news
　　　　To Love, who sent me to this place.

　　　　When that was said, away she flew,
　　　　The goddess who had come to us.
248　　The nymphs, though, who were filled with joy,
　　　　In voices delicate and sweet
　　　　Began a sort of melody
　　　　(And here do not think I am telling lies)
252　　That made them seem, to hear their song,
　　　　Like angels, or like sortilege.
　　　　　　And thus the goddess took her leave,
　　　　Who through the workings of her grace
256　　Had brought the company good cheer,
　　　　Such news had she revealed to them.
　　　　Now they show honor to her ways,
　　　　To her, as they adorn themselves
260　　With roses—in their hair, bosoms,
　　　　And arms—and promise perfect faith,
　　　　As written in the vow that they
　　　　Had sworn and so well recognized.
264　　　　Now when they had had their fill of cheer
　　　　As they preferred, as time was spent
　　　　In singing, laughing happily,
　　　　Without a hint of grief or gloom,
268　　They begged their leave as they arose
　　　　And carried off each valued rose.
　　　　Now I, who surely was not sad,
　　　　Remained in that great residence
272　　In which the gathering had been,
　　　　Where I had not had a single care.
　　　　And so, the hour grown late, the time
　　　　Arrived to take oneself to bed.

276 Mais la deesse qui m'ama,
Sienne merci, et me clama
Sa belle suer de cuer eslit,
M'ot appresté un trop beau lit,
280 Blanc comme noif, encourtiné
Richement et bien ordonné,
En belle chambre toute blanche,
Comme la noif qui chiet sur branche;
284 Pour ce l'ot fait, je n'en doubt mie,
Que je suis a Dyane amie,
La deesse tres honnouree,
Qui toudis de blanc est paree.
288   La me couchay seulette et nue,
Et m'endormy. Lors une nue
Si m'apparu en mon dormant.
Clere et luisant; de ce formant
292 Me merveillay que pouoit estre.
De la nue, qui fu a destre
Costé du lit, luisant et clere,
Comme en esté temps qui esclere,
296 Yssi une voix gracïeuse,
Trop plaisant et trop amoureuse.
           Adonc ou que dormisse ou non,
La voix m'appella par mon nom;
300 Si me dist lors, «Amie chiere,
Qui m'as amee et tenu chiere
Toute ta vie, bien le sçay,
Car souvent t'ay mise a l'essay,
304 Je suis la deesse loyale
De la haulte ligne royale
De Dieu, qui me fist et fourma,
Et de ses rigles m'enforma.
308 Or m'entens, m'amie certaine,
Et je te diray qui me maine.
           «Tu scez comment en ta presence
Je vins presenter par plaisance
312 76v°   Nagueres les roses jolies,
Qui en nul temps ne sont palies,
De par vraie Amour, qui conduit
Ceulz qui de bien faire sont duit,
316 Qui encor devers toy m'envoye

276　The goddess, though, who loved me well
　　　(All praise to her!) and called me her
　　　Sister in sensibility,
　　　Had made a lovely bed for me,
280　As white as snow and richly draped,
　　　Arranged so carefully and placed
　　　Within a splendid chamber, white
　　　As snow that lies upon the branch.
284　She had done it thus, I have no doubt,
　　　Because I am Diana's friend,
　　　The greatly honored deity,
　　　Appareled always all in white.[35]
288　　　　Alone, unclad, I went to bed
　　　And fell asleep. But then a cloud
　　　Appeared before me as I slept,
　　　Brilliant and glowing. Greatly did
292　I wonder what, indeed, it was.
　　　Then from the cloud, upon the right
　　　Beside the bed, shining and bright,
　　　Like lightning in the summertime,
296　There issued forth a charming voice,
　　　Pleasurable and filled with love.
　　　　　　Perceiving not whether I slept,
　　　The voice addressed me by my name,
300　And thus it spoke to me: "Dear friend,
　　　Who have loved me well and cherished me
　　　For all your life, as well I know,
　　　For I have often tested you:
304　I am the faithful goddess of
　　　The high and royal lineage
　　　Of God, who formed and fashioned me,
　　　And inculcated His commands.
308　So hear me out, devoted friend,
　　　I will tell you what has brought me here.
　　　　　　"You know that just before, I came
　　　With greatest pleasure where you were,
312　There to present the roses fair
　　　That in no season lose their bloom.
　　　I represented Love, who guides
　　　All those who are skilled in doing good,
316　Who sends me once again to you

    (Messagiere de ceste voye
    Lui plaist que soye par usage)
    Et voulentiers fais le message.
320   «Amours se plaint trop fort et duelt
    D'une coustume qui trop suelt
    Estre en mains lieux continuee;
    Bien vouldroit qu'elle fust muee,
324   Car elle est male, laide, et vilz,
    Et vilaine, je te plevis,
    Et par especial en ceulx
    Qui ne doivent estre pareceux
328   D'acquerir toutes bonnes meurs
    Pour plus acroistre leurs honneurs:
    C'est es nobles et es gentilz
    Hommes qui doivent ententis
332   Estre a mieulx valoir qu'autre gent;
    Bonté leur siet mieulx que or ne argent.
    Mais des vilains ne fais je force,
    Car ceulx ne font bien fors a force,
336   N'on ne les pourroit amender
    Pour leur ennorter ne mander,
    Car la condicion vilaine,
    Qui pis flaire que male alaine,
340   Si est trop fort a corrigier;
    Trop est fort cil vice a purgier.
    J'appelle vilains ceulz qui font
    Villenies qui les deffont;
348   Je n'entens pas par baz lignaige
    Le vilain, mais par vil courage.
       «Mais cellui qui noble se fait
    De lignie trop se deffait
352   Se sa noblesse en villenie
    Tourne, dis je voir ne le nye;
    Si font plus qu'autres a reprendre
    S'on les puet en vilains faiz prendre.
356   Et pour ce dis, ce n'est pas bourde,
    Qu'en lait fait n'en parolle lourde
    Tout nobles homs, s'il aime pris,
    Se doit garder d'estre repris,
360   Car trop en vauldroit mains senz faille,
    Tout feust il bien preux en bataille.

(As messenger upon this route
It suits him that my service be)
And willingly I bring this word.

320   "Love so profoundly grieves and sighs
About a custom that is maintained
Too well and in so many parts.
He would indeed prefer it changed,

324   For it is evil, ugly, low,
And vulgar, I can certify,
Especially when found in those
Who should not spare an effort toward

328   Acquiring fine, well-mannered ways
So that their honor may increase.
The word is meant for gentlemen
And nobles, who should set their minds

332   Toward being better than the rest:
Good befits them more than silver
Or gold. My care is not common folk,
Whose good is accomplished through sheer force,

336   Who cannot be altered, either through
One's exhortation or command,
Because the common circumstance
(Which smells much worse than breath that is foul)

340   Is much too hard to rectify,
A vice that is just too strong to purge.
I call those "common" who commit
Vulgarities which bring them low.

348   By "common" I do not mean low birth,
But rather lowly heart and mind.
"A man who claims nobility
Through lineage undoes that claim

352   Should he reduce his noble state
To commonness, I do not deny.
A man like that earns more reproof
If he is caught at lowly deeds.

356   That is why I say, it is not false,
Each noble, if he cares for worth,
Must guard himself against reproach
For ugly deed or vulgar word.

360   He would be a much less worthy man,
However great his battle skill.

          Car la prouesse seulement
          Ne gist pas ou grant hardement
364   D'assaillir ne de soy defendre
          Contre aucun qui le vueille offendre,
          Car ce sont prouesses de corps.

          Mais certes mieulx valent encors
368   Les bontez qui viennent de l'ame,
          Ce ne me puet nÿer nulle ame.
          C'est vaillantise et grant prouesse
          Quant un noble cuer si s'adresse
372   Qu'en vertus il soit bien propice
          Et eschever et fuïr vice,
          Ne qu'on ne puist trouver en lui
          Riens dont puist mesdire nullui,
376   Se n'est a tort ou par envie;
          Car n'est en ceste mortel vie
          Homme qui soit de touz amez,
          Ne de toutes gens bons clamez.
380 77rᵒ   Ce fait Envie qui s'efforce
          D'abatre loz; n'y face force
          Bon homme, ains face toudiz bien,
          Car loz vaincra, je te di bien.
384   Et s'un tel homme ainsi apris
          Peut aussi d'armes avoir pris,
          Tant que renommee tesmoingne
          Qu'en tout bien faire s'embesoingne,
388   Et qu'en riens ne soit recrëant,
          Un tel vassal, je te crëant,
          Est bien digne de loz acquerre,
          Se bon est en paix et en guerre,
392   Et juste et loyal en tous cas.
          Et o lui ait pour advocas
          Courtoisie, qui si l'enseingne
          Que de gentil porte l'enseingne
396   En fait, en dit, et en parolle,
          Senz orgueil, qui maint homme affolle.
          Si ait hault cuer et haulte emprise:
          Ce n'est pas l'orgueil qu'on desprise
400   Que d'avoir si haultain courage
          Qu'on ne daingnast faire viltage,

For valor is not found alone
Residing in the bravery
364 To make assaults and mount defense
Against some foe who would bring attack,
For those are but the body's feats.

Now certainly of greater worth
368 Is goodness coming from the soul;
No one can tell me otherwise.
It is valor and great bravery
When noble heart directs itself
372 To favor virtue, all the while
Fleeing from vice, avoiding it,
So no one may discover there
Something to slur, unless it be
376 In error or through jealousy.
For in this mortal life there is not
A man who will be loved by all,
Nor one whom all consider good.
380   That is Envy's doing, who attempts
To harm great fame; a worthy man
Should pay no heed, but just do good.
For honor will win out, I say.
384 And if a man who is learned in those things
Can also have esteem at arms,
So much that his renown attests
He cares to do all that is right,
388 In nothing is he cowardly:
A man like that, I promise you,
Deserves indeed to win high praise,
If he is good in peace and war,
392 And fair and true in every case.
And with him may his counselor
Be Courtesy, who would teach him so
He would bear the mark of noble style
396 In deed, in word, and in his speech,
Avoiding pride, so often man's
Demise. Thus let his thoughts aim high,
And his endeavors; pride like this
400 Is not the sort one scorns—having
A mind so high that it will not stoop

Et que l'en aime les haultaines
Choses contraires aux vilaines.
404 Telz choses sont appartenans
Aux nobles, et que soustenans
Soient justice en tout endroit
Et toute bonté; c'est leur droit.
408   «Mais pour revenir au propos,
Pour quoy vins ça sur ton repos,
Par le commandement mon maistre
Amours, qu'au monde Dieu fist naistre,
412 Et de quoy se deult et complaint,
Et dont par moy a toy se plaint:
C'est de la coustume perverse,
Qui l'onneur de mainte gent verse,
416 De mesdire, que Dieux mauldie,
Par qui mainte femme est laidie
A tort et a grant desraison,
Et maint bon homme senz raison,
420 Qui queurt ores plus qu'onques mais.
Ce fait Envie, qui tel mais
Apporte d'Enfer pour donner
Aux gens et tout empoisonner
424 Et occire de double mort
Qui a si fait vice s'amort.
Mesdire, qui bien y regarde,
C'est tel glaive et si faite darde
428 Que meismes cil qui le balance
Occist et cil sur qui le lance.
Mais aucunes fois plus blecié
Demeure cil qui l'a lancié
432 Que ne fait cil sur qui le rue,
Ou soit en maison ou en rue,
Et son ame plus griefment blece,
Et son honneur et sa noblesse,
436 Que ne fait souvent l'encusé.
Et tel s'est maintes foiz rusé
D'autre qui mieulx de soy valoit
Pour ce que son bien lui douloit.
440 Et tel diffame autrui souvent
Qui est plus seurpris, je m'en vent,
Du mesmes meffait et tachié

To vile pursuits, a mind that loves
The lofty things and not the low.
1404 ndeed, such qualities belong
To noblemen; and may they keep
The cause of justice everywhere,
And goodness; that is their rightful task.
408   "Returning to my subject, though,
The reason I have disturbed your sleep,
Upon command of Love, my lord,
Whom God has brought into the world,
412 To say just why he grieves and mourns,
And thus through me laments to you—
That tiresome habit is the cause,
By which so many people lose
416 Their honor—it is this slandering
(God curse it!) which dishonors scores
Of women wrongly, senselessly,
And many worthy men as well,
420 It is more so now than ever before.
That is Envy's work, who brings this dish
From Hell to serve it up above,
To poison everything about,
424 And bring a double death to him
Who is drawn to such malevolence.
For slander, when one ponders it,
Is like a lance or javelin
428 That kills the man who launches it
As well as him at whom it is aimed.
For sometimes he who is thrown the jab
Is left more wounded than the man
432 At whom the damage has been aimed,
Behind closed doors or on the street.
He wounds his soul more grievously,
His honor, his nobility,
436 More often than the man who is blamed.
Many a time has he accused
Another, one of greater worth:
How hard to bear the other's wealth,
440 And often, too, the man who slurs
Some other man is guiltier
Of just the same misdeed, I am sure,

Qu'il dit que l'autre est entechié.
444 77v°   Si est faulte de congnoissance,
Et d'Envie vient la naissance,
Car nul ne vouldroit que tel verve
On deist de lui, quoy qu'il desserve.
448   Mais chascun puet estre certain
Qu'il est un juge si certain
Qui tout congnoist et hors et ens,
Tout scet et tout est cler vëans;
452   Si rendra a chascun desserte
De bien ou de mal, chose est certe.
             «Trop font mesdisans a haïr,
Et leur compaignie a fuïr
456   Plus que de gent bataillereuse;
Plus male et trop plus perilleuse
Est compaignie, et plus nuysant,
D'omme jangleur et mesdisant:
460   Qui male compaignie hante
Ne puet que du mal ne se sente,
Et avec les loups fault huler,
Et de leur peau soy affuler.
464   Et quant je di homs, j'entens famme
Aussi, s'elle jangle et diffame,
Car chose plus envenimee,
Ne qui doye estre moins amee,
468   N'est que langue de femme male
Qui, soit a certes ou par gale,
Mesdit d'autrui, moque ou ramposne.
Et se mal en vient, c'est aumosne
472   A celle qui s'i acoustume,
Car c'est laide et orde coustume.
N'a femmes n'affiert a mesdire;
Ainçois, quant elles oyent dire
476   Chose qui face autrui dommage,
Abaissier doivent le langaige
A leur povoir, ou elles taire,
S'autre chose ne peuent faire.
480   Car avoir doit, en verité,
Doulceur en femme, et charité.
S'autrement font, c'est leur contraire,
Car bien siet a femme a point taire.

Than he maintains the other is.
444 The fault is one of judgment, and
     In Envy lie its origins.
     For no one wants capricious things
     Said of himself, whatever he
448 Deserves. But we may feel assured
     That there exists a Judge so sure
     He knows the inside and the out,
     He knows it all and sees it all,
452 He will render what each one deserves
     Of good or ill, that is to be sure.
          "Detestable are gossipers,
     Their company is more to be fled,
456 Than even that of warring folk.
     More evil and more dangerous
     And harmful is the company
     Of gossip-hawking, smirching men.
460 Whoever spends his time with bad
     Companions cannot avoid their stench:
     In league with wolves, one howls and wears
     Their skin. And when I say
464 A man, I mean a woman, too,
     Should she spread gossip and untruth;
     For nothing is more poisonous,
     Nor should be less belovèd than
468 An evil woman's wagging tongue,
     Which slurs, insults, or ridicules,
     In fun or with intent to harm.
     If ill results, that is alms to her
472 Who makes a habit of such ways.
     An ugly and a vile pursuit,
     Misspeaking ill-suits womankind.
     Instead, whenever women hear
476 Some word that harms another's name,
     They must extinguish all such talk
     If they can, or themselves be still,
     If nothing else is possible.
480 For women must, in truth, possess
     A gentleness and charity;
     If they do else, it is not their way;
     A well-bred silence suits their style.

484   Mais pour ce que ceste coustume
        Court en mains lieux qu'Envie alume,
        Vouldroit bien Amours errachier
        D'entre ceulz qu'il aime et tient chier;
488   C'est des nobles a qui tel tache
        Trop messiet, s'elle s'i atache,
        Car si preux n'est, je l'ose dire,
        Que, s'il a renom de mesdire,
492   Qu'il n'en soit partout moins amé,
        Moins prisié, et jangleur clamé.
        Mais sur toutes autres diffames
        Het Amours qu'on parle des fammes
496   Laidement en les diffamant.
        Ne veult que ceulz qui noblement
        Se veulent mener pour acquerre
        Pris et honneur en mainte terre
500   Soient de tel tache tachié,
        Car c'est maufait et grant pechié,
        Et pour estrapper tel verjus
        M'envoya bonne Amour ça jus
504   Atout l'Ordre belle et nouvelle,
        De quoy j'apportay la nouvelle
        Present toy n'a gueres de temps.
        Mais encor veult, si com j'entens,
508 78r°   Amours que ceste chose soit
        Publiee, comment qu'il soit,
        Et qu'on le sache en maint pays
        Afin que mesdit soit haÿs
512   En toutes pars ou noble gent
        Sont d'acquerre loz diligent.
        Si veult qu'ayes legacion
        De faire en toute nacion
516   Procureresses qui povoir
        Ayent, s'elles veulent avoir,
        De donner l'Ordre delittable
        De la belle rose agreable,
520   Avec le veu qui appartient.
        Mais Amours veult, bien m'en souvient,
        Que nulle ne soit establie
        A donner l'Ordre gente et lie
524   S'elle n'est dame ou demoiselle

484	Because this custom, though, sweeps through
	The many places set aflame
	By Envy, Love would like to pluck
	Away the ones he cherishes.
488	It is nobles who are suited least
	To being blamed for such a stain.
	For none is so fine, I dare to say,
	That he will not be loved less by all
492	If he is known to spread untruth;
	Less prized, and called a slanderer.
	Above all calumny that Love
	Hates most is defamation and
496	Base talk concerning womankind.
	He does not want the ones who try
	To act with dignity, to earn
	Esteem and worth in many lands,
500	To have this stain attach to them;
	For that is a sin, and wrongly done.
	To stop those acid-dripping tongues,
	The god of Love has sent me down
504	To bring the Order, fine and new,
	The one whose news I publicized
	Before you not so long ago.
	And further, as I understand,
508	The god of Love would like that this
	Be broadcast, in whatever way,
	Made known about, in many lands,
	So slandering will be disliked
512	In every place where noblemen
	Apply themselves to earning praise.
	To you he gives the mission of
	Ordaining ladies, deputies
516	In every realm, and they would be
	Empowered, should they wish it so,
	To give the charming Order out,
	The Order of the pleasing Rose,
520	Hearing the vow that goes with it.
	But Love desires, I well recall,
	That none be named to give the high
	And joyful Order, lest she be
524	An honored lady or a maid

D'onnour, courtoise, franche et belle;
Toutes sont belles quant bonté
A la beauté plus seurmonté.
528   «Ainsi auras par ce couvent
Ceste charge dorenavant.
        Si l'envoye par toute terre
Ou noble gent poursuivent guerre
532   Aux dames, de qui renommee
Est de leur grant bonté semee.
A celles veult et te commande
Bonne Amour par moy, et te mande,
536   Que tu commettes le bel Ordre
Ou nulz ne puet par droit remordre.
Et combien que j'aye apportees
Les roses qui seront portees
540   Des bons, a qui je les donnay
(Et de telles assez en ay,
Car en mon vergier sont cueillies),
Ne veult pas Amours que faillies
544   Els soient es autres contrees
Ou telles ne sont encontrees;
Car quiconques d'orfaverie,
D'or, d'argent, ou de brouderie
548   De soye, ou d'aucune autre chose,
Mais que soit en façon de rose,
Portera l'Ordre qui donnee
Sera de la dame ordonnee
552   De par toy pour l'Ordre establir,
Il souffist; et pour acomplir
Ceste chose voy ci les bulles:
Ou monde n'a pareilles nulles,
556   Si tesmoing la commission.
Cil Dieu qui souffri passion
Te maintiengne toudiz en l'euvre
        D'estude qui grant sc̈ience euvre,
560   Et t'otroit son saint Paradis.
Je m'en vois et adieu te dis».
Adonc est elle esvanoÿe.
Je m'esveillay toute esbahye,
564   Ne vy ouvert huys ne fenestre.
Merveillay moy que ce pot estre;

Of breeding, fair, and courteous.
For women all are beautiful
When goodness passes loveliness.
528 "By reason of this covenant,
You will have this charge forevermore.
     Thus send it out to every land
Where noble people war against
532 The ladies, whose renown is spread
By virtue of the good they do.
To them good Love commands and wants
And orders you, through me, to give
536 The lovely Order to their care,
Where none, by rights, can challenge it.
And though I brought a fine supply
Of roses which the good will wear,
540 To such I proffered them just now
(And though I have got enough of them,
For in my orchard is where they are plucked),
Yet Love desires that roses not
544 Be lacking in the other lands
Where such as these cannot be found.
If men who will wear the Order's badge,
Bestowed by ladies you have ordained
548 So that the Order may exist,
Will wear their roses worked in gold,
In silver, or embroidered silk,
Provided they have been rendered in
552 The rose's shape—that will suffice.
And that you may complete your task,
The bull I now shall pass to you;
There is nothing like it in the world,
556 The mandate testifies to that.
May God who knew the Passion now
Sustain you at that studying,
     Which brings great learning in its wake.
560 And may you reach His Paradise.
Now do I leave, and say adieu."
At that, she disappeared. I woke
In great astonishment. Seeing
564 No door or window left ajar,
I wondered what this could have been;

Si me pensay que c'estoit songe.
Mais ne le tins pas a mençonge
568   Quant coste moy trouvay la lettre
De la deesse au royal sceptre
Qu'elle mist dessus mon chevet,
Coste moy, puis volant s'en vet.
572 78v°   Par grant entente prises ay
Les bulles et moult y musay,
Car j'avoye lumiere d'oile.
Je me levay et la chandoile
576   Alumay adonc senz tarder
Pour mieulx la bule regarder.
Mais oncques ne vy en ma vie
Si de beauté lettre assouvie!
580   Merveilles os, je vous plevy,
De la grant beauté que g'i vy.
Estrange en est moult la maniere:
Le parchemin de fin or yere,
584   Et les lettres furent escriptes
De fin azur, non trop petites
Ne trop grans, mais si bien formees
Que mieulx ne peust. Non pas rimees
588   Ne furent, mais en belle prose
La contint l'Ordre de la Rose.
Le laz en fu de soye azure
Et le seel, de belle mesure,
592   Fut d'une pierre precïeuse
Resplandissant, et gracïeuse.
Le dieu d'Amours fut d'une part;
Les piez ot sur un lïepart.
596   De l'autre part fut la deesse,
De Loyauté dame et princesse.
Les empraintes moult merveilleuses
En furent, et trop gracïeuses,
600   Et bien sembla de si belle estre
Que n'estoit pas chose terrestre.
Si leuz la lettre senz y point
Faillir, et notay chascun point.
604   Lye fu de la vision,
Et d'avoir tel commission,
Car combien que je ne le vaille,

At first I thought it was a dream,
But then I knew it was no lie:
568   I found the letter next to me,
The one the sceptered goddess placed
Upon my bed, quite near my head,
Who then departed through the air.
572   With great desire I took the bull,
And gazed at it full length and breadth
Within the light my oil-lamp gave.
I left my bed without delay
576   And lit the candelabrum there,
The better to inspect the bull.
Never before had I beheld
A letter done so splendidly!
580   I marveled, I can tell you well,
To see the beauty I observed.
Its fashioning was greatly strange:
The parchment was of finest gold,
584   The letters were composed in fine
Blue azure; they were not too small
Nor yet too big, but formed so well
That no one could improve on them.
588   Nor was it rhymed—a lovely prose,
Contained the Order of the Rose.
Its braided strings were azure silk,
Its beautifully proportioned seal
592   Was made resplendent by a gem,
A precious, pleasing stone to see.
The god of Love was on one side,
Upon a leopard were his feet,
596   The goddess had the other part,
Lady and Princess Loyalty.
The modeling was marvelous
And very fair to look upon.
600   Its essence seemed so fine, indeed,
No earthly thing could it have been.
I read the letter, missing not
A jot, and noted every bit.
604   The sight of it, the thought that I
Was charged with it, delighted me.
I scarcely merit it at all—

Ay je desir que nul ne faille.
608 Et pour ce moy, qui suis commise
A ce, ne doy estre remise
De faire si bien mon devoir
Que je n'en doye blasme avoir.
612 Et pour ce ay je fait ce dittié
Ou j'ay tout l'estat appointtié,
Et mis la fourme et la maniere,
Comme il avint et ou ce yere,
616 Afin qu'on le sache en tous lieux.
   Si soient tous jeunes et vieux
Desireux d'estre retenus
En l'Ordre; maiz n'y entre nulz
620 S'il ne veult bien son devoir faire,
Car il se pourroit trop meffaire.
Aussi aux dames amoureuses,
Qui de tout bien sont desireuses,
624 J'entens de l'amour ou n'a vice,
Mal, villenie, ne malice;
Car quiconques le die ou non,
En bonne amour n'a se bien non.
628 Et a celles generaulment
Qui aiment honneur bonnement,
Soit en ce regne ou autre part,
Qui ont les cuers de noble part,
632 De par la deesse je donne
Le plain povoir et habandonne
De donner l'Ordre gracïeux
A tous nobles et en tous lieux
636 79r° Ou bien employé le verront
A ceulz qui avoir le voulront.
Mais s'aucun le prent et le jure,
Et puis aprés il s'en parjure,
640 Cellui soit tenu pour infame,
Haÿ de tout homme et de famme,
Car ainsi le veult la deesse
Qui ceste chose nous adresse.
644 Si feray fin, il en est temps,
Priant Dieu quë aux escoutans,
Et a ceulz qui liront mes dis,
Doint bonne vie et Paradis.

Still, I am eager that no one fail.
608　And since the charge is placed with me
　　To act, I must not be remiss
　　At doing what I should; and thus,
　　I will not be blamed for careless work.
612　And so I have written down this tale
　　In which I have entered all the facts
　　And told the shape and way of it,
　　Just how it happened, where it was,
616　So every place can know of it.
　　　　　May everyone, the young and old
　　Alike, desire to be enrolled
　　Within the Order, but, may none
620　Enlist who will not fulfill his vow,
　　For he could cause enormous harm.
　　For ladies, therefore, who are in love,
　　Who hope for every good result,
624　I destine uncorrupted love,
　　No evil, villainy, or spite;
　　Whoever may agree or not,
　　In true love there is naught but good.
628　Now for those women everywhere
　　Who cherish honor most of all,
　　In this domain or other realms,
　　Women whose hearts are nobly born,
632　In service to the goddess, I
　　Bestow complete authority
　　To give the lovely Order out
　　To nobles, and in places where
636　　　They think they will see it well-employed
　　By those sincerely wanting it.
　　But if a person takes the vow
　　And later violates his word,
640　May he be seen as one disgraced,
　　Despised by women and by men,
　　For thus the goddess wishes it,
　　Who has imparted this to us.
644　　　And so I will end, the time has come,
　　While asking God to grant good life
　　And Paradise to those who hear
　　And those who will read my poetry.

648   Escript le jour Saint Valentin
        Ou mains amans, trés le matin,
        Choisissent amours pour l'annee;
        C'est le droit de telle journee».
652   De par celle qui ce dittié
        A fait par loyale amittié.
        S'aucun en veult le nom savoir,
        Je lui en diray tout le voir:
656   Qui un tout seul cry crieroit,
        Et la fin d'aoust y mettroit,
        Së il disoit avec une yne,
        Il sauroit le nom bel et digne.
660   Cy fine le Dit de la Rose

648 Composed this day, Saint Valentine's,[36]
 When lovers, early in the day,
 Select their sweethearts for the year,
 For that is the warrant of this day.
652 From her who wrote this little tale,
 Composed in loyal comradeship.
 If someone wants to know her name,
 I will tell the truth of it outright:
656 If he utters a single cry,
 Then adds the month of August's end,
 And if he says it with an -een
 He will know the fine and worthy name.
660 Here ends the Tale of the Rose.

4. 1401 or 1402: Pierre d'Ailly, Le jardin amoureux (1351–1420)[37]

Pierre d'Ailly's authorship of this work, which was erroneously attributed
to either Jean Gerson or the bishop of Cambrai, was confirmed convincingly
by Pierre-Yves Badel in 1976.[38] Through a comparative study of d'Ailly's
sermon, *Ille vos docebit omnia* (delivered on Pentecost, 1402), and the *Jardin*,
Badel shows the thematic and narrative similarities between the two "texts."[39]
This being said, of greater interest to us in the present context are the Christian
substitutions for the elements of Jean de Meun's own "jardin amoureux" in
the *Roman*. Although d'Ailly relies on Guillaume de Lorris for the narrative
structure, the target of his criticism is Jean de Meun's immoral depiction of
the god of Love and the surrounding allegories. In d'Ailly's eyes, the true
"art d'aimer" is explained in Holy Scripture, and the true God of Love is the
Christian God; the true beloved is the pious soul. Because the *Jardin* enjoyed
considerable popularity in its time, I have chosen to include it in its entirety
save for the "chansonnette amoureuse" which concludes it. The text is extant
in seventeen manuscripts dating from 1423 to the end of the fifteenth century
and in four incunabulae (1476, 1506, 1515–25, 1528).

Text:

La jardin amoureux de l'âme
En l'abbaye de devote religion fondee.

En ce mondain desert est le jardin d'amoureuse consolacion
ou le vray Dieu d'amours habite; c'est le jardin gracieux ou habite
5 le doulx Jesus et ouquel il appelle sa mie quant il dit ou livre des
chansonnettes amoureuses: *Veni in ortum meum, soror mea, sponsa
mea.* Viens, dit il, en mon jardin, ma doulce suer et ma chiere
espouse. Ceste doulce voix et ceste chansonnette amoureuse chante
melodieusement Jhesucrist, le loyal amant, en appellant a soy la
10 sainte ame qu'est de luy amouree par ardent charité; et la nome
sa suer et son espouse; sa suer par consanguinité de nature, et son
espouse par affinité de grace; sa suer par la semblance de nature
humaine que il prist en la vierge Marie, et son espouse par la beauté
de grace divine qu'elle prent de Dieu le pere; sa suer par le lignage
15 naturel, et son espouse par mariage espirituel. Helas, bien doit celle
estre louee et benoicte qui est de si grant lignage et en si hault mariage qu'elle est nomé suer et espouse du grant roy du ciel et du haut
empereur du monde. Vecy doncques petites parolles et pleines de
grant sentence, embrasee de ardent amour et arrousee de amoureuse
20 doulceur.

Le second chapitre de la saincte ame qui oyt la voix de son
amy dit ainsi:

Translation:

    The Soul's Garden of Love.

    Created in the abbey of pious religion.

       In this worldly desert lies the Garden of loving consolation, where the true God of Love resides. It is the merciful garden,[40] where

5   sweet Jesus resides and to which He calls His beloved when He says in the book of little love songs: veni in hortum meum, soror mea, sponsa mea. Come, He says, to my garden, my sweet sister and my dear spouse. Jesus Christ, the loyal lover, sings melodiously in this sweet voice, and with this little love song calls to Himself the holy

10   soul who is enamored with Him through ardent charity. And He calls her His sister and spouse: His sister by natural consanguinity, and His spouse through affinity in grace; His sister for the resemblance to human nature which He acquired from the Virgin Mary, and His spouse for the beauty of divine mercy which she receives from God

15   the Father; His sister from natural lineage, and His spouse through spiritual marriage. Alas, she who comes from such great lineage and noble marriage must be venerated and blessed and called sister and spouse of the great King of Heaven and the high Emperor of the World. Here, then, are small words full of great meaning, kindled by

20   desirous love and nourished by love's tenderness.

       The second chapter of the holy soul who hears the voice of her beloved reads as follows:

Quant la sainte ame amie du doulz Jhesucrist est ainsi amoureusement appelee de son amy, a la voix de sa doulce chanson elle
25   euvre ses oreilles par diligente entention et resveille son cuer par
fervente cogitacion, et lieve son chief par grant admiration. He
Dieu, dit elle, j'ai oy la voix de mon amy; j'ai oy le son de cellui
que j'aime; he, tres doulz Jhesus, ta voix a sonné a mes oreilles,
ton son a resveillee mon cuer las; ou te queray je, ou te trouveray
30   je? Lors court elle des piez de bonne affection, et quiert la voie de
juste operation, et vient au jardin de vraie perfection; et de la grant
ardeur qu'elle a de courir, de querir et d'entrer, elle fremit, tressault
et chancelle; et de l'ardent desir qu'elle a de son amy trouver, son
cuer soupire, ses yeulx larmoient et sa face palit; car son amoureux
35   desir ne lui sueffre son amy sans ennui longuement actendre, ne
sa si longue demeure paciamment dissimuler; mais elle ne puet
si legierement courre ne si parfaictement querir ne si hastivement
trouver comme son cuer desire, car les piez sont faibles et lassez et
la voie est aspre et estroite, et le jardin ou son amy habite est ferme-
40   ment enclos et clozement fermez. Or oez comment, vous qui par
amour amez.

Le tiers est des piez de la saint ame qui sont faibles et lassez.

Les piez de la saincte ame qui est de Jhesucrist amie sont les
pensees et les affections qui la portent vers son amy, mais ils sont
45   faibles et lassez se ils ne sont bien oingts et confortez de la doulce
oille de grace, car ilz sont souvent ferus et hurtez contre les dures
pierres des diverses temptations que les trois adversaires de l'ame
lui jettent au devant pour faire ses piez trebuches. Ces trois adversaires sont le monde, la char et le diable. Le monde jette les pierres
50   de richesses temporelles, la char jette les pierres de délices corporelles, et le diable jette les pierres de falaces espirituelles. Helas, a
peine puet nul passez parmi ces pierres sans ses piez blecez et sans
clochier ou trebuchier, dont le prophete dit en soy complaignant
que sept fois le jour chiet; et pour cest empeschement la sainte ame
55   est retardee d'aler vers son amy et de si legierement courir coin son
cuer desire.

Le quart chapitre est de la voie du jardin qui est estroite et
aspre.

Mais quant elle puet par le sauf conduit de Dieu eschapper
60   des voies du monde, de la char et du dyable et retraire ses piez des
pierres de leurs temptacions, lors quiert la voie de juste operation,
et la treuve estroite et aspre par austere affliction. Car ceste voie
est close et environnee d'une haie plaine d'espines et garnie de

When the holy soul, beloved of sweet Jesus Christ is called so
lovingly to her beloved, she opens her ears with diligent attention
25   to the voice of His sweet song and awakens her heart with fervent
cogitation, lifting up her head in great admiration. God, she says,
I heard the voice of my beloved, I heard the sound of Him whom I
love; very sweet Jesus, Your voice rang in my ears, the sound of You
awakened my weary heart; where shall I search for You, where shall
30   I find You? Then she runs with feet of great affection, seeking the
path of righteous action, and comes to the garden of true perfection.
And from the great desire she has to run, to search, and to enter, she
trembles, jumps, and staggers; and from the ardent desire she has to
find her friend, her heart sighs, her eyes fill with tears, and her face
35   grows pale; for her loving desire does not permit her to wait long
for her friend without vexation, nor to pretend patiently not to notice
His long absence. However, she cannot run as easily nor search as
perfectly nor find Him as hastily as her heart desires, for her feet are
weak and weary, the path is rough and narrow, and the garden where
40   her beloved resides is securely enclosed and tightly secured. Now
hear how,[41] you who love for love.

The third concerns the feet of the holy soul, which are weak
and weary.

The feet of the holy soul, the beloved of Jesus Christ, are the
45   thoughts and affections which carry her toward her beloved. But
they are weak and weary, if they are not well anointed and soothed
by the sweet oil of mercy, for they are often injured and strike the
hard stones of the various temptations thrown in her path by the
soul's three adversaries in order to make her feet stumble. These
50   three adversaries are the World, the Flesh, and the Devil. The world
throws stones of temporal wealth; the flesh, stones of carnal delights; and the devil throws stones of spiritual deception. Alas, one
can hardly pass between these stones without injuring one's feet and
without limping or stumbling. It is for this reason that the prophet
55   says to himself, lamenting, that he sins seven times a day.[42] Because
of this hindrance, the holy soul is delayed in going toward her beloved and in running as easily as her heart desires.

The fourth chapter concerns the garden's path, which is narrow and rugged.

60   But when through God's safe guidance she is able to escape
the paths of the world, of the flesh, and of the devil, and to pull
her feet away from the stones of temptation, then she will search
for the path of righteous action, and will find it narrow and rugged

65 pointures. Ceste est la voie de vraie penitence qui est poignant par
contriction, mais elle est florissante par confession et fructifiant par
satisfaction; comme cy a merveilleuse haie et precieuse espine qui
si bel florit et fructifie, qu'elle porte les vrais fruits de penitence
qui par especial medicine sont recommandez et louez en la sainte
70 evangile. O, espinette, espinette, moult est ta pointure doucette, car
plus parfont point au cuer et plus tost donne garison; et moult est
ce fruit gracieux qui puet curer la plaie et saner la maladie de tout
pechié mortel. Sans ce fruit gouster, ne puet nul pelerin par ceste
voie passer car il est necessaire pour sa maladie garir, pour santé
acquerir, et pour sa vie soustenir; et est molt doulz et gracieux quant
75 il est bien assavouré, ja soit ce que au commencement il soit sur et
amer.
    Le quint chapitre est de la closture du jardin.
    Quand la sainte ame est entree en la voie de juste operation et
elle a gousté du fruit de penitence pour avoir en son pelerinage es-
80 pirituelle reffection, lors elle vient au jardin de vraie perfection pour
trouver son amy et avoir a luy vertueuse consolation. Mais ce jardin
est fermement enclos et closement fermés, car il est de ung fort mur
encloz et environneez. C'est le mur de dure austerité, fondé dessus
parfonde humilité, eslevé par haulte povreté, fortifié de patience et
85 de benignité, pour resister contre les hurs d'adversité et les vents
de prosperité. De la force et de la haultesse de ce mur la sainte ame
moult se merveille; et quant elle se sent lassee et travailliee et elle
ne voit comme elle puist oultre passer et dedens entrer, lors la belle
se sied au pié du mur et ploure et soupire et maine grant douleur.
90 Mais quant elle a donné un pou de repos a son corps, elle prent
confort en son cuer et se lieve, et tant quiert et tant cerche que pour
sa diligence elle vient a la porte.
    Le VIe chapitre est de la garde du jardin.
    La treuve elle une tres reverende et redoubtee dame qui a par
95 certains signes perceu sa venue et par sa courtoisie lui a la porte ou-
verte. C'est dame obedience qui est garde du jardin et tient les clefs
de discretion, la verge de correction, et le baston de pugnition; les
clefs pour clore et ouvrir et pour faire les bons entrer et les mauvais
yssir; la verge et le baston pour les forfais corrigier et pugnir; et
100 pour bouter hors oysiveté la fole et pechié le villain avec toute leur
compagnie. Ceste verge et ce baston sont deplaisans aux orgueil-
leux, et aux humbles gracieux et plaisans dont le saint prophete dit
que ceste verge et cest baston lui ont fait consolacion.

from severe affliction. For this path is enclosed and surrounded by
65   a hedge, full of thorns covered with sharp points. This is the path of
true penitence, which is thorny from contrition, but it is in bloom
from confession and bearing fruit from satisfaction. What a marvelous shrub and precious thorn, so beautifully flowering and bearing
fruit that it carries the true fruits of penitence, which are lauded in
70   the Holy Gospel as special medicine! O, little thorn, little thorn,
your point is very sweet, for the more deeply you penetrate the
heart, the sooner you will bring healing to it. And very sweet is the
merciful fruit which can heal the wound and illness of all mortal
sin. Without tasting this fruit no pilgrim can take this path, for it is
75   necessary in order for his illness to heal, for him to acquire health,
and to sustain his life. And once it has been well savored, it becomes
very sweet and merciful, though it is sour in the beginning.
      The fifth concerns the garden's gate.
      Once the holy soul has started upon the path of righteous ac-
80   tion and has tasted the fruit of penitence in order to have spiritual
repose during her pilgrimage, then she will come to the garden of
true perfection in order to find her beloved and to obtain from Him
virtuous consolation. But the garden is securely enclosed and tightly
secured, for it is enclosed and surrounded by a strong wall. This is
85   the wall of harsh austerity, built upon profound humility, erected
by great poverty, and fortified by patience and goodwill, so that it
will resist the attacks of adversity and the winds of prosperity. The
holy soul marvels greatly at the strength and height of this wall.
And when she feels weary and exhausted and does not see how she
90   will be able to cross over it and enter inside, the beauty then sits at
the foot of the wall, and cries and sighs and feels great pain. But
when she has given her body a brief rest, she finds comfort in her
heart and stands up; and she searches so earnestly that through her
diligence she reaches the gate.
95   The sixth chapter concerns the guardian of the garden
      There she finds a very reverend and renowned lady who has
perceived her arrival through certain signs and has courteously
opened the door to her. This is Lady Obedience, the guardian of the
garden, who holds the keys of discretion, the rod of correction, and
100   the staff of punishment: The keys are used to lock and unlock the
door, and to let the good enter and to chase away wrong-doers; the
rod and the staff are used to correct and punish errors and to chase
away Idleness,[43] the foolish, and Sin, the villain, along with their
whole entourage. This rod and staff are unpleasant for the haughty,

Le VIIe chapitre est des quatre damoiselles de dame obedi-
105   ence.

Quant la sainte ame voit dame obedience et son estat et sa
maniere, forment le doubte et vers elle humblement se humilie
et s'encline. Et celle lui demande: qui estes vous qui cy venez, et
quelle occasion vous mene? Je suis, dit elle, une povre pelerine
110   qui ay oy la voix de mon amy et viens pour obeir a lui. Estes vous
doncques, dit la dame, celle qui est du Dieu d'amour amee et en
son jardin appelee? S'il est ainsi, bien soyez vous venue. Lors la
prent par la main destre et lui fait jurer et promettre qu'elle vivra en
obedience ne rien ne fera sans autorité et licence; et celle lui promet
115   liement et s'offre joyeusement a sa doctrine et a sa discipline. Et
tantost la dame la recoit doucement et lui baille quatre demoiselles
pour lui accompagner; ce sont les quatre nobles vertus cardinaulz,
c'est assavoir prudence pour lui enseigner, temperance pour lui
chastier, force pour lui garder, justice pour lui gouverner. Lors ces
120   quatre belles damoiselles la prennent en garde et en commande et
sans dangier et sans refus la seuffrent passer la porte et entrer au
jardin.

Le VIIIe chapitre est de la grant beaute du jardin en general.

Quand la saint ame se voit dedens entree, moult est liee et
125   joyeuse; et tant est hastive et desirant de trouver son amy que
a peine peut elle contenir sa maniere. Mais les demoiselles qui
l'accompagnent la contraignent d'avoir amoderance et la font coye-
ment aler et par tous les lieux du jardin ordonnement proceder pour
la beauté regarder et la bonté en considerer. Lors voit elle paintures
130   luisans, herbes verdoyants, flours resplendissans, arbres ombraians,
fruits reconfortans, fontaines bruyants, oiseillons chantans, amies et
amants joyeusement esbanoyans.

Le IXe chapitre est de la peinture du jardin en especial.

Mais de toutes les choses qui sont tant beles et plaisantes, la
135   sainte ame premierement regarde et diligemment considere les nobles peintures qui sont au mur du jardin soubtillement figurees. La
voit elle les œuvres de la divine sapience, les merveilles de la sainte
escrıpture, les histoires de la Bible, les enseignements des evang-
iles, les miracles de Jhesucrist, les fais des apostres, les victoires
140   des martyrs, les vertus des confesseurs, les louanges des vierges, les
vies des Peres, les dis des sains hommes, les exemples des sages et
generalement la puet elle veoir tout ce qui appartient a la doctrine
espirituelle de son sauvement. O comme icy a noble painture qui
contient telle doctrine a qui ne se puet comparer la mondaine phi-
145   losophie ne quelleconque science humaine.

105   and merciful and pleasant for the humble. Therefore the holy
        prophet says that this rod and this staff have given him consolation.
            The seventh chapter concerns the four maidens of Lady Obe-
        dience.[44]
            When the holy soul sees Lady Obedience and her status and
110   manner, she fears her greatly; she humbles herself and bows. Lady
        Obedience asks: Who are you who come here, and what brings you
        here? I am, she says, a poor pilgrim who has heard the voice of
        her beloved, and I have come to obey Him. Are you, then, says the
        Lady, the one who is loved by the God of Love and who has been
115   called into His garden? If so, I welcome you. She then takes her by
        the right hand and makes her swear and promise that she will live
        in obedience and will do nothing without authorization and permis-
        sion. And she promises loyally, offering herself joyously to Lady
        Obedience's doctrine and discipline. And soon the Lady receives her
120   gently and gives her four maidens to accompany her. They are the
        four noble cardinal virtues, namely, Prudence to teach her, Temper-
        ance to chastise her, Strength to watch over her, Justice to govern
        her. Then the four beautiful maidens take her safely under their
        guard and command and, not refusing her, allow her to pass through
125   the gate and enter the garden.
            The eighth chapter concerns the great beauty of the garden in
        general.
            When the holy soul sees that she has entered inside the gar-
        den, she is very happy and joyous, and in such a hurry to find her
130   beloved that she can scarcely contain herself. But the maidens who
        accompany her compel her to be moderate, and make her walk qui-
        etly and proceed properly through all areas of the garden so that she
        may see all its beauty and goodness. There she sees luminous paint-
        ings, green grass, splendid flowers, shady trees, energizing fruit,
135   thundering fountains, singing birds, and lovers amusing themselves
        joyously.
            The ninth chapter concerns in particular the paintings inside
        the garden.
            Yet of all the very beautiful and pleasant things, the holy soul
140   looks first at and diligently considers all the noble paintings which
        are skillfully depicted on the garden wall.[45] Here she sees the works
        of divine sapience, the wonders of the Holy Scripture, the stories of
        the Bible, the teachings of the Gospels, the miracles of Jesus Christ,
        the deeds of the apostles, the victories of the martyrs, the virtues of
145   the confessors, the veneration of the virgins, the lives of the holy
        fathers, the maxims of saintly men, the examples of the wise; and in

Le Xe chapitre des herbes, des fleurs, des arbres et des fruits.

Apres ce que la sainte ame est par ceste painture suffisamment
endoctrinee, elle procede plus avant au jardin pour sentir la plaisante
odeur des herbes et des fleurs et la tres grant doulceur des arbres et
150   des fruits. La, voit elle la terre de nostre mortelle corruption culti-
vee de spirituelle correction et diligemment labouree par vertueuse
exercitation, et doulcement arrosee par divine inspiration. En cette
terre naissent les herbes de humble meditation, les arbres de haulte
contemplation, les fleurs de honeste conversation, les fruits de
155   saincte perfection, et generalement la croissent les biens de grace en
si grande abondance que a peine les pourroit humain entendement
nombrer ou langue raconter. En ces biens prent la sainte ame doulce
pasture et grande refection. Elle se siet dessus la verdure des herbes,
elle se repose sous l'ombre des arbres, elle cueille les fleurs, elle
160   gouste les fruits et par especial de toutes flours et de tous fruits elle
queut la violette de vraie charité qui croit sous l'herbette de basse
humilité; si en fait ung chapelet pour soy parer et pour mieulx plaire
a son amy. Moult est ce chapelet bel et gracieux, et sur tous autres
paremens plaisant au Dieu d'amour et mesmement que on queut
165   l'herbe menue. Et a la doulce violette est ensemble meslee pour
accroissement de beauté la rose vermeillette de charnelle virginité et
la rose blanchette de spirituelle netteté. O tres doulx Dieu; bien doit
estre celle louee et beneye qui peut a son amy tel chapelet presenter
et de telles florettes luy environner. C'est le present qu'il demande a
170   ses amies quant il dit ou livre des Cantiques: fillettes de Jerusalem,
garnissez moi de florettes, environnez moi de pommettes car je lan-
guis d'amourettes. O com cy a gracieuse requeste et tres amoureuse
complainte. Helas, helas, trop seroit le cuer felon et despiteux qui ce
don ne presenteroit a ce loyal amoureux qui pour amer est langou-
175   reux.

Le XIe chapitre est de l'arbre de la croix.

Et pour ce la sainte ame forment se peine et travaille de son
amy trover pour lui offrir et donner le present gracieux des belles
fleurs d'onnesteté et des bons fruits de sainteté. Si quiert tant et
180   carche, qu'elle trouve le precieux arbre de vie. C'est l'arbre de la
sainte croix ou le Dieu d'amour languit d'amoureux martyre et ou il
souffrit mort amere. C'est ou il etendit les bras et ou offrit sa bouche
pour sa mie acoler et baisier. C'est ou il ouvrit son cuer et ou il es-
pandit son sang pour s'amour montrer et declairier. La voit la sainte
185   ame les signes evidens et l'amoureuse langueur et la langoureuse
douleur de son amy. Et quant elle apercoit qu'il est ainsy douloureusement mort pour l'amour d'elle, lors est elle plus que oncques

short, she can see everything that pertains to the spiritual doctrine of her salvation. O, what noble paintings, containing such a doctrine, to which neither worldly philosophy nor any other human science

150   can compare.

The tenth chapter, concerning the grass, the flowers, the trees, and the fruit.[46]

After the holy soul has been sufficiently indoctrinated by this painting, she proceeds further into the garden in order to smell the

155   pleasant odor of grass and flowers, and the intense sweetness of trees and fruit. There she sees the earth of our mortal corruption cultivated by spiritual correction and diligently plowed by virtuous exercise, and softly watered by divine inspiration. In this earth grow the grasses of humble meditation, the trees of great contemplation,

160   the flowers of honorable conversation, the fruit of holy perfection; and in short, the goods of mercy grow in such abundance that human understanding can scarcely count them nor can human speech describe them. In these goods the holy soul finds sweet restoration and great repose. She sits down on the green grass, rests in the

165   shade of the trees, picks flowers, tastes the fruit, and of all the fruits and flowers, she especially gathers the violet of true charity, which grows under the little plot of grass of deep humility. She makes a garland out of them with which to adorn herself in order to better please her beloved. This garland is very beautiful and graceful, more

170   so than any other adornment pleasing to the God of Love, particularly because it is made with lowly grass. And so that the garland will be even more beautiful, the sweet violet is combined with the red rose of carnal virginity and the white rose of spiritual purity. O very sweet God; she who can present such a garland to her beloved

175   and surround Him with such flowers must be praised and blessed. This is the gift He asks of His many beloveds when He says in the *Canticles*: little daughters of Jerusalem, adorn Me with flowers, surround Me with little apples,[47] for I long for love songs. Oh, what a gracious request, what a very impassioned lament. Alas, alas, the

180   heart which would deny this gift to this loyal lover, who so longs to love, would be all too felonious and spiteful.

The eleventh chapter concerns the tree of the Cross.

Therefore, the holy soul struggles hard and labors to find her beloved, in order to offer and give Him the merciful present of

185   the beautiful flowers of honor and the good fruit of holiness. She searches so diligently that she finds the precious tree of life. It is the tree of the holy Cross, where the God of Love languished in loving martyrdom and where He suffered a bitter death. It is where He

mais enamouree et plus embrasee d'amour, car elle est ferue ou cuer
et forment naffree dung dart amoureux, c'est a dire de l'amoureuse
190   compassion du doulz Jhesucrist, dont elle soupire et gemit et sy
font en larmes et en pleurs; et en larmoyant chiet au pied de la
croix. Et ainsi comme en defaillant piteusement se complaint et
garmente fort: Henuy lasse, dit elle, ou aurai je confort puisque mon
amy est mort? Las, c'estoit ma vie; comment pourrai je doncques
195   vivre puisque ma vie est morte? O arbre de la croix, pourquoy es
tu nommé arbre de vie? mieulx devrais tu avoir nom arbre de mort,
puisque en toi est morte la vie mortelle. O immortelle et pardurable
vie, comment es tu ainsi a mort livree? O tres dolz Jhesus et tres
glorieux martyr d'amour, trop as m'amour cher achetee quant pour
200   bien aimer tu as langui de mort amere. O langoureuse mort, trop
m'est amere ta mémoire quant tu m'as toulu la doulceur de ma vie.
O Jesus, ma tres doulce amour, et ma tres amoureuse doulceur; las
ou te trouverai je pour a toy faire present des flourettes de bonne
amour et de bonne odour, et des pommettes de bonne savour que je
205   t'ay oy demander pour reconforter ta douleur et ta mortelle langour.
O douloureuse langour de mon amy, trop me fais douloureusement
languir se tu ne me fais brefvement morir, car je ne quiere vivre sans
lui a nul jour.
       Le XIIe chapitre est des trois dames qui confortent la sainte
210   ame de la mort de son amy.
       Ainsi se complaint la sainte ame de son amy; et quant le Dieu
d'amour oit sa complainte, il a de sa douleur pitié et lui envoye
trois dames pour lui réconforter. Ce sont les trois vertus theologaux;
c'est assavoir foy pour lui fortifier, esperance pour lui aider, charité
215   pour lui solacier. Et lors ces trois nobles dames la confortent moult
doucement. Amie, dient elles, nous sommes de vostre amy mes-
sager et vous dirons de lui bonnes nouvelles. Il est la sus au ciel, et
nous envoie a vous ca jus en terre. Si vous mande par nous que plus
n'ayez tel desconfort pour sa langueur ne pour sa mort, car par sa
220   mort vous aurez vie, par sa langueur vous aurez joie, par sa douleur
vous aurez soulas, et par sa peine aurez repos. Et se quant a present
vous ne le veez, ne se maintenant ne l'avez a vostre talent, de ce ne
devez vous avoir impatience; car s'il est de vous absent corporelle-
ment et vous ne le veez maintenant fors en samblance obscure, si le
225   verrez vous apres face a face clerement. Or soyez donc confortee;
soyez lie, et demenez joie car foy vous temoigne, esperance nous
promet, charité vous assure que se vous amez vostre amy loyaument
et se vous lui gardez l'amoureux present jusques a la fin de cette

190 spread His arms and offered His mouth to His beloved to caress and kiss. It is where He opened His heart and spilled His blood to show and declare His love. Here the holy soul sees the obvious signs and the passionate languor and the languorous pain of her beloved. And when she perceives that He died such a painful death out of love for
195 her, she is more than ever before enamored with him and kindled with love, for she has been struck in the heart and pierced by a tender arrow,[48] in other words, by loving compassion for sweet Jesus Christ, for whom she sighs and suffers and bursts into sobs and tears. Weeping, she falls at the foot of the Cross. And thus, faltering compassionately, she cries out and laments loudly: alas, she says;
200 where shall I find comfort now that my beloved is dead? Alas, this was my life. How can I live now that my life is dead? O tree of the Cross, why are you called the tree of life? You ought to be called the tree of death, since mortal life is dead within you.

O immortal and eternal life, how can you be delivered thus
205 unto death? O very sweet Jesus and very glorious martyr of love, You bought my love at too great a price when out of great love You languished in bitter death. O languorous death, too bitter is the memory of when you took from me the sweetness of my life. O Jesus, my very sweet love and my very loving sweetness; alas,
210 where shall I find You in order to offer You the sweet-smelling little flowers of virtuous love and the delicious little apples I heard You request, to ease Your pain and mortal languor? O painful languor of my beloved, you will make me languish too painfully if you do not let me die shortly, for I do not wish to live without Him one single
215 day.

The twelfth chapter concerns the three ladies who comfort the holy soul over the death of her beloved.

In this way the holy soul laments her beloved. When the God of Love hears her lament, He takes pity on her pain and sends three
220 ladies to comfort her. They are the three theological virtues, namely, Faith to strengthen her, Hope to help her, and Charity to comfort her. Then the three noble ladies comfort her very tenderly. Friend, they say, we are messengers of your beloved, and we will tell you His good news. He is up there in heaven, and sends us here to earth.
225 Through us He asks you to no longer feel sad, either for His languor or for His death, for you have life because of His death, joy because of His languor, solace out of His affliction, and rest as a result of His pain. And if you do not see Him at present or have Him in your company enough, you ought not to be impatient for these things,

230 mortelle vie, finablement vous verrez son cher viaire et baiserez
sa doulce bouche, et aurez avec lui joie sans fin, joie pardurable,
joie sans desconfort de tous maulx assuree, vie sans mort et de tous
biens garnie. Car il mesme dit en la sainte escripture que œil ne vit
ne oreille ne oy, ne cuer ne donne, ne ne puet comprendre les biens
qu'il a appareillez a ses loyaulx amis et amies. Quant la sainte ame

235 oit ces nouvelles: hélas, dit elle, et quant venra la mort, et quant
venra le jour qu'elle me separera de mon corps; certes je desire estre
du corps separee et estre avec Jhesucrist.

Le XIIIe est des fontaines et des ruisseaulx du jardin.

Mais quant cestes trois dames par leurs ardentes paroles et

240 par leurs amoureuses promesses ont la sainte ame ainsi esprise et
embrasee d'ardant desir et d'amoureuse flamme, lors l'adrecent aux
doulces fontaines du jardin pour rafreschir et arroser sa grant ardeur,
et pour adoulcir et attremper l'ardente soif de son desir. Et la trouve
elle la doulce fontaine de grace de laquelle sourdent et naissent sept

245 ruisseaulx qui sont les sept sacremens de Jhesucrist, et sept autres
qui sont les sept dons du saint Esperit. La treuve elle la doulce
fontaine de misericorde qui se moultiplie et s'espart en sept ruisseaulx qui sont sept œuvres espirituelles, et en sept autres qui sont
sept œuvres corporelles. Et quant ces ruisseaulx de sept œuvres de

250 misericorde passent par la fontaine de grace, il en sourt et sault une
belle eau moult roide et moult clere et legiere. C'est l'eaue vive saillant en vie pardurable, si comme Jhesucrist disoit a la Samaritaine.

O Dieu, comme c'est bien sailli et bien monté de bas en
hault quant creature humaine pour faire les œuvres de misericorde

255 en ceste povre vie mortelle monte en la haulte vie du royaume du
ciel. O tres doulx Jhesus, bien seront benois si comme tu promets
en l'evangile ceulx qui pour telles œuvres faire seront de toi ap-
pelés pour venir au hault royaulme qui leur est appareilliez des le
commencement du monde. O roy souverain, comme puet saillir et

260 monter lassus au royaulme du ciel cette eau de grace et de misericorde qui cours ca jus en terre. Comme puet saillir si hault l'eau qui
sourt si bas, et comme puet œuvre terrienne de humaine creature
monter ou royaume celeste de Dieu son createur. Certes ce ne pourroit estre fait fors par la grant vertu de ta bonté infinie, car de toy qui

265 es bon sans mesure, de toy qui es de tous biens la fontaine, viennent
et descendent du ciel en terre les fontaines et les ruisseaulx de grace
et de misericorde, et tu les fait par ta vertu monter de bas en hault et
retourner a toy qui es leur originale et principale naissance.

Or sont donc moult doulces les fontaines; moult sont doulz

230   for He is absent from you in the flesh, and you can now see Him
only in obscurity, but later you will see Him face to face. Therefore,
be comforted now; be joyous, for Faith is your witness, Hope your
promise, and Charity your guarantee that if you love your beloved
faithfully and keep the love you now have for Him until the end of
235   your mortal life, you will at last see His dear face and kiss His sweet
mouth, and you will have unending joy with Him, without sorrow,
and life without death and full of all good things. For He Himself
says in the Holy Scripture that the eye does not see, the ear does
not hear, the heart does not give, and cannot comprehend the good
240   that He has given to His loyal friends. When the holy soul heard this
news: Alas, she said, when death comes, and when the day comes
when death separates me from my body, I desire to be separated
from my body and to be with Jesus Christ.

          The thirteenth chapter concerns the fountains and streams of
245   the garden.[49]

          Yet when these three ladies had instructed the holy soul with
their ardent words and their tender promises, and had seized her
with ardent desire and passionate fervor, they guided her to the
sweet fountains of the garden to cool and assuage her great desire
250   and to quench and calm the ardent thirst of her desire. There she
finds the sweet fountain of mercy, from which there flow seven[50]
streams, which are the seven sacraments of Christ, and seven more,
which are the seven gifts of the Holy Spirit. There she finds the
sweet fountain of mercy, which multiplies and divides into seven
255   streams, which are the seven spiritual works, and into seven more
which are the seven corporeal works. And when these seven streams
of the seven works of mercy pass by the fountain of mercy, a beautiful jet shoots from the fountain, very straight and very clear and
buoyant. It is the living water which swells forth into eternal life, as
260   Christ said to the Samaritan woman.

          O God, how excellently it courses up, ascending from below
as do human creatures when they perform works of mercy in this
poor mortal life, climbing to the exalted life of the heavenly kingdom. O very sweet Jesus, blessed are those who, as You promise
265   in the Gospel, will for such deeds be called to Your high kingdom,
which has been prepared for them since the beginning of the world.
O sovereign King, how can this water of grace and mercy which
flows on earth leap and climb up to the heavenly kingdom? How can
water which runs so low jump so high, and how can the terrestrial
270   work of a human creature climb to the heavenly kingdom of God,

270   les ruisseaulx qui ainsi sourdent et naissent de toy qui es de vraie
       doulceur plain. Et pour ce en est la sainte ame doulcement arrousee
       et abondamment abreuvee; la elle est arrousee pour la grant ardeur
       refreschir; la elle est abrevee pour son ardente soif adoulcir; et de
       la lui vient doulce rosee de piteuse compassion; de la lui descent
275   doulce pluie de parfaite devotion; la sent elle la doulce goutte de
       divine inspiration; la voit elle et boit la doulce eaue de vraie conso-
       lation.
             Le XIVe chapitre est des oiseillons qui volent et chantent au
       jardin.
280   Ainsi prent la sainte ame doulce refection es fontaines et es
       ruisseaulx de ce jardin gracieux; mais moult lui accroissent son sou-
       las et sa joie le doulz chant des oiseaulx qui volent et chantent. Ce
       font les ames devotes qui volent de bas en hault en montant de la vie
       active en la vie contemplative, en deslessant les basses choses terre-
285   niennes pour avenir aux choses celestiennes. Ce font les oyseillons
       qui de terre volent au ciel en ostant les plumes de leurs cogitations
       hors mondaine occupation et en mouvant les ailes de leurs affections
       par divines meditations. Ainsi volent legierement et montent haulte-
       ment les ames devotes. Mais en volant et en montant elles chantent
290   tres doulcement et dient amoureusement chansons espirituelles, en
       donnant au Dieu d'amour louanges et exaltations, en lui rendant
       grâces et benedictions. C'est le doulz et amoureux chant de par-
       faite oroison faite en vraie devotion qui commence a basse voix de
       secrete confession, et moyenne en hault son de discrete exultation,
295   et finablement persevere en ton de jubilation. Ce chant est moult
       melodieux car il est moult doulcement chanté plus par grace que par
       nature; n'il n'y a descort ne demesure, ne faulse ne fainte musique,
       mais il y a plein assent entre le cuer et la bouche et concordance
       parfaite entre la voix et la pensee.
300   Le XVe chapitre est des amies et des amans qui joyeusement
       apprennent l'art d'aimer.
             Au son de cette mélodie viennent amies et amants joyeuse-
       ment esbanayer en faisant joie spirituelle, sans leesce desordon-
       nee; la assemblent les amoureux leur amoureuse compaignie et
305   demainent joyeuse vie en pensant et parlant d'amour; la mettent soy
       a genoilz pour faire au Dieu d'amour hommage, et a son amoureux
       servage se rendent par obeissance; la viennent ils a son escole pour
       oyr la loy amoureuse ou l'art d'amer est tout enclose. C'est l'escole
       de Jhesucrist ou il apprent la loi divine qui contient l'art et la doc-
310   trine de Dieu amer sur toutes choses et son prochain comme soy

his Creator. Surely, this could not be done but by the great virtue of
Your infinite goodness, for the fountains and streams of grace and
mercy come from You, who are good beyond measure and who are
the fountain of all that is good; and by Your virtue You cause them
275 to climb from bottom to top, returning them to You, their first and
principal source of origin.

Thus, the fountains are now very sweet; the streams are very
sweet, which burst and spring from You, who are full of true sweetness. And with this, the holy soul is gently assuaged and her thirst
280 abundantly quenched. Here her great ardor is cooled down; here
her great thirst is calmed; and from here the sweet dew of merciful
compassion comes to her; from here the soft rain of perfect piety
descends; here she tastes the sweet drop of divine inspiration, here
she sees and drinks the sweet water of true consolation.

285 The fourteenth chapter concerns the little birds[51] which fly and
sing in the garden.

In this way, from the fountains and streams of the merciful
garden the holy soul takes sweet repose, yet her solace and joy are
increased still more by the sweet song of the birds which fly and
290 sing. These are the pious souls, flying from up high from below,
climbing from the active life to the contemplative life by leaving
behind lowly terrestrial things in order to attain the things of heaven.
They are the little birds which fly from the earth to the sky, shedding
the feathers of their cogitations of worldly preoccupation and mov-
295 ing the wings of their affection through divine meditation. Thus the
pious souls fly deftly and ascent to great heights. And as they fly and
climb, they sing very sweetly, and lovingly recite spiritual songs, of-
fering praise and exaltation to the God of Love by blessing Him and
giving Him thanks. It is the sweet and loving song of perfect prayer
300 made in true piety, which begins in a low voice of secret confession,
then acquires a loud tone of cautious exultation, and finally continues into a song of jubilation. This song is very melodious, for it is
sung very sweetly, more by means of grace than by nature.

There is neither discord nor false or affected rhythm or music,
305 but the heart and mouth are in full harmony and there is perfect
concordance between voice and thought.

The fifteenth chapter concerns lovers who joyfully learn the
art of love.[52]

At the sound of this melody, lovers joyfully arrive and amuse
310 themselves in spiritual joy, free of undue excess. There, lovers assemble their loving company and lead a joyous life, thinking and

mesme. C'est l'art de bien amer, laquelle ne peut savoir humaine
creature par raison naturelle se elle n'est domptee et enseignee
par foy de divine escripture. Ceste art ne sceurent oncques Virgille
ne Ovide ne les autres qui enseignerent a folement ou faulsement
315   aimer, et a folement honorer Cupido, le faulx dieu d'amour, et sa
fole mere Venus.

A ceste faulx amour fuir, forment nous semont et encline foy,
maistresse de vraye amour: fuyez, fuyez, dit elle, fuyez, loyaulx
amans, fuyez l'escole perilleuse, fuyez l'art faulse et mentongiere,
320   fuyez la doctrine perverse qui apprend l'amour haineuse pleine de
pechies et d'ordure. Mais venez au doulz Jhesucrist qui vous appelle
en son escole; venez au maistre souverain qui vous apprend bien
amer d'amour loyal sans vilenie. Lors viennent les bons escoliers
et fuient toute amour mondaine pour acquerir l'amour divine. Mais
325   ils ne sont pas tous semblables en discipline ne en perfection. Ainsi
sont moult differens en souffisance et en condition car aucuns sont
commencans, les autres profitans et les autres parfaits. Les com-
mencants fuient l'escole par paour de pugnicion, les prouffitans par
ardeur d'acquerir retribution et les parfaits par fine amour et franche
330   dilection. Ce sont les trois estats des vrais estudians d'amour qui
s'estudient et entendent a Dieu amer entierement de cuer, de ame et
de pensee.

Le XVIe chapitre est de la sainte ame qui de joie chante les
louanges du Dieu d'amour.

335   Quant la sainte ame voit ceste belle compaignie qui est de
son amy ainsi enamouree, moult lui plaist et moult lui delicte car
elle n'est pas pleine de fole jalousie; ains desire que son amy soit
amé de tous et que tous soient de lui amez comme soy mesmes; et
pour ce qu'elle puisse les cuers amoureux a cette amour attraire elle
340   se peine et efforce de son amy louer et doulces loanges lui dire et
raconter; et de la joie qu'elle prent en loant son amy et en racontant
les grans biens qui viennent de l'amour de lui, elle est contrainte de
chanter cette chansonnette amoureuse:…

315

speaking about love. They kneel to pay homage to the God of Love, and vow obedience to His impassioned servitude. Here, they come to His school to hear the law of love, in which the whole art of love is contained.[53] It is the school of Christ, where He teaches them the divine law, which includes the art and doctrine of loving God above all things and loving one's neighbor as oneself. It is the art of loving well, which no human being can know through natural reasoning without being taught by divine Scripture through faith. This art was

320

never known to Virgil, Ovid, or any of the others who taught people to love foolishly or falsely and to foolishly honor Cupid, the false god of Love, and his foolish mother, Venus.

That we may flee this false love, Faith, mistress of true love, forcefully summons us and makes us bow down: Flee, flee, she

325

says, flee, faithful lovers, flee the perilous school, flee the false and lying art, flee the perverse doctrine which teaches heinous love full of sin and filth.[54] Instead come to sweet Jesus, who calls you to His school; come to the sovereign Master, who teaches you to love with a love that is faithful and free of villainy. Then the good pupils

330

come, fleeing all worldly love in order to obtain divine love. But they are not all equal in discipline or perfection. Hence, they are very different in ability and condition, for some are beginners, others are advancing in skill, and others have obtained perfection. The beginners flee the school for fear of punishment, the intermediate

335

pupils for fear of retribution, and the perfected ones for courtly love and noble and open enjoyment. These are the three levels of the true students of love, who practice and listen in order to love God with all their heart, soul, and mind.

The sixteenth chapter concerns the holy soul, who from joy

340

sings the praises of the God of Love.

When the holy soul sees this beautiful company thus enamored with her beloved, it pleases and delights her greatly, for she is not filled with foolish jealousy. She desires for her beloved to be loved like this by all, and for all to be loved by Him as they love

345

themselves. And so that she may attract loving hearts to this love, she labors hard and endeavors to praise her beloved with sweet praises; and from the joy she derives from praising her beloved and in telling of the great good which comes from loving Him, she feels compelled to sing this little song of love:...

5. *May 18, 1402: Jean Gerson's (1363–1429) Treatise against the Roman de la rose*[55]

In 1395 Jean Gerson succeeded his former teacher, Pierre d'Ailly, in the position of Chancellor of the University of Paris. It was, however, in his position as Dean of the church of St. Donatien at Bruges, which he held in parallel with his chancellorship, that he felt the urgency for moral and educational reform within the institutional Church. After his return to Paris in 1401, he accepted preaching responsibilities at the church of St. Jean de Grève, where his much-cited series of sermons, the "Poenitemini" were pronounced in the winter of 1402.[56] Although the actual contact and sharing of moral views between Christine de Pizan and Jean Gerson remains speculation, it is interesting to note that Gerson's treatise appeared just over a month prior to de Pizan's first publication of the epistles as part of her collected works on June 23, 1402.

Text:

180r°   Le traictié d'une vision faite contre Le Ronmant de la rose par le
        Chancelier de Paris
                Par ung matin n'a gaires en mon veillant me fut advis que mon
        cuer ysnel s'envola—moienans les plumes et les esles de diverses
5   pensees—, d'ung lieu en aultre, jusques a la court sainte de Cres-
        tienté: illuec estoit Justice Canonique la droituriere seant sus le
        throne d'equité, soustenu d'une part par Misericorde, d'autre part
        par Verité. Justice en sa main destre tenoit le sceptre de remunera-
        cion; en la senestre l'espee tranchant de pugnicion: ot les yeux vif,
10   honnourables et plus resplandissans que n'est la belle estele journal,
        voir que le soleil. Belle fu sa compaingnie, car d'une part estoit son
        tres saige conseil et tout a l'anviron se tenoit sa noble chevalerie et
        baronnie de toute Vertus (qui sunt filles de Dieu proprement et de
        Franche Volenté), comme Charité, Force, Attrempance, Humilité et
15   aultres a grant nombre. Le chief du conseil et come le chansselier
        estoit Entendement Soubtil, joint par compaingnie ferme a dame
        Raison la sage: ses secretaires furent Prudence et Science. Foy, la
        bonne crestienne, et Sapience, la divine et celestienne, furent de
        l'estroit conseil: en leur aide estoient Memoire, Providence, Bon
20   Sentement et autres plusseurs. Eloquance Theologienne, qui
180v°   fu de moyen langaige et atranpé, // se portoit pour l'advocat de la
        court. Le promoteur des causes avoit non Conscience, quar rien
        n'est qu'elle ne saiche et raporte.
                Ainsi comme je me delitoie par grande admiracion a res-
25   garder tout le bel arroy de ceste court de Crestienté et de Justice la
        droituriere, se va lever, comme me sembla, Conscience, qui de son

Translation:

One morning when I was barely awake, I realized that my heart,
equipped with feathers and wings made of various thoughts, had
been flying hurriedly from one place to the next until it had reached
the holy court of Christianity. Here was Canonical Justice the
5   righteous, seated on her throne of equality, supported on one side by
Clemence and on the other by Truth. In her right hand Justice held
the scepter of reward, and in her left the sharp spear of punishment.
She had vigilant eyes, honorable and shinier than the most beautiful
summer day, shinier even than the sun. Her entourage was beauti-
10 ful, for on one side there was her very wise Council and all around
her were her noble chivalry and barony of all Virtues (who, to be
sure, are the daughters of God and of Free Will), such as Charity,
Strength, Temperance, Modesty, and numerous others. The Council's head, acting as chancellor, was Skilled Understanding, in close
15 companionship with Lady Reason the wise;[57] her secretaries were
Prudence and Knowledge. Faith, the good Christian, and Sapience,
the divine and celestial, were part of this intimate Council. Their
satellites were Memory, Providence, Good Judgment, and several
others. Theological Eloquence, who was moderate and temperate in
20 speech, occupied the position of court advocate. The defender of the
cases was called Conscience because there is nothing she does not
know and report.

As I enjoyed and greatly admired all this beautiful array of the
court of Christianity and Justice the righteous, it seemed to me that
25 Conscience was about to rise. It was her responsibility to defend the
cases of the court, together with Right, who acted as the master of
petitions. In her hand and bosom Conscience held several petitions,
among them one which, if I remember correctly, recounted word for
word this lamentable complaint of Chastity, the very beautiful, the
30 very pure, who would never dare think such villainous filth:

TO JUSTICE the righteous, who represents God on earth,
and to the entire religious, pious, and Christian court: I, Chastity,
your loyal subject, implore you and beg humbly that the intolerable

office promeut les causes de la court, aveuc Droit qui pour maistre
des requestes se porte. Conscience tint en sa main et en son saing
plusseurs supplicacions: entre les aultres en y ot une qui mot a mot,
30   bien m'en remembre, contenoit ceste complainte pitable de Chasteté
la tres belle, la tres pure, qui onques ne daigna neiz panser aucune
villainne ordure:

A Justice la droituriere, tenant le lieu de Dieu en terre, et a
toute sa religieuse court devote et crestienne. Supplie humblement
35   et se complaint Chasteté, vostre feable subjecte, que remede soit mis
et provision briefve sus les forfaitures intollerables, lesquelles m'a
fait et ne cesse de fere ung qui se fait nommer le Fol Amoureux. Et
sont telz les articles:

LE PREMIER ARTICLE

40   Ce Fol Amoureux met toute sa paine a chassier hors de la terre
moy—qui n y ay coulpe—et mes bonnes gardes ausy: qui sont Honte, Paour et Dangier le bon portier, qui ne oseroient ne daingneroient
ottroyer nes ung villain baisier, ou dissolus resgars, ou ris atraiant,
ou parolle legiere. Et ce il fait par une Vielle maudite pieur que
45   dyable, qui ensaingne, monstre et enhorte comment toutes juesnes
filles doivent vendre leurs corps tost et chierement sans paour et
sans vergoingne, et que elles ne tiengnent compte de decepvoir ou
parjurer mais que elles ravissent tousjours aucune chose; et ne fas-
sent force ou dangier de se donner hastivement, tant que elles sont
50   belles, a toutes villainnes ordures de charnalité, soit a clers, soit a
lays, soit a prestres, sans differance.

LE SECOND ARTICLE

Il vuelt deffandre mariaige, sans exepcion, par •i• Jalous souspes-
sonneux, hayneux, chagrineux et malendrius, et par luy meesmes
55   et par les dis d'aucuns mes adversaires: et conseille plus tost a se
pandre ou se noyer ou a fere pechiés qui ne font a nommer que se
joindre en mariaige et blasme toutes fames—sans quelconque en
oster—,pour les rendre hayneuses a tous les hommes tellement que
on ne les vuelle prandre en foy de mariaige.

60   LE TROISAIME ARTICLE

Il blasme juesnes gens qui se donnent en religion: pour ce, dit il,
que tousjours tendent a en issir, de leur nature. Et cecy est en mon
prejudice, quar je suis donnee especiaument a religion.

LE •IIIIᴱ• ARTICLE

65   Il giette par tout feu plus ardent et plus puant que feu gregois
ou de souffre: feu de paroles luxurieuses a merveille, ordes et
deffendues—aucunefois ou non de Venus ou de Cupido ou de Ge-

infringements which someone by the name of the Foolish Lover has
imposed and does not cease to impose upon me be remedied without further delay. These are the accusations:

THE FIRST ACCUSATION

This Foolish Lover puts all his effort into trying to chase me from
the earth, I who am guilty of nothing, and with me my good guards,
Shame, Fear, and Danger—the good door guards, who would not
dare nor deign to grant a single shameful kiss, a dissolute gaze, a
provocative laugh, or a lecherous utterance. And the Foolish Lover
does this by means of a slanderous Duenna worse than the devil
himself who teaches, shows, and exhorts all young girls how to sell
their bodies early and at a high price, without fear or shame. Further, they should not worry about deceiving or betraying, provided
they can gain something by doing so. As long as they are beautiful,
they should not resist giving themselves freely to any kind of carnal
filth—to clerics, laymen, or priests, without distinction.

THE SECOND ACCUSATION

He wishes to prohibit marriage, without exception—through his
own words and those of a Jealous Husband, who is suspicious,
vengeful, disgruntled, and evil-minded as well as through the letters of my adversaries. He advises people to drown themselves or
to commit unspeakable sins rather than to engage in marriage. He
accuses all women, without exception, of being vengeful toward all
men, to such an extent that one would never wish to take a woman
in marriage.

THE THIRD ACCUSATION

He insults young people who take their vows because (he says) by
nature, they will always try to leave the religious life. And this is
directed at me, because I am particularly devoted to religion.

THE FOURTH ACCUSATION

He ignites flames more ardent and foul than a Greek fire or a sulfu-
rous one: A fire of astonishingly lecherous words, which are repugnant and prohibited. Sometimes they are pronounced in the name
of Venus or Cupid or Genius, sometimes in his own name, through
which my beautiful houses and edifices and my sacred temples of
human souls are set on fire and burned. And I am rudely cast aside.

THE FIFTH ACCUSATION

He defames Lady Reason, my good mistress, by throwing her into
such a rage, provoking such villainous blasphemy, that she advises
others to speak blatantly and coarsely like the goliards,[58] with no
shame whatsoever, however abominable and shameful a thing may

35

40

45

50

55

60

65

70

nius, souventefois en son propre non—par quoy sont arses et brulees
mes belles maisons et habitacions et mes temples sacrés des ames
70   humainnes; et en suis boutee hors villainnement.
LE •V^E• ARTICLE

Il diffame dame Raison, ma bone maistresse, en ly metant sus telle
raige et tel villain blaspheme que elle conseille parler nuement,
deslaveement et gouliardement sans honte de toutes choses, tant
75   soient abhominables et honteuses a dire ou fere, mesmement entre
persones tres dissolues et adversaires a moy. Helas! Et s'il ne me
vouloit espargnier, que ly a meffait Raison? Mais ainsy est. Certes il
prent guerre a toutes vertus.
LE •VI^E• ARTICLE

80   Quant il parle des choses saintes et divines et esperituelles, il mesle
tantost paroles tres dissolues et esmovans a toute ordure; et toutevois ordure ja n'entrera en paradis tel come il descript.
LE •VIIE• ARTICLE

Il promet paradis, gloire et loyer a tous ceulx et celles qui acom-
85   pliront les œuvres charnelles, mesmement hors mariaige; car il
conseille en sa propre persone et a son exemple essayer de toutes
manieres de fames sans differance, et maudit tous ceulx et celles
qui ainssy ne le feront,—au moins tous ceulx qui me receveront et
retendront.
90   LE •VIIIE• ARTICLE

Il, en sa persone, nomme les parties deshonnestes du corps et les
pechiés ors et villains par paroles saintes et sacrees, ainssy comme
181r° // toute tele euvre fut chose divine et sacree et a adourer, mesmement hors mariaige et par fraude et violence; et n'est pas content
95   des injures dessusdictes s'il les a publiees de bouche, mais les a fait
escripre et paindre a son pouoir, curieusement et richement, pour
atraire plus toute persone a les veoir, ouÿr et recepvoir. Encores y a
pis: car afin que plus subtivement il deceust, il a mesley miel avec
venin, succre avec poison, serpens venimeux cachiés soubz herbe
100   vert de devocion: et ce fait il en assemblant matieres diverses, qui
bien souvent ne font gueres a son propos si non a cause dessusdicte,
et pour ce qu'il fut mieulx creu et de plus grande auctoritey de tant
que il sambleroit avoir plus veu de choses et plus estudié.

Si vous suppli, dame Justice, de hatif remede et convenable
105   provision sus toutes ces injures,—et autres trop plus que ne contient
ceste petite supplicacion, mais son livre en fait foy trop plus que
mestier ne fust.

Aprés que ceste supplicacion de Chasteté fut leue distintee-
ment et en appert, illeuc peussiés vous apercevoir tout le conseil

75   be to say or do, even for those who are very dissolute and who are my opponents. Alas! If he did not wish to spare me, what did Reason do to harm him? But so be it. Indeed, he declares war against all virtues.

THE SIXTH ACCUSATION

80   When speaking about holy, divine, and spiritual things he mixes in dissolute and moving words with all kind of filth, yet the filth he describes will never be allowed into paradise.

THE SEVENTH ACCUSATION

He promises paradise, glory, and laurels to all men and women

85   who will fulfill carnal works, even outside of marriage, because he advises them to follow his example, trying out all kinds of women, without distinction, and he condemns those men and women who will not follow suit—or at least all those who receive and accept me.

THE EIGHTH ACCUSATION

90   In his own name, he names all the shameful body parts and villainous sins using holy and sacred words, as if these works were divine and sacred and to be worshipped through fraud and violence and even outside of marriage. He is not satisfied with simply enunciating the above-mentioned insults, but has them written down and embel-

95   lished as much as possible in a luring and lavish manner in order to attract everyone to see, hear, and accept them. The matter becomes still worse, since in order to deceive more skillfully, he mixes honey with venom, sugar with poison; there are venomous serpents hidden beneath the green grass of piety. He does this by assembling various

100   topics which often have nothing to do with his argument, aside from the above-mentioned objective, and thus one believes him more easily and attributes greater authority to him, so that it seems as though he has seen and studied more than he in fact has.

       I implore you, Lady Justice, to accord this matter the appropri-

105   ate attention and bring about a swift remedy for all these insults, and others which I left out of this little petition, but to which his book attests more than is necessary.

       After Chastity's petition was read distinctly and openly, one could see by the expression and demeanor of the entire Council and

110   all the noble chivalry that they clearly seemed indignant. Nevertheless, since they were wise and temperate, they said that his case would be heard. But since the Foolish Lover, who stood accused, was absent (he had already passed on to the high place from which no one returns), it was asked whether he had spokespersons or sup-

115   porters of any kind in the court of Christianity.[59]

110   et toute la noble chevalerie qui, a leur chiere et leur samblant, bien
       apparoient estre indignés. Neantmoins, comme sages et attrempés
       dirent que partie seroit oÿe. Mais pour ce que le Fol Amoureux qui
       estoit accusey n'y estoit pas (il avoit ja trespassé le hault pas duquel
       nulz ne revient), on demanda s'il avoit en la court de Crestienté
115   procureurs ou faulteurs ou bien veullans quelquonques.
           Lors veissiés, a une grant tourbe et une flote de gens sans
       nombre, josnes et vieulx de tous sexes et de tous ages, qui—sans
       garder ordre, a tort et a travers—vouloient, l'ung excuser, l'autre
       le deffendre, l'autre le loer; l'autre demandoit pardon a cause de
120   jonesse et de folie, en aleguant que il s'en estoit repenti quant il
       escript depuis: «J'ay fait, dit il, en ma jonesse maint dit par vanité»;
       l'autre le soustenoit pour ce qu'il avoit esté tel et si notable clerc et
       biau parleur sans pareil en franssois; aucuns pour ce que il avoit dit
       si proprement la verité de tous estas, sans espargnier nobles ou non
125   nobles, pays ou nacion, siecle ou religion.
           Et quel mal est ce, dit l'ung des plus avisés, quel mal est ce,
       je vous pry, se cest home de tel sens, de tel estude et de tel renon
       a volu composer ung livre de personnaiges ouquel il fait par grant
       maistrise chascun parler selond son droit et sa proprieté? Ne dit pas
130   le prophete en la persone d'ung fol que Dieu n'est pas? Et le saige
       Salemon ne fist il en especial tout son livre *Ecclesiastes* en ceste
       maniere, par quoy on le sauve de cent et cent erreurs qui la sont
       en escript? S'il a parley legierement, c'est la condiccion de Venus
       ou de Cupido, ou d'ung fol amoureux, lequel il vuelt representer.
135   Et ne parla Salemon en ses *Cantiques* en guise des amoureux par
       parolles qui pouroient atraire a mal? Neantmoins on le lit. S'il dit ou
       personnaige de Raison que tout se doit nommer par son non, soient
       veus ses motifs: voirement quel mal est es nons, qui ne l'i entent?
       Les nons sont nons come autres; puis donques que une mesme
140   chose s'entent par ung non ou par ung aultre, que doit chaloir par
       quel non on la donne a entendre? C'est certaing que en nature n'y
       a riens lait. Seule laidure est de pechié, duquel toutefois on parle
       ung chascun jour par son droit non, comme de murtre, de larrecin,
       de fraudes et de rapines. En la parfin, s'il a parlé de paradis et des
145   choses devotes, pour quoy le blasme on de ce de quoy il doit estre
       loé? Et prenons qu'aucun mal fust en son livre, n'est point doubte
       que trop plus y a de bien: praingne chascun le bien et laisse le mal!
       Il proteste par exprès qu'il ne blasme que les mauvais et les mau-
       vaises, et qui se sant coulpable, si s'en amende. Mais aussy n'est il
150   saige qui ne faille a la fois: neis mesmes le grant Omer falli; et qui

Then one could see a huge crowd of people, young and old of both sexes and all ages who in an unruly fashion and in complete disorder wished either to acquit, defend, or praise him. Some asked that he be forgiven on account of his youth and folly claiming that

120 he had since repented by writing, "In my youth I composed, he said, many a text out of vanity."[60] Others supported him because he had been such an illustrious cleric and beautiful rhetorician, unequaled in the French language, and others, in turn, for having spoken the absolute truth about all estates without sparing nobles or common-

125 ers, country or nation, lay or religious life.

And, pray, tell me what evil is there, said one of the most clever ones, what evil is there if this man of such understanding, learning, and renown wished to compose a book in which, in a masterful way, he makes every character speak according to his

130 right and signification? Does the prophet not say in the name of a foolish person that God does not exist? And does the wise Solomon not construct his entire book *Ecclesiastes* in this manner, which was the reason why he was acquitted for the hundreds and hundreds of errors which it contains? If he spoke lecherously, it is because of

135 the nature of Venus or Cupid or a foolish lover whom he seeks to represent. Did Solomon in his *Canticles* not speak in the guise of lovers in a manner which could attract evil? He is read nonetheless. If he has the character of Reason say that everything must be called by name, we must look at his motivation: Truly, what evil is there

140 in names, if no evil is intended? These names are names like any others; therefore, if a thing is understood by one name or another, why is it important by which name it is understood? It is certain that there is nothing ugly in Nature. Only ugliness itself contains sin, of which one speaks every day in calling it by its name, such as mur-

145 der, theft, fraud, and pillaging. In the end, if he speaks of paradise and pious things, why is he insulted for that for which he ought to be praised? And let us assume that his book does contain some sins; there is no doubt that the good outweighs the bad. So let us all take the good and ignore the bad! He purposely declares that he repri-

150 mands only sinners, both men and women, and that those who feel guilty should repent. Indeed, there is no one so wise that he does not err at times: Even the great Homer erred. What should incite this wise court of Christianity to forgiveness and mercy still more is that Saint Augustine and other theologians erred in some things, yet they

155 are not accused or condemned for it, but rather honored. Truly, one who insults this rose called *Le Roman de la rose* must indeed have a beautiful rose in his own garland!

plus doit encliner a pardon et a beninité ceste saige court de Crestienté, nous avons que saint Augustin et autres docteurs pres que tous
errerent en aucuns poins, qui toutefois ne sont pas pour tant accusés
181v° // ou condampnés, mais honnourés. Et vraiement il doit avoir belle
155   rose en son chappel qui ceste rose blasme qui se dit *Le Ronmant de
la Rose!*
         A ces paroles y sambla bien aux amis et fauteurs du Fol
Amoureux que sa cause fust toute gaingnié sans y savoir respondre. Et soubzrioient les ungs aux autres et s'entreresgardoient ou
160   chuchilloient ou faisoient signes divers, quant Eloquance Theologienne (qui est advocat de la court crestienne), a la requeste tant
de Conscience come de Chasteté sa bien amee et a cause de son
office, se leva en piés a belle contenance et maniere attrempee; et
par grande auctorité et digne gravité, il, comme saige et bien apris
165   depuis qu'il ot ung pou tenue sa face encline bas en guise d'ung
home aucunement pansif, se sousleva meurement et seriement, et
en tournant son resgart a Justice et environ tout son barnaige, ouvry
sa bouche, et a voix raisonnant doulce et moyenne, telement commensa sa parole et sa cause:
170   –Je vouldré bien, au plaisir de Dieu—lequel vous representés
ycy, dame Justice—, que l'aucteur que on accuse fust present en
sa persone par retournant de mort a vie: ne me seroit ja besoing de
multiplier langaige ne d'ocuper la court en longue accusacion; car je
tiens en bonne foy que ynellement, volentiers et de cuer il confes-
175   seroit son erreur, demanderoit pardon, crieroit mercy et paieroit
l'amende. Et ad ce presumer m'esmeuvent plusseurs apparances,
nommeement cele qu'aucuns ont allegué: que des son vivant il s'en
repenti: et depuis ditta livres de vraye foy et de sainte doctrine. Je
li en fais tesmoingnaige: dommage fu que fole jeunesse ou aultre
180   mauvaise inclinacion deseu ung tel clerc a tourner nicement et trop
volagement a tele legiereté reprovee son subtil engin, sa grande
estude et fervent, et son beau parler en rimes et proses: voulsist Dieu
que meulx en eust usé!
         Helas! bel amy et subtil clerc! Et n'estoient donques assés folz
185   amoureux au monde sans toy mettre en la tourbe? N'y avoit il qui
les menast et aprist en leur soties sans ce que tu te donnasses leur
capitainne, ducteur et maistre? Folz est qui foloye, et folie n'est pas
sens: trop veult estre blasmé qui se diffame et prant l'office d'ung
diffamé; pour vray, tu estoies digne d'autre maistrise et d'autre of-
190   fice. Vices et pechiés, croy moy, s'aprannent trop de legier: n'y fault
maistre quelconque; nature humainne, par especial en jeunesse, est

After hearing these words it seemed to the friends and supporters of the Foolish Lover that his case was clearly won, without
160 his having had to defend his own actions. Some smiled and looked
at one another or whispered or exchanged various gestures when
Theological Eloquence (who is the Christian court's advocate)—at
the request of Conscience as well as of Chastity her beloved, and in
compliance with her duty—rose to her feet in a tempered and digni-
165 fied manner. With great authority and worthy severity, he,[61] with his
face wisely lowered like that of a man who is somewhat pensive,
rose sternly and serenely, and, turning toward Justice and her entourage, opened his mouth to begin his speech and to present case in a
soft and temperate voice:
170 –In order to please God—whom you represent here, Lady
Justice—I would like the author who stands accused to be present
in person and to return from the dead: I would then have no need
to speak unnecessarily or to keep the court occupied with a long
accusation, because I am very confident that without further ado,
175 voluntarily and sincerely, he would confess his error and ask for
forgiveness, cry for mercy and pay his repentance. I have come to
this assumption based on several conjectures, namely, one which
has been alleged by others: that he repented during his lifetime and
thereafter wrote books of true faith and holy doctrine. I attest to this:
180 It was regrettable that foolish youth and other sinful inclinations
deceived such a cleric into naively and flightily applying his skilled
mind, his great and fervent knowledge and his eloquent rhetoric, in
rhyme and prose, to such reproachful lechery. God, would that he
had used them better!
185 Alas! Beautiful friend and skilled cleric! Were there not
already enough foolish lovers in the world without your joining the
crowd? Were there not already those who guided and instructed
them in their foolishness without your declaring yourself their
captain, teacher, and master? Foolish is he who acts foolishly, and
190 folly is not rational; he who defames himself wishes to be insulted,
and assumes the position of one who is defamed. To tell the truth,
you were worthy of a different occupation and position. Believe
me, vices and sins are learned all too easily; no teacher of any sort
is necessary. Human nature, especially in youth, is far too prone to
195 falter and to slide and succumb to the filth of any carnality. It was
scarcely necessary for you to drag them there or to push them into
it by force. Who is more readily taken or inflamed by the fire of
villainous pleasures than the human heart? Why then did you blow

trop encline a trebuchier et a glassier et cheoir en l'ordure de toute
charnalité: n'estoit besoing que tu les y tirasses ou a force boutas-
ses. Qui est plus tost empris ou enflanmé au feu de vilains plaisirs
195   que sunt les cuers humains? Pour quoy donques souffloies tu ce feu
puant par les vens de toute parole legiere et par l'auctorité de ta persone et ton exemple? Se tu ne doubtoies alors Dieu et sa vanjance
que ne te faisoit sage et avisé la pugnicion qui fu prise de Ovide?
L'onneur de ton estat au mains t'an eust retrait. Tu eusse eu honte, je
200   ne doubte mie, d'avoir esté trové en plain jour publiquement en lieu
de foles fames qui se vendent et de parler a elles come tu escrips.
Et tu fais pis; tu enhortes a pis: tu as par ta folie—quant en toy
est—mis a mort et murtri ou empoisonné mil et mil personnes par
divers pechiées, en encores fais de jour en jour par ton fol livre. Et
205   ja n'en yés a excusser sur la maniere de ton parler par personnaiges,
come je proveray cy apprés clerement: mais je ne puis mie tout dire
a une fois.

        O Dieu tout bon et tout puissant! Et se tu, Fol
Amoureux—puis qu'ainsy te vuelt on nommer—, se tu avoies
210   repantance en ta vie de mains dis (lesquelz tu avois fais en ta jonesse par vanité), pour quoy les lessoies tu durer? Ne devoient eulx
pas estre brullés? C'est trop mauvaise garnison que de venin ou de
poison a une table, ou de feu entre oille et estoupes. Qui ara geté
ung feu partout et il ne l'oste, comment sera il quite des maisons qui
215   en seront arses? Et qui est pieur feu et plus ardent que le feu de luxure? queles maisons sont plus precieuses que les aimes humainnes
182r° (comme est bien contenue en la supplicacion de // dame Chasteté)?
Car elles doivent estre temple sacré du Saint Esperit. Mais qui plus
art et enflemme ces ames que paroles dissolues et que luxuryeuses
220   escriptures et paintures? Nous veons que bonnes, saintes et devotes
parolles, paintures et escriptures esmuevent a devocion, come disoit
Pitagoras: pour ce sont fais les sermons et les ymages es esglises;
trop plus legierement, par le contraire, les mauvaises tirent a dissolucion. N'est cil qui ne l'espreuve, et les ystoires plusseurs le
225   monstrent.

        Mais, bel ami (je parle sans cause a toy, qui n'es pas ycy et
auquel desplaisoit tout ce fait et desplairoit, come j'ay dit, se tu
estoies present,—et se lors tu ne l'eusses sceu tu l'as apris depuis, a
tes griefs cousts et despans, au mains en purgatoire ou en ce monde
230   par penitance), tu diras par aventure que tu ne fus pas maistre de
ravoir ton livre quant il fu publié; ou par aventure te fu il amblé sans
ton sceu autremant; je ne le say. Tant sai je que Berengier, disciple

200 into this fire reeking of the winds of lecherous speech, using the
authority and example of your person? If, indeed, you did not fear
God and His vengeance, did not the punishment which Ovid had to
endure make you wise and reasonable? The honor of your situation
should at least have restrained you. I have no doubt that you would
have been ashamed if you had been seen publicly in the company of
205 prostitutes, speaking to them in the way you suggest in your writings. You do worse; you exhort to worse: Through your folly, which
is great, you have killed, murdered, or poisoned thousands and
thousands of people through various sins, and you continue to do
so day after day with your foolish book. Nor can you be acquitted
210 simply because you have your characters speak for you, which I will
hereafter prove beyond any doubt. However, I cannot say everything
all at once.

O most benevolent and almighty God! If you, Foolish Lover—since this is how you choose to be addressed—did in your life
215 repent of the many works which you in your youth wrote out of
vanity, why did you let them prevail? Should they not have been
burned? Venom or poison on a table, or flames between oil and
straw are far too dangerous a defense. He who spreads fire everywhere and does not extinguish it; how can he be acquitted of having
220 set so many houses on fire? And which fire is worse and more
ardent than the fire of lechery? Which houses are more precious
than human souls (clearly expressed by lady Chastity's petition)?
For they must be the sacred temple of the Holy Spirit. What ignites
these souls more than dissolute speech and frivolous writings and
225 images? We see that good, holy, and pious speech, images and writings encourage piety, as Pythagoras said: It is for this purpose that
sermons and images are produced in the churches.[62] On the contrary,
the sinful ones encourage dissoluteness far too easily. There is not
anyone who cannot attest to this and many stories show it.

230 But dear friend (I speak to you in vain, you who are not here,
and who, as I say, were displeased and would be displeased by this
case were you indeed present. And if you did not know it then, you
have learned it since, through painful scourges and punishment in
purgatory at least, or in this world through penitence), you will say
235 perhaps that you had no control over retracting your book once it
was published, or that it was taken away accidentally without your
knowledge; I do not know. Conversely, I do well know that on the
day of the Appearance of Our Lord, Berengier—former disciple
of Peter Abelard, to whom you make frequent reference—in the

jadis de Pierre Abalart—lequel tu remambres souvent—, quant
vint a l'eure de la mort, la ou verité se monstre qui aura bien fait,
235   et estoit le jour de l'Aparicion Nostre Seigneur; lors en souspirant:
«Mon Dieu, dist Berengier, tu apperras au jour d'uy a moy a ma
salvacion—come j'ay esperance—pour ma repentance; ou a ma
dure dampnacion—come je doubte—pour ce que ceulx lesquelz j'ay
deceu par mauvaise doctrine, je n'ay peu ramener a droite voie de
240   la verité de ton saint sacrement». Par aventure ainsi dis tu. Briefment ce n'est point jeu: et n'est plus perilleuse chose que de semer
mauvaise doctrine es cuers des gens, en tant que la peinne de ceulx
mesmement qui sont dampnés en acroit de jour en jour; et s'ilz sont
en purgatoire, leur delivrance s'en empeesche et retarde. De Sale-
245   mon, qui fu le plus saige du monde, doubtent les docteurs s'il est
sauvés. Pour quoy? Pour ce qu'avant sa mort il ne fist destruire les
temples aux ydoles, lesquelz il avoit fais par la fole amour des fames estranges. La repantance n'est pas souffissant quant on ne oste
l'occasion de ses propres pechiés et des aultres a son pouoir.

250   Neantmoins, quoy que ce soit de ta repentance (s'elle fu
acceptee de Dieu ou non,—je desire que oy), je ne parle fors du
fait en soy et de ton livre; et quar tu ne le deffans point—comme
saige—, je tourneray toute ma querelle contre ceulx qui oultre ton
propre jugement et ta volantey, en grief prejudice de ton bien, de ton
255   honour et salut, quierent, soit a tort, soit a travers, soustenir—non
pas soustenir, mais alaidir et acroistre!—ta vanité. Et en ce te con-
fondent en toy cuidant deffandre; et te desplaisent et nuysent en te
voulant voulant complaire,—a la samblance du medecin oultraigeux
qui vuelt garir et il occist, et du nice advocat qui cuide aidier son
260   maistre et il destruit sa cause.

        Je, par le contraire, rendray ce servise a ton ame et ly feray
ce plaisir ou cest allegement a cause de ta clergie et estude, que je
reprandray ce que tu desires du tout en tout estre repris. Et quelle
ignorance est celle ycy, o biaux amis!—mais quelle fole oultre-
265   cuidance de vous, lesquelz je voy et oy ycy parler, de vous qui
voulés excuser de toute folie ou erreur cil qui se condampne, cil
qui porte en son front le tiltre escript de sa condampnacion? Voire!
de sa condampnacion: ne me resgardés ja! Il se porte par vostre
dit meismes pour ung fol amoureux. Vraiement, quant j'auroie dis
270   plusseurs diffames d'ung tel acteur, je ne ly puis gueres pis imposer que de le nommer fol amoureux: ce non emporte trop grant
fardel et pesant fais de toute lubricité et de charnalité murtriere de
toutes vertus, bouteresse de feu par tout ou elle puet. Ainsy le dirent

240   hour of his death, when Truth reveals those who lived morally, said
with a sigh, "My God, said Berengier, today you appear either for
my salvation and repentance, as I hope, or for my cruel damnation,
as I fear; for I could not bring back to the rightful path of the truth
of your holy sacrament those whom I deceived through my sin-
245   ful doctrine."[63] Perhaps you speak thus. Suddenly, it is no longer a
game: There is nothing more perilous than planting sinful doctrine
in people's hearts, in that their suffering, especially that of those
who are damned, grows daily, and if they are in purgatory, their
deliverance will be impeded and delayed. The theologians have their
250   doubts as to the salvation of Solomon, who was the wisest person
in the world. Why? Because before his death he did not destroy the
temples of idolatry which he had built through his foolish love of
pagan women. Repentance is not sufficient unless one tries as much
as possible to avoid committing sins oneself and causing sins for
255   others.

        Nevertheless, regardless of your repentance (whether God
accepted it or not; I hope he did), I speak only of the case itself
and of your book. Since, wisely, you do not forbid it, I will address
my polemic to those who—against your own judgment and will,
260   gravely tarnishing your worth, honor, and salvation—wish unjustly
to uphold your vanity, not only to uphold it but to vilify and increase
it. They erroneously think that they are defending you, when all they
do is to displease and harm you, all the while wishing to please you,
like the insolent doctor who wishes to heal but kills, and the stupid
265   lawyer who thinks he is helping his master but ends up destroying
his case.

        I, on the other hand, because of your erudition and knowl-
edge will render your soul this service and grant it this pleasure or
alleviation. I will criticize all that you ask me to. What ignorance is
270   here, o beautiful friends! What foolish pride you manifest, you who
are present here and whom I hear speak. You who wish to exempt
from all folly and error the one who condemns himself, who bears
the title of his condemnation on his face? Indeed, of his condemnation: Never look at me! He appears as a foolish lover because of
275   your very words. Truly, if I had repeatedly defamed such an author,
I could not impose on him a worse fate than to call him a foolish lover: This name carries too heavy a burden and is heavy with
all lubricity and carnality, slaying all virtues, and igniting flames
wherever it can. Thus spoke Plato, Archyta of Tarentum, Cicero, and
280   others.[64] Who long ago destroyed Troy[65] the Great through fire and

Platon, Architas Tarentin, Tulle et aultres. Qui craventa jadis par
275   feu et flanme Troye la grand? Fol amoureux. Qui fist lors destruire
plus de cent mil gentilz homes, Hector, Achilles, Priaint et aultres?
Fol amoureux. Qui chassa hors jadis de Ronme le roy Tarquinius et
toute sa lignie? Fol amoureulx. Qui deçoit par fraudes et par par-
juremens desloyaulx honnestes filles et religieuses sacrees? Fol
280 182vº amoureulx. Qui oublie Dieu et sains et saintes et paradis // et sa fin?
Fol amoureulx. Qui ne tient compte de parens ou d'amis quelconques ou de quelconque vertus? Fol amoureulx. Dont viennent
conspiracions civiles, rapines et larressins pour fole largesse nourir,
bastardie ou suffocacion d'enfens mors nés, haynes aussy et mort
285   des maris, et a brief dire tout mal et toute folie? C'est par fol amoureulx.

Mais je voy bien par ce tiltre et par ce blasme vous le voulés
excuser de ses folies, pour ce qu'en fol ne doit on querir se folie
non. En non Dieu, voire, beaulx amis! mais au fol doit on monstrer
290   sa folie; et plus quant il est saige et fait le fol; et plus se c'est ou tres
grief mal d'ung grant païs et en la destruccion villainne de bonnes
meurs et de dame Justice et de toute sa noble court de Crestienté.
Vous veés commant dame Chasteté s'en plaint. Honte et Paour
et dame Raison ma maistresce s'en doellent, et briefment tout le
295   conseil et la noble chevalerie des saintes vertus—bien le veés a leur
maintieng—, s'en indignent forment. Et pour quoy non? Pour ce,
dirés vous, que cest acteur ne parle point, mais aultres qui sont la
introduis. C'est trop petite deffence pour si grant crime. Je vous de-
mende: se aucun se nommoit adversaire du roy de France et sus ce
300   non et come tel li faisoit guerre, ce non le garderoit il d'estre traytre
et de la mort? Vous ne dirés pas. Se en la persone d'ung herite ou
d'ung Sarrazin—voire du deable—, aucun escript et semme erreurs
contre la Crestienté, en sera il escusey? Aultrefoys ung le voust
fere, qui tantost fu contraint a soy rappeller et corrigier par ung des
305   chanceliers de l'esglise de Paris en plainne sale et audience; nonpourquant parlast il entre clers entendens quant il disoit: «Je parle
comme Juif».—«Et tu rapelleras come Crestien», dit le chancelier.

Aucun escripra libelles diffamatoires d'une personne, soit de
petit estat ou non—soit neis mauvaise—, et soit par personnaige: les
310   drois jugent ung tel estre a pugnir et infame. Et donques que doivent
dire les lois et vous, dame Justice, non pas d'ung libelle, mals d'ung
grant livre plain de toutes infamacions, non pas seulement contre
homes, mais contre Dieu et tous sains et saintes qui ainment vertus?
Respondés moy! seroit un a ouïr qui diroit a ung prince ou a ung

flames? The Foolish Lover. Who caused the death of more than one
hundred thousand noble men, Hector, Achilles, Priam, and others?
The Foolish Lover. Who long ago chased King Tarquin[66] and his
entire lineage out of Rome? The Foolish Lover. Who deceives hon-
285   orable girls and veiled nuns through fraud and perjury? The Foolish
Lover. Who forgets God and male and female saints, and paradise
and its outcome? The Foolish Lover. Who neglects parents, friends,
and all virtues? The Foolish Lover. Who causes civil conspiracies,
pillaging, and theft, with the intent of nourishing foolish liberality,
290   bastardy, or abortion, as well as the hatred and death of husbands—
in short, all that is evil and entirely foolish? It is the Foolish Lover.

      Yet I see clearly that with this designation and reproach you
wish to forgive his follies because in a foolish person one ought
to seek nothing but foolishness. In God's name—indeed, beautiful
295   friends! Yet the foolish person must be shown his foolishness, even
more so when he is wise but acts foolishly, and even more so if his
foolishness causes great harm to a country and causes the villainous
destruction of good morals and of Lady Justice and her entire noble
court of Christianity. You see how Lady Chastity complains about
300   it. Shame, Fear, and my mistress, Lady Reason, are pained by it,
and in short the entire council and the noble chivalry of holy virtues
are very indignant, as you can clearly see by their behavior. And
how could they not be? You will say to this that this author does not
speak himself, but through others who are presented by him. This is
305   too insignificant a defense for so great a crime. I ask you: If someone called himself an adversary of the king of France and waged
war under that title, would that protect him from treason and death?
You will say no. If a heretic or a Saracen or even the devil planted
errors against Christianity in his writings, would he be pardoned?
310   Once, someone who attempted to do this was immediately forced by
one of the chancellors of the Church of Paris to recant and to rectify
his statement before a full room and an episcopal audience. Nonetheless, he spoke to learned clerics when he said, "I speak as a Jew."
"And you will recant as a Christian," said the chancellor.

315   Whoever writes defamatory libels about a person of low or
high estate, even a bad person, and even by way of other characters, the law will find such a person just as guilty and disgraceful.
Therefore, what must the laws say—and you, Lady Justice—not of
a libel, but of a long book full of infamy, not only against mankind
320   but against God and all male and female saints who love virtue?
Answer me this: Would there be someone who would say to a prince

315 signeur: «Vraiement, sire, je vous dis en la persone d'ung jaloux
ou d'une vieille ou par •i• songe que vostre fame est tres mauvaise
et forfait son mariaige: gardés vous bien et de riens en elle ne vous
fiés; et a vos filles, qui sont tant josnes et belles, je conseille a tantost soy abandonner a toute euvre charnelle, et a tout home qui leur
320 volra bon pris donner». Dittes moy, vous, beaulx amis, estes vous
tant effrontés et peu sachans que vous jugissiés que tel home on ne
pugniroit mie? que on le soustenroit, oyroit et excusseroit? et plus
encores, se oultre les parolles il envoyoit livres ou paintures!

    An surplus, lequel est pis: ou d'ung crestien clere preschier en
325 la persone d'ung Sarrasin contre la foy, ou qu'il amenast le Sarrazin qui parlast ou escripst? Toutefois jamais ne seroit souffert le
segond oultraige; si est toutefois pis le premier (c'est a dire le fait
du Crestien), de tant que l'ennemy couvert est plus nuisable que
l'appert,—de tant que plus tost et plus familierement on le ressoit et
330 oyt et croit. Je bailleray du venin envelopé de miel; ung en mourra:
en seray je quitte? Je ferray en baisant; je occiray en enbrassent:
en seray je delivre? Je diray publiquement a une devote personne:
«Vraiement vos envieulx et hayneulx dient que vous estes ypo-
crite papelart et que vous estes larron et murtrier et se euffrent a le
335 prouver»: seray je excusé de ce diffame? Ung dissolus mauvais fera
et dira toute lubricité qui se peust trouver entre home et fame devant
une pucelle en disant: «Ne fay pas ainsy come tu nous vois fere,
ainsy et ainsy; regarde bien!»: sera tel a soustenir? Certes non, quar
chasteté, renommee, oeul et la foy n'ont point de jeu, et sont choses
340 trop de legier a blecier et corrompre.

    Mais j'entens bien ce que vous murmurés ensemble: vous
dictes, comme par avant l'ung de vous allega, que Salemon et David
ont ainssy fait. C'est ycy trop grant outraige pour excuser ung fol
amoureulx, accuser Dieu et ses sains et les mener a la querelle; mais
345 ne se puet faire: je voulroie bien que ce Fol Amoureulx n'eust usé
de ces personnaiges fors ainssy que la sainte Escripture en use, c'est
assavoir en reprouvant le mal, et tellement que chascun eust ap-
183r° perceu le reproche du // mal et l'aprobacion du bien, et—qui est le
principal—que tout se fist sans excés de legiereté. Mais nennin voir.
350 Tout semble estre dit en sa persone; tout semble estre vray come
Euvangille, en especial aux nices folz amoureulx auxquelz il parle;
et, de quoy je me dueil plus—tout enflamme a luxure, meismement
quant il la samble reprouver: neis les bien chastes, s'ilz le daingnoi-
ent estudier, lire ou escouter, en vaurroient pis.

355   Dient les docteurs que les *Cantiques* Salemon, soient eulx
certes bien sobres, ne se lisoient anciennement fors par ceulx qui

or a lord, "Truly, Sir, I tell you in the guise of a jealous husband or a duenna or a dream that your wife is evil and sins against marriage: Be watchful and do not place any trust in her; and I counsel your

325 daughters who are so young and beautiful to relinquish themselves immediately to any carnal activity and to any man who is willing to offer a good price for them." Tell me, you, beautiful friends, are you so ignorant and unwise as to suggest that such a man would not be punished—that he would be supported, listened to, and forgiven?

330 And what is more, if in addition to his words he also sent books or images!

To continue, which is worse: If, in the guise of a Saracen, a Christian cleric were to preach against faith, or if he were actually to bring the Saracen, who would himself speak or write? In any case,

335 the second insult would never be tolerated. The first is worse (that is, the case of the Christian), in that the enemy in disguise is worse than the enemy who is discernible, since one accepts, listens to, and believes the former more readily. I will conceal venom in honey and someone will die. Will I be acquitted? I will strike while I kiss, kill

340 while I embrace. Will I be allowed to go free? To a pious person I will say publicly, "Truly, those who despise and envy you say that you are a hypocrite and a thief and a murderer, and they are prepared to prove it." Will I be forgiven for this defamation? A dissolute sinner will in front of a young maiden perform and utter any lewdness

345 possible between a man and a woman, saying, "Do not repeat what you see us do in such and such a way; pay close attention!" Will this be allowed? Of course not, because Chastity, Renown, Eye, and Faith do not take this lightly and are all too easily wounded and corrupted.

However, I hear well what you are mumbling to each other:

350 You say, as one of you alleged earlier, that Solomon and David acted in this way. This is too great an insult, to forgive a foolish lover for denouncing God and His saints and drawing them into the argument. This cannot be done: I very much wished that this Foolish Lover had used these characters only in the way Holy Scripture does, that is,

355 with the intent of refuting evil so blatantly that everyone would grasp the reproach of evil and the approval of good, and—this is essential—that all this had been done without an excess of frivolity. Alas, this is not the case. Everything seems to be said by him; everything seems to be true as the Gospel, especially when he addresses the

360 insensate foolish lovers. And what pains me more is that lechery ignites everywhere, even when he seems to refute it; and even the very chaste, if they dared study, read, or listen to it, would be worse off for it.

avoient trante ans ou plus, affin qu'ilz n'y entendissent quelconque
malvaise charnalitey. Jeunes gens donques nices et volaiges, que
feront eulx a ung tel livre—mais un ung tel feu!—plus enflammant
360 que feu grigoys ou que fournaise a voirre? Au feu! bonnes gens, au
feu! Ostés le, pour Dieu, ostés! Fuyés vous tost! sauvés vous et vous
en gardés saigement, vous et vos enfens! C'est le remede; meilleur
n'y a: qui ne fuit le peril, il y trebuchera et y sera pris comme le rat
au lardon et loups en la louviere, ou le papillon au feu de la chan-
365 doille pour sa clartey, ou les folz ou les enfens aux espees cleres ou
aux charbons vifs pour leur beauté, qui ne les oste de fait.
Sy vous dictes que dedens sont des biens plusseurs, en est, je vous
pry, pour ce le mal dehors? en est le feu se non plus perilleux?
L'amesson nuit il mains aux poissons s'il est couvert de l'ammorse?
370 Une espee, s'elle est ointe de miel, fiert elle se plus avant non? Mais
en surplus, sont faillies ailleurs bonnes et pures doctrines sans mel-
leure de mauvaistié? Que ce soit neccessaire aucune bone envelopee
de la mauvaise garder et tenir chiere et louer, je dis que Mahom-
met par tres grande et avisee malice mella les verités de nostre loy
375 crestienne avec ses ordes erreurs. Pour quoy? Pour attraire plus tost
les Crestiens a sa loy et pour couvrir ses oultraiges. Et ne dit pas
le deable plusseurs verités a la fois, et par demoniaques et par ses in-
vocateurs les magiciens et aussy les herites? Mais ce n'est que pour
decepvoir plus couvertement: si est une mauvaise doctrine de tant
380 pire quant plus y a de bien, et pis vault.
Creés moy—non pas moy mais l'apostre saint Pol et Seneque
et experiance!—que mauvaises paroles et escriptures courrumpent
bonnes meurs et font devenir les pechiés sans honte et ostent toute
bone vergoingne, qui est en jeusnes gens la principal garde de toutes
385 bones condicions contre tous maulx. Josne persone sans honte est
toute perdue. Pour quoy fu Ovide, grand clerc et tres ingenieux
poette, geté en dur exil sans retourner? Il meisme tesmoingne que
ce fut pour son *Art d'amour* miserable, laquelle il avoit escripte
ou temps Octovien l'empereur. Nonpourquant fist il ung livre a
390 l'encontre, *Du remede d'amours;* Ovide eust bien seu parler par
songe ou personnayge s'excusacion en eust attendu par ce.
O Dieu! o sains! o sainctes! o devote court de crestienne religion! o les meurs du temps present! Entre les paiens ung juge paien
et incredule condampne ung paien qui escript doctrine attraiant a
395 fole amour, et entre les Crestiens et par les Crestiens tele et pieur
euvre est soustenue, alosee et deffendue! En bone foy, je ne pouroie
assés dire l'indignité et l'erreur de ceste chose: parolle me fault a la

The theologians say that Solomon's *Canticles*, as temperate
365   as they may be in themselves, were read only by those aged thirty
years and over in order that readers would not interpret any sinful
carnality into them. Therefore, what shall young people, insensate
and fickle, do with such a book—no, with such a fire more incendi-
ary than a Greek fire or a glass oven? Fire! Good people, fire! Ex-
370   tinguish it, by God, extinguish it! Flee, all of you! Save yourselves
and behave wisely, you and your children! This is the cure; there is
no better one: He who does not flee peril will succumb to it and will
be pulled toward it like the rat to the lard and the wolves to the trap
or the butterfly to the brightness of the candle flame, or fools and
375   children—unless they are removed from danger—to the beauty of
shiny swords and gleaming coals.

If you say that many good things are contained in it, I ask you,
do these good things then expunge the evil within it? Does this not
increase the peril of fire? Does a hook harm fish less if it is covered
380   with bait? Does a sword if dipped in honey penetrate less than if it
is not? Moreover, have other good and pure teachings which are not
mingled with evil consequently failed? Is it worth it to keep, honor,
and venerate any goodness, if one must wrap it in evil as did Mohamed with clever malice when he mixed the truth of our Christian
385   doctrine with his filthy errors. Why? In order to more easily attract
Christians to his doctrine and to cover up his insults. And does the
devil not express several truths at once, through demoniacs as well
as through his enchanters, magicians, and heretics? Yet he does so
only to better disguise his deceit: The more good sinful teaching
390   contains, the better he considers it, and the more harmful it is.

Believe me (not me, but Seneca and the Apostle Saint Paul, as
well as experience!)[67] that sinful words and writings corrupt good
morals and quash the shame out of sins and any moral prudishness
from all young people, for whom it serves as the chief protection
395   against all evil. A young person without shame is completely lost.
Why was Ovid, great cleric and very ingenious poet, thrown into
harsh exile with no possibility of return? He himself attests that
it was because of his sinful *Ars amatoris*, which he wrote when
Augustus was emperor. And yet he composed a book to counter it,
400   the *De remedia amatoris*, and spoke skillfully through dreams or
characters which led him to believe that he would be forgiven for his
error.

O God! O male and female Saints! O pious Christian Court!
O moral customs of today! Among the pagans, a pagan and

reprouver. Et que tele œuvre soit pieur que celle d'Ovide, certes je
le maintieng; car *L'Art d'amour*, laquelle escript Ovide, n'est pas
400   seulement toute enclose ou dit livre, mais sont translatés, assemblés
et tirés come a violance et sans propos autres livres plusseurs, tant
d'Ovide come des autres, qui ne sont point moins deshonnestes et
perilleux (ainssy que sont les dis de Heloys et de Pierre Abelart et
de Juvenal et des fables faintes—toutes a ceste fin maudite—de
405   Mars et de Venus et de Vulcanus et de Pigmalion et de Adonis et
autres). Ovide par exprés protesta qu'il ne vouloit parler des bonnes
matronnes et dames mariees, ne de celles qui ne seroient loisyble-
ment a amer. Et vostre livre fait il ainsy? Il reprent toutes et blasme
183v°   toutes, mes-// prise toutes, sans aucune exepcion. Au moins, puis
410   qu'il se maintenoit crestien et qu'il parloit des choses celestiennes
a la fois, pour quoy n'excepta il les glorieuses saintes pucelles et
autres sans nombre qui jusques a souffrir tres durs tourmans et mort
crueuse garderent chasteté ou temple de leur cuer? Pour quoy ne
garda il ceste reverence a la sainte des saintes? Mais nennin! Il es-
415   toit fol amoureux; si n'en avoit cure; si n'en voloit aucune excuser,
affin de baillier plus grant hardement a toutes de soy habandonner;
ne pooit cecy mieux acomplir que par faire entendant aux fames que
toutes sunt telles et qu'elles ne s'en pouroient garder.
            Necessité n'a loy. Diex! quelle doctrine—non pas doctrine,
420   mais blaspheme et heresie!—; ainssy s'efforce il de monstrer que
jeunes gens jamais ne seront fermes et estables en une religion, qui
est faulce doctrine et contre experience. Mais qui se voulroit arester
a tout reprandre ce qui est mal mis ou dit livre, le jour iroit plus tost
a fin que la querelle; et pouroit aussy par aventure la trop grande
425   particularité plus nuyre a bonnes meurs que pourfiter a la cause:
je pouroie cheoir ou vice que je reprans. Si abregeray ma parole et
ne diray plus que des articles contenus en la supplicacion de dame
Chasteté presentés par Conscience; et desja je me sans delivres
d'aucuns articles les plus legiers: si est temps que je descende aux
430   plus griefs et plus inexcusables. La chose est grande, dame Justice:
soit ententif vostre conseil a les oïr diligemment pour y pourveoir
astivement.
            Certes en ce dit livre—se livre se doit dire—bien a lieu le
proverbe commun: «En la fin gist le venin». La moquerie d'Orace
435   a ycy lieu, du paintre qui fait une tres belle fame ou chief et fenist
en poisson (on dit teles estre les Arpiees, qui ont visaige vierge,
mais ventre et autres parties tres ordes). Las! quelle ordure y est la
mise et assemblee! quelz blasphemes y sont dis! quelle dyablie y
est semee! Avoir tantost parlé de Dieu, de paradis, du doulz aignel

405   unbelieving judge condemns a pagan who writes a doctrine which
       attracts foolish love, and among Christians and by Christians such a
       book—and worse—is supported, praised, and defended! I could not
       in good faith adequately express my indignity and the magnitude of
       the error in this case: Speech fails me in my attempt to refute it. And
410   I truly maintain that this work is worse than Ovid's, because not
       only is Ovid's entire *Ars amatoris* contained in this book, but many
       other books by Ovid and others (which are no less dishonorable and
       perilous, as are the writings of Heloise and Pierre Abelard, Juvenal,
       and such fictive fables as those about Mars, Venus, and Vulcan, Pyg-
415   malion, Adonis, and others, all to the same sinful end) are translat-
       ed, assembled, and pulled together without rhyme or reason.[68] Ovid
       declared purposely that he did not wish to speak about respectable
       older women and married ladies nor those who could be loved law-
       fully. Does your book do that? He criticizes all, insults all, despises
420   all without exception. Since he claimed to be a Christian, and since
       at the same time he spoke of celestial things, why did he not at least
       exclude the glorious holy virgins and countless others, who, in order
       to preserve their chastity in the temples of their hearts, endured very
       cruel torture and death? Why did he not keep the holiest of all saints
425   in reverence? But no! He was a foolish lover, for which there was
       no cure. He wished to exclude none of them, in order that he might
       entice all of them to give themselves to men. He could have done
       this in no better way than to teach women that they are all alike and
       that they could not withstand their own natures.
430   Necessity has no law. God! What a doctrine—not a doctrine,
       but rather blasphemy and heresy! He makes a point of showing
       that young people are never constant and steadfast in their religion,
       which is wrong and discounts what we know from experience. The
       day would come to a close sooner than this quarrel if one were to
435   stop and criticize all that is sinful in this book. And incidentally, the
       greatest detail could harm good conduct more rather than furthering
       it: I myself could fall prey to the vice which I refute. I will abridge
       my speech and comment only on the accusations contained in Lady
       Chastity's petition, presented by Conscience; I feel that I have
440   already dealt with some of the most insignificant ones. It is now
       time that I came to the worst and the least forgivable. The matter is
       grave, Lady Justice: May your Council be attentive in hearing them
       diligently, in order to reach a speedy decision.
           It is undoubtedly true that the following proverb applies to this
445   book, if one can call it a book: "In the conclusion lies the venom."[69]
       Horace's mockery is appropriate here, of the painter who creates

440   tres chaste, de la belle fontenelle, et puis en la persone de l'auteur
        soudainnement et d'ung tenant recité sa tres dissolue vie—de
        laquelle n'est tant deshoneste qui n'en eust honte!—, enhortés tous
        a ainssy fere, a s'abandonner a toutes fames, pucelles ou non, pour
        essaier de tout! Et—qui est la some du mal—il dit teles choses estre
445   sactuares et euvres sacrees et adoureés! Il eust mieulx dit execrables
        et dampnables et detestees, ou—que diroie je ycy?—pour vray, c'est
        grande abhominacion d'i panser tant seulement: ja ma bouche n'en
        sera enordie de plus en dire, ne vos oreilles saintes grevees ne ceste
        court empuentee de l'escouter.
450   Si vous pry neantmoins que prejudice n'en soit fait a ma
        cause; et s'il est vray ce que saint Augustin dit—et oy—,que «mains
        mal n'est pas mesprisier la parole sainte de Dieu que le corps Jhesu
        Crist», il n'a point fait moins de irreverence a Dieu d'ansy parler et
        entouillier villainnes choses entre les parolles divines et consacrees
455   que s'il eust getté le precieux corps Nostre Seigneur entre les piés
        de pourceaulx ou sur ung fiens. Pensés quel oultraige, quelle hyde et
        quel erreur! Il n'eust mie pis fait de getter le teuxte des Euvangilles
        ou l'imaige du cruxefis en une grant fange orde et parfonde! Dit Ar-
        istote (recite Seneque) que on ne se doit onques tenir tant reveram-
460   ment et honestement come quant on parle de Dieu: et cil ycy gette
        ensemble en une ville boe et une ordure la pierre precieuse et sainte
        de la verité crestienne parlant de Dieu! Je l'argue ycy: ou il creoit
        ce qu'il disoit de paradis (come je tiens—las donques!), et que ne
        pensoit il a ce qu'il creoit; s'il ne le creoit, il estoit faulx herite
465   faintif. Ainssy argue je de sa vie dissolue,—de laquelle il se glorifie
        et vente.
            En oultre je perleroie—se n'estoit ce que aucunement se
        peust plus sauver—, je parleroie comment en la persone, mainte-
        nant de Nature, maintenant de Genius (selond ce que a proposé
470   Chasteté—et c'est vray), il enhorte et commande sans differance
184r°   user de toute charnalité, et maudit toux ceulx et // celles qui n'en
        useront; et ja de mariaige ne sera faicte mencion—qui toutes fois
        par nature est ordonné—, ja n'y ara sobresse de parler gardee: et
        promet paradis a tous qui ainssy le feront. Or est fol qui ne le croit,
475   qui n'ansuit telle doctrine, qui ne la chante par tout. Vray est que
        ceste ficcion poetique fut corrumpuement estraitte du grant Alain, en
        son livre qu'il fait *De la plainte Nature;* car aussy tres grant partie
        de tout ce que fait nostre Fol Amoureulx n'est presques fors trans-
        lacion des dis d'autruy. Je le sçay bien: il estoit humble qui daignoit
480   bien prandre de ses voisins et se hourdoit de toutes plumes, come de
        la cornaille dient les fabbles,—mais pou me meut cecy; je reviens

a very beautiful woman's head with a fish's body (these beings are called harpies, who have the face of a virgin but a stomach and other parts which are very ugly).[70] Alas! What filth has been gathered and

450   put here! What blasphemous words it contains! What diabolic spell has been implanted in it when first he spoke of God, paradise, the sweet and very chaste Lamb, and the beautiful little fountain, only to recount suddenly, in one stretch and in the person of the author himself, his very dissolute life—exhorting everyone to follow suit, to

455   give oneself to all women, maidens or not, in order to try out every-thing (this is so dishonorable that anyone would be ashamed)! And here is the height of evil: He claims that such things are sanctuaries and are sacred and worshipped works! He should have called them execrable, damnable, and detestable, or—how can I say this, for in

460   truth it is a great abomination to even think about it—my mouth shall not be contaminated further, nor your holy ears burdened, nor this court sullied in hearing such things.

        I ask, nonetheless, that prejudice not be brought against me. If it is indeed true that Saint Augustine said, as I have heard, that "it

465   is just as evil to tarnish the body of Christ as the holy doctrine of God,"[71] he [the Foolish Lover, i.e., Jean de Meun] committed no less irreverence toward God in speaking thus and in weaving such villain-ous things in among holy and divine words than had he thrown the body of Our Lord among pigs' feet or on a dung heap. Think what

470   an insult, what a hydra, and what an error! He could not have done worse had he thrown the Gospel or the image of the crucifix into a great, deep garbage heap! Aristotle said (quoted by Seneca) that one must never behave as reverently and honorably as when speaking of God, and yet when he is speaking of God, this author throws the

475   holy and precious stone of Christian truth into vile mud and filth![72] I denounce him: Either he believed what he said about paradise (as I maintain, alas!) and did not think about what he believed; or, if he did not believe it, he was a hypocrite and a heretic. Thus, I denounce him based on his dissolute life, of which he boasts and brags.

480   Moreover, if indeed he could still save himself, I would speak about how, sometimes in the character of Nature, sometimes in the character of Genius (according to what Chastity has claimed, and it is true), he exhorts and recommends the use of any carnality, without exception, and condemns all those men and women who do not make

485   use of it. At no time does he mention marriage—which is ordained by Nature, after all—or the sobriety of discreet speech. Instead, he promises paradise to all who follow this advice. Now, anyone who does not believe him, who does not follow this doctrine, who does

a Alain et dy que par personnaige quelconque il ne parla onques en
tele maniere: a tart l'eust fait; tant seulement il maudit et repreuve
les vices contre nature. Et a bon droit; aussy fais je: maudis soient

485   qui ne s'en tendront, et Justice les arde! Mais ce n'est pas qu'il enhorte a pechié quelconque pour fuire ung pechié: ce seroit sote sirur-
gie vouloir une plaie par une aultre garir et feu par feu estaindre. Et
qui ces euvres et oultraiges veult excuser par Nature qui parle, je
respons pour vous, dame Nature, que onques vous ne concillastes

490   pechié, onques ne voulsistes que persone fist contre aucuns des dis
commandemens (lesquelx nous appellons vos commandemens)
les conmandemans de Nature; dire le contraire seroit erreur en la
foy (c'est assavoir dire que selonc droit de nature euvre naturelle
d'omme et de fame ne fust pechié hors mariaige).

495   Dame Justice, j'ay longuemant parlé—je le sens bien voir
quant au temps, mais tres briefment quant a la grandeur du forfait—, conbien que a vous et a vostre tres saige et avisé conseil,
qui comprenés tout a brief langaige, qui haiés tant toute villainne
ordure, qui savés toutes lois et drois et qui piessa avés oÿ parler de

500   ceste cause ce qui est dit—sans grande curiosité (car je say a qui je
parle, et devant qui, et pour qui)—: ce qui est dit doncques pouroit
assés souffrir pour condampner le dit livre et l'escommenier, come
on a fait des autres qui sont nuysans a nostre foy et a bones meurs,
come les apostres le firent aux nouviaux convertis. (Ainssy mesme-

505   ment le firent les anciens des livres d'ung poete dit Archiloqus, nonpourquant fussent eux de grande maistrise; mais ilz nuisoient plus a
bones meurs des josnes gens qu'ilz n'en profitoient a leurs engiens,
conme est ycy proprement.)

            Si establiroie ycy ma fin, se non que dame Raison la saige et

510   ma bone maistresse me fait ung signe d'encores parler: n'est pas
merveille, car son honeur grandement y depent. Bien se seust deffendre, c'est chose clere, mais pour ce que j'ay commencié, et veult
a son plaisir que je continue, voulantiers le feray et assés brief,—et
plus que le crime ne requerroit.

515   Se cest erreur desraisonnable—o vous qui ycy estes pour le
Fol Amoureulx, lequel impose a Raison la raige (n'est ce pas raige
dire que on doye parler nuement et baudement et sans vergoingne,
tant soient deshonnestes les parolles au jugement de toutes gens,
nes de ceulx qui seroient sans loy ou sans vergoingne?)—, se cest

520   erreur, di je, ne fust de piessa reprouvé par les anciens philozophes,
cest acteur ou vous qui le deffendés—mais accusés!—ne fuciés pas
tant a blasmer. Mais ce est verité que des avant l'advenement de

490 not sing it everywhere is foolish. It is true that this fictive poetry was taken corruptly from the great Alanus's book *De planctu naturae*,[73] because a very large portion of what our Foolish Lover does is merely a translation of other authors' works. I know it well: He who deigned to take from his neighbors and to decorate himself with all sorts of feathers is humble, like the crow of the fables.[74] But this

495 does not move me much. I return to the case of Alanus, and state that he never spoke like this through any character. He was wrong to do this, only when he condemned and reproved vices against Nature. And rightly so! I condemn those who do not adhere to this, and Justice will punish them! Not that he exhorts people to any kind of

500 sin in order to flee sin: that would be a silly endeavor to wish to heal one wound with another or to wish to extinguish fire with fire. And whoever wishes to excuse these matters and insults because they are articulated by Nature, I answer in your stead, Lady Nature, that you at no time intended to recommend sin, that you at no time wished

505 anyone to act against the Ten Commandments (which we call your commandments), Nature's commandments. To speak to the contrary would be an error in faith—that is to say that according to Nature's law the natural activity between a man and a woman was not a sin outside of marriage.

510 Lady Justice, I have spoken at length, and feel that the amount of time it has taken is right, yet it is only brief given the magnitude of this crime, although you and your wise and clever council understand everything easily even if it is succinctly put: You despise all villainous filth, you know all laws and rights, and you have heard

515 about this matter before. (I know to whom I am speaking, before whom and for whom.) That which has been said should easily suffice, then, to condemn this book, and to excommunicate it as has been done with others who are harmful to our faith and good morals, as did the apostles with the newly converted. (Thus did even the

520 Ancients with the books of a poet named Archilochus,[75] their great mastery notwithstanding. But they did harm to the good morals of young people more than they helped their character, which is the case here also).

I would end here if Lady Reason, my wise and good mistress,

525 were not indicating to me that I should continue to speak, which is not surprising since her honor largely depends on it. Obviously, she could quite ably defend herself. However, since I have started and she wishes me to continue, I will do so gladly and rather succinctly, no more than the crime necessitates.

Jhesu Crist, Tulle, en son livre *Des offices,* et autres philosophes

184v° (et depuis, les sains docteurs, // come vous poués encores lire

525   et savoir) ont reprouvé ceste folie: mais aussy bonne coustume,
qui vault nature, la mesprise, la ressoingne et despitte. Comment donques se peut soustenir baillier a dame Raison ung tel
personnaige—ainssy come ceulx qui ainssy ne le font fussent hors
du sens et de raison!—comme parlast Raison, non mie la saige,

530   mais l'assotee et la souillarde! En non Dieu! ce personnaige eust
mieulx appartenu a pourceaulx ou a chiens que a Raison; et ce ne
contrueve pas ce dit de moy, car aucuns anciens qui se nommoient
philozophes furent appellés chiens pour ceste imfame doctrine,—et
ne fu pas Chain maudit et fait villain serf pour ce seulement qu'il

535   regarda sans couvrir les parties secretes de Noé son pere? Cest
erreur aussy estoit jadis l'erreur des Turlupins, en maintenant que
c'estoit l'estat d'ignosance et de souverainne perfection en terre.
Comment pouoit on imposer chose plus desraisonnable a Raison?
Comment se pouoit donner plus grant hardement a tous desraison-

540   nables que de fere Raison ainssy parler, mesmement que en parlant
elle recite choses mignotes enclinans a toute legiereté. Or bailliés,
bailliés vos filles et vos enfans a tel docteur, et s'elles ne sunt assés
saiges, envoyés les a l'escolle de telle Raison! Aprenés les a tous
maulx—s'elles n'en sevent assés trouver par elles—, et les batés

545   s'elles ne parlent des choses selonc ce que Raison commande! Mais
an surplus, par ce meismes motif on prouveroit que on doit aler
nus et fere nus tout et par tout sans avoir honte; et croy qu'ainsy
le soustenroit selonc sa position. Or voise, qui ainssy le maintient,
parmy les rues pour esprouver comment Raison le deffendra d'estre

550   huyés et abayé et ordoyé!

      Encor se Raison eust parlé a ung sage clerc et entendent
la nature des choses, ou a ung grant theologien qui seut comment, se ne fust pechié originel, riens ne nous tournast a honte, il
eust excusacion telle quelle: il peust alleguer la nudité de Eve et

555   Adan,—combien que ce n'est mie pareil pour l'estat d'innocence
et pour le nostre. (Et y a telle differance come de sain a malade:
ung vin qui ne nuyroit a ung saing fera hors du sens ung qui tramblera fievrés: ainssy est que veoir ou oïr aucunes choses charnelles
nuement et selonc leur premier estat esmouveroit les pecheurs

560   regardans a tres villains desirs, et pour l'esta d'innocence n'eust pas
ainssy esté: tout cecy apert, car avant pechié Eve et Adan estoient
nus sans honte, puis pecharent, et tantost se mussierent et couvrirent
a grant vergoingne.) Et n'est ja besoing de demander pour quoy une

530   If this irrational error—O all of you who are here on behalf
          of the Foolish Lover, who causes Lady Reason's madness (is it not
          madness to say that one must speak plainly and bawdily, without
          prudishness, even though the words are dishonorable in the judg-
          ment of all who are not lawless or shameless?)—if, I say, this irra-
535   tional error was not reproved by the ancient philosophers, ought not
          this author or you who defend him (accuse him instead!) be equally
          insulted? Yet the truth is that before the coming of Christ, Cicero,
          in his book *De Officiis*,[76] and other philosophers (and since then the
          holy Church Fathers, as you may still read and learn) have rebuked
540   this foolishness. Also, good morals worthy of Nature itself despise,
          dread, and detest it. How is it possible, then, to portray Lady Reason
          in such a way and to portray those who do not follow this Reason
          as having lost their minds and judgment? To have her speak, not
          as the wise one, but as dim-witted and filthy! In the name of God!
545   This character should be portrayed by swine or dogs rather than by
          Reason. I am not inventing this, because the Ancients who called
          themselves philosophers were called dogs for this sort of infamous
          doctrine. And was Ham not condemned and made a common serf
          solely because he saw the exposed secret parts of Noah, his father?[77]
550   In former times, this error was also the error of the Turlupines[78] who
          maintained that such was the state of innocence and ultimate perfec-
          tion on earth. How could one impute an even more irrational thing
          to Reason? How could all the irrational people together find enough
          courage to make Reason speak thus, especially since she speaks of
555   coquette things, inviting frivolity. Give, now, just give your daugh-
          ters and children to such a teacher, and if they are not well enough
          behaved, send them to the school of such a Reason! Teach them all
          possible evil, if they cannot find enough by themselves, and beat
          them if they do not speak of things the way Reason commands it!
560   Yet what is more, one could similarly prove that one should go
          naked and do everything naked everywhere without feeling shame.
          I think that he would support this, based on his position. Now, let
          us see who maintains this publicly in the streets in order to prove
          that Reason will protect him from being scorned, shouted at, and
565   covered with filth!
              Moreover, if Reason had spoken to a wise cleric who under-
          stood the nature of things, or to a great theologian who knew that
          if it had not been for original sin we would not have come to know
          shame, he would have given the justification plainly. He could have
570   blamed Eve and Adam's nudity, although their state of innocence is

565 maniere de parler est a reprouver plus que l'autre quant on dit une
mesme chose; sa et la ne convient ja que je m'areste pour en rendre
cause naturelle: experience assés le monstre: c'est pour la fantasie
qui plus s'esmeut, et la fantasie est celle qui fait tout le desir. De
ce vient que dame Oyseuse est portiere de Fole Amour, car elle ne
treuve point l'imaginacion et la fantasie de la persone occupee; si

570 li envoye charnelz desirs d'une fasson et d'autres: pour tant n'est
tel remede come de soy occuper en aucune bone besoingne. De
ce avient que une persone melencolieuse et maladive et de chetive
complexion sera a la foys plus ardenment temptee de charnalité que
une personne sainne et sanguine riant et se jouant. Et tout vient de la

575 fantasie: quelle merveille se ung feu couvert de cendres ne brule pas
si tost come le sentier a nus? Ainssy est de choses charnelz nuee-
ment dictes ou resgardees.

Mais je reprans mon propos et dy que se le personnaige de
Raison eust parlé a sage clerc et rassis, aucune chose fust. Mais

580 non! il parle a Fol Amoureux. Et ycy garda mal l'acteur les riegles
de mon escolle (les riegles de rhetorique), qui sont de regarder cil
qui parle et a qui on parle, et pour quel tamps on parle. Et n'est pas
le deffault ycy seulement, car es autres lieux plusseurs il atribue a
la personne qui parle ce qui ne le doit appartenir (come il introduit

585 Nature parlant de paradis et des misteres de nostre foy, et Venus qui
jure par la char Dieu). Mais de ce ne tien ge compte, conbien que
c'est faulte a tel—lequel aucuns veulent tant essaucier dessus tous
aultres presque qui onques furent—: je me dueil trop pour dame
Raison et pour Chasteté de ce que il a fait dire par Raison la sage a

590 ung fol amoureux teles gouliardies; auquel par avant Cupido, qui
se dit Dieu xd'amours, avoit deffandus tous villains parlers et ors
185r° et tous // blasmes de fames,—come se Cupido fust plus chaste et
raisonnables que dame Raison et Chasteté!

O Dieu! je faulx: ne fu pas ung mesmes acteur; ainsois fu cil

595 sus le commencement duquel cest acteur de qui je parle edifia tout
son ouvraige. Piessà les fondemens estoient gettés par le premier,
et de sa propre main et matiere sans mendier sa et la, et sans y
assambler tel viltey de boe et de flache puante et orde comme est
mise ou sommillon de cest ouvraige. Je ne say se le sussesseur

600 le cuidait honourer: s'il le creoit pour vray il fu deceu; car a ung
commencement qui par aventure se porroit assés passer selond
son fait—mesmement entre Crestiens—, il adjousta tres orde fin
et moien desraisonnable contre Raison, laquelle fin et moiens nes
les mescreans en leur chose publique (come j'ay dit d'Octovien et

not the same as ours. (The difference is the same as that between a healthy and an infirm person: A wine which would harm a healthy person would send a person already shivering with fever out of his mind. So it goes when sinners see or hear carnal things in plain and
575 natural language; it awakens very villainous desires. However, this was not the case during the state of innocence: It is clear that before sinning, Eve and Adam were naked and felt no shame, then they sinned, and immediately thereafter hid and covered themselves, feeling great shame.) It is not necessary to ask why a certain manner
580 of speaking should be more reproved than another when the same idea is expressed. In either case, I need not stop now to explain the natural cause of this, since experience shows it clearly enough: It is because the imagination is more agitated, and all desire is the result of imagination. Thus it follows that Lady Idleness is the gate-keeper
585 of Foolish Love, because the latter cannot reach the imagination of one who is busy. In one way or another she kindles in him carnal desire. It is for this reason that there is no better cure than to busy oneself with some worthy task. It follows that a melancholic or sickly person of weak temperament will be more ardently tempted
590 by carnality than a healthy, sanguine, happy person. Everything originates in the imagination: Is it surprising that a fire covered in ashes does not burn as quickly as an open one? It is the same with carnal things which are plainly said or directly gazed upon.

       However, I will take up my argument and say that if the char-
595 acter of Reason had spoken to a wise and established cleric, none of this would have occurred. But no! He[79] speaks to the Foolish Lover. Here, the author has observed poorly the rules of my school (the rules of rhetoric) which are to take into account who is speaking, with whom one is speaking, and for how long one will speak. He
600 not only commits this error here, but also in several other places, where he attributes to the character speaking that which does not belong to him (as when he portrays Nature as speaking about paradise and the mysteries of our faith, and Venus as swearing on the flesh of God). But I will not consider this, although it is one of his
605 errors which some wish to place above all others that ever were. I am too greatly aggrieved for Lady Reason and Chastity, and that he made Reason, the wise one, utter such obscenities to a foolish lover, whom Cupid (who claims to be the God of Love) had previously forbidden all villainous speech and places, as well as the rebuke of
610 women. As if Cupid were more chaste and reasonable than Lady Reason and Chastity!

605   des philozophes) onques n'ont peu souffrir ne soustenir. Les sains
       docteurs meismement ont corrigié leurs dis et amendés,—tant ne
       soit pareil ycy et la.

           Si conclus devant vous et vostre noble court, dame Justice
       Canonique, que provision doit estre mise par arrest et sans contredit
610   de partie a ce defaut. Riens je ne conclus contre la personne de
       l'aucteur,—a Dieu bien s'en conviengne—, mais du deffault, qui
       est trop grant, je parle. Conment trop grant default? Je l'ay dessus
       monstré et le repete en brief: trop grant en occasions de erreurs, en
       blaphemes, en venimeuses doctrines, en destruccions et desolacions
615   de povres ames crestiennes, en illicite perdicion de tamps qui est
       tant precieux, au prejudice de Chasteté, en la disipacion de loy-
       aulté hors mariaige et ens, ou dechassement de Paour et de Honte,
       ou diffame de Raison, ou grant deshonneur de vous, dame Justice
       Canonique, et de vos loys et drois, et de toute ceste religieuse court
620   de toute Crestienté, voir de tous bons,—voir des mauvais, qui en
       deviennent pieurs!

           Si soit ung tel livre osté et exterminé sans jamais en user, par
       especial es parties esquelles il s'abonne des personnaiges diffamés
       et deffandus, comme de Vielle dampnee—laquelle on doit justicier
625   ou pilory—, de Venus (c'est a dire de Luxure, qui est pechié mor-
       tel), et de Fol Amoureulx—lequel on ne doit point laissier foloier a
       son plaisir: on ne li porroit fere plus grant contraire ne plus le haïr.

           Si est ma demande a Dieu plaisant; a vous, dame Justice, rai-
       sonnable; a toute vostre court, agreable; et aux folz amoureulx—tant
630   y reclaimment il a present—, tres prouffitable et amoureuse, et quant
       ilz seront garis, sera tres plaisant et delitable. Et affin qu'aucun ne
       cuide ou ne se plaingne que je accuse autre chose que les vices et
       non pas les persones, je fais ou non de Chasteté et de Conscience
       une telle requeste et conclusion contre toute paintures ou escriptures
635   ou dis qui esmeuvent a Lubricité; car trop y est encline de soy nostre
       fragilité sans la pis enflanmer et trebuchier ou parfont des vices,
       loing des vertus et de Dieu,—qui est nostre gloire, nostre amour,
       nostre salut, joye et felicité.

           Eloquance ot fenie quant je n'aperceu l'eure que mon cuer
640   ravola come il estoit voley; et sans riens oïr de la sentence, je me
       trouvay en mon estude a la vespree, l'an de grace mil •IIII^C• et •ii•,
       le •xviiie•. jour de may. La trouvay bien aultre matiere pour mon
       cuer occuper, que plus ne fust ainsy volage: et fu la matiere de la
       Benoite Trinité en unité divine et simple, puis du Saint Sacremant
645   de l'autel, etc.

O God! I am mistaken: It was not one and the same author, but
rather the one who composed the opening on which this author, of
whom I speak here, built his entire work. Long ago the foundations
615 were erected by the former with his own hands and substance without stealing from here and there and without constructing such filth
out of the stinking, rotting mud hole with which this work is burdened. I do not know whether the successor wished to honor him.
If it was thus, he was deceived, because to a beginning—which,
620 incidentally, could well have been passed off as his own argument,
particularly among Christians—he added a very filthy ending and an
irrational section in the middle, against Reason, which not even the
pagans would have tolerated or supported publicly, as I have said
about Augustus and the philosophers. Although the two cases are
625 not the same, for even the holy Church Fathers have rectified their
works and repented.

I conclude before you and your noble court, Lady Canonical Justice, that provisions must be made against this offense by
unanimous decree. I conclude nothing against the author's person,
630 which will be dealt with by God, but I speak of the offense, which
is too great. In what way is it too great? I have shown this above and
will repeat it briefly: There are too many errors, blasphemies, and
venomous teachings; there is too much destruction and desolation of
poor Christian souls and illicit perdition of time, which is precious,
635 and there is prejudice against Chastity; there is the dissipation of
loyalty outside and within marriage, the casting aside of Fear and
Shame, the defamation of Reason, and great dishonor of you, Lady
Canonical Justice, and of your laws and rights, and of the entire
religious court of all Christianity, even of all good people—and even
640 bad people, who become worse through this!

Such a book ought to be expunged and exterminated without
ever being used again, especially the parts where he promulgates
defamed and forbidden characters, such as the Duenna, who is
damned and must be brought to justice at the pillory, Venus (that is,
645 Lechery, which is a mortal sin), and the Foolish Lover, who must
not be allowed to act as foolishly as he pleases. He could not be any
more offensive nor could one hate him more.

May my petition please God, be rational to you, Lady Justice,
and agreeable to your entire court, as well as profitable and loving
650 to foolish lovers and pleasant and delightful to them once they are
cured, much as they may object to it at present. And in order that no
one may think or complain that I make accusations about anything

655

660

665

other than the vices, not the people themselves, I am drafting a petition and conclusion in the name of Chastity and Conscience against all depictions or writings which promote lubricity. Because our fragility is already tempted enough by Nature without being kindled further and pushed toward vices and away from virtues and from God, who is our glory, our love, our salvation, our joy, and our felicity.

Eloquence ceased when I noticed the time, and my heart returned, just as it had taken flight. And without having heard the sentence, I found myself again in my study at Vespers, in the year of our Lord 1402, the 18th day of May. There I found plenty of other matters to occupy me, so that I was not as agitated, namely, the subject of the Blessed Trinity in divine and simple unity, and of the Holy Sacrament of the altar, etc.

6. End of Summer, 1402: Pierre Col's Reply to Christine de Pizan's and Jean Gerson's Treatises[80]

Although Pierre Col's epistle clearly is a rebuttal not only to Christine de Pizan but also to Jean Gerson's treatise, the latter was not among the intended recipients. In fact, it seems that Jean Gerson received a copy of this reply through a third party. After having read it, he certainly was quick to respond in the form of an epistle in Latin, the *Talia de me* written in December 1402.[81] Christine, for her part, had already sent her reaction in her letter dated October 2, 1402.[82]

Text:
185r° La response maistre Pierre Col, Chanoine de Paris aux deux traitiés
precedens
Aprés ce que je oÿ parler de ton hault entendement, cler engi-
en, et de ton eloquance melodieuse, je desiré tres ardemment veoir
5   de tes epistres et autres telz chosettes: si est aprés grant sollicitude
d'enquerir venue entre mes mains une certaingne tienne espistre,
addrecee, a mon advis, a ung mien seigneur et maistre especial, mon
seigneur le prevost de Lisle, laquelle si commance: «Reverance,
185v° honneur», etc., et par laquelle tu t'efforces de reprandre // ce tres
10   devolt catholique et tres eslevey theologien, ce tres divin orateur et
poete et tres parfait philozophe, maistre Jehan de Meun, en aucunes particularités de son livre de la *Rose*, pour lequel louer je n'ose
ouvrir la bouche, ne que je feroye avancié mon pié pour entrer en
ung abisme. Car selonc ce que nous lison de Herode, qui pourfita
15   plus aux Imnocens par hayne en les faisant occirre qu'il n'eust peu
fere par amour, pareillemant toy et aultres—qui s'eufforcent comme
toy a impugner ce tres noble escripvain Meun—le loués plus en le
cuidant blasmer que je ne pouroye le louer pour y user tous mes
membres,—fussent ilz ores tous convertis en langues: tant pour la
20   rudesse de mon engin, grosseur d'entendement, labile memoyre et
langaige mal ordonné, come plus vraiemant pour l'abbisme multi-
pliee de biens qui y sont nondisibles a home, lesquelz vous faictes
avertir en le cuidant blasmer.
Toutefois je, confiant de verité, par les raisons de luy, meismes
25   me efforceray de respondre aux tiennes, plus polies de langaige que
ton langaige n'est poly de raison des aultres, ses adversaires, par
moy veues ou oÿes, dont je ne puis avoir memoire. Et ne me soit
imputey, a presumpcion ou arogance: ce ne le me fait mie faire en
verité: mais pour ce que entre les aultres disciples du dit Meun je
30   desirre estre au moins le manre, et que les raisons que tu amainnes
encontre—se raisons doivent estre nommees—sont telles qu'il n'est

Translation:

The reply by Master Pierre Col, Chancellor of Paris, to the two previous treatises

After having heard of your high intelligence, clear mind, and melodious eloquence, I wished ardently to see other epistles and similar little things which you had written. After making avid inquiries, I finally obtained a certain one of your epistles, addressed, I think, to one of my lords and esteemed masters, my lord the provost of Lille, which begins as follows: "Reverence, honor," etc. In it you make a point of criticizing this very pious Catholic and highly learned theologian, this very divine orator and poet, and accomplished philosopher, Master Jean de Meun, with respect to some parts of his book of the *Rose,* which, to praise it I dare not open my mouth, any more than I would move my foot toward an abyss. Given what we read about Herod, who, by having the Innocents killed, did them more good through his hatred than he could have out of love, similarly you and others who, like you, try to attack this very noble writer, Meun, have praised him more by insulting him than I could praise him even if I were to use all my wits, had they all been converted into tongues. Not for the dullness of my intellect, lack of sophistication and eloquence, and my weak memory, but especially for the wealth of good things about this man, which are too numerous to express yet to which you draw attention, all the while thinking that you are insulting him.

In any case, I, loyal to the truth of his arguments, will attempt to respond to your own, which are more polite in language than those of the others, his adversaries whose arguments I have seen or heard but cannot recall. I pray I shall not be accused of presumption or arrogance, which, in truth, is not what motivates me to do this; it is instead that among the disciples of Meun, I wish at least to be the smallest, and that the arguments which you bring forth against him—if indeed they can be called arguments—are such that they never necessitate a response from the most advanced disciples of the aforementioned Meun, but from those who are average ones or closer to the bottom. They are also loyal to the great cause which I wish

ja besoing, je ne dis pas des plus avanciés disciples du dit Meun
mais des moyens ou assés pres au dessoubz qu'ilz y respondent,
confiant aussy du grant droit que je vueil soustenir, ja soit ce que
35   trop se soustiengne de leur meismes: mais j'en fais mon escu. Et me
pardonne se je parle par «tu», car je le fais pour monstrer que ceste
mienne responce vient par bonne amour, c'est assavoir pour toy
ramener a droite voye; et auxi pour parler plus proprement selonc
que nos anciens maistres ont parley.
40   Premierement tu, sans raison, commences au chapistre de
Raison et dis qu'elle nomme les secrés membres d'omme par leur
propre non. Et respons a tel argument que Diex fist les choses:
donc sont elles bonnes: donc les puet on bien nommer. Vraiement
ce dis tu: «Je confesse que Dieu crea toutes choses pures et nettes
45   venans de soy; n'adonc en l'estat d'ignocence n'eust esté laidure
de les nommer. Mais par la polucion de pechié devint homme immonde…»; et fais exemple de Lucifer, qui fut premierement bel et
le non bel, «qui puis par pechié fu rameney a orrible laidesse, par
quoy le non, tout soit il de soy bel, si donne il erreur aux oyans…».
50   Oultre du dis que «le non ne fait pas la deshonnesteté de la chose,
mais la chose fait le non deshonneste». Ycy resembles tu le pellican:
tu te tues de ton bec. Par ta foy! se la chose fait le non deshonneste,
quel non pues tu baillier a la chose qui ne soit deshonneste, se la
chose ne se change come le non?
55   Mais je viens a ce que tu dis que en l'estat d'ingnocence
estoit licite de nommer les secrés membres, et que Dieu les forma
en tel estat. Je te demande se tu parloies des secrés membre d'ung
enfant de deux ou de trois ans—car tu ne niroyes pas que Dieu ne
nous forme trestous—, les oseroies tu bien nommer par leur pro-
60   pre non? Se tu dis que non, toutevoies est il en l'estat d'ignocence,
sans polucion en fait et en pansee. Et ne vault riens si repliquer du
pechié originel, car il vint par inobedience. Et se la polucion de nos
premiers parans fait le non des secrés membres si lait qu'on ne les
puisse licitement nonmer, je dy que par plus fort raison on ne dev-
65   roit pas nommer yceulx nos premiers parens: car ce sunt ceulx qui
pecherent, et non pas membres. Se tu dis que oy (c'est assavoir c'on
puisse nommer les secrés membres d'ung enfant), je te prie que tu
nous desclaires l'aage jusques auquel il est [licite] de les nommer, et
auxi s'on peut nommer par leur non les membres secrés d'un aagié
70 186rº home chaste et vierge toute sa vie; pareillement des // mambres
pareilz aux membres secrés qui sont es bestes mues, se tu les oseroies nommer—car ceulx ne pechent point—, affin qu'apraingnes

35   to defend, though it defends itself well enough. Nevertheless, I shall
    fulfill my duty. Forgive me if I address you by the informal "you,"
    which I do in order to show that my response stems from kindness
    in the attempt to bring you back to the right path and also to speak
    more properly according to the ways of our ancient masters.

40   First, for no reason, you begin with the chapter of Reason,
    saying that she calls the secret male parts by their correct names.
    My response to such an argument is that God made all things, hence
    they are good and can therefore be named. To be exact, you say, "I
    admit that God created all things coming from Him to be pure and

45   proper; therefore in the state of innocence there could have been no
    ugliness in naming them. Yet it was through the corruption of sin
    that mankind became unclean...." You cite Lucifer as an example,
    who at first was beautiful, as was his name, "which then was re-
    duced to terrible ugliness through his sin. This means that the name,

50   beautiful as it may be in itself, terrifies those who hear it because
    of its association with the person...." Elsewhere you say that "the
    name does not make the thing shameful but it is the thing which
    makes the name shameful." Here, you resemble the pelican: You
    kill yourself with your own beak. By your faith! If the thing makes

55   the name shameful, what name can you give the thing which is not
    shameful, if the thing does not change as does the name?

        However, I will move on to your statement that in the state of
    innocence it was licit to name the secret parts and that God made
    them in such a state. I ask you, if you were speaking of the secret

60   parts of a child of two or three—since you would not deny that
    God forms us all very early on—would you dare call them by their
    proper names? If you say no, [I will say] that, after all, this hap-
    pened in a state of innocence, without corruption in act and thought,
    and that it is worthless to reply that it had to do with original sin

65   because this came from disobedience. And if the corruption of our
    first parents does indeed render the name of the secret parts so ugly
    that one cannot name them licitly, I say that more importantly one
    ought not to name our first parents, because it is they who sinned,
    not their parts. If your answer is yes (that is, that one may name the

70   secret parts of a child), I ask you to specify the age until which it is
    licit to name them, and also whether one may call by their proper
    names the secret parts of an elderly man who has been chaste and
    a virgin all his life. Similarly, in your attempt to teach Reason and
    Meun's disciples how one ought to speak, would you dare to name

75   the equivalent body parts belonging to dumb animals—because they

75
a Raison et aux disciples du dit Meun comment on doit parler. En
verité l'Amant, ou chapistre de Raison, fait plus d'argumens et de
plus fors la moitié que tu ne fais: auxquelx Raison respons: et toutevoies tu ne respons pas aux raisons d'icelle meisme, laquelle chose
tu deusses fere avant que tu la reprisses. Si n'est plus besoing de te
respondre quant ad ce.

80
Mais j'ay veu ung escript fait en maniere d'une plaidoierie en
la court sainte de Crestienté, en laquelle estoit Justice Canonique
establie come juge et les Vertus entour elle come son conseil, duquel
le chief et conme chancellier estoit Entendement Subtil, joint par
compaingnie a dame Raison, Prudence, Science et autres come
secretaires, Eloquence Theologienne come advocat de la court; et

85
le promoteur des causes estoit Conscience, lequel promoteur ont
fait lever et presenter une requeste pour Chastetey contenant ceste
forme: «A Justice la droituriere, tenant le lieu de Dieu en terre,
et a toute sa religieuse court devote et tres crestienne. Supplie
humblement et se complaint Chasteté, vostre feable subjecte, que

90
remede soit mis et provision briefve sur les forfaitures intollerables,
lesquelles m'a fait et ne cesse faire ung qui se fait nommer le Fol
Amoureux». Et met aprés huit ou nuef articles.

Or en verité je cuide congnostre la persone qui celle plaidoierie a compilee, et me doubte qu'il ne parle de Fol Amoureulx come

95
clerc d'armes et ne li desplaise: car par ma foy je tiens qu'ainsy
come il meismes, quant il prescha en Greve le jour de la Trinité,
dist que icelle Trinité nous veons et cognoissons en umbre et come
par ung mirouer, ainssy voit, entent et parle d'ung fol amoureux;
car je panse qu'il ne le fut onques, ne n'y ot onques pensee: en tant

100
que je oseroie dire qu'il contoit mieulx la Trinité qu'il ne fait Fol
Amoureux, aussi y a il plus pansé. Et pour yce j'eusse cause assés
de dire a toute celle plaidoirie, qu'il n'y fault point respondre: car
tout le plaidoié est fondé sur ung fol amoureulx, et l'aucteur ne sceit
qu'est fol amoureux. Et ne vault riens de dire que ja soit ce qu'il

105
ne soit fol amoureux, si entent il par aventure mieulx que tel—l'est
ou a esté—; ce puet estre, mais j'ose bien dire que s'il meismes
l'eust esté et ne le fust a present, il entendist mieux la moitié qu'il
ne fait: car trop plus a experience de ne say quelle puissance que
n'a meismes l'effait de vive voix. Toutevoies la verité et le bon

110
droit sont telz et si clers pour celluy qu'il appelle Fol Amoureux
qu'il ne me grevera riens respondre aux particulieres raisons que
propose dame Eloquance Theologienne, come on li mé seure; car
par ma foy elle nel se pansa onques, la bone dame, come je diray cy

certainly have not sinned. Truly, in the chapter of Reason, the Lover
has more numerous and by far more forceful arguments than you
do, to which Reason responds. Yet you, in turn, do not respond to
her arguments, which you should have done before criticizing her.
80   Hence, it is not necessary to respond to you further on this subject.

However, I have seen a text in the form of a petition in the
holy court of Christianity where Canonical Justice was established
as judge and the Virtues surrounded her as her Council, the head and
Chancellor of which was Sound Judgment, joined by the company
85   of Lady Reason, Prudence, Knowledge, and others as secretaries.
Theological Eloquence was the court advocate, and the defender
of the cases was Conscience. They presented a request on behalf
of Chastity, containing the following statement: "To Justice the
righteous, who represents God on earth, and to the entire religious,
90   pious, and Christian court. I, Chastity, your loyal subject, implore
you and complain humbly that the intolerable infringements which
someone by the name of the Foolish Lover has imposed and does
not cease to impose upon me be remedied without further delay."
And eight or nine accusations follow.
95   Now, in truth, I think I know the person who compiled this
petition,[84] and have the suspicion that he speaks of the Foolish Lover
as an ordained cleric, which must cause him discontent. For, by my
faith, I maintain in accordance with what he said when he preached
at the Place de Grève on the day of the Trinity, that we see and know
100   this Trinity as a shadow, like a mirror.[85] And it is thus that he sees
and understands a foolish lover, because, I think, he has never been
one nor has he ever thought about it, so that I dare say that he not
only knows the Trinity better than he does the Foolish Lover but has
also thought more about the former. Therefore, I would have reason
105   enough to say that it is not necessary to respond to this [entire] complaint, because it is founded entirely on the case of a foolish lover,
and the author does not know what a foolish lover is. Moreover,
there is no point in saying that although he has never been a foolish
lover, he understands perhaps better than one who is or has been
110   one. Certainly, I dare say that even if he had been one and was no
longer one he would understand a great deal more than he does: For
experience has much more power than that which one is simply told.
Nevertheless, for the one whom he calls the Foolish Lover, truth and
righteousness are so clear that I have no difficulty responding to the
115   particular charges which Theological Eloquence has brought against
him. For, by my faith, she never did think it through, the good lady,

115 aprés,—presupposé encore que le dit Meun eust esté fol amoureux
par aucun temps.

     Premierement donc dame Eloquance Theologienne dist
que maistre Jehan de Meun porte en son front le tiltre escript de
sa condampnacion par ce mot «Fol Amoureux», en disant: «Qui
craventa jadis par feu et flame Troye la grant? Fol Amoureux. Qui
120 fist destruyre lors plus de cent mil gentilz homes, Hector, Achilles, et autres? Fol Amoureux. Qui chassa hors de Ronme le roy
Tarquinius? Fol Amoureulx… »; et d'autres similitudes parelles. Je
demande a dame Eloquance se cest argument tent a blasmer estre
fol amoureulx, ou a blasmer le livre de la *Rose* pour ce qu'un qui fut
125 fol amoureulx l'a fait. Si tent a blasmer fol amoureux, je n'y respons
point: car je confesse que c'est folie et sans raison que de l'estre; et
ne fault ja qu'on s'efforce de plus blasmer Fol Amoureux que fait le
livre de la *Rose.* Avise bien qui le lit: ne dit il pas du Deu d'amours:
«C'est le dieu qui tous les desvoye… »? Et depuis:
130   Mais de la fole amour se gardent,
           tant les cuers esprennent et ardent…
           C'est ce qui la pel t'amaigroie…

           … son cuer mis en amour de fame,
135   dont maint ont perdu corps et ame…

           C'est l'amour qui souffle et atise
           la brese qu'i t'a ou cuer mise…

140   Quiconques a Raison s'accorde
           jamais par amours n'amera…

186vº   //…que ceulx qui plus le hantent
           en la fin plus s'en repantent…
145 et en plus de cent autres lieux que je laisse pour cause de brieté, si
non ung ver, qui souffisoit assés pour tous, c'est assavoir:
           Maint y perdent, bien dire l'os,
           sens, temps, chatel, corps, ame, los.
Or espluchent hardiement ce «los» ceulx qui plus veulent blasmer
150 Fol Amoureulx que maistre Jehan de Meun ne fait, et je croy qu'i
n'y troveront que rengier. Et quant maistre Jehan de Meun appelle
les secrés membres de fame «saintuaires» et «reliques», il le fist
pour monstrer la grant folie qui est en Fol Amoureux: car ung fol
amoureux ne pense a autre chose que a ce bouton; et est son dieu, et
155 l'aoure come son dieu. Aussi en ce pas la y faingny poetiquemant,

as I will demonstrate hereafter—assuming again that the aforementioned Meun was a foolish lover at some point.

120 First, then, Lady Theological Eloquence states that Master Jean de Meun has the title of his condemnation, "Foolish Lover," written across his face, when she says, "Who long ago destroyed Troy the Great through fire and flames? The Foolish Lover. Who caused the death of more than one hundred thousand noble men, Hector, Achilles, Priam, and others? The Foolish Lover. Who long

125 ago chased King Tarquin[86] and his entire lineage out of Rome? The Foolish Lover..." and other such things. I ask Lady Eloquence whether this argument attempts to insult foolish lovers or the book of the *Rose* because it was made by a foolish lover. If it is supposed to insult foolish lovers, I will not respond, because I admit that be-

130 ing a foolish lover is foolish and irrational. And it is not necessary to try to insult the Foolish Lover more than the book of the *Rose* already does. Whoever may read it, consider it well: Does he not say of the God of Love, "He is the God who leads them all astray..."?[87] And then he says,

135 But may they stay away from foolish love,
which sets hearts on fire and burns them...
This is what has shriveled your skin...

...who gave his heart to the love of a woman,
140 where many have lost body and soul...

It is love that blows and kindles
the embers which have been put in your heart...

145 Whoever adheres to Reason
will never love passionately...

...so that those who chase [love] most
will repent most in the end...
150 and in addition to this there are one hundred other places, which I will leave out for brevity's sake but for one verse which could suffice for all, namely:
Many lose there, I dare say,
sense, time, castle, body, soul, reputation.

155 Now, those who wish to insult the Foolish Lover more than Master Jean de Meun has already done may examine this "reputation" closely, but I think they will find only reindeer there.[88] And when Master Jean de Meun calls the female secret parts "sanctuaries"

et aux poetes et paintres a tousjours esté licence pareille de tout
faindre, comme dit Orace. Si n'est ce pas si mal appellé c'on pouroit
bien dire, d'appeller les secrés mambres ceintuaires: car les portes et
les murs d'unne citey, selonc les loys, sont appellés saintes pour ce
160   que s'on y commet force ou les trespasse sans congié, il y a peinne;
ainssy est il des secrés membres de fame: il y a peinne, qui y fait
force ou qui sans force indeuement les trespasses. Et si dit la Bible
que on souloit saintifier les secrés manbres de fenme.
        Mais se l'argument tant a blasmer le livre de la *Rose* pour ce
165   qu'un qui fut fol amoureux l'a fait, je me merveille commant dame
Eloquance ne fait premierement ses conclusions contre Salmon,
David et aultres folz amoureux qui furent trop devant Meun, des-
quelz les livres sont meslés en la sainte Escripture et les paroles ou
saint mistere de la Messe. Qui fist tuer Urie le bon chevalier par
170   traïson, pour commettre adultere avec sa fame? Fol amoureux. Qui
fist edifier temples aux ydoles pour l'amour de fames estranges?
Fol Amoureulx. Et trop d'autres, que je trespasses. Contre ceulx
cy deust premieremant parler dame Eloquence, se son argument
protestast. Mais nannin voir. Ne lisons nous pas que saint Pierre et
175   saint Pol, aprés leur pechié, furent plus fermes en la foy, et plusseurs autres pareillement? Je dy que maistre Jehan de Meun, puis
qu'il fut fol amoureux, fu tres fermes en raison: car de tant qu'il
congnut mieux la folie qui est en fole amour par experience, de
tant la desprisa il plus et loua Raison. Et quant il fist ce livre de la
180   *Rose* il n'estoit plus fol amoureux, ains s'en repantoit de l'avoir
esté, comme il appert par ce qu'il sceut si bien parler de Raison: s'il
ne l'eust congnue, amee et entendue, il n'en eust ainssy seu parler
comme il en parla,—et toutevoies il est vray que Fol Amoureux ne
la congnoist, aime, ou entent. Et si dit en chapistre de Nature, quant
185   il parle de paradis, que les choses du vergier Deduit ne sont que
fanfelues; et de la fontainne Narcisus dit:
        Dieux! que bone fontainne et sade,
        ou li sain devienent malade…
et qu'elle enivre de mort les vifs. Conment pouoit il mieux monstrer
190   qu'il n'estoit pas fol amoureux et qu'il amoit Raison que en blasment le vergier Deduit et les choses qui y sont, et en louant Raison
et mettant ung aultre parc (ung autre parc ou vergier), ouquel il figure si notablement la Trinitey et l'Incarnacion par l'escharboucle et
par l'olive qui prant son acroissement de la rousee de la fontainne,
195   etc.? Des qu'il commensa a escripture, il entre en raison; et Dieu
sceit combien il se tient: a painne se peut il oster (aussy ne s'i estoit
gaires tenu le premier aucteur). Et ne cuide pas que ce qu'il dit en

160 and "relics,"[89] he does so in order to show the great foolishness of
the Foolish Lover. For a foolish lover thinks of nothing but this
rosebud. It is his god, and he adores it as his god. Moreover, in this
particular passage he dissimulates poetically, and, as Horace says,
it has always been the prerogative of poets and painters to dissimu-
165 late everything.[90] It is not so bad, one might say, to call these secret
parts sanctuaries, because the gates and walls of a city are according
to the laws called holy, because it takes strength to open them or
because trespassing them without permission will be punished. It is
the same with the secret parts of a woman: He who enters there by
force or without force, but unduly, will be punished. And the Bible
170 speaks about the custom of sanctifying the secret parts of women.

Yet if the reason for refuting the *Rose* is based on the fact that
it was made by a foolish lover, I am astonished that Lady Eloquence
does not make her arguments first against Solomon, David, and
other foolish lovers who far preceded Meun and whose books may
175 be found in Holy Scripture and their words in the holy sacrament
of Mass. Who had Uriah the good knight slain for treason in order
to commit adultery with his wife?[91] The Foolish Lover. Who out
of love for foreign women had temples erected for the worship of
idols? The Foolish Lover. And many others, which I will skip. Lady
180 Eloquence should speak against them first if she wishes to declare
her argument publicly. But this is not the case. Do we not read that
Saint Peter and Saint Paul, having been sinners, were more steadfast in their faith, like many others also? I say that Master Jean de
Meun, since he was a foolish lover, was very steadfast in his cause:
185 For the better he knew through experience the folly which lies in
foolish love, the more he despised it and praised Reason. And when
he made the book of the *Rose,* he was no longer a foolish lover and
repented for having been one, it seems, because he knew to speak
so well of Reason. Had he not known, loved, and understood her,
190 he would not have spoken as he did. Conversely, it is true that the
Foolish Lover does not know, love, or understand her. In the chapter
of Nature, when he speaks of paradise, he declares that the things in
the Garden of Delight are merely foolish. And of Narcissus's fountain, he says:
195 God! What a good and enticing fountain,
Where the healthy become sick…
and that it intoxicates the living with death. How better could he
show that he was not a foolish lover and that he loved Reason than
to insult the Garden of Delight and the things it contains and to
200 praise Reason and introduce another park (another park or garden)

son *Testament*: «J'ay fait en ma jonesse maint dit par vanitey», qu'il
entende de ce livre de la *Rose;* car vraiement come je [ne] monstre-
200   ray mais, il entendoit d'aucunes balades, rondiaux et virelais que
nous n'avons pas par escript,—au moins moy.

          Mais venons a ce qui fait a ton propos. Dame Eloquance,
adressant ses parolles a ceulx qui soustiennent ce Fol Amoureux, dit
ainssy: «N'est ce pas, fait elle, rage dire que on doye parler nue-
205   ment et baudement et sans vergoingne, tant soient deshonnestes les
paroles au jugement de toute gent…» etc. Ha! dame Eloquance! On
vous impose cy mal reciter vostre fait principal sur quoy vous fon-
dés tous vos argurnans ensuivans: mais n'en sachiés mal gré a celluy
qui ce fait, car je tieng veritablement qu'i ne le fait pas
210 187r° essienment. // Certes il a eu pou plaisance a ce tres noble livre de
la *Rose,* par quoy il l'a pou veu ou noyant,—ou, come je cuideroie
mieux, [pour] ce qu'i l'a pou veu, y a il desplaisance. Je ne doubte
point que si l'eust veu et releu par fois souvent recordees, que
de tant come son entendement passe tant d'autres que je ne say
215   lesquelz non, de tant plus le louast, prisast, amast et honnourast.
Veés ci, veés ci les parolles que dit Raison:
          Biaux amis, je puis bien nommer,
          sans moy fere mal renommer,
          appertement par propre non
220   chose qui n'est se bone non.
          Voire du mal seurement
          puis je bien parler proprement, etc.
Il ne dit pas c'on en doye parler; il dit qu'on en puet parler: ce n'est
pas tout ung, devoir et pouoir. Je confesse que querir occasion de
225   parler de l'euvre de nature en laquelle se fait la pollucion qu'aucuns
tant abhominent et se soubtiver a en parler diversement pour le
plaisir c'on y auroit trop, ce seroit mal fait; et ainsy l'entent Tulle
ou livre *Des offices,* et les autres philozophes qui pareillement en
parlerent. Mais quant on parle de plusseurs choses diverses, et sans
230   y venir par affeccion particuliere on descent aux secrés menbres, on
en puet parler proprement: et ainssy en parle maistre Jehan de Meun
ou chapitre de Raison. Et par Dieu! une fois en convient il parler au
moins: quant on leur meist non premierement; et on ne meist pas
le non premierement pour en parler a celle fois seulement et non
235   jamais aprés. Et s'il est licite d'en parler par propre non en nul cas,
il est licite d'en parler en la maniere que Raison en parle: aussy
les nomme la sainte Escripture par leur propre non; et tres proprement pareillement les loys en plusseurs lieux. En oultre, les secrés

where he so illustriously depicts the Trinity and the Incarnation through the carbuncle, and the olive which grows from the dew of the fountain, etc.? He embraced reason as soon as he began his writ-ing, and God knows how much he adheres to her. He could hardly

205 tear himself away from her (which is why he was not very loyal to the first author). And do not believe, when he says in his *Testament*, "In my youth I composed many a text out of vanity," that he refers to the book of the *Rose*. For, truly, as I will not show further, he referred to *ballades*, *rondels*, and *virelais* which we do not have in

210 writing; at least I do not.

But let us get to your point! Lady Eloquence, addressing in her speech those who support this Foolish Lover, says, "Is it not, she says, a great outrage to claim that one must speak bluntly, bawdily, and shamelessly, regardless of how shameful the words are in the

215 eyes of all others…" etc. Ha! Lady Eloquence! You are forced to erroneously stating your main argument, on which all your ensuing arguments are based. But do not hold a grudge against the one who accuses you, because I am convinced that he does not do it purpose-ly. Surely, he took little pleasure in reading this very noble book of

220 the *Rose,* because he saw little or nothing of it, or, as I would like to think, it is because he saw only a little that he could not find plea-sure in it. I do not doubt at all that, had he seen and reread it several times thoroughly—particularly since his intelligence surpasses that of so many others that I cannot imagine whose it does not surpass—

225 he would have praised, loved, and honored more. Let us see here, let us see here Reason's speech:

Beautiful friends, I may certainly name,
without acquiring bad renown,
openly by its proper name

230 a thing which does not have a good name.
Truly, I may certainly
speak in proper terms of evil, etc.

He does not say that one *must* speak about it but that one *may* speak about it. Must and may are not the same thing. I admit that it would

235 be sinful to seek the opportunity to speak of the work of Nature, in which the corruption of some is abominable, as it would be to speak about such things ingeniously and in different ways in order to gain great pleasure. This is how Cicero in his *De Officiis* understands it, as do other philosophers who speak about it in a similar fashion. But

240 when one speaks about several different things and, in the process, arrives quite inadvertently at the subject of the secret parts, one is

240   membres sont necessaires et utiles et proufitables et biaux et bons:
encor deffent la Bible que home a qui on les a coupés n'entre en
l'eglise, et la les nomme elle tres proprement. Ne je ne croy pas que
Jhesu Crist eust membre qu'on ne pouist nommer honnestement.
Toy et tes complices aussy les nommés par leur seurnon, lesquelz
seurnons, par ce que les propres nons sunt communs a diverses
245   choses, furent trouvés pour plus specifier ycelles. Et si ne parle pas
Raison de l'euvre en laquelle est pollucion, mais nomme les membres ad ce et autres choses deputés.

             Non pour tant se ces nons desplaisent a aucuns, ne desplaisent
il a chascun (je dis cecy pour ce que dame Eloquance dit: «… tant
250   soient deshonnestes les parolles au jugement de toutes gens»); n'il
ne faut ja dire que bone coustume defent d'en parler proprement.
Se la coustume est bonne ou mauvaise, je m'en tais; mais dire que
fames n'ont pas acoustumé d'en parler ainsy plainnement, dame
Eloquance n'en aura pas les gans. Car ou chapitre de Raison est dit:
255   Se fames nes nomment en France,
             ce n'est fors desacoustumance;
et dit « en France » notablement, pour ce que son livre est en franssois, et si puet estre qu'ailleurs qu'an France fames les nomment
proprement. Encor suis je esbahis de la coustume, car fames nom-
260   ment bien leurs secrés membres par leur propre non: ilz ne veulent
nommer ceulx des hommes; si ne voy je pas qu'il soient plus honnestes que ceulx des hommes.

             Voire, mais (ce dit dame Eloquance) il garda mal les regles
de rethorique; car il deust avoir resgardé a qui Raison parloit: s'elle
265   eust parlé a un clerc ou theologien, «aucune chose feust»; mais elle
parloit a ung fol amoureux, qui par telz parolles peut estre esmeu
a charnalité—ce que ne seroit ung grant clerc ou theologien—, et
semble par ses paroles qu'estre clerc, philozophe, ou theologien et
fol amoureux ne se sueffrent pas ensemble, ains sont incompatibles.
270   Hélas! il en va bien autrement, et est alé et ira—dont c'est dom-
mages—, come de David et Salemon et autres (aucuns docteurs
meismes dient que Salemon fist les *Cantiques* pour l'amour de la
fille Pharaon; si fut il tenu le plus sage qui fust devant luy ne de
son tamps). Brief, on y amenroit plus de mil exemples de gens
275   qui furent clers et folz amoureux, car il s'antresueffrent auxi bien
ensemble qu'estre clerc et chevalereux, come furent Pompee, Julius
Cesar, Cipion, Tulle et autres. Mais je croy pour ce que cil qui celle
plaidoierie a compilee est clerc, philozophes et theologien, sans
estre fol amoureux, qu'i cuide qu'ausy soit il des autres. Et n'est il

able to speak about them properly. And this is how Master Jean de
Meun speaks about them in the chapter of Reason. And by God! It
is appropriate to mention them at least once as long as one does not
245 overstress their importance. And this is not the case, since he mentions them by name only once and then never again. If it is licit to
speak about them using their proper names in that case, the way in
which Reason speaks about them is also licit. Moreover, Holy Scripture also calls them by their proper names, as do the laws in several
250 places. In addition, the secret parts are necessary, useful, helpful,
beautiful, and good: The Bible forbids men who have been castrated
to enter the Church and the secret parts are clearly named there. Nor
do I believe that Jesus Christ had parts which could not be named
honorably. You and your partisans also name them by their surnames,
255 because proper names are common for various things, so the surnames are more specific. And Reason does not speak of the work of
corruption, but names the parts belonging to this and other things.

     Yet if some dislike these names, not everyone does (I say this
because Lady Eloquence says, "…the words are so terribly shameful
260 in the eyes of everyone"); nor must one say that good practice prohib-
its people to speak about them in proper terms. Whether this custom
is good or bad, I shall be quiet about it. But to say that women are
not in the habit of speaking about them overtly does not give Lady
Eloquence much credit. For it is written in the chapter of Reason:
265   If women do not name them in France,
    it is only for loss of the custom.
and it says specifically "in France" because his book is in French.
Therefore, women might name them properly elsewhere. Further, I
am astonished by this custom, because women do indeed call their
270 secret parts by their proper names. It is those of men which they do
not wish to name, although I do not see that theirs are more honorable
than those of men.

     Moreover, (Lady Eloquence says) he observed the rules of
rhetoric poorly, because he should have considered with whom
275 Reason was speaking: If she had spoken with a cleric or theologian,
"that would have been one thing." However, she was speaking with
a foolish lover, who could have been incited to carnality—which a
great cleric or theologian would not have been. Her speech seems
to suggest that being a cleric, philosopher, or theologian on the one
280 hand and a foolish lover on the other are irreconcilable and incompat-
ible. Alas! Quite the contrary is true, was and will be, as it was for
David and Solomon and others—so this is wrong (some theologians

280   pas possible que il meismes, ou tamps a venir, soit fol amoureux?
        Par Dieu si est! Si n'en seroit il ja moins clerc, au moins au com-
        mansement de la fole amour. Aussy ne s'esmeut pas ung home a
        folement amer pour nommer deux ou trois membres secrets—de par
        Dieu!—puis qu'il les fault ainssy nonmer. Quant Raison les nonme
285 187v° elle presche au Fol Amoureux qu'il s'os- // tast de la Fole amour,
        et en parlant de diverses choses vint a propos de parler des secrés
        membres: vrayement s'il eust tousjours ainsy esté auccupé, Oyseuse
        ne luy eust ja ouvert l'uis du vergier; encore—non obstant qu'il fust
        desja fol amoureux—le fist Raison esmouvoir de s'en oster, comme
290   le Dieu d'amours luy reproche. Et que maistre Jehan de Meun ou
        chapistre de Raison ne descendi pas a parler des secrés membres
        pour affeccion qu'il y eust a en parler nuement et baudement, mais
        pour ce qu'il vint a propos et pour monstrer la folle a ceulx qui dient
        qu'il n'est licite d'en parler en nul cas par propres nons, appert par
295   ce que ailleurs ou il parle de l'euvre de nature ne le nomme il pas
        par propre non (comme ou chapistre d'Ami et de la Vielle, esquelz il
        nomme le «jeu d'amous», la «besongne d'amours», et «ce tripot»).
        Si ne fault ja dire qu'il garda mal les regles de rethorique, car il
        monstre evidemmant qu'il les avoit naturelement et par estude: j'ose
300   dire que qui le lit et entent, il entendra avec maistre Jehan de Meun
        ne devoir autremant parler qu'il parla. Et quant dame Eloquance dit
        qu'il atribue a Nature parler de Dieu, je dy que elle le puet et doit
        faire, et que la chamberiere peut bien parler a son maistre; et pareil-
        lement saint Augustin, ou livre de *Seul parlers,* la ou il fait l'ame
305   devote demander a la terre et aux autres elemans s'ilz estoient son
        dieu, et qu'il respondent que non et qu'elle le quiere plus hault, dit
        aprés que les responces de choses sont la testacion de Dieu. Aussy
        veult monstrer Meun qu'il estoit naturel et crestien en parlant de
        Nature, et sy estoit poete, come j'ay dit, par quoy il laissoit de tout
310   parler par ficcion.
            Voire, mais (fait dame Eloquance) ce Fol Amoureux fait dire
        a Raison ce que par avant Cupido deffent. Et puis fait une meniere
        de se reprandre: «O dya! fait elle, ce ne fu pas ung meisme aucteur,
        mais cil sur le commensement duquel cestuy Meun edifia son
315   ouvraige»: les fondemans estoient bons et nes, et cestuy y fist ung
        sommillon de fange.
            Certes vescy trop bien dit! A quel fin est ce, je luy pry, que
        Cupido baille du bouton (c'est a dire qu'il aviengne a l'exceucion
        fole amoureusse)? Et veuci trop contradiccion: il blasme Raison qui
320   chastie l'Amant d'estre fol amoureux, et loue Cupido qui ensaingne
        comment on en venra a chief.

even say that Solomon wrote the *Canticles*[92] out of love for Pharaoh's
daughter, yet he was considered the wisest person of all time). In
285 short, one could cite more than one thousand examples of people who
were clerics and foolish lovers at once, because being both a cleric
and chivalrous—as were Pompey, Julius Caesar, Scipio, Cicero, and
others—is indeed very much reconcilable. I believe that he who compiled this complaint is a cleric, philosopher, and theologian without
290 being a foolish lover, and assumes that this is also the case for others.
And is it not possible that he, too, will in the future be a foolish lover?
By God, yes, of course! At least at the beginning of foolish love, he
would not be any less a cleric. Moreover, a man is not moved to love
foolishly simply by hearing the name of two or three secret parts—by
295 God!—since they must be named in such a way. When Reason names
them, she preaches to the Foolish Lover to desist from foolish love,
and by speaking about several matters, she arrives at the subject of
speaking about secret parts. Truly, if he had already been preoccupied
with this, Idleness would never have opened the gate to the garden
300 for him. Furthermore, despite the fact that he may already have been
a foolish lover, Reason made him desist from this, for which the God
of Love reproaches her. And in the chapter of Reason, Master Jean
de Meun did not lower himself to speak of the secret parts out of a
desire to speak plainly and bawdily, but because the topic comes up
305 and also to show the foolishness of their statement to those who say
it is never licit to speak about these parts in proper terms. This is
obvious when elsewhere he speaks about Nature's work and does not
name them properly (for example, in the chapter of the Friend and
the Duenna, where he refers to the "game of love," the "task of love,"
310 and "this dance"). One must not say that he observes poorly the rules
of rhetoric, since he obviously shows that he mastered them naturally
and through study. I dare say that whoever reads and understands it,
will agree with Master Jean de Meun, that he could not have spoken
differently than he did. When Lady Eloquence says that it is Nature's
315 responsibility to speak about God, I say that she can and must do so;
the chambermaid surely has the right to speak to her master. Similarly, when in the book of the *Soliloquies*[93] Saint Augustine has the
pious soul ask the earth and the other elements if they are his god, and
they answer in the negative and ask him to seek higher, he then says
320 that the responses of natural things are attestations of God's existence.
Moreover, Meun wishes to show that it was natural and Christian to
speak about Nature, and as a poet, as I have said, he had everyone
speak fictionally about everything.

Mais tu ne peus taire, ce dis tu, de ce que Raison dit que en
la guerre amoureuse, «Mieulx vault decepvoir que deceus estre»;
et argues: «Dont s'ensuit il que tous deux sont bons: qui ne puet
325   estre.» Par mon serement, se tu te fusses deportee d'escripre cest
argument ce fust ton honneur; il n'est pas a mettre en escript: non,
c'est pour les enfans d'escole en peinne et defaut d'autres, quant ilz
sont plusseurs a arguer sur une mesme proposicion. Et ne dit pas
Jhesu Crist que mieux fust a Judas s'il n'eust onques esté, qu'avoir
330   traï son maistre? Il s'ensuyroit par ton argument que tous deux
fussent bons. L'en ne doit pas prandre ainssy les mos a la letre,
mais selonc les mos precedans et l'entendement de l'aucteur. Le
ver sans moyen precedant ces quatre que tu as allegués est: «Mais
ce sont li moins deceu»: je croy que ce n'est pas a dire que bon soit
335   decevoir. En oultre je dy qu'il me vaulroit mieux—c'est a dire qu'il
me greveroit moins—faire samblant de toy amer pour moy aasier
charnelement de ton corps qu'il ne feroit pour celle meisme fin
que j'en fuisse fol amoureux, pour quoy j'en perdisse mon estude,
«sans, temps, chastel, corps, ame, los» (come dit est). Car tous les
340   maux qui s'ensuivent par le premier cas s'ensuyent par le second,
mais non pas tous ceulx qui s'ensuivent par le second s'ensuyent par
le premier. Toutevoies tien je que ces quatre vers: «Car adés vault
il mieux, biau mestre», etc., et aucuns autres, sont adjoustés: dont
ceux qui ce font mesprannent trop, car je ne voy pas c'on y peust
345   adjouster n'y oster sans empirer.
       Or alons oultre. «Quelle deshonnesteté a il (ce dit dame Elo-
quence et toy aussy) en ce chapistre de Vielle! Qu'i puet on noter
fors toute laidure»? Et pariellement ou chapistre de Jalousie. Et
188r° voulroies // bien en avoir trouvé qui te peust soulre—par quoy ton
350   entendement fust rasadiés—«a quoy peuent estre proufitable tant de
parolles deshonnestes qui en ce livre sont….» Mais, fais tu, «je ne
condampne pas l'aucteur en toutes pars du dit livre… »; comme se
tu voulsisses dire que tu le condampnes en ce en quoy tu le reprens,
et te fais juge, aprés ce que tu as parlé par oppinion ou presumpcion
355   oultrageuse. O tres fole oultrecuidance! O parole trop tost yssue et
sans avis de bouche de fame, qui condampne home de si hault entendement, de si fervant estude, qui a si grant labeur et meure deliberacion a fait si tres noble livre comme celluy de la *Rose,* qui passe
aussy tous autres qui onques fussent en langage ou il escript son
360   livre: duquel, quant tu l'aras leu cent fois se tu entens la greigneur
partie, tu n'employas onques mieulx temps ne ton entendement!
Vraiement celuy qui a compillee la plaidoierie dame Eloquance a

Indeed, but (says Lady Eloquence) this Foolish Lover has
325 Reason say that which Cupid has already forbidden. Then she tries
to redeem herself: "Well, she says, it was not one and the same
author but the one on whose opening this Meun built his work." The
foundations were good and pure, and he made a heap of mire out
of it. Certainly, this is very well said! I ask her to what end Cupid
330 would give away the rosebud, in other words to what end would he
help this plan of foolish love to succeed. And herein lies too great a
contradiction: He reprimands Reason, who chastises Lover for being
a foolish lover, and praises Cupid, who teaches one how to achieve
this goal.
335 But you say that you cannot be silent about Reason's statement that in the amorous war "it is better to deceive than to be deceived," and you argue, "It follows that both are good, which cannot
be." Upon my oath, if you had abstained from writing this argument,
it would have been to your honor. It is not something that should be
340 put in writing. No, this is for school children, who for lack of others
all debate the same proposition. Does Jesus Christ not say that it
would have been better for Judas had he never lived, than to have
betrayed his Master? From your argument it would follow, then, that
both are good. One ought not to take the words literally in this way,
345 but to understand them according to what precedes them, and according to the author's understanding. The verse which immediately
precedes the four which you cite is "But they are the ones who are
the least deceived." I do not think this means that deception is good.
In addition, I say that I would prefer—that is, it would cause me less
350 pain—to pretend that I loved you in order to enjoy your body than it
would to lose my learning, "sense, time, soul, body, and reputation"
over it (as is written). For all the evil which ensues from the first
case ensues equally from the second, but not all that ensues from
the second ensues from the first. Nevertheless, I maintain that these
355 four verses ("For it is always better, dear Master," etc.) and some
others are interpolated. Therefore, those who do this misunderstand
greatly, because I do not see how one could add or take away anything without harming the text.
Now, let us move on! "What dishonor there is in the chapter
360 of the Duenna (as Lady Eloquence says, and as you, too, say)! What
appalling filth can be noted there?" And likewise in the chapter of
Jealousy. And you would very much have liked to find someone
who could explain to you—this would have appeased your intellect—"to what end so many dishonorable words which are in this

esté plus preudent et gracieux que tu n'as, car il dit a la fin du plaid-
oyé qu'il n'oÿ point de sentence rendre. Mais quoy! Selonc ce que
365   dit Terence: «Veritey engendra hayne, et flaterie amis», je me doubte
pour ce qu'il dit verité que tu le vuelles mordre; mais je te conseille
que tu gardes tes dens.

Je respons a dame Eloquance et a toy par ung meisme moyen,
et dy que maistre Jehan de Meun en son livre introduisy personnaig-
370   es, et fait chascun personnaige parler selonc qui luy appartient: c'est
assavoir le Jaloux comme jaloux, la Vielle come la Vielle, et pareillement des autres. Et est trop mal pris de dire que l'aucteur tiengne
les maulx estre en fame que le Jalous, en faisant son personnaige,
propose; non fait, certes, mais il recite ce que tous les jours ung
375   jaloux dit de toutes fames, pour monstrer et corrigier la tres grant
desraisonnableté et passion desordenee qui est en home jaloux. Et
la cause pour quoy ung jaloux dit (c'est a dire qui le muet a dire
tant de maulx de toutes fammes et non pas seulement de la sienne),
c'est a mon avis que regulierement ung chascun homme marié,
380   avant qu'il soit jaloux, cuide avoir la milleur fame, ou au moins
auxi bone comme il en soit point. Et vient ceste cuidance, come je
tieng, partie pour l'amour qu'il a a elle—et chose amee n'est pas
de legier mescrue—, laquelle amour vient pour ce que la famme est
sienne et nos choses nous samblent plus belles et meilleurs que les
385   estranges; partie aussy pour ce que fame en la presence de son mary
se maintient le plus bel et simplement qu'elle peut,—supposé qu'en
son absence elle se tiengne baudement. «Et pour ce, comme dit saint
Jherome en une sienne espistre, ung chascun seut savoir le darrenier
les maulx de son ostel». Je croy bien qu'il y a d'autres raisons as-
390   sés, mais toutevoyes quelque raison qu'il y ait, experience monstre
ce que j'ay devant dit, c'est assavoir que l'omme, avant qu'il soit
jaloux, [cuide] sa fame la meilleur ou auxi bonne come il en soit
point, mesmement quant a chasteté. Et c'est bien fait d'ainsy cuidier
en mariaige, parmy la moderacion terencienne (c'est assavoir «sans
395   riens trop»), car autrement n'y auroit paix entre gens mariés: et fut
le moyen par quoy Aspasia mist accort entre Xenophon et sa fame,
comme recite Tuelle en sa *Rethorique.* Pour ce dont quant Jalousie
survient a ung mary, et souspessonne mal en celle qu'il tenoit par
avant pour si bonne que maleur n'y [a]—supposé qu'elle n'y ait
400   coulpe, comme il avient bien souvent—, inanimement, [en] celle
fureur et passion desordenee de jalousie qui propremant est appellee mal felon, dit il que toutes sont teles. Et c'est ce que dit Aristote
en sa *Rethorique:* que qui a ung mauvais voisin, il cuide que tous

365 book can possibly be advantageous…." But you say, "I do not
condemn the author for all parts of this book…." As if you wished
to say that you condemn him only for that for which you reprimand
him, and you put yourself in the role of judge after you have spoken
out of prejudice and foolish pride. O very foolish pride! O speech
370 uttered too soon and without counsel, from the mouth of a woman
who condemns a man of such high intellect, of such fervent learning, who through such great labor and mature deliberation made
so very noble a book as that of the *Rose,* which exceeds all others
ever written in the language in which he wrote this one, and through
375 which, once you will have read it one hundred times, if you understand most of it, you will never have put your intellect to a better
use! Truly, he who compiled the complaint of Lady Eloquence was
more prudent and gracious than you, because at the end of the complaint he said that he did not intend to render punishment. And yet,
380 as Terence said, "Truth engenders hatred and flattery friends." I have
the feeling that it is because he speaks the truth that you wish to take
a bite out of him. But I advise you to keep your teeth to yourself.

  I respond to Lady Eloquence and to you in the same way and
say that in his book Master Jean de Meun introduced characters
385 which he had speak according to their designation, that is, the Jealous Husband as a jealous person, the Duenna as a Duenna, and so
on with the others. It is therefore a grave error to say that the author
maintains that evil lies only in women, as the Jealous Husband
suggests, in accordance with his character. This is surely wrong, yet
390 he simply recites what a Jealous Husband would say of all women
every day, in order to show and to correct the very great irrationality
and unruly passion which resides in a jealous man. And the reason
a jealous husband says this (that is, the reason he is moved to utter
so much evil about all women and not just his own), is, in my view,
395 that every married man usually thinks (before becoming jealous)
that he has the best wife, or at least one as good as any other. And I
maintain that this thought is born out of love for her, since a loved
thing is not easily shunned. This love arises, then, because the
woman is his, and our own things seem more beautiful and better
400 to us than those of others. It also arises because a woman conducts
herself in the most beautiful and innocent manner when she is in the
presence of her husband. Let us suppose that she behaves bawdily in his absence. "Because of this, as Saint Jerome says in one of
his epistles,[94] every husband will be the last to learn what evil has
405 befallen his home." I certainly think that there are enough other rea-

es autres soient telz. S'ung chevalier a renon d'estre le plus fort, le
405   plus appert, le plus hardy et le mieulx avisé en armes d'ung royaume
et pour tel le tiengne chascun, et il vient chevalier estrangier qui le
desconfesse chevalereusement, on tenroit qu'il n'est autre chevalier
d'icelluy royaume que l'estrangier n'eust desconfit; et paroillement
juge ung jaloux sur toutes fames quant il tient la sienne pour abatue,
410   en especial ceulx qui plus ont cuidé et tenu leurs fames bonnes et
chastes avant que jalousie y survenist.

Or aux similitudes dame Eloquance. «Se ung se nomme adver-
188v° saires du // roy de France (ce dit dame Eloquance), et soubz ce non
il li fait guerre…; se en la persone d'ung Sarrazin… ung home seme
415   erreurs en la foy, en sera il excusé»? Et d'autres pareilles, qui tant
soit pou ne sont a propos. Je li demande: pour tant, se Salluste recite
la conjuracion de Catiline encontre la chose publique de Ronme, en
est il pour ce coulpable? pour tant, se Aristote recite les oppinions
des anciens philozophes contenans erreurs en philosophie, est il
420   semeur d'erreurs en icelle? pour tant, se la sainte Escripture recite
les abominables pechiés de Soudome et Gomorre, enorte elle yceulx
ensuir? Quant tu vas au sermon, n'ois tu pas aux prescheurs respondre les vices que tous les jours font homes et fames, affin qu'ilz
aillent le droit chemin? En bone foy, damoiselle, si fait: on doit
425   ramentevoir le pié de quoy on cloche pour plus droit aler!

Ha! dame Chasteté! est ce le louyer que vous voulés rendre
a maistre Jehan de Meun, qui tant vous a prisee et toutes autres
vertus, et blasmés tous vices, come entendement humain le puet
concepvoir? Voire, come entendement humain le puet concepvoir:
430   n'en soubzriés ja! Je dy que qui bien lit ce livre—et souvent pour le
mieux entendre—, il y trouvera ensaignemans pour fouir tous vices
et ensuir toutes vertus. Et ne dit il pas en chapistre du Jaloux que
> nul qui vive chastement
> ne peut venir a dampnement…
435   et ou chapistre de Raison:
> Celuy, qui va dely querant,
> sces tu qu'il se fait? Il se rent
> comme serfs et chetif et nices
> du prince de trestous les vices…
440   et que
> …c'est de tous maulx la racine
> si come Tulle le determine…

410   sons, but whatever reason there may be, experience shows that what
I said earlier, namely that any man, before becoming jealous, thinks
that his wife is the best or is as good as any, especially with regard
to chastity. And this is how one should consider marriage, within the
Terencian moderation (that is, "without too much of anything"),[95]
for otherwise there could never be peace among two married people.
This is how Aspasia[96] brought agreement to Xenophon[97] and his
wife, as Cicero cites in his *Rhetoric*. Therefore, when Jealousy
strikes a husband, who suspects sinful behavior in the one whom

415   he previously thought so good that there could be no ill fortune (let
us suppose that she is innocent, as often happens), he is befallen by
such furor and unruly jealous passion that he calls her an evil felon,
and also says this about all other women. As Aristotle states in his
Rhetoric, he who has a bad neighbor thinks that all the others are

420   bad, too.[98] If a knight said to be the strongest, most apt, bravest, and
cleverest in arms in the whole kingdom were defeated in battle by a
foreign knight, one would think that there must be no other knight
in the kingdom who could not be defeated by this foreigner. Similarly, a jealous man judges all women if he thinks that his own wife

425   has succumbed—especially those men who were convinced, before
jealousy struck, that their wives were good and chaste.

Now to Lady Eloquence's analogies: "If someone called
himself an adversary of the king of France (says Lady Eloquence)
and waged war under that title… if a Saracen… planted errors

430   against the Christian faith, would he be forgiven?" And other such
examples, which are hardly on the topic. I ask her: If Sallust quotes
the conspiracy of Catiline against the Republic of Rome, is he guilty
of it? And, if Aristotle quotes opinions of the ancient philosophers
which contain philosophical errors, is he the creator of these errors?

435   Moreover, if Holy Scripture cites the abominable sins that took
place in Sodom and Gomorrah, does it exhort others to follow them?
When you go and listen to a sermon, do you not hear the preach-
ers respond to the vices which men and women commit every day,
in order to lead them onto the right path? In good faith, my lady, it

440   is so: One must not remind human nature of the foot with which it
limps!

Ha! Lady Chastity! Is this the praise you wish to render
Master Jean de Meun who holds you and all other virtues in such
high esteem and reprimands all the vices which the human intellect

445   can conceive? Indeed, yes, all those which the human intellect can
conceive. Do not smile about it! I say that whoever reads this book

> Jeunesce met hommes es folies,
> es bobans, et es ribaudises
445   es luxures et es oultraiges…

et pour plus blasmer vices dit que «li mauvais ne sont pas home»;
et ou chapistre du Jaloux dit que tous les vices firent saillir Povreté
d'enfer pour venir en terre; et de Honte dit qu'elle refrene et
dompte. Encor parle il plus contre les hommes que contre contre les
450 fames: ne reprant il, ou chapistre de Nature, vint et six vices dont
hommes est entechiés,—et en tant d'autres lieux que je trespasse,
que c'est sans nombre (ou chapistre de Nature, que clers abandon-
nés a vices doivent estre plus pugnis que gens lais et simples; et
que gentillesce gist en vertus, entre lesquelz vertus il met dames
455 honnorer et damoiselles)! Par Dieu! ce n'est pas blasmer le sexe femenin! (je dy cecy contre ton excusacion mise es darreniers mos de
ton epistre): saint Ambroise, en ung sien sermon, le blasme plus (le
sexe femenin); car il dit que c'est ung sexe usagié a decevoir. Vraiement aussy fais tu: tu blasmes plus que Meun quant tu dis que s'en
460 lisoit le livre de la *Rose* devant les roynes, princesses et autres grans
dames, il leur convenroit couvrir leur face de honte rougie. Car pour
quoy rougiroient ilz? Il samble qu'ilz se sentiroyent coulpables des
vices que le Jaloux recite de fame.
    N'il ne blasme pas religion come luy met sus dame Elo-
465 quance. Il est bien vray qu'il dit que Ypocrisie

> …trahist mainte region
> par habit de religion…

il ne dit pas «par religion», mais «par l'abbit de religion». Car come
il dit,
470   Qui de toison dam Celin
> en lieu de mantel sebelin
> sire Ysangrin affubleroit, etc.

et c'est ce que dame Eloquence et toy avés dit par autres mos,
c'est assavoir de mesler miel avec venin pour plus nuyre. Et quant
475 dame Eloquance dit qu'il dit que jeunes gens ne sont point estables
en religion, je dy que quant ung jeune home entre en religion par
jeunesce et non pas par devocion qu'il n'est pas fermes en icelle; et
c'est ce que dit maistre Jehan de Meun ou chapistre de la Vielle, et
veés cy les propres parolles:
480   Aussy vous dy [ge] que li hom,
> quant il entre en religion
> et vient aprés qu'il s'en repent,
> par pou que de dueil ne se pent.

well—and often—in order to understand it better, will find lessons
on how to flee from every vice and to follow every virtue. Does it
not say in the chapter of the Jealous Husband that,

450
       those who live chastely
       will not be damned;
and in the chapter of Reason
       He who seeks pleasure,
       do you know what happens to him? He will become
455
       a wretched and stupid serf
       of the prince of all vices;
and
       ...it is the root of all evil
       as Cicero defines it...[99]
460

       Youth drives men to follies,
       to frivolities, ribaldries,
       lechery, and excess...
and in order to rebuke vices, he says that "the bad ones are not part
465
of man(kind)." In the chapter of the Jealous Husband, he says that
all the vices made Poverty jump out of hell in order to come to
earth, and of Shame he says that she restrains and controls people.
And he speaks more against men than against women. In the chapter
of Nature, does he not refute twenty-six vices which tarnish men,
470
as well as in many other places, which I will skip because they are
countless (in the chapter of Nature he says that clerics who have
fallen prey to vice must be punished more severely than laypeople
and innocent people, and that nobleness sleeps in virtue—and he
includes the virtue of honoring ladies and maidens)! By God! This
475
does not insult the female sex! (I say this in response to the accusation you write in the last words of your epistle.) In one of his sermons, Saint Ambrosius[100] insults it more (the female sex) for he says
it is a sex accustomed to deceiving. In fact, you do the same: You
insult more than just Meun when you say that if one were to read
480
the book of the *Rose* before queens, princesses, or other bourgeois
ladies it would be appropriate for them to cover their faces, blushing
with shame. Why would they blush? It seems they would feel guilty
of the vices which the Jealous Husband recounts of women.
      Neither does he insult religion, as Lady Eloquence alleges. It
485
is very true that he says that Hypocrisy,
       ...betrays many a region
       in the guise of religion....

485 Et ainsy appert qu'i presuppose qu'i parle d'omme qui se repent
d'estre entré en religion, — comme il avient souvent. Lors dit il
aprés que

> … ja si grans solers n'aura
> ne ja si faire ne saura
> grant chaperon ne grant aulmuce,
490 > que Nature ou cuer ne se muce, etc.

et ung pou aprés dit:

> Ainssy est il, biaux filz, par m'ame,
> de tout homme et de toute fame
> quant a naturel apetit, etc.

495 Il est certaing que natures apetit d'omme n'est pas de soy obligier a
ne mengier jamais de char, ou estre chaste ou povre toute sa vie, ou
189r° soy tenir // tousjours a une fame, ne pareillement d'unne fame a se
tenir tousjours a ung home. Comme propose mesmes dame Eloquence, nostre fragilité est encline aux vices; vuelt elle pour ce louer
500 les vices? Nannil! Aussy se maistre Jehan de Meun dit que naturel
appetit n'est pas a religion mais au contraire, ne vuelt il pas par ce
blasmer religion et louer son contraire.

Mais tu me diras a cecy que je recite les bonnes paroles et
non les mauvaises, lesquelles esmuevent a lubricité et ensaingnent a
505 prandre le chastel Jalousie; et dame Eloquance dit qu'il veult bouter
hors Chasteté de toutes fames. Je respons et te dy qu'en toutes
manieres de guerre c'est plus grant aventaige d'estre deffendeur
qu'asaillant, mais c'on en soit par avant avisé. Et presupposé se
Jalousie a fait fere ung fort chastel et y a mis bonnes gardes pour le
510 garder et ce chastel a esté pris par une certaingne maniere d'assault,
se maistre Jehan de Meun a escripte la maniere comment il fu pris,
ne fait il plus grant aventaige aux gardes du chastel de leur avoir
enseingné par ou il fu pris—pour eulx en garder dorenavent pour
estouper le trou par ou ce fu ou y mettre meilleurs gardes—qu'il ne
515 fait a ceulx qui le vouldroient assaillir? Par Dieux! si fait, presup-
posey ce que j'ay dit avant: que c'est avantaige que d'estre deffendeur; et meismement qu'il escript la maniere du prandre en
langaige commun a homes et fanmes, jeunes et vielz, c'est assvoir
en franssois.

520 Ovide, quant il escript *L'Art d'amours,* il escript en latin,
lequel n'entendent fammes: et ne le bailla qu'aux assaillans pour
aprandre a asaillir le chastel: c'estoit la fin de son livre, sans parler
par personnaiges (mais il, come Ovide, bailla tous ses ansaingne-
mans). Pour ce, moyennant la tres enorme jalousie des maris ron-
525 mains, fut il exillié—que ay je dit, moiennant!—certainnement ce fu

He does not say "by religion" but "in the guise of religion." For he says,

490   Who would put the fleece of Dame Belin
         on Sir Isengrin[101]
         instead of a sable mantel, etc.

This is what you and Lady Eloquence have said using other words, namely, mixing honey with venom in order to do more damage. And
495 when Lady Eloquence says that he says young people are not steadfast in religion, I say that when a young man takes his vows because he is young and not out of piety, he is not steadfast. And this is what Master Jean de Meun says in the chapter of the Duenna. Let us look here at the exact words:

500   I also tell you that the man
         who takes his vows
         and then later comes to regret it
         is almost ready to hang himself out of sorrow.

It is apparent, therefore, that he presupposes a man who regrets hav-
505 ing taken his vows, as often happens. He then goes on to say that,
         ...he will never have shoes large enough
         nor will he know how to make
         hood or cowl large enough
         for Nature to remain hidden in his heart, etc.
510 and a little later he says
         By my soul, it is thus, beautiful son,
         with every man and every woman
         when it comes to natural appetite, etc.

It is certain that a man's natural appetite is not to force himself
515 never to eat meat, nor to be chaste and poor all his life, nor to remain loyal to one woman, nor is it for a woman to remain loyal to one man. As even Lady Eloquence suggests, our weakness draws us to the vices. Does she wish to praise the vices by saying this? Not at all! Likewise, if Master Jean de Meun says that natural appetite is
520 not part of religion but the opposite, it is not that he intends to insult religion and to praise its opposite.

But you will tell me in response to this that I recount the good words and not the bad, those which encourage lubricity and teach one to conquer the castle of Jealousy. Lady Eloquence says that he
525 wishes to chase Chastity out of all women. I respond, and tell you that in any war it is always more advantageous to be the defender than the assailant, but only if one has been informed of the attack beforehand. And let us suppose that Jealousy has had a strong castle

commensement, moyen et fin pour quoy il fu exillié—si le fu—que
la jalousie tres enorme et felonne des maris ronmains! Comme j'ay
oÿ dire a ceulx qui ont esté par pays, la fenme du moins jaloux du
pays d'Ytalie et de Rommenie est plus estroit tenue que la fame du
530   plus jaloux de France. Et pour ce, s'Ovide fu exillié, par jalousie
ce feust; come ung home, pour escripre contre la foy, si se rapelle,
ne sera point exillié, mais son livre sera ars: et le livre pour lequel
Ovide fu exillié dure, dura et a duré en toute Crestienté; et si se rap-
pella aussy Ovide en faisant le livre de *Remede d'amours.* Vraiment
535   je n'entens point comment cest exillement se soustienge par raison:
je dy que si un livre est cause d'exillier son aucteur, le livre doit
estre estre premierement exillié. Mais a propos de ce que dit dame
Eloquance Theologienne, «qu'un vin qui ne nuyra a ung sain fera
hors du sens ung qui tramblera fievrés», parieillement di je qu'un re-
540   gart fait par la fournie ou la fame d'ung Ronmain ou Ytalyen donra
occasion au mary, come j'ai oÿ dire, de l'empoisonner et ainssy le
murdrier mauvaisement, la ou ung baisier en France ne donroit pas
occasion de tenser sa fame, ou au mains la ferir. Si ne fault ja dire
que maistre Jehan de Meun ne mist pas tant seulement en son livre
545   *L'Art d'amours* que Ovide fist; mais de biaucop d'autres aucteurs,
car de tant come il recite diverses manieres d'assaillir, de tant advise
il plus les gardes du chastel pour eulx en deffendre: et a celle fin le
fist il. En verité je cognois home fol amoureux, lequel pour soy oster
de fole amour a emprunté de moy *Le Ronmant de la Rose,* et luy ay
550   oÿ jurer par sa foy que c'est la chose qui plus li a aidié a s'en oster.
(Je di cecy pour ce que tu quiers: «Quans en sont devenus hermites
ou entrés on religion», et [dis] qu'i print grant painne pour noyant.)
Encore qui plus est, la Vielle que dame Eloquance et toy blasmés
tant, avant qu'ele presche a Belaqueil, dit on protestant:
555   Je vous dy bien avant le cop,
ne vous vueil pas en amour mettre,
189vº   // mais s'oubz en voulés entremettre,
je vous mosteray voulantiers
et les chemins et les santiers
560   par ou je deüsse estre allee, etc.
et aprés dit expressement a Bellaqueil que ce qu'elle luy presche,
c'est affin qu'il n'y soit deceus:
Et qu'il est sot certainnement
qui pour jurer croit nul amant.
565   Et s'il y a paroles qui samblent plus baudes, ou plus diffamans le
sexe feminin, il recite les aucteurs qui dient ycelles, car come il dit,

530 built and has put in place good guards to guard it and that this castle
has been conquered by a certain kind of attack. If Master Jean de
Meun described the way in which it was taken, does he not give the
castle's guards a greater advantage than those who wished to attack
it, by having taught them how they were taken? For henceforth
they will be better able to guard its gaps or to place more guards
535 there. By God! Indeed, let us consider again what I said earlier:
that the defender has the advantage, particularly since he writes in
a language common to men and women, young and old, that is, in
French.

Ovid, when he wrote the *Ars amatoris*, he did so in Latin,
540 which women do not understand. And he gave it only to the assailants, in order that they might learn how to lay siege to the castle.
This was the objective of his book, without speaking through
characters (but he, like Ovid, presented all his lessons himself). For
this and due to the extreme jealousy of Roman husbands Ovid was
545 exiled. What am I saying—"due to"! This was surely the beginning,
middle, and end of why he was exiled, yes, because of the extreme
and very cruel jealousy of Roman husbands! As I have heard tell
from those who have been to that country, the wife of the least jealous Italian and Roman husband is more strictly kept than the wife
550 of the most jealous husband of France. Hence, if Ovid was exiled,
it was due to jealousy. It is like the case of a man exiled for writing
against the Christian faith: If he recants he will not be exiled, but
his book will be burned. Yet the book for which Ovid was exiled
lives on and will live on, as it has throughout all Christianity, even
555 though Ovid did in fact recant by producing the book the *Remede
d'amours*. Truly, I do not understand how this act of exile can possibly be sustained rationally. I say that if a book is the cause for
exiling its author, the book itself must first be exiled. But about that
which Lady Theological Eloquence says, "that a wine which would
560 harm a healthy person would send a person already shivering with
fever out of his or her mind." It is thus, I say, with a glance by a
female relative or wife of a Roman or Italian man, which gives him
the opportunity, as I have heard tell, to poison her, and, consequently, to murder her evilly, whereas a kiss in France would not be occa-
565 sion enough to scold one's wife, or at least not to beat her. One must
never say that in his book Master Jean de Meun borrowed only from
Ovid's *Ars amatoris* but from many other authors also, because the
more he recounts the many means of attack, the more he teaches the
guards of the castle to defend it. This is the aim of the book. In fact,

il n'y fait «riens fors reciter»; si me samble c'on deust premierement blasmer les aucteurs que les reciteurs d'iceulx, comme j'ay
desja dit. Mais tu me diras: pour quoy les recitoit il? Je di qu'il le
570   faisoit pour plus ansaingnier les portiers et a garder mieulx le chastel; et aussy qu'i sont a son propos. Car son propos fu de poursuir
la matiere commensee et touchee par Guillaume de Lorris, et en
ce faisant parler de toutes choses selonc leur estat au proufit de
creature humainne, tant a l'ame come au corps. Pour ce parle il de
575   paradis et de vertus: pour les suir; et des vices, pour les fouir; et de
tant come il parle de vices et vertus d'enfer et paradis pres a pres
l'ung de l'autre, monstre il plus la beauté des uns et la laidure des
autres. Et ce qu'il dit ou chapistre de jalousie et de la Vielle et an autres lieux touchans le fait d'amours, il le fist en poursuyant l'euvre
580   commencee par Guillaume de Lorris.

Ne Genius ne promet pas paradis aux folz amoureulx, come
li met sus dame Eloquance; car il parle de ceulx qui exercitent
bonnement les œuvres de Nature: ce n'est pas tout ung, exerciter
les euvres de Nature bonnement et estre fol amoureux. Ne Nature
585   ne Genius n'enortent pas c'on soit fol amoureux, mais ilz enortent suyvre les euvres de Nature, lesquelz sont licites d'exercier,
c'est assavoir pour continuer l'espesse humainne et pour delaissier
l'euvre contraire a nature, qui est abhominable a plus exprimer. Et
combien que je n'ose ne vueil dire que exercer l'euvre de Nature a
590   ces deux fins
dessusdictes tant seulement hors de mariaige ne soit pas pechié,
toutevois ose je dire que il est permis icelle exercer a ces deux fins
en l'estat de mariaige. Et c'est ce que dit maistre Jehan de Meun ou
chapistre de la Vielle:
595   Pour ce fist par les mariaiges,
par les conseilz des hommes saiges…

pour oster dissolucions
et contemps et occisions
600   et pour aidier les norretures
dont il ensemble les cures…
Par Dieu! ce n'est pas blasmer mariaige, dire qu'il fut ordenés par
sages gens! Mais je te diray que saint Augustin en dit en son livre
des *Confessions*: «Bonne chose est a home ne touchier fame»; et,
605   «Qui est sans famme espousee, il panse aux choses qui sont de Dieu
pour luy plaire; mais cil qui est joint par mariaige panse les choses
qui sont du monde pour plaire a sa fame.» Je te ramentoy cecy, et a
ceulx qui veullent aprandre et corrigier par leur langaige, sans rai-

570   I know a foolish lover who borrowed the *Roman de la rose* from me
in order to rid himself of foolish love. I heard him swear on his faith
that this was the thing which most helped him rid himself of it. (I say
this because you ask, "When did this make them hermits or take their
vows," and I say that he suffered great pain for nothing.)

575   What is more, the Duenna whom you and Lady Eloquence insult
so greatly says in protest, before preaching this to Fair Welcoming:

      I will gladly tell you at the outset,

      that I do not wish you to be in love

      but if you wish to get involved in it

580   I will gladly show you

      the roads and the paths

      along which I ought to have gone, etc.

and afterwards she purposely says to Fair Welcoming that she is
preaching to him in order that he might not be deceived:

585   And he who believes any lover's oath

      surely is a fool.

      And if there are words which seem more bawdy or defaming of
the female sex, it is because he quotes the authors who spoke them.
For, he says, he "merely quotes." It seems to me that above all one

590   ought to reprimand the authors whom he cites, as I have already said.
Yet you will say to me, why did he cite them? I say that he did so in
order to teach the guards to better guard the castle, and also because
their words fit with his subject, which was to pursue the matter begun
by Guillaume de Lorris and in doing so to speak of all things accord-

595   ing to their natural condition for the benefit of human beings, in soul
as much as in body. It is for this reason that he speaks of paradise and
virtues, in order to follow them; and of vices, in order to flee from
them. And by speaking of vices and virtues, of hell and paradise one
next to the other, he better shows the beauty of the one and the ugli-

600   ness of the other. What he says on the topic of love in the chapters of
Jealousy and the Duenna, as well as elsewhere, he says in order to
continue the work begun by Guillaume de Lorris.

      Nor does Genius promise paradise to foolish lovers, as Lady
Eloquence alleges, because he is speaking of those who practice the

605   works of Nature dutifully. To practice the works of Nature dutifully
and to be a foolish lover are not the same thing. Neither Nature nor
Genius exhorts anyone to be a foolish lover, but they exhort people
to follow the works of Nature, the practice of which is licit, that is,
to propagate the human species and to refrain from work contrary to

610   Nature, which is abominable, to express it more precisely. Although I
neither dare nor wish to say that to practice the work of Nature in the

610 son, aucteur—lequel soit notable et non repris par avant—, combien
qu'il puet estre qu'il saiche mieulx que le ramenteveur: mais il n'est
si mauvais sourt que cil qui ne vuelt oÿr.

Il samble donques que se l'euvre de nature est licite en aucun
cas, qu'elle n'est pas mauvaise de soy, mais par aucun consequant.
Se Genius amonneste a suyre les euvres de Nature meismemant
615 a ces deux fins que j'ay dites—et il est licite a les excerciter, au
moins par mariage, en promettant paradis a ceulx qui les suyront
bonnemant («mais qu'ilz se gardent bien des vices», car ce sont
ses propres mos)—, je n'y voy point de mesprison. Et pour ce que
chascun n'a pas leu le livre de la *Rose,* je reciteray ycy les propres
620 mos de Genius, et me soit pardonné se je suis trop prolix en recitant
ores et autreffois les propres mos du livre; deux causes le me font
fere: l'une si est affin c'on ne cuide que je die chose qui ne soit ou
190rº livre, pour ce que mains // sont qui ne le lisent point, come j'ay dit;
l'autre raison est que je ne pouroye en prose aussi briefment reciter
625 une chose come maistre Jehan de Meun la dit en rime leonine. Veés
cy donques les mos de Genius:

> Et qui de bien amer se painne
> sans nulle pensee villainne,
> et qui loyaulment s'i travaille,
630 > floris en paradis s'en aille.
> Mais qu'il se face bien confés,
> j'en praing sur moy tretout son fés,
> de tel pouoir comme jel puis prandre.

Et pour recapituler son sermon dit:

635 > Pansés de Nature honorer,
> servés la par bien labourer;
> et se de l'autruy riens avés,
> rendés le, se vous le savés,
> et se vous rendre ne poués
640 > les biens despendus ou joués,
> aiés en bonne voulenté,
> quant des biens aurés a planté.
> D'occision nul ne s'aprouche,
> nettes aies les mains et bouche,
645 > soyes loyal, soies piteux,
> lors yras ou champ delicteux,
> par trace l'aignelet suyant, et cetera.

C'est en brief la recapitulacion de tout le sermon Genius et son
entencion des choses qu'il a devant dictes. Et puis que c'est son en-

above-mentioned objectives is not a sin outside of marriage, I do
dare say that within the state of marriage it is permissible to practice
them with these two objectives in mind. And that is what Master
615   Jean de Meun is saying in the chapter of the Duenna,
        Marriage was created
        on the advice of wise men...

        In order to prevent trouble,
620   fights, and murders
        and to help the offspring
        for whom one has joint responsibility...
     By God! To say that it was instituted by wise men does not
insult marriage! I will tell you that in his book of the *Confessions,*
625   Saint Augustine confirms this when he states, "For a man it is a
good thing not to touch a woman," and, "He who is not married to
a woman thinks upon divine matters, in order to please God, but he
who is joined in marriage thinks upon worldly things, in order to
please his wife."[102] I remind you of this, you and those who—with-
630   out cause—wish by their language to teach and to correct the author,
who is renowned and has never before been refuted, although it is
quite possible that he knows this better than I. No one is more deaf
than one who does not wish to hear.
     Therefore, it seems that if the work of Nature is licit in some
635   cases, it is not bad in itself but because of certain consequences. If
Genius encourages us to follow the works of Nature especially with
those two objectives in mind which I have mentioned (and it is licit
to practice them, at least within marriage, and to promise paradise
to those who adhere to them dutifully, "but they must refrain from
640   vices," because these are his own words), I see no error in this. And
because not everyone has read the book of the *Rose,* I shall cite here
Genius's own words and shall be forgiven if I am too prolix when I
cite, here and elsewhere, the exact words of the book. I do this for
two reasons: First, in order that one will not think that I am saying
645   things which are not in the book, for numerous are they who do not
read it, as I have said; and the other reason is that I could not recount as briefly in prose a matter which Master Jean de Meun states
in leonine rhyme. Here, then, are Genius's words:
        He who strives to love well
650   with no villainous thought
        and who works at it loyally,
        will be decorated with flowers when he goes to paradise.

650   tencion, quant tu l'as leu tout au long—et ceulx qui le reprannent—,
       que n'y prenés vous garde?
        Si ne me puis assés esmervillier comme persone l'ose blasmer—je
       ne dy pas seulement li, mais ceulx qui prisent et aimment son livre
       de la *Rose*. Quant a moy, en bone verité je desire plus estre des
655   blasmés et repris par prisier et amer le livre de la *Rose* que je ne
       fais estre soubtilz blasmeurs et repreneurs d'icelluy. Et sachent tuit
       cil qui le reprannent qu'il reste encore •vii• mille, que ne ploieret
       onques le genoul devant Baal, qui sont tous presets de le deffendre.
       S'il eust esté du tamps d'entre vous qui le blasmés, je deisse que
660   vous eussiés hayne particulere a sa personne; mais vous ne le veistes
       onques: si ne puis ymaginer dont ce vient, sinon pour la tres ele-
       vee haultesse du livre, plus hable a recepvoir les vens de souffles
       envieux. Car ygnorance n'en est point cause en telz y a, s'elle ne
       venoit toutevoies par pou lire le dit livre de la *Rose;* ou par aven-
665   ture faingnés vous blasmer le dit livre pour cause de l'essaucer par
       esmouvoir les escoutans les paroles a le lire, et vous savés bien que
       qui le lira, il trouvera le contraire de vos escrips et tous ensaingne-
       mans tres notables: et en ce cas les repreneurs devroient estre tenus
       assés pour excusés, car la fin et leur entencion seroit bonne, quelque
670   moyen qu'il y eust.
              Si te prie, femme de grant engin, que tu gardes l'onneur que
       tu as pour la hautesse de ton entendement et langaige bien ordené;
       et que s'on t'a loué pour ce que tu as tirey d'un boulet par dessus
       les tours de Nostre Dame, ne t'essayes pour tant a ferir la lune d'un
675   boujon pesant: garde que tu ne rassambles le corbel, lequel, pour
       ce que on loua son chant, se prist a chanter plus fort qu'il n'avoit
       acoustumé et laissa cheoir sa bouchié. Et pour toutes solucions prie
       a tous et a toutes qui le veulent reprendre ou blasmer en quelque
       part que ce soit, qu'i le lisent avent quatre fois du mois—et a
680   loisir—pour mieulx l'entendre; et je pren leur lecture bien entendue
       pour solucion. Et s'ilz n'en veulent riens fere, qu'ilz advisent la fin a
       laquelle il escript son livre, et qu'ilz lisent son excusacion sans estre
       affecté au contraire; et je ne doubte pas qu'ilz ne le tiengnent pour
       excusé, car il n'y fault autre excusacion ne responce que celle qu'i
685   met droitement devant le commencement de l'assault. Car la seule-
       ment parle il come aucteur et la come aucteur dit que
              … nul ne doit fame despire,
                 si n'a cuer des mauvais le pire…
       et si fait protestacion que ce n'est pas s'entencion
690   de parler contre home vivant,

And if he is well confessed,
I will take all his deeds upon me
655   with all the power invested in me.
And to recapitulate his sermon:
Think to honor Nature,
serve her by laboring well;
and if you receive something from someone else,
660   pay it back, if you can,
and if you cannot do so
because you have spent or gambled the goods away,
have good will,
when you will have accumulated goods.
665   No one can brush against murder,
and keep hands and mouth clean,
be loyal and compassionate,
and you will go to the delightful field,
following the path of the Lamb, etc.
670   This, in short, is the recapitulation of Genius's entire sermon and the message of what precedes it. And since this is his message, if you and those who reprimand him have read it in its entirety, why do you not pay attention to it?

    I cannot marvel enough that someone dares to insult him, and
675   I do not mean only him, but all those who respect and love his book of the *Rose*. As for me, truthfully, I desire more to be among the insulted and refuted for praising and loving the book of the *Rose* than to be among its skillful critics and refuters. And all those who refute it should know that seven thousand still remain who will not
680   bend their knee before Baal, and who are all prepared to defend it. If he had lived at the time of those who insult him, I venture to say that you would have particularly hated his person. But you have never seen him. Thus, I cannot imagine where this hatred comes from, save from the extreme excellence of his book, more prone to
685   receiving the winds of envy. For ignorance is not the cause, unless it stems from your sketchy reading of the book of the *Rose*; or did you perhaps feign insult of this book in order to glorify it, thereby encouraging the listeners of your words to read it, because you know well that whoever reads it will find the opposite of what you
690   have written against it and will find very renowned lessons in it. In that case, the refuters would be held in sufficiently good standing to be forgiven, because their objective and intention would be good, whichever means they used.

            sainte religion suiant
            ou qui [sa] vie use en bone euvre,
            de quelque robe qu'il se cuevre…
      et que s'il y a paroles trop baudes ou trop foles, que

695   …ce requeroit (sa) matiere
            qui vers telz parolies (le) tire
            par les propretés de soy…
      et qu'il n'y fait «riens fors reciter»; et generalment dit qu'il ne dist
      onques riens qui ne fust «pour ensaingnement», c'est assavoir pour
700   ung chascun avoir congnoissance de luy meismes et d'autres; et
   190v° finablement // que s'il y a
            …parole
            que Sainte Esglise tiengne a fole…
      qu'il est tout prest de l'amender.
705   Si m'esbahis par trop quant il metoit ce los en la bouche dame
      Eloquance Theologienne et de tous ceulz de la court de sainte Crest-
      ienté d'aviser s'il y avoit en son livre que reprandre, qu'il ont ainssy
      laissié dormir par l'espasse de cent ans ou plus et tant qu'il est
      maintenant publié par toute Crestienté et—qui plus est—translaté
710   en estranges langaiges. Mais je croy qu'ilz t'atendoient, toy et les
      autres qui le veulent reprandre: car je say de vray que par devant n'a
      esté persone qui l'eust seu reprandre. Si sont piessa les quatre ordres
      mandiens, entre lesquelz a eu de tres nobles clers, lesquelz n'avoient
      pas petite auctorité envers le pape et les princes et princesses tem-
715   porelz, et lesquelx il ne flata mie grandement. Or resgardés quel
      promoteur que de Conscience, qui laisse dormir une cause l'espace
      de cent ans! Par le corps Dieu! On ne fait point d'onneur a toute
      celle court sainte de Crestienté de li mettre asseure telle negligence;
      et en especial a dame Eloquance Theologienne, qui propose mal son
720   fait principal et emprant mauvaise querelle en la faisant maintenir
      et parler par la maniere que les maistres de rethorique ont baillié
      en leurs livres, ce qui n'apartient a dame Eloquance Theologienne,
      come dit saint Augustin ou quart de *Doctrine crestienne*. En bonne
      foy on li vouloit fere emprandre dure province a dame Eloquance. Si
725   ne li pouoit on trop baillier d'ayde. Mais je say bien leur responce:
      ilz diront qu'ilz n'y panserent onques.
        Toutevoyes pri je a toute celle benoite court qu'ilz pardonnent
      a celuy qui ce leur a imposé; car je say certainnement qu'il tent a
      bonne fin, c'est assavoir celle meismes a quoy tend maistre Jehan
730   de Meun. Vray est que je ne le pouroye excuser du tout, qu'i n'y ait
      mesprenture en les imputer si negligens, et vouloir fere emprandre
      mauvaise querelle—mais non pas par malice: car je tiens que en

I beg you, woman of high intelligence, to keep the honor
695   which you have as a result of your elevated understanding and
eloquent language. And though you have been praised for firing a
shot over the towers of Notre-Dame, do not, however, attempt to
destroy the moon with a heavy cannon. Be wary of resembling the
crow who, having been praised for its singing, sang even louder
700   than was its custom and let its food fall from its mouth.[103] And to be
granted any forgiveness, I ask that all those men and women who
wish to reprimand and insult him for any part of his book to read it
at least four times—and at leisure—in order to better understand it.
Of course I am willing to regard their reading of this book as a form
705   of absolution. If they wish to do nothing, I ask that they consider the
objective of his book and that they read his apology without being
fixated on the opposite point of view. I have no doubt that they will
not consider him to be forgiven, because no apology nor response is
necessary other than the one which directly precedes the beginning
710   of the attack. For only in this instance does he speak in the voice of
the author, and as such he says that,

> ...no one must insult women,
> unless he has the meanest of hearts

and the author declares that it is not his intention to

715
> speak against any living man,
> who adheres to the holy religion
> or who uses his life in order to do good deeds,
> no matter with which cloak he covers himself

and that if his words are too bawdy or foolish, it is that,

720
> ... his subject matter demanded it
> which pulled him toward such words
> through their own inherent quality...

and that all he is doing is "merely quoting." In general, he says that
at no time did he do anything that was not "for teaching"—in other
725   words, so that everyone might gain knowledge about himself and
about others. Finally, he says that if there are indeed

> ...words
> which the Holy Church considers foolish,

he is certainly willing to retract them.
730   It amazes me greatly when he left it up to the mouth of Lady
Theological Eloquence and to everyone of the holy court of Christianity to consider whether there was anything to be criticized in his
book, since they let it sleep for one hundred years or more so that it
is now published all over Christendom and—what is more—trans-
735   lated it into foreign languages. But I think that they waited for you

li n'an a point, ou si pou come en home vivant—, mais par ce tant
seulement qu'il a pou veu ce noble livre de la *Rose* (cointement ce

735   qu'il en a veu). Veulliés luy donques pardonner, vous, dame Justice
Canonique, Raison, Eloquance, Conscience et les autres barons
de la court sainte Crestienté, et luy commender en penitance de ce
forfait que il lise tout au lonc et au ley et a loisir ce tres noble livre
de la *Rose* trois fois en l'onneur de celle Benoite Trinitey en unité;

740   laquelle nous ottroit a tous toison si blanche que nous puissiens,
avec le dit de Meun, brouter de herbes qui sont ou parc a l'aignelet
saillant.

Amen.

and those who wish to criticize him, for I know with certainty that
there was previously no one who saw it fit to reprimand him. There
were the four mendicant orders,[104] among whose members there
were very noble clerics with high authority toward the Pope, and
740   contemporary princes and princesses whom he did not particularly
flatter. Now, let us look at what sort of defender Conscience is, who
allows this matter to sleep for the duration of a century! By God's
body! No honor is bestowed upon this entire court of Christianity
for evidencing such negligence, especially not on Lady Theological
745   Eloquence, who presents her principal argument poorly and incites
a malicious quarrel by sustaining it and by speaking in a way such
as that outlined by the master rhetoricians in their books, which,
however, does not apply to Lady Theological Eloquence, as Saint
Augustine says in the forth book of his *De doctrina christiana*.[105]
750   I am convinced that they wished to make it very difficult for Lady
Eloquence, without granting her much help. But I know their answer well: They will say that this thought never occurred to them.

Nonetheless, I ask that this entire blessed court forgive him
who imposed himself on them, because I know with certainty that
755   he did so with good intentions, namely, the ones which are also in
keeping with those of Master Jean de Meun. It is true that I could
not forgive him at all for his error of imputing such negligence on
them and for wishing to incite a malicious quarrel—but not out of
wickedness, because I maintain that there is none in him, or as little
760   as in any living man. Yet he did this only because he had seen little
of this noble book of the *Rose* (to express it prudently). Therefore, I
ask you to forgive him, you, Lady Canonical Justice, Reason, Eloquence, Conscience, and the other barons of the holy court of Christianity, and to impose as his penitence for this crime the reading of
765   this noble book of the *Rose* in its entirety and at his leisure, three
times, in the honor of the Blessed Trinity in unity, who grant us all
a fleece so white that we may, together with de Meun, feed upon the
grass which can be found in the park of the gambolling lamb.

Amen.

7. July/August, 1402: Epistle 154 by Jean de Montreuil[106]

The message to counteract or to stop the detractors of the *Roman de la rose* becomes increasingly insistent, in particular since Christine de Pizan dared to include the *Debate Epistles* in the publication of the first edition of her collected works (completed on June 23, 1402).[107] This is a significant event in the history of the Debate because with her publication Christine now takes the epistolary polemic out of its private sphere making it accessible to a wider public. As Eric Hicks and Ezio Ornato have argued, thus far the participants of the Quarrel have succeeded in preserving their anonymity before the public. Christine, by publishing her dossier, or perhaps by sending it to such illustrious persons as the Queen Isabeau de Bavière and Guillaume de Tignonville, changes that and Jean de Montreuil and Gontier Col are now disclosed as ardent partisans of the controversial *Roman*.[108] Several speculations have been voiced as to the recipient of this particular letter but no identity can be proven definitively.[109]

Text:

107 v° Ut sunt mores hominum et affectus varii, dicam sinistra indicia. Audies, vir insignis, et videbis pariter in contextu cuiusdam mee rescriptionis in vulgari, quam inique, iniuste et sub ingenti arrogantia nunnulli in precellentissimum magistrum Johannem de Magduno invehunt et delatrant, precipue mulier quedam, nomine Cristina, ut

5 dehinc iam in publicum scripta sua ediderit: que licet, ut est captus femineus, intellectu non careat, michi tamen audire visum est Leuntium grecam meretricem, ut refert Cicero, que «contra Theofrastum, philosophum tantum, scribere ausa fuit». Asserentes obtrectatores predicti eundem ingenuissimum virum passibus in multis perclaris-

10 simi operis sui de *Rosa* erravisse et loquutum extitisse insolenter ut petulans: primo scilicet in capitulo Rationis, eam, ut aiunt, loqui supra personatus faciens dignitatem; consequenter Zelotipum excessive; et in sui tractatus seu libri decisione, ubi Amans iuveniles suas exprimit passiones indecenter, pernimiumque, ut subiungunt,

15 ac lubrice. «O tempora! o mores!», «Vix enim apud me sum», ut ait Therencius: tantum opus, talem virum—cui similem non tulit etas nostra, nec, ut auguror, secula ulla restituent—sic detractionis conspiciens unguibus lacerari, mortuo inconsideratissimi verba facientes,—quos vivens solo nutu oppido compressisset, qui de

20 personatuum varietate non discernunt, seu notant quibus passioni-
108r° bus moveantur aut induantur affectibus, et quem ad finem quave // dependentia aut quamobrem sint loquuti, nec quod demum satirici is instructor fungitur officio, quo respectu plura licet que aliis actoribus prohibentur.

Translation:

I must make some unfavorable observations on how the behavior
and emotions of men are changeable. You will see, excellent man,
and you will equally see in the context of a particular response in
the vernacular, how unfairly, unjustly and with what enormous
arrogance serveral people inveigh against and denounce the most
5   excellent teacher Jean de Meun, especially a certain woman named
Christine, who has brought out in succession her writings in public;
and although she does not lack intellect, according to female capac-
ity, it seems to me, however, that I hear Leontium, the Greek whore,
who, as Cicero reports, "dared to write against as great a philoso-
10   pher as Theophrastes."[110] These detractors mentioned above claim
that this most brilliant man in many passages of his outstanding
work on the *Rose* has erred and spoken insolently and petulantly;
first, in the section of Reason, making her speak, as they say, beyond the dignity of her character, then that of the Jealous Husband,
15   who speaks in an exaggerated fashion, and then, at the end of his
treatise or book, where the Lover articulates his juvenile passions
indecently, excessively, and as they add, obscenely. "O the times!
the morals!"[111] As Terence says "I am hardly at home"[112] seeing how
such a work, such a man—whose equal our age cannot bring and
20   future centuries, I predict, will not produce—are torn apart by the
claws of detraction. These reckless people—who do not discern the
variety of characters nor notice with what passions they are moved
or what emotions they take on or to what end or in what context or
why they speak, or finally that this teacher discharges the office of
25   a satirist, in which respect many things are permitted which are forbidden to other authors—quarrel with a dead man who in life would
have crushed them with a single nod.

      I would indeed argue openly against these critics as freely
as possible, if I did not know with authority how many outstanding
30   members of the military and clerical profession have been hitherto
born to suffer the stain of this accusation, nor is it such that the loftiest
minds can avoid the barking of such dogs or the bites of the envious.
He who was both king and prophet observed that "the mouth of those
who speak iniquities cannot be closed."[113] Indeed, as the opinion of
35   Livy states, "the greater the glory, the closer is envy."[114] But what
bothers me the most is that some of the detractors of this romance,
which should rather be called a mirror of or discourse on human life,
have only examined it superficially or read it in passing. In fact others, if they have studied it strenuously, are, believe me, hardly able

25   In hos siquidem maledicos exclamarem quam libenter, nisi
         autoritate comperissem quotquot usquam nati sunt militaris cleri-
         monieque professionis excellentiores talis semper iacture maculam
         subiisse: nec est quod alta pretereant ingenia canum latratum talis-
         modi aut morsuram invidorum, rege simul et propheta contestante
30   non posse «obstrui os loquentium iniqua», quippe cum, iuxta Livii
         sententiam, «quo gloria maior, eo propior invidia». Sed me nimis
         urit quod tales existunt nostri detractores quorum aliqui roman-
         tium huiusmodi, quod potius vite humane speculum dici debet aut
         discursus, viderunt summotenus aut legerunt in transitu, ut referunt;
35   alii vero, qui tametsi enixe studuerint, minime, credi michi, tante
         rei sunt capaces aut susceptibiles misterii. Daque quod istorum
         aliquis opus id attentius viderit et toto nervorum conatu proces-
         sus incubuerit lectioni, ut intelligere concessum sit: eundem tamen
         ordinis vocatio sic inducit, aut exigit professio, ut aliter loquatur ac
40   sentiat,—vel talis est qui ad continuationem speciei humane—qui fi-
         nis libri est—redditur forsitan inutilis. Quis igitur talium non deferat
         protinus iudicio!—qui profecto, ut ait Petrarcha, «quod nesciunt, aut
         negligunt, in aliis reprehendunt».
             Quasobres, frater carissime, industriam tuam rogandam esse
45   velim—quatinus tu qui, ut sentio, eundem philosophum et poetam
         ingeniosissimum, ut meritus est, veneraris, diligis, atque colis et
         in suo genere dicendi ceteros excellis buius regni—contra istos
         declames maledicos altissona fortiter musa tua, taliter baculo tue
         disertie defensando doctorem istum morum optimum, si mens ta-
50 108vᵒ men elevetur a sensibus, quod agnoscant quid sit // in eum dicere tot
         scientificis munitum discipulis et amicis potentibus decoratum.
             Vale, meque preceptori meo magistro Johanni Venatoris sup-
         pliciter recommenda, et parce quod tibi per «tu» confidenter sum
         loquutus. Hoc enim ex lectione antiquorum didisci: singularem
55   personam plurali numero alloqui non deberi.

40 to understand such a work or be open to its mysteries. And granting that one of these critics would read this work more attentively and would brood over the reading with all the effort of his mental power and be able to understand it, then, however, the voice of his order would lead him, or his profession would require that he speak and feel

45 otherwise—unless he is a man who is perhaps useless for the continuation of the human species, which is the end of this book. Who among these people (who, in fact, as Petrarch says, "reproach in others what they do not know or what they neglect"),[115] would not then on the spot defer this to judgment?

50 For these reasons, my most loving brother, I would ask for your diligence—as far as you can, who, I know revere, love, and worship this most ingenious philosopher and poet, as he deserves, and who surpass others of this kingdom in this art of speaking—ask you to speak out publicly against these critics with your intrepidly

55 sublime Muse such that you defend with the rod of your eloquence this outstanding student of human behavior, so that if their mind is elevated to their senses, they will understand what it means to speak against a man defended by learned disciples and distinguished with powerful friends.

60 Take care and send my greetings to my preceptor and teacher Jean Le Veneur,[116] and forgive me if I have spoken to you with the familiar pronoun, for I have learned from reading the ancients that a single person should not be addressed in the plural.

8. After October 30, 1402: Pierre Col Replies to Christine de Pizan[117]

This unfinished letter was addressed to Christine by Pierre Col at an unknown date after October 30, 1402, which is the date of reception of Christine's letter by Pierre Col.

Text:

199r° A Fame de hault entendement, damoiselle Cristine de Pizan

        Combien que tu aies proposé de n'escrire plus reprehension ou blasme contre la compilacion du *Romant de la Rose*—come sage et ravisee qui ses et appersois que humainne chose est de pechier, mais perseverance est euvre de deable—, pour tant ne retarderas tu
5 ma plume qu'elle ne te rescripve; car aprés tant de reprehencions et duplicacions par toy proposees et escriptes contre si notable escrivain, raison de droit et bonne coustume ensemble m'ottroient replique, qui comme disciple du dit escrivain ay fait une seule responce,—combien qu'il n'en fust besoing, pour ce que selonc que
10 mon petit entendement le peut concepvoir, la seule lecture de tes evasions est assés solucion. Et n'ofusquent en riens la verité que je soustiens, ne tache aucune empraingnent a la tres clere renommee maistre Jehan de Meun tes palliacions extravagans et ornemens de langaige: et croy que pour ceste cause t'a laissié a respondre le
15 prevost de Lisle. Je mesme en fu esmeus par aucun espace de temps de ne te respondre point, et pour ce aussy que j'avoye bien ailleurs ou entendre. Toutes voyes par maniere d'esbat pour aprandre et moy excerciter, je responderay a aucuns fais particuliers et evasions mises en ton epistre responsive a moy presentee le .xxxᵉ. jour
20 d'octobre. Et te prie que tu tiengnes pour repetees mes excusacions mises en mon aultre responce.

        Ja soit ce que tu dis ung pou devant la fin de ta darreniere response que ce n'est mie honneur de soy prandre a toy, que es le plus foyble partie, et qu'on deust «derompre la grose tige», non pas soy
25 arester aux petites branches (veu que de ton oppinion sont plusseurs «sages docteurs…grans princes de ce royaume et chevaliers…»), si n'ay je sceu personne qui l'ait blasmé par avant toy ne par aprés, se non celuy qui a composé la plaidoierie dame Eloquance; et toutevoyes me reprans tu de ce que j'ay ozé reprandre a euvre de si no-
30 table clerc: qui sonne contradiccion; et ne te desplaise, ci et ailleurs tu trebuches en la fosse que tu m'avoyes appareillie, c'est assavoir de dit et desdit, quant tu dis c'on se deust prandre aux autres, et tu me reprans de ce que je n'y suis provis.

Translation:

> To a woman of elevated understanding, Lady Christine de Pizan
>
>   Although you declared that you would stop writing any more words of blame or reproach against the compilation of the *Roman de la rose*, as would a wise and reasonable person who knows that it is human to sin and that perseverance is the devil's work, you, none-
>
> 5   theless, do not delay my quill in provoking a response. For after so much criticism and repetition, which were declared and written by you against this illustrious writer, reason of righteousness and good moral practice together demand my reply. As a disciple of this writer, I have responded only once, although there was no need for
>
> 10   this, because as my small intelligence can see, one reading of your evasive arguments is absolution enough. Moreover, your extravagant ramblings and flowery language do not in any way obfuscate the truth which I uphold, nor do they tarnish the reputation of the very renowned cleric Master Jean de Meun. I think it is for this reason
>
> 15   that the provost of Lille has not answered you. I, myself, was for quite some time uninclined to answer you, not to mention that I was preoccupied elsewhere. In any case, for the benefit of the debate and to learn and to practice, I will respond to some particular arguments and excesses which you include in your epistle presented to me on
>
> 20   the 30th day of October. I ask you to keep in mind the justifications of my other response.
>
>   Although you say shortly before the end of your last response that it is not honorable to attack you, the weakest member, and that one ought to "rip out the biggest branch," instead of stopping at the
>
> 25   little branches (given that many "wise theologians…, great princes of this kingdom, and knights…" share your opinion), I know of no one who has insulted him either before or after you, except for the one who composed the petition by Lady Eloquence. And in any case, you criticize me for having dared to criticize the work of this
>
> 30   renowned cleric: What a contradiction. And may it not displease you, but here and there you slide into the very ditch which you had dug for me, namely, in making and then retracting your statement that we must attack the others. Yet you criticize me for having done this very thing.

35   Quant je panse a celle petite branchette il me souvient du proverbe commun que l'en dit: «Ce blasme te vault ung grant los». O Doulx Dieu tres glorieux! quantes gens sont qui jamais n'appetissent leur los ou se blasment aucunement, se n'est pour eulx magnifier! Vescy que tu t'appelles petite branchette, et toutes voyes….

35   When I think of that little twig, I am reminded of the common proverb which says, "This insult will bring you great reputation." O sweet, glorious God! There are many people who have never craved fame or who insult themselves solely to magnify their own glory! Here you call yourself a little twig, and yet….

9. December 1402: A Letter by Jean Gerson[118]

This letter coincides with the series of sermons *Poenitemini* held at the Place-de-Grève in December, 1402[119] and constitutes Jean Gerson's swift reply to Pierre Col's treatise.

Text:

131v°   // Talia de me scribis, vir erudite et frater in Christi caritate dilectis-
         sime, qualia michi nequaquam usurpo; neque enim me tali dignor
         honore: horreo potius hanc laudem dum inter nugas, ymmo—parce
         frater vera dicenti—inter insanias falsas memorata miscetur. Fit
         nichilominus ut vel in mediis occupacionibus tibi rescribere non dif-
5   ferat, tum zelus meus redamare debens atque morem gerere tibi qui
         me diligere, non dico simulas—seorsum hec a te fictio—, sed vere
         monstras; tum pretera spes qua confido te ei fidem non denegaturum
         quem tantopere commendaveris; tum denique professio mea debens
         erroribus et viciis quantum valet obniti, que iam effecit ut sub invo-
10   lucro quodam nuper ediderim gallico sermone, quantum diei cursus
         tulit, orationem non contra Insanum Amatorem sed adversus scripta,
         verba et picturas ad illicitos amores amariores morte sollicitantes,
         stimulantes et urgentes.
             Porro neque repetiturus sum, neque in latinum versurus elo-
15   quium ea que ibidem disputata legisti: illic peroratum satis arbitror
         scripta, verba et picturas provocatrices libidinose lascivie penitus
         excecrandas esse et a re publica christiane religionis exulandas,— t
         hoc quidem apud omnem intellectum, qui et catholica fide illustra-
         tus est, et nequaquam viciosa passione corruptus. Apud illos vero,
20   qualis oracio persuadere sperabitur, qui suaderi nolunt, quibus suus
         error placet, quos excecavit malicia eorum qui dati sunt in repro-
         bum sensum, qui avertunt occulos suos ne videant in finem, qui
         denique illud severissimum maledictionis genus incurrunt ut mala
         consuetudine delectentur, ut blandiatur menciaturque iniquitas sibi?
25   Inter quales te numerare nec debeo, frater carissime: et ut nunquam
         debiturus sim supplex oro.
             Proposui autem decerpere aliqua eorum que scriptum
         tuum hesterno sero monstratum corrigenda delendaque continet.
         Quid dico aliqua! cum fere omnia—tecum loquor frater—sint in
30   hoc vel in illo culpanda. Propterea scriptum illud mox ut ipsum
         receperis—si quid in me est consilii—flamma rapax absumet, aut
         laceratum minutatim perget in oblivionem sempiternam. In primis
         tamen te tuique similes ammonitos velim, ne sapienciorum actorum
132r°   ignoranciam habere vos concludat tanta huius actoris // vix inter

Translation:

You write things about me, learned man and dearest most beloved brother in Christ, which I can in no way claim for myself; nor do I consider myself worthy of such honor; I dread this praise—forgive me for speaking the truth—when it is mixed together with such trifles—in fact, with such mad lies. All the same, it happens that my
5   writing back to you cannot be delayed in the midst of my business: first my zeal requiring me to love you in return and to indulge you who, I say, does not pretend to love me—this pretense is far removed from you—but you truly show this. Next, the longstanding hope which makes me confident you will not deny credence to the one
10 whom you have praised so much; then, finally, my profession requiring me to struggle as vigorously as can be against errors and vices so that I recently published in French in the form of an allegory which takes place as a plea for the duration of one day, not against a foolish lover but against writings, words and pcitures which rouse, stimulate,
15 and encourage illicit loves more bitter than death.

In turn, I shall not repeat nor translate into Latin the things under dispute which you have read there: I judge that I have sufficiently demonstrated that the writings, words, and pictures which are provocative in libidinous and lascivous ways ought to be utterly
20 abhorred and banished from Christendom—and this applies in fact to every intellect which is enlightened by the Catholic faith and which is in no way corrupted by a vicious passion. What kind of appeal can be hoped to persuade those who do not wish to be convinced, who are content with their error, who are blinded by the malice of those
25 who give in to base sentiment, who turn their eyes away in order not to see their end, and finally who encounter this most severe kind of evil-speaking that they delight in this evil custom so that their iniquity flatters and deceives them? I must not count you among these people, my most beloved brother, and I pray never to have to do so.
30 I have proposed, however, to gather some of the things which must be corrected or deleted in your writing which I was shown yesterday evening. What do I mean when I say "some"? For almost all—I speak to you as a brother—are reproachable in one way or another. For this reason, a violent flame should consume this writing shortly
35 after you receive it back—if there is any wisdom in me—or it should

35   mediocres numerandi tamque yperbolica admiracio, quem multi
      superant quantum delphinis balena britannica maior, et quantum
      inter virgulta cupressi. Tu vero tibi nunc attende quale precipicium
      paraverit attemptata tractacio materie theologice.
            Dicis itaque quod puer biennis aut triennis sit in statu inno-
40   cencie. Hec est heresis Pelagii, quam asserens pertinaciter hereticus
      est censendus. Ea insuper multa que ad dissolucionem indissolu-
      bilis racionis agitasti, plus et plus te circumligant nodis eiusdem
      heresis, exemplo avium laqueatarum viscove suo se volutancium:
      adeo anxium noxiumque est obniti veritati. Legatur non ego sed
45   Augustinus in *De Nuptiis et concupiscencia,* presertim in secundo
      libro: videbitur quod dico. Putasti tamen arbitror quod putare non
      debueras: puerum ideo esse in statu innocencie, vel quia ignorans
      est, vel peccati actualis nundum reus. Sed originalem corruptelam
      morbide concupiscencie advertere mens tua debuerat, que ab ea ut
50   omnes pessundatur.
            Dicis id quod te scripsisse miror si non pudet et penitet te:
      amator, inquis, insanus solus bene iudicat de huiusmodi viciosa,
      ymmo furiosa passione; alienus vero ab ea (qualem me esse
      tu dicis, ego non dico), eam non nisi «in speculo et enigmate»
55   recognoscit,—quasi videlicet oporteat omnes qui de viciis recte
      incorrupteque iudicaturi sunt ut eisdem prius viciis corrumpantur.
      Longe aliter est: nullus de viciosis operibus fert iudicium perver-
      sius quam ipsi talium febrili egritudine aut letali morbo «corrupti et
      abhominabiles facti in studiis suis»: exempla a sensualitate suppe-
60   tunt multa. «Male verum examinat omnis corruptus iudex», inquit
      Flaccus.
            Sed quod addis membra secreta mulierum sanctificata olim
      ex more fuisse, nescio qualis te Biblia docuerit nisi forte tu aliam
      a nostra te penes habueris,—aut si non movet te seducitque illud
65   Luce: «Omne masculinum adaperiens vulvam, sanctum Domino vo-
      cabitur». Quid, oro, sanctum Domino vocabitur? Si siles, respondeo:
      primogenitus.
            Ceterum actor tuus et pene Deus tuus plurima bona, inquis,
      scripsit, plurima valde supra communem doctorum omnium intelli-
70   genciam, quorum lectio non nisi decies repetita cognoscitur. Quid si
      eciam mala plurima nimis et multo plus plurima commiscuit bonis
      istis contraria? Quid reliquum est dicere nisi eum more insani ama-
      toris insanisse, variasse, discordasse et, juxta therencianum verbum,
      voluisse «cum racione insanire»?

sink into eternal oblivion having been torn up into tiny shreds. To begin, I would like however to admonish you and those like you, lest an admiration so excessive of this author who hardly deserves to be counted among the mediocre because it causes you to be ignorant

40 of wiser authors. In fact, many surpass him like the great whale of Brittany surpasses the dolphins, and the cypress trees the shrubs in a hedge. But now you must pay attention to the precipice which your attempted treatment of theological matters has prepared.

You say that a two- or three-year-old child is in the state of

45 innoncence. This is Pelagian heresy, [120] and whoever asserts this is to be censured as a persistent heretic. Many things besides this which you adduced to irrefutable arguments wrap you more and more in the knots of this heresy like birds tossing themselves around in nets on birdlime: so troublesome and harmful it is to struggle against

50 the truth. You should read not me but Augustine in *De nuptiis et concupiscentia* [On marriage and lust], especially the second book: You will see what I am saying. Yet, you thought, I take it, what you should not have thought: The child was in a state of innocence because either it was ignorant or not yet guilty of actual sin. But your

55 mind should have taken notice of the original sin of sickly concupis- cence, and how all things are destroyed by it.

You said this, and I wonder that you were not ashamed or re- morseful for having written this. You said that only the Foolish Lover can judge this vice, or rather this furious passion correctly, whereas

60 the one who is ignorant of it (as you, not I, hold me to be) recog- nizes it only "in a glass darkly"[121]—as though it were necessary for all of those who rightly and justly judge these vices have first to be corrupted by the same vices. In fact, it is quite the opposite: No one can pass judgment on the works of vice more falsely than those who

65 have been "corrupted and made unclean in their studies"[122] by such a feverous sickness and fatal disease, as Horace said.[123]

But you add that the private parts of women were once sancti- fied by ancient custom, and I do not know what Bible has taught you this unless you have at your place one quite different from ours—or

70 perhaps this passage from Luke has prompted you and led you astray? "Every male who opens the vulva will be called holy to the Lord."[124] What, I pray, shall be called holy to the Lord? If you do not answer, I will: The first-born.

But you say, your author—and almost your God—has writ-

75 ten many good things, indeed many things which by far exceed the common intelligence of all doctors, which are only understood after

75 132v°   Propterea opus illud chaos informe recte // nominatur, et
              babilonica confusio et brodium quoddam almanicum et Protheus in
              omnes se formas mutans,—tale demum cui dici possit illud pueris
              decantatum: «Conveniet nulli qui secum dissidet ipse».
                   Sane quod de theologis introducitur, quos labi refers in amo-
80   rem quandoque insanum (quemadmodum michi ipsi comminaris—a
              quo malo me avertat non Cupido falsus sed verus dilectionis Deus!),
              istud positum michi visum est magis ad diffamacionem theologorum
              quam pertinenter ad rem, et ut fortassis sub umbra culpe maioris in
              theologis isti sua crimina vel solarentur vel absconderent vel probar-
85   ent. Nam si Tullius, cum virum eloquentem describeret, dixit eum
              esse virum bonum dicendi peritum, multo amplius cum theologum
              nomino, virum debeo intelligere bonum, sacris litteris eruditum.
                   Age rursus, si tuus actor non ex affectione inhoneste loquutus
              est, da racionem quis eum impulerit ea introducere ex quibus Racio
90   tam obsceno illotoque sermone loqueretur.
                   Amplius vero culpatur actor tuus, non quod introduxerit
              Naturam de Deo loquentem, sed quod taliter loquentem de hiis mis-
              teriis que sola revelacio gratuita et supernaturalis ministratur.
                   Et quia me, in opusculi mei impugnacione, cum insigni
95   femina miscuisti, quero si virilis illa femina cui tuus sermo
              dirigitur—quamquam ita confuso ordine ut nunc ab ea ad Elo-
              quenciam Theologicam, nunc econverso raptim migret—, si illa,
              inquam, virago arguit erroneum hoc pro proverbio positum: «Melius
              est decipere quam decipi», nonquid non recte redarguit? Ostendit
100   evasionis tue tam anxia et ficta meditacio quod magno racionis
              aculeo urgebat te mulier, quando ad hoc confugisti ut diceres in hac
              parte librum addicione subdola deturpatum,—quod qua ratione scire
              potueris, nec dicis nec video.
                   Illud subinde mulier hec prudenter attulit quod ad lecturam
105   actoris tui erubescerent regine—erubescerent ingenia bene morata
              ingenuoque pudore predita—, quale tuum esse eciam scripta tua
              velis nolis ostendunt: nichil enim ibi obscenum loqui potuit bona
              indoles tua. Nullum quippe consequens est eas personas taliter
              agentes se propterea de criminibus suspectas ostendere: ymmo vero
110 133r°   si erubescunt // magis salva res est, ut therencianus sermo dicit.
                   Non attingam omnia: alioquin linea fere quelibet eliminanda
              occurreret,—ut cum dicis non esse naturalem appetitum hominis
              coniungi matrimonialiter solum virum cum muliere unica et solam
              cum unico. Hoc enim et falsum est et uni ex dictis tuis inconsonum
115   dum Genium nature deum deffendis, quia, inquis, de sola matrimo-
              niali copula loquebatur.

being read ten times. But what if he has mixed together too many bad
things and others which are contrary to the good? What remains to
say except that he has gone mad like the Foolish Lover, that he has
80   changed his mind and contradicted himself, following the words of
Terence, that he has wanted to "go mad with reason"?[125] For this reason that work is rightly called a formless chaos, a Babylonian confu-
sion, some kind of German soup, and a Proteus changing himself into
every shape, precisely that which can be said that schoolboys should
85   avoid, "something which disagrees with itself can never agree with
anyone else."[126]

Indeed, what has been posited about theologians who, you
claim, at one time or another have fallen into such a foolish love
(with which you threaten me, and may the true God of Love and not
90   the false Cupid turn me away from this evil) seems to me more pertinent to defaming theologians than to proving your case, as though
perhaps under the guise of a great guilt among theologians they
would mitigate or conceal or make acceptable their crimes. For if
Cicero says, describing the eloquent man as a good man and experi-
95   enced in speaking, I must know him as a good man learned in Holy
Scripture when I speak of a theologian.

Then again, if your author did not speak impurely out of inclination, give me the reason which made him introduce those things
about which Reason speaks in such an obscene and unclean language.
100   Your author can indeed be broadly blamed, not because he
introduces Nature speaking about God, but that he had Nature speak
in such a way about these mysteries which only free and supernatural
revelation affords.

And since in your attack on my short work you have brought
105   me together with that remarkable woman, I ask you if this manly
woman to whom your words are addressed— although in such a
confused order that now you wander hastily from her to Theological Eloquence and then back again—I ask you if this manly woman
has demonstrated the error contained in the proverb "it is better to
110   deceive than be deceived"? Has she not indeed proved this to be
untrue? The awkward and made up reflections in your feeble excuse
show that the woman has pricked you with the great barb of reason
when you take recourse by saying that the book has been disfigured
by a deceitful addition in this part—and neither do you say nor do
115   I see by what means you could know this. Shortly afterwards this
woman prudently showed that queens blush when they read your
author—and all well-mannered minds endowed with intelligence

Similiter quale est illud quod turpitudinem actoris hac pictura
celare putaveris, quod malum docuit ut cognitum vitaretur, quod
preterea unus tibi notus philocaptus remedium sibi ex hoc melleo
120   toxico velud tyriacam de veneno confecerit! Omnia quippe talia
frivola sunt.

Illud quoque parum catholice alegatum est dixisse quosdam
Cantica canticorum ob laudem filie Pharaonis edita: nam qui dixit
irreligiose mentitus est.

125   Illud vero magis subdolum videtur dum contendendo vis indu-
cere recursum ad librum esse faciendum: «Non habet liber, inquis,
per omnia sicut sonat eius impugnacio». Nolo contra niti; malo dare
victas manus, malo subcumbere, quam tam improba contagiosaque
lectio repetatur.

130   Porro finis scripti tui notat illos curvasse genua coram Baal
a quibus liber iste spretus viluit. Dicam libere quod sencio: ista
introductio vel depravat sentenciam et viciosa est, vel tamquam
scandalosa, iniuriosa et falsa heresimque sapiens in fide et moribus
radenda est denique, si serio dictum est.

135   Tu nunquam preconiis tuis tantumdem extollere parvitatem
meam potueras quantum vituperas dum confingit tua forte libertas
mecum loquendi ea me scripsisse que scripsi quatenus homines,
quos scimus niti in vetitum, flamma maior exureret animaretque
ad lecturam libri huius repetendam,—quasi videlicet professionem
140   meam commutaverim in mendacium, et sit officium meum ficte
agere in doctrina morum et michi ipsi, more actoris tui - ymmo
christiane religioni!—dissidere, corde insuper et corde loqui. Moriar
priusquam ista umquam fictione palliatus inveniar. Vide potius ne
133vº   actorem tuum iste dolus // infecerit: dum enim amoris carnalis indu-
145   cit vituperia—cuius laudes sepius extollit—, quidni secundum tuam
noticiam faciles ad illum animos proniores reddere studuerit?

Quid de protestacione illa actoris tui loquar quam pro
velamine quodam sue feditati superinducere conatus est: Nichil,
inquit, ipse de meo posui: se ergo recitatorem non actorem profite-
150   tur. Quamobrem nolite vos, admiratores sui, laudem ei tribuere si
bene dixit, sicut non vult maledicta sua in probrum eius versa iri si
quedam arguenda transtulerit. Nolite preterea tanto contra nos odio
excandescere, neque tam ampullosis verbis buccisque tumentibus in
nos declamare si liber iste pro sua parte culpatur: non enim personas
155   sed scripta, quisquis ilia confecerit, infamamus, nisi forte minis-
trator pocionis toxicate, eciam ab alio composite, non inde culpa
carere iudicandus estimatur. Quale est iterum, Deus optime, prote-

120 and shame would blush as well—and even your writings show this whether you admit it or not, for your innate good character was unable to say anything obscene there. However, it does not follow that people acting this way show themselves suspect of crimes for this reason. On the contrary, if they blush, the more all is well, as Terence's comment makes clear.

125 I will not touch on everything: Otherwise it would be necessary to strike almost any line you could choose—as where you say that it is not a natural desire of man to be joined in marriage, with one man having a single wife, one woman a single husband. For this is false and in disagreement with one part of your writings when you defend Genius as the God of Nature, since, as you say, he spoke 130 only about the marriage bond. The same is the case when you think you can conceal the ugliness of your author with this picture: that he taught evil so that, once recognized, it could be avoided, that one of your acquaintances, smitten by love, concocted for himself a remedy from this poisonous honey as one brews an antidote from 135 venom. In fact, such arguments are worthless.

It is also hardly Catholic to claim, as some have said, that the Song of Songs was written in praise of the Pharaoh's daughter, for whoever says this is lying impiously. Indeed, the deception is clearer when in the course of arguing you want to claim that one should go 140 back to the book: "The book, you say, does not at all contain what the criticism of it claims." I do not want to exert myself against this, I prefer to surrender, I prefer to concede defeat than to reread something so morally unsound and polluted.

Moreover, the end of your work claims that those who have re-
145 jected this scorned book have bent their knee before Baal. I will tell you freely what I feel: This claim either distorts the meaning, and is vicious, or it is all the more scandalous, injurious, and false, and maintains a heresy against the faith and morals, and finally should be expunged if it was expressed seriously.

150 With your public statements you could never praise my insignificance as much as you criticize it, while your supposed freedom to speak with me claims that I have written these things so that the fire will burn all the more intensely and inspire men—whom we know are inclined to the forbidden—to read and reread this 155 book—as though I had changed my profession into lying and as though my duty would be to pretend to disagree with moral doctrine and even with myself—following the pattern of your author—and to disagree with the Christian religion and to say the opposite of

stari unum et eodem contextu protestacioni sue obvium fieri? Istud
certe non est excusare se sed taliter agere ut dicatur: «Ex ore tuo te
160   judico, serve nequam».

Tandem vero ego te nunquam, o christiana curia, animo lesi
neque verbo. Tu non omnia potes delicta corrigere fateor: alio-
quin quid divine iusticie in futuro servaretur? Sufficit in multis
redargucio per leges et edicta communia: sicut contra simoniam,
165   furta, homicidia, adulteria, ita contra hanc contagiosissimam male
loquendi vel scribendi licenciam, presertim ubi publicus accusator
invenitur nullus. Nichilominus habitatores tuos ecclesiasticos multos
ego neque super libris multis Ovidii, neque super magicis figmentis,
neque nominatim super hoc libro et aliis conservatis in multorum
170   perniciem excusare propono: illos excuso quos officium nullum ad
dampnandum constringebat, et qui pro sua parte, verbo vel scripto,
generaliter aut specialiter, ut ego nunc et multi pridem, talia repro-
barunt.

Neque pretereundum censeo quod scribunt Actus Apostolo-
175 134r° rum omnes converses noviter ad fidem qui fuerant // curiosa sectati
combussisse libros suos valoris denariorum quinquaginta millium.
Ecce coram Deo quia non mentior, et per si quid in me est cui dare
fidem dignum ducis affirmo si solus esset liber actoris tui michi
proprius, valens mille libras et amplius, ego prius darem eum flamm-
180   mis rapacibus exurendum quam venderem taliter publicandum.
Vide quantum afficiar, ymmo vero non afficiar ipsum relegere, non
quidem ex ignorancia sicut tu reputas—quamquam in me multa
sit—, sed pro mea et aliorum consciencia. Itaque memini me pridem
gustasse iam ab adolescentia fontes illos omnes aut fere omnes a
185   quibus actoris tui dicta velud rivuli quidam male traducti prodierunt:
Boecium, Ovidium, Therencium, Juvenalem, Alanum, et de Sancto
Amore, Abelardum cum sua Heloyde, Marcianum Capellam et si
qui sunt alii; scito preterea quod codicellum unum cuius titulus est
Itinerarium mentis in Deum, a domino Bonaventura, quem uno die
190   perlegi, ego toti libro tuo—ymmo et decem talibus!—in profundi-
tate sciencie opponere non dubitaverim: et tu ad intelligendum hunc
librum nos adeo brutos et ebetes esse diiudicas!

Attamen pro hac commonicione tua, ut relegam et sic intelli-
gam, ego vicem reddo: lege, frater, et iterum relege quartum librum
195   *De doctrine christiana;* ille enim aliquanto plus affert difficultatis
quam liber tuus in vulgari. Animadvertes, crede michi, non esse factam iniuriam tirannicam Eloquencie si eam theologie sociaverimus:
pudebit te forsan audacie allegandi ea que non plene prospexeris.
Augustinus plane tibi reclamat, tum expressissimis verbis ibidem

160   what I believe. I would rather die than ever be found in such a cloak of fiction. Look instead whether this trick has tainted your author: for while his censure applies to carnal love, whose praises he often sings, did he not in fact really endeavor—following your conception—to make those souls already impelled toward it even more inclined?

165   What should I say about this claim of your author that he tried to cover his shame with some veil? He said that he had shown nothing of himself and thus claims to be a narrator and not a protagonist. For this reason, you his admirers, should not praise him if he spoke well just as he did not wish that his slanders become a source of shame for himself, in case he brought across something objection-

170   able. Moreover, stop flaring up in hatred against us and railing at us with such blown-up words and puffed-up cheeks if this book is accused in its own right, for we do not attack the reputation of persons but of writing, whoever wrote it, unless perhaps the person who administers a poisoned drink—even one concocted by someone else—is

175   not considered fit for a trial to determine his innocence. Once again, what is this, good God, to witness one thing and in this same context of testifying, act in a contrary way? This certainly cannot be sued in self-defense, rather acting like this recalls the saying "I have condemned you from your own mouth, worthless servant."[127]

180   At last, indeed, o court of Christianity, I have never offended you in spirit or in word. I confess you cannot correct all the defects, otherwise what would be left in the future for divine justice? In many matters a conviction through laws and common edicts suffices; just as with simony, theft, homicide, adultery, so it is with this most polluted

185   license of speaking or writing in an evil way, especially where no public accuser comes forward. Nonetheless, I cannot excuse many of your Churchmen when they write about Ovid's many books or about magical fictions or specifically about this book and others which contain so much ruin for many. I excuse those whom no duty has forced

190   to act as censors and who for their part reproach similar matters, spoken or written, in general or in specifics, as I do now and as many have done previously.

     Nor do I believe that what is written in the Acts of the Apostles should go unnoticed: that the new converts to the Faith who had

195   practiced magic burnt their books with a total value of fifty-thousand pieces of silver. With God as my witness that I am not lying, and I swear by that which you consider credible in my person, if a single book of your author belonged to me—worth a thousand pounds or more—I would cast it into the greedy flames so that it be burnt rather

200   than sell it so that it could be made public as such. See how much

200   (4 *o De doctrina christiana,* in ipso operis vestibulo), tum factis
           operum suorum tantis eloquencie viribus elaboratorum; quamquam
           temperate modestia loqutus sum, si adverteris, dum Eloquenciam
           Theologicam mediocri sermone loquentem esse introduxi, curiosita-
           tem quasi michi iamiam opponendam vigilanter excludens.
205   134 v°   // Postremo cessent ioci, frater optime et melioris cause pa-
           trocinio dignissime; taceat interim libido vel vincendi vel garriendi.
           Veniamus ad rem seriam religiosamque. Assero tibi, si scirem ger-
           manum meum composuisse talem librum atque publicasse, penitere
           autem super hoc premonitus et animadversus sufficienter finaliter
210   recusasse, ego non plus pro eo in hac impenitentia mortuo quam pro
           dampnato preces offerrem Domino Nostro Jesu Christo,—in quo
           bene vale, tradens te deinceps salubrioribus castioribusque studiis
           neque dans occasionem scandali simplicibus. Et si quid asperius
           dictum fortassis offenderit, da veniam mee fidel, multum de te pre-
215   sumenti quia multum diligenti. Denique totum tum veritatis catho-
           lice zelo tum desiderio ad salutem tuam deputatum habe.
                Et oremus pro invicem ut salvemur.

I am moved—or rather, in fact am *not* moved—to reread this, and indeed not out of ignorance as you argue—although my ignorance is great—but for the sake of my conscience and that of others. For I remember that I previously enjoyed, already in my adolescence, all

205   these sources, or almost all, from whom the writings of your author proceeds like many diverted streams: Boethius, Ovid, Terence, Juvenal, Alain de Lille, Guillaume de Saint Amour, Abelard with his Heloise, Martianus Capella, and all the others: Moreover, you should know that I would not doubt that a short manuscript entitled

210   *Itinerarium mentis in Deum* [The Mind's Journey to God] by Saint Bonaventura—which I read in one day—can be compared favorably with respect to the profundity of its learning with all of your book—or even with ten more like it! And you decide that we are too brutish and dull to understand this book.

215   However, for the sake of your reminder that I should reread it in order to understand it, I will turn the tables: Read, brother, and read again the fourth book of *De doctrina christiana*, for it presents more difficulty than your book in the vernacular. You will notice it, believe me, that I have made no oppressive injury to Eloquence

220   when I associate it with theology. Perhaps you will be ashamed that you have so boldly adduced things which you have not fully examined. Augustine gives a clear retort to you not only in the most explicit words there (Book Four of the *De doctrina christiana*, at the beginning of this part of the work) but also in the deeds of his works

225   elaborated with such a force of eloquence; I have indeed spoken with tempered modesty, if you notice, when I have Theological Eloquence speak in a middle style, avoiding anything excessive which could be taken against me.

Finally, let the jokes stop, my best brother, more deserving of

230   a better cause to defend; may the desire to conquer or to talk nonsense be still in the meantime. Let us proceed to a more serious and religious matter. I maintain to you, if I knew that my brother had written and published such a book, and had finally refused, although forewarned and sufficiently informed, to repent for this, I would of-

235   fer for him, having died in this impenitence, no more prayers to Our Lord Jesus Christ than for a damned soul, our Lord in whom I bid farewell to you who should devote yourself in the future to healthier and chaster studies and of no cause for scandal to the simple-minded. And if perhaps something said here more harshly offends

240   you, please forgive my good faith, which has greatly presumed on you since it springs from a deep love. Finally, allot your time to the ardent love of the Catholic Faith and the desire for your salvation.

And let us pray for each other's salvation.

10. *December 1402–March 1403: Sermons of the Series Poenitemini by Jean Gerson*[128]

The following passages are excerpts from sermons preached by Jean Gerson in the church St.-Jean-en-Grève. The series of sermons on the seven capital sins is entitled *Poenitemini* and lasts from December 3, 1402, the first advent, until March 18, 1403. The passages quoted are those where Gerson explicitly refers to the *Roman de la rose*.

Before beginning with the actual sermons, Jean Gerson announces the outline of his series to his congregation in his first sermon which took place on December 10, 1402, the second Advent.

Texts:

27v°   Regarder des choses par dehors es bestes ou es paintures ou ailleurs qui sont deshonnestes, est ce pechié? Je respon comme par avant. C'est fort par especial que lire livres esmouvans a luxure ne soit pechié mortel, et ceulx qui les retiennent devroient estre contrains par leurs confesseurs les ardre ou dessirer, que aulx ou aultres n'y

5 28r°   pechassent plus (comme est Ovide ou je ne sçay quel // Matheol, ou partie du *Rommant de la Rose,* ou rondeaux et baladez ou chanssons trop dissolues). Si jugés quelle penitence doivent faire ceulx qui les font et publient, sus quoy j'en ay escript plus a plain; parellement dy je des paintures ordes et deshonestes….

10   Est tenue la personne ramener a bonne voye l'autre qu'elle a deceu par son fait ou par ses parolles? Je respon que oy, de tout son pooir; et ce on il doit chargier en penitence. Et ce je fais en toute personne. Notés comment yci parlera encontre *Le Rommant de la Rose* qui veult en la personne de Raison que on parle gouliarde-

15   ment. Telz paroles enflamment a luxure, et c'est pour quoy elles sont a deffendre: notéz, Seneque *(turpia, etc.)*; Aristote (7° *Politice);* Noé et Chan; Tulle; saint Augustin; notés le peril du rommant et samblables, etc.; et la laidure de la fin, etc. *(videatur finis);* notés de l'enfant qui retint bien le mal du rommant; notés qu'il est dampné

20   s'il ne s'est repenti; notés que sa paine croit la paine assessoire et accidentele.

Translation:

To look upon things which are dishonorable, other than those pertaining to beasts or in images or elsewhere—is this a sin? I reply as I did before. In fact, it is especially astonishing that reading books which encourage lechery is not a mortal sin, and those who own them ought to be forced by their confessors to burn or shred them in
5   order that they or others will not sin anymore (such as Ovid, or I do not know which passage by Matheolus,[129] or the *Roman de la rose*, or *rondels* and ballades or songs which are too dissolute). Those who produce and publish them must decide upon the kind of penitence, a topic on which I have written extensively. I say the same
10   about filthy and dishonorable images….

      Is the person who has deceived another in deed or word urged to bring him or her back to the right path? My answer is yes, with all his power, and indeed, this ought to be one's penitence, which I apply to anyone. Note that the *Roman de la rose* contradicts this,
15   where the character of Reason speaks in the manner of goliards. These words incite people to lechery, which is why they must be forbidden. Note Seneca (*turpia*, etc.),[130] Aristotle (*7º Politice*);[131] Noah and Ham,[132] Cicero,[133] Saint Augustine;[133] note the peril of the romance and others, etc.; and the ugliness of the conclusion, etc.
20   (*videatur finis*); note the child who remembers well the evil of the romance, note that he is damned if he does not repent, note that his suffering increases the incidental suffering.

***

On December 24, the fourth Advent, the preacher replies to three complaints
by "Foolish Lovers":

Text:

52r° Est ce la maindre pechié qui fait briser la foy de mariage, etc., suc-
ceder batars, embler les corps, etc., emprisonner, se tuer, mourir par
desespoir, murtres d'enfans? Notéz Architas Tarantinus. Qui fait
briser, ordoier sacrements? Qui fait personne bestiale? Qui fait hors
du sens et a la fois mourir? *Nota de 1ᵃ.* Qui fait oublier Dieu et ses

5 jugemens, et par male coustume cheoir en enfer? Dit *Le Romant
de la Rose* que c'est le mandre pechié de quoy corps de femme
soit entechié, etc. (la cause: pour ce que a tous autres maulx elle
s'abandonne). Notéz contre ceulx qui tournent a erreurs les femmes
pour en abuser et les font herites. *Cape penitentiam:* hatéz vous de

10 52v° prandre penitence tandis // que temps en est; prenéz le seur, etc.;
repentéz vous, etc.…

53v° 　　　Bouche demande se chançons sont licites. Raison dicerne: ou
elles sont honnestes et en temps et en lieu; ordes et luxurieuses; ou
fausses et herites; ou hors temps et lieu et a mal d'autrui, comme es

15 54r° eglises. Les •iii• derrains poins sont pechiéz et a // deffendre. Notéz
que la voix de la femme est comme des serainnes, lesqueles Ulicés
passa en estoupant ses oreilles.

　　　Bouche demande se proprement parler des menbres honteux
et de tout ce pechié est chose desraisonnable. Et argue que non:

20 premierement par l'auctorité du *Roumant de la Rose*; secondement
par les raisons qui y sont: car les mos de soy ne sont point lais, et se
les choses sont laides c'est pour le pechié, et pechié est aussi bien en
murtre et larcin, desquel on parle bien.

　　　Yci respont raison que parler proprement des choses se peut

25 faire ou commancement par gouliardie; ou appert par soy enflamer
a luxure; ou par maniere de personnaige; ou par maniere de doctrine entre gens saiges et adviséz et qui ne quierent fors la verité des
choses.

　　　Premierement ne se doit faire, et dire le contraire est erreur;

30 comme qui diroit que on devroit aler nus; comme qui voudroit excuser Chan de ce qu'il ne covrit son pere: c'est l'erreur des philosophes qui pour ce furent dis chiens. Aristote le deffant ou •viiᵉ• de
Politiquez; Seneque dit*: Turpia ne dixeris* (lait dire atrait lait

54v° faire). Saint Augustin dit que c'est erreur se partir de // soy mesmes;

35 Tulle en *De officiis;* on l'apelle langaige ors et delavéz; saint Pol dit
que pluseurs choses qui se font a part ne font nes a nommer «*corrumpunt bonos mores*», etc.). Ceulx qui dirayent le contraire, je

Translation:

Is it truly the least of the sins if it shatters the faith in marriage, etc., creates bastardy, violates bodies, etc., imprisons, kills, causes death out of desperation, and results in the murder of children? Note Architas Tarantinus.[134] Who shatters, tarnishes sacraments? Who turns people into beasts? Who acts irrationally and consequently dies?

5 *Nota de 1* [a].[135] Who causes God and His judgment to be forgotten and descends into hell through evil conduct? The *Roman de la rose* says that that which tarnishes the body of a woman, etc., is the least of sins (why? because she gives in to all other evils). Rebuke those who lead women into error in order to take advantage of them and

10 to make them heretics. *Cape penitentiam*: make haste to repent while there is still time; be sure of it, etc.; repent, etc....

Mouth asks whether songs are licit. Reason discerns: Either they are honorable, timely, and in their proper place; filthy and lecherous; or false and heretical; or untimely and out of place, and

15 as evil for those elsewhere as they are for churches. The last three items are sinful and must be forbidden. Note that a woman's voice is like that of the sirens, which Ulysses blocked out by covering his ears.

Mouth asks whether it is unreasonable to speak in proper

20 terms of shameful parts and of that entire sin. I argue that it is not: First, based on the authority of the *Roman de la rose*, second, based on the reasons given in it—for words in themselves are not ugly, and if the things are ugly it is because of the sin, and there is also sin in murder and theft, of which one certainly speaks.

25 Here Reason responds that one can speak of things properly, either first in the manner of the goliards, or to entice oneself openly to lechery, or by means of a character or a doctrine shared by wise and skilled people who seek nothing but the truth in things.

First, this must not be done, and to say the opposite is a

30 mistake. Like one who says that one ought to walk around naked, like one who would like to forgive Ham for not having covered his father. This is the error the philosophers made, which is why they were dogs. Aristotle forbids it in the seventh book of his *Politics*, Seneca says: *Turpia ne dixeris* (speaking filthily attracts filth). Saint

35 Augustine says that it is wrong to be untrue to oneself; in Cicero's *De officiis* it is called ugly and unwashed language; Saint Paul says that certain things which are done in private must not be named

voudroie que eulx mesmes apreissent ainsi leur filles a parler selond
Raison.

40   La seconde raison et maniere ne se peut excuser: meismement
entre gens mariéz doit estre honesté gardee.

Tiercement ne se doit faire en publique pour les causes dessusdictes, et aussi doit estre verité et honnesteté gardee es personnages.

La quarte maniere se peut faire et la quinte en aucun cas,
45   comme ung malade se monstrera tout nus a ung medecin pour soy
gairir. Et si maistre Jehan de Meun entendoit ainsi il avoit droit:
mais il failli en ce qu'il feist parler Raison a ung Fol Amoureux;
secondement en ce qu'il enhortoit parler communement femmes et
autres; tiercement en ce que il publia son livre a jeunes gens qui en
50   abusoient; quartement en ce que ces raisons monstrerent aussi que
on devroit aler nus. Si diz pour respondre que les mos sont lais pour
le mal qui en vient et lequel on y entant, comme sont aussi
55r°   les regars des femmes nues pour // le desir mauvais qui s'en ensuit.
Notéz saint Augustin *De nuptiis et concupiscientia,* et le proverbe
55   commun: y n'y a mal qui ne lui entant.

Ostéz, bonnes gens, ces livres d'entre vos filles et enfants! Car
ilz prandront le mal et laisseront le bien. Exemple de l'enfant, etc.
Notéz quelle est la fin. Notéz des autres: de Ovide qui en fut en exil;
notéz de Matheole le sot.

60   Je di •iii• ascercions: la premiere, que se je avoie ung *Roumant
de la Rose* qui fust seul et vaulsist mil livres, je l'ardroie plus tost
que je le vendisse pour publier, ainsi comme il est; secondement,
se je savoie qu'il ne s'en feust repenti, je ne prieroie pour lui nez
que pour Judas,—et acroissent ceulx qui le lisent en mal la paine a
65   icellui s'il est dampné ou en Pugatoire; tiercement, se je confessoie
personne qui en abusast, je lui conmanderoie effacer plusieurs choses ou du tout le geter hors. Ainsi des paintures ordes et qui enflamment, ou sont faictes pour les amies et amis folz, etc.

("*corrumpunt bonos mores*," etc.). Those who would claim the opposite, I would like them to teach their daughters to speak as Reason
40   does.

The second reason and practice cannot be forgiven: Even
among married people, respect must be maintained.

The third reason must not be exercised in public for the above-
mentioned reasons, and truth and respect must be maintained in
45   people.

The fourth may be done, and the fifth in some cases, such as
that of an infirm person who will show himself naked to a doctor in
order to be cured. And if Master Jean de Meun meant it in that way,
he was correct. Yet he failed in having Reason speak to a foolish
50   lover; second, in exhorting women and others to speak commonly;
third, in making his book available to young people, who have
misused it, fourth, in that these reasons also show that one ought to
go naked. I say this to respond to the argument that words are ugly
because of the evil that ensues and which one deduces from them,
55   such as the gazes of naked women which awaken evil desire. Note
Saint Augustine's *De nuptiis et concupiscientia* and the common
proverb: Evil lies in the intention.

Good people, take these books away from your daughters and
children! For they will espouse what is evil and leave what is good.
60   The example of the child, etc. Note the conclusion. Note that of others: that of Ovid, who was exiled; note Matheolus, the stupid.

I mention three assertions: The first, that if I had a copy of the
Roman de la rose which was the only one and which was worth as
much as one thousand books, I would burn it rather than selling it
65   for publication as it is. Second, if I knew that he had not repented, I
would not pray for him any more than I would for Judas—and those
who read it for the wrong intention increase his suffering, whether
he is damned or in Purgatory. Third, if I confessed someone who
misused it, I would recommend that several things be effaced or that
70   the entire book be thrown away. The same applies to filthy images
and images which are enticing or made for foolish lovers of both
genders, etc.

***

Poenitemini V preached on December 31, 1402 deals with conjugal chastity. According to Jean Mourin and Eric Hicks, this excerpt is in fact part of a second version of this particular sermon which was never delivered publicly (only the first version was). Since this version contains a refutation of the *Roman,* Jean Gerson must have opted not to make it public, because, in light of the recent epistolary exchange between Christine de Pizan, Pierre Col, and Jean Gerson himself, he undoubtedly would have felt obligated to render a public condemnation of Jean de Meun's work.[137]

Text:

51v°   Devotez gens, ainsi comme je pensoye l'autrier a ceste matere, je senti que dedens le secret de mon cuer se levoit une disputacion, a sçavoir laquelle chasteté estoit plus a recommander; ou virginité, ou mariage, ou viduité? Mais avant toutes chosez je supposay que chascune de ces fillez de chasteté estoient bonne et a loer; car je sçay bien
5   que aucuns herites ont voulu condampner l'estat de virginité, les autres l'estat de mariage, et les autres ne tenoient compte de quelconque chasteté, mais looyent Luxure et disoient qu'elle estoit selon nature. *Le Roman de la rose* le fait dire a Genius qui se dit dieu de nature, et puiz la personne de l'aucteur encore le dit plus ordement en la fin. Et
10   aprés ceste supposicion je mis ceste conclusion: que virginité pour ce temps est plus a loer quant est de soy, et puiz viduité, et puiz mariage. L'autre conslusion est que chascune de ces chastetéz doit loer et honnorer l'autre sans orguel, car aucunes personnes en mariage se sauvent mielx que les autres aucunes des •ii• estas.
15   Vous plaist il que je vous oevre •i• peu les raisons que soloyent faire les herites—et encore font aucuns—contre ces •iii• estas et contre la supposicion que j'ay mise? Je croy que vous le vouléz bien. Et je le feray le plus entendiblement que je pourray et bien briefment, une raison contre chascun estat.
20 52r°   Que vault virginité, ont dit aucuns, quant le monde faurroit // se chascun estoit vierge? Je respon yci que ceste chose n'est point a douter que chascun se tiegne en l'estat de virginité, et se le cas avenoit que Dieu le vausist, lors seroit voirement la fin du monde, car une foiz doit elle venir. En oultre je dy que il ne faut pas pour ce,
25   se mariage est necesaire, que virginité soit mendre ou a blasmer. Qui est chose plus necessaire que sont aucuns mestiers, comme bergiers ou couturiers ou fourniers? Neantmoins se une personne eslit a estre clerc ou bourgeois, il ne convient pas dire qu'elle face mal ou qu'elle ne face le mielx: pareillement est en nostre propos. Tiercement je dis
30   que pour ce tempz de grace et pour ceste loy a laquelle peuent estre amenéz touz autres peuples par baptesme, mariage n'est pas tant necessaire comme au commencement du monde ou en l'encienne loy, qui comprenoit seulement les Juifs.

Translation:

Pious people, as I was thinking upon this matter the other day, I felt that deep in my heart a debate arose, namely, on the topic of which sort of chastity was more commendable: virginity, marriage, or widowhood? Above all, I assumed that every one of these paths of chastity was good and to be praised, because I know well that

5 some heretics have wished to condemn the state of virginity, others marriage, and others, in turn, have not taken any form of chastity into account, but have praised Lechery instead and said that this was in compliance with Nature. The *Roman de la rose* has Genius say it, the so-called god of Nature, and then at the end the author in his

10 own person says it in filthy terms. And after that assumption I came to this conclusion: that virginity, taken alone, is to be praised more, then widowhood, and then marriage. The other conclusion is that each of these forms of chastity must praise and respect the others without pride, for some people fare better in marriage than do others

15 in the other two situations.

Would you like me to explain a little the reasons which the heretics usually used, and which some still do, against these three situations and against the assumption I have put forth? I think you would like me to do this. And I shall do it as comprehensibly and

20 briefly as possible, one reason against each status.

What is virginity worth, some have said, if the world would perish if everyone were a virgin? I respond here that observance of the state of virginity by everyone is not at all to be feared, and if it were indeed the case, God would condone it, and the end of the

25 world would truly be upon us, as it will inevitably be at some point. In addition, I say that this is no reason to insult virginity or to claim it to be less merely because marriage is necessary. What can be more necessary than certain professions, such as shepherd or tailor or baker? Nevertheless, if a person chooses to become a cleric or a

30 burgher, it is not appropriate to say that he or she has fared better or worse than others. It is the same with our case. Third, I say that in this time of mercy and in this doctrine, to which all people may be brought through baptism, marriage is not as necessary as it was at the beginning of the world or at the time of the Old Testament,

35 which only applied to Jews.

11. 1403–1404: Epistle 152 by Jean de Montreuil[138]

In this letter addressed to an unidentified person, Jean de Montreuil expresses his hope that two of his texts will be received more favorably than one of his compositions in the vernacular, his "Proverbes." Eric Hicks has identified these two texts as first epistle 118 and second epistle 154 which is closely linked to epistle 152.[139]

Text:

Epistle 152

106v°   Ex quo nuce ille nostre quadam sub ligatura in vulgari, reverende
      pater, non dignantur vestre submitti visioni, temptare est animus de
      solutis. Ecce igitur, preceptor mi, que pridem non minori cum im-
      petu quam nuge huiusmodi edite sunt, duas mitto epistolas: alteram
      commendatitiam florentissimi operis illius de *Rosa,* alteram super
5   eodem, satire formam tenentem, in eum qui sic, alio licet ex capite,
      vos impetit. Quasquidem peto poscoque et obtestor non tam viles et
      abiectas censeri ut non mereantur grandia agenda vestra paulisper
      alternare; sed gaudeam insipidas et ieiunas predictas scriptiones,
107r° in vestre sapientie aula in transitu, ut aiunt, refici, neu // querulas
10   redire, veluti *Proverbia,* de contemptu. Socrates, omnium doctis-
      simus Apollinis responso, «cum pueris ludere non erubescebat»;
      Scipio Affricanus Censorinusque Cato, tanti viri, lapillos in arena
      connumerare gestiebant. Vos vero regulas discipuli ad nauseam
      usque contempnetis, et quem ad studium provocare debetis allectu,
15   ad proficientie desperationem inducetis! Absit ab humanitate vestra,
      absit a paterna dilectione et benivolentia singulari! Barbarorum
      mores isti sint, non vestri. Ad neminem adhuc, quod audierim,
      egistis isto modo: et Johannes hoc primus baculo ferietur? Primus
      huic subicietur infortunio? Et quem patronum et alumpnum habere
20   confidebam, vehementissimo potiar despectore? Non credam, pater
      mi, etiam si ipse Cicero suaderet, nec autumem: quin verius favoris
      applausum directionemque ab innata vestre caritatis bonitate pre-
      stolabor, que sic me oculo benevolentie contempletur ut novum non
      cogar ad azilum recurrere, sed indulgentiam quam semper optavit
25   piis supplicationibus prepositus Insule consequatur. «Et si quod pec-
      catum fuerit, corrigemus te iudice», istud monente Therentio.
         Bene valete.

Translation:

Since, reverend father, our trifles rhymed in the vernacular are not worth being submitted to your view, I am of a mind to try with prose. Therefore, my teacher, I am sending two letters which were composed on the previous day with no less verve than my trifles in verse: the one is a commendation of this glittering work of the *Rose*,

5 the other on the same subject, written as a satire against the man who has gone after you so much, of course for other reasons. I ask, beg, and entreat you not to judge them so vile and abject that they do not merit being interchanged for a short time with your more serious business; but I would be glad if these empty and barren

10 writings were recast by passing through the court of your wisdom and not come back—like our *Proverbs*—full of contemptuous complaints. Socrates was judged the most learned of all in Apollo's answer "because he did not blush to play with young boys"; and such great men like Scipio the African and Cato the Censor were

15 delighted to count small stones in the sand. You would even have scorned in disgust the exercises of your own pupil whom you should urge on to study with enticement and instead lead to despair regarding his progress. May this be far removed from your humanity, from your paternal affection, and singular kindness. This behavior would

20 suit barbarians, not you. As far as I have heard, you have never acted this way with anyone. And Jean de Meun will be the first to bear this stick? The first to endure this misfortune? And where I was sure to have a master and disciple, I now gain a savage critic! I would not believe this, my father, even if Cicero himself tried to persuade

25 me, nor could I ever agree: instead I would expect the applause and direction of your favor springing from the innate goodness of your love, which contemplates me with a kind eye, so that I am not forced to run to a new refuge, but will seek the indulgence which the Provost of Lille has always sought with pious prayers. As Terence

30 admonishes, "and if there were some fault, we will correct it with you being the judge."

Take care.

Notes

1.   Unless otherwise stated, translations are my own. Those excerpts and texts, which also appear
      in Eric Hicks's *Le débat sur le Roman de la rose* (Geneva: Satlkine, 1996), have been closely
      checked against that edition.
2.   For the transcription of the epistles I used Ezio Ornato's edition, *Opera*, vol. 1 (Turin: Giap-
      pichelli, 1963), and manuscript Paris, Bibliothèque Nationale lat. 13062 which is an autograph
      manuscript. Reprinted with the permission of Slatkine Reprints from Eric Hick's edition, 27-45.
      Jean de Montreuil's letters have been preserved in a second manuscript, Vat. Reg. lat. 332, also
      an autograph manuscript. For further information on the codicology and manuscript history I
      refer to the edition by Ezio Ornato and to Eric Hicks and Ezio Ornato, "Le débat sur *le Roman
      de la rose*," *Romania* 98 (1977): 35–64, 186–219.
3.   Eric Hicks and Ezio Ornato retrace the circumstances that led to the provost's correspondence
      in their two articles, "Le débat" and "Le débat, suite," *Romania* 98 (1977): 35–64, 186–219.
4.   *Opera*, 144–45, *Le débat*, 28
5.   Ibid., 177–78, *Le débat*, 28-30.
6.   *Buc.* 3.31: "tu dic mecum quo pignore certes," and 49: "Numquam hodie effugies, veniam
      quocumque vocaris."
7.   Christine de Pizan uses this image in her letter to Pierre Col (chap. 3.7, 157) as does Jean de
      Meun himself in the *Roman de la rose*.
8.   The word *imitator* has been translated literally from the Latin (imitator) implying that Jean
      de Montreuil sees Jean de Meun as the imitator of a literary tradition, namely that of Roman
      Antiquity, and Ciceronian rhetoric in particular.
9.   *Opera*, 178–79, *Le débat*, 29-31 .
10.   Terence, *And.* 68: "Veritas odium parit."
11.   *Opera*, 179–81, *Le débat*, 32-35.
12.   This is a reference to both Christine's explicit (chap. 3.4, 131) and Gerson's implicit judgment
      of the *Roman*.
13.   What follows in this paragraph is an adaptation of Lacantius's *Divinae Instituiones*.
14.   *Le débat*, liii.
15.   *Opera*, 181–82, *Le débat*, 36.
16.   The word *minutam* in the Latin is in all likelihood one of the earliest attributions for the term
      with the meaning of a rough draft or protocol.
17.   *Opera*, 182–83, *Le débat*, 38-40.
18.   Horace, *Ars poet.*, 309.
19.   Terence, *And.*, 505.
20.   "in eternum," *Ps.*, 116. 2.
21.   Seneca, *Ad Lucil.*, 120. 19.
22.   "Delictum meum," *Ps.*, 31. 5.
23.   *Ps.*, 118. 162.
24.   Eric Hicks speculates that the reason for the omission of this dedicatory epistle from the Harley
      manuscript was motivated by Guillaume de Tignonville's fall into disgrace in 1407 when he
      ordered the hanging of a student without waiting for the proper judgment. As a punishment
      for this outrageous act he was forced to kiss the cadaver of his victim on the mouth. I used
      manuscript BN fr. 12799 and *Le débat*, 7–8 for the transcription of this letter.
25.   *Le débat*, 198.
26.   Jean de Montreuil addresses a letter in Latin to him which proves that they knew each other.
      The letter has been edited by Ezio Ornato, *Opera. Epistolario*, vol. 1.
27.   Christine's plea for support by the queen and Tignonville must be understood in judicial terms.
      Let us not forget that both Gontier and Pierre Col demanded that she recant her views on the
      Roman. The support by persons of authority such as the queen and the provost of Paris would
      consequently be crucial protection for Christine.

28. As has been pointed out by Eric Hicks and others, the *Debate Epistles* do indeed represent Christine's first work in prose (except for the "allegories" and the "glosses" of the *Epistre Othea*) and set the stage for her subsequent writings (*Le débat*, 198, n. 8).

29. In addition to Maurice Roy's edition of this text, *Œuvres poétiques de Christine de Pizan*, 3 vols (1886, 1891, 1896; repr. New York: Johnson, 1965), 2:29–48, Thelma Fenster and Mary Carpenter Erler have edited and translated the *Dit de la rose* in their above-mentioned work: *Poems of Cupid, God of Love. Christine de Pizan's Epistre au dieu d'Amours* and *Dit de la Rose, Thomas Hoccleve's The Letter of Cupid*, with George Sewell's *The Proclamation of Cupid* (Leiden: Brill, 1990). I am indebted to Thelma Fenster and Mary Carpenter Erler for graciously allowing me to reproduce their edition and translation. The editors chose to translate the octosyllables of the poem in unrhymed iambic tetrameter. This translation is reproduced here, with slight modifications. Again, more significant changes are annotated in the appendix. The extant manuscripts are:

    a. Chantilly Condé 492 (anc. 1667) (fols 67vo–79ro)—base manuscript

    b. BN f. fr. 12779 (Mouchet, suppl. fr. 6259)

    c. BN f.fr. 604, anc. 7087, de la Mare 413

30. James Laidlaw, "Christine de Pizan: A Publisher's Progress," *Modern Language Review* 82, no.1 (1987): 37–75; 56.

31. *Le débat*, xlvi; my translation.

32. For a succinct synopsis of the poem, I refer to Fenster and Carpenter Erler's edition, 15–16. The following works offer critical insight into this poem: Patricia Stäblein-Harris, "Orléans, the Epic Tradition, and the Sacred Texts of Christine de Pizan," in *Reinterpreting Christine de Pizan*, ed. Earl Jeffrey Richards (Athens: University of Georgia Press, 1992), 272–84; Lori Walters, "Fathers and Daughters: Christine de Pizan as Reader of Male Chivalric Orders and Traditions of Clergie in the Dit de la Rose," in *Reinterpreting Christine de Pizan*, 63–76; Kevin Brownlee, "Discourses of the Self: Christine de Pizan and the *Rose*," *Romanic Review*, 79, no.1 (1988): 199–221; and Charity Cannon Willard, "Christine de Pizan and the Order of the Rose," in *Ideals for Women in the Works of Christine de Pizan*, ed. Diane Bornstein (Kalamazoo, MI: University of Michigan Press, 1981), 51–67.

33. As mentioned before, "Christine and her contemporaries dated the beginning of the year at the movable feast of Easter, following a practice introduced more than two centuries earlier by King Philip Augustus. Since she dates the dinner party and the time of composition in January and February, respectively, for her the year would still be 1401" (*Poems of Cupid*, 129). The actual date of composition is 1402.

34. It cannot be proven that such an order actually existed. Conversely, we can say with certainty that similar chivalric orders did indeed exist, such as Marshal Boucicaut's Order of the White Lady on the Green Shield of which Guillaume de Tignonville was a member and cofounder. We can therefore safely say that Christine used an existing cultural practice for the fictive framework of her poem.

35. The color white is a reference to Diana's chastity.

36. Again, Christine takes advantage of a propitious moment for proclaiming female honor by chosing this saint's day for the real or fictitious moment of composition of her poem.

37. Pierre-Yves Badel offers two hypotheses on the date of composition of the *Jardin amoureux*, which are May 14, 1402, or July/August 1401. See his article, "Pierre d'Ailly, *auteur du Jardin amoureux*," *Romania* 97 (1976): 369–81.

38. Msgr. Glorieux included the *Jardin* in his edition of Jean Gerson's *Oeuvres complètes de Jean Gerson,* 7 vols. (Tournai: Desclée, 1960), 1:144–54.

39. See Badel, "Pierre d'Ailly." For a detailed analysis of the commonalities between Pierre d'Ailly's and Jean de Meun's works, see Badel, "Pierre d'Ailly,." I am gratelul to Renate Blumenfeld-Kosinski for sending me her article "Jean Gerson and the *Debate on the Romance of the Rose*" (in *The Companion to Jean Gerson,* ed. Brian Patrick McGuire, Leiden: Brill, 2006), 317–56, where she also discusses this topic. I have used Msgr. Glorieux's edition of the text. The translation is my own.

40.   Guillaume de Lorris's Garden of Delight has been replaced here with the merciful garden or the Garden of Mercy.

41.   The sentence in the original reads: "Or oez comment..." which is also incomplete. For authenticity's sake, I left it incomplete in the translation also.

42.   This is a proverb from the Book of Proverbs (24: 16): "Le juste pèche sept fois par jour."

43.   Lady Idleness is the gatekeeper in the *Roman* who holds a mirror as a symbol of her allegorical meaning.

44.   Parallel to the *Roman* are the merry dancers who are joined by Lover after he enters the garden.

45.   The allegories depicted on Guillaume Lorris's garden wall, on the other hand, are sins and negative attributes such as Hatred, Felony, Villainy, Avarice, Envy, Sadness, and so forth.

46.   These are all elements which are also described in the *Roman* when the lover walks through the Garden of Delight.

47.   The apples in the *Roman* are bright red pomegranates.

48.   In the *Roman*, Lover is pierced by five arrows which the god of Love shoots in order to make him succumb to his loyal service.

49.   The allusion here is clearly to the fountain of Narcissus in Guillaume's *Roman*. At the same time we are also reminded of the beautiful fountain from which three jets emanate in Jean de Meun's continuation.

50.   The symbolic number has been changed from three to seven in order to account for the prominence of the number seven in the Catholic doctrine (for example, the seven sacraments).

51.   The birds' song is depicted in great detail in Guillaume de Lorris's *Roman*.

52.   This chapter is of course the most obvious criticism of Jean de Meun's parallel doctrine, his "art of love."

53.   This is reminiscent of the famous couplet "Ce est li romanz de la rose/Ou l'art d'amours est tout enclose."

54.   This advice is an almost literal quote of Christine de Pizan's urgent counsel in her letter to Pierre Col, see chap. 3.7, 274, repeated by Jean Gerson in his treatise against the *Roman*, see chap. 4.5, 443.

55.   This treatise was published on May 18, 1402. It is extant in a total of eight manuscripts:
      a. BN fr. 1563, fols 180ro-185ro—base manuscript
      b. BN fr. 1797
      c. BN fr. 3887
      d. BN fr. 24839
      e. BN fr. 1556
      f. BN Nouv. Acq. Fr. 10.059
      g. Troyes, Bibliothèque municipale ms. 929
      h. Montpellier, Faculté de Médecine H 368
      See also, *Le débat*, 58–87.

56.   For further biographical information I refer to Diana E. Adams Smith, *Some French Works of Jean Gerson. An Introduction and Translation*, PhD diss. (University of South Carolina, October 1976). For excerpts from his sermons *Poenitemini*, see no. 10 of this chapter. I also refer to *The Companion to Jean Gerson*, ed. Brian Patrick McGuire (Leiden: Brill, 2006).

57.   The frequent mentioning of Lady Reason and the incessant attempt by Gerson to rehabilitate this allegory to the noble function which has been assigned to her by God is also the topic of his 149 line dialogue titled "Ecole de la raison" (see chap. 3 note 39).

58.   Goliards were wandering students and clerics famous for their satirical verses and poems in praise of drinking and debauchery.

59.   The Foolish Lover in this case is Jean de Meun himself.

60.   Pierre Col in his reply to Christine de Pizan and Jean Gerson quotes this sentence again (see 317 of this chapter) which is taken up, in turn, by Christine in her letter to Pierre (chap. 3.7, 149).

61.   Although the allegory of Eloquence Theologienne is feminine, the personal pronoun switches to the masculine "il."

62. In Seneca, *Ad Lucil.*, 15.94.42.

63. According to Eric Hicks, Gerson confuses Abelard's student and the famous Bérenger de Tours (†1098) (*Le débat*, 211). Gerson repeats this exemplum in his third sermon of the series *Poenitemini* (Contre la luxure) which he held on December 17, 1402: "Vous savez que office d'ennemy est nuire a autrui; et ce quiert luxure en mil manieres. Notez de Terquinius, et de ceulx qui se delitent mal mener petis enfans; et la question que il les doivent ramener, et comment. Et des confesseurs. Notez Berangier. A la parfin c'est certain qu'elle fait ordes les voies de Dieu et puantes a aucuns ennemis, etc." [You know that it is the enemy's task to harm others and that is what lechery seeks to do in a thousand ways. Remember Tarquin and those who take evil pleasure in misleading little children; and the problem of how to bring them back. And of the confessors: Remember Bérengier; in the end it is certain that lechery tarnishes the ways of God and infects the enemy, etc.] (*Jean Gerson. Oeuvres complètes*, 7 vols., 2:825; my translation).

64. Quoted in Cicero, *De senect.*, 12.41: "Haec…locutum Archytam Nearchus Tarentinus…. "

65. See also *Poenitemini II* in *Oeuvres complètes*, 7.812: "Luxure mist en feu et flamme la belle cité de Troye la grande" [Lechery set the beautiful city of Troy the Great on fire and in flame] (my translation).

66. This is a reference to the speech of the Jealous Husband in the *Roman*: «Si feroit il, par foi, Lucrece,/Ja soit ce qu'el se soit occise/Pour ce qu'afforce l'avoit prise/Li filz au roi Tarquinius./ N'onc, ce dist Tytus Livius,/Mariz ne peres ne paranz/Ne li porent estre garanz/Pour pene que nus i meïst,/Que devant eus ne s'oceïst». [By my faith, he would do the same with Lucretia, even though she killed herself because King Tarquin's son took her by force. According to Titus Livius, no husband or father or relative could prevent her, in spite of all the trouble that they undertook, from killing herself in front of them] (my translation). Tarquinius Superbus was, in legend, the son or grandson of Tarquinius Priscus and son-in-law of Servius Tullius. Through a revolt against him Lucretia was raped by Tarquin's son Sextus. The Tarquin family was expelled from Rome, and the monarchy at Rome was abolished (509BC). Gerson repeats this exemplum in *Poenitimini III*, 7:825. This is a prominent exemplum to underline female virtue and strength and was already mentioned by Pierre Ceffons (chap. 1.D.1 and the anonymous author of the *Ménagier de Paris*, chap. 1.D.4). Christine de Pizan uses it in the *Livre de la cité des dames* for example (2:xliv).

67. "Corrumptus mores bonos colloquia mal" (Saint Paul, I Cor. 15:33). For the quote by Seneca, see *Poenitemini* 4. 213, this chapter: "Turpia ne dixeris."

68. These are references to examples cited by Jean de Meun.

69. Eric Hicks has identified this proverb as "En la queue gist le venin" with reference to the scorpion [The venom lies in the tail], in Langlois, *Proverbes communs*, no. 235 (*Le débat*, 213).

70. *Ars poetica*, 1–5.

71. Gerson's reference is to the Admonitio ut silentium in ecclesia proebeatur, sermon CCC, al. 26 ex. *Homilis* 50.

72. As pointed out by Eric Hicks, Gerson will repeat this double quote a few days later in his sermon *Videmus* (*Le débat*, 213).

73. Jean de Meun's alleged plagiarism of Alain de Lille *De planctu naturae* is a longstanding criticism of his work, see Winthrop Wetherbee, "The Literal and the Allegorical: Jean de Meun and the *De Planctu Naturae*," *Medieval Studies* 33 (1971): 264–91; and more recently, Friedrich Wolfzettel, "Jean de Meun, 'ancien' ou 'moderne'?" *Etudes médiévales* 1 (1999): 235–44.

74. Aesop's fable.

75. Hicks identifies the source of this anecdote as taken from Valerius Maximus, Fact. et dict. mem., 6. iii.Ext. 1: "Noluerunt enim ea liberorum suorum animos imbui, ne plus moribus noceret quam ingeniis prodesset." Christine makes a very similar allusion in her *Fais et bonnes meurs* (see *Le débat*, 213–14).

76. *De Officiis*, 1.35.126–28.

77. Ham, one of Noah's sons, fell victim to his father's drunkenness. The disrespect it provoked in his son caused the father to lay a curse on Ham's son Canaan.

78. See Christine McWebb, "Heresy and Debate: Reading the *Roman de la Rose*," *Aevum* 77 (2003): 545–56.
79. This is a switch from *Reason* to "il," that is, the author/narrator.
80. Since this letter is not included in manuscript Harley 4431, I used BN fr. 1563 as my base manuscript, as did Eric Hicks in *Le débat* (88–112). In BN fr. 1563, this letter occupies fols 185ro–190vo.
81. See no. 9 of this chapter. See also Eric Hicks's arguments in *Le débat*, xlix.
82. Chap. 3.7.
83. See chap. 3, n. 39.
84. As indicated by Hicks, Gerson was appointed chancellor of Notre-Dame de Paris on July 13, 1395 which would make Pierre Col, who took the oath on June 21, 1389, his colleague in the chapter (*Le débat*, 216).
85. For a detailed listing and analysis of Jean Gerson sermons, I refer to Louis Mourin, *Jean Gerson. Prédicateur français* (Bruges, Belgium: De Tempel, 1952). The reference here is to the series of sermons entitled *Poenitemini* which the Chancellor pronounced in December,1402.
86. See note 66.
87. All translations of passages from the *Roman de la rose* are my own.
88. This must be a proverbial expression which I have not been able to identify.
89. See chap. 3, n. 24.
90. Ars poet., 9–10: "Pictoribus atque poetis/quidlibet audendi simper fuit aequa potestas." Jean de Montreuil uses this same quote in letter 154, this chapter, no. 7.
91. OT 2 Sam., 11:12; 1 Kings 1:2: Husband of Bathsheba who was killed by David, Bathsheba's seducer.
92. According to Hicks, it was Theodore of Mopsueste who professed this opinion (*Le débat*, 218).
93. Sol. 30.d. Gerson quotes this passages also in his sermon *Videmus*: "Belle suer, je te diray, respond Raison. J'ai cherché par mer et par terre, par l'air et par le ciel et ay demandé a la terre se elle estoit mon Dieu...tout [s]'est escrié a haulte voix: Dieu nous a faiz; les ydolatres et les payens faillent; nous ne sommes point Dieu; querez le ailleurs et au dessus de nous." [Beautiful sister, I will tell you, replies Reason. I looked on water and on land, in the air and the sky and asked earth if she was my God...all cried out loud: God made us; saracens and pagans misguide us, we are not God. Search for him elsewhere and above us.] (Louis Mourin, *Six sermons*, 156; my translation) (see also *Le débat*, 219).
94. *Ep.* CXLVII, "Ad Sabinianum" (PL, vol 22.1203).
95. Well known inscription at the temple of Delphe (*And.* 61 "Ne quid nimis").
96. Aspasia was the mistress of the Athenian statesman Pericles and a vivid figure in Athenian society in the fifth century BC. Cicero, *Rhet.* 1.31–32, 51–52.
97. Born of a wealthy Athenian family, Xenophon grew up during the great war between Athens and Sparta (431–404 BC).
98. *Rhet.* 2.21 (1395b): "A maxim, as has been said, is an assertion of a generality, and people enjoy things said in general terms that they happen to assume ahead of time in a partial way; for example, if some one had met up with bad neighbors or children, he would accept a speaker's saying that nothing is worse than having neighbors...."
99. This is a reference to the speech of the Duenna in the *Roman de la rose*.
100. I was unable to identify the specific sermon.
101. One of Aesop's fables.
102. *Confessions*, 2.2.3.
103. This is a reference to Aesop's fable of the fox and the crow.
104. In other words, the Franciscans, the Dominicans, the Augustinians, and the Carmelites. For a full account of the quarrel which inspired the most virulent passages of False Seeming's discourse, see John Moorman, *A History of the Franciscan Order. From Its Origin to the Year 1517* (Oxford: Oxford University Press, 1968), 127–31; and Michel-Marie Dufeil, *Guillaume*

de Saint-Amour et la polémique universitaire parisienne, 1250–1259 (Paris: Picard, 1972).

105. De doctrina christiana 4.1.2: "Primo itaque expectationem legentium, qui forte me putant rhetorica daturum esse praecepta quae in scholis saecularibus et didici et docui, ista praelocutione cohibeo…."

106. *Opera,* 220–22., *Le débat*, 42–45.

107. No autograph manuscript exists of this edition. However, three manuscripts have been identified as reproducing its content fairly accurately: Paris, BN fr. 12779, Chantilly, Musée Condé, ms. 492–93 and BN fr. 604 (see *Le débat*, lviii).

108. "Le débat sur le Roman de la rose, suite," 205–206.

109. See in particular, "Le débat sur le Roman de la rose, suite," 207–210.

110. See chap.5, n. 29.

111. This phrase is often used by Cicero ("O tempora").

112. And., 937.

113. "os loquentium" Ps., 62. 12.

114. Livii sententiam. Ab urbe cond., 35.10. 5.

115. Sen., XVIII, 3 (letter to Boccaccio).

116. Unfortunately, I have not been able to identify this person.

117. It is extant only in BN fr. 1563. In *Le débat*, 152–54.

118. For the transcription I used the *Oeuvres complètes*, 2:65–70 as well as Paris, Bibliothèque Mazarine ms. 940, fols 131vo–134vo. In *Le débat*, 161–75.

119. For a selection of excerpts, see no. 10.

120. Pelagianism or Pelagian Heresy was a fifth-century Christian heresy taught by Pelagius (354–418), a monk and theologian, and his followers that stressed the essential goodness of human nature and the freedom of the human will. Pelagius was concerned about the slack moral standards among Christians, and he hoped to improve their conduct by his teachings. Rejecting the arguments of those who claimed that they sinned because of human weakness, he insisted that God made human beings free to choose between good and evil and that sin is a voluntary act committed by a person against God's law. Celestius, one of his disciples, denied the church's doctrine of original sin and the necessity of infant Baptism. Pelagianism was opposed by Saint Augustine. Condemned by two councils of African bishops in 416, and again at Carthage in 418, Pelagius and Celestius were finally excommunicated in 418. See *Saint Augustine's De nuptiis et concupiscencia*, 2.3.9.

121. I Cor. 13.12. See also Pierre Col's letter to Christine de Pizan and Jean Gerson where the former refers to Jean Gerson's sermons at the Place de Grève (no. 6, 311).

122. Ps., 13.1: "Corrupti sunt, et abominabiles facti sunt in studiis suis."

123. See Horace, Sat., 2.2.8–9.

124. Luc., 2.23.

125. Terence, Eun.61–63: "…incerta haec si tu postules/Ratione certa facere, nihilo plus ages/Quam si des operam ut cum ratione insanias."

126. Dist. Cat., 1.4.2.

127. Luc., 19.22.

128. For the transcription of these passages I used manuscript BN fr. 24842, fols 8vo–35vo, and *Oeuvres complètes*, 7:810–41, nos. 369–71. In *Le débat*, 178–85. They also appear in manuscript BN fr. 24840. For more information on codicology and the chronology and content of the sermons, I refer to Louis Mourin, *Jean Gerson. Prédicateur français,* in particular 138–47.

129. See for example chap. 1.D.2.

130. As identified by Eric Hicks, this is a reference to the Libellus de moribus attributed to Saint Martin of Braga (†580): "Turpia ne dixeris, paulatim enim pudor per verba discutitur" (*Le débat*, 231).

131. *Pol.*, 7.15.

132. See no. 5, this chapter n. 77.

133. Ibid., 285.

134. Ibid.
135. Ibid.
136. This is a reference to the first sermon in the series.
137. As explained by Eric Hicks in *Le débat,* 183–84.
138. *Opera*, 218–19, *Le débat*, 40–42.
139. In *Le débat*, xl.

Chapter Five

The Debate after the Debate
and French Humanism

That Christine de Pizan pursued her criticism of Jean de Meun's work well beyond 1402 is now commonplace.[1] In this chapter I have identified her explicit references to the *Roman* from 1403 beginning with the *Livre de la mutacion de Fortune* to about 1410. Laurent de Premierfait's *De casibus virorum illustrium* concludes my compilation projecting forward at the same time to a new current in French literary history which is the beginning of humanism.

A. Christine de Pizan—1403–13

1. 1403: Le livre de la mutacion de Fortune[2]

Part autobiography, part chronicle, part philosophical reflection on such issues as human destiny and divine predetermination versus free will, the *Livre de la mutacion de Fortune* is one of Christine's most influential works. Like several of her other texts, such as the *Chemin de lonc estude*, the *Epistre Othea,* or the *Avision-Cristine*, it recounts in pedagogical fashion the author's own history and that of the world and her adoptive country, France. Renate Blumenfeld-Kosinski describes it as follows: "we find a universal history, 'read' from the wall paintings in Fortune's castle and transmitted by Christine, prefaced by an allegorical version of Christine's own life and a moral evaluation of the different parts of society."[3] In the passage below, Christine warns her readers of corrupt advisers to the prince, and compares their dishonest practices to the allegory of False Seeming of Jean de Meun's *Roman.*

Text:

46rº	Croy qu'ici vi plusieurs pervers,
	Tout fussent ilz fourré de vairs,
	Et dont Dieu scet la conscience;
4	Mais, bien croy que grant escience
	Et malice porent avoir
	De trouver maniere d'avoir
	Finance; d'ou qu'elle venist,
8	N'en chaloit, mais qu'on la tenist.
	Et tout treuve l'en, es histoires
	De Romme autentiques et voires,
	Que ceulx de Romme conseillers,
12	Ou avoit de bons chevaliers,
	Povres communement estoient,
	Car a nullui le sien n'ostoient;
	Le bien commun leur souffisoit,
16	Mais au propre nul ne visoit.
	Et tant qu'ainsi les Rommains firent,
	Empires et regnes conquirent,
	Mais, tres qu'au bien propre tacherent,
20	Leurs plus grans honneurs estancherent.
	A ce ne prenoient pas garde
	Maint maulx conseiller, que feux arde!
	Dont je y vi de faulses gens
24	En grant honneur, plus diligens
	De propres prouffis acquerir
	Que des prouffis communs querir,
	Assimulans avoir vertus;
28	Les vi, n'estourdis, ne testus,
	Ains, par semblans, coys et rassis.
	Ha! Com grans coups donnoient cilz,
	Par leurs semblans couvers et faulx,
32	Enveloppez de grans deffaux,
	Et quel peril ambicieux
	Est que d'omme malicieux
	Et caut, qui proprement scet faindre,
36	Beau parler, coulourer et paindre!
	Se grant mauvaistié y habonde,
	C'est pour pervertir tout un monde
	A pou et royaumes et gens.
40	Qui se sçaroit, tant fust sachens,

Translation:

      I think that I saw many corrupt people,
      All covered in vair,
      Of whom God knows the scruples;

4   But, I surely think they will possess
      Great skill and ruse
      To find ways to
      Enrich themselves; where

8   They find wealth, they do not care,
      But they do care about holding on to it.
      The authentic and true
      Histories of Rome,[4]

12   Are full of this;
      That those who counseled Rome
      Or had good knights,
      Were commonly poor

16   Because they did not take themselves as exceptions.
      The common good sufficed
      And their own good they sought not.
      And the more the Romans did this

20   Conquering empires and reigns
      Yet as soon as they strove for their own good
      An end to their honor they put.
      Of this they did not take heed,

24   Of the many evil councillors: let fire torch them!
      There I saw many false people
      In great honor, more diligent
      To acquire their own profit

28   Than to seek the common good,
      Simulating virtue,
      I saw them, neither confused nor narrow-minded,
      But feigning coyness and skill.

32   Ha! The great blows they dealt,
      By means of their false cloaks[5]
      Enveloped in great faults;
      And what tempting peril

36   It is for a cunning and sly man
      Who knows how to feign astutely,
      To speak, adorn, and depict eloquently!
      Such great evil abounds there,

40   It could be enough to corrupt the whole world,

De tel cedicieur garder?
Je croy nul, a droit regarder,
Car trop a de soubtilz engins
44   En felons et d'agus engins.
Ne faut ja faindre faulx semblant,
Plus deceveur que lierre emblant,
Soubz Mendians ou Jacobins
48   Et freres qui vont en chappins,
Com fist Meun, jadis, ou *Rommant*
De la Rose, parlant d'amant,
Car ycy fu il plus perfaict
52   Le fauls semblant, en dit et fait,
Et trop plus perilleux, sans doubte,
Qu'en ceulx, qui ne se meslent goute
De gouvernements temporeulx,
56   Ains feroit on bien pou pour eulx;
Mais ceulx ci du fait se mesloient
Du gouvernement, ou mesloient,
Par leur tres faulses couvertures,
60   Des faulx contras et grans laidures,
Mais pour leur malice infinie,
Par qui ert gastee et honnie
Mainte personne, bien savoient
64   Leurs fais couvrir, car ilz faignoient
Que pour le mieulx trestout feïssent
46v°   Et que tout mal contrat heïssent.
Devant les princes se moustroient
68   Tieulx, mais les gens qui les hantoient,
Qui avoient a eulx a faire,
Sçavoient plus de leur affaire,
Car plumez, a tort, et a droit,
72   Y estoient, en tout endroit,
Sanz conscience et sanz regart
A pitié, en quelconque esgart.
Et pour ce qu'Escripture dit
76   (Ce que un proverbe ne desdit)
Que «l'en ne doit porter honneurs,
Fors a ceulx qui ont bonnes meurs»
Que cuidez vous qu'il me faisoit
80   Grant mal et qu'il me desplaisoit
Qu'il couvenoit grant honneur faire

And kingdoms and people.
Who would know to guard themselves,
From such seducers,
44   So clever are they?
No one, I think, to be exact,
For in felons there is too much
Skillful ability and sly wit.
48   No worse deceiver has there ever been
Than False Seeming,
Who was more deceiving than ranking ivy,
Among Mendicants and Jacobins,[6]
52   And friars who wear capes,
As Meun said a long time ago
In the *Romance of the Rose*, speaking of lovers.
For here False Seeming was more perfect
56   In word and deed,
And, without a doubt, much more perilous
Than those who do not interfere with
Worldly government.
60   Yet precious little would be done for them.
However, those who did meddle
In government, or
Through their deceptive camouflage,
64   In false agreements and great filth,
And for their unending ruses,
With which they have spoiled and dishonored
Many a person: They knew well
68   To cover their deeds, for they feigned,
And pretended, that it was for the good of all
And that they despised any foul agreement.
Before the princes they would feign
72   Thus, only those who pursued them,
Who had dealings with them,
Knew more of their affairs,
For crooks were here and there;
76   They were everywhere,
Without scruple or regard
Or pity for no one.
And the Scripture says
80   (Which a proverb does not deny)
That "one need honor no one

A ces gens de si faulx affaire,
Genous enclins a eulx parler,
84   Et « monseigneur» les appeller!
Et Dieu scet quel compte tenoient
Des povres gens, quant la venoient,
Pour quelque afaire qu'a eulx eussent!
88   Ne sembloit pas que ilz les deussent
Nez tant seulement regarder!
De leur besongnes retarder
N'estoient lent un an ou .II.,
92   Par quoy je y en vi maint d'eulx
Les poursuivre, a moult grant hachee,
Pour ce qu'avoient empeschee
Leur chevance; ne a delivre
96   N'en pouoient estre delivre;
Dont faisoient trotter aprés
Eulx ces povres, un an ou pres.
Et quant leur veoye telz meurs,
100   Disoye qu'a joennes, n'a meurs,
Pleust a Dieu que l'en ne portast
Honneur, fors a ceulx qu'on notast
Estre vertueux et sanz triches,
104   Et non mie ainsi aux plus riches!
Si mettroit chacun peine a estre
Virtueux, pour haulcier son estre.

But one of good morals."[7]
What think you of the great pain
84   It caused me, and how it displeased me
That such great honor was often expressed
For those of false dealings,
Knees bent when people spoke to them,
88   And they were called "Sir"!
And God knows what regard
They had for poor people, when they saw them coming
For some affair!
92   It seemed that they only had to look at them:
They would delay their tasks,
Fall behind by a year or two,
Which is why I saw many of them
96   Chasing the poor with enormous axes,
Because they had hindered
Their profit: since they did not deliver,
They themselves could purchase nothing.
100   So they made these poor people
Trot after them, one year or almost.
And when you see such morals,
Tell the young people: morals these are not.
104   It would please God not to honor them,
Except those whom one knows
To be of virtue and without trickery,
And not only because they are the wealthiest!
108   If only all people made an effort to be
Virtuous, in order to improve their situation!

2. 1404–1405: *Le livre de la cité des dames*[8]

Probably the most popular and well-studied of Christine's prose works, the *Livre de la cité des dames* has long been read as a continuing effort by the author to refute Jean de Meun's controversial work.[9] There are two explicit references to the *Roman de la rose* (excerpts 1, 2), both of which attest to the lively anti-feminine discourse taking place during and before Christine's lifetime. I have included excerpt 3 because of its succinct, albeit implicit, summary of the misogynist discourse reminiscent of the discourse of the Jealous Husband in Jean de Meun's *Roman*. Although excerpt 4 does not mention the *Roman de la rose*, Lady Righteousness reminds Christine and the reader that she had already clearly voiced her opinions on the matter in the *Epistre au dieu d'Amours* as well as in the *Debate Epistles*.

Text:

Book 1, Chapter 2

291r°   Ci dit Cristine comment .iij. dames lui apparurent et comment celle
        qui estoit devant l'arraisonna premiere et la reconforta d'un desplai-
        sir que elle avoit.
                En celle dolente pensee ainsi que je estoie, la teste bais-
5   see comme personne honteuse, les yeulx plains de larmes, tenant
        ma main soubz ma joe accoudee sus le pommel de ma chayere,
        soubdainement sus mon giron vi dessendre un ray de lumiere si
        comme se le souleil fust, et je, qui en lieu obscur estoie ou quel, a
        celle heure, souleil royer ne peust, tressailli. Adoncques si comme
10   se je fusse resveillee de somme et dreçant la teste pour regarder dont
        tel lueur venoit, vi devant moy, tout en estant, .iij. dames couron-
        nees de tres souveraine reverence, desquelles la resplandeur de leurs
        cleres faces enluminoit moy mesmes et toute la place. Lors se je fus
        esmerveillee, nul nel demand, considerant sur moy l'uys clos et elles
15   la venues. Doubtant que ce feust aucune fantasie pour me tempter,
        fis en mon front le signe de la croix, remplie de tres grant paour.
                Adonc celle, qui premiere des trois estoit, en sousriant, me
291v°   prist ainsi a arraisonner: «Fille chere ne t'espouvantes, // car nous
        ne sommes mie cy venues pour ton contraire, ne faire aucun en-
20   combrier, ains pour toy consoler comme piteuses de ta turbacion et
        te giter hors de l'ignorance, qui tant avugle ta mesmes congnois-
        sance que tu deboutes de toy ce que tu ne scez de certaine science,
        et ajoustes foy a ce que tu ne scez ne vois ne congnois autrement
        fors par pluralité d'oppinions estranges. Tu ressembles le fol, dont
25   la truffe parle, qui en dormant au molin fu revestu de la robe d'une
        femme et au resveiller, pour ce que ceulx qui le moquoyent lui

Translation:

Christine describes how three ladies appeared to her and how the
one who was in front spoke first and comforted her in her pain.

    So occupied with these painful thoughts, my head bowed in
shame, my eyes filled with tears, leaning my cheek on my hand, el-

5   bow propped on the pommel of my chair's armrest, I suddenly saw
a ray of light fall on my lap, as though it were the sun. I shuddered
then, as if wakened from sleep, for I was sitting in a shadow where
the sun could not have shone at that hour. And as I lifted my head
to see where this light was coming from, I saw three crowned ladies

10   standing before me, and the splendor of their bright faces shone on
me and throughout the entire room. Now no one would ask whether
I was surprised, for my doors were shut and they had still entered.
Fearing that some phantom had come to tempt me and filled with
great fright, I made the Sign of the Cross on my forehead.[10]

15   Then she who was the first of the three smiled and began to
speak, "Dear daughter, do not be afraid, for we have not come here
to harm or trouble you but to console you, for we have taken pity
on your distress, and we have come to bring you out of the ignorance which so blinds your own intellect that you shun what you

20   know for a certainty and believe what you do not know or see or
recognize except by virtue of many strange opinions. You resemble
the fool in the prank who was dressed in women's clothes while
he slept; because those who were making fun of him repeatedly
told him he was a woman, he believed their false testimony more

25   readily than the certainty of his own identity. Fair daughter, have
you lost all sense? Have you forgotten that when fine gold is tested

tesmoignoient que femme estoit, crut mieulx leur faulx dis que la
certaineté de son estre. Comment, belle fille, qu'est ton sens de-
venu? As tu doncques oublié que le fin or s'espreuve en la fournase
30   qui ne se change ne meut de ses vertus, ains plus affine de tant plus
est martelé et demené en diverse façons? Ne scez tu que les tres
meilleurs choses sont les plus debatues et les plus arguees? Se tu
veulx aviser mesmement aux plus haultes choses qui sont les ydees,
c'est assavoir les choses celestielles, regardes se les tres plus grans
35   philosophes qui ayent esté que tu argues contre ton mesmes sexe en
ont point determiné faulx et au contraire du vray et se ilz reppunent
l'un l'autre et reprennent, si comme tu mesmes l'as veu ou livre
Methaphisique, la ou Aristote redargue et reprent leurs oppinions
et recite semblablement de Platon et d'autres. Et nottes derechef se
40   saint Augustin et autres docteurs de l'Eglise ont point repris mesmement Aristote en aucunes pars, tout soit il dit le prince des philosophes et en qui philosophie naturelle et morale fu souverainement.
Et il semble que tu cuides que toutes les paroles des philosophes
soient article de foy et que ilz ne puissent errer. Et des poetes dont
45   tu parles, ne scez tu pas bien que ilz ont parlé en plusieurs choses
en maniere de fable et se veulent aucunefois entendre au contraire
de ce que leurs diz demonstrent? Et les peut on prendre par une
figure de grammaire qui se nomme *antifrasis* qui s'entent, si comme
tu scez, si comme on diroit tel est mauvais, c'est a dire que il est
50   bon, aussi a l'opposite. Si te conseille que tu faces ton prouffit de
leurs dis et que l'entendes ainsi, queque fust leur entente es lieux ou
ilz blasment les femmes. Et par aventure que cellui homme qui se
nomma Matheolus en son livre, l'entendi ainsi, car maintes choses
y a lesquelles qui a la letre tenir les vouldroit, ce seroit pure heresie.
55   Et la vituperacion que dit, non mie seulement lui, mais d'autres et
mesmement le *Rommant de la Rose,* ou plus grant foy est adjoustee
pour cause de l'auctorité de l'aucteur de l'ordre de mariage, qui est
saint estat digne et de Dieu ordené, c'est chose clere et prouvee par
l'experience que le contraire est vray du mal qu'ilz proposent et
60   dient estre en ycellui estat a la grant charge et couple des femmes.
Car ou fu oncques trouvé le mari qui tel maistrise souffrist avoir a sa
femme que elle eust loy de tant lui dire de villenies et d'injures
292r° comme yceulx mettent que femmes // dient? Je croy que quoyque tu
en ayes veu en escript que oncques de nul de tes yeulx n'en veys si
65   sont mençonges trop mal coulourees. Si te dis en concluant, chere
amie, que simplece t'a meue a la present oppinion. Or te reviens a
toy mesmes, reprens ton sens et plus ne te troubles pour tieulx fanfelues, car saches que tout mal dit si generaument des femmes empire
les diseurs, non pas elles mesmes ».

in the furnace, it does not change or vary in strength but becomes purer the more it is hammered and handled in different ways? Do you not know that the best things are the most debated and the most
30 discussed? If you wish to consider the question of the highest form of reality, which consists in ideas or celestial substances, consider whether the greatest philosophers who have lived and whom you support against your own sex have ever resolved whether ideas are false and contrary to the truth. Notice how these same philosophers
35 contradict and criticize one another, just as you have seen in the *Metaphysics* where Aristotle takes their opinions to task and speaks similarly of Plato and other philosophers. And note, moreover, how even Saint Augustin and the Doctors of the Church have criticized Aristotle, in certain passages, although he is known as the prince of
40 philosophers in whom both natural and moral philosophy attained their highest level. It also seems that you think that all the words of the philosophers are articles of faith, that they could never be wrong. As far as the poets of whom you speak are concerned, do you not know that they spoke on many subjects in a fictional way[11] and that
45 often they mean the contrary of what their words openly say? One can interpret them according to the figure of grammar called *antiphrasis*, which means, as you know, that if you call something bad, in fact, it is good, and also vice versa. Thus I advise you to profit from their works and to interpret them in the manner in which they are
50 intended in those passages where they attack women. Perhaps this man, who called himself Matheolus in his own book, intended it in such a way, for there are many things which, if taken literally, would be pure heresy.[12] As for the attack against the estate of marriage which is a holy estate, worthy and ordained by God—made not only
55 by Matheolus but also by others and even by the *Romance of the Rose* where greater credibility is averred because of the authority of its author, it is evident and proven by experience that the contrary of the evil which they posit and claim to be found in this estate through the obligation and fault of women is true. For where has the
60 husband ever been found who would allow his wife to have authority to abuse and insult him as a matter of course, as these authorities maintain?[13] I believe that, regardless of what you might have read, you will never see such a husband with your own eyes, so badly colored are these lies. Thus, in conclusion, I tell you, dear friend, that
65 simplemindedness has prompted you to hold such an opinion. Come back to yourself, recover your senses, and do not trouble yourself anymore over such absurdities. For you know that any evil spoken of women so generally only hurts those who say it, not women themselves."

Text:

Book 2, Chapter 25

334r°   Dit Cristine a Dame Droiture contre ceulx qui dient que femmes ne
        scevent riens celer, et la responce que lui fait est de Porcia, fille de
        Catho.

                «Dame, je congnois certainement maintenant, et autrefoiz l'ay
5   apperceu, que grant est l'amour et la foy que maintes femmes ont eu
        et ont a leurs maris. Pour ce je me donne merveille d'un lengage que
        cuert assez communement entre les hommes et mesmement maistre
        Jehan de Meun trop fort l'afferme en son *Rommant de la Rose*, et
        autres aucteurs aussi le font, que homme ne die a sa femme chose
10   que il vueille celer et que femmes ne se scevent taire».
        Responce: «Amie chiere, tu dois savoir que toutes femmes ne sont
        mie sages et semblablement ne sont les hommes, par quoy se un
334v°   homme a aucun scavoir, // il doit bien voirement aviser quel sens sa
        femme a et quel bonté, ains qu'il lui die gaires chose qu'il vueille
15   celer, car peril y peut avoir. Mais quant un homme sent qu'il a une
        femme bonne, sage et discrete, il n'est ou monde chose plus fiable
        ne qui tant le peust reconforter.
                «Et que femmes fussent si pou secretes comme yceulx veulent
        dire, et ancore a propos de femmes amantes leurs maris, n'ot mie
20   celle oppinion jadis a Romme le noble homme Brutus, mari de
        Porcia. Celle noble dame Porcia fu fille de Cathon le Mendre qui
        neveu estoit au grant Catho. Son dit mari, qui la senti tres sage,
        secrete et chaste, lui dist l'entencion que il avoit, lui et Cassien,
        qui estoit un autre noble homme de Romme, de occire Julius Cesar
25   au conseil, laquelle chose la sage dame, avisant le grant mal qui
        en vendroit, de tout sa puissance lui desconseilla et desloua. Et du
        soucy de ceste chose fu a si grant meschef que toute nuit dormir
        ne pot. Le matin venu, quant Brutus yssoit de sa chambre pour aler
        parfournir son emprise, la dame, qui moult voulentiers l'en destour-
30   nast, prist le rasoir du barbier, si comme pour trancher les ongles et
        le laissa cheoir. Puis fist maniere de le reprendre et tout de gré le se
        ficha en la main, par quoy ses femmes, qui navree la virent, si fort
        s'escrierent que Brutus retourna. Et quant bleciee la vit il la blasma
        et dist que ce n'estoit mie son office de ouvrer de resouer, mais au
35   barbier. Et elle lui respondi qu'elle ne l'avoit pas fait si follement
        comme il pensoit, car ce avoit elle fait tout de gré pour essayer com-
        ment elle se occiroit se l'emprise qu'il avoit faicte venoit mal pour
        lui. Mais cellui ne s'en laissa oncques et ala et occist tantost apres,

Translation:

Christine speaks to Lady Rectitude against those men who say that
women do not know how to conceal anything. The response made
by Lady Rectitude deals with Portia, Daughter of Cato.

My lady, now I know for certain what I had suspected ear-
5   lier, that many women have shown, and show, great love and faith
toward their husbands. For this reason I am amazed at the opinion
which circulates quite commonly among men—even Master Jean de
Meung argues strongly (too strongly in fact!) in his *Romance of the
Rose,* along with other authors as well—that a man should not tell
10   his wife anything which he wishes to conceal and that women are
unable to be silent."

"Dear friend," she replied, "you must know that all women are
not wise—nor all men, for that matter—so that if a man possesses
such wisdom, he must seriously consider what sense and what
15   goodness his wife has before he tells her anything which he might
want to hide, for he may be running a risk. But when a man feels
he has a good, wise, and discreet wife, there is nothing in the world
more trustworthy, nor is there anyone who could comfort him more.

"The noble Roman Brutus, husband of Portia, never shared the
20   opinion that women are as indiscreet as these men claim and that
women love their husbands so little. This noble lady Portia was the
daughter of Cato the Younger, who was the nephew of Cato the Elder. Her husband, who felt that she was quite wise and chaste, told
her of the intention which he and Cassius, another Roman noble-
25   man, had to kill Julius Caesar in the senate. Considering the great
evil which would arise from this action, the wise lady tried with all
her might to dissuade him and advise him against the deed. Because of her worry over this matter, she was so upset that she could
not sleep all night long. When morning came, Brutus was leaving
30   his room to carry out his plan, and Portia, who would have gladly
turned him away from the deed, took a barber's razor, as if to cut her
nails, dropped it, and then as she pretended to pick it up, she delib-
erately struck herself in the hand with it, whereupon her women servants, seeing her wounded, cried out so loudly that Brutus returned.
35   When he saw her wounded, he reproached her and remarked that it
was not her office to use a razor, but a barber's. She replied that she
had not acted as foolishly as he thought, but had done so deliber-
ately to try out a way to kill herself if his plan miscarried. Neverthe-

40

45

entre lui et Cassien, Julius Cesar. Mais ilz en furent exillez et en fu
puis occis Brutus, nonobstant qu'il s'en fust fuy hors de Romme.
Mais quant Porcia sa bonne femme sceut sa mort, tant fu grande
sa douleur qu'elle renonça a joye et vie. Et pour ce que on lui tolli
couteaulx et toute chose dont occire se peust, car on veoit bien ce
que faire vouloit, elle ala au feu et prist charbons ardans et les avala,
et ainsi se ardi et estaigni. Et par celle voye, qui fu la plus estrange
dont oncques autre mourust, fina la noble Porcia».

less, Brutus did not allow himself to be dissuaded, and departed.
40 Shortly afterward he killed Caesar, who stood between Cassius and himself. All the same, both were exiled; then Brutus was killed, although he had fled Rome. When his good wife Portia learned of his death, her grief was so great that she abjured both joy and life. And since all knives or anything sharp with which she could kill
45 herself had been taken from her, for it was obvious what she wanted to do, she went to the fire, took burning coals, swallowed them, and burned herself to death. In such a strange way—the strangest way in which anyone ever died—the noble Portia ended her life."

Text:

Book 2, Chapter 47

343v° Preuves contre ce que on dit de l'inconstance des femmes, parle
      Cristine et puis Droitture lui respont de l'inconstance et fragilité
      d'aucuns empereurs.
                 «Dame, certes, merveilleuse constance, force et vertu et
5   fermeté me racontez de femmes. Que pourroit on plus dire des plus
      fors hommes qui oncques furent? Et toutevoyes, sur tous les vices
      que hommes, et mesmement les livres, dient estre en femmes, crient
      tous d'une voix sur elles que variables et inconstans sont, muables
      et legieres et de fraisle courage, flechissans comme enfans, ne qu'il
10   n'y a aucune fermeté. Sont doncques ces hommes si constans que
      varier leur soit comme hors de tout leur usage ou pou commun, qui
344r° tant accusent femme de muableté // et d'inconstance? Et certes, se
      ilz ne sont bien fermes, trop leur est lait d'accuser autrui de leur
      mesmes vice ou d'i demander la vertu que ilz ne scevent avoir».
15   Responce: «Belle doulce amie, n'as tu pas tousjours ouy
      dire que le fol apperçoit trop bien la petite bucherie en la face de
      son voisin, mais il ne se donne de garde du grant tref qui lui pent
      a l'ueil? Si te monstreray grant contradicion en ce que les hom-
      mes tant dient de la variacion et inconstance des femmes. Il est
20   ainsi que tous generaument afferment que femmes par nature sont
      moult fresles. Et puisque ilz accusent de fragilité les femmes, il est
      a presupposer que ilz se reputent estre constans ou, a tout le moins,
      que les femmes ne le soient pas si comme eulx. Et il est voir, toute-
      voyes, que ilz demandent aux femmes trop plus grant constance que
25   ilz mesmes ne scevent avoir, car eulx qui se dient tant estre fors et
      de noble condicion, ne se pevent tenir de cheoir en plusieurs tres
      grans deffaulx et pechez, non mie tous par ignorence, mais par pure
      malice, ayant congnoissance que ilz mesprennent. Mais de tout
      ce ilz s'excusent et dient que c'est humaine chose que de pecher,
30   mais quant il avient que aucunes femmes cheent en aucune deffail-
      lance (et dont eulx mesmes sont cause par leur grant pourchas et de
      longue main), adonc c'est toute fragilité et inconstance, selon leurs
      diz. Mais comme il me semble a droit juger, puis que tant fraisles
      les reputent, ilz deussent aucunement supporter leur fragilité et non
35   pas reputer a elles estre grant crisme ce que ilz tiennent a eulx estre
      petit deffault. Car il n'est tenu en loy ne trouvee en nulle escripture
      que il leur loise a pecher, ne que aux femmes ne que vice leur soit
      plus excusable. Mais de fait ilz se donnent tele auctorité que ilz ne

Translation:

> Refutation of the inconstancy of women. Christine speaks, and then Rectitude answers her regarding the inconstancy and weakness of certain emperors.
>
> "My lady, you have given me a remarkable account of the marvel-
> 5 ous constancy, strength, endurance, and virtue of women. What more could one say about the strongest men who have lived? Men, especially writing in books, vociferously and unanimously claim that women in particular are fickle and inconstant, changeable and flighty, weak-hearted, compliant like children, and lacking all stam-
> 10 ina. Are the men who accuse women of so much changeableness and inconstancy themselves so unwavering that change for them lies outside the realm of custom or common occurrence? Of course, if they themselves are not that firm, then it is truly despicable for them to accuse others of their own vice or to demand a virtue which they
> 15 do not themselves know how to practice."
>
> She replied, "Fair sweet friend, have you not heard the say-
> ing that the fool can clearly see the mote in his neighbor's eye but pays no attention to the beam hanging out of his own eye? Let me point out to you the contradiction in what these men say concern-
> 20 ing the variability and inconstancy of women: since they all gener-
> ally accuse women of being delicate and frail by nature, you would assume that they think that they are constant, or, at the very least, that women are less constant then they are. Yet they demand more constancy from women than they themselves can muster, for these
> 25 men who claim to be so strong and of such noble condition are un-
> able to prevent themselves from falling into many, even graver faults and sins, not all of them out of ignorance, but rather out of pure malice, knowing well that they are in the wrong. All the same, they excuse themselves for this by claiming it is human nature to sin.
> 30 When a few women lapse (and when these men themselves, through their own strivings and their own power, are the cause), then as far as these men are concerned, it is completely a matter of fragility and inconstancy. It seems to me right, nevertheless, to conclude—since they claim women are so fragile—that these men should be some-
> 35 what more tolerant of women's weaknesses and not hold something to be a crime for women which they consider only a peccadillo for themselves. For the law does not maintain, nor can any such written opinion be found that permits them and not women to sin, that their

40   veulent supporter les femmes, ains leur font et dient, plusieurs en y
     a moult d'oultrages et de griefs, ne ilz ne les daignent reputer fortes
     et constans quant elles endurent leurs durs oultrages. Et ainsi a tous
     propos veulent avoir les hommes le droit pour eulx et les .ij. bous de
     la couroie. Et de ce as tu assez souffisamment parlé en ton *Epistre*
     du Dieu d'Amours.

45   «Mais a ce que tu m'as demandé se les hommes sont tant fors
     et tant constans que ilz ayent cause de blasmer autrui d'inconstance,
     se tu regardes depuis les aages et temps ancians jusques aujourd'uy,
     je te di que par les livres et par ce que tu en as veu en ton aage et tous
     les jours peus veoir aux yceulx, non mie es simples hommes ne de bas
50   estat. Mais des plus grans tu pourras veoir et congnoistre la perfeccion,
     la force, et la constance qui y est, voire generaument en la plus grant
     partie, combien que il en soit de sage, constans et fors, et il en est bien
     besoing.

          «Et se tu veulx que je t'en donne preuves et de pieça et du
55   temps d'ores, pour ce que, ainsi que se es courages des hommes
     ne eust aucune inconstance ne varieté, ilz accusent tant les femmes
     de cellui vice, regardes es estas des plus poissans princes et des
     greigneurs hommes, qui est chose impartinent plus que es aultres.
344v° Que te puis je dire des imperiaulx? Je te // demande ou fu oncques
60   courage de femme tant fraisle, tant paoureux ne si malostru ne
     moins constant que fu cellui de l'empereur Claudien? Il estoit tant
     variable que tout quanque il ordenoit a une heure, il despeçoit a
     l'autre, ne quelconques fermeté n'estoit trouvee en sa parole. Ils
     s'accordoit a tous conseulx. Il fist occire sa femme par sa folie et
65   cruaulté, et puis au soir demanda pourquoy elle ne se aloit coucher.
     Et a ses famillers, a qui il avoit fait trancher les testes, manda que ilz
     se venissent jouer avecques lui. Cestui estoit tant de chetif courage
     que adés il trembloit ne de nul ne se fioit. Que t'en diroie? Toutes
     maleurtez de meurs et de courage furent en ce chetif empereur. Mais
70   a quoy te dis je de cestui? Fu il seul en l'empire seant plain de tel
     fragilité? Thibere l'empereur, de combien valut il mieulx? Toute in-
     constance, toute varieté, toute lubrieté, n'estoit elle en lui plus qu'il
     n'est trouvé de nulle femme»?

40   vice is more excusable. In fact these men allow themselves liberties
      which they are unwilling to tolerate in women and thus they—and
      they are many—perpetrate many insults and outrages in word and
      deed. Nor do they deign to repute women strong and constant for
      having endured such men's harsh outrages. In this way men try in
      every question to have the right on their side—they want to have it

45   both ways! You yourself have quite adequately discussed this prob-
      lem in your *Epistre au Dieu d'Amour*.

         But as for your question whether men are so strong and so
      constant that they are justified in accusing others of inconstancy, if
      you consider, starting with wise men in Antiquity up to the present,

50   I can tell you that, from books and from what you have seen in your
      own time and what you can see every day with your own eyes, not
      in simple men nor in those of low estate but in the most prominent,
      indeed, generally in the majority of them, you will be able to ob-
      serve their perfection, strength, and constancy and to see how many

55   wise, constant, and strong men there are and how great the need for
      them is.

         "And if you want me to give you proof, from the past and
      present, of why they accuse women so often of this vice, as well
      as whether inconstancy or fickleness are found in men's hearts,

60   consider the state of the most powerful princes and greatest men
      which is more shameless than that of others. What can I say about
      the emperors? Let me ask you where there was ever a woman's
      heart so frail, so fearful, so utterly vulgar, and so inconstant as
      that of Emperor Claudius?[14] He was so changeable that he would

65   countermand orders which he had given an hour before, nor was he
      consistent in his pronouncements. He could agree to every bit of
      advice. In his madness and cruelty he had his wife killed, and that
      same evening asked why she had not come to bed. And he would
      summon retainers whom he had had beheaded to come and enter-

70   tain him. He was so weakhearted that he constantly shook with fear
      and he trusted no one. What more can I tell you about him? Every
      misfortune of mores and emotions were combined in this servile
      emperor. But why am I telling you about him? Was he the only one
      filled with such weakness who ever ruled over the empire? Was the

75   emperor Tiberius any better?[15] Were not inconstancy, fickleness, and
      lust more clearly apparent in him than in any woman whatsoever?"

Text:

Book 2. Chapter 54

351r°   Demande Cristine a Droiture se c'est voir ce que plusieurs hommes
        dient que si pou soit de femmes loyalles en la vie amoureuse, et la
        response de Droiture.

             En procedant oultre, je, Cristine, dis derechef ainsi «Dame, or
5   passons oultre ycestes questions, et yssant un petit hors des ter-
        mez, continuez jusques ycy. Moult voulentiers vous feroie aucunes
        demandes, se ja savoie que ennuyer ne vous en deust, pour ce que la
        matiere sur quoy je parleroie, quoyque la chose soit fondee sur loy
        de nature, yst aucunement hors de l'atrempement de raison».
10   Et celle a moy respondi: «Amie, dis ce que il te plaira, car le
        disciple qui pour apprendre demande au maistre ne doit estre repris
        se il enqiuert de toutes choses».
             «Dame, il cuert au monde une loy naturelle des hommes aux
        femmes et des femmes aux hommes, non mie loy faicte par es-
15   tablissement de gens, mais par inclination charnelle, par laquelle ilz
        s'entreaiment de tres grant et enforciee amour par une fole plai-
        sance, et si ne scevent a quelle cause ne pourquoy tele amour l'un de
        l'autre en eulx se fiche. Et en ycelle amour, qui est assez comune et
        que on appelle la vie amoureuse, dient communement les hommes
20   que femmes, quoy que elles promettent, y sont moult pou arrestees
        en un lieu et de pou d'amour et a merveilles faulses et faintes, et
        que tout ce leur vient de la legiereté de leur courage. Et entre les
        autres aucteurs qui de ce les accusent, Ovide, en son livre *De l'art
        d'amours*, leur donne moult grant charge. Et dit cellui Ovide, et
25   semblablement les autres, quant assez ont blasmees sur celles cho-
        ses les femmes, que ce qu'ilz en mettent en leurs livres, tant des
        meurs decevables d'elles comme leurs mauvaistiez, que ilz le font
351v°pour // le bien publique et commun, adfin de aviser les hommes de
        leurs cautelles pour mieulx les eschever, si comme du serpent mucié
30   soubz l'erbe. Si vous plaise, chiere dame, m'apprendre de ceste
        chose le vray».
             Responce: «Amie chere, quant est ad ce qu'ilz dient que si
        decevables soient, ne scay a quoy plus t'en diroie, car toy mesmes
        as assez souffisamment traitié la matiere tant contre cellui Ovide,
35   comme contre autres, en ton *Epistre du dieu d'amours* et es *Epistres
        sus le 'Rommant de la Rose'*. Mais sur le point que tu m'as touchié
        que ilz dient que pour le bien commun le firent, je monstreray que
        pour ce ne fust ce mie, et voycy la raison: autre chose n'est bien

Translation:

Christine asks Rectitude whether what many men say is true, that so few women are faithful in their love lives; and Rectitudes's answer:

Proceeding further, I, Christine, again spoke, "My lady, let us now move on to other questions and for a short while go beyond

5   the topics developed up to now, for I would like to ask you several questions, if I were sure that they would not bother you, since the subject I want to discuss goes somewhat beyond the temperament of reason."

She replied to me, "Friend, ask what you like, for the disciple

10   who must ask the master questions in order to learn ought not to suffer reproof for inquiring about everything."

"My lady, a natural behavior of men toward women and of women toward men prevails in the world which is not brought about by human institutions but by the inclination of the flesh, and

15   in which men and women love one another with a very strong love strengthened in turn by foolish pleasure. And they do not know for what reason and to what end such a mutual love is implanted in them. Men usually claim that women, in spite of everything they promise regarding this widespread passion usually called one's

20   'love life,' are rarely constant, not very loving, and amazingly false and fickle. All of this stems from the frivolousness of their hearts. Among other Latin authors who level this charge is Ovid, who makes serious accusations in his *Ars amatoria.* When he finishes his attack, Ovid (as well as others) says that everything contained

25   in his books regarding women's deceptive manners and malice was for the benefit of the common good, in order to warn men about women's ruses so that they could better avoid them, like the snake hidden in the grass. If you would, dear lady, teach me the truth of this matter."[16]

30   She replied, "Dear friend, as for the charge that women are deceitful, I really do not know what more I can say to you, for you yourself have adequately handled the subject, answering Ovid and the others in your *Epistre au Dieu d'Amour* and your *Epistres sur le Roman de la Rose.*[17] But, as for the point you mention that these

35   men attack women for the sake of the common good, I can show you that it has never been a question of this. And here is the reason: the common good of a city or land or any community of people is nothing other than the profit or general good in which all members,

40 commun ou publique en une cité ou pays ou communité de peuple
fors un prouffit et bien general, ouquel chacun, tant femmes comme
hommes, participent ou ont part. Mais la chose qui seroit faicte en
cuidant proffiter aux uns et non aux autres, seroit appellé bien privé
ou propre, et non mie publique. Et ancore moins le seroit le bien que
on touldroit aux uns pour donner aux autres et tele chose doit estre

45 appellee non mie seulement bien propre ou privé mais droicte extorcion faite a autrui en faveur de partie et a son grief pour soustenir
l'autre. Car ilz ne parlent point aux femmes en elles avisant que
elles se gardent des agais des hommes. Et toutevoies est ce chose
certaine que tres souvent et menu ilz deçoivent les femmes par leurs

50 cautelles et faulx semblans. Et n'est mie doubte que les femmes sont
aussi bien ou nombre du peuple de Dieu et de creature humaine que
sont les hommes, et non mie une autre espece, ne de dessemblable
generacion, par quoy elles doyent estre forcloses des enseignemens
moraulx. Doncques, je conclus que se pour le bien commun le

55 feissent, c'est assavoir des .ij. parties, ilz eussent aussi bien parlé
aux femmes que elles se gardassent des agais des hommes comme
ilz ont fait aux hommes que ilz se gardassent des femmes. Mais a
laisser aler ycestes questions, et en suivant l'autre, c'est assavoir que
femmes ne soient mie de si pou d'amour la ou leur cuer s'applique

60 et que plus y font arrestees que ilz ne dient, me souffira de le te
prouver par exemple, par deduisant en tesmoing partie de celles qui
jusques a la mort y ont perseveré. Et premierement te diray de la
noble Dido, royne de Cartage, dont cy dessus a esté parlé de sa grant
valeur, quoyque toy mesmes en tes dittiez autrefois en ayes parlé».

women as well as men, participate and take part. But whatever is
40   done with the intention of benefiting some and not others is a matter of private and not public welfare. Even less so is an activity in
which one takes from some and gives to others, and such an activity
is perpetrated for the sake of private gain, and at the same time it
constitutes, quite simply, a crime committed for the benefit of one
45   person and to the disadvantage of the other. For they never address
women nor warn them against men's traps even though it is certain
that men frequently deceive women with their fast tricks and duplicity. There is not the slightest doubt that women belong to the people
of God and the human race as much as men, and are not another
50   species or dissimilar race, for which they should be excluded from
moral teachings. Therefore, I conclude that if these men had acted
in the public good—that is, for both parties—they should also have
addressed themselves to women and warned them to beware of
men's tricks just as they warned men to be careful about women.
55   But leaving behind these questions and pursuing the others, that is
whether women who so little love where they set their hearts and
whether women are more constant than these men claim, it will be
enough for me to deduce the point for you from examples of women
who persevered in their love until death. First, I will tell you of the
60   noble Dido, queen of Carthage, whose great value I discussed above
and which you yourself have spoken of earlier in your works."[18]

3. 1405: Le livre de l'advision Cristine[19]

Christine's autobiographical dream-vision represents, together with the *Mutacion* and the *Othea*, a quasi-epic account of contemporary society and history. More accurately, however, the polysemic structure of the text suggests a semiotic richness of superimposed layers of meaning, and has been situated by the editors within the genre of the "songe politique," together with such works as the *Songe du vergier* (1378) and Alain Chartier's *Quadrologue invectif.*[20] The reference to the *Roman de la rose* is enunciated by Lady Opinion, who in Book 3 will be replaced by a more authoritarian voice in the form of Lady Philosophy. Lady Opinion's speech constitutes a reminder that it was she who engendered the exchange that became the [D]ebate about the *Roman de la rose*.

Text:

Book 2, Chapter 21 and 22

50r°   Encore parle l'ombre
        Que dis tu? Souffist il? T'ay assez conté du fait de mes puissances, desquelles ne pourroies en ta vie, comme autre fois t'ay dit, tous les examples ouir, tant en y a et si divers sont? Sces tu encore
5   qui je suis? Et moy a elle:- Dame, congnoistre vous cuidasse, maiz les raisons contradictoires que me narrez vaciller me font en vostre congnoiscence.
        Car, se bien entendu l'ay, tres au premier me deistes que, la ou verité est attainte, ne pouez arrester; et toutesvoie bien sçay et suis
10   certaine que en maint cas m'avez pure verité yci endroit clarifiee. Si ne sçay entendre comment ce puist estre que chose doubteuse tesmoing puisse estre de verité pure. Et elle a moy:- Fille, euvre le sens de ton entendement et escoutes et notes. Car je te promet que, quoy qu'autre fois en divers cas te fusse menterresse, en cestui cy
15   t'ay dit verité se bien l'entens, et ne m'y contredis s'il te recorde de ce qu'ay dit, c'est assavoir que cause suis moiennant estude et entendement de faire attaindre les choses vraies. Mais bien est vray que aussitost qu'ataintes sont, je me depars en cellui cas ne plus n'y arreste. Et qu'il soit voir, ainsi l'as esprouvé, car, non obstant que
20   ces choses t'aye dictes, non pas moy les t'ay certifies mais les sens
50v° par le moien d'estude qui raporté // l'a ton entendement, lequel par raison est certain que ainsi soit. Pour ce en ce cas de toy me partiray, et en lieu te remandra certaineté.
        Et par plus gros example ne te souvient il de moy et de ma
25   congnoissance par les divers cas que je t'ay fait mettre en termes et faire plusieurs lectures? Ne fus je celle qui mist le debat entre les

Translation:

The shadow speaks again:

"What do you say? Does this suffice? Have I told you enough
about the fact of my powers, concerning which you might not hear
all the examples in your lifetime, as I already said to you, there are
5   so many and so varied? Do you know who I am yet?" And I said to
her "Lady, I might have thought I knew you, but the contradictory
arguments that you have told me make me hesitate about know-
ing you. For if I have completely understood it, from the very first
you told me that where truth is attained you cannot stay; yet I well
10   know and am certain that in many matters you have clarified the
absolute truth here for me. I do not understand how this can be: that
a doubtful thing may bear witness to unadulterated truth." And she
said to me, "Daughter, open the sense of your understanding and
hear and take note. For I promise you that although at other times
15   in various matters I may have been untruthful, in this one I have
told you the truth— you listen well to it, and do not contradict me
if I remind you of what I said, that is, that I am the cause through
the means of study and understanding of making the truth obtained.
But it is indeed true that as soon as it is obtained, I depart from that
20   case, nor do I stay there any longer. And that this must be true, you
have proved; for despite these things that I told you, I myself have
not confirmed them for you, but intelligence by means of study has
brought it to your understanding which by reason is certain this
must be so. Therefore, in this case, I will leave you and instead,
25   leave you certainty.

"And through weightier examples do you not remember me
and my knowledge by the various accounts that I had you write

clers, disciples de Maistre Jehan de Meun—comme il s'i appel-
lent—, et toy sur la compillacion du *Romant de la Rose*, duquel
entre vous contradictoirement escripsistes l'un a l'autre, chascune
30   partie soustenant ses raisons, si comme il appert par le livret qui en
fut fait?

Chapter 22: Respont Cristine a l'ombre

Adonc, comme mon entendement apperceust par clere congnoissance qui estoit celle qui tant arraisonnee m'avoit, je dis ainsi:
35   «Ha! Dame Opinion puissant et forte, voirement vous dois je
moult bien congnoistre, car tres m'enfance oz je vostre acointance.
Et certainement je congnois et confesse vostre auctorité estre de
grant vigueur et puissance. Et quoy que vous soiez blasmee souven-
tesfois, qui bien de vous use ne puet errer, et mal pour cellui en qui
40   vous n'estes saine. Mais puisqu'il vous a pleu de vostre grace tant
m'onnorer qu'a moy si clere evidenment vous estes manisfestee, me
racontent vos grans proprietez, encore vous requier que a anui ne
vous soit de me declairer aucunes demandes. Et elle a moy:- Fille,
dis ce qu'il te plaist.
45   -Dame, puisqu'il est ainsi que de vous vient la premiere in-
vencion des œuvres humaines bonnes ou males, rudes ou soubtilles
selon la disposicion des entendemens, comme dit avez, plaise vous
me certifier se es choses par vous engendrees en moy—lesquelles a
mon pouoir par le moien d'estude et de telle science et entende-
50 51r° ment comme j'ay—qui en mes compillacions // et volumes sont
declairees, se en aucune chose y ay erré, comme si saige ne soit qui
aucune fois ne erre. Car, s'ainsi estoit, mieulx vouldroie tart que
jamais les amender.

Et elle a moy:- Amie chiere, soies en paix. Car je te dis que
55   non pour tant t'ay je blasmee de ce que prerogative de honneur volz,
comme je ay dit devant, donner a Fortune, et moy, comme je soie
principe, y oublias, faulte n'y a, non obstant que par moy maint s'en
debatent diversement: car les aucuns dient que clercs ou religieux
les te forgent et que de sentement de femme venir ne puissent. Mais
60   ce sont les ignorans qui ce dient, car ilz n'ont pas congnoissance
des escriptures qui de tant de vaillans femmes sages plus que toy et
lettrees, et meismement prophetes, qui ou temps passé ont esté, font
mencion; et comme Nature ne soit amendrie de sa puissance, encore
en peut estre. Les autres dient ton stille estre trop obscur et que on
65   ne l'entent, si n'est si delictable. Et ainsi diversement le fais aux
ungs louer et aux autres reprimer de loz, comme chose quelconques
estre a tous agreable soit impossible. Mais tant te dis que verité, par

down and make commentaries about? Was I not the one who
brought about the debate among the clerics—disciples of Jean de
30   Meun as they call themselves—and you concerning the compilation
of the *Roman de la rose*, about which you wrote each other from
opposite positions, each party maintaining his or her arguments, just
as it appears in the small book written about it?"
Chapter 22: Christine's reply to the shadow:
35   Then, as my mind discerned with clear understanding who
was the one who had conversed with me for so long, I spoke thusly:
"Oh! strong and powerful Dame Opinion, truly, I should know
you quite well, for I have been acquainted with you since childhood! And certainly I know and acknowledge that your authority
40   is quite vigorous and strong. Although you are often blamed, he
who uses you well cannot err; and it is bad for those in whom you
are unsound. But since it pleased you by your grace to honor me so
much that you are so clearly revealed to me, telling me of your great
properties, I still ask [you], if it does not weary you, to answer some
45   questions for me." And she said to me: "Daughter, say what you
please."
"Lady, since it is that from you comes the first invention
of human deeds—good or bad, crude or subtle, according to the
disposition of the understanding, as said—please certify for me if in
50   the matters you engendered in me by you—which, in as far as I was
able, I acquired through the means of study and such learning and
understanding as I possess—which are expressed in my compila-
tions and volumes, if I have erred in any matter; for there is no sage
that sometimes does not make mistakes. For if it was so, I should
55   prefer to correct them later than never."
And she told me, "Dear friend, be at peace. For I tell you no.
Even if I accused you of wanting to bestow the preeminent honor on
Fortune, as I said before, of forgetting about me, as I am the principal one, there is no fault there, even though because of me many
60   people argue about them in various ways; for some say that clerics
or monks forged them for you and that they could not come from
the intelligence of a woman. But those who say this are ignorant,
for they do not know the Scriptures which mention so many valiant
women—wiser than you and literate—and even the prophets who
65   lived in the times past, and since Nature is not diminished in her
power, this can even yet be so. Others say that your style is too obscure and that they cannot understand it, so it is not very enjoyable.
Thus variously I cause some to praise and others to repress praise

le tesmoing de l'experience, ne seuffre le blasme avoir effait sur le
loz. Si te conseil que ton œuvre tu continues, comme elle soit juste,
70   et ne te doubtes d'errer en moy. Car tant que je seray en toy fondee
sur loy, raison et vray sentement, tu ne mesprendras es fondacions
de tes œuvres es choses plus voir semblables, non obstant de plusieurs les divers jugemens, les ungs par moy simplement, les autres
par Envie. Car je t'acertaine que, quant elle et moy sommes ensem-
75   ble, adonc se font les tres faulx jugemens, ne il n'est si bon qui y
soit espargné. Et adonc suis je perilleuse quant Envie me gouverne.
51v° Si faisons la personne avuglee es autrui choses et en son // meismes
fait, qui en soy nous a. Si lui rongions le cuer ne reposer ne le lais-
sons et vouloir lui donnons de faire mains maulx qui acomplis sont
80   aucune fois. Et mal est gouverné cil qui chiet entre noz mains, ja si
bon ne sera ne si puissant.
Ne veames nous jadis les portes de Romme au preux Julius Cesar,
qui tant victorieux s'en retournoit, et au derrenier tant pourcha-
çames qu'il fu occis? Assez de telles en avons faictes n'il n'est si
85   sage qui garder s'en saiche. Si t'ay assez narré de mes aventures, et
atant souffise. Car, par ce que je donne a croire a l'un que une
chose est bonne et bien faite ou que elle est vraie, et a l'autre tout le
contraire—dont sourdent batailles et mains debas—, la prolixité de
mes narracions si racontee pourroit aux lisans a anuy tourner. Et si
90   te prophetise que ceste lecture sera de plusieurs tesmoingnee
diversement. Les ungs sur le langaige donront leur sentence en
plusieurs manieres: diront qu'il n'est pas bien elegant, les autres que
la composicion des materes est estrange. Et ceulx qui l'entendront
en diront bien. Et le temps a venir plus en sera parlé qu'a ton vivant.
95   Car tant te dis je encore que tu es venue en mauvais temps. Car les
sciences ne sont pas a present en leur reputacion, ains sont comme
choses hors saison. Et qu'il soit vray, tu en vois pou qui a celle
cause soient en la maison de Fortune surhauciez. Maiz, aprés ta
mort, venra le prince plain de valeur et sagesce qui par la relacion
100 de tes volumes desirera tes jours avoir esté de son temps et par grant
desir souhaidera t'avoir veue. Si me suis a toy descripte; or diffinis
de moy ce qu'il t'en semble.
     Et moy a elle:- Dame, comme la desceipcion de vous meismes
52r° m'en apprengne la diffinicion, // je dis que, comme parfaictement
105 ore vous congnoisse, que vous voirement estes d'Ignorance fille,
adhesion a une partie, en doubtant tousjours de l'autre. Et de ce je
m'avise ce que de vous dist Aristote ou premier livre de *Posteres*,
que cellui qui vous a doubte tousjours qu'autrement puis estre que

as anything that pleases everyone is impossible. But I tell you this
70   much: truth, by the testimony of experience, does not let censure
affect reputation. I advise you then to continue your work, as it is
valid, and do not suspect yourself of failing because of me. For
inasmuch as I will be founded in you on law, reason, and true judgment in you, you will not err in the foundations of your work in the
75   matters which seem most truthful, in spite of the many and various
judgments some from me alone, others from Envy. For I assure you
that when she and I are found together then very false judgments
are made, nor is there any so good that it is spared. And thus I am
dangerous when Envy directs me. We make the person blind in other
80   things and in his own action in whom we are. So we gnaw at his
heart, leave him no rest, and make him long to do many evil things,
which sometimes come to pass. Ill-governed is the one who falls in
our hands, however good he may be or however powerful.
          "Did we not refuse the gates of Rome once to mighty Julius
85   Caesar, who returned there flushed with triumph, and pursue [him]
until he was finally killed?[21] We are responsible for many such
deeds, nor is anyone wise enough to know how to protect himself
from us. I have told you enough then about my adventures; and at
this point, let it suffice. For since I make one person believe that one
90   thing is good and well done or that it is true and another believes
the opposite—from which arise many controversies and many
conflicts—the prolixity of my stories, if recounted here, might bore
the readers. And so I prophesy to you that several people will bear
witness to this commentary in different ways. Some will give ver-
95   dicts on your language in different ways; they will say it is not very
elegant, others that the composition of the material is strange. And
those who will understand it will speak well of it. In times to come,
more will be said of it than in your lifetime. For this much I tell you
again: you have come at a bad time. For the sciences are not highly
100   esteemed at present but are like things out of season.[22] And that
this is true, you see few who because of this are raised to Fortune's
house. But after your death, there will come a prince, full of valor
and wisdom, who—because of the content of your books—will
wish you had lived in his time and will greatly long to have known
105   you. So I have described myself to you. Now declare exactly what
you think I am." I told her, "Lady, since your own description teaches me the definitive response, I say I must know you perfectly now,
that you are truly the daughter of Ignorance—attached to one side in
perpetual mistrust of the other. And in this, I am counseled by what

ce qu'il pense, comme vous soiez non certaine. Et saint Bernard
110   aussi dit ou .Ve. chappitre de *Consideracion* que vous estes ambigue
et pouez estre deceue. Si dis et conclus que vous estes adhesion a
une partie, laquelle adhesion est causee de l'apparence d'aucune
raison prouvable, soit que l'oppinant ait doubte de l'autre partie, soit
que non. De vostre puissance je dis que, pour l'ignorance qui est
115   es hommes, que par vous est plus le monde gouverné que par grant
savoir».

　　　Explicit la seconde partie du Livre de l'Advision de Cristine

110 Aristotle says about you in the first book of the *Prior Analytics*,[23] that he who has you fears always that it may be otherwise than he thinks since you are uncertain. And Saint Bernard also says in the fifth chapter of the *De consideratione* that you are ambiguous and can be deceived.[24] Consequently I say and conclude that you are an

115 attachment to one party, which attachment is caused by the appearance of some provable argument, whether or not the one holding the opinion questions the other side. And concerning your power I say that because of the ignorance which is in man, the world is governed more by you than by great learning."

120 Here ends the second part of the book of Christine's *Vision*

4. 1408–13: Autres Ballades: Rondel and Ballade XXXVII[25]

The two poems that follow are part of an array of rondels and ballades on varying subjects, which reflect Christine's political and social concerns in the years between 1408 and 1413. Very little has been written specifically on Ballade XXXVII and the preceding rondel.[26] In *Christine de Pizan. Her Life and Works. A Biography*, Charity Cannon Willard describes this collection of poems as follows: "Between the two ballade cycles [the *Cent ballades* and the *Cent ballades d'amant et de dame*], there was a group of poems entitled *Autres ballades* (*Ballades on Various Subjects*), fifty-three in all and generally poems of circumstance...."[27] The rondel and ballade XXXVII clearly express Christine's ongoing criticism of Jean de Meun's *Roman*. The rondel immediately follows a letter addressed to the Queen Isabeau de Bavière (ballade XXXVI), for whom Christine worked as a lady in waiting at the time. On the other hand, it is unclear to whom this plea for support is addressed.

Text:
Rondel

Mon chier Seigneur, soyez de ma partie!
Assailli m'ont à grant guerre desclose
4   Les aliez du Rommant de la Rose
Pour ce qu'à eulx ne me suis convertie.

Bataille m'ont si cruelle bastie
Que bien cuident m'avoir ja presqu'enclose,
8   Mon chier Seigneur, soyez de ma partie!

Pour leur assaulx ne seray alentie
De mon propos, mais c'est commune chose
Que l'en cuert sus à qui droit deffendre ose;
12   Mais se je suis de sens pou advertie,
Mon chier Seigneur, soyez de ma partie!

Ballade XXXVII

Jadis avoit en la cité d'Athenes
16   Fleur d'estude de clergie souvraine;
Mais, non obstant les sentences certaines
De leur grant sens, une erreur trop villaine
Les decevoit, car plusieurs divers dieux

Translation:

> My dear lord, be on my side:
> I have been attacked in an open war
> By the allies of the *Roman de la rose*,
4 > For I did not convert to their camp.
>
> They mounted such a cruel battle
> That they thought they had me almost contained,
> My dear lord, be on my side.
>
8 > I will not be slowed down by their assault.
> Yet it is common knowledge
> That one is assailed if one dares to defend what is right.
> If I am mistaken,
12 > My dear lord, be on my side.

Ballade XXXVII

> In the city of Athens, there once was
> A flowering of study of souverain learning;[28]
16 > But despite the sound judgment
> Of their great intelligence, a terribly base error
> Deceived them, for they claimed that many different gods
> There were. This is what some of them preached as best they could,
20 > When they ought to have known

20   Aouroient, dont aucuns pour leur mieulx
        Y preschierent qu'ilz devoient savoir
        Qu'il n'est qu'un Dieu, mais mal en prist à cieux;
        —On est souvent batu pour dire voir.

24   Aristote le très sage, aux haultaines
        Sciences pront, d'icelle cité, plaine
        De tel erreur, fu fuitis; maintes peines
        Il en souffri; Socrates qui fontaine
28   De sens estoit; fu chacié de cil lieux;
        Plusieurs autres occis des envieux
        Pour verité dire; et appercevoir
        Peut bien chascun que, partout soubz les cieulx,
32   On est souvent batu pour dire voir.

        Se ainsi va des sentences mondaines;
        Pour ce le di que plusieurs ont attaine
        Sur moy, pour tant que paroles très veines,
36   Deshonneur et diffame incertaine,
        Reprendre osay, en jeunes et en vieulx,
        Et le Rommant—plaisant aux curieux—
        De la Rose, que l'en devroit ardoir!
40   Mais pour ce mot maint me sauldroit aux yeulx.
        On est souvent batu pour dire voir.
        Princes, certes, voir dire est anieux
        Aux mençongeurs qui veulent decevoir,
44   Pour ce au pere voit on mentir le fieulx.
        On est souvent batu pour dire voir!

That there was only one God; but they were badly dealt with.
One is often beaten for speaking the truth.

Aristotle, the wise, steeped in the
24   High Sciences, was chased away from that city,
Full of such error; Socrates
Suffered great pain, who possessed
The fountain of understanding. He was chased from this place,
28   And many others were killed, by those who were jealous,
For having told the truth; and everyone
Can easily ascertain
That everywhere under the sun,
32   One is often beaten for speaking the truth.

Such is the state of worldly judgments;
I say this because many have assailed me
For I dared refute many very vain words,
36   Dishonest and possibly defamatory
For young and old,
And the *Roman de la rose*
Which pleases the curious,
40   Ought to be burned!
But for these words, many jumped on me;
One is often beaten for speaking the truth.[29]
Prince, truly it is bothersome to tell the truth
44   In the eye of the liars who wish to deceive;
Because of this, one sees a son lie to a father:
One is often beaten for speaking the truth.

5. 1410: *Le livre de fais d'armes et de chevalerie*[30]

This instructional treatise has puzzled Christine scholars, who are uncertain
as to why she felt the need to compose a manual on warfare. Charity Cannon
Willard speculates that "the duke of Burgundy's plan for the dauphin's [Louis
de Guyenne] military education was certainly the inspiration for this manual
on warfare."[31] More importantly, in my view, she notes that at the time of
composition of the *Fais d'armes*, Christine's adversary in the debate, Jean de
Montreuil, "wrote the first version of a treatise entitled *A Toute la Chevalerie*....
He presented a version in Latin to Louis of Guyenne in 1408 and offered an
extended French version several years later."[32] Both authors seem to have felt
the need to boost the morale of the French troops at that crucial period of the
Hundred Years War. I would argue, however, that in addition to nationalistic
motivations, the composition of this manual also shows the continued contact
between Christine and Jean de Montreuil. Thus, it is not surprising that Christine
takes yet another opportunity to revive her opinions on the *Roman de la rose*
and to remind her opponent of her views.

The excerpt in question is the first chapter of book 3 of the *Livre des fais
d'armes*. Christine's reference to Jean de Meun's *Roman* serves as an authen-
tication of her own work, which, as many have argued, confirms yet again that
she made a point of applying the same literary and authorial principles which
were valid for male clerical authors of her time. Naturally, it is all the more
telling that she specifically mentions the *Roman* and Jean de Meun as examples
of the acceptability of copying from others.

Text:

49r°	Ainsi que j'etendoyra entrer en ceste iiie partie du present livre, mon
	entendement aucques lasse de la pesanteur de la matere et labour
	des precedens parties. Adonc surprise de somme en mon lit couchiée
	m'apparut en dormant par semblance une creature si comme en la
5	fourme d'un tres sollempnel homme habit de chiere et de mantil
	d'un pesant ancien saige auttorisé qui ainsi me dist: Chiere amie,
	Christine de laquelle en fait ou en pensée de labour nulle heure ne
	cesse de excuse d'estude pour laquel cause et en contemplacion
	de l'amour que tu as aux choses que lettres pueent demonster par
10	especial en exortacion de toutes nobles œuvres et meurs vertueux
	fust venuz pour estre en ton ayde en la present œuvre de cestui livre
	de chevalerie et de faiz d'armes ou par grant diligence mue par bon
	vouloir tant tu t'ocupes. Et pour ce en confortant le bon desin que
	as de donner matere aux chevaliers et nobles qui le pouvoient ouir
15	d'eux employer et plus embellir es faiz que noblesse requierent;
	c'est assavoir au dit excercice d'armes tant ou labour de corps

Translation:

       While I was waiting to begin work on the third part of this
book and my brain was weary from the great weight of the first two
parts, there appeared before me, as I lay drowsily in bed, someone
resembling a solemn man in clerical garb;[33] he spoke to me as a

5   right authorized judge might, saying: "Dear friend Christine, whose
love of deed and thought result in the labor of studying, which is
ceaseless, in consideration of the great love you have for things
represented by letters, especially in exhortation of all noble works
and virtuous conditions, I have come here to lend a hand in the

10   composition of this present book of knighthod and deeds of arms,
with which you have occupied yourself very diligently and with
goodwill. Therefore, in conformity with your great desire to give
material to all knights and other noble men who can read or hear
it, for employment and improvement in accomplishing those deeds

15   required of them, which is to say, the aforesaid exercise of arms, by
physical training of the body and according to the rights authorized

comme es droiz qu'il leur conviennent selon les loix est bon que tu
cueilles sur l'arbre de batailles qui est en mon jardin aucuns fruiz
et que si ceulx tu sembles sy t'encroistra vigueur et force a mieulx
20   pouoir par achever la pesanteur de ton dit œuvre. Et pour bastir ediffice par tirant aux diz de Vegece et des autres dont jusques ycy t'es
aydée te convient retrenchier les branches d'icelluy arbre prendre le
meilleur et sur celluy merrain fonder partie de ton dit ediffice auquel
parfaire je comme maistre et tu soyes disciple y seray en ton ayde.
25   Ces choses oyés me sembloit adonc que ainsi lui disoye: O digne
maistre, je cognois que tu es celluy estude que j'aim et tant ay aymé
depuis je viens ne me souvient. Et par laquel vertu et frequantacion
ay las a dieu grace achevées maintes belles emprises. Certes de ta
compaignie suis tres joyeuse, mais comme ne doie desplaire au
30   maistre se le disciple desireux d'apprendre forment questions. Te
prie que me dies se reprouche pouvra estre a mon œuvre ce que
m'as conseillé user du dit fruit arme chevalerie adcerete. Respons
49v° que de tant est une œuvre tesmoignée par plus de gent // tant plus
est autentique. Et pour ce se aucuns en murmurent selon l'usaige
35   des mesdisans disant que autrepart part menders; je leur respons
que c'est commun usaige entre mes disciples de eulx entredoner et
departir des fleurs que ils prennent en mes jardins diversement et
tous ceulx qui s'en aydent ne les ont pris premier cueillies. Comment ne s'ayda pas Jehan de Meun en son livre de la rose des diz de
40   Lorris et semblablement d'autres sy n'est point de reprouche a me
est louenge quant bien et proprement sont appliquiez et sage est sa
maistrise et est signe savoir sur son veu et vise de mains livres. Mais
la ou mal a propos on feroit servir choses ailleurs prinses, la se voit
le vice. Sy faiz hardiement et ne te doubtes car ton œuvre est bonne
45   et sy te certiffie que de mant saige seras louée.

by written law, it is good for you to gather from the Tree of Battles
in my garden some fruit that will be of use to you, so that vigor
and strength may grow within you to continue work on the weighty
20   book. In order to build an edifice that reflects the writings of Vegetius and of other authors who have been helpful to you, you must cut
some branches of this tree, taking only the best, and with this timber
you shall set the foundation of this edifice. To do this, I as master
will undertake to help you as disciple."

25   Having heard these things, it seemed to me that said to him:
"O worthy Master, I know that you are one whose work I admire
greatly and have admired as long as I can recall; your haunting and
virtuous presence has already helped me, thanks be to God, to bring
to a successful conclusion many fine undertakings. Certainly, I am
30   very glad to have your company. But it ought not to displease the
master if the disciple, desirous of learning, asks questions. I pray
you tell me if my work can be reproached for your counseling me to
make use of the aforesaid fruit."

          "Dear friend, in this matter I reply that the more a work is seen
35   and approved by people, the more authentic it becomes. Therefore,
if anyone should murmur, according to the ways of detractors, saying that you took material from others, I answer them by saying that
it is common usage among my disciples to exchange and share the
flowers they take from my garden individually. And even though
40   they help themselves, they are not the first to do so. Did not Master
Jean de Meun make use of the works of Lorris, and likewise of other
writings in his *Roman de la rose*? It is therefore not a rebuke, but a
lawful and praiseworthy matter when material is suitably applied,
wherein is the mastery of the material, for therein is the indication
45   of having seen and read many books. But it is wrong to take material without acknowledgment; therein is the fault. So do boldly what
you have to do and do not doubt that your work is good. I assure
you that it shall be commended and praised by many a wise man."

B. The Beginnings of French Humanism

The Italian humanist influence becomes more pronounced as the fourteenth century progresses, and Petrarchian tendencies are quite discernable in the argumentation of both the proponents and the opponents of the *Roman de la rose*. It is for this reason that I have included one postdebate reference that elucidates the embryonic French humanism at that time: Laurent de Premierfait, in his translation of Boccaccio's *De Casibus*, includes two lengthy passages referring to the *Roman*, which clearly are reminiscent of Petrarch and the humanist tradition.[34]

1. Laurent de Premierfait (1360/70?–1418)

There is no indicative information as to the date of birth of this writer. However, as Carla Bozzolo has pointed out, he was in all likelihood of the same generation as Jean Gerson and Nicolas de Clamanges.[35] A native of the Champagne region, he had a close friendship with de Clamanges, as well as with Jean de Montreuil, with whom he shared admiration for Jean de Meun's *Roman*. Another author who greatly influenced Laurent de Premierfait's literary interests is Boccaccio: During the years 1411 and 1414, de Premierfait translated the *Decameron* from the Florentine language into Latin, then into French, with the help of Antonio d'Arezzo. In 1409 he added a translation of a second work of Boccaccio's: the *De casibus virorum illustrium,* titled *Des cas des nobles hommes et femmes.* There are two brief additions to this translation in which the author refers to Jean de Meun's *Roman de la rose*: The first is a concise version of the myth of Narcissus, wherein the latter, proud of his own beauty, vows to fall in love only with a woman as beautiful and young as himself:

1409: De casibus virorum illustrium[36]

Text:

Comme doncques il, qui se adonna a chacer par les forests aux
bestes sauvaiges en defuiend la compaignie des hommes, se feust
enamouré d'une femme moult belle appellee Echo, laquelle cog-
noissant l'orgueil de Narcisus ne se voult point abandonner a lui,
5   fors que en lui rendend une parole pour l'aultre; comme Narcisus
donques, aveugle en son propre jugement selon lequel il desprisoit
chascun au resgard de soy mesme, un jour entre les aultres eust
longuement chassié aux bestes parmi une forest et, pour relever son
traveil par repos et pour appaiser la soif et torcher la sueur, feust
10   venu en un lieu umbraigeux de celle forest pres duquel estoit une
fontainne tele et ainsi descripte comme le noble poete Jehan Clopinel de Meun la figura par vers en son *Livre de la Rose*; et pour tant
plus n'en parle....

Translation:

> Now he who gave himself to hunting wild beasts in the forest, flee-
> ing the company of men, had fallen in love with a very beautiful
> woman named Echo. She who knew of Narcissus's haughtiness did
> not want to give herself to him other than to exchange words with
> 5 him. Narcissus, then—blind in his judgment of himself, according
> to which he despises everyone in comparison to himself—one day,
> after having hunted beasts in a forest for a long time, and in order
> to unburden himself of his work through rest and quench his thirst
> and calm his sweat, came to a shadowy place in his forest, close to
> 10 which there was a fountain such as is depicted by the noble poet
> Jean Clopinel de Meun in verse in his *Book of the Rose*, so I will
> speak no more of it....[37]

1409: De casibus virorum illustrium[38]

This second addition is a work in praise of Dante, and reflects the emerging humanism in France. More importantly, it could also be read as a last attempt to help the vindication of Jean de Meun's *Roman* and, by extension, of Jean de Montreuil's arguments during the Debate.

Text:

Pour ce toutevoies que j'ay parlé de Dant noble poete florentin, savoir affiert que cestui Dant, qui environna les regions du monde et enquist et conversa les hommes renommez en sciences divines et humaines, entre plusieurs nobles et anciannes citez il enscrcha
5   Paris, en laquele lors estoient et encore sont trois choses les plus resplendissans et notables qui soient en quelconque aultre partie du monde, c'est assavoir le general estude de toutes sciences qui sont figure de paradis terrestre; secondement les nobles eglises et aultres lieux sacrez garnis d'ommes et femmes servens jour et nuyt a Dieu
10   qui sont figure de paradis celeste; tiercement les deux cours judici-aires qui aux hommes discribent la vertu de justice, c'est assavoir Parlement et Chastellet qui portent la figure par moitié de paradis et d'enfer. Cestui poete Dant, entre plusieurs volumes nouveaulx estans lors a Paris, rencontra le noble *Livre de la Rose,* en quoy
15   Jehan Clopinel de Meung, homme d'engin celeste, peigny une vraye mappemonde de toutes choses celestes et terriennes. Dant donques, qui de Dieu et de Nature avoit receu l'esperit de poetrie, advisa que ou *Livre de la Rose* est descript le paradis des bons et l'enfer des mauvais en langaige françois, voult, en langaige florentin, soubz
20   aultre maniere de vers rimoiez, contrefaire au vif le beau *Livre de la Rose* en ensuivant tel ordre comme fist le divin poete Virgile ou .VIe. livre que l'en nomme *Eneyde.* Et, pour ce que le poete Dant, selon sa profession, dampnoit et reprenoit les vices et les hommes vicieux, il, qui estoit bien nobles et bien meritz, fut dechaciez de
25   Florence et forsbannis d'illec et mourut en la cité de Ravennes.

Translation:

         In any case, I have spoken of Dante, the noble Florentine poet,
         because it is important to know that Dante, who circled the regions
         of the world and researched and conversed with men renowned in
         the divine and human sciences, singled out Paris from among many

5   noble and ancient cities where three of the most resplendent and
         remarkable things could and still can be found which can be found
         also in other parts of the world: namely, the study of all sciences
         which make up terrestrial paradise, second, the noble churches and
         other sacred places adorned with men and women who serve God

10   day and night and who are part of heavenly paradise, and third,
         the two judicial courts which describe the virtue of Justice to men,
         namely, the Parliament and Castle, which bear the sign of paradise
         and hell. This poet, Dante, discovered among several new vol-
         umes which were in Paris at that time the noble *Book of the Rose*,

15   in which Jean Clopinel de Meun, a man of celestial intelligence,
         depicts a veritable *mappa mundi* of all things heavenly and worldly.
         Dante, who was given the spirit of poetry by God and Nature, rea-
         soned that in the *Book of the Rose*, paradise for the good and hell for
         the bad are described in the French language, and so in his lifetime

20   he wanted to imitate, in the Florentine language and in a different
         rhymed verse, the beautiful *Book of the Rose*, following an order
         such as the divine poet Virgil did in the sixth book, called *Aenead*.
         And the poet Dante, in line with his calling, damned and refuted
         the vices and vicious men; he, who was very noble and meritori-

25   ous, was chased from Florence and banished, and died in the city of
         Ravennes.

Notes

1. On this topic, see Mary Anne Case, "Christine de Pizan and the Authority of Experience," in *Christine de Pizan and the Categories of Difference*, ed. Marilynn Desmond (Minneapolis: University of Minnesota Press, 1998), 71–87; Marilynn Desmond and Pamela Sheinghorn, *Myth, Montage, Visuality in Late Medieval Manuscript Culture: Christine de Pizan's Othea* (Ann Arbor: Michigan University Press, 2001); David Hult, "The *Roman de la rose* and the querelle des femmes," in *Cambridge Companion to Medieval Women's Writing*, ed. Carolyn Dinshaw and David Wallace (Cambridge, UK: Cambridge University Press, 2003), 184–94; Christine McWebb, "The *Roman de la rose* and the *Livre des trois vertus*: The Never-Ending Debate," in *Au Champ des escriptures. IIIe Colloque international sur Christine de Pizan*, ed. Eric Hicks (Paris: Champion, 2000), 309–24; Helen Solterer, *The Master and Minerva: Disputing Women in French Medieval Culture* (Berkeley: University of California Press, 1995).

2. The only existing edition is that of Suzanne Solente ed., *Le livre de la mutacion de fortune par Christine de Pisan. Publié d'après les manuscrits*, 3 vols. (Paris: Picard, 1959). The passage reproduced here can be found in 2: ll. 5537–642. The translation is my own. Extant manuscripts:

   a. Bibliothèque royale de Bruxelles 9509 (1403) is the only manuscript which contains this text in its complete form—base manuscript for Solente's edition

   b. Chantilly, Musée Condé 494

   c. Munich, Staatsbibliothek, gall. II (incomplete)

   d. BN f. fr. 603

   e. The Hague, Koninklijke Bibliotheek ms. 78 D42, 170fols

   f. Chantilly, Musée Condé 493

   g. BN f.fr. 604

   h. BN f.fr. 25430 (only contains part IV, V)

   i. Private Collection: M. Pierre Bérès, 179fols, formerly in library of Sir Sidney Cockerell

   j. Bibl. de l'Arsenal, ms. 3172 (only contains first five parts)

   k. BN nouv. acq. fr. 14852, 2fols

3. "Christine de Pizan and the Political Life in Late Medieval France," in *Christine de Pizan: A Casebook*, ed. Barbara Altmann and Deborah McGrady (New York: Routledge, 2003), 9–24; 11. Other relevant analyses have been done by Kenneth Varty, "Christine's Guided Tour of the Sale merveilleuse: On Reactions to Reading and Being Guided round Medieval Murals in Real and Imaginary Buildings," in *Christine de Pizan 2000*, ed. John Campbell and Nadia Margolis (Amsterdam: Rodopi, 2000), 163–73; Lori J. Walters's two pieces, "Fortune's Double Face: Gender and the Transformations of Christine de Pizan, Augustine, and Perpetua," *Fifteenth-Century Studies* 25 (2000): 97–114; and "Translatio Studii: Christine de Pizan's Self-Portrayal in Two Lyric Poems and in the *Livre de la mutacion de Fortune*," in *Christine de Pizan and Medieval French Lyric*, ed. Earl Jeffrey Richards (Gainesville: University Press of Florida, 1998), 155–65; Kevin Brownlee, "Hector and Penthesilea in the *Livre de la mutacion de Fortune*: Christine de Pizan and the Politics of Myth," in *Une femme de lettres au moyen âge*, ed. Liliane Dulac and Bernard Ribémont (Orléans, France: Paradigme, 1995), 69–82; and "The Image of History in Christine de Pizan's *Livre de la Mutacion de Fortune*," in *Contexts: Style and Values in Medieval Art and Literature*, ed. Daniel Poirion and Nancy Freeman Regalado (New Haven, CT: Yale University Press, 1991), 44–56; and Joël Blanchard, "Christine de Pizan: Les Raisons de l'histoire," *Le Moyen Age: Revue d'Histoire et de Philologie* 92 (1986): 417–36.

4. Christine's reference to the histories of Rome is undoubtedly inspired by her reading of the *Histoire ancienne jusqu'à César*.

5. This is an allusion to the passage of False Seeming in the *Roman de la rose* where he dresses in the cloak of the itinerant monk in order to give his mocking discourse on the mendicant orders satirical clout.

6. The topic of virtue and honor of the mendicant orders was much debated in the Middle Ages. For a discussion of this issue in the context of the debate, I refer to the Introduction and to chap. 1.C.

7. Eccl. 10:31.
8. The latest edition is *La città delle dame*, ed. Patrizia Caraffi and Earl Jeffrey Richards (Milan: Luni editrice, 2001). Earl Jeffrey Richards, trans., *The Book of the City of Ladies*, rev. ed. (New York: Persea Books, 1998). I am grateful to both authors for their permission to reproduce the excerpt and its translation. Both used Harley 4431 as their base manuscript. There are twenty-five extant manuscripts of this text. Rosalind Brown-Grant has also published a translation, *The Book of the City of Ladies* (Harmondsworth, UK: Penguin, 1999).
9. This work has provoked by far the most prolific outpouring in Christinian scholarship. I will limit my references strictly to those which deal primarily with the *Livre de la cité des dames* in the context of the debate about the *Roman de la rose*, such as David Hult, "The *Roman de la rose*, Christine de Pizan, and the querelle des femmes," in *The Cambridge Companion to Medieval Women's Writing*, ed. Carolyn Dinshaw and David Wallace (Cambridge, UK: Cambridge University Press, 2003), 186–94; E. Jeffrey Richards, "Christine de Pizan and Medieval Jurisprudence," *Contexts and Continuities: Proceedings of the IV International Colloquium on Christine de Pizan* (Glasgow July 21–27, 2000), ed. Angus J. Kennedy, 3 vols (Glasgow: Glasgow University Press, 2002), 3: 747–66; Christine McWebb, "The *Roman de la Rose* and the *Livre des trois vertus*: The Never-Ending Debate," in *Au champ des escriptures*, 309–24; Rosalind Brown-Grant, *Christine de Pizan and the Moral Defence of Women: Reading Beyond Gender* (Cambridge, UK: Cambridge University Press, 1999); Josephine Donovan, *Women and the Rise of the Novel, 1405–1726* (London: Macmillan, 1999); Earl Jeffrey Richards, "Rejecting Essentialism and Gendered Writing: The Case of Christine de Pizan," in *Gender and Text in the Later Middle Ages*, ed. Jane Chance (Gainesville: University Press of Florida, 1996), 96–131; and, tangentially, Judith Kellogg, "Transforming Ovid: The Metamorphosis of Female Authority," in *Christine de Pizan and the Categories of Difference*, 181–194; Maureen Cheney Curnow, "La Pioche d'inquisicion: Legal-Judicial Content and Style in Christine de Pizan's *Livre de la cité des dames*," in *Reinterpreting Christine de Pizan*, ed. Earl Jeffrey Richards et al. (Athens, GA: University of Georgia Press, 1992), 157–72; Maureen Quilligan, *The Allegory of Female Authority: Christine de Pizan's Cité des dames* (Ithaca, NY: Cornell University Press, 1991); Susan Schibanoff, "Taking the Gold out of Egypt: The Art of Reading as a Woman," in *Gender and Reading: Essays on Readers, Texts, and Contexts*, ed. Elizabeth Flynn and Patrocinio P. Schweickart (Baltimore: Johns Hopkins University Press, 1986), 83–106.
10. The setting for the appearance of the three Virtues makes it clear that Christine is truly experiencing their visit, that she is not dreaming like Lover, the protagonist of the *Roman*, and consequently that her experiences are more truthful than Lover's. The appearance of Reason, Rectitude, and Justice recalls the appearance of Lady Philosophy to Boethius at the opening of the *De consolatione,* as though Christine's work were a kind of "consolation" for ladies. At the same time, Reason's appearance is also reminiscent of that of Virgil to Dante at the opening of the *Commedia*, a work which Christine claimed to have introduced to France.
11. Though Christine has yet to mention the *Roman*, this dismissal of the testimony of poets can be seen as a direct attack on the *Roman* whose opening, "maintes genz dient qu'en songes/n'a se fables non et mensonges" [many people say that there are only fables and lies in dreams], anticipates the *Roman*'s valorization of the higher truth of poetry.
12. See chap. 1.D.2.
13. This is a quasi-literal quote from Christine's letter to her opponent in the Debate, Jean de Montreuil (chap. 3.5, 126 and 125–127).
14. The comment on the inconstancy and weakness of the Emperor Claudius and other Roman emperors presents a slight departure from the author/narrator's normal line of argument: in general she demonstrates the virtues of women without reference to the vices of men.
15. Adopted son of Augustus, Tiberius is remembered as a reclusive, inefficient ruler whose reign was marked by terror and mayhem.
16. The comparison of a woman to a snake comes up frequently in the Debate correspondence; for example, in Christine's letter to the provost of Lille where the former quotes Genius's words from the *Roman*, "Flee, flee from women, the evil serpents hidden under the grass!" (chap. 3.4, 130, 131).

17. Christine explicitly connects her observations on the fidelity of women in love to her earlier remarks in the Quarrel to the *Roman*, one additional piece of evidence that Christine viewed the *Cité* as a continuation of the Debate.

18. In order to escape marriage Dido is said to have stabbed herself in front of the people.

19. I have used Christine Reno and Liliane Dulac's edition, *Le livre de l'advision Cristine* (Paris: Champion, 2001) for the original, and for the translation *The Vision of Christine de Pizan* by Glenda McLeod and Charity Cannon Willard (New York: Brewer, 2005). This translation draws from an earlier translation by McLeod, *Christine's Vision* (New York: Garland, 1993). Further, an earlier translation exists by Sister Mary Towner, *Lavision-Christine: Introduction and Text* (New York: AMS Press, 1969). With permission to reprint by Champion and AMS Press. There are three extant manuscripts of the text:

      a. Ex-Phillipps 128 (private collection): This manuscript is particularly interesting because it is the only one which includes the now well-studied prologue, a metatextual commentary on the author's conception and use of allegory. For an edited version of this prologue, see Christine Reno, "The Preface to the Avision-Christine in ex-Philipps 128," in *Reinterpreting Christine de Pizan*, 207–27. This is the base manuscript used for the edition of the text.

      b. BN f.fr. 1176

      c. Bruxelles, B.R. 10309. This manuscript has only limited usefulness because of the many errors it contains.

20. *Le livre de l'advision Cristine*, xxi.

21. This is a reference to the attempt by Metellus to refuse the gates of Rome to Caesar. This incident is told in the *Faits des Romains*, which supposedly succeeds the *Histoire ancienne jusqu'a Cesar*, to which Christine refers frequently.

22. In her *Livre du corps de policie*, Christine criticizes the poor standards for princely education.

23. Aristotle, *Prior Analytics*, 89a3.

24. In all likelihood, Christine took the passage in Aristotle's *Prior Analytics* and the one of book 5 of the *De consideratione* of Saint Bernard from the "Opinio" in *Catholicon*. It is possible, however, that Christine knew Saint Bernard's work directly, one of the few authors she recommends to her son in the *Enseignemens moraux* (see *Le livre de l'advision Cristine*, 174–75).

25. There are two editions of these poems: first, *Oeuvres poétiques* (1:249–51) by Maurice Roy, who used BN f.fr. 835 as his base manuscript. I used Harley 4431 for reasons of consistency. Variants in BN f.fr. 835 are noted in the Appendix. The second, more recent edition is by Kenneth Varty, *Christine de Pisan, Ballades, Rondeaux, and Virelais* (Leicester, UK: Leicester University Press, 1965),118–19; Varty, too, used the Harley manuscript. In addition, Raymond M. Thomassy reproduces the Rondel in his *Essai sur les écrits politiques de Christine de Pizan: suivi d'une notice littéraire et de pièces inédites* (Paris: Debécourt, 1838), 108–109. I would also like to point out here that Sandra Hindman erroneously claims that Roy used the Harley manuscript as his base manuscript for the edition (see "The Composition of the Manuscript of Christine de Pizan's Collected Works in the British Library: A Reassessment," *The British Library Journal* 9, no. 2 (1983): 93–123, n. 1, 122). Translations are my own.

26. Lori Walters discusses it in the framework of a topos study of translatio studii in "Translatio studii: Christine de Pizan's Self-Portrayal in Two Lyric Poems and in the *Livre de la mutacion de Fortune*," in *Christine de Pizan and Medieval French Lyric*, ed. Earl Jeffrey Richards (Gainesville: University Press of Florida, 1998), 155–67. See also Danielle Roch, "La structure des Autres balades de divers propos de Christine de Pizan, ou la quête inachevée de l'harmonie du monde," *Romania* 1–2, no.123 (2005): 222–35.

27. Charity Cannon Willard, *Christine de Pizan. Her Life and Works. A Biography* (New York: Persea Books, 1984), 61.

28. According to Kenneth Varty, "The beginning of this ballade is borrowed from the beginning of Aristotle's Metaphysics where one may read 'All men have a natural desire for knowledge.' This maxim was well known in Christine's day, when Aristotle was revered as the greatest of all thinkers" (*Ballades*, 160).

29. As Lori Walters has shown, Christine's evocation of the persecution of Aristotle and Socrates for having foretold the coming of Christ creates a string of intertextual links between this ballade and, retrospectively, the *Debate Epistles* and the *Cité des dames*: "In the dispute over the *Rose*, Jean de Montreuil had compared Christine to Leontium, the Greek prostitute who had dared to criticize Theophrastus. Christine responded to this criticism in the *Cité des Dames*, I.30.3, by redefining Leontium as a philosopher.... If Christine portrays herself as a Leontium figure in the *Cité*, she goes even further in poem 37 where she presents herself as an avatar of Athena/Minerva—indeed, I am tempted to say, as a kind of precursor of the Blessed Virgin Mary—whose character and wisdom outshine the beleaguered male philosophers for whom Christine proposes female counterparts." "Translatio Studii," 160. See also Nadia Margolis, "Christine de Pizan: The Poetess as Historian," *Journal of the History of Ideas* 47 (1986): 361–75; 366.

30. No edition exists to date; however, three manuscripts have been identified by C. C. Willard as being more or less contemporary with the work, Brussels, Bibliothèque Royale MS 10476, BN f. fr. 603, and a third manuscript which "appeared in a sale recently is also an early copy but bears no indication of its original owner," *The Book of Arms and Chivalry* (University Park: Pennsylvania State University Press, 1999), 2. For the transcription of the excerpt I used BN f.fr. 603. The excerpt occupies fol. 49ro–49vo. C. C. Willard and Sumner Willard used Brussels, Bibliothèque Royale MS 10476 for the translation of this work, of which I reproduce pages 143–44. This work is extant in about twenty manuscripts, which attests to its considerable popularity as an instructional manual on warfare. It is particularly interesting to note that the recent discovery of an early German translation shows that its popularity transcended national borders. As of yet, this manuscript has not been edited. For a description see Wolfram Scheider-Lastin, "Christine deutsch. Eine Übersetzung des *Livres des fais d'armes et de chevalerie* in einer unbekannten Handschrift des 15. Jahrhunderts," *Zeitschrift für deutsches Altertum und deutsche Literatur* 125 (1996): 187–201. Also Danielle Buschinger, "Christine de Pizan en Allemagne," in *Contexts and Continuities*, 1:171–73.

31. *Christine de Pizan. Her Life and Works* (New York: Persea Books, 1984), 183.

32. *Christine de Pizan*, 181. Montreuil's treatise can be found in *Opera: l'œuvre historique et polémique*, ed. N. Grévy, E. Ornato, G. Ouy (Turin: Giappichelli, 1975), 91–135.

33. As noted by the translators, "the personage introduced here is undoubtedly Honoré Bouvet (or Bonet), the author of the *Arbre des batailles* (The tree of battles), the treatise on warfare written probably shortly before 1390 and dedicated to King Charles VI.... Christine's borrowing all comes from book IV of his work, and her use of the dialogue to present the problems under discussion cleverly simplifies them" (143).

34. For a more detailed investigation into this topic, I refer to Carla Bozzolo, ed., *Un traducteur et un humaniste de l'époque de Charles VI, Laurent de Premierfait* (Paris: Publications de la Sorbonne, 2004).

35. Ibid., 17.

36. Cited in Badel, 486, and based on manuscript BN fr. 226, which is the base manuscript for the edition published by P. M. Gathercole, *Des cas des nobles hommes et femmes* (Chapel Hill: University of North Carolina Press, 1968). The excerpt can be found on page 168 of this edition which only comprises book 1 of the translation. The translation is my own.

37. Is it merely through negligence that Laurent de Premierfait attributes the narration of this myth to Jean de Meun rather than to Guillaume de Lorris?

38. MS fr. 226, fol. 268vo. Cited in Badel, 486. My translation.

Appendix

Variants

Variants have been provided only where more than one manuscript was con-
sulted for the transcription of the passage in question or where an existing
translation of a text was modified by me.

Chapter Two

References are to line numbers in the English translation. The changes noted
are with respect to Fenster and Carpenter Erler's translation.

B.1. 4 The son of Venus, goddess powerful!; 48 faking; 88 It is not a good;
129 get their part; 193–194 When God on high created angels, made/The
cherubim, archangels, seraphim…; 220–222 Who'd rather want to lose
their worldly wealth/Than be accused or blamed of deeds like that/For
anything, nor captured in the act; 284 And there he lays to women nasty
ways; 368–369 In which he teached them and openly/Elucidates the
way to trick the girls; 533 Their judgment's poor, the sentence very bad;
569–570 Their judgment's poor, the sentence very bad; 598–599 Whose
body was already, summing up,/Among the things of earth the noblest
one

Chapter Three

References are to line numbers in the original. The variants noted are with
respect to manuscript BN f. fr. 12779.

1. 9 de *omitted;* 24 loisible ne a souffrir; 28 come cy; 33 fait soubz vostre
saige
2. 3 esquelles dictes paroles; 6 Cristine *omitted*; 7 aucunement *omitted*; 9 le
dit prevost envoya a la dicte Cristine; 11 lequel dit clerc; 14 a elle ycelle;
15 come la dicte
3. 1 Maistre Gontier Col *omitted*; 5 et *omitted*; 23 de Meun *omitted*; 45 en
ceste compilacion; 46 Quant ad; 53 maistre *omitted*

4.   3 et Prevost de Lille *omitted*; 15 soustenant ycellui; 37 devant dit; 39 elle *omitted*; 74 estre deboutee; 81–82 ne fait la deshonnesteté de la chose; 97–98 car trop est pire le vice de propre malice que cellui de simple ignorance *omitted*; 105 desiréz a; 114–115 parla par la bouche Jeremie; 126 qu'il; 127 a *omitted*; 129 Et *omitted*; 130–131 bien serait; 170 mors, pendus; 184 ne de quoy; 188 ne *omitted* prier; 193 n'en; 143 ne quel; 194 de mariage *omitted*; 196–197 prouffitable mais vrayement; 210 ja a esté; 210 vaillans femmes; 243 raison et honte; 247 ce que raison et honte doit reffraindre, aux bien ordonnéz, seulement le penser; encore plus, j'ose dire que mesmes les goliars auroient horreur de le lire ou oïr en publique en places honnestes et devant personnes que ilz reputassent vertueuses; 253 ne apprent *omitted*; 255–256 autre estrange chose feust devenuz ce seroit matiere; 257 Et sans faille; 276 d'aucune; 278 puis dire; 326 excepcion tout

5.   2 Maistre Gontier Col *omitted*; 5 la divine; 12 et *omitted* magnifeste; 13 trop grant *omitted*; 26–27 je me mecte a escrire encontre tes faulses; 36 Le tien Gontier Col *omitted*

6.   1 Cristine *omitted;* 1 Cy aprés s'ensuit la responce, envoyee, au dit maistre Gontier Col; 6 reprimer et; 14 m'apparut…adrecié a un subtil clerc; 15 moye se confere; 19–20 comme *omitted* passionné; 25 Ha! hault entendement ingenieux; 29 soit bien; 33 de vray; 46 plus *omitted*; 47 tant est; 57 publiquement *omitted*

References are to line numbers in the original. The variants noted are with respect to manuscript BN f. fr. 1563.

7.   1 Pierre Col; 3–4 entendre des choses; 7–8 souventefois sont esmeues diverses questions; 22 meu sus la compilacion du; 30 Reverance et honneur; 38 Vierge Marie; 43 come tu m'escrips; 58 grossement *omitted*; 59 n'est ja; 67–68 pour ce que la fin pour quoy j'en parleroye ne seroit pas deshonneste; 69 je *omitted*; 76–77 je te demande que tu me dise se ung anfant; 87 ce *omitted*; 92 ne mucierent; 97 et estiper; 98 etc.; 99 une *omitted*; 99–101 en la tres vraye, juste et raisonnable oppinion contre la compilacion du dit *de la Rose*; 101 tres grans; 121 la court sainte de Crestienté; 140 quoy tu te tiens; 153 y *omitted*; 161 n'en senti; 165 est a; 170 *The repetition of* a moy *omitted*; 176 qu'elle puist; 178 ou pour plus grant; 181 mie *omitted*; 206 que on; 210 et par; 225 de charnalité; 232 yci en droit; 233 on ne; 251 nomment bien; 261 maistre *omitted*; 265 mie *omitted*; 266 d'en ester; 271 *The repetition of* par Dieu! *omitted*; 272 que honte ne t'en garde *omitted*; 273 la desconfit; 277 honneste; 294 ja affollement amer; 304 mieux li; 313 il a failly; 320 six fois plus; 325 Sés tu comment; 326 et les; 330 et entremeslent divers metaulx et matieres

omitted; 334 et a la; 338 en est; 344 sera respondre, et deffendra; 348 deux bons; 358–359 solucions respondre, et deffendra; 359 Et mervilleusement; 368 encore et; 369 la sienne doctrine; 370 deceu et c'est assavoir decevance; 371 dit de; 375 car n'est ce; 377 dire hardiment; 382 en bien; 383 consideres ung pou; 387 les histoires *omitted*; 387 dame Discorde; 390 seroit; 392 en mauvais effait!; 405 lui *omitted* en; 413 les condicions pour *omitted*; 414 tourner aux condicions; 415 doivent bien; 416 Et aussy; 426 autres mains; 426 Si n'en; 427 corps, ame; 427 de ce telz; 429 me diras yci; 431 mesmement qui sont; 435 te *omitted*; 436 on s'en; 438 je ne lay point; 439 de deux; 442 de decepveur; 446 moquerres; 447 sont les fais; 443–444 je puis que dire; 448 *The repetition of* ce *omitted*; 448 en la fin; 461 je le vouloye; 462 dis *omitted*; 471 tres bien; 474 t'en passes; 480 est *omitted*; 483 t'en passes; 484 homme, home; 486 ravales par; 498 me *omitted*; 499 et car; 507 les *omitted* luy fault; 507 de bien; 512 et tant de; 523 tu veulz; 523 on se garde; 524 des gens; 541 l'oppinion; 542 s'ilz; 547 aultre; 550 es livres; 558 on te; 559 qui sonne; 567 et aux; 571 ainssy feras; 576 par avant; 585 l'acteur; 611 pour *omitted* coulpables; 612–613 c'est maudit et mal raporté; 617 y *omitted*; 618 A quoy puet est bonne telle lecture qui honnestement ne puet estre leue en leur presance?; 629 et tu dis voir; 629 bonnes parolles; 638 assaillis; 647 tu ne; 652 en toute maniere; 656 faulce monoye; 667 tu ja; 676 Et comment dya! tu dis…; 693 de tele semence; 696 demeure racine; 697 et *omitted*; 699 que de bien; 703 dont *omitted*; 704 n'eschappent; 708 decevoir *omitted*; 710–711 lui *omitted* a ja; 716 tu eusses presté; 718 a Boesce; 720 que tu ne luy ayes baillié; 723 je oy; 733 telle povre; 743 en *omitted*; 744 puis si dit; 746 ce c'on; 748 appercevoit de la; 752 qui ait dit mal; 765 qu'en leur; 767–768 suivre et des vices, pour les fuir; 776 n'excerciteront; 780 la beatitude de paradis; 783 grant *omitted*; 784 et *omitted* plus; 789 et ou tu pourras plus proufiter; 792 le faist; 792 lui a donner; 797 dessusdictes; 798 tout ung ce fere; 802 Nature et; 804 amoureux *omitted*; 811 point c'est; 812 court contre val; 813 qu'i; 814 ne; 814 los; 816 de *omitted* mariage; 821 en celle; 821 ains dist plainnement et a la lectre: « Toutes pour tous et tous pour toutes » *replaces* maniere; 842 si *omitted*; 843–844 mariage en ce que il dit tant estre de contentions et d'ennuyeux obprobres que il n'est nul, tant; 845 qui ne; 852 mais de celluy; 852 qui y est; 853 du monde pour plaire a sa fame; 855 qu'i; 858 ainsi *omitted*; 861 te *omitted*; 861 une autre grant; 862 de mot en mot; 865 que *omitted* pour ce; 868 et vas; 869–870 qu'il dit permy le mal; tu n'oublies mie que il dist; 874 vela le bien; 876 n'avons; 877 qu'i; 882 gart; 885 parti; 900 estrepey et; 905 elettes; 909 ne *omitted*; 910 a louer; 911 maintes matieres; 912 herreur; 914–915 Tu ressambles Helouye du Paraclit; 916 appellee de maistre Pierre Abalart

que estre royne couronnee; si appert bien que les voulantés qui mieux
plaisent ne sont pas toutes raisonnables; 930 habille; 934 nulle envie;
936 avoir *omitted*; 937 je te promet n'y ay aucune; 938 oste ne; 939 soye
par; 943 et beaux; 948 sa *omitted*; 948 et d'ampirement de; 956 loué; 958
la lune du ciel d'ung boujon; 960 bouchee; 964 lancié comme; 965 sus
omitted; 966 bouchee; 967 savoir chose de; 969 et exerciter *omitted*; 970
ce *omitted*; 984–985 sachiés mal gré; 997 elle attendoit; 1000 une petite
pointelette; 1005 qu'i pourra et quant; 1010 mieulx a; 1025 Cristine de
Pizan

Chapter Four

References are to line numbers in the English translation. The changes noted
are with respect to Fenster and Carpenter Erler's translation.

3.   158 For they were gathered, and loyally meant; 202 And to that flower,
called a rose premier; 218–219 For seed that he has sown among us here/
From which we're on the way, I hope to see; 298 Not heeding if I slept
or not; 318 It pleases him my service be; 491–496 That if he's known
to spread untruth,/He will not be loved the less by all,/Less prized and
called a slanderer./Above all other calumny/It is talk of women basely
done,/Defaming them, that Love hates most

Chapter Five

References are to line numbers in the original. The variants noted are with
respect to manuscript BN f. fr. 835.

4.   (Rondel) 5 je ne suis convertie

Bibliography

Primary Sources

Altmann, Barbara, ed. *The Love Debate Poems of Christine de Pizan (Le livre du Debat de deux amans, Le livre des Trois jugements, Le Livre du Dit de Poissy)*. Gainesville: University Press of Florida, 1998.

Baird, L. John, and John R. Kane, trans. *La querelle de la rose. Letters and Documents*. Chapel Hill: North Carolina Studies in the Romance Languages and Literatures, 1978.

Bétemps, Isabelle, Michèle Guéret-Laferté, Nicolas Lenoir, Sylvain Louis, Jean Maurice, and Carmelle Mira, eds. *La consolation de la Philosophie de Boèce. Dans une traduction attribuée à Jean de Meun d'après le manuscrit Leber 817 de la Bibliothèque municipale de Rouen*. Rouen, France: Les Publications de l'Université de Rouen, 2004.

Brereton, Georgina E., ed. *Le mesnagier de Paris*. Paris: Livre de poche, 1994.

Brown-Grant, Rosalind, trans. *The Book of the City of Ladies*. Harmondsworth, UK: Penguin, 1999.

Buzzetti Gallarati, Sylvia, ed. *Le Testament Maistre Jehan de Meun: un caso letterario*. Alessandria, Italy: Ed. dell'Orso, 1989.

Calin, William, ed., trans. "Deschamps's 'Ballade to Chaucer' Again, or the Dangers of Intertextual Medieval Comparatism." In *Eustache Deschamps, French Courtier-Poet, His Work and His World*, edited by Deborah M. Sinnreich-Levi, 73–84. New York: AMS Press, 1998.

Caraffi, Patricia, and Earl Jeffrey Richards, eds. *La città delle dame*. Milan: Luni Editrice, 1997.

Coopland, G.W, ed. *Le songe du vieil pelerin*. 2 vols. Cambridge, UK: Cambridge University Press, 1969.

Dulac, Liliane, ed. "L'Epistre a la reine." In *Christine de Pizan*, edited by Liliane Dulac and Jean Dufournet. Special issue, *Revue des langues romanes* 92, no. 2 (1988): 253–64.

Dunn, Charles, and Harry W. Robbins, trans. *The Romance of the Rose*. Syracuse, NY: Syracuse University Press, 2002.

Fenster, Thelma S., and Mary Carpenter, eds., trans. *Poems of Cupid, God of Love. Christine de Pizan's Epistre au dieu d'Amours and Dit de la Rose, Thomas Hoccleve's The Letter of Cupid, with George Sewell's The Proclamation of Cupid*. Leiden: Brill, 1990.

Gathercole, P.M. *Des cas des nobles hommes et femmes*. Chapel Hill, NC: 1968.

Glorieux, Palémon Msgr, ed. *Jean Gerson. Œuvres complètes*. Paris: Desclée, 1960–.

Grévy, N., and Ezio Ornato, G. Ouy, eds. *Opera. Jean de Montreuil*. 3 vols. Turin: Giappichelli, 1975.

Hamel, A.G. van, ed. *Les lamentations de Matheolus et le Livre de Leesce de Jehan Le Fèvre, Edition accompagnée de l'original latin des Lamentations*. 2 vols. Paris: Bouillon, 1892, 1905.

Hasenohr-Esnos, Geneviève, ed. *Respit de la mort, Respit de la mort par Jean le Fèvre*. Paris: Picard, 1969.

Hicks, Eric, ed. *Le débat sur le Roman de la rose*. Geneva: Slatkine Reprints, 1996.

Hicks, Eric, and Thérèse Moreau, eds. *Livre des fais et bonnes meurs du sage roy Charles V.* Paris: Stock, 1997.

Kennedy, Angus J., ed. "La lamentacion sur les maux de la France de Christine de Pisan." In *Mélanges de la langue et littérature françaises du moyen âge et de la Renaissance offerts à Monsieur Charles Foulon,* vol. 1, 177–85. Paris: Institut de français, Université de Haute-Bretagne, 1980.

Kosta-Théfaine, Jean-François. "L'Epistre a Eustace Morel de Christine de Pisan." *Le moyen français* 38 (1996): 79–91.

Kraft, Christine. *Die Liebesgarten-Allegorie der "Echecs amoureux."* Frankfurt/Main: Peter Lang, 1977.

Laborde, Le Comte A. de, ed. *Les manuscrits à peintures de la Cité de Dieu de Saint Augustin.* 3 vols. Paris: Rahir, 1909.

Laurie, Ian S., and Deborah M. Sinnreich-Levi, eds. *Eustache Deschamps. Selected Poems.* New York: Routledge, 2002.

Lecoy, Félix, ed. *Le roman de la rose.* 3 vols. Paris: Champion, 1965.

Lettenhove de, Kervyn, ed. *Poésies de Gilles li Muisis,* 2 vols. Louvain: Lefever, 1882.

McLeod, Glenda K., and Charity Cannon Willard, trans. *The Vision of Christine de Pizan.* New York: Brewer, 2005.

Ornato, Ezio, ed. *Opera,* 3 vols. Turin: Giappichelli, 1963-81.

Poirion, Daniel, and Jean Dufournet, eds, trans. *Le roman de la rose.* Paris : Flammarion, 1999.

Power, Eileen, trans. *The Goodman of Paris (Le ménagier de Paris). A Treatise on Moral and Domestic Economy by a Citizen of Paris, c. 1393.* London: Routledge, 1992.

Reno, Christine, and Liliane Dulac, eds. *Le livre de l'advision Cristine.* Paris: Champion, 2000.

Richards, Earl Jeffrey, trans. *The Book of the City of Ladies.* New York: Persea, 1982.

Rossetti, Domenico, ed. *Poesi minori del Petrarca.* 3 vols. Milan, 1831–34.

Roy, Maurice, ed. *Oeuvres poétiques de Christine de Pisan.* 3 vols. New York: Johnson, 1965. First published 1886, 1891, 1896 by Firmin Didot, Paris.

Saint-Hilaire, Auguste Queux de, and Gaston Raynaud, eds. *Oeuvres complètes. Eustache Deschamps.* 11 vols. 1966.First published 1878–1903 by Didot, Paris.

Solente, Suzanne, ed. *Le livre des fais et bonnes meurs su sage roy Charles V.* 2 vols. Geneva: Slatkine Reprints, 1977. First published 1936–40 by Champion, Paris..

———. *Le livre de la mutacion de fortune par Christine de Pisan. Publié d'après les manuscrits,* 3 vols. Paris: Picard, 1959.

Stürzinger, J. J., trans. *Le pèlerinage de la vie humaine de Guillaume de Deguileville.* London: Nichols and Sons for the Roxburghe Club, 1893.

Tarnowski, Andrea, ed. *Le livre du chemin de long estude.* Paris: Lettres gothiques, 2000.

Thomassy, Raymond M, ed. *Essai sur les écrits politiques de Christine de Pisan: suivi d'une notice littéraire et de pièces inédites.* Paris: Debécourt, 1838.

Varty, Kenneth, ed. *Christine de Pisan, Ballades, Rondeaux, and Virelais.* Leicester, UK: Leicester University Press, 1965.

Ward, Charles Frederick, trans. *The Epistles on the Romance of the Rose and Other Documents in the Debate.* Chicago: University of Chicago Press, 1911.

Willard, Charity Cannon, and Eric Hicks, eds. *Livre des Trois vertus.* Paris: Champion, 1989.

Willard, Charity Cannon, and Sumner Willard, trans. *The Book of Arms and Chivalry.* University Park: Pennsylvania State University Press, 1999.

Williamson, Joan B., ed. *Le livre de la vertu du sacrement de mariage.* Washington, D.C.: The Catholic University of America Press, 1993.

Secondary Sources

Adams Smith, Diana E. "Some French Works of Jean Gerson. An Introduction and Translation." PhD diss., University of South Carolina, October 1976.

Altmann, Barbara. "Trop peu en sçay: The Reluctant Narrator in Christine de Pizan's Works on Love." In

Chaucer's French Contemporaries: The Poetry/Poetics of Self and Tradition, edited by Barbara Altmann and Barton Palmer, 217–49. New York: AMS Press, 1999.

———. "Hearing the Text, Reading the Image: Christine de Pizan's *Livre du Debat de Deux Amans.*" In *Au champ des escriptures. IIIe Colloque international sur Christine de Pizan,* edited by Eric Hicks, Diego Gonzalez, and Philippe Simon, 693–708. Paris: Champion, 2000.

Amblard, Paule. *Le pèlerinage de vie humaine: le songe très chrétien de l'abbé Guillaume de Digulleville: ouvrage réalisé à partir du manuscrit 1130 de la Bibliothèque Sainte-Geneviève à Paris.* Paris: Flammarion, c1998.

Aubert, Félix. *Le Parlement de Paris. De Philippe le Bel à Charles VII (1314–1422). Sa compétence, ses attributions.* Geneva: Slatkine, 1977.

Badel, Pierre-Yves. "Pierre d'Ailly, auteur du *Jardin amoureux.*" *Romania* 97 (1976): 369–81.

———. *Le roman de la rose au XIVe siècle. Etude de la réception de l'oeuvre.* Geneva: Droz, 1980.

———. "Lectures alchimiques du *Roman de la Rose.*" *Chrysopoeia: Revue de la Société d'Étude de l'Histoire de l'Alchimie* 5 (1992–96): 173–90.

Bakker, J. J. M. "Syncategorèmes, concepts, équivocité: Deux questions anonymes, conservées dans le ms. Paris, B.N., lat. 16.401, liées à la sémantique de Pierre d'Ailly (c. 1350–1420)." *Vivarium* 34 (1996): 76–131.

Beer, Jeanette. "Patronage and the Translator: Raoul de Presles's *La cité de Dieu* and Calvin's *Institution de la religion Chrestienne* and *Institutio religionis Christianae.*" In *Translation and Transmission of Culture between 1300 and 1600,* edited by Jeanette Beer and Kenneth Lloyd-Jones, 91–142, Kalamazoo, MI: Medieval Institute Publications, 1995.

Blamires, Alcuin. *The Case of Women in Medieval Culture.* Oxford: Clarendon Press, 1997.

Blamires, Alcuin, Karen Pratt, and Marx, C. William, eds. *Woman Defamed and Woman Defended: An Anthology of Medieval Texts.* Oxford: Clarendon Press, 1992.

Blanchard, Joël. "Christine de Pizan: Les raisons de l'histoire." *Le Moyen Age: Revue d'Histoire et de Philologie* 92 (1986): 417–36.

Blumenfeld-Kosinski, Renate. "Jean Le Fevre's Livre de Leesce: Praise or Blame of Women?" *Speculum* 69, no.3 (1994): 705–25.

———. "Satirical Views of the Beguines in Northern French Literature." In *New Trends in Feminine Spirituality. The Holy Women of Liège and their Impact,* edited by Juliette Dor, 237–49. Brussels: Brepols, 1999.

———. "Christine de Pizan and the Political Life in Late Medieval France." In *Christine de Pizan: A Casebook,* edited by Barbara Altmann and Deborah McGrady, 9–24. New York: Routledge, 2003.

———. "Jean Gerson and the Debate on the *Romance of the Rose,*" *A Companion to Jean Gerson,* ed. Brian P. McGuire. Leiden: Brill, 2006, 317–356.

Bozzolo, Carla, ed. *Un traducteur et un humaniste de l'époque de Charles VI. Laurent de Premierfait.* Paris: Publications de la Sorbonne, 2004.

Brown-Grant, Rosalind. *Christine de Pizan and the Moral Defense of Women. Reading Beyond Gender.* Cambridge, UK: Cambridge University Press, 1999.

Brownlee, Kevin. "Discourses of the Self: Christine de Pizan and the Rose." *Romanic Review,* 79, no. 1 (1988): 199–221.

———. "The Image of History in Christine de Pizan's *Livre de la Mutacion de Fortune.*" In *Contexts: Style and Values in Medieval Art and Literature,* edited by Daniel Poirion and Nancy Freeman Regalado, 44–56. New Haven, CT: Yale University Press, 1991.

———. "Literary Genealogy and the Problem of the Father: Christine de Pizan and Dante." In *Dante Now: Current Trends in Dante Studies,* edited by Theodore J. Cachey, 205–35. Notre Dame, IN: University of Notre Dame Press, 1995.

———. "Hector and Penthesilea in the *Livre de la mutacion de Fortune*: Christine de Pizan and the Politics of Myth." In *Une femme de lettres au moyen âge,* edited by Liliane Dulac and Bernard Ribémont, 69–82. Orléans, France: Paradigme, 1995.

Brownlee, Kevin, and Sylvia Huot, eds. *Rethinking the Romance of the Rose: Text, Image, Reception.* Philadelphia: University of Pennsylvania Press, 1992.

Buschinger, Danielle. "Christine de Pizan en Allemagne." In *Contexts and Continuities. Proceeding of the Fourth International Colloquium on Christine de Pizan (July 2000)*, edited by Angus J. Kennedy et al., 171–73. Glasgow: University of Glasgow Press, 2002.

Case, Mary Anne. "Christine de Pizan and the Authority of Experience." In *Christine de Pizan and the Categories of Difference*, edited by Marilynn Desmond, 71–87. Minneapolis: University of Minnesota Press, 1998.

Cheney Curnow, Maureen. "La Pioche d'inquisicion: Legal-Judicial Content and Style in Christine de Pizan's *Livre de la cité des dames.*" In *Reinterpreting Christine de Pizan*, edited by Earl Jeffrey Richards et al., 157–72. Athens, GA: University of Georgia Press, 1992.

Delaruelle, Etienne. "La translation des reliques de Saint Thomas d'Aquin à Toulouse (1369) et la politique universitaire d'Urbain V." *Bulletin de littérature ecclésiastique* 56 (1955): 129–46..

Delisle, Léopold. *Recherches sur la librairie de Charles V, Roi de France, 1337–1380. Partie II: Inventaire général des livres ayant appartenu aux Rois Charles V et Charles VI et à Jean, Duc de Berry.* Amsterdam: van Heusden, 1967.

Desmond, Marilynn. "The *Querelle de la Rose* and the Ethics of Reading." In *Christine de Pizan: A Casebook*, edited by Barbara K. Altmann and Deborah L. McGrady, 167–80. New York: Routledge, 2003.

Desmond, Marilynn, and Pamela Sheinghorn. *Myth, Montage, Visuality in Late Medieval Manuscript Culture: Christine de Pizan's Othea.* Ann Arbor: Michigan University Press, 2001.

Donovan, Josephine. *Women and the Rise of the Novel, 1405–1726.* London: Macmillan, 1999.

Douais, Célestin. *Les reliques de saint Thomas d'Aquin, Textes originaux.* Paris: Librairie Vve Ch. Poussielgue, 1903.

Dufeil, Michel-Marie. *Guillaume de Saint-Amour et la polémique universitaire parisienne, 1250–1259.* Paris: Picard, 1972.

Faral, Edmond. *Histoire littéraire de la France.* Paris: Imprimerie nationale, 1962.

Fenster, Thelma. "Did Christine Have a Sense of Humor? The Evidence of the Epistre au dieu d'amours." In *Reinterpreting Christine de Pizan*, edited by E. Jeffrey Richards, 23–36. Athens: University of Georgia Press, 1992.

Ferrier, Janet. "Seulement pour vous endoctriner: The Author's Use of Exempla in *Le Menagier de Paris.*" *Medium Aevum*, 48 (1979): 77–89.

Fleming, John V. *The Roman de la rose. A Study in Allegory and Iconography.* Princeton, NJ: Princeton University Press, 1969.

———. *Reason and the Lover.* Princeton, NJ: Princeton University Press, 1984.

Fiumi, Lionello. "La fortune de Dante en France de Christine de Pisan à Saint-John Perse." *Bulletin de la Société d'Etudes dantesques du Centre universitaire méditerranéen* 16 (1967): 33–45.

Furr, Grover, "France vs. Italy, French Literary Nationalism in 'Petrarch's Last Controversy' and A Humanist Dispute of ca. 1395." In *Proceedings of the Patristic, Medieval and Renaissance Conference.* 4 (1979): 115–25.

Green, Karen. *The Woman of Reason: Feminism, Humanism and Political Thought.* Cambridge, UK: Polity Press, 1995.

Guenée, Bernard. "Pierre d'Ailly (1351–1420)." In *Entre l'église et l'état: quatre vies de prélats français à la fin du moyen âge (XIIIe–XVe siècle)*, 125–299. Paris: Gallimard, 1987.

Gunn, Alan M. F. *The Mirror of Love, A Reinterpretation of "The Romance of the Rose."* Lubbock, TX: Texas Technical Press, 1952.

Hanley, Sarah. "Identity Politics and Rulership in France: Female Political Place and the Fraudulent Salic Law in Christine de Pizan and Jean de Montreuil." In *Changing Identities in Early Modern France*, edited by Michael Wolfe, 78–94. Durham, NC: Duke University Press, 1997.

Heller-Roazen, Daniel. *Fortune's Face: The Roman de la Rose and the Poetics of Contingency.* Baltimore: Johns Hopkins University Press, 2003.

Hicks, Eric. "Situation du débat sur le *Roman de la rose.*" In *Une femme de lettres au moyen âge. Etudes autour de Christine de Pizan*, edited by Liliane Dulac and Bernard Ribémont, 51–67. Orléans, France: Paradigme, 1995.

Hicks, Eric, and Ezio Ornato. "Le débat sur le *Roman de la rose.*" *Romania* 98 (1977): 35–64, 186–219.

Hindman, Sandra. "The Composition of the Manuscript of Christine de Pizan's Collected Works in the British Library: A Reassessment." *The British Library Journal* 9, no. 2 (1983): 93–123.

Hult, David. *Self-Fulfilling Prophecies: Readership and Authority in the First Roman de la rose.* Cambridge, UK: Cambridge University Press, 1986.

———. "Language and Dismemberment: Abelard, Origen, and the *Romance of the Rose.*" In *Rethinking the Romance of the Rose. Text, Image, Reception,* edited by Kevin Brownlee and Sylvia Huot, 101–30. Philadelphia: University of Pennsylvania Press, 1992.

———. "Words and Deeds: Jean de Meun's *Romance of the Rose* and the Hermeneutics of Censorship." *New Literary History. A Journal of Theory and Interpretation* 28, no. 2 (1997): 345–66.

———. "The *Roman de la rose*, Christine de Pizan, and the *querelle des femmes.*" In *The Cambridge Companion to Medieval Women's Writing,* edited by Carolyn Dinshaw and David Wallace, 184–94. Cambridge, UK: Cambridge University Press, 2003.

Huot, Sylvia. "Seduction and Sublimation: Christine de Pizan, Jean de Meung and Dante." *Romance Notes* 25, no. 3 (1985): 361–73.

———. *The Romance of the Rose and Its Medieval Readers: Interpretation, Reception, Manuscript Transmission.* Cambridge, UK: Cambridge UniversityPress, 1993.

———. "The Miroir de mariage: Deschamps Responds to the Roman de la rose." In *Eustache Deschamps, French Courtier-Poet, His Work and His World,* edited by Deborah M. Sinnreich-Levi, 131–44. New York: AMS Press, 1998.

Kellogg, Judith. "Transforming Ovid: The Metamorphosis of Female Authority." In *Christine de Pizan and the Categories of Difference,* edited by Marilynn Desmond, 181–94. Minneapolis: University of Minnesota Press, 1998.

Kelly, Douglas. *Internal Difference and Meanings in the Roman de la rose.* Madison: University of Wisconsin Press, 1995.

Kennedy, William J. *The Site of Petrarchism, Early Modern National Sentiment in Italy, France and England.* Baltimore: Johns Hopkins University Press, 2003.

Krueger, Roberta. "Christine's Anxious Lessons. Gender, Morality, and the Social Order from the *Enseignemens* to the *Avision.*" In *Christine de Pizan and the Categories of Difference,* edited by Marilynn Desmond, 16–40. Minneapolis: University of Minnesota Press, 1998.

———. "'Nouvelles choses': Social Instability and the Problem of Fashion in the *Livre du chevalier de La Tour Landry,* the *Ménagier de Paris,* and Christine de Pizan's *Livre des trois vertu.*" In *Medieval Conduct,* edited by Kathleen Ashley and Robert Clark, 49–85. Minneapolis: University of Minnesota Press, 2001.

Laidlaw, James. "Christine de Pizan: An Author's Progress." *Modern Language Review* 78, no. 3 (1983): 532–50.

———. "Christine de Pizan: A Publisher's Progress." *Modern Language Review* 82, no. 1 (1987): 37–75.

Langlois, Ch.-V. *La vie en France au moyen âge. De la fin du XIIe au milieu du XIVe siècle d'après des moralistes du temps.* Geneva: Slatkine Reprints, 1970.

Langlois, Ernest. *Les manuscrits du Roman de la rose, description et classement.* Geneva: Slatkine Reprints, 1974.

Margolis, Nadia. "Christine de Pizan: The Poetess as Historian." *Journal of the History of Ideas* 47 (1986): 361–75.

McWebb, Christine. "The *Roman de la rose* and the *Livre des trois vertus:* The Never-Ending Debate." In *Au Champ des escriptures. IIIe Colloque international sur Christine de Pizan,* edited by Eric Hicks, 309–24. Paris: Champion, 2000.

———. "Heresy and Debate: Reading the *Roman de la Rose.*" *Aevum* 77 (2003): 545–56.

———. "Hermeneutics of Irony: Lady Reason and the *Romance of the Rose.*" *Dalhousie French Studies* 69 (2004): 3–14.

Minnis, Alastair. *Magister Amoris, The Roman de la Rose and Vernacular Hermeneutics.* Oxford: Oxford University Press, 2001.

Moorman, John. *A History of the Franciscan Order. From Its Origin to the Year 1517.* Oxford, 1968.

Mourin, Louis. *Jean Gerson. Prédicateur français.* Bruges, Belgium: De Tempel, 1952.

Müller, Franz Walter. *Der Rosenroman und der lateinische Averroismus des 13. Jahrhunderts* Frankfurt: Klostermann, 1947.

Nabert, Nathalie. "Christine de Pizan, Jean Gerson et le gouvernement des âmes." In *Au champ des escriptures. IIIe Colloque international sur Christine de Pizan,* edited by Eric Hicks, Diego Gonzalez, and Philippe Simon, 251–68. Paris: Champion, 2000.

Nouvet, Claire. "Writing (in) Fear." In *Gender and Text in the Later Middle Ages,* edited by Jane Chance, 279–305. Gainesville: University Press of Florida, 1996.

Pascoe, Louis B. "Theological Dimensions of Pierre d'Ailly's Teaching on the Papal Plenitude of Power." *Annuarium Historiae Conciliorum* 11 (1979): 357–66.

———. "Pierre d'Ailly: histoire, schisme et Antichrist." In *Genèse et débuts du Grand Schisme d'Occident: [Colloque international tenu à] Avignon, 25–28 septembre 1978,* edited by Michel Hayez, 615–22. Paris: CNRS, 1980.

Piaget, Arthur. "Chronologie es Epistres sur le Roman de la rose." In *Etudes romanes dédiées à Gaston Paris.* Paris: Bouillon, 1891, 114–22.

Poirion, Daniel. "Les mots et les choses selon Jean de Meun." *L'information littéraire* 26 (1974): 7–11.

———. "De la signification selon Jean de Meun." In *Archéologie du signe,* edited by Lucie Brind'Amour and Eugene Vance, 165–85. Toronto: Pontifical Institute of Medieval Studies, 1983.

Potansky, Peter. *Der Streit um den Rosenroman.* Munich: Fink, 1972.

Pratt, Karen. "The Strains of Defense: The Many Voices of Jean Lefèvre's *Livre de Leesce.*" In *Gender in Debate from the Early Middle Ages to the Renaissance,* edited by Thelma S. Fenster and Clare A. Lees, 113–34. New York: Palgrave, 2002.

Quilligan, Maureen. *The Allegory of Female Authority: Christine de Pizan's Cité des dames.* Ithaca, NY: Cornell University Press, 1991.

Ribémont, Bernard. "Christine de Pizan et la figure de la mère." In *Christine de Pizan 2000. Studies on Christine de Pizan in Honour of Angus J. Kennedy,* edited by John Campbell and Nadia Margolis, 149–62. Amsterdam: Rodopi, 2000.

Ricci, Pier Giorgio. "La cronologia dell'ultimo 'certamen' petrarchesco." *Studi Petrarcheschi* 4 (1951): 47–59.

Richards, Earl Jeffrey. *Dante and the Roman de la rose: An Investigation into the Vernacular Narrative Context of the Commedia.* Tübingen: Niemeyer, 1981.

———. "Christine de Pizan and Dante: A Reexamination." *Archiv für das Studium der Neueren Sprachen und Literaturen* 222 (1985): 100–11.

———. "Rejecting Essentialism and Gendered Writing: the Case of Christine de Pizan." In *Gender and Text in the Later Middle Ages,* edited by Jane Chance, 96–131. Gainesville: University Press of Florida, 1996.

———. "*Glossa Aurelianensis est quae destruit textum*: Medieval Rhetoric, Thomism and Humanism in Christine de Pizan's Critique of *the Roman de la Rose.*" *Cahiers de Recherches Médiévales (XIIe–XVe s.)* 5 (1998): 247–63.

———. "The Lady Wants to Talk: Christine de Pizan's *Epistre a Eustace Mourel.*" In *Eustache Deschamps, French Courtier-Poet. His Work and His World,* edited by Deborah M. Sinnreich-Levi, 109–22. New York: AMS Press, 1998.

———. "Christine de Pizan and Medieval Jurisprudence." In *Contexts and Continuities. Proceeding of the Fourth International Colloquium on Christine de Pizan (July 2000),* edited by Angus J. Kennedy et al., 747–66. Glasgow: University of Glasgow Press, 2002.

Robertson, D.W. *Preface to Chaucer.* Princeton, NJ: Princeton University Press, 1962.

Roch, Danielle. "La structure des *Autres balades de divers propos* de Christine de Pizan, ou la quête inachevée de l'harmonie du monde." *Romania* 1–2, no.123 (2005): 222–35.

Scheider-Lastin, Wolfram. "Christine deutsch. Eine Übersetzung des *Livres des fais d'armes et de chevalerie* in einer unbekannten Handschrift des 15. Jahrhunderts." *Zeitschrift für deutsches Altertum und deutsche Literatur* 125 (1996): 187–201.

Schibanoff, Susan. "Taking the Gold out of Egypt: The Art of Reading as a Woman." In *Gender and Reading: Essays on Readers, Texts, and Contexts,* edited by Elizabeth Flynn and Patrocinio P. Schweickart, 83–106. Baltimore: Johns Hopkins University Press, 1986.

Solterer, Helen. *The Master and Minerva: Disputing Women in French Medieval Culture.* Berkeley: University of California Press, 1995.

Stäblein-Harris, Patricia. "Orléans, the Epic Tradition, and the Sacred Texts of Christine de Pizan." In *Reinterpreting Christine de Pizan,* edited by Earl Jeffrey Richards, 272–84. Athens: University of Georgia Press, 1992.

Stakel, Susan. *False Roses: Structures of Duality and Deceit in Jean de Meun's Roman de la Rose.* Stanford, CA: Anma Libri, 1991.

Szittya, Penn R. "The Antifraternal Tradition in Middle English." *Speculum* 52 (1977): 287–313.

Thijssen, J. M. M. H. *Censure and Heresy at the University of Paris 1200–1400.* Philadelphia: University of Pennsylvania Press, 1998.

Trapp, D. "Peter Ceffons of Clairvaux." *Recherches de théologie ancienne et médiévale* 24 (1957): 101–54.

Varty, Kenneth. "Christine's Guided Tour of the Sale merveilleuse: On Reactions to Reading and Being Guided round Medieval Murals in Real and Imaginary Buildings." In *Christine de Pizan 2000,* edited by John Campbell and Nadia Margolis, 163–73. Amsterdam: Rodopi, 2000.

Walters, Lori. "Fathers and Daughters: Christine de Pizan as Reader of Male Chivalric Orders and Traditions of *Clergie* in the *Dit de la Rose.*" In *Reinterpreting Christine de Pizan,* edited by E. Jeffrey Richards, 63–76. Athens: University of Georgia Press, 1992.

———. "*Translatio Studii*: Christine de Pizan's Self-Portrayal in Two Lyric Poems and in the *Livre de la mutacion de Fortune.*" In *Christine de Pizan and Medieval French Lyric,* edited by Earl Jeffrey Richards, 155–65. Gainesville: University Press of Florida, 1998.

———. "Fortune's Double Face: Gender and the Transformations of Christine de Pizan, Augustine, and Perpetua." *Fifteenth-Century Studies* 25 (2000): 97–114.

Wetherbee, Winthrop. "The Literal and the Allegorical: Jean de Meun and the *De Planctu Naturae.*" *Medieval Studies* 33 (1971): 264–91.

Willard, Charity Cannon. "A Re-examination of *Le Debat de deux amans,*" *Les bonnes feuilles* 3 (1974): 73–88.

———. "Christine de Pizan and the Order of the Rose." In *Ideals for Women in the Works of Christine de Pizan,* edited by Diane Bornstein, 51–67. Kalamazoo: University of Michigan Press, 1981.

———. "A New Look at Christine de Pizan's *Epistre au dieu d'Amours.*" In *Seconda Miscellanea di studi e ricerche sul Quattrocento francese,* edited by Jonathan Beck and Gianni Mombello, 71–92. Chambéry/Turin: Centre d'études franco-italien, 1981.

———. *Christine de Pizan. Her Life and Works.* New York: Persea Books, 1984.

———. "Raoul de Presles's Translation of Saint Augustine's *De civitate dei.*" In *Medieval Translators and Their Craft,* edited by Jeanette Beer, 329–46. Kalamazoo, MI: Medieval Institute Publications, 1989.

Wolfzettel, Friedrich. "Jean de Meun, 'ancien' ou 'moderne'?" *Etudes médiévales* (1999): 235–44.

Zimmermann, Albert, ed. *Die Auseinandersetzungen an der Pariser Universität im XIII. Jahrhundert.* Berlin: Walter de Gruyter, 1976.

Index